Effective Human Relations

Interpersonal and Organizational Applications

TWELFTH EDITION

Effective Human Relations

Interpersonal and Organizational Applications

BARRY L. REECE, EMERITUS
Virginia Polytechnic Institute and State University

SOUTH-WESTERN
CENGAGE Learning·

Australia • Brazil • Japan • Korea • Mexico • Singapore • Spain • United Kingdom • United States

SOUTH-WESTERN
CENGAGE Learning·

Effective Human Relations:
Interpersonal and Organizational
Applications, **Twelfth Edition**
Barry L. Reece

Senior Vice President, LRS/Acquisitions &
Solutions Planning: Jack W. Calhoun

Editorial Director, Business & Economics:
Erin Joyner

Senior Acquisitions Editor: Michele
Rhoades

Developmental Editor: Josh Wells

Marketing Manager: Jon Monahan

Art and Cover Direction, Production
Management, and Composition:
PreMediaGlobal

Media Editor: Rob Ellington

Senior Manufacturing Planner:
Ron Montgomery

Executive Marketing Communications
Manager: Jason LaChapelle

Cover Image: © Henk Meijer/Alamy

Rights Acquisitions Specialist, Text and
Image: Amber Hosea

For product information and technology assistance, contact us at
Cengage Learning Customer & Sales Support, 1-800-354-9706

For permission to use material from this text or product, submit all
requests online at **www.cengage.com/permissions**
Further permissions questions can be e-mailed to
permissionrequest@cengage.com

Library of Congress Control Number: 2012946938

ISBN-13: 978-1-133-96083-6

ISBN-10: 1-133-96083-9

South-Western
5191 Natorp Boulevard
Mason, OH 45040
USA

Cengage Learning is a leading provider of customized learning
solutions with office locations around the globe, including Singapore,
the United Kingdom, Australia, Mexico, Brazil, and Japan. Locate your
local office at: **www.cengage.com/global**

Cengage Learning products are represented in Canada by
Nelson Education, Ltd.

For your course and learning solutions, visit **www.cengage.com**

Purchase any of our products at your local college store or at our
preferred online store **www.cengagebrain.com**

Printed in the United States of America
1 2 3 4 5 6 7 16 15 14 13 12

To Vera Marie Reece
Our loving wife and mother. Thank you for the support and endless
love you give to both of us.
Barry L. Reece and Monique E. Reece

Brief Contents

Contents

About the Authors

BARRY L. REECE is Professor Emeritus at Virginia Polytechnic Institute and State University. Prior to joining the faculty at Virginia Tech, he held faculty positions at Ellsworth Community College and the University of Northern Iowa. Over the years, he has served as visiting professor at the University of Iowa, University of Missouri, University of Nebraska, University of Northern Colorado, and Wayne State College. He is the author or co-author of six college textbooks that have been through a total of 40 editions since 1980.

Barry received his Ed.D. from the University of Nebraska. He has been actively involved in teaching, research, consulting, and designing training programs throughout his career. He has conducted more that 500 workshops and seminars devoted to leadership, human relations, communications, sales, customer service, and small business operations. He has received the Excellence in Teaching Award for classroom teaching at Virginia Tech and the Trainer of the Year Award presented by the Valleys of Virginia Chapter of the American Society for Training and Development.

Barry currently divides his time between writing textbooks, writing poetry, and working on various projects for the Veterans for Peace organization. He lives near Chapel Hill, North Carolina, with his wife Vera and a spirited Lakeland terrier named Anna.

MONIQUE REECE, Contributor to the twelfth edition, has held the position of Affiliated Executive Faculty at the Institute for Leadership and Organizational Performance at the University of Denver teaching in both the Executive MBA and Professional MBA programs.. She has also served as an Executive Education faculty member at the Daniels College of Business, University of Denver; online faculty for Colorado State University; and is a Lecturer for universities and organizations.

Monique has more than 25 years of teaching, consulting, and executive management experience, working with both Fortune 500 companies and fast-growing entrepreneurial businesses in the U.S., Europe, Asia, and South America. She is the founder of MarketSmarter LLC (www.MarketSmarter.com), a consulting and training firm that helps companies improve business strategy, marketing, and organizational culture to inspire innovation, employee commitment, and customer loyalty. She formerly served as Executive Vice President at Jones Knowledge and as Director of Global Market Development and Corporate Planning at Avaya.

Monique is the author of ***Real-Time Marketing for Business Growth: How to Use Social Media, Measure Marketing and Create a Culture of Execution***, coauthor of ***Market Smarter Not Harder***, and a former columnist for The Denver Business Journal. She currently serves on the Chief Marketing Officer Council (CMO) Academic Liaison Board. She lives in Denver, Colorado and Santa Fe, New Mexico.

Preface

Those who enter the work force today encounter a work/life landscape that is more complex and unpredictable than at any other time in history. The mastery of interpersonal relationship skills gives us the self-confidence needed to achieve success in our highly competitive work force. People who have effective interpersonal skills are more likely to be hired and more likely to receive promotions. People skills become more important the higher you rise in the organization.

Effective Human Relations: Interpersonal and Organizational Applications, twelfth edition, continues to be one of the most practical and applied textbooks available. The revision process involved a review of over 1,000 articles that appeared in *Fast Company, Inc.* magazine, *The Wall Street Journal, Fortune, Harvard Business Review, Health & Spirituality*, and several other journals. The authors have also reviewed numerous best-selling books and research reports written by scholars who are searching for what is true, right, and lasting in the field of interpersonal relations.

BUILDING ON PREVIOUS STRENGTHS

Effective Human Relations: Interpersonal and Organizational Applications, twelfth edition, continues to be one of the most widely adopted human relations texts available today. It has been successful because the authors continue to build on strengths that have been enthusiastically praised by instructors and students.

- The **"total person" approach** to human relations continues to be a dominant theme of this new edition. We continue to believe that human behavior at work and in our private lives is influenced by many interdependent traits such as emotional balance, self-awareness, integrity, self-esteem, physical fitness, and healthy spirituality. This approach focuses on those interpersonal relationship skills needed to be well-rounded and thoroughly prepared to handle a wide range of human relations problems and issues.
- This edition, like all previous editions, provides the reader with an in-depth presentation of the **seven major themes of effective human relations:** Communication, Self-Awareness, Self-Acceptance, Motivation, Trust, Self-Disclosure, and Conflict Resolution. These broad themes serve as the foundation for contemporary human relations courses and training programs.
- **Self-assessment and self-development opportunities** are strategically placed throughout the entire text. One of the few certainties in today's rapidly changing workplace is the realization that we must assume greater responsibility for developing and upgrading our own skills and competencies. In many cases, self-development begins with self-awareness. A deficit in self-awareness can be damaging to one's personal relationships and career success.
- A hallmark of this edition, and of all previous editions, is the use of many **real world examples** of human relations issues and practices. These examples build the reader's interest and promote understanding of major topics and concepts. Many of the organizations cited in the twelfth edition have been recognized by the authors of *The 100 Best Companies to Work For, The 100 Best Corporate Citizens, 100 Best Companies for Working Mothers*, and *America's 50 Best Companies for Minorities*.

The twelfth edition also includes companies who have received the *Top Small Work-place Award* given by the *Wall Street Journal.*

STAYING ON THE CUTTING EDGE—NEW TO THIS EDITION

The twelfth edition of *Effective Human Relations: Interpersonal and Organizational Applications* has been updated to reflect the growing importance of the human element in our service-oriented, information-saturated, global economy. It is a practical text designed to help students achieve the insight, knowledge, and relationship skills needed to deal with a wide range of people-related problems. Staying on the cutting edge requires improvements in every edition.

Major Changes and Improvements

These significant changes and improvements can be found in the twelfth edition:

- Every chapter features a new opening vignette.
- Every chapter includes a new Career Insight that provides practical tips for job-hunters and career changers.
- There are 14 new Human Relations in Action boxed inserts.
- There are 12 new Total Person Insights.
- Twenty-four of the chapter cases are new.
- There are 14 "How To" boxed inserts that emphasize application of key concepts.
- Social media and its impact on communication is included throughout the text.
- New research about positive psychology, and its practical application to organizational and personal communication, is added.
- The significance of a thriving company culture is prominent throughout the text.
- Coverage of generational differences has been updated and expanded.
- Over 40 new photo and cartoon images enhance the learning process.
- Every chapter has been updated to include new real-world and international examples.

CHAPTER ORGANIZATION

This book is divided into six parts. **Part 1, "Human Relations: The Key to Personal Growth and Career Success,"** provides a strong rationale for the study of human relations and reviews the historical development of this field. One important highlight of Chapter 1 is a detailed discussion of the major developments influencing behavior at work. This material helps students develop a new appreciation for the complex nature of human behavior in a work setting. The communication process—the basis for effective human relations—is explained from both an individual and organizational level in Chapter 2. Social media and its impact on communication is discussed in this chapter.

Part 2, "Career Success Begins with Knowing Yourself," reflects the basic fact that our effectiveness in dealing with others depends in large measure on our self-awareness and self-acceptance. We believe that by building high self-esteem and by learning to explore inner attitudes, motivations, and values, the reader will learn to be more sensitive to the way others think, feel, and act. Complete chapters are devoted to such topics as communication styles, building high self-esteem, personal values and ethical choices, attitude formation, and motivation.

Part 3, "Personal Strategies for Improving Human Relations," comprises four chapters that feature a variety of practical strategies that can be used to develop and maintain good relationships with coworkers, supervisors, and customers. Chapters on constructive self-disclosure, learning to achieve emotional control, building stronger relationships by applying the fundamentals of positive psychology, and developing a professional presence are featured in this part of the text.

In **Part 4, "If We All Work Together…,"** the concepts of team building and conflict resolution are given detailed coverage. Because employers are increasingly organizing employees into teams, the chapter on team-building leadership strategies (Chapter 12) takes on major importance. The chapter on conflict resolution (Chapter 13) describes several basic conflict resolution strategies, discusses ways to deal with difficult people, and provides an introduction to the role of labor unions in today's work force.

Part 5, "Special Challenges in Human Relations," is designed to help the reader deal with some unique problem areas—coping with personal and work-related stress, working effectively in a diverse work force, and understanding the changing roles of men and women. The reader is offered many suggestions on ways to deal effectively with these challenges.

Part 6, "You Can Plan for Success," features the final chapter, which serves as a capstone for the entire text. This chapter offers suggestions on how to develop a life plan for effective human relations. Students will be introduced to a new definition of success and learn how to better cope with life's uncertainties and disappointments. This chapter also describes the nonfinancial resources that truly enrich a person's life.

TOOLS THAT ENHANCE THE TEACHING/LEARNING PROCESS

The extensive supplements package accompanying the twelfth edition of *Effective Human Relations: Interpersonal and Organizational Applications* includes a variety of new and traditional tools that will aid both teaching and learning. The supplements emphasize learning by doing.

STUDENT SUPPORT

Management CourseMate

This robust website includes interactive games, quizzes, streaming videos, PowerPoint® slides, and more, and is designed for use in conjunction with the text to enhance learning and broaden student understanding.

INSTRUCTOR SUPPORT

Instructor's Resource Manual

The Instructor's Resource Manual, found on the Instructor CD and protected instructor website, includes two parts. Part One contains, for each chapter, a Chapter Preview, Purpose and Perspective, Presentation Outline, Suggested Responses to Critical Thinking and Skill Development Challenges, Answers to Try Your Hand exercises, and additional application exercises. Part Two contains Instructional Games.

Test Bank

The Test Bank contains 20 True/False, 20 Multiple Choice, 10 Completion, 10 Short Answer/Essay, and 5 Short Case Multiple Choice questions. The Microsoft Word® version of the Test Bank can be found on the Instructor CD and protected instructor website. The enhanced electronic version of the Test Bank, powered by ExamView, is found on the Instructor CD and allows instructors to streamline assessments from start to finish.

PowerPoint® Slides

These dynamic slides are available on the instructor companion website and Instructor CD. The instructor slides follow the structure of the chapter and facilitate in-class discussion of key concepts. Additional talking points and non-text material are included in the instructor version of the slides. The student versions of the slides are available on the CourseMate website.

DVD

The video package consists of several segments that illustrate chapter concepts using examples from real-world companies. Teaching notes and suggested uses for the segments are included in the DVD Guide found on the Instructor CD and instructor website.

Instructor Companion Website

The instructor companion website includes electronic Instructor's Manual files, electronic Test Bank files, PowerPoint® slides, and a DVD Guide.

Instructor's Resource CD

This Instructor CD includes the Instructor's Resource Manual, ExamView software, Test Bank files, DVD Guide, and PowerPoint® slides.

THE SEARCH FOR WISDOM

The search for what is true, right, or lasting has become more difficult because we live in the midst of an information explosion. The Internet is an excellent source of mass information, but it is seldom the source of wisdom. Television often reduces complicated ideas to a sound bite. Books continue to be one of the best sources of knowledge. Many new books, and several classics, were used as references for the twelfth edition of *Effective Human Relations: Interpersonal and Organizational Applications*. A sample of the books we used to prepare this edition follows:

How Full Is Your Bucket? by Tom Rath and Donald O. Clifton

A Whole New Mind by Daniel H. Pink

Now Discover Your Strengths by Marcus Buckingham and Donald O. Clifton

The Success Principles by Jack Canfield

The Leadership Challenge by James M. Kouzes and Barry Z. Posner

The Sedona Method by Hale Dwoskin

The Art of Happiness by the Dalai Lama and Howard C. Culter

Be Your Own Brand by David McNally and Karl D. Speak

Civility—Manners, Morals, and the Etiquette of Democracy by Stephen L. Carter

Complete Business Etiquette Handbook by Barbara Pachter and Majorie Brody

Creative Visualization by Shakti Gawain

Do What You Love … The Money will Follow by Marsha Sinetar

Emotional Intelligence by Daniel Goleman

The Speed of Trust by Stephen M. R. Covey

The Four Agreements by Don Miquel Ruiz

Getting to Yes by Roger Fisher and William Ury

How to Win Friends and Influence People by Dale Carnegie

The Human Side of Enterprise by Douglas McGregor

I'm OK—You're OK by Thomas Harris

Minding the Body, Mending the Mind by Joan Borysenko

Multicultural Manners—New Rules of Etiquette for a Changing Society by Norine Dresser

The 100 Absolutely Unbreakable Laws of Business Success by Brian Tracy

1001 Ways to Reward Employees by Bob Nelson

Psycho-Cybernetics by Maxwell Maltz

Self-Matters: Creating Your Life from the Inside Out by Phillip C. McGraw

The 7 Habits of Highly Effective People by Stephen Covey

The 17 Essential Qualities of a Team Player by John C. Maxwell

The Carrot Principle by Adrian Gostick and Chester Elton

The Six Pillars of Self-Esteem by Nathaniel Branden

Spectacular Teamwork by Robert R. Blake, Jane Srygley Mouton, and Robert L. Allen

Working with Emotional Intelligence by Daniel Goleman

The Five Dysfunctions of a Team by Patrick Lencioni

The Happiness Advantage by Shawn Achor

Happier by Talben-Shahar

Real-Time Marketing for Business Growth by Monique Reece

Peak by Chip Conley

Delivering Happiness by Tony Hsieh

Positivity by Barbara Fredrickson

StrengthsFinder 2.0 by Tom Rath

Crucial Conversations by Kerry Patterson, Joseph Grenny, Ron McMillian, Al Switzler

Fierce Conversations by Susan Scott

Who Moved My Cheese? by Spencer Johnson

ACKNOWLEDGMENTS

Many people have contributed to *Effective Human Relations: Interpersonal and Organizational Applications*. Throughout the years, the text has been strengthened as a result of numerous helpful comments and recommendations. We extend special appreciation to the following reviewers and advisors who have provided valuable input for this and prior editions:

James Aldrich, North Dakota State School of Science

Thorn Amnotte, Eastern Maine Technical College

Garland Ashbacker, Kirkwood Community College

Sue Avila, South Hills Business School

Linda Babcock, Santa Monica Community College

Shirley Banks, Marshall University

Rhonda Barry, American Institute of Commerce

Kenneth Bell, Ellsworth Community College

James A. Bliven, Haskell Indian Nations University

C. Winston Borgen, Sacramento Community College

Jane Bowerman, University of Oklahoma

Jayne P. Bowers, Central Carolina Technical College

Kathy Broneck, Pima Community College

Charles Capps, Sam Houston State University

Lawrence Carter, Jamestown Community College

Cathy Chew, Orange County Community College

Barbara Ching, Los Angeles City College

John P. Cicero, Shasta College

Anne C. Cowden, California State University Sacramento

Michael Dzik, North Dakota State School of Science

Jim Elias, Muscatine Community College

John Elias, University of Missouri

Patrick G. Ellsberg, Lower Columbia College

Marilee Feldman, Kirkwood Community College

Debra Fells, Mesa Community College

Mike Fernsted, Bryant and Stratton Business Institute

Dave Fewins, Neosho County Community College

Dean Flowers, Waukesha County Technical College

Jill P. Gann, Ann Arundel Community College

M. Camille Garrett, Tarrant County junior College

Roberta Greene, Central Piedmont Community College

Ralph Hall, Community College of Southern Nevada

Sally Hanna-Jones, Hocking Technical College

Daryl Hansen, Metropolitan Community College

Carolyn K. Hayes, Polk Community College

John J. Heinsius, Modesto junior College

Stephen Hiatt, Catawba College

Jan Hickman, Westwood College

Larry Hill, San Jacinto College—Central

Bill Hurd, Lowe's Companies, Inc.

Chie Ishihara, Riverside Community College

Lisa R. Jackson, Schoolcraft College

Thomas Jay, Flathead Valley Community College

Dorothy Jeanis, Fresno City College

Marlene Katz, Canada College

Robert Kegel, Jr., Cypress College

Karl N. Kelley, North Central College

Vance A. Kennedy, College of Mateo

Marianne Kozlowski, Evergreen State College

Kristina Leonard, Westwood College

Deborah Lineweaver, New River Community College

Thomas W. Lloyd, Westmoreland County Community College

Jerry Loomis, Fox Valley Technical College

Roger Lynch, Inver Hills Community College

Edward C. Mann, The University of Southern Mississippi

Paul Martin, Aims Community College

James K. McReynolds, South Dakota School of Mines and Technology

Herb Meyer, Scott Community College

Russ Moorhead, Des Moines Area Community College

Marilyn Mueller, Simpson College

Erv J. Napier, Kent State University

Barbara Ollhoff, Waukesha County Technical College

Leonard L. Palumbo, Northern Virginia Community College

James Patton, Mississippi State University

C. Richard Paulson, Mankato State University

Naomi W. Peralta, The Institute of Financial Education

William Price, Virginia Polytechnic Institute and State University

Shirley Pritchett, Northeast Texas Community College

Linda Pulliam, Pulliam Associates Chapel Hill, N.C.

Erin Rea, University of Michigan

Lynne Reece, Alternative Services

Jack C. Reed, University of Northern Iowa

Lynn Richards, Johnson County Community College

Khaled Sartawi, Fort Valley State University

Robert Schaden, Schoolcraft College

Mary R. Shannon, Wenatchie Valley College

J. Douglas Shatto, Muskingum Area Technical College

Dan Smith, Dept. Ohio Business College

Kaischa Smith, Northwestern Michigan College

Marilee Smith, Kirkwood Community College

Camille Stallings, Pima Community College

Lori Stearns, Minnesota West Community Technical College

Cindy Stewart, Des Moines Area Community College

Rahmat O. Tavallali, Wooster Business College

Jane Tavlin, Delgado Community College

V. S. Thakur, Community College of Rhode Island

Linda Truesdale, Midlands Technical College

Wendy Bletz Turner, New River Community College

David Wang, Gateway Technical College

Greg Watson, Eastern Arizona College

Marc Wayner, Hocking Technical College

Tom West, Des Moines Area Community College

Steven Whipple, St. Cloud Technical College

Burl Worley, Allan Hancock College

Over 200 business organizations, government agencies, and nonprofit institutions provided us with the real-world examples that appear throughout the text. We are grateful to those organizations that allowed us to conduct interviews, observe workplace environments, and use special photographs and materials.

The partnership with Cengage Learning has been very rewarding. Several members of the staff have made important contributions to this project. Sincere appreciation is extended to Acquisitions Editor Michele Rhoades, Associate Development Editor Josh Wells, Media Editor Rob Ellington, Editorial Assistant Tammy Grega, and Production Manager Kim Kusnerak.

Barry L. Reece

Monique Reece

Effective Human Relations

Interpersonal and Organizational Applications

PART 1

Human Relations: The Key to Personal Growth and Career Success

CHAPTER 1
Introduction to
Human Relations

CHAPTER 2
Improving Personal and
Organizational Communications

Jupiterimages/Comstock Images/Getty Images

CHAPTER PREVIEW

LEARNING OBJECTIVES

After studying Chapter 1, you will be able to

1-1 Explain the nature, purpose, and importance of human relations.

1-2 Identify major developments in the workplace that have given new importance to human relations.

1-3 Identify major forces influencing human behavior at work.

1-4 Review the historical development of the human relations movement.

1-5 Identify seven major themes that serve as the foundation for effective human relations.

Introduction to Human Relations

TIP OF THE ICEBERG | WORKING FOR THE BEST

Each year, a list of the 100 best companies to work for is published in *Fortune* magazine. *Fortune* partners with the Great Place to Work Institute to conduct an extensive employee survey of corporate America. Job seekers need to study the list carefully because these are companies where morale is high and interpersonal relationships are characterized by a high level of trust and camaraderie.

America's best companies represent a wide range of industries such as software, finance, retailing, hospitality, and manufacturing. Some firms appear on the list almost every year:[1]

SAS Institute

Whole Foods Market

Edward Jones

Marriott International

The Methodist Hospital System

Zappos.com

SAS, the world's largest privately owned software company (5,629 employees), is a 14-year veteran of the Best Companies list. SAS has been ranked number one twice. The company has kept and added benefits when other companies are cutting jobs, pay, and perks. SAS offers a state-of-the-art fitness center, an on-site health center, flexible work schedules, and day care for children.[2]

Fortune magazine also publishes an annual ranking of the World's Most Admired Companies. These are companies that actually believe that employees are their most valuable asset. The most admired firms are more likely to keep people employed—even in a depressed economy.[3]

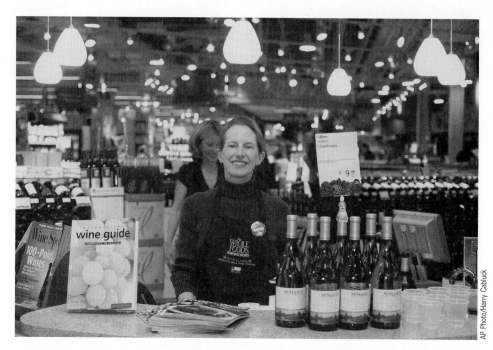

Consistently ranked as one of the Top 100 Companies to work for by *Fortune magazine*, Whole Foods Market focuses on the satisfaction of both its customers and its employees.

TECHNICAL SKILLS AREN'T ENOUGH

1-1   A lack of technical skills is not the primary reason new hires fail to meet employer expectations and experienced workers falter on the road to career success. Today's best companies want new hires to be strong in two areas: technical skills and interpersonal skills. Interpersonal skills, sometimes described as soft or people skills, fall into two categories:[4]

Personal qualities: Treating others with sensitivity, making the right ethical choices, emotional control, ability to work as a team member, etc.

Thinking skills: Ability to engage in creative problem solving, make appropriate decisions, apply critical listening skills, etc.

Interpersonal skills are as learnable as computer programs or a new electronic messaging system. And, interpersonal skills can enhance a résumé and a job interview.

Human Relations Defined

1-2   The term **human relations** in its broadest sense covers all types of interactions among people—their conflicts, cooperative efforts, and group relationships. It is the study of *why* our beliefs, attitudes, and behaviors sometimes cause relationship problems in our personal lives and in work-related situations. The study of human relations emphasizes the analysis of human behavior, prevention strategies, resolution of behavioral problems, and self-development.

Major Developments that Give New Importance to Human Relations

Every organization depends on three essential factors: people, process, and technology. The first success factor is people.[5] Personal and interpersonal effectiveness set the stage for career success. Studies indicate that communication and interpersonal skills are highly rated by nearly all employers who are hiring new employees.

Several important developments in the workplace have given new importance to human relations. Each of the following developments provides support for human relations.

- *The labor market has become a place of churning dislocation caused by the heavy volume of mergers, acquisitions, business closings, bankruptcies, downsizings, and outsourcing of jobs to foreign countries.* Executives often view downsizing as an important step toward profitability. Restructuring efforts often result in low morale and mistrust of management. Employees who remain after a company reduces its ranks also suffer; they often feel demoralized, overworked, and fearful that in the next round of cuts they will be targeted.[6]

- *Changing work patterns create new opportunities and new challenges.* Throughout the past few years, the United States has embraced a flexible labor force. Data reported by the Bureau of Labor Statistics indicates that about 26 percent of working Americans have *nonstandard* jobs. The largest group of people in this category is temporary or part-time workers. Another large segment of the nonstandard workforce are self-employed. When enterprising persons are laid off by corporations, they increasingly become independent consultants, contractors, landscape gardeners, carpenters, and tax consultants.[7]

- *Organizations are increasingly oriented toward service to clients, patients, and customers.* We live in a service economy where relationships are often more important than products. Restaurants, hospitals, banks, public utilities, colleges, airlines, and retail stores all must now gain and retain the patronage of their clients and customers. In any service-type firm, there are thousands of "moments of truth"—those critical incidents in which customers come into contact with the organization and form their impressions of its quality and service.

> *We live in a service economy where relationships are often more important than products.*

- *Workplace incivility is increasingly a threat to employee relationships.* In this information-based, high-tech, speeded-up economy, we are witnessing an increase in workplace incivility. Rude behavior in the form of high-decibel cell phone conversations, use of profanity, or failure to display simple courtesies such as saying "thank you" can damage workplace relationships. Incivility is the ultimate career killer.

- *Many companies are organizing their workers into teams in which each employee plays a part.* Organizations eager to improve quality, improve job satisfaction, increase worker participation in decision making and problem solving, and improve customer service are turning to teams.

  Although some organizations have successfully harnessed the power of teams, others have encountered problems. One barrier to productivity is the employee who lacks the skills needed to be a team member. In making the transition to a team environment, team members need skills in group decision making, leadership, conflict resolution, and communications.[8]

- *Diversity has become a prominent characteristic of today's work force.* A number of trends have contributed to greater work force diversity. Throughout the past two decades, participation in the labor force by Asian Americans, African Americans, and Hispanics has increased; labor force participation by adult women has risen to a record 60 percent; the employment door for people with physical or mental impairments has opened wider; and larger numbers of young workers are working with members of the expanding 50-plus age group. Within this heterogeneous work force, we will find a multitude of values, expectations, and work habits. The major aspects of work force diversity are discussed in Chapters 15 and 16.

Total Person Insight

"It is teamwork that remains the ultimate competitive advantage, both because it is so powerful and so rare."

Source: Patrick Lencioni, *The Five Dysfunctions of a Team* (San Francisco: Jossey-Bass, 2002), p. vii.

These developments represent trends that will no doubt continue for many years. Many other developments have also had an unsettling impact on the U.S. work force in recent years. In 2001, the economy was jarred by the collapse of several hundred dot.com companies. The World Trade Center terrorist attack on September 11, 2001, crippled the airline and aerospace industries. In 2002, public trust in the corporate establishment was shaken by a wave of corporate scandals that involved Enron, Tyco, Merrill Lynch, Arthur Anderson, WorldCom, and many other companies. In 2007, our economy slumped into a recession triggering a sharp rise in unemployment and underemployment.

The Challenge of Human Relations

To develop and apply the wide range of human skills needed in today's workplace can be extremely challenging. You will be working with clients, customers, patients, and other

Figure 1.1 ■ Major Relationship Management Challenges

workers who vary greatly in age, work background, communications style, values, cultural background, gender, and work ethic.

Human relations is further complicated by the fact that we must manage three types of relationships (see Figure 1.1). The first relationship is the one with ourselves. Many people carry around a set of ideas and feelings about themselves that are quite negative and in most cases quite inaccurate. People who have negative feelings about their abilities and accomplishments and who engage in constant self-criticism must struggle to maintain a good relationship with themselves. The importance of high self-esteem is addressed in Chapter 4.

human
RELATIONS
in Action

DEFINING TALENT AT PWC

PricewaterhouseCoopers has 175,000 employees working in 154 countries. The company provides a wide range of audit, tax, and advisory services. Dennis Nally, CEO, says having technical skills is important but that's almost a given these days. *Talent* is having the right softer skills in terms of being able to work in a collaborative environment, teaming with people, communicating well, and demonstrating sensitivities to cultural diversity.

Source: Javier Espinoza, "PwC's CEO Switches Tactics to Keep Millennials," *Wall Street Journal*, July 11, 2011, p. B4.

The second type of relationship we must learn to manage is the one-to-one relationships we face in our personal and work lives. People in the health-care field, sales, food service, and a host of other occupations face this challenge many times each day. In some cases, racial, age, or gender bias serves as a barrier to good human relations. Communication style bias, a topic that is discussed in Chapter 3, is another common barrier to effective one-to-one relationships.

The third challenge we face is the management of relationships with members of a group. As already noted, many workers are assigned to a team on either a full-time or a part-time basis. Lack of cooperation among team members can result in quality problems or a slowdown in production.

The Influence of the Behavioral Sciences

The field of human relations draws on the behavioral sciences—psychology, sociology, and anthropology. Basically, these sciences focus on the *why* of human behavior. Psychology attempts to find out why *individuals* act as they do, and sociology and anthropology concentrate primarily on *group* dynamics and social interaction. Human relations differs from the behavioral sciences in one important respect. Although also interested in the why of human behavior, human relations goes further and looks at what can be done to anticipate problems, resolve them, or even prevent them from happening. In other words, this field emphasizes knowledge that can be *applied* in practical ways to problems of interpersonal relations at work or in our personal life.

Human Relations and the "Total Person"

The material in this book focuses on human relations as the study of *how people satisfy both personal and work-related needs.* We believe, as do most authors in the field of interpersonal relations, that such human traits as physical fitness, emotional control, self-awareness, self-esteem, and values orientation are interdependent. Although some organizations may occasionally wish they could employ only a person's physical strength or creative powers, all that can be employed is the **total person**. A person's separate characteristics are part of a single system making up that whole person. Work life is not totally separate from home life, and emotional conditions are not separate from physical conditions. The quality of one's work, for example, is often related to physical fitness or one's ability to cope with the stress created by family problems.

Many organizations are beginning to recognize that when the whole person is improved, significant benefits accrue to the firm. These organizations are establishing employee development programs that address the total person, not just the employee skills needed to perform the job. Gregg Appliances, Inc., an appliance and electronics retail chain, offers employees education programs that help them cope with marital stresses.[9] International Business Machines has launched a program to combat childhood obesity among employees' children.[10] Some organizations offer lunchtime seminars on financial planning, parenting skills, and other topics.

Total Person Insight

"The rules for work are changing, and we're all being judged, whether we know it or not, by a new yardstick—not just how smart we are and what technical skills we have, which employers see as givens, but increasingly by how well we handle ourselves and one another."

Source: Anne Fisher, "Success Secret: A High Emotional IQ," *Fortune*, October 26, 1998, p. 293.

The Need for a Supportive Environment

Some persons in leadership positions do not believe that total person development, job enrichment, motivation techniques, or career development strategies help increase productivity or strengthen worker commitment to the job. It is true that when such practices are tried without full commitment or without full management support, there is a good chance they will fail. Such failures often have a demoralizing effect on employees and management alike.

A basic assumption of this book is that human relations, when applied in a positive and supportive environment, can help individuals achieve greater personal satisfaction from their careers and help increase an organization's productivity and efficiency.

human
RELATIONS
in Action

RÉSUMÉ PREPARATION

You are in the process of preparing a résumé that will be used in conjunction with several upcoming job interviews. Assume that you cannot include any past employment experience, training programs, degrees, awards, or community service. The only data you can put on your résumé are the interpersonal skills that you have developed. How would you select and document these critical transferable skills?

Source: Adapted from Marshall Goldsmith, "Nice Guys Can Finish First," *Fast Company*, November 2004, p. 123.

THE FORCES INFLUENCING BEHAVIOR AT WORK

1-3   A major purpose of this text is to increase your knowledge of factors that influence human behavior in a variety of work settings. An understanding of human behavior at work begins with a review of the six major forces that affect every employee, regardless of the size of the organization. As Figure 1.2 indicates, these are organizational

Figure 1.2 ■ Major Forces Influencing Worker Behavior

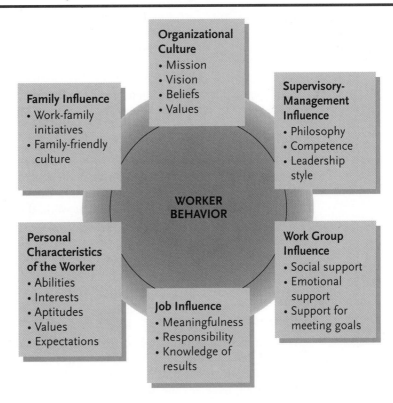

culture, supervisory-management influence, work group influence, job influence, personal characteristics of the worker, and family influence.

Organizational Culture

Every organization, whether a manufacturing plant, retail store, hospital, or government agency, has its own unique culture. The **organizational culture** is the collection of shared values, beliefs, rituals, stories, and myths that foster a feeling of community among organizational members.[11] The culture of an organization is, in most cases, the reflection of the deeply held values and behaviors of a small group of individuals. In a large organization, the chief executive officer (CEO) and a handful of senior executives will shape the culture. In a small company, the culture may flow from the values held by the founder.[12]

Enron Corporation, the second-largest company in U.S. history to file for bankruptcy, maintained a corporate culture that pushed everything to the limits: business practices, laws, and personal behavior. This culture drove Enron to dizzying growth, but it eventually collapsed under the weight of greed, deception, and corruption.[13]

By contrast, Google, the popular Internet search engine, has developed a culture that emphasizes customer service. One slogan summarizes the Google philosophy: "Focus on the user and all else will follow."[14] Google ranks near the top of *Fortune's* Best Companies to Work For list.

In the new economy, almost every source of organizational success—technology, financial structure, and competitive strategy—can be copied in an amazingly short period of time.[15] However, making customers the center of the company culture can take years.

Supervisory-Management Influence

It is no exaggeration to say that supervisors and managers are the spokespersons for the organization.

Supervisory-management personnel are in a key position to influence employee behavior. It is no exaggeration to say that supervisors and managers are the spokespersons for the organization. Their philosophy, competence, leadership style, and integrity establish the organization's image in the eyes of employees. Each employee develops certain perceptions about the organization's concern for his or her welfare. These perceptions, in turn, influence such important factors as productivity, customer relations, safety consciousness, and loyalty to the firm.

Work Group Influence

In recent years, behavioral scientists have devoted considerable research to determining the influence of group affiliation on the individual worker. This research has identified three functions of group membership. First, it can satisfy *social needs*. When employees feel more connected to their colleagues at work, they are generally more productive.[16] Many people find the hours spent at work enjoyable because coworkers provide needed social support. Second, the work group can provide the *emotional support* needed to deal with pressures and problems on or off the job. Finally, the group provides *assistance in solving problems* and *meeting goals*. A cohesive work group lends support and provides the resources we need to be productive workers.

Job Influence

Work in modern societies does more than fulfill economic needs. When we find meaning and fulfillment in our jobs, we become more complete as human beings.[17] As one organizational consultant noted, work has taken center stage in the lives of most people: "We spend most of our waking hours doing our jobs, thinking about work, and

A work group can be a positive influence in employees' lives when group members offer each other job assistance and emotional support.

getting to and from our workplaces. When we feel good about our work, we tend to feel good about our lives. When we find our work unsatisfying and unrewarding, we don't feel good."[18] Unfortunately, many people hold jobs that do not make them feel good. Many workers perceive their jobs to be meaningless and boring. Some workers experience frustration because they feel powerless to influence their working conditions.

Personal Characteristics of the Worker

Every worker brings to the job a combination of abilities, interests, aptitudes, values, and expectations. Worker behavior on the job is most frequently a reflection of how well the work environment accommodates the unique characteristics of each worker.

Identifying the ideal work environment for today's work force is difficult. A single parent may greatly value a flexible work schedule and child care. The recipient of a new business degree may seek a position with a new high-tech firm, hoping to make a lot of money in a hurry. Other workers may desire more leisure time, and some workers seek job security.

Coming into the workplace today is a new generation of workers with value systems and expectations about work that often differ from those of the previous generation. Today's better-educated and better-informed workers value identity and achievement. They also have a heightened sense of their rights.

Family Influence

A majority of undergraduates and those currently employed name balancing work and personal life as their top career goal.[19] Most people want time for family, friends, and leisure pursuits. However, finding employers who truly support work/life balance can be difficult, especially during a slowing economy.

The number of dual-income families has doubled since 1950. Both parents have jobs in over 60 percent of married-couple homes. When both partners are working long hours, it may be difficult to balance career and family choices. Some long-standing work and family problems include a lack of quality, affordable child care, inflexible work schedules, and time management problems. These issues will be discussed in Chapter 16.

THE DEVELOPMENT OF THE HUMAN RELATIONS MOVEMENT

1-4   The early attempts to improve productivity in manufacturing focused mainly on trying to improve such things as plant layout and mechanical processes. But, over time, there was more interest in redefining the nature of work and perceiving workers as complex human beings. This change reflected a shift in values from a concern with *things* to a greater concern for *people*. In this section, we briefly examine a few major developments that influenced the human relations movement.

The Impact of the Industrial Revolution

The Industrial Revolution marked a shift from home-based, handcrafted processes to large-scale factory production. Before the Industrial Revolution, most work was performed by individual craft workers or members of craft guilds. Generally, each worker saw a project through from start to finish. Skills such as tailoring, carpentry, and shoemaking took a long time to perfect and were often a source of pride to an individual or a community. Under this system, however, output was limited.

The Industrial Revolution had a profound effect on the nature of work and the role of the worker. Previously, an individual tailor could make only a few items of clothing in a week's time; factories could now make hundreds. However, the early industrial plants were not very efficient because there was very little uniformity in the way tasks were performed. It was this problem that set the stage for research by a man who changed work forever.

Taylor's Scientific Management

In 1874, Frederick W. Taylor obtained a job as an apprentice in a machine shop. He rose to the position of foreman, and, in this role, he became aware of the inefficiency and waste throughout the plant. In most cases, workers were left on their own to determine how to do their jobs. Taylor began to systematically study each job and break it down into its smallest movements. He discovered ways to reduce the number of motions and get rid of time-wasting efforts. Workers willing to follow Taylor's instruction found that their productivity increased.[20]

Frederick W. Taylor started the **scientific management** movement, and his ideas continue to influence the workplace today. Critics of Taylor's approach say that the specialized tasks workers perform often require manual skills but very little or no thinking.

Total Person Insight

"You can only get so much more productivity out of reorganization and automation. Where you really get productivity leaps is in the minds and hearts of people."

Source: James Baughman quote from Frank Rose, "A New Age for Business?" *Fortune*, October 8, 1990, p. 162.

Mayo's Hawthorne Studies

Harvard Business School Professor Elton Mayo and his colleagues accidentally discovered part of the answer to variations in worker performance while conducting research in the mid-1920s at the Hawthorne Western Electric plant, located near Chicago. Their original goal was to study the effect of illumination, ventilation, and fatigue on production workers in the plant. Their research, known as the **Hawthorne studies**, became a sweeping investigation into the role of human relations in group and individual productivity. These studies also gave rise to the profession of industrial psychology by legitimizing the human factor as an element in business operations.[21]

After three years of experimenting with lighting and other physical aspects of work, Mayo made two important discoveries. First, all the attention focused on workers who participated in the research made them feel more important. For the first time, they were getting feedback on their job performance. In addition, test conditions allowed them greater freedom from supervisory control. Under these circumstances, morale and motivation increased and productivity rose.

Second, Mayo found that the interaction of workers on the job created a network of relationships called an **informal organization**. This organization exerted considerable influence on workers' performance.

Although some observers have criticized the Hawthorne studies for flawed research methodology, this research laid the foundation for the field of organizational behavior.[22]

From the Great Depression to Today

During the Great Depression, interest in human relations research waned as other ways of humanizing the workplace gained momentum. During that period, unions increased their militant campaigns to organize workers and force employers to pay attention to such issues as working conditions, higher pay, shorter hours, and protection for child laborers.

After World War II and during the years of postwar economic expansion, interest in the human relations field increased. Countless papers and research studies on worker efficiency, group dynamics, organization, and motivational methods were published. Douglas McGregor, in his classic book *The Human Side of Enterprise,* argued that how well an organization performs is directly proportional to its ability to tap human potential.[23] Abraham Maslow, a noted psychologist, devised a "hierarchy of needs," stating that people satisfied their needs in a particular order. Later, Frederick Herzberg proposed an important theory of employee motivation based on satisfaction. Each theory had considerable influence on the study of motivation and is explored in detail in Chapter 7.

Since the 1950s, theories and concepts regarding human behavior have focused more and more on an understanding of human interaction. Eric Berne, in the 1960s, revolutionized the way people think about interpersonal communication when he introduced transactional analysis, with its "Parent-Adult-Child" model. At about the same time, Carl Rogers published his work on personality development, interpersonal communication, and group dynamics.

Peter Drucker, often described as the greatest management thinker and writer of all time, influenced organizational behavior for a period of 60 years. He originated the view of the corporation as a human community built on trust and respect for the worker. He made clear there is "No business without a customer," a simple concept that created greater support for customer services.[24]

BIG-BOOK BLOCKBUSTERS

Each year, between 4,000 and 5,000 new books claiming to be about business are published. Here is a list of five heavyweights that have had a major impact on the way we view interpersonal relations:

- *The One Minute Manager* by Kenneth Blanchard and Spencer Johnson. (Published in 1982 and still making best-seller lists.)

- *Reengineering the Corporation* by Michael Hammer and James Champy. (A *BusinessWeek* reviewer said, "May well be the best-written book for the managerial masses since *In Search of Excellence*.")

- *Built to Last* by Jim Collins. (According to *USA Today*, it's "one of the most eye-opening business studies since *In Search of Excellence*.)

- *In Search of Excellence* by Tom Peters and Robert Waterman. (Described by the *Wall Street Journal* as "one of those rare books on management that are both consistently thought provoking and fun to read.")

- *How to Win Friends and Influence People* by Dale Carnegie. (Published in 1936 and still a best seller.)

Source: Adapted from Ryan Underwood, "A Field Guide to the Gurus," *Fast Company*, November 2004, p. 104.

There is no doubt that management consultants Tom Peters and Robert Waterman also influenced management thinking regarding the importance of people in organizations. Their best-selling book *In Search of Excellence*, published in 1982, describes eight attributes of excellence found in America's best-run companies. One of these attributes, "productivity through people," emphasizes that excellent companies treat the worker as the root source of quality and productivity. The editors of *Fast Company* magazine say that *In Search of Excellence* "fired the starting gun in the race to the New Economy."[25]

We have provided you with no more than a brief glimpse of selected developments in the human relations movement. Space does not permit a review of the hundreds of theorists and practitioners who have influenced human relations in the workplace. However, in the remaining chapters, we do introduce the views of other influential thinkers and authors.

MAJOR THEMES IN HUMAN RELATIONS

1-5   Seven broad themes emerge from the study of human relations. They are communication, self-awareness, self-acceptance, motivation, trust, self-disclosure, and conflict resolution. These themes reflect the current concern in human relations with the twin goals of (1) personal growth and development and (2) the achievement of organizational objectives. To some degree, these themes are interrelated (see Figure 1.3), and most are discussed in more than one chapter of this book.

Communication

It is not an exaggeration to describe communication as the "heart and soul" of human relations. **Communication** is the means by which we come to an understanding of ourselves and others. To grow and develop as persons, we must develop the awareness and the skills necessary to communicate effectively. Communication is the *human* connection. That is why the subject is covered in more than one section of this book. In

Figure 1.3 ■ Major Themes in Human Relations

Communication

Conflict resolution

Self-awareness

EFFECTIVE HUMAN RELATIONS

Self-disclosure

Self-acceptance

Trust

Motivation

Chapter 2, we explore the fundamentals of both personal and organizational communication. It is these fundamentals that provide the foundation for all efforts to improve communication. Chapter 3 provides an introduction to communication styles and outlines several practical tips on how you can cope with communication style bias. Chapter 8 explains how constructive self-disclosure, an important form of personal communication, can be used to improve human relationships.

Self-Awareness

One of the most important ways to develop improved relationships with others is to develop a better understanding of ourselves. With increased **self-awareness** comes a greater understanding of how our behavior influences others. The late Stephen Covey, author of *The Seven Habits of Highly Effective People,* says that self-awareness enables us to stand apart and examine the way we "see" ourselves, as well as to see other people.[26]

> *The importance of self-awareness is being recognized by an increasing number of authors, trainers, and educators.*

The importance of self-awareness is being recognized by an increasing number of authors, trainers, and educators. Daniel Goleman, author of the best-selling book *Emotional Intelligence,* has given us new insights into the importance of self-awareness. Goleman says IQ accounts for only about 20 percent of a person's success in life. The rest, he says, you can credit to "emotional intelligence." Of all the elements that make up emotional intelligence, Goleman asserts, self-awareness is the most important. He notes that a deficit in self-awareness can be damaging to one's personal relationships and career.[27] Self-awareness is discussed in greater detail in the chapters that are featured in Part 2.

human
RELATIONS
in Action

LIFE CHANGING MEETING

Jim Collins, best-selling author, recalls a life-changing meeting with Peter Drucker. Collins says Drucker altered the direction of his life by focusing the discussion around one simple question: "What do you want to contribute?"

Self-Acceptance

The degree to which you like and accept yourself is the degree to which you can genuinely like and accept other people. **Self-acceptance** is the foundation of successful interaction with others. In a work setting, people with positive self-concepts tend to cope better with change, accept responsibility more readily, tolerate differences, and generally work well as team members. A negative self-concept, however, can create barriers to good interpersonal relations. Self-acceptance is crucial not only for building relationships with others but also for setting and achieving goals. The more you believe you can do, the more you are likely to accomplish. Chapter 4 explains why high self-esteem (complete self-acceptance) is essential for effective human relations. That chapter also helps you identify ways to achieve greater self-acceptance.

Motivation

Most people who engage in the study of **motivation** seek answers to two questions: "How do I motivate myself?" and "How do I motivate others?" If you are really committed to achieving peak performance, you must motivate yourself from within.[28] Inner drives for excellence can be very powerful. Chapter 4 will help you identify the priorities and values that motivate you. To motivate others, you need to understand time-proven, well-researched theories and well-established motivation strategies. Chapter 5 will help you identify the priorities and values that motivate you. Chapter 7 explores the complex nature of human motivation, particularly of self and others, and examines various motivation strategies. In Chapter 10, you will learn how incentives and various positive reinforcement methods serve as external motivators.

Trust

Trust is the building block of all successful relationships with coworkers, customers, family members, and friends. There is compelling evidence that low levels of trust in a work force can lead to reduced productivity, stifled innovation, high stress, and slow decision making.[29] When a lack of trust exists in an organization, a decline in the flow of information almost always results. Employees communicate less information to their supervisors, express opinions reluctantly, and avoid discussions. Cooperation, so necessary in a modern work setting, deteriorates. When a climate of trust is present, frank discussion of problems and a free exchange of ideas and information are encouraged. The concept of trust is discussed in Chapters 8 and 12.

Self-Disclosure

Self-disclosure and trust are two halves of a whole. The more open you are with people, the more trust you build. The more trust there is in a relationship, the safer you feel to disclose who you are. Self-disclosure is also part of good communication and helps eliminate unnecessary guessing games. Managers who let their subordinates know what is expected of them help those employees fulfill their responsibilities. Chapter 8 emphasizes the need of individuals to verbalize the thoughts and feelings they carry within them and provides many practical suggestions on how to use constructive self-disclosure.

Conflict Resolution

Conflict in one form or another surfaces almost daily in the lives of many workers. You may experience conflict during a commute to work when a careless driver cuts

Vincent Yu/AP Photos

Conflict can be difficult to resolve in a productive way when a lot is at stake, as when Costa Rica's Coach Alexandre Guimaraes argued with an opposing coach during the 2002 World Cup soccer game.

you off at a freeway exit ramp. If your job includes supervisory-management responsibilities, you will spend a great deal of time in **conflict resolution**, attempting to resolve conflicts among members of your staff. As a team member, you may assume the role of mediator when other team members clash. Conflict also surfaces when working parents attempt to balance the demands of both work and family. Stressful conditions at home often interfere with work performance, and on-the-job pressures create or magnify problems at home.[30] The ability to anticipate or resolve conflict can be an invaluable skill. Although Chapter 13 deals specifically with the topic of conflict resolution, the chapters devoted to communication, achievement of emotional control, and team building provide many valuable suggestions on how conflict can be handled constructively.

HUMAN RELATIONS: BENEFITS TO YOU

As previously noted, the work force is currently characterized by downsizing, mergers, buyouts, business closings, and other disruptive forces. We are seeing more emphasis on quality products and quality services. In addition, diversity has become a more prominent characteristic of today's work force. These conditions will very likely continue in the new millennium. One of the best ways to cope with these changes is to develop and apply the interpersonal skills needed for success in today's working world.

Many leaders think that courses in human relations are important because very few workers are responsible to themselves alone. These leaders point out that most jobs today are interdependent. If people in these jobs cannot work effectively as a team, the efficiency of the organization will suffer.

LOOKING BACK: SUMMARY OF LEARNING OBJECTIVES

1. **Explain the nature, purpose, and importance of human relations.**

   The healthy functioning of any organization, large or small, depends on teamwork. Effective human relations are the very foundation of teamwork. Human relations, when applied in a positive and supportive environment, can help increase an organization's productivity and efficiency.

2. **Identify major developments in the workplace that have given new importance to human relations.**

   The restructuring of America from an industrial economy to an information economy has had profound implications for the study of human relations. Several major developments in the workplace have given new importance to this branch of learning. Some of these developments include churning dislocation in the labor market, changing work patterns, the need for higher service standards, increasing workplace incivility, greater reliance on team-based structures, and work force diversity.

3. **Identify major forces influencing human behavior at work.**

   A key purpose of this text is to increase understanding of major factors that influence human behavior in a variety of work settings. These include organizational culture, supervisory-management influence, work group influence, job influence, personal characteristics of individual workers, and family influence.

4. **Review the historical development of the human relations movement.**

   Early attempts to improve productivity in manufacturing focused on such things as plant layout and mechanical processes. With the passing of time, there was more interest in redefining the nature of work and perceiving workers as complex human beings. Two landmarks in the study of motivation and worker needs are Frederick Taylor's work in scientific management and Elton Mayo's Hawthorne studies. Later research by Douglas McGregor, Frederick Herzberg, Carl Rogers, Peter Drucker, and others contributed greatly to our understanding of how to achieve productivity through people.

5. **Identify seven major themes that serve as the foundation for effective human relations.**

   Seven major themes emerge from a study of human relations: communication, self-awareness, self-acceptance, motivation, trust, self-disclosure, and conflict resolution. These themes reflect the current concern in human relations with personal growth and satisfaction of organization objectives.

KEY TERMS

human relations, 4
total person, 8
organizational culture, 10
scientific management, 12
Hawthorne studies, 13

informal organization, 13
communication, 14
self-awareness, 15
self-acceptance, 16

motivation, 16
trust, 16
self-disclosure, 16
conflict resolution, 17

CAREER INSIGHT

The daily news sources are constantly reporting on mergers, business closings, downsizing, and changing business trends. With so much uncertainty in the job market, you need to devote time to answering the following questions:

1. What are your career goals? Although you will no doubt change careers several times, now is the time to carefully study career options.

2. What transferable skills do you currently possess? What skills need to be developed? "Millions of people make a career-change each year without going back to school," says Richard N. Bolles, author of the best-selling book, *What Color is Your Parachute*.[31]

TRY YOUR HAND

1. In his book, *The Success Principles*, Jack Canfield describes 50 principles that will increase your confidence, help you tackle daily challenges, and teach you how to realize your ambitions. Number one on his list is "Take 100% responsibility for your life." This includes the quality of your relationships, your health and fitness, your income, your career success—everything! He says most of us have been conditioned to blame events outside of our life for those parts of our life we dislike. Reflect on your life up to this point and identify situations in which you blamed someone or something else for your failure to achieve a goal or improve in some area. Do you see any situations in which you felt justified in blaming others or refused to take risks?[32]

2. Human relations and the *total person* concept are interwoven in the 17 chapters of this text. Progressive organizations recognize that most employees are striving to satisfy both personal and work related needs. They also recognize that employees display a wide range of interrelated human traits such as emotional control, values orientation, and self-awareness.
   a. Analyze the importance of creating an organizational culture that meets the needs of the *total person*.
   b. Many organizations that have been selected for *Fortune* magazine's list of 100 best companies to work for in America provide benefits that meet the needs of the total person. Brainstorm with classmates the benefits you will seek throughout your employment career.

3. Companies featured in *Fortune*'s list of the 100 best companies to work for in America are characterized by openness, fairness, camaraderie among employees, job security, opportunities for advancement, and sensitivity to work/family issues. These companies are concerned about the total person, not just the skills that help the company earn a profit. Here are some of the companies that have made the "best companies" list:

Company	Location	Type of Business
NetApp	Sunnyvale, CA	Storage & Data Management
Zappos.com	Henderson, NV	E-Commerce Retailer
Edward Jones	St. Louis, MO	Financial Services
DreamWorks	Glendale, CA	Animation
Marriott International	Washington, DC	Hotel Chain
Quicken Loans	Detroit, MI	Online Mortgage Lender

Develop a profile of two of these companies by visiting their websites and reviewing the available information. Also, visit Hoover's Inc. website, a resource that provides access to profiles of thousands of companies. Additional information on each of these companies may be found in *Bloomberg Businessweek*, *Forbes*, *Fortune*, and other business publications.

CRITICAL THINKING CHALLENGE

To achieve a better understanding of the major themes in human relations, complete the sentences below. Work quickly and don't worry too much about the ending. Sentence completion exercises can be powerful vehicles for self-discovery and personal growth.

■ To become more self accepting I need to…

■ To build a more trusting relationship with others, I need to…
■ My greatest strength in the area of communication is…
■ To grow in the area of self-awareness, I need to…
■ I am motivated to give my best when…

SELF-ASSESSMENT EXERCISE

For each of the following statements, circle the number from 1 to 5 that best represents your response: (1) strongly disagree (never do this); (2) disagree (rarely do this); (3) moderately agree (sometimes do this); (4) agree (frequently do this); (5) strongly agree (almost always do this).

A. I accept the premise that within an organization all work is influenced by relationships.	1	2	3	4	5
B. I accept the view that major developments in the workplace have given new importance to the study of human relations.	1	2	3	4	5
C. I view human relations as the study of how people satisfy both personal and work-related needs.	1	2	3	4	5
D. I understand the major forces influencing worker behavior.	1	2	3	4	5
E. I can explain the major themes that emerge from the study of human relations.	1	2	3	4	5

After identifying your response to each item, select an attitude or skill you would like to improve. Prepare a written goal and then describe the steps you will take to achieve this goal.

YOU PLAY THE ROLE

The college you attend offers career counseling, job placement assistance, and help finding summer internships. You plan to meet with a career counselor and seek help finding a summer internship with a well-established company. You will be meeting with a class member, who will assume the role of career counselor. The purpose of this meeting is to give the counselor some basic information about your career plans and the type of company you would like to work for. Before the meeting, prepare a written outline of information you plan to present during the meeting. Base your notes on your academic studies and your current employment interests. The outline should focus on the following areas:

- Define what type of work would be most meaningful.
- Describe what type of organizational culture would be most appealing to you.
- Identify what you find to be the basic rewards of work.

BELOW THE SURFACE | CAMPUS LIFE AT SAS

At the beginning of this chapter, we introduced SAS Institute, a very successful software company located in Cary, North Carolina. SAS sells software that helps organizations analyze and mine vast amounts of data to predict customer preferences and other trends.

Visit the 300-acre SAS campus and you will discover one of the most perk-friendly workplaces in the world. Feeling stress? Visit the weight room, billiards hall, sauna, or swim in the Olympic-size pool. You might also consider a walk through the oaken woods or a visit to the meditation garden. Need basic health care? Visit the health-care center staffed by four physicians, 10 nurse practitioners, nutritionists, physical therapists, and a psychologist.[33]

The architect of this rare corporate culture is Jim Goodnight, former professor at North Carolina State

University. He takes pride in the low rate of employee turnover and the high morale among his workers. Goodnight plans to continue adding employee benefits while many other companies are cutting jobs, pay, and perks. During an interview with *Fortune* magazine editors he said, "My chief assets drive out the gate every day. My job is to make sure they come back."[34]

QUESTIONS

1. We noted in this chapter that when the whole person (total person concept) is improved, significant benefits accrue to the firm. In what ways has SAS embraced the total person concept?

2. How might a smaller company, with fewer resources, embrace the total person concept?

CLOSING CASE — IN SEARCH OF WORK/LIFE BALANCE

A growing number of workers do not feel there's a healthy balance between work and personal life. Some are tired of working 10- to 12-hour days and weekends. Many want a better balance between work and family. These employees search for companies that offer family-friendly features such as flexible scheduling, telecommuting, and child care. Each year *Working Mother* magazine publishes a list of the 100 best companies for working mothers. Let's look at two of the companies that made the 2011 list.[35]

- *American Express* This financial services company describes its commitment to the health of its employees as a "core business value." Employees who want to lose weight, screen for medical conditions, or reduce stress can consult with nurses, health coaches, dietitians, and physicians at company sponsored wellness clinics. The company offers seminars on eating well and cafeterias with nutritious meals.

- *Bain & Company* This Boston based management consulting firm offers all employees flexible schedules and the opportunity to work off-site. Women may reduce their work schedules by 40 percent and still be considered for promotions. The firm offers fully paid maternity leave for up to 12 weeks.

QUESTIONS

1. What are some of the economic benefits that justify the family-friendly services offered by these two companies?

2. Some companies develop work/life programs that focus primarily on employees who have children. What are the advantages and disadvantages of this approach?

CHAPTER 1 ENDNOTES

1. Milton Moskowitz, Robert Levering, and Christopher T. Kaczyk, "100 Best Companies to Work For," *Fortune*, February, 2011, pp. 91–101.
2. David A. Kaplan, "The Best Company to Work For," *Fortune*, February 8, 2010, pp. 57–64.
3. Geoff Colvin, "Opinion," *Fortune*, March 22, 2010.
4. Heidi R. Perreault, "What Makes the Soft Skills so Hard," *The Delta Pi Epsilon Journal*, Fall, 2006, pp. 125–127.
5. Gerhard Gschwandtner, "The Magic Formula for Sustainable Success," *Selling Power*, June 2006, p.10.
6. Joann S. Lublin, "Mergers Often Trigger Anxiety, Lower Morale," *Wall Street Journal*, January 16, 2001, pp. B1, B4; Daniel Roth, "How to Cut Pay, Lay Off 8,000 People, and Still Have Workers Who Love You," *Fortune*, February 4, 2002, pp. 63–68.

7. James O'Toole and Edward C. Lawler, III, "A Piece of Work," *Fast Company*, June 2006, p. 88; Peter Cog, Michelle Conlin, and Moira Herbst, "The Disposable Worker," *Bloomberg Businessweek*, January 18, 2010, pp. 33–39.

8. Jeff Pettit, "Team Communication: It's in the Cards," *Training & Development*, January 1997, p. 12.

9. Rachel Emma Silverman, "Working on Your Marriage—at Work," *Wall Street Journal*, May 31, 2007, p. 1.

10. William M. Bulkeley, "IBM to Help Pay for Plans to Curb Childhood Obesity," *Wall Street Journal*, October 24, 2007, p. D4.

11. Robert Kreitner, *Management*, 9th ed. (Boston: Houghton Mifflin, 2004), p. 304.

12. Allan A. Kennedy, interview by, in "The Culture Wars," *Inc.*, 20th Anniversary Issue, 1999, pp. 107–108.

13. Anita Raghavan, Kathryn Kranhold, and Alexei Barrionuevo, "How Enron Bosses Created a Culture of Pushing Limits," *Wall Street Journal*, August 26, 2002, p. B1.

14. David A. Price, "How Google Got Going," *Wall Street Journal*, July 12, 2011, p. A13.

15. Jeffrey Pfeffer, *The Human Equation* (Boston: Harvard Business School Press, 1998), p. 293.

16. Sue Shellenbarger, "Along with Benefits and Pay, Employees Seek Friends on the Job," *Wall Street Journal*, February 20, 2002, p. B1.

17. "Great Expectations," *Fast Company*, November 1999, p. 224.

18. Betsy Jacobson and Beverly Kaye, "Balancing Act," *Training & Development*, February 1993, p. 26.

19. Sue Shellenbarger, "Job Candidates Prepare to Sacrifice Some Frills and Balance—For Now," *Wall Street Journal*, November 21, 2001, p. B1; Stephanie Armour, "Workers Put Family First Despite Slow Economy, Jobless Fears," *USA Today*, June 6, 2002, p. 38; "Work-Life Balance Tops Pay," *USA Today*, March 13, 2008, p. 1B.

20. Alan Farnham, "The Man Who Changed Work Forever," *Fortune*, July 21, 1997, p. 114; Cynthia Crossen, "Early Industry Expert Soon Realized a Staff Has Its Own Efficiency," *Wall Street Journal*, November 6, 2006, p. B1.

21. Bradley J. Rieger, "Lessons in Productivity and People," *Training & Development*, October 1995, pp. 56–58.

22. "A Field Is Born," *Harvard Business Review*, July/August 2008, p. 164.

23. Jim Collins, "The Classics," *Inc.*, December 1996, p. 55.

24. John A. Byrne, "The Man Who Invented Management," *BusinessWeek*, November 28, 2005, pp. 97–106.

25. Thomas J. Peters and Robert H. Waterman, Jr., *In Search of Excellence: Lessons from America's Best-Run Companies* (New York: Harper & Row, 1982), p. 14; Tom Peters, "Tom Peters' True Confessions," *Fast Company*, December 2001, p. 80.

26. Stephen R. Covey, *The Seven Habits of Highly Effective People* (New York: Simon & Schuster, 1989), pp. 66–67.

27. Richard Koonce, "Emotional IQ, A New Secret of Success," *Training & Development*, February 1996, p. 19; Cary Cherniss and Daniel Goleman, eds., *The Emotionally Intelligent Workplace* (San Francisco: Jossey-Bass, 2001), pp. 13–26.

28. Denis Waitley, *Empires of the Mind* (New York: Morrow, 1995), p. 133.

29. Michael Crom, "Building Trust in the Workplace," *The Leader*, October 1998, p. 6; Ron Zemke, "Can You Manage Trust?" *Training*, February 2000, pp. 76–83; Steven M.R. Covey, *The Speed of Rust*, New York: Free Press, 2006, pp. 3–6.

30. Harold H. Bloomfield and Robert K. Cooper, *The Power of 5* (Emmaus, Pa.: Rodale Press, 1995), p. 61.

31. Richard N. Bolles, *What Color is Your Parachute?*, Berkeley, CA: Ten Speed Press, 2004, pp. 8–11.

32. Jack Canfield, *The Success Principles* (New York: Harper Collins, 2005), pp. 3–18.

33. David A. Kaplan, "The Best Company to Work For," *Fortune*, February 8, 2010, pp. 57–64.

34. Alan M. Wolf, "Fortune smiles: SAS is No. 1 place to work," *News & Observer*, January 22, 2010, p. 1B and 7B.

35. "The 100 Best Companies for Working Mothers List 2011." [cited 29 December 2011]. Available from workingmother.com; INTERNET.

Yamada Taro/Digital Vision/Getty Images

Improving Personal and Organizational Communications

TIP OF THE ICEBERG | COMMUNICATION BREAKDOWN

W hen Tony Hayward took over oil giant BP PLC, he vowed that safety would be his top priority. The company had experienced a series of disastrous accidents that tarnished the firm's safety record. Three years later he would preside over one of the worst industrial disasters in history. The *Deepwater Horizon*, a giant offshore drilling rig the size of a sports arena, was consumed in flames. Crew members were abandoning ship—leaping from the main deck, falling 70 feet into the sea. After burning for 36 hours, the *Deepwater Horizon* sank, snapping the mile-long pipe that ran between the drilling rig and the well head at the bottom of the sea. Over 200 million gallons of oil poured into the gulf before engineers could figure out a way to stop the flow.[1]

The *Deepwater Horizon* blowout has become one of the most scrutinized maritime disasters in history. Eleven crew members lost their lives and the worst offshore oil spill in U.S. history caused massive environmental damage. What went wrong? An in-depth investigation by *Fortune* magazine revealed a philosophy that focused too much on *personal safety* (reducing slips and falls) and too little on *process safety* (avoiding a deadly explosion). BP had strict guidelines preventing employees from carrying a cup of coffee without a lid—but no standard procedure for how to conduct a key test that might have prevented a well blowout. Process safety practices focus on major hazards and risks that must be fully understood by BP engineering and line operating personnel. These practices require a greater understanding of the communication process.[2]

CHAPTER PREVIEW

LEARNING OBJECTIVES

After studying Chapter 2, you will be able to

2-1 Explain the communication process.

2-2 Identify and explain the filters that affect communication.

2-3 Identify ways to improve personal communication, including developing listening skills.

2-4 Understand how communications flow throughout an organization.

2-5 Learn how to effectively use communication technologies.

Better communication between BP's management and employees regarding process safety measures might have prevented the Deepwater Horizon disaster in the Gulf of Mexico.

COMMUNICATION IN AN INFORMATION ECONOMY

The new millennium has ushered in the age of information, led by rapid advances in electronic communication. Within many organizations we are seeing the flattening of hierarchies (fewer layers of management) and greater use of teams. This means that more rank-and-file staff members need to be able to collect, evaluate, and exchange information.[3] Later in this chapter, we will discuss corporate blogs, instant messaging, text messaging, and other forms of electronic communication. We will also discuss various social media platforms that enhance the exchange of information.

The Battle for Our Attention

Maggie Jackson, author of *Distracted: The Erosion of Attention and the Coming Dark Age*, says today's tech-savvy worker is often distracted by the constant flow of information from electronic sources. As the speed and volume of information increases, so do the number of distractions. Many workers say that frequent interruptions and the need to engage in multi-tasking rob them of time to think. More information does not necessarily make us more knowledgeable. Ms. Jackson says critical thinking, problem-solving, reflection, and focused communications are critical to personal and career success.[4]

THE COMMUNICATION PROCESS

2-1   Many people take communication for granted. When they write, speak, or listen to others, they assume that the message given or received is being understood. In reality, messages are often misunderstood because they are incomplete or because different people interpret messages in different ways. The diversity of today's work force calls for a greater understanding of how to communicate effectively, through technology or face-to-face, with people from different cultures, countries, and lifestyles.

Impersonal Versus Interpersonal Communication

In a typical organization, the types of communication used to exchange information can be placed on a continuum ranging from "impersonal" on one end to "interpersonal" on the other.[5] **Impersonal communication** is a one-way process that transfers basic information such as instructions, policies, and financial data. Generally, organizations use this information-delivery process when they use electronic bulletin boards or memos as quick, easy ways to "get the word out." Their effectiveness is somewhat limited because there is little, if any, possibility for the person receiving the information to clarify vague or confusing information.

Interpersonal communication is the exchange of information between two or more people. Such words as *share, discuss, argue,* and *interact* refer to this form of two-way communication. Interpersonal communication can take place in meetings, over the phone, in face-to-face interviews, or even during classroom discussions between instructors and students. If interpersonal communication is to be effective, some type of **feedback**, or understood response, from the person receiving the information is necessary. When this exchange happens, those involved can determine whether the information has been understood in the way intended. This is one of the reasons many employees prefer person-to-person meetings, telephone calls, or Web conferencing services offered by GoToMeeting or Meetup.

Sender—Message—Receiver—Feedback

Effective communication is a continuous loop that involves a sender, a receiver, the message, and feedback that clarifies the message.[6] To illustrate, suppose your friend phones from your neighborhood convenience store and asks for directions to your home. You give your friend the appropriate street names, intersections, and compass directions so that he can drive to your door without getting lost. When your friend repeats his understanding of your directions, you clarify any misunderstandings, and he drives directly to your home. A simplified diagram of this communication process would look like Figure 2.1.

Figure 2.1 ■ Diagram of a Simple Communication Process

Figure 2.2 ▪ Diagram of More Complex Communication Process

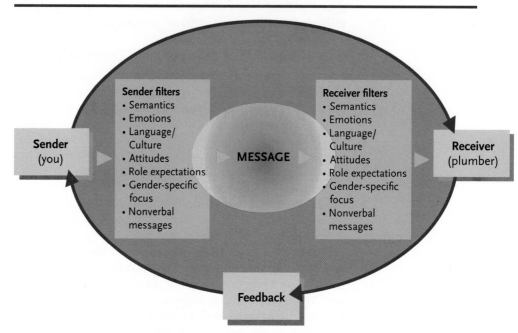

Now suppose you are late for an appointment, and the plumber you had requested three days ago calls you from her cell phone and asks directions to your house. She explains that she has gotten lost in this neighborhood before, and it is obvious that English is her second language. The communication process becomes much more complicated, as shown in Figure 2.2. As your message travels from you to your plumber, it must pass through several "filters," each of which can alter the way your message is understood. Most communications flow through this complex process.

COMMUNICATION FILTERS

2-2   Messages are sent—and feedback is received—through a variety of filters that can distort the intended message (see Figure 2.2.). When people are influenced by one or more of these filters, their perception of the message may be totally different from what the sender was attempting to communicate. Both sender and receiver must be keenly aware of these possible distortions so that they can intercept any miscommunication.

Semantics

We often assume that the words we use mean the same things to others, but this assumption can create problems. **Semantics** is the study of the relationship between a word and its meaning(s). Words have associated meanings and usages. We can easily understand what words like *typewriter*, *computer*, or *envelope* mean. But more abstract terms, such as *cloud computing*, *downsizing*, or *internal customers*, have less precise meanings.

New buzzwords surface frequently. Just about the time people understood the meaning of *rightsizing* and *downsizing*, the term *unsiloing* was introduced to make a simple, but important point: Managers should encourage cooperation across departments and share resources. Sometimes buzzwords confuse or cover up what someone is actually saying.[7]

People who have communicated extensively via Internet chat rooms, blogs, and text messaging often assume that their jargon, or cyberlingo, will be understood by everyone. However, when cyberlingo is used in the mainstream of communication within organizations, it can be confusing to those who are unfamiliar with "words" such as BTW (by the way), or GMTA (great minds think alike).[8] The impact of generational differences on interpersonal communications will be discussed in future chapters.

Language and Cultural Barriers

The needs of a multicultural work force are getting more attention today because of globalization and employers' growing support for cultural diversity among their workers. The culture in which we are raised strongly influences our values, beliefs, expressions, and behaviors. **Culture** can be defined as the accumulation of values, rules of behavior, forms of expression, religious beliefs, and the like, for a group of people who share a common language and environment. Culture helps shape just about every aspect of our behavior and our mental processes. Culture is frequently associated with a particular country; but actually, most countries are multicultural. African Americans, Hispanic Americans, Asian Americans, and American Indians represent a few of the subcultures within the United States.[9]

The ability to interpret human actions, gestures, and speech patterns in a foreign culture is called **cultural intelligence** or CQ. A person with a high CQ quickly analyzes an unfamiliar cultural situation and then responds appropriately.[10] Management professors P. Christopher Earley and Elaine Mosakowski have studied more than 2,000 managers in 60 countries. They have identified three sources of cultural intelligence.[11]

Head. Before visiting a foreign country, learn as much as possible about the host country's customs, religion, politics, morals, social structure, food, table manners, and the roles of men and women.

Body. You can win the respect of foreign hosts, guests, or colleagues by showing you understand their culture. The way you shake hands, order coffee, or accept a gift can demonstrate, to some degree, you have already entered their world.

Heart. Adapting to a new culture is much easier when you have confidence in yourself. In Chapter 4, we introduce *self-efficacy*, the belief that you can achieve what you set out to do. A major source of *self-efficacy* is the experience of mastery in your area of specialization.

HOW TO SPEAK IOWAN

One solution to the doctor shortage in rural America is to enlist physicians from Egypt, India, and other countries. At Mercy Medical Center in Mason City, Iowa, about one-third of the physicians are foreign-born. The administration was concerned that there might not be a social or emotional connection between patients and international physicians. With help from professors at the University of Northern Iowa, the hospital developed a training course entitled "Topics for Small Talk with Iowans." The foreign born doctors learned about Iowa's history and traditions, crops, climate, and sporting interests. So, if a patient makes reference to a mixed marriage, the person might be referring to a University of Iowa *Hawkeye* tying the knot with an Iowa State University *Cyclone*.

Source: Miriam Jordan, "Learning to Speak Iowan: Corn, Pigs, Cyclones and Hawkeyes," *Wall Street Journal*, September 9, 2011, pp. A1 and A16.

Emotions

Strong emotions can either prevent people from hearing what a speaker has to say or make them too susceptible to the speaker's point of view. If they become angry or allow themselves to be carried away by the speaker's eloquence, they may "think" with their emotions and make decisions or take action they regret later. Three-time Indianapolis 500 winner Helio Castroneves used a Twitter rant to complain about a penalty imposed during a race. He called IndyCar race director Brian Barnhart a "circus clown." He was fined $30,000 and put on probation.[12]

Detaching yourself from another's feelings and responding to the content of the message is often difficult. It is hard to realize that another person's emotional response is more likely about fear or frustration than it is about you as an individual. Many jobs require that employees remain calm and courteous regardless of a customer's emotional state. Emotional control is discussed extensively in Chapter 9.

Attitudes

Attitudes can be a barrier to communication in much the same way as emotions. The receiver may have a negative attitude toward the sender's voice, accent, gestures, mannerisms, dress, or delivery. These negative attitudes create resistance to the message and can lead to a breakdown in communication. Perhaps the listener has an established attitude about the speaker's topic. For example, a person who is strongly opposed to abortion will most likely find it difficult to listen with objectivity to a prochoice speaker. Keep in mind, however, that an overly positive attitude can also be a barrier to communication. When biased in favor of the message, the listener may not effectively evaluate the speaker's information. More is said about the power of attitudes in Chapter 6.

Role Expectations

Role expectations influence how people expect themselves, and others, to act on the basis of the roles they play, such as boss, customer, or subordinate. These expectations can distort communication in two ways. First, if people identify others too closely with their roles, they may discount what the other person has to say: "It's just the boss again, saying the same old thing." A variation of this distortion occurs when we do not allow others to change their roles and take on new ones. This often happens to employees who are promoted from within the ranks of an organization to management positions. Others may still see "old Chuck" from accounting rather than the new department head.

Second, role expectations can affect good communication when people use their roles to alter the way they relate to others. This is often referred to as "position power." For example, managers may expect employees to accept what they say simply because of the authority invested in the position. When employees are not allowed to question the manager's decisions or make suggestions, communication becomes one-way information giving.

Gender-Specific Focus

Gender roles learned throughout childhood can influence the way men and women communicate. After all, boys and girls do grow up in different worlds, and they are conditioned to approach communication in different ways. As adults, women are more likely to view conversation as an opportunity to establish rapport, make connections, and negotiate joint relationships. Men are more likely to view conversation as an opportunity to maintain status, exhibit skill and knowledge, and preserve independence. Men are more likely to perceive conversation as a form of competition during which they must negotiate to gain the upper hand.[13] Chapter 16, "The Changing Roles of Men and Women," discusses specific strategies you can use to communicate more effectively with those whose gender differs from your own.

Nonverbal Messages

When we attempt to communicate with another person, we use both verbal and nonverbal communication. **Nonverbal messages** are "messages without words" or "silent messages." These are the messages (other than spoken or written words) we communicate through facial expressions, voice tone, gestures, appearance, posture, and other nonverbal means. Research indicates that when two people communicate, nonverbal messages convey much more impact than verbal messages. This chapter limits its discussion to the form of nonverbal communication commonly referred to as "body language." Physical appearance, another powerful form of nonverbal communication, is discussed in Chapter 11.

Many of us could communicate more clearly, more accurately, and more credibly if we became more conscious of our body language. We can learn to strengthen our communications by making sure our words and our body language are consistent. When our verbal and nonverbal messages match, we give the impression that we can be trusted and that what we are saying reflects what we truly believe. If your spoken message and your body language are mismatched, the person receiving the message will respond to the nonverbal message every time.[14] If a manager says to an employee, "I am very interested in your problem," but then begins to look at her watch and fidget with objects on her desk, the employee will most likely believe the nonverbal rather than the verbal message.

AFP/AFP/Getty Images

Say Ni Hao (Hello) to Home Depot employees who are preparing for work at a store located in Beijing. The world's largest home improvement retailer must embrace lots of cultural adaptation if it is to achieve success in China.

You can improve your communication by monitoring the nonverbal messages you send through your eye contact, facial expressions, gestures, and personal space.

Eyes transmit more information than any other part of the body.

Eye Contact. Eyes transmit more information than any other part of the body. Because eye contact is so revealing, people generally observe some unwritten rules about looking at others. People who hold direct eye contact for only a few seconds, or avoid eye contact altogether, risk communicating indifference. However, a direct, prolonged stare between strangers is usually considered impolite, even potentially aggressive or hostile. Continuous eye contact is especially offensive in Asian and Latin American countries. As a general rule in North America, when you are communicating in a business setting, your eyes should meet the other person's about 60 to 70 percent of the time.

human
RELATIONS
in Action

HOW TO COMMUNICATE WITH AUTHENTICITY AND CHARISMA

Step One: Being Open

When you approach a group meeting or an interview, your manner should be relaxed—no different than if you were talking to a family member or a good friend.

Step Two: Being Connected

Your nonverbal messages should orient you toward the audience; zero in or their issues and problems.

Step Three: Being Passionate

How are you connected with your own feelings and emotions? How do you feel about the content of the material you present?

Step Four: Listening

Authentic and charismatic communication requires that you listen to your audience. Tune in and stay tuned in.

Source: Nick Morgan, *Trust Me—Four Steps to Authenticity and Charisma*, San Francisco, CA, Jossey-Bass, 2009, pp. 30–32.

Facial Expressions. If you want to identify the inner feelings of another person, watch facial expressions closely. A frown or a smile will communicate a great deal. We have all encountered a "look of surprise" or a "look that could kill." Most of our observations are very accurate. However, facial expressions can be intentionally manipulated. When a person is truly happy, the muscles used for smiling are involuntarily controlled by the body's limbic system. When you force a smile, the cerebral cortex (under voluntary control) activates and the person appears to have a "fake" look when he or she smiles. That is why actors often recall a past emotional experience to produce the emotional state they want.[15] If we are able to accurately assess the facial expressions of others and draw conclusions accordingly, we can be sure that others are doing the same to us.

Gestures. Gestures send messages to people about how you are reacting to them and to the situation in which you find yourself. They often add an element that is perceived as a lively speaking style that keeps the attention of others. In some cultures, if you fail to

Figure 2.3 ■ Same Sign, Different Meanings

OK SIGN
France: You're a zero;
Japan: Please give me coins;
Brazil: an obscene gesture;
Mediterranean countries: an obscene gesture.

THUMBS-UP
Australia: Up yours;
Germany: The number one;
Japan: The number five;
Saudi Arabia: I'm winning;
Ghana: An insult;
Malaysia: The thumb is used to point rather than the finger.

THUMB AND FOREFINGER
Most countries: money;
France: Something is perfect;
Mediterranean: a vulgar gesture.

Source: "Same sign, different meanings" (graphic) by Sam Ward from *USA Today*, March 14, 1996, p. 7c. Reprinted by permission.

gesture, you may be perceived as boring and stiff.[16] Be aware that some gestures that may be common in one culture may have dramatically different meaning to people from another culture. The examples in Figure 2.3 illustrate how the same gesture can have very different meanings.

Personal Space. Research conducted by Edward Hall provides evidence that people use the space around them to define relationships. It is possible to make others uncomfortable by standing too close to them or too far away from them. A customer may feel uncomfortable if a salesperson stands too close. A job applicant may feel uncomfortable if the interviewer maintains a distance of several feet. Hall identified four "zones" of comfortable distances that help us understand this nonverbal effect on others:[17]

1. *Intimate distance* includes touching to approximately 18 inches from another person. Most people will respond with defensiveness when strangers intrude into this territory.
2. *Personal distance* ranges from 18 inches to 4 feet. This distance is usually reserved for people we feel close to, such as spouses or close friends.
3. *Social distance* is 4 to 12 feet and is used for most business meetings and impersonal social gatherings. Business can be conducted with a minimum of emotional involvement.
4. *Public distance*, which usually involves one-way communication from a speaker to an audience, is 12 to 15 feet.

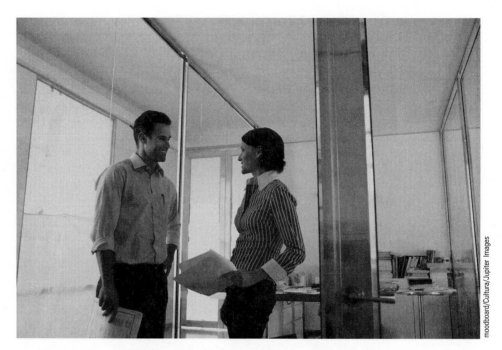

A social distance of about four feet is appropriate for most business meetings, perhaps a little less if the businesspeople know each other well and feel comfortable with one another.

Americans should realize that the distances Hall describes may be different when they are attempting to effectively communicate with those from another culture. For example, Asians are accustomed to close contact.

Who Is Responsible for Effective Communication?

The sender and the receiver share *equal* responsibility for effective communication. The communication loop, as shown in Figure 2.2, is not complete if the message the receiver hears, and acts upon, differs from the one the sender intended. When the sender accepts 100 percent of the responsibility for sending a clear, concise message, the communication process begins. But the receiver must also accept 100 percent of the responsibility for receiving the message as the sender intended. Ideally receivers should provide senders with enough feedback to ensure that an accurate message has passed through all the filters that might alter it.

HOW TO COMMUNICATE POSITIVE NONVERBAL MESSAGES

- Tune into your body language. Check for deeply ingrained habits (twisting your hair).
- Exhibit good posture. Stand tall (no slouching) and sit erect.
- Maintain proper eye contact. Look people in the eye, but don't stare them down.
- Avoid negative gestures. Don't cross your arms or wring your hands.
- Sound enthusiastic and interested. The tone of your voice has a great effect on the words you speak.

Source: Barbara Pachter, *When the Little Things Count*, Cambridge, MA, DaCapo Press, 2006, pp. 55–57.

HOW TO IMPROVE PERSONAL COMMUNICATION

2-3 Now that you understand the communication process and the various filters messages must pass through, you can begin to take the necessary steps to improve your own personal communication skills.

Send Clear Messages

Send clear, concise messages with as little influence from filters as possible so that you can avoid being misunderstood. Miscommunication can easily be avoided if both parties follow these simple rules:

- *Use clear, concise language.* Avoid slang, jargon, or complex, industry-specific semantics that the receiver might not understand. Tailor your messages to your receivers by using words and concepts they understand.
- *Use repetition.* When possible, use parallel channels of communication. For example, by sending an e-mail and making a phone call, you not only gain the receiver's attention through dialogue but also make sure there is a written record in case specific details need to be recalled.
- *Use appropriate timing.* An important memo or e-mail may get no attention simply because it is competing with more pressing problems facing the receiver. When you need someone's cooperation, be acutely aware of his or her schedule and workload so that you can avoid causing any inconvenience or frustration.
- *Consider the receiver's preferences.* Some people prefer to receive information via e-mail, and others prefer telephone calls or face-to-face contact. Monitor and discover the preferences of those you communicate with on a regular basis, and adjust your communications with them accordingly.

Develop Effective Listening Skills

We may be born with the ability to hear, but we have to *learn how to listen.* We may think we are good listeners, but the truth is that most people don't listen at all. Too often we simply speak and then think about what we are going to say next, rather than concentrating on what the other person is trying to say.

Effective listening skills can greatly enhance your personal and job-related communication. When someone says "You are a good listener," you have received one of the highest forms of praise.

Active Listening. **Active listening** is fueled by curiosity and requires your complete concentration on what you are hearing, body language that exhibits your listening attitude, and feedback as to what you think the speaker is trying to tell you. In some cases, a simple statement such as "Please tell me more about that" will help you become an active listener. Susan Scott, author of *Fierce Conversations,* offers this advice: "Dig for full understanding. Use paraphrasing and perception checks; don't be satisfied with what's on the surface."[18] When you become an active listener, you will make fewer mistakes, learn new information, and build stronger relationships.

If you would like to pursue additional resources to help you become a better listener, access the information available through the International Listening Association website. In addition, carefully examine Table 2.1, How to Be an Active Listener, and make every effort to implement its recommendations when you are interacting with others. You may be surprised by the impact you can make.

Table 2.1 ■ How to Be an Active Listener

1. *Develop a listening attitude.* Regard the speaker as worthy of your respect and attention. Maintain good eye contact and lean slightly forward. Don't rush the speaker. Be patient and refrain from planning what to say in response until the speaker has finished talking.

2. *Give the speaker your full attention.* This is not easy because the messages you hear are often spoken at a much slower rate than you are able to absorb them. This allows your mind to roam. Your senses are constantly receiving extraneous information that may divert your attention.

3. *Clarify by asking questions.* If something is not clear because the speaker has referred to a person or an event that you are not familiar with, ask him or her to back up and explain. If you want the speaker to expand on a particular point, ask open-ended questions such as "How do you feel about that?" or "Can you tell us some ways to improve?"

4. *Feed back your understanding of the speaker's message.* Paraphrase, in your own words, your understanding of what the speaker has just said: for example, *"Do you mean...?" "Am I right in assuming that we should...?" "What I hear you saying is..."* or *"In other words, we...."*

Critical Listening. To add depth to your active listening skills, consider honing your critical listening skills. **Critical listening** is the attempt to see the topic of discussion from the *speaker's* point of view and to consider how the speaker's perception of the situation may be different from your own. To improve your ability to critically view new information, be sure to listen for evidence that challenges, as well as confirms, your own point of view. This is especially important when there is no opportunity for feedback, such as when you are viewing "tabloid" television, listening to network TV news "sound bites," or reading Internet blogs. Analyze the source of the information and determine its validity and credibility. Critical listening skills will help you avoid perpetuating erroneous information simply because you heard it through gossip, saw it on TV, or read it on a blog.

All of the communications filters identified in Figure 2.2 tend to distort your ability and willingness to listen, so activating your critical thinking/listening skills will take some effort.

To help you in this skill development process, ask yourself the following questions:

■ Does the speaker's reasoning make sense?
■ What evidence is being offered to support the speaker's views?
■ Do I know each point to be valid based on my own experience?
■ Is each point based on a source that can be trusted?[19]

For some people, critical listening at a meeting is very difficult. They fear that if they sit in silence, everyone will assume they have nothing to say. It's fine just to listen and learn at a meeting. Quality of participation should matter more than quantity.[20]

Empathic Listening. Another dimension to becoming a better listener involves empathy, which means understanding another person's feelings. Many workers today face serious personal problems and feel the need to talk about them with someone. They do not expect specific advice or guidance; they just want to spend some time with an empathic listener. Stephen Covey, the noted author and consultant, described

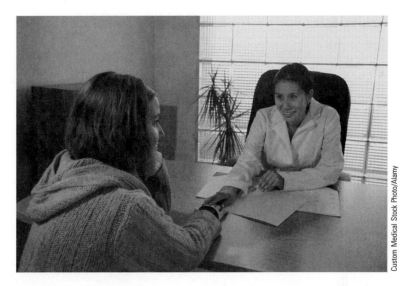

Empathic listening is an essential skill for business, whether you're a salesperson listening to a customer or a manager listening to an employee.

empathic listening as listening with your ears, your eyes, and your heart.[21] If you want to practice empathic listening, adopt the following practices:

- *Avoid being judgmental.* Objectivity is the heart and soul of empathic listening. The person is communicating for emotional release and does not seek a specific response.
- *Acknowledge what is said.* You do not have to agree with what is being said, but you should let the person know you are able to understand his or her viewpoint.
- *Be patient.* If you are unable or unwilling to take the time to hear what the person has to say, say so immediately. Signs of impatience send a negative message to the person needing to talk.[22]

We live in a culture where empathic listening is quite rare. Interrupting has become all too common as people rush to fill every gap in the conversation. Nevertheless, empathic listening is greatly valued by those with personal or work-related problems—people want to spend time with a good listener.[23]

---

human
RELATIONS
in Action

THE POWER OF SILENCE

Each conversation we have with a coworker, a customer, or a significant other can enhance or weaken the relationship. A conversation that has the power to truly transform a relationship requires some silence. Yet, for most Americans, silence in a conversation is almost unendurable. Interrupting the other person or responding too quickly with little or no thought can weaken a relationship. Every important conversation requires moments of silence—time to reflect on what the other person has said and consider our response. During most conversations, do you use silence to improve communication? Analyze your response.

Source: Susan Scott, *Fierce Conversations* (New York, Viking, 2002), pp. 156–157. Chapter 7 is entitled "Let Silence Do the Heavy Lifting."

COMMUNICATIONS IN ORGANIZATIONS

2-4   The healthy functioning of any organization, large or small, depends on effective communication. Most organizations establish formal channels or structures through which communication travels. However, an informal channel, commonly referred to as the grapevine, provides a major communications link.

Formal Channels: Horizontal and Vertical

Most organizations establish a formal structure through which official information travels. **Horizontal channels** are used to move information among people on the same level of authority, such as all the store managers of a national retail clothing store chain, all department chairpersons within a college, or all the administrative assistants within an organization. **Vertical channels** move information up and down through all levels of authority within an organization. A message from the president of the organization will move down to the vice president(s), then to the manager(s), and then to the workers. Communicating down vertical channels is fairly routine. Communicating back up can be more difficult because managers fail to encourage the upward flow of information from subordinates.

When formal communication channels are working effectively, everyone authorized to initiate and receive companywide communications will receive the same information in a timely manner. If the level of trust among those sending and receiving the information is fairly high, these messages will usually be understood, believed, accepted, and acted on. If the level of trust is low, however, workers will tend to put more faith in rumors, even if such information conflicts with the formal message.

Informal Channel: The Grapevine

Messages passed through the horizontal and vertical channels can usually be tracked through linear paths, but the pathway of rumors may look more like a cobweb interwoven throughout the organizational chart. The **grapevine**, the informal communication channel, carries unofficial information and exists in every organization. It can have either positive or negative effects. Many times, the grapevine will clarify orders sent through the formal channels. At times, however, messages that move through the grapevine may be exaggerated, distorted, or completely inaccurate. These rumors develop quickly when at least two conditions exist in an organization: high degrees of anxiety and a great deal of uncertainty. To quell rumors, top management has to communicate in a timely and honest way.[24]

Rumors about individuals, or gossip, in the workplace can undermine morale, weaken authority, ruin reputations, and leave even the best teams decimated in its wake. When gossip reaches excessive levels, there are two common causes: lack of clarity from management on key issues and poor channels for problem solving.[25] Management needs to work hard to anticipate issues that might stimulate rumors and gossip.

Modern Internet and communication technologies have vastly and instantly extended the reach of the grapevine. Workplace rumors and gossip now spread faster than ever. And e-mail messages and blogs leave an electronic trail that can be read by anyone at any time.[26]

Improving Upward Communication

Every effort should be made to encourage upward communication. **Upward communication**, the process of encouraging employees to share their feelings and ideas with their managers, is one of the most effective ways to improve organizational communication and is common among the best companies to work for in America. Employees with limited power are naturally very cautious about discussing mistakes, complaints, and failings with a more powerful person. However, when managers demonstrate the desire to listen to their subordinates, ideas, suggestions, and complaints begin to flow upward. They recognize that improving communications will inevitably help build trust among all employees, regardless of their position in the organization.

COMMUNICATION TECHNOLOGIES

2-5 The percentage of time people spend using traditional forms of communication such as letters, phone calls, and face-to-face conversations has been eroded by the need to use faster, more convenient communication technologies. Text messaging, instant messaging, tweets, e-mail, and Web conferencing have changed the way workers stay connected in a work setting. What's driving this change? There are several factors at play:

- *Growth of the **virtual office**.* Thanks to high-speed and wireless Internet access millions of workers now enjoy the "anytime, anywhere" office.
- *Virtual offices*, networks of workers connected by the latest technology, appeal to members of our mobile work force.
- *Cost effectiveness.* The low cost of technology-based communication is unsurpassed. It costs very little to share information with many people on a local or global basis. The rising cost of travel has influenced how people choose to communicate.
- *Globalization.* As more and more organizations serve customers on several continents, or need to communicate with employees working in several different countries, technology-based communication enables more efficient communication across time zones.

In all the frantic speed with which information now flows, many people forget that communication still must be carefully created before it is transmitted. If the message is not handled properly or is poorly written, the sender risks being misunderstood or giving the impression he or she is poorly educated or careless.

Social Media

The term **social media** refers to the use of Web-based and mobile technologies to turn communication into an interactive dialogue. A common thread running through all definitions of social media is a blending of technology and social interaction.[27]

The rapid growth of social media has given every individual the ability to interact and influence colleagues, customers, companies, and society with words, videos, and music through the media channels they choose to use. Although Facebook, Twitter, LinkedIn and YouTube are the most popular social media networks, there are dozens of others that cater to specific niches. Some companies choose to develop their own social network platforms to increase communication across teams or among groups of people who work on a project or share common interests.

Social media has increased the demand for employees who can write with clarity and understand the rules of etiquette that apply to users of various media platforms. Once a comment is posted it is etched in history forever. No matter how "private" a message is intended to be, it can be forwarded and shared with virtually anyone. Some people become so enthusiastic about what they can do with these technologies that they forget the impact their actions can have on their careers. Think before you post![28] Figure 2.4 summarizes the important social media principles.

Figure 2.4 ▪ Social Media Principles

Listen. Social media is all about listening to what people are saying, what is important to them.

Learn. Social media requires an insatiable appetite for learning. It can spark new ideas and give you insight and perspective.

Engage. "Social" means engagement. If your goal is to build a huge following of friends or followers, you must ask: What is the objective?

Transparency. Social media is incredibly transparent. What you do and say is visible to the world.

Live by the golden rule. "Do unto others as you would have them do unto you" is a principle to live by every day.

Give more than you take. Early social media pioneers could have had an attitude of scarcity, but thankfully, they didn't. Share information freely to help others and believe that what goes around comes around.

Brand authenticity. Consistency of brand promise (personal or commercial) is important across all media platforms.

Source: Monique Reece, *Real-Time Marketing for Business Growth*, Upper Saddle River, NJ, Pearson Education, 2010, p. 238.

Mobile Communication

The ability to communicate instantly with anyone in the world, where, when, and how you desire, is driven by mobile communication. Smart phones, cell phones, iPads, and tablets are a few of the growing number of mobile devices that function as small computers. Just as most people wouldn't even consider leaving home without their keys and wallet, they won't leave home without at least one of these devices. Throughout the day, they will be used for e-mail, texting, searching the web, playing games, watching movies, listening to music, shopping, and dozens of other activities driven by an individual's personal communication preference.

Despite the growing variety and complexity of mobile communication devices, the basics of communication etiquette are as important as ever. Communication needs to change based on whom you are communicating with, and the situation. Abbreviated messages (OMG, LOL) are okay to use with friends but considered inappropriate in many business environments. Although texting and e-mails are usually brief when using a small device like an iPhone, take a few seconds to check spelling and reread your message to avoid embarrassing mistakes.

Voicemail etiquette is also important. Be sure your recorded message is professional, includes your full name, and tells the caller when they can expect to have calls returned. If you won't be answering calls for an extended period of time, let callers know this and who they can contact regarding urgent matters during your absence. When you are connected to another person's voice mail, slowly state your full name, *a brief explanation of what information or action you need from that person* (the component most often neglected), your phone number, and the best time to reach you. All four components are necessary to avoid phone tag. Then if the receiver reaches your voice mail when calling back, he or she can simply leave you a voice message with the information you wanted. The communication loop is complete.

E-mail

Members of Generation Y often describe e-mail as "so last millennium." They prefer the instant gratification that comes with the use of instant messaging, and text messaging. However, e-mail is still popular, especially for business messages that require persuasion, permanence, or formality. When you use e-mail, follow these guidelines:

Know Your Company's Policies. Most organizations monitor their employees' e-mail carefully. Keep in mind that even deleted messages live on indefinitely in the company's hard drives and may resurface. E-mail that might be sexually offensive could be considered sexual harassment and have serious ramifications. Avoid sending personal e-mail messages on company time.

Create an Appropriate E-mail Address. Carefully design your e-mail address to give the impression you want to convey. Addresses such as Crazylady@_____.com or Partyboy@_____.com may be acceptable for personal e-mail but should never be used in a business setting.

Use the **Subject:** *Line.* This brief introduction to your message will cue the receiver as to the content of your message. Busy readers glance at the subject line and decide when and whether to read the message. Avoid use of a one-word subject such as *important, update,* or *issue.*

Compose Clear, Concise Messages. The authors of *Send,* a combination stylebook and etiquette manual for e-mail users, say their title is intended to be an acronym, guiding us to improved e-mail use. Messages should be **S**imple, **E**ffective, **N**ecessary, and aimed at getting something **D**one. A message written in simple conversational language takes less time to write and is more pleasant to read. Tell readers what action you want them to take.[29]

Recognize E-mail Limitations. The missing element in e-mail and other electronic communication is *rapport,* that bonding state that is easier to establish in person or by phone. Facial expressions, tone of voice, gestures—important social cues—are missing in e-mail.[30] Readers will not be able to tell if you are serious or being sarcastic, prying or simply curious, angry or merely frustrated. After creating your message, reread it as a stranger might. If words or phrases might be misconstrued, rewrite it so as to make clear *exactly* what you mean to say (see Figure 2.5).

Figure 2.5 ▪ E-Mail Best Practices

- Do not send e-mail when you are angry or exhausted.
- When a face-to-face meeting is necessary, do not use e-mail as a substitute.
- When receiving large amounts of e-mail, selectively choose which ones you want to read by scanning the subject lines.
- Make every attempt to create e-mail messages that are concise and error-free.
- Do not use e-mail to share rumors or gossip or to say anything sensitive or critical that touches on someone's job competence.
- Don't use company computers for personal matters.
- Don't send anything you wouldn't want published.

Source: Adapted from Mary Ellen Guffey and Dana Loewy, *Business Communications: Process and Product,* Mason, OH, South-Western Cengage Learning, 2011, pp. 196–197.

Blogs

A **blog** is a discussion or information site, usually written by one person, used to communicate perspectives and information about certain topics. Some blogs are integrated into a company website, others are posted separately on a platform like Wordpress and reflect views of the CEO. Blogs are often used to keep interested subscribers, customers and employees informed. Readers often leave feedback, so some blogs serve as a form of communication and market research.

Some companies encourage employees to create their own blog. At SAS Institute more than 600 employees have their own internal blogs. One employee writes the "Smells Like a Log" blog which describes unusual uses for the SAS programming language. Leaders at SAS believe that blogs conferring a wide range of topics have helped develop a culture of cohesion.[31]

LOOKING BACK: SUMMARY OF LEARNING OBJECTIVES

1. **Explain the communication process.**

   The age of information has given us major advances in technology-based communication. However, successful communication in a work setting requires human involvement. The diversity of today's work force calls for a greater understanding of how to communicate effectively. Impersonal one-way communication methods can be used effectively to share basic facts, policies, and instructions. If feedback is necessary, rely on interpersonal communication that involves a two-way exchange. As noted in this chapter, two-way communication is often a complex process.

2. **Identify and explain the filters that affect communication.**

   Messages are sent—and feedback is received—through a variety of filters that often distort the messages. Figure 2.2 provides a summary of the most common filters that can challenge both senders and receivers of messages. For example, body language conveys information through eye contact, facial expressions, gestures, and the use of personal space. When you are influenced by one or more of these filters, the message you receive may be totally different from what the sender was attempting to communicate.

3. **Identify ways to improve personal communication, including developing listening skills.**

   The sender and the receiver share equal responsibility for effective communication. Therefore, both sender and receiver should take the necessary steps to improve their personal communication skills. Individuals can make their messages clearer by choosing words carefully, using repetition, timing the message correctly, and considering the receivers' preferences. Personal communication can also be improved by the use of active, critical, and empathic listening skills.

4. **Understand how communications flow throughout an organization.**

   Effective communication in organizations unifies group behavior, builds teamwork, and contributes to improved productivity. Formal communication channels can be vertical or horizontal. The grapevine uses an informal approach to rapidly transmit information, but rumors or gossip may have a negative effect if the information is untrue. Progressive organizations are constantly searching for ways to improve upward communication. They recognize that frontline employees are often in the best position to recommend ways to improve the organization.

5. **Learn how to effectively use communication technologies.**

   Memos, letters, phone calls, and face-to-face conversations have been replaced, in many situations, by technology-based communication alternatives. Virtual offices, networks of workers connected by the latest technology, are now quite common. These communication technologies are time efficient and cost-effective for organizations. However, the increase in the use of e-mail, text messaging, Twitter, mobile communication, and other high-tech communication methods can create human relations problems. The rapid growth of social media has given every individual the ability to interact with colleagues, customers, and friends.

KEY TERMS

impersonal communication, 25
interpersonal communication, 25
feedback, 25
semantics, 26
culture, 27
cultural intelligence, 27

nonverbal messages, 29
active listening, 33
critical listening, 34
empathic listening, 35
horizontal channels, 36
vertical channels, 36

grapevine, 36
upward communication, 36
virtual office, 37
social media, 37
blog, 40

CAREER INSIGHT

Business dealings in North America tend to be characterized by informality. Yet, too much informality during the job interview process can create problems. For example, addressing someone by their first name during the interview would be a mistake. And watch the lingo. Tory Johnson, president of New York-based *Women for Hire Inc.*, thought she had found a qualified and enthusiastic intern for her small recruiting firm. Then she received the candidate's thank-you note, which included words such as *hiya* and *thanx*, along with several exclamation points and a smiley-face emoticon. Johnson was put off by the shorthand language and decorative symbols.[32]

TRY YOUR HAND

1. During the next week, study the listening habits of students in another class in which you are enrolled. Keep a journal of your observations by identifying the nonverbal behaviors you witness. Are there barriers to effective communication between the instructor and the student? How do you believe the students' nonverbal behaviors might affect the relationship between the instructor and the students?

2. Print out the most recent e-mails that you have sent or received and bring them to class. Analyze their effectiveness in terms of the e-mail tips in this chapter. Did the messages violate any of the tips? If so, which ones? How could these messages be improved?

3. Many times, we take the conversation away from others and make it our own. This practice not only wastes time, but is a major relationship killer. Here is how it works: At the beginning of the conversation, you tell the other person about a problem you are dealing with and, before you finish the story, the other person says, "I know what you mean," and then describes a personal experience that may or may not have anything to do with your problem. Once the other person takes over the conversation, a valuable exchange of ideas is probably lost. During the next week, monitor your conversations with friends, family members, and coworkers. How often did the other person attempt to take the conversation away from you? How often did you attempt to take over the conversation?[33]

4. Assume that you are currently employed by Toyota International in their Information Technology Department with offices in several countries around the globe. Next week, you will travel to Poland and Greece to check on the installation of new telecommunications equipment. Your manager told you that *most* of the people you will work with speak English. However, you want to be prepared to greet people and say "yes," "no," "thank you," and "goodbye" in the languages of the countries you will visit. Go to *http://www.travlang.com*, scroll down and select "Foreign Languages for Travelers." Then follow the two steps for the language of your choice and click on the option "basic words." Select, record, and practice the appropriate words.

   Now go to *http://www.kwintessential.co.uk/resources/country-profiles.html* and click on the country that corresponds with the language you learned in the exercise above. Learn more about the country's social customs, such as rules and taboos of doing business, verbal and nonverbal communication techniques, decision-making techniques, and meeting, gift-giving, and dining etiquette.

CRITICAL THINKING CHALLENGE

1. As you build your human relations skills, it is very important to establish an acute sensitivity to the impact communication filters have on your interpersonal relationships at home and at work. Review Figure 2.2, and identify the communication filters that were in place during a recent face-to-face conversation, argument, or confrontation you had with another person. Did any of these filters interfere with your ability to send or receive the information being transmitted during the exchange? Evaluate how, if you were to repeat the interaction with this person, you could reduce the impact of these filters and thereby improve your ability to effectively communicate the messages you were sending and receiving.

2. A close friend and respected financial advisor employed by a brokerage services company sent you the following e-mail message: "It appears that your employer is planning to close one or two distribution centers within the next few months. I will let you know if I receive more specific information." Should you share this information with friends who work at your distribution center? Why or why not?

SELF-ASSESSMENT EXERCISE

Completion of this self-assessment will provide you with information needed to develop goals for self-improvement. Circle the number from 1 to 5 that best represents your response to each statement: (1) strongly disagree (never do this); (2) disagree (rarely do this); (3) moderately agree (sometimes do this); (4) agree (frequently do this); (5) strongly agree (almost always do this).

A. I am able to send clear, concise verbal messages.	1	2	3	4	5
B. When people talk, I listen attentively and frequently use active listening skills.	1	2	3	4	5
C. I am conscious of how I express nonverbal messages (facial expression, tone of voice, body language, and so on) when communicating with others.	1	2	3	4	5
D. I understand the flow of communication in organizations and the positive and negative influence of informal communication.	1	2	3	4	5
E. I can describe the role of social media and other forms of digital media in the changing world of personal and professional communication.	1	2	3	4	5

After recording your response to each item, select an attitude or skill you would like to improve. Prepare a written goal and then describe the steps you will take to achieve this goal.

YOU PLAY THE ROLE

This role-play exercise is designed to enhance your awareness of the filters that can alter or aid a message between a sender and a receiver in the communication process. Review Figure 2.2 *Diagram of More Complex Communication Process* before you begin this activity. Select a partner and be prepared to discuss specific information about your present or past work situation. Assume the role of sender and share these ideas with the receiver. Did your message match what the receiver understood? What filters lead to parallel communication, and what filters lead to distortion? After you have discussed the complexity of the communication process, change roles; you are now the receiver and the receiver is the sender.

BELOW THE SURFACE | IMPROVING SAFETY PRACTICES AT BP

At the beginning of this chapter, you were given a brief introduction to one of the worst industrial disasters in history. The Deepwater Horizon blowout killed 11 people and set off the worst off-shore oil spill in U.S. history. Investigations conducted after the accident indicate that problems had plagued the well for weeks before the blowout. A survey of workers in the weeks before the oil rig exploded showed that many of them were concerned about safety practices and feared reprisals if they reported mistakes or other problems to corporate-level personnel based in Houston. Workers also voiced concerns about equipment reliability, maintenance that was not completed, and unsafe behaviors on the rig.[34]

QUESTIONS

1. Over 100 employees were living and working on the Deepwater Horizon when it exploded. What steps could have been taken to give these workers a greater voice in accident prevention? What filters are likely to distort upward communication?

2. As noted at the beginning of this chapter, top management was focused too much on *personal safety* and too little on *process safety*. Why would top management embrace this safety philosophy?

CLOSING CASE | SHOULD EMPLOYERS RESTRICT SOCIAL MEDIA USE?

Just one Tweet, photo, e-mail, video, or post on Facebook can permanently damage a person's reputation, and cause significant loss to companies and their investors. At a Dominos pizza store one employee filmed another doing unappetizing things to food that was intended for a customer, then posted the video on YouTube. Domino's stock quickly plummeted by 10 percent.

Social media is powerful, and it's important to understand the repercussions before making a hasty comment one might later regret. Even a one sentence post made on Facebook can cause an employee to be fired. Roy Rhone, Jr., a Frito-Lay warehouse employee was fired after writing on Facebook he was "a hair away from setting it off in that b—."[35]

Companies want to know what their customers and employees are saying about them, so as the popularity of social media has skyrocketed, so has the number of social media monitoring tools. Some search tools like Google Alerts are easy to use, free, and available to anyone. Simply enter a name, company, or topic and you can receive daily alerts about the search term. Other social media monitoring tools like Radian6 and Hearsay are robust, scouring the Internet deep and wide to find what people are saying and report the status of their social reputation score.

Some business leaders who think little is being said about their companies are surprised to learn how much is actually being said. When one big company made this claim, Hearsay CEO, Clara Shih, said the tool turned up an astonishing 60,000 different social media pages where employees mentioned or discussed company matters (not including the thousands of employee profiles on LinkedIn).[36] Yes, Big

Brother is not restricted to government; it has spread to corporate environments, too.

Where should a company draw the line with respect to social media use by its employees?

QUESTIONS

1. Imagine you are the CEO of your own company and answer the following questions:

   ■ What policies, if any, would you put in place for employees using social media? Defend your reasons, pro or con.

   ■ If an employee makes disparaging comments on her Facebook page about the company, should she be fired?

2. Go to http://www.google.com/alerts and sign up for two Google alerts on search terms that are interesting to you, such as a person, company, sports team, etc. Request daily alerts delivered to your e-mail. Evaluate the number of comments made on your search term, and note how many are positive or negative.

CHAPTER 2 ENDNOTES

1. Peter Elkind and David Whitford, "An Accident Waiting to Happen," **Fortune**, February 7, 2011, pp. 105–132; Russell Gold and Casselman, "On Doomed Rig's Last Day, A Divisive Change of Plan," **Wall Street Journal**, August 26, 2010, pp. A1 and A6.

2. Ibid.

3. Mary Ellen Guffey and Dana Loewy, **Business Communication: Process and Product**, Mason, OH: South-Western Cengage Learning, 2011, pp. 188–189.

4. Maggie Jackson, **Distracted: The Erosion of Attention and the Coming Dark Age** (New York: Prometheus Books, 2008), p. 14; "Maggie Jackson's Call for Focus—Fighting Back in an Age of Distractions," **A Buzzflash Interview**, June 30, 2008 [cited 30 June 2008]. Available from http://blog.buzzflash.com/interviews/115; INTERNET; David Robinson, "What Were We Talking About?," **Wall Street Journal**, June 12, 2008, p. A15.

5. John Stewart and Gary D'Angelo, **Together—Communicating Interpersonally** (New York: Random House, 1988), p. 5.

6. For more information on the components of communication, see Scot Ober, **Contemporary Business Communication**, 5th ed. (Boston: Houghton Mifflin, 2003), pp. 5–9.

7. Carol Hymowitz, "Mind Your Language: To Do Business Today, Consider Delayering," **Wall Street Journal**, March 27, 2006, p. B1.

8. Cai Shaoyao, "Cyberlingo—A Jargon Not for General Use," **Shanghai Star**, January 6, 2005 [cited 26 October 2005]. Available from http://app1.chinadaily.com.cn/star/2005/0206/vo2-3.html; INTERNET; Julie Martin, "Cyberlingo! BRB? ROTFL? LOL? It's Greek to Me" [cited 26 October 2005]. Available from http://www.goodchatting.com/articles/archives/000006.php; INTERNET.

9. Douglas A. Bernstein, Louis A. Penner, Alison Clarke-Stewart, and Edward J. Roy, **Psychology**, 7th ed. (Boston: Houghton Mifflin, 2006), pp. 23–24.

10. Christopher Earley and Elaine Mosakowski, "Cultural Intelligence," **Harvard Business Review**, October 2004, p. 139.

11. Christopher Earley and Elaine Mosakowski, "Cultural Intelligence," pp. 141–142.

12. Reported in **Autoweek**, October 17, 2011, p. 107.

13. Deborah Tannen, **You Just Don't Understand: Men and Women in Conversation** (New York: Ballantine Books, 1990), pp. 24–25, 85; Mary Ellen Guffey and Dana Loewy, **Business Communication: Process and Product**, p. 101.

14. Nick Morgan, "How to Become an Authentic Speaker," **Harvard Business Review**, November 2008, pp. 62–63.

15. Don Clark, "Communication and Leadership," July 17, 2005, pp. 9, 10 [cited 27 October 2005]. Available from http://www.nwlink.com/donclark/leader/leadcom.html; INTERNET.

16. Ibid., p. 7.

17. William B. Gudykunst, Stella Ting-Toomey, Sandra Sudweeks, and Lea Stewart, **Building Bridges: Interpersonal Skills for a Changing World** (Boston: Houghton Mifflin, 1995), pp. 315–316. "Playing Keepaway," **Psychology Today**, June 2007, p.15.

18. Susan Scott, **Fierce Conversations: Achieving Success at Work and in Life, One Conversation at a Time** (New York: Viking, 2002), pp. 156–157.

19. Michael Toms, "Dialogue—the Art of Thinking Together—Sparks Spirit of 'Aliveness' in Organizations," **The Inner Edge**, August/September 1998.

20. Leigh Buchanan, "The Office," **Inc.**, October 2006, p. 140.

21. Stephen R. Covey, *The Seven Habits of Highly Effective People* (New York: Simon & Schuster, 1989), pp. 240–241.

22. C. Glenn Pearce, "Learning How to Listen Empathically," *Supervisory Management*, September 1991, p. 11.

23. Robert Epstein, "Waiting," *Psychology Today*, September/October 2001, p. 5.

24. Jared Sandberg, "Ruthless Rumors and the Managers Who Enable Them," *Wall Street Journal*, October 29, 2003, p. B1.

25. Bruce Clarke, "How to Deal with Office Gossip," *News & Observer*, April 3, 2011, p. 3E.

26. Robert Kreitner, *Management*, 10th ed. (Boston: Houghton Mifflin Company, 2007), p. 349.

27. Monique Reece, *Real-Time Marketing for Business Growth*, pp. 235–238; a definition of social media appears in Wikipedia, the free online encyclopedia.

28. Barbara Pachter, *Greet! Eat! Tweet!*, Cherry Hill, NJ: Pachter and Associates, 2010, pp. 121–122.

29. John Derbyshire, "To: Emailers, Subject: Etiquette," *Wall Street Journal*, March 21, 2007, p. P10; Robert Kreitner, *Management*, 10th ed. (Boston: Houghton Mifflin, 2007), p. 362.

30. Marina Krakovsky, "Caveat Sender—The Pitfalls of E-mail," *Psychology Today*, March/April 2004, pp. 15–16.

31. David A. Kaplan, "The Best Company to Work For," *Fortune*, February 8, 2010, p. 62.

32. Sarah E. Needleman, "Informal Lingo Might Put Off Job Recruiters," *The News & Observer*, August 3, 2008, p. 49.

33. This exercise is based on information taken from Scott, *Fierce Conversations*, pp. 117–118.

34. Ian Urbina, "Oil Rig Workers Fretted About Safety," *News & Observer*, July 22, 2010, pp. 1A and 11A.

35. Melanie Trottman, "For Angry Employees, Legal Cover for Rants," *Wall Street Journal*, December 2, 2011, p. B1.

36. David Kirkpatrick, "Social Power and the Coming Corporate Revolution," *Forbes*, September 26, 2011, p. 78.

PART 2

Career Success Begins with Knowing Yourself

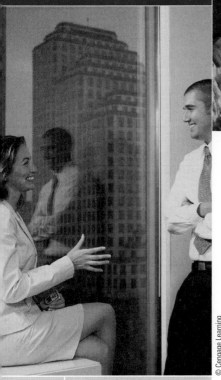

CHAPTER 3

Understanding Your Communication Style

TIP OF THE ICEBERG | THE SKILL OF MIRRORING

M ost of us enjoy reading profiles of well-known business leaders, athletes, actors, and politicians. When Daniel Akerson was named the new CEO of General Motors, he was described as brash, blunt, and demanding. Jeff Bezos, founder and CEO of Amazon.com has been described as the happy extrovert. Indra Nooyi, CEO of PepsiCo, is an inspirational leader who can relate to people from the boardroom to the front line.

Career success depends, in large part, on our ability to relate to people who vary a great deal in terms of their thoughts, feelings, and actions. Camille Wright Miller, an experienced trainer, consultant, and author has worked with many effective leaders over the years. She says many of these leaders have the ability to "mirror" the behaviors of persons they communicate with. Psychologists and sociologists use the term **mirroring** to describe a situation where one person intentionally matches the communication style of the person he or she is meeting with.[1]

In many cases, subtle shifts in how you present yourself can increase the comfort level of the other person. If you participate in a job interview, observe key elements of the person's communication style. If the person speaks slowly and seems to deliberately select each word, consider slowing your own speech pattern. Your goal is not to manipulate the other person, nor mimic the person, but to avoid a situation where the other individual is distracted by differences.

© Cengage Learning

CHAPTER PREVIEW

LEARNING OBJECTIVES

After studying Chapter 3, you will be able to

3-1 Understand the concept of communication style and its effect on interpersonal relations.

3-2 Discuss the major elements of the communication style model.

3-3 Identify your preferred communication style.

3-4 Improve communication with others through style flexing.

49

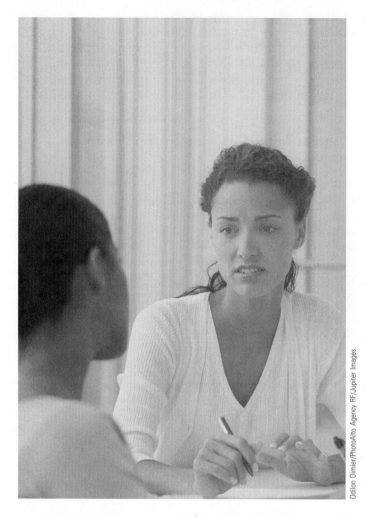

Mirroring, as you see here, is a great way to help the person you're talking to feel more comfortable, which improves communication.

Odilon Dimier/PhotoAlto Agency RF/Jupiter Images

COMMUNICATION STYLES: AN INTRODUCTION

3-1   Have you ever wondered why it seems so difficult to talk with some people and so easy to talk with others? Can you recall a situation where you met someone for the first time and immediately liked that person? Something about the individual made you feel comfortable. You may have had this experience when you started a new job or began classes at a new school. A major goal of this chapter is to help you understand the impact your communication style has on the impression others form of you. This chapter also provides you with the information you will need to cope effectively in today's workplace, which is characterized by greater diversity and more emphasis on teamwork.

human
RELATIONS
in Action

COMPETENT COMMUNICATORS

Competence in communicating starts with an understanding that we all have our own styles of communication—and different styles affect everything we hear and say.

Source: Eric F. Douglas, *Straight Talk*, Palo Alto, CA: Davies-Black Publishing, 1998, p. 1.

Communication Style Defined

The impressions that others form about us are based on what they observe us saying and doing. They have no way of knowing our innermost thoughts and feelings, so they make decisions about us based on what they see and hear.[2] The patterns of behavior that others can observe can be called **communication style**.

Each person has a unique communication style. By getting to know your style, you can achieve greater self-awareness and learn how to develop more effective interpersonal relations. Accurate self-knowledge is truly the starting point for effectiveness at work. It is also essential for managing the three key relationships described in Chapter 1: relationships with self, with another person, and with members of a group. If your career objective is to become a supervisor or manager, you will benefit by being more aware of your employees' communication styles. Job satisfaction and productivity increase when employees feel that their leaders understand their personal needs and take these into consideration.

Communication-Style Bias

Accurate self-knowledge is truly the starting point for effectiveness at work.

Your communication style is the "you" that is on display every day—the outer pattern of behavior that others see. If your style is very different from the other person's, it may be difficult for the two of you to develop rapport. **Communication-style bias** is a state of mind that most of us experience from time to time, but we may find it difficult to explain the symptoms. For example, a purchasing agent was overheard saying, "I do not know what it is, but I just don't like that sales representative." The agent was no doubt experiencing communication style bias but could not easily describe the feeling.

Personality and Your Communication Style

Psychologists generally view **personality** as a unique pattern of enduring thoughts, feelings, and actions that characterize a person.[3] Scholars and researchers agree that personality is relatively stable, changing in only subtle ways over time. Our style of communicating, on the other hand, is an acquired behavior. Modifying your communication style is a skill that can be learned. Once you learn it, it's a skill you can use all your life.[4]

Fundamental Concepts Supporting Communication Styles

This may be your first introduction to communication styles. Therefore, let's begin by reviewing a few basic concepts that support the study of this dimension of human behavior.

1. *Individual differences exist and are important.* Length of eye contact, use of gestures, speech patterns, facial expressions, and the degree of assertiveness people project to others are some of the characteristics of a personal communication style. We can identify a person's unique communication style by carefully observing these patterns of behavior.[5]
2. *Individual style differences tend to be stable.* The basics of communication style theory were established by Swiss psychiatrist Carl Jung. In his classic book *Psychological Types*, he states that every individual develops a primary communication style that remains quite stable throughout life. Each person has a relatively distinctive way of responding to people and events.[6]

3. *There is a limited number of styles.* Jung observed that people tend to fall into one of several behavior patterns when relating to the world around them. He describes four behavior styles: intuitor, thinker, feeler, and sensor.[7] Those in the same behavior category tend to display similar traits.

4. *A communication style is a way of thinking and behaving.* It is not an ability but instead a preferred way of using the abilities one has. This distinction is very important. An *ability* refers to how well someone can do something. A *style* refers to how someone likes to do something.[8]

5. *To create the most productive working relationships, it is necessary to get in sync (mirror) the behavior patterns (communication style) of the people you work with.*[9] The ability to identify another person's communication style and to know how and when to adapt your own preferred style to it, can give you an important advantage in dealing with people. Learning to adapt your style to fit the needs of another person is called "style flexing," a topic that is discussed later in this chapter.

Total Person Insight

CLICKING SHAPES OUR LIVES

Whether it's at a party or at work, we all know what it feels like to "click" with another person. New research suggests that clicking plays a significant role in determining our career success.

Source: Ori Brafman and Rom Brafman, "Etc. Social Studies," *Bloomberg Businessweek*, June 20, 2010, pp. 72–73.

THE COMMUNICATION STYLE MODEL

3-2   This section introduces a model that encompasses four basic communication styles. This simple model is based on research studies conducted during the past 70 years and features two important dimensions of human behavior: dominance and sociability. As you study the communication style model, keep in mind that it describes your *preferences*, not your *abilities*.

The Dominance Continuum

In study after study, those "differences that make a difference" in interpersonal relationships point to dominance as an important dimension of style. **Dominance** can be defined as the tendency to display a "take-charge" attitude. Every person falls somewhere on the **dominance continuum**, illustrated in Figure 3.1. David W. Johnson in his book

Figure 3.1 ■ Dominance Continuum

Low dominance   High dominance

Source: From Manning, Gerald L., Michael Ahearne, Barry L. Reece, *Selling Today: Partnering to Create Value*, 12th, © 2012. Reproduced by permission of Pearson Education, Inc., Upper Saddle River, New Jersey.

Reaching Out—Interpersonal Effectiveness and Self-Actualization states that people tend to fall into two dominance categories: low or high.[10]

1. *Low dominance.* These people are characterized by a tendency to be cooperative and eager to assist others. They tend to be low in assertiveness and are more willing to be controlled by others.
2. *High dominance.* These people give advice freely and frequently initiate demands. They are more assertive and tend to seek control over others.

The first step in determining your most preferred communication style is to identify where you fall on the dominance continuum. Do you tend to be low or high on this scale? To answer this question, complete the dominance indicator form in Figure 3.2. Rate yourself on each scale by placing a checkmark at a point along the continuum that represents how you are perceived by *others*. If most of your checkmarks fall to the right of center, you rank high in dominance. If most fall to the left of center, you are low in dominance.

Another way to assess the dominance dimension is to ask four or five people who know you well to complete the dominance indicator form for you. Their assessment may provide a more accurate indication of where you fall on the continuum. Self-assessment alone is sometimes inaccurate because we often lack self-insight.[11] Once you have received the forms completed by others, try to determine if a consistent pattern exists. (Note: It is best not to involve parents, spouses, or close relatives. Seek feedback from coworkers or classmates.)

Where Should You Be on the Dominance Continuum?

Is there any best place to be on the dominance continuum? Not really. Successful people can be found at all points along the continuum. Nevertheless, there are times when people need to act decisively to influence the adoption of their ideas and communicate their expectations clearly. This means that someone low in dominance may need to become more assertive temporarily to achieve an objective. New managers who are low in dominance must learn to influence others without being viewed as aggressive or insensitive. The American Management Association offers a course entitled "Assertiveness Training," which is designed for individuals who want to exercise a greater influence on others, get their suggestions across more effectively, and resolve conflict situations decisively yet diplomatically.[12]

People who are high in dominance must sometimes curb their desire to express strong opinions and initiate demands.

People who are high in dominance must sometimes curb their desire to express strong opinions and initiate demands. A person who is perceived as being extremely strong-willed and inflexible will have difficulty establishing a cooperative relationship with others.

human
RELATIONS
in Action

SUCCESS OR FAILURE IS UNRELATED TO ANY STYLE

Your style is not based on how you see yourself. Your style is based on other people's perceptions of you—regardless of how much or how little those perceptions match your own self-image. Self-knowledge is the beginning of wisdom.

Source: Robert Bolton and Dorothy Grover Bolton, *People Styles at Work*, New York: American Management Association, 1996, p. 13.

Figure 3.2 ■ Dominance Indicator Form

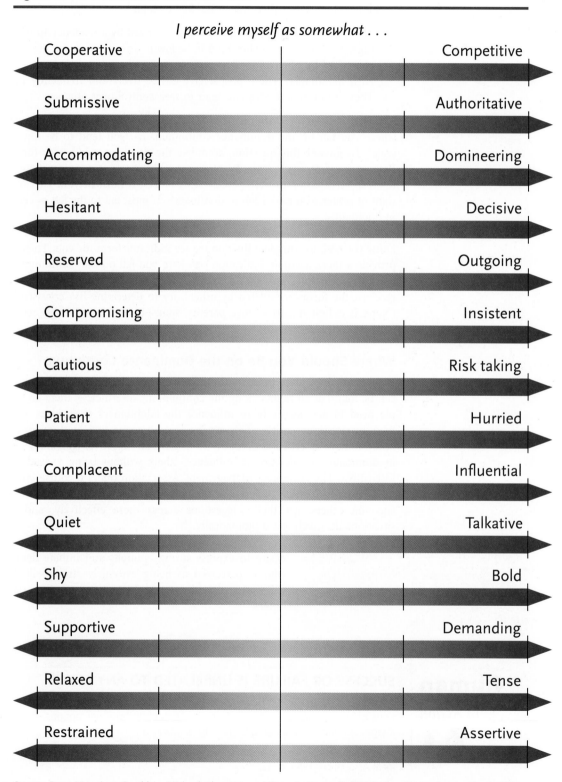

Figure 3.3 ■ Sociability Continuum

High sociability

Low sociability

Source: From Manning, Gerald L., Michael Ahearne, and Barry L. Reece, *Selling Today: Partnering to Create Value*, 12th, © 2012. Reproduced by permission of Pearson Education, Inc., Upper Saddle River, New Jersey.

The Sociability Continuum

Have you ever met someone who was open and talkative and who seemed easy to get to know? An individual who is friendly and expresses feeling openly can be placed near the top of the **sociability continuum.**[13] The continuum is illustrated in Figure 3.3. **Sociability** can be defined as the tendency to seek and enjoy social relationships.

Sociability can also be thought of as a measure of whether you tend to control or express your feelings. Those high in sociability usually express their feelings freely, whereas people low on the continuum tend to control their feelings. The person who is classified as being high in sociability is open and talkative and likes personal associations. The person who is low in sociability is more reserved and formal in social relationships.

The second step in determining your most preferred communication style is to identify where you fall on the sociability continuum. To answer this question, complete the sociability indicator form shown in Figure 3.4. Rate yourself on each scale by placing a checkmark at a point along the continuum that represents how you are perceived by others. If most of your checkmarks fall to the right of center, you are high in sociability. If most fall to the left of center, you are low in sociability.

The sociability indicator form is not meant to be a precise instrument, but it will provide you with a general indication of where you fall on each of the scales. You may also want to make copies of the form and distribute them to friends or coworkers for completion. (Remember, it is advisable not to involve parents, spouses, or close relatives in this feedback exercise.)

Where Should You Be on the Sociability Continuum?

Where are successful people on the sociability continuum? Everywhere. There is no best place to be. People at all points along the continuum can achieve success in an organizational setting. Nevertheless, there are some commonsense guidelines that persons who fall at either end of the continuum are wise to follow.

Figure 3.4 ■ Sociability Indicator Form

I perceive myself as somewhat . . .

Disciplined	Easygoing
Controlled	Expressive
Serious	Lighthearted
Methodical	Unstructured
Calculating	Spontaneous
Guarded	Open
Introverted	Extroverted
Aloof	Friendly
Formal	Casual
Reserved	Attention seeking
Cautious	Carefree
Conforming	Unconventional
Subdued	Dramatic
Restrained	Impulsive

Source: From Manning, Gerald L., Michael Ahearne, and Barry L. Reece, *Selling Today: Partnering to Create Value*, 12th, © 2012. Reproduced by permission of Pearson Education, Inc., Upper Saddle River, New Jersey.

A person who is low in sociability is more likely to display a no-nonsense attitude when dealing with other people. This person may be seen as impersonal and business-like. Behavior that is too guarded and too reserved can be a barrier to effective communication. Such persons may be perceived as unconcerned about the feelings of others and interested only in getting the job done. Perceptions are critical in the business world, especially among customers. Even a hint of indifference can create a customer relations problem.

People who are high in sociability openly express their feelings, emotions, and impressions. They are perceived as being concerned with relationships and therefore are easy to get to know. At times, emotionally expressive people need to curb their natural exuberance. Too much informality can be a problem in some work relationships. The importance of adapting your style to accommodate the needs of others is discussed later in this chapter.

Four Communication Styles

The dominance and sociability continua can be combined to form a rather simple model that will tell you more about your communication style (see Figure 3.5).

The **communication style model** will help you identify your most preferred style. Dominance is represented by the horizontal axis and sociability by the vertical axis. The model is divided into quadrants, each representing one of four communication styles: emotive, directive, reflective, or supportive. As you review the descriptions of these styles, you will likely find one that is "most like you" and one or more that are "least like you."

Emotive Style. The upper-right-hand quadrant combines high sociability and high dominance. This is characteristic of the **emotive style** of communication (Figure 3.6).

Figure 3.5 ■ When the dominance and sociability dimensions are combined, the framework for communication style classification is established.

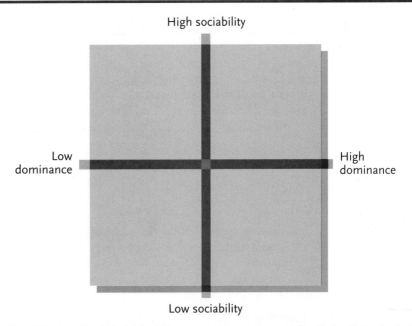

Source: From Manning, Gerald L., Michael Ahearne, and Barry L. Reece, *Selling Today: Partnering to Create Value*, 12th, © 2012. Reproduced by permission of Pearson Education, Inc., Upper Saddle River, New Jersey.

Figure 3.6 ■ The emotive style combines high sociability and high dominance.

High sociability

EMOTIVE

Low dominance

High dominance

Low sociability

Source: From Manning, Gerald L., Michael Ahearne, and Barry L. Reece, *Selling Today: Partnering to Create Value*, 12th, © 2012. Reproduced by permission of Pearson Education, Inc., Upper Saddle River, New Jersey.

You can easily form a mental picture of the emotive type by thinking about the phrases used earlier to describe high dominance and high sociability. A good example of the emotive type of person is comedian Jay Leno. Ellen DeGeneres, talk-show host, and Suze Orman, noted authority on money management, also project an outspoken, enthusiastic, and stimulating style. Rachael Ray, host of several Food Network cooking shows, displays the emotive style. She is animated, frequently laughs at herself, and seems to like an informal atmosphere.

Here is a list of verbal and nonverbal clues that identify the emotive person:

1. *Displays spontaneous, uninhibited behavior.* The emotive person is more apt to talk rapidly, express views with enthusiasm, and use vigorous hand gestures. David Letterman, late night talk show host, and Richard Branson, the founder of Virgin Atlantic Airways, fit this description.
2. *Displays the personality dimension described as extroversion.* Extroverts typically enjoy being with other people and tend to be active and upbeat. The emotive person likes informality and usually prefers to operate on a first-name basis.
3. *Possesses a natural persuasiveness.* Combining high dominance and high sociability, this person finds it easy to express his or her point of view dramatically and forcefully.

Directive Style. The lower-right-hand quadrant represents a communication style that combines high dominance and low sociability—the **directive style** (Figure 3.7). Martha Stewart and Donald Trump project the directive style. Tom Peters, the hard-driving

Figure 3.7 ■ The directive style combines high dominance and low sociability.

Source: From Manning, Gerald L., Michael Ahearne, and Barry L. Reece, *Selling Today: Partnering to Create Value*, 12th, © 2012. Reproduced by permission of Pearson Education, Inc., Upper Saddle River, New Jersey.

management consultant, easily fits the description of this communication style. All these people have been described as frank, assertive, and very determined. Some behaviors displayed by directives include the following:

1. *Projects a serious attitude.* Senator John McCain projects the directive style.
2. *Expresses strong opinions.* With firm gestures and a tone of voice that communicates determination, the directive projects the image of someone who wants to take control. Judge Judith Sheindlin of the *Judge Judy* television show and Phillip McGraw, known to television viewers as "Dr. Phil," display this behavior.
3. *May project indifference.* It is not easy for the directive to communicate a warm, caring attitude. He or she does not find it easy to abandon the formal approach in dealing with people.

Reflective Style. The lower-left-hand quadrant of the communication style model features a combination of low dominance and low sociability. This is the **reflective style** of communication (Figure 3.8).

The reflective person is usually quiet, enjoys spending time alone, and does not make decisions quickly. The late physicist Albert Einstein fits this description. He once commented on how he liked to spend idle hours: "When I have no special problem to occupy my mind, I love to reconstruct proofs of mathematical and physical theorems that have long been known to me. There is no goal in this, merely an opportunity to indulge in the pleasant occupation of thinking."[14]

Figure 3.8 ■ The reflective style combines low dominance and low sociability.

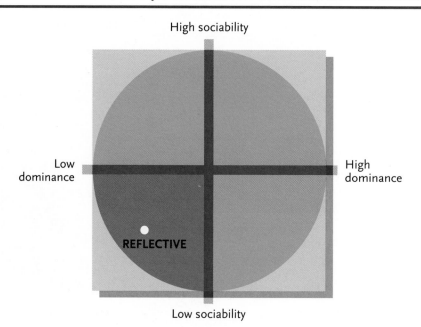

Source: From Manning, Gerald L., Michael Ahearne, and Barry L. Reece, *Selling Today: Partnering to Create Value*, 12th, © 2012. Reproduced by permission of Pearson Education, Inc., Upper Saddle River, New Jersey.

Captain Chesley "Sully" Sullenberger was at the controls of his Airbus A320 when it suffered a bird strike en route from New York to Charlotte, North Carolina. After the loss of both engines he executed an emergency landing on the Hudson River. After several interviews with Captain Sullenberger, a *Wall Street Journal* reporter described him as "...a precise, methodical, cerebral man who carefully chooses his words."[15] These are the characteristics of the reflective communication style. Some of the behaviors characteristic of this style are as follows:

1. *Expresses opinions in a disciplined, deliberate manner.* The reflective person does not seem to be in a hurry. He or she expresses measured opinions. Emotional control is a common trait of this style.
2. *Seems to be preoccupied.* The reflective person is rather quiet and may often appear preoccupied with other matters. As a result, he or she may seem aloof and difficult to get to know.
3. *Prefers orderliness.* The reflective person prefers an orderly work environment. At a meeting, this person appreciates an agenda. A reflective person enjoys reviewing details and making decisions slowly.

Supportive Style. The upper-left-hand quadrant combines low dominance and high sociability—the **supportive style** of communication (Figure 3.9). People who possess this style tend to be cooperative, patient, and attentive.

Figure 3.9 ■ The supportive style combines low dominance and high sociability.

High sociability

SUPPORTIVE

Low dominance   High dominance

Low sociability

Source: From Manning, Gerald L., Michael Ahearne, and Barry L. Reece, *Selling Today: Partnering to Create Value*, 12th, © 2012. Reproduced by permission of Pearson Education, Inc., Upper Saddle River, New Jersey.

The supportive person is reserved and usually avoids attention-seeking behavior. Additional behaviors that commonly characterize the supportive style include the following:

1. *Listens attentively.* Good listeners have a unique advantage in many occupational settings. This is especially true of loan officers, sales personnel, and supervisors. The talent comes more naturally to the supportive person.
2. *Avoids the use of power.* Supportive persons are more likely to rely on friendly persuasion than power when dealing with people. They like to display warmth in their speech and written correspondence. Neil Armstrong, Apollo 11 crew member, and Julia Roberts, actress, display these behaviors.
3. *Makes and expresses decisions in a thoughtful, deliberate manner.* Supportive persons appear low-key in a decision-making role. Meryl Streep, Paul Simon, Meg Ryan, Kevin Costner, the late Princess Di, and Mary Tyler Moore all display characteristics of this style.

INTERNATIONAL MARKET FOR FOUR-STYLE TRAINING

Although four-style programs were initially created and marketed in the United States, they have become a global phenomenon. Wilson Learning, a pioneer in four-style training for over 40 years, is doing business in 45 countries. Inscape Publishing, the company that developed the popular DiSC learning instrument over three decades ago, reports that more than 40 million people worldwide have completed DiSC four-dimension workshops.

Source: "A Global Profiling Tool" (Wilson Learning Corporation: Eden Prairie, Minn., 1999); Tom Ritchey, *I'm Stuck, You're Stuck* (San Francisco: Berrett-Koehler, Inc., 2002), p. 5.

IDENTIFYING YOUR PREFERRED COMMUNICATION STYLE

3-3 A college professor enrolled in a four-style training program offered by Wilson Learning Corporation. After completion of a communication style assessment instrument, he learned that his preferred style was *reflective*. At first, the professor had doubts about the validity of the instrument. Over the years he had made many classroom presentations and viewed himself as an *emotive*. We must avoid stereotyping or "pigeon holing" persons who work in various occupations. Not all scientists are *reflective* and not all salespeople are *emotive*.

Did you find one particular communication style that is most like yours? If your first attempt to identify your most preferred style was not successful, do not be discouraged. No one conforms completely to one style. You share some traits with other styles. Also, keep in mind that communication style is just one dimension of personality. As noted previously, your personality is made up of a broad array of psychological and behavioral characteristics. It is this unique pattern of characteristics that makes each person an individual. *Communication style* refers only to those behaviors that others can observe.

Did you discover a communication style that is least like yours? In many cases, we feel a sense of tension or discomfort when we have contact with persons who speak or act in ways that are at odds with our communication style. For example, the person with

Rachael Ray, host of several television cooking shows, often expresses her views dramatically and impulsively. The *emotive* person likes to create a social relationship quickly and usually feels more comfortable in an informal atmosphere.

a need for orderliness and structure in daily work may feel tension when working closely with someone who is more spontaneous and unstructured.

Online Assessment of Your Communication Style

You can gain additional insight into your communication style by accessing the product support website for this book at www.cengagebrain.com and clicking on the Online Assessment of Your Communication Style link. After completing the assessment, you will be provided with a profile indicating your most preferred communication style.

Variation Within Your Communication Style

Communication styles also vary in intensity. For example, a person may be either moderately or strongly dominant. Note that the communication style model features zones that radiate outward from the center, as illustrated in Figure 3.10. These dimensions might be thought of as **intensity zones**.

Zone 1. People who fall within Zone 1 will display their unique behavioral characteristics with less intensity than people in Zone 2. This means that it may be more difficult to identify the preferred communication style of people in Zone 1. They will not be as obvious in their gestures, tone of voice, speech patterns, or emotional expressions. You may have trouble picking up the right clues to identify their communication style.

Zone 2. People who fall within Zone 2 will display their behavioral characteristics with greater intensity than those in Zone 1. For example, on the following dominance continuum, Sue, Mike, Harold, and Deborah each fall within a different zone.

Figure 3.10 ■ Communication Style Intensity Zones

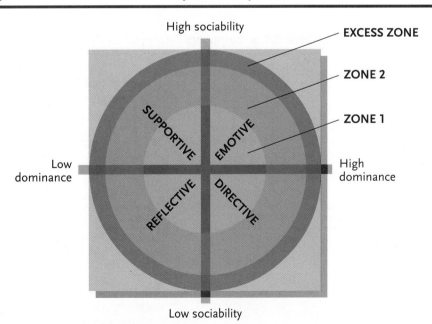

Source: From Manning, Gerald L., Michael Ahearne, and Barry L. Reece, *Selling Today: Partnering to Create Value*, 12th, © 2012. Reproduced by permission of Pearson Education, Inc., Upper Saddle River, New Jersey.

In terms of communication style identification, it is probably easier to distinguish between Sue and Deborah (who are in Zone 2) than between Mike and Harold (who are in Zone 1). Of course, the boundary line that separates Zone 1 from Zone 2 should not be viewed as a permanent barrier. It is important to understand that under certain conditions, people will abandon their preferred style temporarily.

You can sometimes observe this behavior change when a person is upset or angry. For example, Sue is a strong supporter of equal rights for women. At school, she hears a male student say, "I think a woman's place is in the home." At that point, she may express her own views in the strongest possible terms. This forcefulness will require temporarily abandoning the comfort of her low-dominance style to display assertive behavior.

Excess Zone. The **excess zone** is characterized by a high degree of intensity and rigidity. It can also be labeled the "danger" zone. When people occupy this zone, they become inflexible and display a lack of versatility (see Table 3.1). Extreme intensity in any quadrant is bound to interfere with good human relations.

> *Inflexible and rigid communication styles are likely to lead to a breakdown in human relations.*

People often move into the excess zone when they are under stress or not feeling well. A person who feels threatened or insecure may also move into the excess zone. Even a temporary excursion into the excess zone should be avoided if at all possible. Inflexible and rigid communication styles are likely to lead to a breakdown in human relations.

Table 3.1 ■ Behaviors Displayed in the Excess Zone

Supportive Style	Attempts to win approval by agreeing with everyone Constantly seeks reassurance Refuses to take a strong stand Tends to apologize a great deal
Directive Style	Is determined to come out on top Will not admit to being wrong Appears cold and unfeeling when dealing with others Tends to use dogmatic phrases such as "always," "never," or "you can't"
Emotive Style	Tends to express highly emotional opinions Is outspoken to the point of being offensive Seems unwilling to listen to the views of others Uses exaggerated gestures and facial expressions
Reflective Style	Tends to avoid making a decision Seems overly interested in detail Is very stiff and formal when dealing with others Seeks to achieve perfection

Tips on Style Identification

To identify a person's communication style, focus your full attention on observable behavior. The best clues for identifying styles are nonverbal. Learn to be observant of people's gestures, posture, and facial expressions, and the rapidity and loudness of their speech.[16] Animated facial expressions and high-volume, rapid speech are characteristic of the emotive communication style. Infrequent use of gestures, speaking in a steady monotone, and few facial expressions are characteristic of the reflective style. Of course verbal messages will also be helpful. If a person tends to be blunt and to the point and makes strong statements, you are likely observing a directive.

We have noted that communication style is determined by where a person falls on the sociability continuum and the dominance continuum. Once you have identified as many verbal and nonverbal clues as possible, use this information to place the person on each continuum. Let's assume that the clues indicate that the person is low in dominance. This means you can automatically eliminate the emotive and directive styles because both are characterized by high dominance. The next step is to place the person on the sociability continuum. If the clues indicate that the person is low in sociability, you automatically eliminate the supportive style. By the process of elimination, you conclude that this person is probably reflective. The authors of *People Styles at Work*, however, warn that your initial perception of another person's style should not be carved in stone. You should continue to collect new information and reassess your initial observations (see Table 3.2).[17]

Keep in mind that different situations bring out different behaviors. If you observe someone participating in a classroom discussion, then later observe the same person relaxing with friends at a local restaurant, you may witness two different behavioral patterns. Getting to know someone is hard work, and it's best not to look for shortcuts.[18]

Table 3.2 ■ How to Read Others

Style identification is based on observation of behavior. Behavior is what a person does that can be *seen* and *heard*. Look for specific clues that are useful in discovering a person's style. Consider these examples:

Directive	Emotive
■ Decides quickly	■ Starts conversations easily
■ Gets right to the point	■ Makes friends easily
■ Takes charge	■ Generally outgoing
■ Moves quickly	■ Persuades others
Supportive	**Reflective**
■ Listens patiently	■ Thinks things through
■ Relates to others warmly	■ Not impulsive
■ Avoids arguments	■ Plans ahead
■ Rarely makes demands of others	■ Detailed reports and messages

Source: Robert Bolton and Dorothy Grover Bolton, *People Styles at Work*, New York: American Management Association, 1996, p. 80–81. Tom Ritchey, *I'm Stuck, You're Stuck*, San Francisco: Berrett-Koehler Publishers, Inc., 2002, p. 78.

VERSATILITY: THE THIRD DIMENSION

3-4   Earlier in this chapter, we described two important dimensions of the communication style model: dominance and sociability. You will recall that these dimensions of human behavior are independent of each other. Now we are ready to discuss versatility, an important third dimension of human behavior.

Persons who can create and maintain interpersonal relations with others, regardless of their communication styles, are displaying versatility. **Versatility** can be defined as acting in ways that earn a social endorsement. Endorsement means simply other people's approval of our behavior. People give us their endorsement when they feel *comfortable* and *non-defensive* with us.[19]

The dimension of versatility is independent of style. This means that the emotive style is no more or less likely to be versatile than is the reflective style. Communication style remains relatively stable throughout life, whereas versatility is changeable.

Versatility is a trait we exhibit ourselves rather than elicit from others. Versatile people recognize that they can control their half of relationships and that it is easier to modify themselves than it is to modify others. The versatile person asks, "What can I do to make it easier for the other person to relate to me?"[20]

Research on versatility conducted by Wilson Learning Corporation indicates that the ability to adapt to another person's communication style greatly improves interpersonal relationships. People are divided nearly equally across the four communication styles, so we share our own style with only one out of four persons we have contact with. Once we develop and apply versatility skills, a greater number of people will feel comfortable and non-defensive in our presence.[21]

Achieving Versatility Through Style Flexing

Getting classified according to communication style doesn't mean you are "typecast" for life. You can always learn to strengthen areas of your most preferred communication

Versatility is a trait displayed by journalist Diane Sawyer, shown here with co-anchor Robin Roberts interviewing Beyoncé. She has the ability to adapt to another person's communication style quite easily. The dimension of versatility is independent of style.

style in order to get along better with others.[22] One way to broaden your personality is to engage in **style flexing**, which is the deliberate attempt to change or alter your style to meet the needs of another person. It is a temporary effort to act in harmony with the behavior of another person's communication style. Style flexing is communicating in a way that is more agreeable to persons of other styles. As noted earlier in this chapter, you can learn to adapt your style to accommodate others.

Total Person Insight

"The process of understanding our behavior and the behavior of others is difficult, time-consuming, and often draining. It is a struggle we will all face on a continual basis."

Source: Bob Phillips and Kimberly Alyn, *How to Deal with Annoying People*, Eugene, Oregon: Harvest House Publishers, 2005, p. 18.

Style Flexing at Work. To illustrate how style flexing can be used in an organizational setting, let's take a look at a communication problem faced by Jeff Walker, buyer of sporting goods for a small chain of sporting goods stores. Jeff's preferred communication style is *emotive*. His immediate supervisor is Rhonda Greenbaum. Her preferred style is *reflective* and tends to approach her work in an orderly, systematic manner. Jeff finds it difficult to curb his stimulating, promotional style and therefore is sometimes viewed as "unstable" by Ms. Greenbaum.

What might Jeff do to improve communication with his supervisor? Jeff is naturally an open, impulsive communicator. During meetings with a reflective person, he should appear less spontaneous, slow his rate of speech, and avoid the use of dramatic gestures. He should try to appear more reserved.

The reflective person admires orderliness, so Jeff should be sure he is well prepared. Before each meeting, he should develop a mental agenda of items that he wants to cover. At the beginning of the meeting he might say, "Ms. Greenbaum, there are three things I want to discuss." He would then describe each item concisely and present information slowly and systematically. This disciplined approach will be appreciated by the reflective supervisor.

Strategies for Adapting Your Style

Once you have identified the dominant style of the other person, begin thinking of ways to flex your style to gain a social endorsement. Remember, you can control your half of the relationship. What can be done to meet the interpersonal needs of the other person? Here are a few general style adaptation strategies:

Flexing to the Emotive Style

- Take time to build a social as well as a business relationship. Leave time for relating and socializing.
- Display interest in the person's ideas, interests, and experiences.
- Do not place too much emphasis on details. Emotive people like fast-moving, inspirational verbal exchanges.
- Maintain a pace that is fast and somewhat spontaneous.

Flexing to the Directive Style

- Be specific, brief, and to the point. Use time efficiently.
- Present the facts logically, and be prepared to provide specific answers to questions.
- Maintain a pace that is fast and decisive; project an image of strength and confidence.
- Messages (written or oral) should be short and to the point.

Flexing to the Reflective Style

- Appeal to the person's orderly, systematic approach to life. Be well organized.
- Approach this person in a straightforward, direct manner. Get down to business quickly.
- Be as accurate and realistic as possible when presenting information.
- Messages (written or oral) should be detailed and precise. The pace of verbal messages should be slow and systematic.

Flexing to the Supportive Style

- Show a sincere interest in the person. Take time to identify areas of common interest.
- Patiently draw out personal views and goals. Listen and be responsive to the person's needs.
- Present your views in a quiet, nonthreatening manner. Do not be pushy.
- Put a priority on relationship building and communication.

In those situations where you are attempting to win the support or cooperation of another person, look and listen for clues that identify the individual's preferred communication style. Once you are able to recognize and adjust to communication styles different from your own, gaining a social endorsement will be much easier.

---

human
RELATIONS
in Action

STEVE BALLMER: EMBRACING THE EXCESS ZONE

Steve Ballmer, CEO of Microsoft, was known as a very demanding executive during his early years with the company. His explosive temper was legendary, and he often put the fear of God into his staff members. He once needed throat surgery because he yelled so much. Later he became more diplomatic and less domineering.

Source: "The Top 25 Managers of the Year," *BusinessWeek*, January 14, 2002, p. 65.

In an organizational setting, style flexing is especially critical when something important is at stake. Let's assume that you are head of a major department in a large hospital. Tomorrow you will meet with the hospital administrator and propose the purchase of new X-ray equipment that will cost a large amount of money. This is a good time to think about the administrator's communication style and consider your style-flexing strategies. Every decision is influenced by both reason and emotion, but the weight given to each of these elements during the decision-making process can vary from one person to another. Often we make the mistake of focusing too much attention on the content of our message and not enough on how to deliver that message.[23]

A WORD OF CAUTION

A discussion of communication styles would not be complete without a few words of caution. It is tempting to put a label on someone and then assume the label tells you everything you need to know about that person. In *The Name of Your Game*, Stuart Atkins says we should be careful not to use labels that make people feel boxed in, type-cast, or judged. He says we should not classify *people*; we should classify their *strengths* and *preferences* to act one way or another under certain circumstances.[24] As noted in Chapter 1, the "total person" is made up of such interdependent traits as emotional control, values orientation, self-esteem, and self-awareness. To get acquainted with the whole person takes time and effort. Atkins makes this observation: "It requires much more effort to look beyond the label, to experience the person as a dynamic process, to look at the fine print on the box and carefully study the ingredients inside the package. We have been conditioned to trust the label and look no further."[25]

> *It is tempting to put a label on someone and then assume the label tells you everything you need to know about that person.*

You must also be careful not to let the label you place on yourself become the justification for your own inflexible behavior. If you discover that your most preferred communication style is reflective and take the position that "others will simply have to get used to my need for careful analysis of data before making a decision," then you are not displaying the characteristics of a versatile person. Try not to let the label justify or reinforce why you are unable to communicate effectively with others.[26]

Strength/Weakness Paradox

As noted previously in this chapter, there is no "best" communication style. Each style has its unique strong points. Supportive people are admired for their easygoing, responsive style. Directives are respected for the thoroughness and determination they display. The stimulating, personable style of emotive persons can be very refreshing. And the emotional control and disciplined nature of reflective persons are almost universally admired.

Problems arise when people overextend or rely too much on the strengths of their style. The directive who is too demanding may be viewed by others as "pushy." The supportive person may try too hard to please others and risk being viewed as "wishy-washy." An emotive person may be viewed as too excitable or not serious enough in a business setting. The reflective person who cannot seem to make a decision without mountains of information may be viewed as too cautious and inflexible. Some people rely too heavily on established strengths and fail to develop new skills that will increase their versatility.

LOOKING BACK: SUMMARY OF LEARNING OBJECTIVES

1. Understand the concept of communication style and its effect on interpersonal relations.

   Communication styles are our patterns of behaviors that are observable to others. Each of us has a distinctive way of responding to people and events. Communication style bias is likely to surface when you meet someone who displays a style distinctly different from your own.

2. Discuss the major elements of the communication style model.

   The communication style model is formed by combining two important dimensions of human behavior: dominance and sociability. Combinations of these two aspects create four communication styles—emotive, directive, reflective, and supportive.

3. Identify your preferred communication style.

   With practice you can learn to identify your communication style. The starting point is to rate yourself on each scale (dominance and sociability) by placing a checkmark at a point along the continuum that represents how you perceive yourself. Completion of the dominance and sociability indicator forms will help you achieve greater awareness of your communication style. You may also want to ask others to complete these forms for you.

4. Improve communication with others through style flexing.

   A third dimension of human behavior—versatility—is important in dealing with communication styles that are different from your own. You can adjust your own style to meet the needs of others—a process called style flexing.

   We must keep an open mind about people and be careful not to use labels that make them feel typecast or judged. Keeping an open mind requires more thought than pigeonholing does.

KEY TERMS

mirroring, 49	sociability continuum, 55	supportive style, 60
communication style, 51	sociability, 55	intensity zones, 63
communication-style bias, 51	communication style model, 57	excess zone, 64
personality, 51	emotive style, 57	versatility, 66
dominance, 52	directive style, 58	style flexing, 67
dominance continuum, 52	reflective style, 59	

CAREER INSIGHT

An organizational consultant noticed something unusual during a visit to a large engineering firm. Most employees wore plastic name tags with large capitalized letters after their names: Sue Banson ENFP or Raymond Bloom INTJ. Every employee in the company had completed the Myers-Briggs personality inventory. Each employees' four-letter personality description was on display so coworkers could quickly understand their personality type. Good idea? This approach will create problems if employees assume the labels of any personality test tells them everything they need to know. The Myers-Briggs personality descriptor is just the tip of the iceberg.

Source: Judith Sills, "When Personalities Clash," *Psychology Today*, November/December 2006, pp. 51–62.

TRY YOUR HAND

1. Jay Leno is a popular late night comedian. Consider the behaviors he displays on his show, and then complete the following exercises:
   a. On the dominance continuum, place a mark where you feel he belongs.
   b. On the sociability continuum, place a mark where you feel he belongs.
   c. On the basis of these two continua, determine Jay Leno's communication style.
   d. In your opinion, does he display style flexibility?
2. Myers-Briggs Personality Types and Jungian Personality Types are two very popular descriptions of the concepts in this chapter. Using your search engine, access the Internet sites that refer to these concepts. Type in "Jungian" + personality profiles to access the Jungian personality types. To access the Myers-Briggs types, type in "Myers-Briggs" + personality profiles. Does the number of queries indicate anything about the validity and popularity of these theories? Examine specific queries about both of these theories. Do you see the relationship between these two theories and the material in this chapter? Each year about 2.5 million Americans complete the Myers-Briggs Type Indicator (M.B.T.I.). Why is this psychological-assessment instrument so popular?
3. Self-awareness is very important. As we get to know ourselves, we can identify barriers to acceptance by others. Once you have identified your most preferred communication style, you have taken a big step in the direction of self-awareness.

If you have not yet determined your most preferred communication style, take a few minutes to complete the dominance indicator form (Figure 3.2) and the sociability indicator form (Figure 3.4). Follow the instructions provided.

4. You have been given the opportunity to complete an online assessment of your communication style (see page 63). After completion of this assessment, you were provided with a profile that indicates your most preferred communication style. In some work or social situations, you may find yourself exhibiting a communication style that is different than your preferred style. Reflect on a situation where you engaged in style flexing. What communication style did you display? Did the movement away from your most preferred style improve communication?

5. Visit the websites of Wilson Learning Worldwide and Inscape Publishing and review the popular communication style training programs offered by each company.

CRITICAL THINKING CHALLENGE

1. After you have determined your own place on the dominance scale, think about your closest coworkers and friends. Who is the most dominant in your circle? Who is the least dominant? Can you recall occasions when either low dominance or high dominance created a barrier to effective interpersonal relations?

2. After you have determined your position on the sociability scale, think about your closest coworkers and friends. Who is the highest on the sociability indicator? Who is the lowest? Can you recall an occasion when high sociability or low sociability created a barrier to effective interpersonal relations?

SELF-ASSESSMENT EXERCISE

For each of the following statements, circle the number from 1 to 5 that best represents your response to each statement: (1) strongly disagree (never do this); (2) disagree (rarely do this); (3) moderately agree (sometimes do this); (4) agree (frequently do this); (5) strongly agree (almost always do this).

A. I have a clear understanding of the two dimensions of human behavior: dominance and sociability.	1	2	3	4	5
B. I can describe the verbal and nonverbal clues that identify each of the four basic communication styles.	1	2	3	4	5
C. I accept the fact that each communication style has its unique strong points and that there is no "best" communication style.	1	2	3	4	5
D. I make a deliberate attempt to change or alter my communication style (style flexing) in order to meet the needs of other persons.	1	2	3	4	5

After identifying your response to each item, select an attitude or skill you would like to improve. Prepare a written goal and then describe the steps you will take to achieve this goal.

YOU PLAY THE ROLE

For the purpose of this role-play, read the Closing Case: Style Flexing and assume the role of Eric Welch, who is described as a quiet, amiable person who displays the supportive communication style.

You will meet with Susan Hernandez, who has set up an appointment to inspect the property you represent. Prior to the role-play, study the chapter material on style flexing and on how to communicate effectively with persons who display the directive communication style. Prepare for the first five to seven minutes of the meeting. How will you present yourself during the initial contact? What would be the best way to get the meeting off to a good start?

BELOW THE SURFACE | APPLYING THE SKILL OF MIRRORING

At the beginning of this chapter, we noted that psychologists and sociologists use the term *mirroring* to describe a situation where one person intentionally matches the communication style of the person who they are talking to. By knowing our own communication style, we are better able to recognize and respond to the other person's style.

When we mirror the person with whom we are speaking, they tend to feel more relaxed and are more likely to open up. Mirroring may involve several aspects of nonverbal communication such as eye contact, facial expressions, gestures, and personal space. Monitoring the behavior of the person you are talking to requires your complete concentration. The use of active listening skills, described in Chapter 2, will be very helpful during the mirroring process.

QUESTIONS

1. Communication-style bias is a state of mind that most of us experience from time to time. How can mirroring help us avoid this form of bias?

2. Let's assume you are preparing for a job interview with a hard-driving department manager who has been described as frank, assertive, and very determined. What behaviors should you display that will enhance your chances of building rapport with this person?

CLOSING CASE | STYLE FLEXING

Eric Welch has been employed at Grant Real Estate for almost two years. Before receiving his real estate license, he was a property manager with a large real estate agency in another community. During his first year with Grant, he was assigned to the residential property division and sold properties totaling $825,000. He then requested and received a transfer to the commercial division.

Three months ago, Eric obtained a commercial listing that consisted of 26 acres of land near a growing residential neighborhood. The land is zoned commercial and appears to be ideally suited for a medium-size shopping center. Eric prepared a detailed prospectus and sent it to Susan Hernandez, president of Mondale Growth Corporation, a firm specializing in development of shopping centers. One week later, he received a letter from Ms. Hernandez requesting more information. Shortly after receiving Eric's response, Ms. Hernandez called to set up an appointment to inspect the property. A time and date were finalized, and Eric agreed to meet her plane and conduct a tour of the property.

Eric is a quiet, amiable person who displays the *supportive* communication style. Friends say that they like to spend time with him because he is a good listener.

QUESTIONS

1. If Ms. Hernandez displays the characteristics of the *directive* communication style, how should Eric conduct himself during the meeting? Be specific as you analyze those behaviors that would be admired by Ms. Hernandez.

2. If Ms. Hernandez wants to build rapport with Eric Welch, what behaviors should she display?

3. It is not a good idea to put a label on someone and then assume the label tells us everything about the person. As Eric attempts to build rapport with Ms. Hernandez, what other personal characteristics should he try to identify?

CHAPTER 3 ENDNOTES

1. Camille Wright Miller, "Mirroring Others Helps You Connect with Them," *The Roanoke Times*, August 24, 2005.
2. Robert Bolton and Dorothy Grover Bolton, *People Styles at Work* (New York: AMACOM, 1996), p. 10.
3. Douglas A. Bernstein, Louis A. Penner, Alison Clarke-Stewart, and Edward J. Roy, *Psychology*, 7th ed. (Boston: Houghton Mifflin, 2006), p. 540.
4. Erik F. Douglas, *Straight Talk*, Palo Alto, CA: Davies-Black Publishing, 1998, pp. 10–11.
5. Tony Alessandra, *Behavioral Profiles: Participant Workbook* (San Diego: Pfeiffer & Company, 1994), p. 12.
6. Robert Bolton and Dorothy Grover Bolton, *People Styles at Work* (New York: AMACOM, 1996), pp. ix–x.
7. Ibid., p. x.
8. Robert J. Sternberg, *Thinking Styles* (New York: Cambridge University Press, 1997), p. 8.
9. Robert Bolton and Dorothy Grover Bolton, *People Styles at Work* (New York: AMACOM, 1996), p. x.
10. David W. Johnson, *Reaching Out—Interpersonal Effectiveness and Self-Actualization*, Boston, MA: Allyn and Bacon, 2003, pp. 82–83. The dominance factor was described in an early book by William M. Marston, *The Emotions of Normal People* (New York: Harcourt, 1928). Research conducted by Rolfe La Forge and Robert F. Suczek resulted in the development of the Interpersonal Check List (ICL), which features a dominant-submissive scale. A person who receives a high score on the ICL tends to lead, persuade, and control others. The Interpersonal Identity Profile, developed by David W. Merrill and James W. Taylor, features a factor called "assertiveness." Persons classified as high in assertiveness tend to have strong opinions, make quick decisions, and be directive when dealing with people. Persons classified as low in assertiveness tend to voice moderate opinions, make thoughtful decisions, and be supportive when dealing with others.
11. Christopher Caggiano, "Psychopath," *Inc.*, July 1998, pp. 77–85.
12. "Assertiveness Training," http://www.amanet.org/seminars; INTERNET.
13. The research conducted by La Forge and Suczek resulted in identification of the hostile/loving continuum, which is similar to the sociability continuum. Their Interpersonal Check List features this scale. L. L. Thurstone and T. G. Thurstone developed the Thurstone Temperament Schedule, which provides an assessment of a "sociable" factor. Persons with high scores in this area enjoy the company of others and make friends easily. The Interpersonal Identity Profile developed by Merrill and Taylor contains an objectivity continuum. A person with low objectivity is seen as attention seeking, involved with the feelings of others, informal, and casual in social relationships. A person who is high in objectivity tends to be indifferent toward the feelings of others. This person is formal in social relationships.
14. "On the Human Side," *Time*, February 19, 1979, p. 75.
15. Jeffrey Zaslow, "What We Can Learn from Sully's Journey," *Wall Street Journal*, October 14, 2009, p. D1.
16. Robert Bolton and Dorothy Grover Bolton, *People Styles at Work* (New York: AMACOM, 1996), p. 87.
17. Ibid.
18. "Ask Dr. E," *Psychology Today*, January/February 2000, p. 28.
19. David W. Merrill and Roger H. Reid, *Personality Styles and Effective Performance* (Radnor, Pa.: Chilton Book, 1981), p. 88.
20. Wilson Learning Corporation, *Growth Through Versatility* (Eden Prairie, Minn.: Wilson Learning Corporation), p. 4.
21. "Versatility: The Key to Sales Performance" (Edina, Minn.: Wilson Learning Worldwide, 2004), pp. 1–4.
22. Bob Reeves, "It Takes All Types," *Lincoln Star*, May 24, 1994, p. 11.
23. Gary A. Williams and Robert B. Miller, "Changing the Way You Persuade," *Harvard Business Review*, May 2002, pp. 65–67.
24. Stuart Atkins, *The Name of Your Game* (Beverly Hills, Calif.: Ellis & Stewart, 1981), pp. 49–50.
25. Ibid., p. 51.
26. Chris Lee, "What's Your Style?" *Training*, May 1991, p. 28.

Marcy Maloy/Digital Vision/Getty Images

Building High Self-Esteem

TIP OF THE ICEBERG | THE DREADED REJECTION LETTER

Each year, about three million high school students apply for admission to one or more colleges. Then they wait, hoping for a positive response. Hundreds of thousands of applicants will receive the dreaded rejection letter. A rejection letter from the school of your dreams can be very devastating—a real blow to your self-esteem.

However, time puts rejection letters in perspective. Meredith Vieira, former *Today* show co-host, received a rejection letter from Harvard during her senior year in high school. At the time she was crushed. Vieira was accepted by Tufts University where she met a mentor who sparked her interest in journalism.[1]

John Schlifske, president of Northwestern Mutual insurance company, recalls coming home from school the day a rejection letter from Yale University arrived: "Mom was all excited and gave it to me." His heart fell when he learned his application had been rejected. An aspiring college football player, "I wanted to go to Yale so badly." Today Schlifske realizes he had a deeper, richer experience at Carleton College in Minnesota. He says he received a "phenomenal" education and became a starter on the football team. Years later, he would discuss the Yale rejection experience with his son Dan who was rejected by one of his top choices, Duke University.[2]

Lee Bollinger, President of Columbia University, was rejected as a teenager when he applied to Harvard. He says the experience confirmed his belief that it was up to him to define his talents and potential. To "allow other people's assessment of you to determine your own self-assessment is a very big mistake."[3]

Feeling sad when you've been rejected after a college or job application is understandable, but there is no need to dwell on the negative. It may be the beginning of some other better opportunity.

YanLev/Shutterstock.com

THE POWER OF SELF-ESTEEM

4-1   The importance of self-esteem as a guiding force in our lives cannot be overstated. Your self-esteem includes your feelings about your adequacy in the many roles you play in life—friend, brother or sister, daughter or son, employee or employer, a student leader, and so on. In this chapter, we will discuss how self-esteem is developed and identify ways to raise your self-esteem. This information will help you realize your full human potential, both individually and as a group member.

> *The importance of self-esteem as a guiding force in our lives cannot be overstated.*

Self-Esteem = Self-Efficacy + Self-Respect

Nathaniel Branden, author of *The Six Pillars of Self-Esteem* and *Self-Esteem at Work,* has spent the past three decades studying the psychology of self-esteem. He states that the ultimate source of self-esteem can only be internal: It is the relationship between a person's self-efficacy and self-respect. Self-efficacy is the learned expectation of success. What we do or try to do is controlled by our perceptions or beliefs about our chances of success at a particular task or problem.

human
RELATIONS
in Action

DON'T ACCEPT A DIMINISHED SENSE OF SELF-ESTEEM

With the recent collapse in the financial, housing, and employment markets, many people are experiencing a diminished sense of self-worth. Most who are experiencing devaluation didn't earn it; they are every bit as competent as they were before the floor fell out from under them. They may need to accept a lower-level position than one's experience dictates, but they need not own a diminished sense of self-esteem.

Source: Peggy La Cerra, "Managing Self-Worth in a Tough Market," *Spirituality & Health*, March–April, 2009, p. 14.

Your perception of your self-efficacy can influence which tasks you take on and which ones you avoid. Albert Bandura, a professor at Stanford University and one of the foremost self-efficacy researchers, views this component of self-esteem as a resilient belief in your own abilities. For example, an administrative assistant who masters a sophisticated computerized accounting system is more likely to tackle future complicated computer programs than is a person who feels computer illiterate and may not even try to figure out the new program, regardless of how well he or she *could* do it.[4]

Self-respect, the second component of self-esteem, is what you think and feel about yourself. Your judgment of your own value is a primary factor in achieving personal and

Ethan Miller/Staff/Getty Images Entertainment/Getty Images

To achieve stardom in the competitive world of country music, Alan Jackson had to value and respect himself in spite of years of disappointment. His music was rejected by all of the major Nashville labels before his "star quality" was finally discovered.

career success. People who respect themselves tend to act in ways that confirm and rein-force this respect. People who lack self-respect may put up with verbal or physical abuse from others because they feel they are unworthy of praise and deserve the abuse. Nathaniel Branden believes that the healthier our self-esteem, the more inclined we are to treat others with respect, goodwill, and fairness, since we do not tend to perceive them as a threat, and since self-respect is the foundation of respect for others.[5]

Self-efficacy and self-respect are central themes of the definition of self-esteem adopted by the National Association for Self-Esteem (NASE). NASE defines self-esteem as "The experience of being capable of meeting life's challenges and being worthy of happiness."[6] It is having the conviction that you are able to make appropriate choices and decisions.

Authentic Self-Esteem

The NASE definition of self-esteem helps us make the distinction between authentic (healthy) self-esteem and false (unhealthy) self-esteem. *Authentic self-esteem* is not expressed by self-glorification at the expense of others or by the attempt to diminish others so as to elevate oneself. Arrogance, boastfulness, and overestimation of your abili-ties are more likely to reflect inadequate self-esteem rather than, as it might appear, too much self-esteem.

HOW SELF-ESTEEM DEVELOPS

4-2   To understand the development of self-esteem, it is helpful to examine how you formed your self-concept. Your self-concept is the bundle of facts, opinions, beliefs, and percep-tions about yourself that are present in your life every moment of every day.[7] The self-concept you have today reflects information you have received from others and life events that occurred throughout childhood, adolescence, and adulthood. You are *consciously* aware of some of the things you have been conditioned to believe about yourself. But many comments and events that have shaped your self-concept are pro-cessed at the *unconscious* level and continue to influence your judgments, feelings, and behaviors whether you are aware of them or not.[8]

Childhood

Researchers in the field of developmental psychology are concerned with the course and causes of developmental changes over a person's lifetime. They pay close attention to *genetic* and *environmental* factors (nature versus nurture).[9] Although space does not per-mit a detailed discussion here of cognitive, social, and emotional development during early childhood, we can state with conviction that developmental experiences during the first few years of life are extremely important. For example, too little attention from nurturing parents and too much television viewing can hinder healthy childhood development.[10]

Because childhood events are retained in your brain, poor performance in school, abusive or uncaring parents, or a serious childhood accident can be defining experiences in your life. Messages from siblings, teachers, and various authority figures can have a lasting impact on your self-concept. These childhood experiences can form the founda-tion for your level of self-esteem that emerges later in life.

Adolescence

The transition from childhood to adulthood can be a long and difficult period. At about age 11, children begin to describe themselves in terms of social relationships and personality traits. Many of the problems of adolescence are associated with challenges to young people's *self-esteem*, their sense of being capable, and worthy of respect.[11]

As adolescents attempt to resolve questions about self-worth, sexuality, and independence, they may "try out" alternative identities. Teens often turn to movies, music videos, and magazines for guidance and attempt to emulate the unrealistic body images and fashions that their peers deem worthwhile. Adolescence can last well into the 20s as each person attempts to develop his or her own unique identity.[12]

As adolescents become more self-conscious, they gradually develop a personal identity as unique individuals. That identity may be affected by their *ethnic identity*—the part of a person's identity that is shaped by the racial, religious, or cultural group to which the person belongs. Adolescents who achieve a clear, positive ethnic identity exhibit higher self-esteem, greater optimism, and more social competence.[13]

WHERE HAVE THE GOOD MEN GONE?

Kay Hymowitz, author of *Manning Up: How the Rise of Women Has Turned Men into Boys*, says today's girls are growing into women and accepting adult responsibilities must faster and more effectively than today's boys. She argues that too many men in their 20s are living in a new kind of extended adolescence. Women now outpace their male peers in getting through college. They are more likely than men to be in grad school and making strides in the workplace.

Source: Kay S. Hymowitz, "Where Have All the Good Men Gone?" *Wall Street Journal*, February 19–20, 2011 (weekend edition), pp. C1–C2.

Adulthood

When you reach adulthood, you are greatly influenced by a time-reinforced self-concept that has been molded by people and events from all your past experiences. You have been bombarded over the years with positive and negative messages from your family, friends, teachers, supervisors, and the media. You may compare yourself to others, as was so common in adolescence, or you may focus on your own inner sense of self-worth. Emmett Miller, a noted authority on self-esteem, says that as adults we tend to define ourselves in terms of the following items.[14]

The Things We Possess Miller says this is the most primitive source of self-worth. If we define ourselves in terms of what we have, the result may be an effort to accumulate more and more material things to achieve a greater feeling of self-worth. The idea that we can compensate for self-doubt and insecurity with our checkbook is widely accepted in America.[15] People who define themselves in terms of what they have may have difficulty deciding "what is enough" and may spend their life in search of more material possessions.

What We Do for a Living Miller points out that too often our self-worth and identity depend on something as arbitrary as a job title. Amy Saltzman, author of *Downshifting*, a book on ways to reinvent (or redefine) success, says, "We have allowed our professional identities to define us and control us."[16] She points out that we have looked to outside forces such as the corporation, the university, or the media to provide us with a script for leading a satisfying, worthwhile life.

Our Internal Value System and Emotional Makeup Miller says this is the healthiest way for people to identify themselves:

> *If you don't give yourself credit for excellence in other areas of life, besides your job and material possessions, you've got nothing to keep your identity afloat during a job layoff or a troubled family relationship. People who are in touch with their real identity weather the storm better because they have a more varied and richer sense of themselves, owing to the importance they attach to their personal lives and activities.*[17]

As an adult, you will be constantly adjusting the level of your self-esteem as you cope with events at work and in your personal life. The loss of a job or being passed over for a promotion may trigger feelings of insecurity or depression. A messy divorce can leave you with feelings of self-doubt. An unexpected award may raise your spirits and make you feel better about yourself.

The Past Programs the Future

Phillip McGraw, better known as "Dr. Phil," has developed a one-sentence guide to understanding the importance of your self-concept: *The past reaches into the present, and programs the future, by your recollections and your internal rhetoric about what you perceived to have happened in your life.*[18] Past experiences and events, which McGraw describes as "defining moments," can influence your thinking for a lifetime and program your future. They get incorporated into your deepest understanding of who you are because they are often the focus of your internal dialogue—a process we call "self-talk." Later in this chapter, we will discuss how to avoid the influence of negative self-talk and build upon positive messages.

Total Person Insight

"How many times do we pay for one mistake? The answer is thousands of times. The human is the only animal on earth that pays a thousand times for the same mistake. The rest of the animals pay once for every mistake they make. But not us. We have a powerful memory. We make a mistake, we judge ourselves, we find ourselves guilty, and punish ourselves.... Every time we remember, we judge ourselves again, we are guilty again, and we punish ourselves again, and again, and again."

Source: Don Miguel Ruiz, *The Four Agreements* (San Rafael, Calif.: Amber-Allen Publishing, 1997), p. 12.

SELF-ESTEEM INFLUENCES YOUR BEHAVIOR

4-3   Your level of self-esteem can have a powerful impact on your behavior. Your sense of *competence* and resulting *self-respect*, the two components of self-esteem, stem from the belief that you are generally capable of producing the results in life that you want by making appropriate, constructive choices. This confidence makes you less vulnerable to the negative views of others. People with healthy self-esteem tend to have a sense of personal worth that has been strengthened through various achievements and through accurate self-appraisal.[19]

Characteristics of People with Low Self-Esteem

> *When we rely too heavily on validation from external sources, we can lose control over our lives.*

1. *They tend to maintain an external locus of control.* People who maintain an external locus of control believe that their life is almost totally controlled by outside forces and that they bear little personal responsibility for what happens to them.[20] When something goes wrong, they have a tendency to blame something or someone other than themselves. Even when they succeed, they tend to attribute their success to luck rather than to their own expertise and hard work. They continually rely on other people to make them feel good about themselves, and therefore need an ever-increasing dose of support from others to keep them going. When we rely too heavily on validation from external sources, we can lose control over our lives.[21]

2. *They are more likely to participate in self-destructive behaviors.* If you do not like yourself, there is no apparent reason to take care of yourself. Therefore, people with low self-esteem are more likely to drink too much, smoke too much, and eat too much. Some may develop an eating disorder such as bulimia or anorexia, often with devastating results.

3. *They tend to exhibit poor human relations skills.* Individuals with low self-esteem may have difficulty developing effective interpersonal skills. Workers with low self-esteem may reduce the efficiency and productivity of a group: They tend to exercise less initiative and hesitate to accept responsibility or make independent decisions, and are less likely to speak up in a group and criticize the group's approach.

Total Person Insight

"The essence of self-esteem is compassion for yourself. When you have compassion for yourself, you understand and accept yourself. If you make a mistake, you forgive yourself."

Source: Matthew McKay and Patrick Fanning, *Self-Esteem*, Oakland, CA: New Harbinger Publications, Inc., 1992, p. 83.

Characteristics of People with High Self-Esteem

1. *They tend to maintain an internal locus of control.* People who believe they are largely responsible for what happens to them maintain an internal locus of control. They make decisions for their own reasons based on their standards of what is right and wrong. They learn from their mistakes, but are not immobilized by them.

2. *They are able to feel all dimensions of emotion without letting those emotions affect their behavior in a negative way.* Although you may not be able to stop feeling the emotions of anger, envy, and jealousy, you can control your thoughts and actions when you are under the influence of these strong emotions. It is okay to have anxious, scared, angry, or depressed feelings—as long as you don't let them stop you from doing what you have to do.[22]

3. *They are less likely to take things personally.* Don Miguel Ruiz, author of the best-selling book *The Four Agreements,* cautions us to avoid taking others' comments personally: "When you make it a strong habit not to take anything personally, you avoid many upsets in your life." He notes that many of these messages come from people who are unable to respect you because they do not respect themselves.[23]

4. *They are able to accept other people as unique, talented individuals.* They learn to accept others for who they are and what they can do. Our multicultural work force makes this attitude especially important. Individuals who cannot tolerate other people who are "different" are less likely to achieve career success in today's labor market.

5. *They have a productive personality.* They are optimistic in their approach to life and are capable of being creative, imaginative problem solvers. They have the ability to evaluate the dynamics of a relationship and adjust to the demands of the interaction. They are able to handle stress in a productive way by putting their problems and concerns into perspective and maintaining a balance of work and fun in their lives.[24]

HOW TO INCREASE YOUR SELF-ESTEEM

4-4   "The level of our self-esteem is not set once and for all in childhood," says Nathaniel Branden. It can grow throughout our lives or it can deteriorate.[25] Healthy self-esteem comes from realizing what qualities and skills you have that you can rely on and then making a plan to build those qualities and skills that you want in the future. The person you will be tomorrow has yet to be created. Your new, higher level of self-esteem will not happen overnight. Such a change is the result of a slow, steady evolution that begins with the desire to overcome low self-esteem.

Search for the Source of Low Self-Esteem

Many people live with deep personal doubts about themselves but have difficulty determining the source of those feelings. They even have difficulty finding the right words to

"Can't you keep your parenting to yourselves?"

Barbara Smaller/CartoonBank.com

describe those negative feelings. People with low self-esteem are less likely to see themselves with great clarity. The self-image they possess is like a reflection in a warped funhouse mirror; the image magnifies their weaknesses and minimizes their strengths. Increasing your self-esteem requires achieving a higher level of self-awareness and learning to accurately perceive your particular balance of strengths and weaknesses.[26]

To start this process, take time to list and carefully examine the defining moments in your life. Pay special attention to those that were decidedly negative, and try to determine how these moments have shaped your current self-concept. Next, make a list of the labels that others have used to describe you. Study the list carefully, and try to determine which ones you have internalized and accepted. Have these labels had a positive or negative influence on your concept of yourself? Phillip McGraw says, "If you are living to a label, you have molded for yourself a fictional self-concept with artificial boundaries."[27]

Living Consciously

Nathaniel Branden says living consciously is the highest manifestation of life—the basic tool of survival. If we don't bring an appropriate level of consciousness to our life, the penalty is a diminished sense of *self-efficacy* and *self-respect*. One barrier to living consciously is the evasion of facts that make us uncomfortable:

"I know I'm living beyond my means, but—"

"I know my children suffer from having too little time with me, but—"

Branden says that to live consciously means to seek awareness of everything that bears on our actions, purposes, values, and goals. Table 4.1 includes a few examples of how we can live consciously.[28]

Take Responsibility for Your Decisions

Psychologists have found that children who were encouraged to make their own decisions early in their lives have higher self-esteem than those who were kept dependent on their parents for a longer period of time. Making decisions helps you develop confidence in your own judgment and enables you to explore options.

The attitude that you must be right all the time is a barrier to personal growth. With this attitude, you will avoid doing things that might result in mistakes. Much unhappiness comes from the widespread and regrettable belief that it is important to avoid making mistakes at all costs.[29] James Dyson, founder and CEO of Dyson Corporation says, "I love this side of wrong thinking—of encouraging people who have ideas to go

Table 4.1 ■ How to Live Consciously

- Reaching out toward relevant facts rather than ignoring them.
- Noticing and confronting my impulses to avoid or deny painful or threatening realities.
- Being concerned to know if my actions are in alignment with my purposes.
- Searching for feedback from the environment so as to adjust or correct my course when necessary.
- Being receptive to new knowledge and willing to reexamine old assumptions.

Source: Nathaniel Branden, *The Six Pillars of Self-Esteem* (New York: Bantam, 1994), p. 72.

see if they work." Dyson made 5,127 prototypes of the bagless vacuum cleaner before he got it right.[30]

Total Person Insight

"Most people think they know what they are good at. They are usually wrong.... And yet, a person can perform only from strength." Peter Drucker

Source: Tom Rath, *Strengths Finder 2.0*, New York: Gallup Press, 2007, p. 15.

Engage in Strength Building

Over the past 30 years, the Gallup International Research and Education Center has researched the best way to maximize a person's potential. One of the most important findings can be summarized in a single sentence: Most organizations take their employees' strengths for granted and focus on minimizing their weaknesses. The research findings suggest that the best way to excel in a career is to maximize your strengths.[31]

The Gallup Organization research has been summarized in *Now, Discover Your Strengths* by Marcus Buckingham and Donald Clifton. The first step toward strength building is to discover your greatest talents. A talent is any naturally recurring pattern of thought, feeling, or behavior that can be productively applied. A strength is a consistent, near perfect performance of an activity; you can see yourself doing it repeatedly, happily and successfully. When Tiger Woods was at the top of his game, he was recognized for his long-game with woods and irons. His ability to chip out of a bunker was inconsistent when compared to other top professionals. Butch Harmon, his coach, encouraged Woods to work on his weakness just enough so that it did not undermine his strengths. Once his bunker play reached acceptable levels, Woods and his coach turned their attention to improving Tiger's dominant strength, his swing.[32]

Strength building also requires the acquisition of knowledge and skill. As we prepare for a career, we must acquire certain factual knowledge. An accountant must know how to prepare a statement of cash flow. Nurses must know how to administer medications with precision. Skill, the application of knowledge, might be thought of as the "doing" part of strength building.[33]

HOW TO IDENTIFY YOUR TALENTS

When we are not doing what we are truly good at, we are not living up to our greatest performance capabilities. One way to identify your dominant talents is to step back and watch yourself as you try out different activities:

- Complete an elective course
- Volunteer to chair a committee
- Accept a part-time job in an area that appeals to you
- Complete an internship
- Attend a career fair

If you flourish in some activities, analyze why this happened.

Source: Marcus Buckingham and Donald O. Clifton, *Now, Discover Your Strengths* (New York: Free Press, 2001), pp. 31–32.

Buckingham's research indicates that the best managers spend 80 percent of their time trying to amplify their employees' strengths.[34] Chances are, however, you will not be working for a boss who encourages strength building. So, be prepared to assume responsibility for identifying your natural talents and building your strengths.

STRENGTHS LIBRARY

These publications will guide you during the strength building process:

Now, Discover Your Strengths, by Marcus Buckingham and Donald O. Clifton

Go Put Your Strengths to Work, by Marcus Buckingham

Strengths Finder 2.0, by Tom Rath

Strengths Based Leadership, by Tom Rath and Barry Conchie

Seek the Support and Guidance of Mentors

A mentor is someone who develops another person through tutoring, coaching, and guidance.[35] In most organizations, mentoring is carried out informally, but formal programs that systematically match mentors and protégés are also common.

Most people who have had a mentoring experience say it was an effective development tool. However, many surveys indicate that only a small percentage of employees say they have had a mentor. In today's fast-paced work environment, where most people have a heavy workload, you must be willing to take the initiative and build a mentor relationship.[36] Warren Bennis, founding chairman of the Leadership Institute at the University of Southern California, states, "Being mentored isn't a passive game. It's nothing less than the ability to spot the handful of people who can make all the difference in your life."[37] Here are some tips to keep in mind.

1. *Search for a mentor who has the qualities of a good coach.* Mentors need to be accomplished in their own right, but success alone does not make someone a good mentor. Look for someone whom you would like to emulate, both in business savvy and in operating style. Be sure it is someone who is absolutely credible, a person you trust enough to talk with about touchy issues.[38]

REVERSE MENTORING

In an effort to help senior executives keep up to date in the areas of technology, social media, and the latest workplace trends, many companies are pairing upper management with younger employees—a practice known as *reverse mentoring*. Cisco Systems, Inc. has started a Gen Y Reverse Mentoring Program and the Young Employee Network at Hewlett-Packard is seeking to formalize reverse mentoring throughout the company.

Source: Leslie Kwoh, "Reverse Mentoring Cracks the Workplace," *Wall Street Journal*, November 28, 2011, p. B7.

2. *Market yourself to a prospective mentor.* The best mentor for you may be someone who is very busy. Sell the benefits of a mentoring partnership. For example, point out that mentoring can be a mutually rewarding experience. Describe specific steps you will take to avoid wasting the time of a busy person. You might suggest that meetings be held during lunch or agree to online mentoring.[39]

Many young workers have felt they know more than their bosses. While this may not always be true, they often do possess current knowledge and skills that could be shared with senior managers through reverse mentoring.

Some progressive companies have initiated *open-source* or *external* mentoring programs. Kathleen Lim was promoted to billing operations manager at Box.net, a $10.7 million cloud computing company in Palo Alto, California. It was her first management job at her first post-college employer. Her most important question was: "How do other organizations do it?" With the help of her boss, the collection manager at Salesforce.com was asked to meet with Lim on an as-needed basis. The Salesforce collection manager agreed to serve as an external mentor. Over the months that followed, Lim received an abundance of information that has helped her develop a successful billing operations department.[40]

Set Goals

Research points to a direct link between self-esteem and the achievement of personal and professional goals. People who set goals and successfully achieve them are able to achieve higher self-esteem. Why? Because setting goals enables you to take ownership of the future. Once you realize that just about every behavior is controllable, the possibilities for improving your self-esteem are endless. Self-change may be difficult, but it's not impossible.

The major principles that encompass goal setting are outlined in Table 4.2. Goal setting should be an integral part of your efforts to break old habits or form new ones. Before you attempt to set goals, engage in serious reflection. Make a list of the things you want to achieve, and then ask yourself this question: What goals are truly important to me? Are these goals realistic? If you set goals that really excite you, desire will fuel your will to achieve them.[41]

Practice Guided Imagery

Guided imagery is one of the most creative and empowering methods for achieving your goals available today. It provides you with a way to harness the power of the mind and

Table 4.2 ■ Goal-Setting Principles

Goal setting gives you the power to take control of the present and the future. Goals can help you break old habits or form new ones. You will need an assortment of goals that address the different needs of your life. The following goal-setting principles will be helpful.

1. *Spend time reflecting on the things you want to change in your life.* Take time to clarify your motivation and purpose. Set goals that are specific, measurable, and realistic. Unrealistic goals increase fear, and fear increases the probability of failure.

2. *Develop a goal-setting plan that includes the steps necessary to achieve the goal.* Put the goal and the steps in writing. Change requires structure. Identify all activities and materials you will need to achieve your goal. Review your plan daily—repetition increases the probability of success.

3. *Modify your environment by changing the stimuli around you.* If your goal is to lose five pounds during a one-month period, make a weight chart so you can monitor your progress. You may need to give up desserts and avoid restaurants that serve huge portions. Gather new information on effective weight-loss techniques, and seek advice from others. This may involve finding a mentor or joining a support group.

4. *Monitor your behavior, and reward your progress.* Focus on small successes, because each little success builds your reservoir of self-esteem. Reinforcement from yourself and/or others is necessary for change. If the passion for change begins to subside, remind yourself why you want to achieve your goal. Be patient—it takes time to change your lifestyle.

imagination to succeed at something. It can be used to help you relax, set goals (like losing weight), or prepare for a challenging opportunity such as interviewing for a new job. Some heart surgeons use guided imagery to calm their patients, which helps speed recovery. Wearing headphones, the patient hears carefully crafted, medically detailed messages that urge the person to relax and imagine themselves in a safe, comfortable place: "Feel the new strength flowing through you, through arteries that are wider and more open, more flexible with smoother surfaces than before."[42]

To visualize means to form a mental image of something. It refers to what you see in the mind's eye. Once you have formed a clear mental picture of what you want to accomplish, identify the steps needed to get there, and then mentally rehearse them. Rehearsal must be followed by *action* to further your goal. Rami Shapior, award-winning author and teacher says, "It isn't enough to think differently, we must *be* different and *do* differently."[43]

Many athletes choreograph their performance in their imagination before competitions. Studies by the U.S. Olympic Training Center show that 94 percent of the coaches use mental rehearsal for training and competitions.[44] Artists rarely begin a work of art until they have an image of what it is they are going to create. Dancers physically and mentally rehearse their performances hundreds of times before ever stepping on stage. The same techniques can be used in the workplace.

Work-Related Visualization Let's assume your team members have asked you to present a cost-saving plan to management. The entire team is counting on you. The visualization process should begin with identifying the steps you will take to get approval of the plan. What information will you present? What clothing will you wear? Will you use PowerPoint or some other visual presentation method? Will you use any printed documents? Once you have identified all important contingencies and strategies for success, visualize the actual presentation. See yourself walking into the room with your chin up, your shoulders straight, and your voice strong and confident. Picture yourself making appropriate eye contact with people in the room. The focus of your preparation should be on things within your control.

HOW TO BREAK OUT OF A SLUMP

Major league pitcher John Smoltz, a former star for the Atlanta Braves, recalls starting a season with a dismal record of 2–11. He contacted sports psychologist Jack Llewellyn for help. With guidance from Llewellyn, Mr. Smoltz learned to recover more swiftly from a bad pitch. He repeatedly watched a two-minute tape Dr. Llewellyn had made of a half-dozen of his *perfect* pitches. Then if he made a bad pitch during a game, he did not step back on the mound until he visualized that positive file in his mind. His confidence restored, Mr. Smoltz posted a 12–2 record for the remainder of the season.

Source: Sue Shellenbarger, "Slumping at Work? What Would Jack Do?" *Wall Street Journal*, October 13, 2010, p. D1.

Use Positive Self-Talk

Throughout most of your waking moments, you talk to yourself. Self-talk takes place in the privacy of your mind. It can be rational and productive, or it can be irrational and disruptive. When the focus of this internal conversation is on negative thoughts, you are usually less productive.[45] Some psychologists refer to these negative thoughts as your inner critic. The critic keeps a record of your failures but never reminds you of your strengths and accomplishments. A major step toward improving your self-esteem is to understand how to respond to the negative influence of your inner critic.[46]

> *Self-talk takes place in the privacy of your mind.*

When your inner critic talks to you, ask yourself, "Who is this voice that is reminding me of my past failures?" (see Figure 4.1). The chances are it is not your current boss or spouse, but someone in your past such as a teacher, coach, harsh parent, or sibling. Recognize that this critical voice is probably no longer relevant and take the necessary steps to replace those negative messages with positive ones.[47] You can create effective, positive self-talk statements for each of your goals by using the following guidelines:

1. Be *specific* about the behavior you want to change. What do you want to do to increase your effectiveness? You should firmly believe that what you want is truly possible.
2. Begin each self-talk statement with a first-person pronoun, such as *I* or *my*. Use a present-tense verb, such as *am, have, feel, create, approve, do,* or *choose*. Don't say, "My ability to remember the names of other people *will* improve." Instead, focus on the present: "I *have* an excellent memory for the names of other people."
3. Describe the results you want to achieve. Be sure to phrase the statement as though you have already achieved what you want:
   - I am in control of my habits.
   - I am confident and optimistic.
   - I am prompt and efficient.
   - I care enough to assert myself when necessary.

This last step is very important. You must focus on what you want, not on what you don't want. State your self-talk in a positive way. If you say "I will control my anger," the

Figure 4.1 ■ The Self-Talk Endless Loop

Source: From Jack Canfield, *The Success Principle: How to Get from Where You Are to Where You Want to Be.* Copyright © 2005. Reprinted by permission.

mind, which quickly creates visual images, focuses on anger. A better choice would be "I will be a more patient, accepting person." The words "patient" and "accepting" create positive images in the mind.

Jack Canfield, author of *Key to Living the Law of Attraction,* says we should avoid sending mixed signals to ourselves and those around us. When you are against something, you may actually be recreating it. So, instead of thinking "I don't want to be late," think "I want to be on time." When you create a self-talk statement, always keep in mind your goal.[48]

Keep in mind that positive self-talk that is truly effective consists of thoughts and messages that are realistic and truthful. It is rationally optimistic self-talk, not unfounded rah-rah hype. Positive internal dialogue should not be a litany of "feel good" mantras; it should be wholly consistent with your authentic self.[49]

ORGANIZATIONS CAN HELP

4-5 Although each of us ultimately is responsible for increasing or decreasing our own self-esteem, we can make that task easier or more difficult for others. We can either support or damage the self-efficacy and self-respect of the people we work with, just as they have that option in their interactions with us. Organizations are beginning to include self-esteem modules in their employee- and management-training programs.

When employees do not feel good about themselves, the result will often be poor job performance. This view is shared by many human resource professionals. Many organizations realize that low self-esteem affects their workers' ability to learn new skills, to be effective team members, and to be productive. Research has identified five factors that can enhance the self-esteem of employees in any organization (see Figure 4.2).[50]

■ *Workers need to feel valuable.* A major source of worker satisfaction is the feeling that one is valued as a unique person. Self-esteem grows when an organization makes an effort to accommodate individual differences, to recognize individual accomplishments, and to help employees build their strengths.

■ *Workers need to feel competent.* Earlier in this chapter, we noted that self-efficacy grows when people feel confident in their ability to perform job-related tasks. One of the best ways organizations can build employee confidence is to involve employees in well-designed training programs.

Figure 4.2 ■ Factors That Enhance the Self-Esteem of Employees

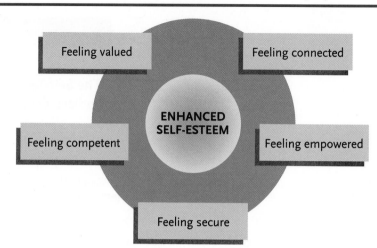

- *Workers need to feel secure.* Employees are more likely to feel secure when they are well informed and know what is expected of them. Managers need to clarify their expectations and provide employees with frequent feedback regarding their performance.
- *Workers need to feel empowered.* Progressive organizations recognize that every employee has something to contribute to the organization and that limiting employees' contributions limits the organization's progress. When all employees are treated with respect and given the latitude for individual action within the defined limits of the organization, they are free to use their creativity and ingenuity to solve problems and make customers happy.
- *Workers need to feel connected.* People are likely to achieve high self-esteem when they feel their coworkers accept, appreciate, and respect them. Many companies are fostering these feelings by placing greater emphasis on mentoring and teamwork. Team-building efforts help promote acceptance and cooperation.

LOOKING BACK: SUMMARY OF LEARNING OBJECTIVES

1. **Define self-esteem and discuss its impact on your life.**

   Self-esteem is a combination of self-respect and self-efficacy. If you have high self-esteem, you are more likely to feel competent and worthy. If you have low self-esteem, you are more likely to feel incompetent, unworthy, and insecure. Self-esteem reflects your feelings of adequacy about the roles you play, your personality traits, your physical appearance, your skills, and your abilities. High self-esteem is the powerful foundation for a successful personal and professional life.

2. **Discuss how self-esteem is developed.**

   A person starts acquiring and building self-esteem from birth. Parents, friends, associates, the media, and professional colleagues all influence the development of a person's self-esteem. Adolescents often depend on social relationships to define their value and may compare themselves to media personalities.

Adults often define themselves in terms of their possessions, jobs, or internal values.

3. **Identify the characteristics of people with low and high self-esteem.**

People with high self-esteem tend to maintain an internal locus of control, manage their emotions, rarely take things personally, accept other people as unique and talented, and have productive personalities. People with low self-esteem tend to maintain an external locus of control, are likely to participate in self-destructive behaviors, and exhibit poor human relations skills. They often rely on the opinions of others to establish their inner self-worth.

4. **Identify ways to raise your self-esteem.**

To build high self-esteem, individuals must accept their limitations, take responsibility for their decisions, engage in strength building, identify their talents, and work with a mentor. Taking responsibility for your decisions and living with the consequences, positive or negative, can also help build self-esteem. Goal setting is an integral part of raising one's self-esteem. Guided imagery and positive self-talk can help overcome the inner critic that often interferes with personal and professional success.

5. **Understand the conditions organizations can create that will help workers raise their self-esteem.**

Many organizations now realize that they need to help build employees' self-esteem and are doing so by making workers feel valuable, competent, and secure. Employers are empowering their employees to use their creativity and ingenuity to solve problems and make customers happy, which allows workers to develop a sense of personal responsibility.

KEY TERMS

self-esteem, 76
self-efficacy, 76
self-respect, 77
self-concept, 78
developmental psychology, 78

external locus of control, 81
internal locus of control, 81
talent, 84
strength, 84
mentor, 85

guided imagery, 86
visualize, 87
self-talk, 88
inner critic, 88

CAREER INSIGHT

Marcus Buckingham, author of *Go Put Your Strengths to Work*, encourages us to discover our strengths and then engage in activities that will strengthen them. He says "Only 17 percent of people spend most of their work day doing things they really like to do." Take time to compile an inventory of activities you have truly enjoyed as a student or an employee. Think about activities that play to your strengths. Chances are you have talents and strengths that can be enhanced and applied with greater enthusiasm. Set some new goals that focus on strength building.

Source: Marcus Buckingham, *Go Put Your Strengths to Work* (New York: Free Press, 2007), pp. 130–134.

TRY YOUR HAND

1. Review Table 4.2, Goal-Setting Principles. Work through each of the four principles in light of something you would like to change in your world. It could be a physical characteristic, such as weight control or beginning an exercise regimen. It might be a component of your personality, such as becoming more confident or assertive. Perhaps you would like to reexamine your career goals. Whatever your choice, write out your plan for change then follow it through.

2. This chapter identified five characteristics of people with high self-esteem. Read each of the statements below and rate yourself with this scale: U = Usually; S = Sometimes.

	U	S
I maintain an internal locus of control.	☐	☐
I am able to feel all dimensions of emotions without letting these emotions affect my behavior in a negative way.	☐	☐
I do not take things personally.	☐	☐
I am able to accept other people as unique, talented individuals.	☐	☐
I feel I have a productive personality.	☐	☐

3. Building your self-esteem is often a do-it-to-yourself project. No one can wrap a package of self-esteem and give it to you for your birthday. If you, or someone you care about, need more support in building this life-skill, visit the National Mental Health Information Center, http://www.mentalhealth.samhsa.gov/publicaitons, and click on *Building Self-esteem—A Self-Help Guide* listed under "Publications." Go to the table of contents and click on *Things You Can Do Right Away—Every Day—to Raise Your Self-Esteem*. Select five activities you would recommend to someone who is experiencing low self-esteem.

CRITICAL THINKING CHALLENGE

Oprah Winfrey says, "Each of us arrives with all we need to feel valued and unique, but slowly that gets chipped away." She is correct, but some life experiences do cause us to increase the value we place on ourselves. After careful reflection on your childhood and adolescence, identify the five events or people who had a significant impact (positive or negative) on your self-esteem. Think of these experiences as "defining moments" in your life.

Source: Oprah Winfrey, "You Are the Dream," *O, The Oprah Magazine*, March 2001, p. 39.

SELF-ASSESSMENT EXERCISE

For each statement, circle the number from 1 to 5 that best represents your response: (1) strongly disagree (never do this); (2) disagree (rarely do this); (3) moderately agree (sometimes do this); (4) agree (frequently do this); (5) strongly agree (almost always do this).

A. I tend to be future oriented and not overly concerned with past mistakes or failures.	1	2	3	4	5
B. I have developed and maintained high expectations of myself.	1	2	3	4	5
C. I accept myself as a changing, growing person capable of improvement.	1	2	3	4	5
D. I have the strength to cope with life's problems and disappointments.	1	2	3	4	5
E. I am able to maintain an internal locus of control.	1	2	3	4	5
F. My goals are clearly defined, attainable, and supported by a plan for achieving each goal.	1	2	3	4	5
G. I constantly monitor my self-talk in order to maintain high self-esteem.	1	2	3	4	5

After identifying your response to each item, select an attitude or skill you would like to improve. Prepare a written goal and then describe the steps you will take to achieve this goal.

YOU PLAY THE ROLE

You have accepted a summer job with Neiman Marcus. Throughout the summer, you will replace sales staff that are on vacation. In addition to earning money to pay next fall's college tuition, you anticipate that this job will help you develop your customer service skills. To maximize the learning opportunities and explore another area within the company, you want to develop a mentor relationship with the assistant store manager. You have an appointment with her tomorrow. In this role-play situation, you will meet with a class member who will assume the role of the assistant store manager who is very busy and has scheduled the meeting to last no more than 15 minutes. During this short period of time, you will need to explain why you need a mentor and market yourself to this prospective mentor. Prior to the role-play activity, review the information on mentoring in this chapter.

BELOW THE SURFACE | YOUR ASSESSMENT REALLY COUNTS!

As noted in the opening vignette, a rejection letter from the college of your dreams can be a real blow to your self-esteem. Two rejection letters from the same school is a major disappointment. Harold Varmus wanted to study medicine at Harvard Medical School, but his application was rejected. He then enrolled in graduate studies in literature at Harvard, but soon decided a career in this field would not be rewarding. He applied again to Harvard Medical School and was again rejected. During the application process the dean chastised him in an interview for being "inconstant and immature," and advised him to enlist in the military. The admission staff at Columbia University Medical School were impressed by Mr. Varmus and made him feel welcome. After graduation, he achieved success in his chosen field, earning the Nobel laureate in medicine.[51]

As noted in the opening vignette, Lee Bollinger, president of Columbia University, was rejected as a teenager when he applied to Harvard. At the time, he was living in a small, isolated town in rural Oregon. Educational opportunities were limited. After being accepted at the University of Oregon, he worked hard to define his talents and his potential. He was determined not to let rejections control his life. Today he says, "To allow other people's assessment of you to determine your own self-assessment is a very big mistake." He says, "The question really is, who at the end of the day is going to make the determination about what your talents are, and what your interests are? That has to be you."[52]

QUESTIONS

1. Throughout life we often allow other people's assessment of us to determine our own self-assessment. What steps can we take to avoid being overly influenced by the views of others?

2. Identify at least two major rejections you have experienced and explain how you coped with each negative experience. Would you change how you responded?

CLOSING CASE   THE MENTORING OF EDWARD

Shoshana Zuboff likes to reflect on some of the special students she taught at the Harvard Business School. Some students, she recalls, "threw themselves at learning as if their lives depended on it." One of those students, Edward, had a troubled past. His parents split up when he was a small boy, and he was on his own much of the time as his mother needed to work. Edward and his mother lived in a neighborhood where drugs and gangs were common. By the sixth grade, he was a drug dealer, and later he ended up in a penitentiary. Then he had the good fortune to meet a judge who offered him two years in a drug rehabilitation program in return for good behavior. After rehab, he got a job, enrolled in a community college, and made the dean's list several times. A counselor encouraged Edward to set his sights high, so he applied and was accepted to an Ivy League school, where he studied business and economics. This success led to his acceptance into the Harvard Business School, where he met Professor Zuboff.

Although Edward had accomplished a great deal since leaving the penitentiary, he felt a growing sense of shame over things he did not know. During one lecture, Professor Zuboff briefly mentioned the name of an author who had written about Auschwitz. After class, Edward asked,

"What is Auschwitz?" Because of his disadvantaged childhood, he had missed out on many learning experiences that most students take for granted. To avoid giving away his deep-seated, inner secret, he mastered many defense strategies to protect his image amongst his peers. Professor Zuboff noted, "he was haunted by the sense of not knowing what he didn't know or how to learn it."

With help from this caring professor and her husband, who agreed to serve as his mentor, Edward began a program of study designed to fill in the gaps in his education. His self-esteem improved greatly as his program of self-improvement unfolded. Today Edward runs a successful consulting firm that focuses on leadership and emotional intelligence.[53]

QUESTIONS

1. Professor Zuboff says Edward was haunted by the sense of not knowing what he didn't know or how to learn it. Is it possible that many employees in today's labor force suffer from that same fear? Explain your answer.

2. Some people can benefit from multiple mentors? What other types of mentors, in addition to Professor Zuboff and her husband, might Edward find helpful?

CHAPTER 4 ENDNOTES

1. Sue Shellenbarger, "At College Admission Time, Lessons in Thin Envelopes," *Wall Street Journal*, March 24, 2010, p. D1.
2. Ibid., p. D2.
3. Ibid.
4. Douglas A. Bernstein, Louis A. Penner, Alison Clarke-Stewart, and Edward J. Roy, *Psychology*, 9th ed. (Wadsworth, Cengage Learning, 2012), p. 575.
5. Nathaniel Branden, *The Six Pillars of Self-Esteem* (New York: Bantam, 1994), p. 7.
6. Robert Reasoner, "The True Meaning of Self-Esteem," National Association for Self-Esteem, Normal, Il. [cited

April 30, 2003]. Available from http://www.self-esteem-nase.org; INTERNET.
7. Phillip C. McGraw, *Self Matters* (New York: Simon & Schuster, 2001), pp. 69–70.
8. Sharon Begley, "Follow Your Intuition: The Unconscious You May Be the Wiser Half," *Wall Street Journal*, August 30, 2002, p. B1; Sharon Begley, "How Do I Love Thee? Let Me Count the Ways—and Other Bad Ideas," *Wall Street Journal*, September 6, 2002, p. B1.
9. Douglas A. Bernstein, Louis A. Penner, Alison Clarke-Stewart, and Edward J. Roy, *Psychology*, 9th ed. (Wadsworth, Cengage Learning, 2012), p. 465.

10. Marilyn Elias, "Short Attention Span Linked to TV," *USA Today*, April 5, 2004, p. A1; Lyric Wallwork Winik, "The Toll of Video Violence," *Parade*, July 22, 2004, p. 15.

11. Douglas A. Bernstein, Louis A. Penner, Alison Clarke-Stewart, and Edward J. Roy, *Psychology*, 9th ed. (Wadsworth, Cengage Learning, 2012), p. 502.

12. Ibid., p. 505.

13. Ibid.

14. Emmett Miller, *The Healing Power of Happiness* (Emmaus, Pa.: Rodale Press, 1989), pp. 12–13. To learn more about Emmett Miller's writings visit http://www.DrMiller.com.

15. Lacey Beckmann, "One More Thing Money Can't Buy," *Psychology Today*, November/December, 2002, p. 16.

16. Amy Saltzman, *Downshifting* (New York: HarperCollins, 1990), pp. 15–16.

17. Miller, *The Healing Power of Happiness*, pp. 12–13.

18. Phillip C. McGraw, *Self Matters* (New York: Simon & Schuster, 2001), p. 73.

19. Robert Reasoner, "The True Meaning of Self-Esteem," National Association for Self-Esteem, Normal, Il. [cited April 30, 2003]. Available from http://www.self-esteem-nase.org; INTERNET.

20. Arthur H. Goldsmith, Jonathan R. Veum, and William Darity, Jr., "The Impact of Psychological and Human Capital on Wages," *Economic Inquiry*, October 1997, p. 817.

21. Hyrum W. Smith, *The 10 Natural Laws of Successful Time and Life Management* (New York: Warner Books, 1994), p. 178.

22. Annie Gottlieb, "The Radical Road to Self-Esteem," *O, The Oprah Magazine,* March 2001, pp. 101–102.

23. Don Miguel Ruiz, *The Four Agreements* (San Rafael, Calif.: Amber-Allen Publishing, 1997), pp. 47–61.

24. James J. Messina and Constance M. Messina, *The SEA's Program Model of Self-Esteem* [cited 9 November 2005]. Available from http://www.coping.org/selfesteem/model.htm; INTERNET.

25. Nathaniel Branden, *The Six Pillars of Self-Esteem* (New York: Simon & Schuster, 2001), p. 33.

26. Matthew McKay and Patrick Fanning, *Self-Esteem*, 2d ed. (Oakland, Calif.: New Harbinger, 1992), p. 42.

27. Phillip C. McGraw, *Self Matters* (New York: Simon & Schuster, 2001), p. 73.

28. Nathaniel Branden, *The Six Pillars of Self-Esteem* (New York: Simon & Schuster, 2001), p. 67–74.

29. Arnold A. Lazarus and Clifford N. Lazarus, *The 60-Second Shrink* (San Luis Obispo, Calif.: Impact Publishers, 1997), p. 40.

30. David Yellen, "Disrupters," *Fast Company*, December 2011, p. 109.

31. Marcus Buckingham and Donald O. Clifton, *Now, Discover Your Strengths* (New York: Free Press, 2001), p. 8.

32. Ibid., pp. 25–27.

33. Ibid., pp. 28–31.

34. Nanette Byrnes, "Start Search," *BusinessWeek*, October 10, 2005, p. 74.

35. Robert Kreitner, *Management*, 11th ed., Mason, OH: South-Western Cengage Learning, 2009, p. 415.

36. Carol Hymowitz, "Today's Bosses Find Mentoring Isn't Worth the Time and Risks," *Wall Street Journal*, March 13, 2006, p. B1.

37. Fiona Haley and Christine Canabou, interviews by, "The Mentors' Mentors," *Fast Company*, October 2003, p. 59.

38. Thomas J. DeLong, John J. Gabarro, and Robert J. Lees, *Harvard Business Review*, January 2008, p. 117.

39. Ginger Adams and Tena B. Crews, "Telementoring: A Viable Tool," *Journal of Applied Research for Business Education*, Vol. 2, No. 3, 2004, pp. 1–4.

40. Leigh Buchanan, "Can You Say Externship?" *Inc.*, October 2011, pp. 110 and 112.

41. Stan Goldberg, "The 10 Rules of Change," *Psychology Today*, September/October 2002, pp. 38–44.

42. Andrew Weil, "Images of Healing," *Dr. Andrew Weil's Self Healing*, November 2003, p. 3; Amy Dockser Marcus, "Heart Surgeons Try Using the Power of Suggestion," *Wall Street Journal*, February 20, 2004, p. D1.

43. Rami Shapiro, "What Do You Think of 'The Secret'"? *Spirituality & Health*, May/June 2007, p. 17.

44. James Bauman, "The Gold Medal," *Psychology Today*, May/June 2000, pp. 62–68.

45. See McGraw, *Self Matters*, for comprehensive coverage of how internal dialogue influences our self-concept.

46. Matthew McKay and Patrick Fanning, *Self-Esteem*, 2d ed. (Oakland, Calif.: New Harbinger, 1992), p. 42.

47. Julie Morgenstern, "Fire Your Inner Critic," *O, The Oprah Magazine*, August 2004, pp. 75–77.

48. Jack Canfield and D.D. Watkins, *Jack Canfield's Key to Living the Law of Attraction* (Deerfield Beach, FL: Health Communications, 2007), pp. 31–34.

49. Phillip C. McGraw, *Self Matters* (New York: Simon & Schuster, 2001), pp. 204–205.

50. Roy J. Blitzer, Colleen Petersen, and Linda Rogers, "How to Build Self-Esteem," *Training & Development*, February 1993, pp. 58–60.

51. Sue Shellenbarger, "At College Admission Time, Lessons in Thin Envelopes," *Wall Street Journal*, March 24, 2010, p. D1.

52. Ibid, p. D2.

53. Shoshana Zuboff, "Only the Brave Surrender," *Fast Company*, October 2004, p.121.

Comstock/Getty Images

Personal Values Influence Ethical Choices

CHAPTER PREVIEW

LEARNING OBJECTIVES

After studying Chapter 5, you will be able to

5-1 Explain how moral intelligence contributes to personal and organizational success.

5-2 Understand how personal values are formed.

5-3 Understand values conflicts and how to resolve them.

5-4 Learn how to make the right ethical decisions based on your personal value system.

5-5 Understand the importance of corporate values and ethical choices.

TIP OF THE ICEBERG | DANGEROUS LIAISONS IN THE WORLD OF INSIDER TRADING

A mor Moffat, wife of IBM executive Robert Moffat, was still in her pajamas when she heard the doorbell ring. One of the five FBI agents standing on the porch said, "Open the door, we're here to arrest Robert Moffat." Moffat, senior vice president of IBM's systems and technology group, often arrived early at IBM headquarters to get a jump on work. His wife called and said he needed to come home immediately. The FBI agents were at his home to arrest him for conspiracy related to insider trading. He would never return to his office again.

Moffat's arrest was a shock to the people who knew him well. The 31-year IBM veteran was a hard working, talented executive who was widely considered a candidate for the CEO position. Danielle Chiesi, former consultant to New Castle Funds LLC, was arrested on the same day as Moffat. She had maintained contact with highly placed sources at tech companies she covered for New Castle. Later, during court proceedings, the public would learn that Chiesi and Moffat had a long-term affair. Information she obtained from Moffat and others was given to several business associates who made millions in the stock market.[1]

Robert Moffat pleaded guilty to passing on confidential information about two companies and was sentenced to six months in prison. He testified that he had not profited financially from his crimes. Ms. Chiesi pleaded guilty to three counts of conspiracy to commit securities fraud and was sentenced to 30 months in prison.[2]

The new generation of workers is coming of age at a time when our culture is placing a great deal of emphasis on self-gratification, the crossing of many moral boundaries, and the breaking of many social taboos. This chapter will help you understand how to make the right ethical decisions based on a value system that embraces honor and integrity. It will help you understand how your values are formed, how to clarify which values are important to you, and how to resolve human relations problems that result when your personal values conflict with others' values.

IBM executive Robert Moffat was convicted of insider trading and sentenced to six months in prison. Businesspeople are frequently faced with ethical and even legal choices, which is why it's essential to have a firm grasp on personal values.

Louis Lanzano/AP Photos

MORAL INTELLIGENCE IN THE WORKPLACE

5-1   Many of America's most successful leaders rank high in the area of moral intelligence. Cognitive intelligence (IQ) is undeniably important, but not sufficient for exceptional performance. **Moral intelligence** is our mental capacity to determine how universal human principles such as responsibility, compassion, forgiveness, and humility should be applied to our personal values, goals, and actions.[3]

Our **character** is composed of personal standards of behavior, including honesty, integrity, and moral strength. It is the main ingredient we seek in our leaders and the quality that earns us respect in the workplace. Former U.S. senator Al Simpson said, "If you have character, that's all that matters; and if you don't have character, that's all that matters, too."[4]

In recent years, we have seen many leaders stray away from the ethical path. Ethical violations hurt individuals, businesses, stockholders, and society. In the early 2000s, our attention was focused on scandals at Enron, Tyco, and WorldCom. Today, a long list of American corporations have faced criminal changes related to unethical or illegal behavior.[5]

Integrity is the basic ingredient of character that is exhibited when you achieve congruence between what you know, what you say, and what you do.[6] When your behavior is in tune with your professed standards and values—when you practice what you believe in—you have integrity. When you say one thing but do something else, you *lack* integrity.

How important is it to be viewed as a person with integrity and a strong sense of character in the eyes of your friends, family members, fellow workers, and leaders?

When you look closely at the factors that contribute to warm friendships, strong marriages, successful careers, and successful organizations, you quickly come to the conclusion that character and integrity are critical.

HOW TO BUILD AND MAINTAIN INTEGRITY

- Recognize that the key mark of integrity in human relations is consistency.
- Resolve to live in truth with yourself and with every person in your life.
- Make promises carefully, then always keep your word.

Source: Brian Tracy, *The 100 Absolutely Unbreakable Laws of Business Success*, San Francisco, CA: Berrett-Koehler Publishers, Inc., 2000, pp. 121–123.

HOW PERSONAL VALUES ARE FORMED

5-2 Hyrum Smith, author of *The 10 Natural Laws of Successful Time and Life Management*, says that certain natural laws govern personal productivity and fulfillment. One of these laws focuses on personal beliefs: Your behavior is a reflection of what you truly believe.[7] **Values** are the personal beliefs and preferences that influence your behavior. They are deep-seated in your personality. To discover what really motivates you, carefully examine what it is you value.

Once you are aware of your value priorities, you are in a better position to plan and initiate life-changing activities.

Table 5.1 details the values clarification process. These five steps can help you determine whether or not you truly value something. Many times you are not consciously aware of what is really driving your behavior because values exist at different levels of awareness.[8] Unless you clarify your values, life events are likely to unfold in a haphazard manner. Once you are aware of your value priorities, you are in a better position to plan and initiate life-changing activities.

Core Values Drive Behavior

Hyrum Smith says that everything starts with your **core values**, those values that you consistently rank higher than others. When you are able to identify your core values, you have a definite picture of the kind of person you want to be and the kind of life you want to have. Anne Mulcahy, former CEO of Xerox Corporation and a mother of two sons, says she and her husband make decisions at home and work based on their core values: "Our kids are absolutely the center of our lives—and we never mess with that."[9] Maura FitzGerald, founder of FitzGerald Communications, Inc., a public relations firm, asks all her employees to adhere to the "FitzGerald Family Values" before accepting a job with her company. All her workers carry with them a wallet-size card listing the organization's basic operating principles, one of which is "Never compromise our integrity—this is our hallmark."[10]

Later in this chapter, we will discuss the powerful influence of core values on organizational success.

Focus on Your Life's Purpose

Jack Canfield, Brian Tracy, and other authorities on the development of human potential emphasize how important it is to define your purpose in life. Canfield says, "Without purpose as the compass to guide you, your goals and action plans may not ultimately

Table 5.1 ■ A Five-Part Valuing Process to Clarify and Develop Values

THINKING
We live in a confusing world where making choices about how to live our lives can be difficult. Of major importance is developing critical thinking skills that help distinguish fact from opinion and supported from unsupported arguments. Learn to think for yourself. Question what you are told. Engage in higher-level thinking that involves analysis, synthesis, and evaluation.

FEELING
This dimension of the valuing process involves being open to your "gut level" feelings. If it doesn't "feel right," it probably isn't. Examine your distressful feelings such as anger, fear, or emotional hurt. Discover what you prize and cherish in life.

COMMUNICATING
Values are clarified through an ongoing process of interaction with others. Be an active listener and hear what others are really saying. Be constantly alert to communication filters such as emotions, body language, and positive and negative attitudes. Learn to send clear messages regarding your own beliefs.

CHOOSING
Your values must be freely selected with no outside pressure. In some situations, telling right from wrong is difficult. Therefore, you need to be well informed about alternatives and the consequences of various courses of action. Each choice you make reflects some aspect of your values system.

ACTING
Act repeatedly and consistently on your beliefs. One way to test whether something is of value to you is to ask yourself, "Do I find that this value is persistent throughout all aspects of my life?"

Source: Howard Kirschenbaum, *Advanced Values Clarification* (La Jolla, CA: University Associates, 1977).

fulfill you." To get from where you are today to where you want to be, you have to know two things: where you stand today and where you want to get to.[11] Once you have identified your core values, defining your purpose in life will be much easier.

human
RELATIONS
in Action

SETTING THE INTENTION

- Observe your thoughts; they become your words.
- Observe your words; they become actions.
- Observe your actions; they become habits.
- Observe your habits; they become your character.
- Observe your character; it becomes your destiny.

Source: *New Dimensions Annual Journal*, Ukiah, CA: New Dimensions Media, 2002, p. 46.

Influences That Shape Your Values

As you engage in the values clarification process, it helps to reflect on those things that have influenced your values, such as people and events of your generation, your family, religious groups, your education, the media, and people you admire.

Generational Influences. Generational influences are among the most powerful forces shaping our values. Generations follow observable historical patterns and thus offer a powerful tool for predicting future workforce attitudes.[12]

Table 5.2 provides a summary of some of the key events and people that have shaped the values of four generations: the Matures, the Baby Boomers, Generation X, and Millennials/Generation Y. Although workers of different ages want basically the same things—meaningful work, respect, and a fair reward for work done well—they can have very different ideas about what these mean. An older Baby Boomer might believe that respect is due when someone spends many years on the job. To a Generation

Table 5.2 ■ People and events have influenced the formation of values for four groups of Americans: Matures, Baby Boomers, Generation X, and Millennials (sometimes called Generation Y). This means that today's work force represents the broadest range of ages and values in American history.

MATURES (BORN 1928–1945)	BABY BOOMERS (BORN 1946–1964)	GENERATION X (BORN 1965–1976)	MILLENNIALS (BORN 1977–2002)	GENERATION ?
Eisenhower	Television	AIDS	Corporate downsizing	It's too early to label or generalize about this generation.
MacArthur	The Cold War	The wellness movement	Ethics scandals	It will be formed by the way historical events and moods shape its members lives.*
The A-bomb	The space race	Watergate	Digital technology	
Dr. Spock	The Civil Rights Act	Glasnost	24/7 economy	
John Wayne	The pill	The Oklahoma	Jeff Bezos	
The Great Depression	The drug culture	City bombing	9/11 terrorist attacks	
World War II	Gloria Steinem	MTV	Wars in Iraq and Afghanistan	
The New Deal	The Vietnam War	The World Wide Web	Income gap	
	JFK and MLK assassinations	Information economy	Globalization	
		Work/Life balance concerns	Employment uncertainty	

*Views expressed by Neil Howe and William Strauss, authors of *Generations: The History of America's Future, 1584 to 2089* and *Fourth Turning: An American Prophecy*.

Xer, respect is expected when someone displays competence. Someone born during the early years of the Baby-Boom generation might be satisfied with feedback during annual or semiannual performance reviews. Generation Xers, as a group, have a need to see results almost daily and receive frequent feedback on their performance. Analyzing the traits of any large population can lead to unfair and unrealistic stereotyping, but generational differences shaped by sociological, political, and economic conditions can be traced to differences in values.[13] This important topic is discussed in several other chapters.

Your Family. Parents must assume many roles, none more important than *moral teacher.* In many families in contemporary society, one parent must assume full responsibility for shaping children's values. Some single parents—those overwhelmed with responsibility for career, family, and rebuilding their own personal lives—may lack the stamina needed to give their children the guidance they need. And in two-parent families, both parents may work outside the home and, at the end of the day, may lack the time or energy to intentionally direct the development of their children's values. The same may be true for families experiencing financial pressures or the strains associated with caring for elderly parents.

Religious Groups. Many people learn their value priorities through religious training. This may be achieved through the accepted teachings of a church, through religious literature such as the Koran and the Bible, or through individuals in churches, mosques, or synagogues who are positive role models.

Religious groups that want to define, instill, and perpetuate values may find an eager audience. Stephen Covey and other social observers say that many people are determinedly seeking spiritual and moral anchors in their lives and in their work. People who live in uncertain times seem to attach more importance to spirituality.[14] Healthy spirituality is discussed in Chapter 17.

human RELATIONS *in Action*

THE DIVORCE GENERATION

"Every generation has its life-defining moments. If you want to find out what it was for a member of the Greatest Generation (Matures), you ask: "Where were you on D-Day?" For Baby Boomers, the questions are: "Where were you when Kennedy was shot?" or "What were you doing when Nixon resigned?" For much of my generation—Generation X, born between 1965 and 1980—there is only one question: "When did your parents get divorced?" Our lives have been framed by the answer. Ask us. We remember everything."

Source: Susan Gregory Thomas, "The Divorce Generation," *Wall Street Journal*, July 9–10, 2011, pp. C1–C2.

Education. Many parents, concerned that their children are not learning enough about moral values and ethical behavior, want character education added to the curriculum. They are concerned about the constant barrage of messages children are getting about behavior in government and corporate America. Research conducted by the Josephson Institute Center for Youth Ethics indicates that parents have reason to worry. The 2010 Report Card on the Ethics of American Youth indicates widespread lying and cheating among teens. The Josephson Institute of Ethics has developed a variety of grassroots training activities involving what it refers to as the six pillars of character: trustworthiness, respect, responsibility, fairness, caring, and citizenship.[15]

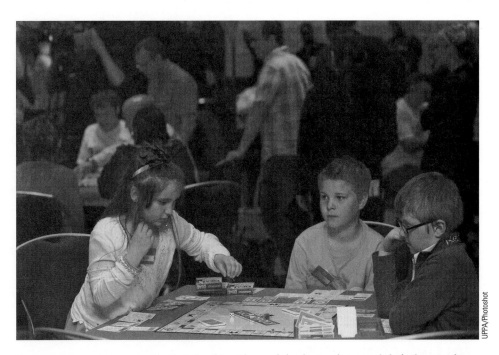

Even at a very young age, people start absorbing ideas and developing their own beliefs about qualities such as trust, respect, and fairness.

The Institute for Global Ethics, or IGE, is dedicated to promoting ethical action in a global context. The Center for Corporate Ethics, or CCE, is a division of the IGE. The CCE has developed tools, techniques, and training programs aimed at reducing the likelihood and risks of ethical lapses. More information can be found on these organizations' websites.[16]

The Media. Mainstream television and many of today's movies seen by young viewers continues to feature a great deal of violence and antisocial behavior. In addition, many young people spend time playing violent video games. Learning can occur not only by doing but also by observing what others do and what happens to them. Learning by watching others is called **observational learning**. There is evidence that exposure to media violence can trigger or amplify viewers' aggressive thoughts and feelings. Too often, media violence provides models that viewers imitate. The vast majority of studies have showed that exposure to media violence results in increased aggressive behavior.[17]

People You Admire. In addition to being influenced by the media, you have probably also done some **modeling**—you have shaped your behavior to resemble that of people you admire and embraced the qualities those people demonstrate. Most employees look to their leaders for moral guidance. Unfortunately, there is a shortage of leaders who have a positive impact on ethical decision making. A survey found that less than half of employees in large organizations think their senior leadership is highly ethical.[18]

Avoiding Values Drift

Once you have examined the various influences on your values and have clarified what is important to you now that you are an adult (see Table 5.1), you also need to be aware of

values drift, the slow erosion of your core values over time—those tiny changes that can steer you off course. When you observe lying, abuse, theft, or other forms of misconduct at work, or feel pressure to make ethical compromises, carefully and intentionally reflect on the values you hold dear and choose the appropriate ethical behavior that maintains your character and integrity. Monitor your commitment to your values and make adjustments when necessary to get your life back on track.

A friend offers to take you to the movies. She says she will save a few dollars by buying senior tickets online. Neither of you is a senior. What do you do?[19] The person you are dating often picks you up in his mother's car which has a handicap license plate. He usually parks in spaces reserved for handicap drivers. Do you say anything? The erosion of your core values can begin with decisions that may seem insignificant.

Total Person Insight

"Every time I've done something that doesn't feel right, it's ended up not being right."
Mario Cuomo, Former Governor of New York

Source: "Sunbeams" *The Sun*, January 2006, p. 48.

VALUES CONFLICTS

5-3   One of the major causes of conflict within an organization is the clash between the personal values of different people. There is no doubt about it; people are different. They have different family backgrounds, religious experiences, educations, role models, and media exposure. These differences can pop out anywhere and anytime people get together. Many observers suggest that organizations look for **values conflicts** when addressing such problems as declining quality, absenteeism, and poor customer service. The trouble may lie not so much in work schedules or production routines as in the mutual distrust and misunderstanding brought about by clashes in workers' and managers' value preferences. The late Peter Drucker, author of *The Practice of Management*, said: "Organizations are no longer built on force but on trust. The existence of trust between people does not mean that they like one another. It means that they understand one another. Taking responsibility for relationships is therefore an absolute necessity. It is a duty."[20]

Internal Values Conflicts

How you resolve internal values conflicts depends on your willingness to rank your core values in the order of their importance to you.

A person who is forced to choose between two or more strongly held values is experiencing an **internal values conflict**. Soon after the World Trade Center was attacked by terrorists, many people began to reexamine their values. Some decided to spend more time with family and friends, thinking that although overtime might be an opportunity to make more income, it was also an obstacle to maintaining a commitment to their family. Some workers also decided that their "work and spend" lifestyle no longer made sense. Before the terrorist attacks, a 28-year-old market research manager described herself as "very driven" and motivated to acquire things. Following September 11 she said, "Maybe I don't need all this stuff."[21]

How you resolve internal values conflicts depends on your willingness to rank your *core values* in the order of their importance to you. Prioritizing your values will help you make decisions when life gets complicated and you have to make difficult choices. If one of your values is to be an outstanding parent and another is to maintain a healthy body, you should anticipate an internal values conflict when a busy schedule requires a choice between attending your daughter's soccer game and your weekly workout at the fitness center. However, when you rank which value is most important, the decision will be much easier.

Values Conflicts with Others

As we have noted, four distinct generations have come together in the workplace. Employees from each generation bring with them different experiences and expectations. Values conflicts are more likely in this environment. These conflicts require effective human relations skills.

How will you handle a tense situation where it is obvious your values conflict with those of a colleague? You may discover your supervisor is a racist and you strongly support the civil rights of all people. One option is to become indignant and take steps to reduce contact with your supervisor. The problem with being indignant is that it burns your bridges with someone who can influence your growth and development within the organization. The opposite extreme would be to do nothing. But when we ignore unethical or immoral behavior, we compromise our integrity, and the problem is likely to continue and grow.[22] With a little reflection, you may be able to find a response somewhere between these two extremes. If your supervisor tells a joke that is demeaning to members of a minority group, consider meeting with her and explaining how uncomfortable these comments make you feel. When we confront others' lapses in character, we are strengthening our own integrity.

human
RELATIONS
in Action

Tony Dungy, the first African-American head coach to win a Super Bowl, and best-selling author of inspirational books, says his favorite verse in the Bible is Matthew 16:26: "What does it profit a man to gain the whole world but forfeit his soul?" Throughout his 30 years in the NFL, he saw a lot of players who earned huge amounts of money and received many accolades but were not happy because they have not directed their lives toward something meaningful.

Source: Matthew Kaminski, "A Coach's Faith," *Wall Street Journal*, September 12, 2009, p. A13.

PERSONAL VALUES AND ETHICAL CHOICES

5-4 **Ethics** refers to principles that define behavior as right, good, and proper. Your ethics, or the code of ethics of your organization, does not always dictate a single moral course of action, but it does provide a means of evaluating and deciding among several options.[23] Ethics determines where you draw the line between right and wrong.

As competition in the global marketplace increases, moral and ethical issues can become cloudy. Although most organizations have adopted the point of view that "good ethics is good business," exceptions do exist. Some organizations encourage, or at least condone, unethical behaviors. Surveys show that many workers feel pressure to violate their ethical standards in order to meet business objectives.[24] Thus, you must develop your own *personal* code of ethics.

Every job you hold will present you with new ethical and moral dilemmas. And many of the ethical issues you encounter will be very difficult. Instead of selecting from two clear-cut options—one right, one wrong—you often face multiple options.[25]

---

human RELATIONS *in Action*

A HIPPOCRATIC OATH FOR BUSINESS

Lawyers have their oath of attorney and doctors have the Hippocratic Oath. Now Masters of Business Administration graduates have the *MBA Oath*, which you can find online. It is hoped that this oath will lay the foundation for a new generation of ethical business leaders. Those who sign the MBA Oath make eight promises. The first promise reads:

I will act with utmost integrity and pursue my work in an ethical manner. My personal behavior will be an example of integrity, consistent with the values I publicly espouse.

Source: Max Anderson and Peter Escher, *The MBA Oath*, New York, New York: Penguin Group, 2010, pp. 6–13; 99.

How to Make the Right Ethical Choices

Unethical acts by employees cost U.S. businesses billions of dollars each year. Employee theft and fraud represent two of the largest loss categories. For small businesses, preventing these losses can be an uphill struggle.[26] The following guidelines may help you avoid being part of this growing statistic.

Learn to Distinguish Between Right and Wrong. Although selecting the right path can be difficult, a great deal of help is available through books, magazine articles, and a multitude of online resources. Support may be as close as your employer's code of ethics, guidelines published by your professional organization, or advice provided by an experienced and trusted colleague at work. In some cases, you can determine the right path by *restraining* yourself from choosing the *wrong* path. For example:

- Just because you have the power to do something does not mean it is the proper thing to do.
- Just because you have the right to do something does not mean it is right to do.
- Just because you want to do something does not mean you should do it.
- Choose to do more than the law requires and less than the law allows.[27]

Don't Let Your Life Be Driven by the Desire for Immediate Gratification. Progress and prosperity have almost identical meanings to many people. They equate progress with the acquisition of material things. One explanation is that young business leaders entering the corporate world are under a great deal of pressure to show the trappings of success—a large house or an expensive car, for example.

Some people get trapped in a vicious cycle: They work more so that they can buy more consumer goods; then, as they buy more, they must work more. They fail to realize that the road to happiness is not paved with Rolex watches, Brooks Brothers suits, and a Lexus. Chapter 17 offers support for finding satisfaction through nonfinancial resources that make the biggest contribution to a fulfilling life.

Make Certain Your Values Are in Harmony with Those of Your Employer. You may find it easier to make the right ethical choices if your values are compatible with those of your employer. Many organizations have adopted a set of beliefs, customs, values, and practices that attract a certain type of employee. Harmony between personal and organizational values usually leads to success for the individual as well as the organization. Enlightened companies realize that committed employees give them their competitive edge and are taking values seriously.

When Tony Hsieh founded Zappos.com, an online shoe retailer, he was determined to create a culture that thrives on unique values and delivers exceptional levels of personalized customer service. Step one was developing a list of core values (see Figure 5.1) that would serve as the foundation for one of the strongest and most unique company cultures in the world. Step two was finding ways to integrate the core values into the employees' everyday behavior.

Since Zappos is "Powered by Customer Service," one of the biggest challenges is finding employees who love working with other people to deliver "Wow!" customer service. New candidates are screened in two interviews. One interview is focused on skills and the other on core values and cultural fit. Once hired, every employee goes through five weeks of training in culture, core values, and customer service. Zappos is

Figure 5.1 ■ Zappos, one of America's most successful online retailers, is guided by these core values.

Zappos Core Values

1. **Deliver WOW Through Service**
   Go the "extra mile" to make sure that the customer is completely taken care of.
2. **Embrace and Drive Change**
   Realize that we are a growing company and that change is inevitable if we are going to stay relevant.
3. **Create Fun and a Little Weirdness**
   To ensure that our customers catch our enthusiasm, we need to create an environment worth passing on… not to mention the importance of not taking ourselves too seriously.
4. **Be Adventurous, Creative, and Open-Minded**
   In a setting that is going to change, an attitude of open-mindedness is key. Besides… who knows when the next big idea is going to hit; think "outside the box."
5. **Pursue Growth and Learning**
   Pushing yourself to the next level benefits the individual and the company as a whole.
6. **Build Open and Honest Relationships with Communication**
   It has been said, "Teamwork makes the dream work." Communication is the key to strong teams moving in the same direction for the common good of the company.
7. **Build a Positive Team and Family Spirit**
   Since the majority of one's week is spent at work, it seems only fitting to create an atmosphere worth coming to.
8. **Do More with Less**
   Money is not always the key to success. Sometimes solving the task at hand with limited resources brings about a greater sense of accomplishment and satisfaction for a "job well done."
9. **Be Passionate and Determined**
   Go for your dreams and desires and don't let anyone or anything stop you from doing what you want to do within the company.
10. **Be Humble**
    The truth is that it is not about me; keeping this in mind makes all of the other Core Values not only possible but attainable.

Source: © 2010 Zappos.com, Inc.

The corporate culture at Zappos is built on a foundation of outstanding customer service, which is why the company tends to attract outgoing, friendly, sociable employees.

now part of Amazon.com, but the fun, productive, and happy culture remains at this successful online shoe retailer.[28]

CORPORATE VALUES AND ETHICAL CHOICES

5-5   When organizations consistently make ethical decisions that are in the best interest of their stakeholders—employees, customers, stockholders, and the community—they are considered good corporate citizens because they are socially responsible. The list "The 100 Best Corporate Citizens" published by *Corporate Responsibility Officer* magazine reminds us that a company can be socially responsible and still achieve excellent earnings. In her *BusinessWeek* article "A Conscience Doesn't Have to Make You Poor," Susan Scherreik interviewed stockholders who invest only in companies that are good corporate citizens. One stated, "I see the damage that many companies do to people's health and the environment by polluting or creating dangerous products. Investing in them makes no sense because these companies won't flourish in the long run."[29]

Corporate Crime

Many organizations have gotten into serious trouble by ignoring ethical principles. In recent years, the media have carried headlines concerning organizations involved in corporate crime. Executives employed by Enron, WorldCom, Adelphia Communications, Tyco International, and other corporations have spent time in prison for criminal acts. Many employees working for these firms lost their jobs and their retirement savings. Some stock holders saw their investments disappear.

Several large corporations have been fined large sums of money for business practices that the U.S. government viewed as detrimental to consumer or employee safety. Merck & Company pleaded guilty to illegal promotion of its pain-killer Vioxx and was fined $950 million. Bank of America paid $335 million to settle allegations that its Countrywide Financial unit discriminated against black and Hispanic borrowers.[30]

Leaders such as Jeffrey Immelt, CEO of General Electric, believe you can fuse high performance with high integrity. He realizes that employees at all levels of the company will be tempted to "make the numbers" by juggling accounts or cutting corners. From day one, he made a stirring call for performance with integrity. General Electric's 220 officers and 600 senior managers were told that failure to create the right culture would result in termination.[31]

Many business leaders say they have difficulty determining the right course of action in difficult "gray-area" situations. And even when the right ethical course of action is clear, competitive pressures sometimes lead well-intentioned managers astray.[32] Tom Chappell, author of *The Soul of a Business*, explains why organizations often have difficulty doing what is morally right and socially responsible: "It's harder to manage for ethical pursuits than it is to simply manage for profits."[33]

How to Prevent Corporate Crime

Establish and Support a Strong Code of Ethics. We have recently seen an increase in ethical initiatives that make ethics a part of core organizational values. **Codes of ethics**, written statements of what an organization expects in the way of ethical behavior, can give employees a clear indication of what behaviors are acceptable or improper.[34] An

"Honesty is the best policy, Fernbaugh, but it's not company policy."

ethics code can be a powerful force in building a culture of honesty, but only if it is enforced without exception. The list of corporate values at Enron Corporation included respect, integrity, communication, and excellence. As events have shown, these values did not prevent unethical conduct at the highest levels of the company. Empty values statements create cynical and dispirited employees and undermine managerial credibility.[35]

---

human
RELATIONS
in Action

TABLE MANNERS

At age 16, Julia Stewart was a waitress at an IHOP. Today she is IHOP's CEO. She does not usually hire anyone without going out to eat with them. She says you can tell a lot about people by the way they act toward the food server: "If you have a complete conversation with me and you never acknowledge the food server, you are being disrespectful and will never work for me."

Source: Julia Stewart, "The Pancake Pusher," *Fortune*, October 15, 2007, p. 48.

Hire with Care. The hiring process used at Zappos provides a model for other organizations. First, identify a guiding set of core values and then find people who have those values. Success hinges on effective hiring interviews. At Umpqua Bank, where every element of the culture is focused on great customer service, potential candidates are interviewed by at least four associates who represent different areas of the bank. Those who are involved in the interviews have completed the "Hire the Best" training programs.[36]

Some companies use integrity tests (also called honesty or character tests) to screen out dishonest people. Two standardized tests designed to measure honesty are the Reid Report (*http://www.reidlondonhouse.com*) and the newer Career Ethic Inventory (*http://www.careerethic.com*). These tests are helpful, but they are not a substitute for rigorous interviewing and reference checks. Résumés that include exaggerations or outright fabrications tell you a lot about the integrity of the applicants.[37]

Provide Ethics Training. Many ethical issues are complex and cannot be considered in black-and-white moral terms. The fact that an action is legal and does not violate a law does not necessarily make the action morally or ethically acceptable.[38] It is for these reasons that ethics training has become quite common. In some cases, the training involves little more than a careful study of the company ethics code and its implications for day-to-day decision making. In other cases, employees participate in in-depth discussions of complex ethical decisions.

Can colleges and universities teach ethics? In the wake of numerous corporate scandals, business schools have been criticized for producing graduates who are obsessed with making money regardless of the ethical consequences. In response to this criticism, business schools are trying a host of new methods including required ethics courses and honor oaths.

Develop Support for Whistleblowing. When you discover that your employer or a colleague is behaving illegally or unethically, you have three choices. You can keep quiet and keep working. You can decide you can't be party to the situation and leave. Or you can report the situation in the hope of putting a stop to it. When you reveal wrongdoing within an organization to the public or to those in positions of authority, you are a **whistleblower.**

Total Person Insight

The honor code at West Point sends a clear message about what the U.S. Military Academy expects of its cadets:

"A cadet will not lie, cheat, steal, or tolerate those who do."

The last five words are the most difficult for most cadets. They have a responsibility to report misbehavior in their fellow cadets.

Source: William McGurn, "Duty, Honor, Football," *Wall Street Journal*, August 23, 2011, p. A11.

FBI attorney Coleen Rowley wrote a memo to FBI director Robert Mueller claiming that the department ignored the pleas of the Minneapolis field office to investigate Zacarias Moussaoui, who was subsequently indicted as a September 11 co-conspirator. Cynthia Cooper informed WorldCom's board of directors that illegal accounting procedures covered up $3.8 billion in corporate losses. Enron vice president Sherron Watkins wrote a letter to Enron chairman Kenneth Lay alerting him to the illegal accounting procedures that misled stockholders about Enron's financial picture. All three of these women tried to keep their concerns "in house" by speaking the truth to executives in a position of power, not to the public. As details exploded in the media, these women were plunged into the public eye. *Time* magazine proclaimed them "Persons of the Year for 2002" and made them national celebrities.[39]

Disclosing wrong-doing can be a daunting experience. Your fellow colleagues may resent the disruption your revelations cause in their lives. They may be impressed with your integrity, but not everyone will be on your side in your struggle to do what is right and ethical. Your efforts may result in months or even years of emotional and financial turmoil. A survey conducted by the National Whistleblower Center in Washington, D.C., showed that half of the whistleblowers were fired because of their actions. Most reported being unable to acquire new jobs because prospective employers perceived them as troublemakers. Others faced demotions or were placed in jobs with little impact or importance.[40]

Each individual must make his or her own decision as to whether the disturbing unethical offense is worth the personal cost. Table 5.3 lists four questions potential whistleblowers should ask themselves before taking action.

VALUES AND ETHICS IN INTERNATIONAL BUSINESS

If the situation is complex on the domestic scene, values and ethical issues become even more complicated at the international level. American business firms are under great pressure to avoid doing business with overseas contractors that permit human rights violations such as child labor, low wages, and long hours in their factories. The 1977 Foreign Corrupt Practices Act and later amendments prohibit U.S. companies from using bribes or kickbacks to influence foreign officials, and many industrial nations have signed a multinational treaty outlawing corporate bribery. But monitoring illegal activities throughout the world is a difficult task. Doing business in the global marketplace continues to be an ethical minefield with illegal demands for bribes, kickbacks, or special fees standing in the way of successful transactions. American businesses acknowledge that it is difficult to compete with organizations from other countries that are not bound by U.S. laws. However, according to the International Business Ethics Institute (*http://www.business-ethics. org*), there has been significant progress in the last few years.

Table 5.3 ■ Whistleblower Checklist

Experts say that people who are thinking about blowing the whistle on their company should ask themselves four important questions before doing so.

1. Is this the only way?

Do not blow the whistle unless you have tried to correct the problem by reporting up the normal chain of command and gotten no results. Make sure your allegations are not minor complaints.

2. Do I have the goods?

Gather documentary evidence that proves your case, and keep it in a safe place. Keep good notes, perhaps even a daily diary. Make sure you are seeing fraud, not merely incompetence or sloppiness.

3. Why am I doing this?

Examine your motives. Do not act out of frustration or because you feel underappreciated or mistreated. Do not embellish your case, and do not violate any confidentiality agreements you may have.

4. Am I ready?

Think through the impact on your family. Be prepared for unemployment and the possibility of being blacklisted in your profession. Last, but not least, consult a lawyer.

Source: Paula Dwyer and Dan Carney, with Amy Borrus and Lorraine Woellert in Washington and Christopher Palmeri in Los Angeles, "Year of the Whistleblower," *BusinessWeek*, December 16, 2002, pp. 107–108.

The federal government has been stepping up its pursuit of cases that involve violations of the Foreign Corrupt Practices Act. IBM recently agreed to pay a $10 million fine for engaging in widespread payment of bribes to vendors in Asia.[41]

LOOKING BACK: SUMMARY OF LEARNING OBJECTIVES

1. **Explain how moral intelligence contributes to personal and organizational success.**

   A strong sense of character grows out of your personal standards of behavior. When you consistently behave in accordance with your values, you maintain your integrity.

2. **Understand how personal values are formed.**

   Your values are the personal importance you give to an object or idea. People's values serve as the foundation for their attitudes, preferences, opinions, and behaviors. Your core values are largely formed early in life and are influenced by people and events in your life, your family, religious groups, your education, the media, and people you admire.

3. **Understand values conflicts and how to resolve them.**

   Internal values conflicts arise when you must choose between strongly held personal values. Value conflicts with others, often based on age,

racial, religious, gender, or ethnic differences, require skilled intervention before they can be resolved.

4. **Learn how to make the right ethical decisions based on your personal value system.**

   Once you have clarified your personal values, your ethical decisions will be easier. You must learn to distinguish right from wrong, avoid the pursuit of immediate gratification, and choose an employer whose values you share. Shared values unify employees in an organization by providing guidelines for behavior and decisions.

5. **Understand the importance of corporate values and ethical choices.**

   Corporate values and ethics on both the domestic and the international levels are receiving increasing attention because of the devastating effect and expense of corporate crime. Many organizations are developing ethics codes to help guide employees' behavior, hiring only those individuals who share their corporate values, offering ethics training opportunities to all employees, and supporting whistle-blowing. As multinational organizations increase in number, the individuals involved will need to consciously examine their values and ethical standards to deal effectively with differing values structures around the world.

KEY TERMS

moral intelligence, 98
character, 98
integrity, 98
values, 99
core values, 99

observational learning, 103
modeling, 103
values drift, 104
values conflicts, 104
internal values conflict, 104

ethics, 105
codes of ethics, 109
whistleblower, 110

CAREER INSIGHT

If you are job hunting, honesty is the best policy. George O'Leary was hired to become the next Notre Dame football coach, then forced to resign five days later when lies about his academic and athletic achievements surfaced. Marilee Jones, an MIT dean, quit when her credentials proved to be inaccurate. When job seekers are struggling to find a job, they find it harder to resist embellishing their resumes or job applications."

A growing number of employers are checking résumé information and these checks often reveal discrepancies.

Résumé fraud is not uncommon, so employers are looking closely at the information you provide. Did you serve as a department head or did you hold a team leader position? Did you major in accounting or complete just two courses in accounting? Was your graduation GPA 3.00 or 2.7? Did you resign from your last position or were you fired? Now is the time to check your résumé and make sure it provides an accurate presentation of your work and education experience.

Anna Prior, "In Job Hunting, Honesty is Still the Best Policy," *Wall Street Journal Sunday*, April 25, 2010, p. 4E.

TRY YOUR HAND

1. Guilt and loss of self-respect can result when you say or do things that conflict with what you believe. One way to feel better about yourself is to "clean up" your integrity. Make a list of what you are doing that you think is wrong. Once the list is complete, look it over and determine if you can stop these behaviors. Consider making amends for things you have done in the past that you feel guilty about.[42]

2. You work for a company where the HR director has been involved in unethical activities. You know that others are also aware of the situation; however, no one is willing to share the director's behavior with upper management. You do not want to be the whistleblower; however, you realize that guilt and loss of self-respect can result when you do or do not do things that conflict with what you believe. Discuss this situation with two or three classmates. Identify pros and cons of becoming a whistleblower.

3. One of the great challenges in life is the clarification of our values. The five-part valuing process described in Table 5.1 can be very helpful as you attempt to identify your core values. Select one personal or professional value from the following list, and clarify this value by applying the five-step process:

   a. Respect the rights and privileges of people who may be in the minority because of race, gender, ethnicity, age, physical or mental abilities, or sexual orientation.

   b. Conserve the assets of my employer.

   c. Utilize leisure time to add balance to my life.

   d. Maintain a healthy lifestyle.

   e. Balance the demands of my work and personal life.

CRITICAL THINKING CHALLENGE

Practice making ethical choices based on your value priorities in the following scenarios.

- You are offered a great job, but you have to relocate to a distant city. Your family agrees that the decision is yours to make, but you know they do not want to move. What do you do?
- You have discovered that your boss lied on her résumé about her academic credentials. She is being considered for a new position in your organization, but you believe you are more qualified than she is. Will you tell the hiring panel about your boss's indiscretion?
- You are taking an online college class and have been offered the final exam from a student who printed a copy for you after taking the exam yesterday. The correct answers are not on the test copy. You are in danger of failing the class and losing your financial aid. Do you accept the document or use it to study for your exam?

SELF-ASSESSMENT EXERCISE

For each of the following statements, circle the number from 1 to 5 that best represents your response to each statement: (1) strongly disagree (never do this); (2) disagree (rarely do this); (3) moderately agree (sometimes do this); (4) agree (frequently do this); (5) strongly agree (almost always do this).

A. I base my personal and professional decisions on clearly defined personal values.	1 2 3 4 5
B. I accept the fact that others' values may differ from mine, and I respect their right to maintain a value system that differs from my own.	1 2 3 4 5
C. I have a clear sense of what is right and wrong, and my character reflects the fundamental strengths of honesty, fairness, service, humility, and modesty.	1 2 3 4 5
D. I maintain my integrity by practicing what I believe in and keeping my commitments.	1 2 3 4 5
E. When I observe unethical practices, I will report them to the appropriate person(s).	1 2 3 4 5

After identifying your response to each item, select an attitude or skill you would like to improve. Prepare a written goal and then describe the steps you will take to achieve this goal.

YOU PLAY THE ROLE

You are currently employed by a pharmaceutical wholesaler that sells prescription drugs to hospitals in a three-county area. Each morning, you help other employees fill orders that arrive via computer or the telephone. Once the orders are completed and loaded into delivery vans, you spend the rest of the day delivering products to hospitals. Although others help fill the orders, you are responsible for the accuracy of each order and for timely delivery. Rob Howard, a fellow employee, performs the same duties, but delivers items to hospitals in a different territory. Over the past two months, you have noticed that he sometimes makes poor ethical choices. For example, the company's reimbursement for lunch is a maximum of $8. Rob packs each day's lunch and never eats at a restaurant. At the end of each week, however, his reimbursement form claims the maximum amount for each meal. Once he bragged about earning an extra $40 each week for meals that were not purchased.

Rob owns a small landscaping business on the side and sometimes uses the company van to transport items to customers. Recently you drove by a Home Depot store and noticed him loading bags of mulch into the company van. At one point you thought about talking with the supervisor about these ethical lapses, but decided to talk with Rob first. Another class member will assume the role of Rob Howard. Try to convince him that some of these on-the-job activities are unethical.

BELOW THE SURFACE | SERVING TIME FOR INSIDER TRADING

At the beginning of this chapter, you were introduced to Robert Moffat and Danielle Chiesi, two persons involved in one of our nation's biggest insider trading cases. They were among a group of 26 people charged in a criminal insider-trading probe; 19 have pleaded guilty. Raj Rajaratnam, billionaire co-founder of the Galleon Group hedge fund, master-minded the insider trading ring that netted his firm $45 million. He gave generous rewards to persons who provided him with illegal insider information. After a lengthy trial, Rajaratnam was found guilty and sentenced to 11 years in prison, the longest-ever term imposed in an insider-trading case.[43]

The prosecution's case relied on FBI wiretaps and confidential informants. In court, U.S. Attorney Jonathan Streeter was able to play numerous phone conversations that showed Rajaratnam traded illegally on more than 35 stocks. During sentencing, the judge said the billionaire investor's crimes "reflect a virus in our business culture that needs to be eradicated."[44]

QUESTIONS

1. Robert Moffat was a rich, powerful IBM executive earning more than $11 million a year. He was married with four children. What motivated him to risk the loss of his job and going to prison?

2. Warren Buffett, chairman of Berkshire Hathaway, is universally regarded as a beacon of integrity. He gives his employees the following ethical mandate: "Lose money for the firm and I will be understanding; lose a shred of reputation for the firm and I will be ruthless." Do you feel this mandate has merit? Should other leaders take the same position?

3. What are some of the lessons current business-school students should take away from the insider trading scandal discussed in this chapter?

CLOSING CASE | PEOPLE AND PURPOSE AT NEW BELGIUM BREWING

New Belgium Brewing Company, based in Fort Collins, Colorado, was founded by a husband and wife team who met over a beer at a friend's house. A year later, they founded their own brewery which has grown to become America's third-largest craft brewery.

After touring several European villages famous for beer, the plan for New Belgium Brewing Company started to take shape. (Touring on a bicycle with fat tires, of course). The new entrepreneurs wanted to create an outstanding beer and minimize the company's footprint on the planet. They prepared a vision statement and a list of core values before they ever sold a bottle of beer. One of the core values reads: *Environmental stewardship: Honoring nature at every turn of the business.* This core value reflects their strong belief in sustainability. As early adopters of the movement toward sustainability, employees voted to make New Belgium Brewing the first 100 percent wind-powered brewery in 1998. The company has set goals to reduce their carbon footprint by 25 percent, reduce water usage by 10 percent, offset eight million car miles by riding bikes, and supporting the onsite recycling center.

An employee ownership plan encourages employees to become more engaged. Employees own about 32 percent of New Belgium through a stock-ownership plan. The company has embraced open-book management practices that include monthly meetings where employees review financial statements, business strategies, and branding plans. They worked hard to create a culture of transparency that fosters trust and respect. The result of New Belgium's passion and purpose tied to business practices is an amazing employee retention rate of 92 percent.[45]

QUESTIONS

1. Carefully review the business practices at New Belgium Brewing Company and determine which of these would be most appealing to you.

2. In 1998 employees at New Belgium Brewing voted to make the company 100 percent wind-powered, even if it meant forfeiting their yearly bonus. Would you support this initiative even if it meant a reduction in your earnings?

3. New Belgium Brewing has created a high-involvement employee culture. What are some of the major benefits of a culture of transparency?

CHAPTER 5 ENDNOTES

1. James Bandler, with Doris Burke, "Dangerous Liaisons at IBM," *Fortune*, July 26, 2010, pp. 66–80; Susan Pulliam and Michael Rothfeld, "Motive for Stock Leak Can Be Respect, Love," *Wall Street Journal*, March 14, 2011, pp. C1 and C3.

2. Chad Bray, "Tipster Gets 30 Months," *Wall Street Journal*, July 21, 2011, p. C3.

3. Doug Lennick and Fred Kiel, *Moral Intelligence*, Upper Saddle River, NJ: Pearson Education, Inc., 2010, p. 7.

4. David Gergen, "Candidates with Character," *U.S. News & World Report*, September 27, 1999, p. 68. The importance of honesty in leadership positions is discussed in James M. Kouzes and Barry Z. Posner, *The Leadership Challenge*, 3rd edition (San Francisco: Jossey-Bass, 2002), pp. 27–28.

5. Ross Tartell, "Can Leadership Ethics Be Learned?" *Training*, May/June 2011, pp. 16–18.

6. Nathaniel Branden, *Self-Esteem at Work* (San Francisco: Jossey-Bass, 1998), p. 35; Brian Tracy, *The 100 Absolutely Unbreakable Laws of Business Success*, San Francisco, CA: Berrett-Koehler Publishers, Inc., 2002, p. 121.

7. Hyrum W. Smith, *The 10 Natural Laws of Successful Time and Life Management* (New York: Warner Books, 1994), pp. 14–15.

8. J. David McCracken and Ana E. Falcon-Emmanuelli, "A Theoretical Basis for Work Values Research in Vocational Education," *Journal of Vocational and Technical Education*, April 1994, p. 4.

9. Sue Shellenbarger, "Some Top Executives Are Finding a Balance Between Job and Home," *Wall Street Journal*, April 23, 1997, p. B1. Anne Mulcahy was named CEO of the year in 2008 by *Tech Her*.

10. Katharine Mieszkowski, "FitzGerald Family Values," *Fast Company*, April 1998, p. 194.

11. Jack Canfield, *The Success Principles* (New York: HarperCollins, 2005), pp. 20–29.

12. Neil Howe and William Strauss, "The Next 20 Years: How Customers and Workforce Attitudes Will Evolve," *Harvard Business Review*, July/August 2007, pp. 41–52.

13. Jeffrey Zaslow, "The Latest Generation Gap: Boomers Are Often Unfairly Lumped Together," *Wall Street Journal*, July 8, 2004, p. 1; Shirley Holt, "Generation Gaps in the Workplace," *The Roanoke Times*, March 27, 2005, pp. 1, 3; Karen Auby, "A Boomer's Guide to Communicating with Gen Y and Gen Y," *BusinessWeek*, August/September 1, 2008, p. 63; Roy Saunderson, "Learning Across the Generations," *Training*, May/June 2011, pp. 78–79.

14. Chris Lee and Ron Zemke, "The Search for Spirit in the Workplace," *Training*, June 1993, p. 21.

15. "The Ethics of American Youth," Josephson Institute of Ethics at (http://www.josephsoninstitute.org). Cited 11 January 12.

16. "About the Institute for Global Ethics," Institute for Global Ethics at (http://www.ethics@globalethics.org). Cited 11 January 12.

17. Douglas A. Bernstein, Louis A. Penner, Alison Clarke-Stewart, and Edward J. Roy, *Psychology*, 9th ed. (Boston: Wadsworth, Cengage Learning, 2012), pp. 227–231.

18. O. C. Ferrell, John Fraedrich, and Linda Ferrell, *Business Ethics*, 5th ed. (Houghton Mifflin, 2002), pp. 123–135.

19. Jancee Dunn, "Now What Do I Do?" *O, The Oprah Magazine*, March 2008, p. 89.

20. John Hollon, "Drucker Knew Best," **Workforce Management**, November 21, 2005, p. 58.

21. Sue Shellenbarger, "In Cataclysmic Times, Workers Need Room to Rethink Priorities," **Wall Street Journal**, September 19, 2001, p. B1.

22. John Beebe, "Conscience, Integrity and Character," **The Inner Edge**, June/July 2000, pp. 9–11.

23. "Making Sense of Ethics." [cited 13 January 2003]. Available from http://www.josephsoninstitute.org/MED/MED-1makingsense.htm; INTERNET.

24. Craig Mindrum, "Business Ethics—Moral Intelligence and *Workforce* Performance," **Workforce Performance Solutions**, March 2006, pp. 28–32.

25. Price Pritchett, **The Ethics of Excellence** (Dallas, Tex: Pritchett & Associates, n.d.), p. 28.

26. "CyberSource® Joins with Association of Certified Fraud Examiners to Support 2002 National Fraud Awareness Week," July 29, 2002. [cited 13 January 2003]. Available from http://phx.corporate-ir.net/phoenix.zhtml?c=94844&p=irol-newsArticle&ID=320302&highlight=; INTERNET. Raymund Flandez, "Stop That Thief," **Wall Street Journal**, June 16, 2008, p. R6.

27. "Making Sense of Ethics" [cited 13 January 2003]. Available from http://www.josephsoninstitute.org/MED/MED-1makingsense.htm; INTERNET.

28. Monique Reece, **Real-Time Marketing for Business Growth**, Upper Saddle River: NJ, Pearson Education, Inc., 2010, pp. 14–16.

29. Susan Scherreik, "A Conscience Doesn't Have to Make You Poor," **BusinessWeek**, May 1, 2000, pp. 204–206.

30. Peter Loftus and Brent Kendall, "Merck to Pay $950 Million Vioxx Settlement," **Wall Street Journal**, November 23, 2011, p. B3; Ruth Simon and Brent Kendall, "B of A Settles Lending Case," **Wall Street Journal**, December 22, 2011, p. C1.

31. Ben W. Heineman , Jr., "Avoiding Integrity Land Mines," **Harvard Business Review**, April 2007, pp. 100–108.

32. Andrew Stark, "What's the Matter with Business Ethics?" **Harvard Business Review**, May/June 1993, p. 38.

33. "Tom Chappell—Minister of Commerce," **Business Ethics**, January/February 1994, p. 17.

34. Ferrell, Fraedrich, and Ferrell, **Business Ethics**, pp. 182–183.

35. Patrick M. Lencioni, "Make Your Values Mean Something," **Harvard Business Review**, July 2002, pp. 5–9.

36. Margery Weinstein, "You're Hired," **Training**, July/August 2011, pp. 34–37. For more information on the importance of cultural fit read Ari Weinzweig, "Ask Ari Weinzweig," *Inc.*, December 2007, p. 84.

37. Anne Fisher, "How Can You Be Sure We're Not Hiring a Bunch of Shady Liars?" **Fortune**, May 26, 2003, p. 180.

38. Michelle Reece, "Business Ethics and the Pharmaceutical Industry," **SPBT Focus**, Fall 2005, p.24.

39. Richard Lacayo and Amanda Ripley, "Persons of the Year," *Time*, December 31, 2002, pp. 32–33.

40. Paula Dwyer and Dan Carney, with Amy Borrus and Lorraine Woellert in Washington and Christopher Palmeri in Los Angeles, "Year of the Whistleblower," **BusinessWeek**, December 16, 2002, pp. 107–108; Michael Orey, "WorldCom-Inspired 'Whistle-Blower' Law Has Weaknesses," **Wall Street Journal**, October 1, 2002, p. B1; R. Scott Oswald and Jason Zuckerman, "Protecting the Whistleblower," **Corporate Responsibility Officer**, January/February 2008, p. 49.

41. Jessica Holzer and Shayndi Raice, "IBM Settles Bribery Charges," **Wall Street Journal**, March 19, 2011, p. B1.

42. Chris Hill and Toby Hanlon, "26 Simple Ways to Change How You Feel," **Prevention**, August 1993, p. 126.

43. Caroline Winter, David Glovin, and Jennifer Daniel, "The Great Hedge Fund Takedown," **Bloomberg Businessweek**, March 14–20, pp. 78–81.

44. Susan Pulliam and Chad Bray, "Trader Draws Record Sentence," **Wall Street Journal**, October 14, 2011, pp. A1–A2.

45. Kelly K. Spors, "Top Small Workplaces," **Wall Street Journal**, October 13, 2008, pp. R1 and R8; "Workplace Awards" [accessed 28 December 2008]. Available from http://www.winningworkplaces.org; INTERNET; "Our Story" [accessed 29 December 2008]. Available from http://www.newbelgium.com; INTERNET.

CHAPTER 6

Attitudes Can Shape Your Life

TIP OF THE ICEBERG | I'M FEELING SAUCY

Panda Express is one of the fastest-growing and most successful restaurant chains in the United States. The Panda Restaurant Group (PRG) is a privately owned, 1,350-location "fast casual" Asian restaurant chain. This success story started in the early 1970s when Andrew Cherng and his chef father arrived as Chinese émigrés. After opening his first restaurant, Cherng worked seven days a week to make it a success. Today, Andrew Cherng and his wife Peggy hold the titles of co-chairman and co-CEO.

Cherng is a strong supporter of self-improvement programs that focus on the *total person*. He urges his employees to eat a well-rounded diet and get plenty of exercise. To be a manager at Panda, you have to be committed to being positive to continuous learning. He is a devotee of Stephen Covey's *Seven Habits of Highly Effective People* and Don Miguel Ruiz's *Four Agreements*.[1]

Cherng sees the company's growth in personal terms. Reaching his goals means better service, better execution, and better environment. Each area requires a human touch. When Panda Express employees make a commitment to self-improvement, they often voice their plan in front of their colleagues at company sponsored training classes. At one meeting, 71 Panda Express managers waited in line to make their public statement. All were wearing orange T-shirts that read "I'm feeling saucy."[2]

The beneficial impact of individual and organizational attitudes is not always easy to measure. However, the correlation between positive attitudes and high performance, low employee turnover, and increased productivity exists in most organizations.

Fast-casual restaurant chain Panda Express deliberately seeks out employees who are positive, engaged, curious, and well-balanced.

THE IMPORTANCE OF ATTITUDES

6-1   **Attitudes** are thoughts that you have accepted as true and that lead you to think, feel, or act positively or negatively toward a person, idea, or event. Social psychologists have studied attitude development intensely over many years. They view attitudes as having three components:[3]

- **Cognitive** This component is a set of beliefs about the attitude object. Many years ago, tobacco companies spent millions of dollars publicizing the pleasure of smoking certain cigarette brands. The health threatening aspects of smoking were not mentioned. Today, the number of adults who smoke has declined steadily because their beliefs have been shaped by accurate information regarding the dangers of smoking.
- **Emotional** The emotional, or *affective* component includes feelings about the object. Every year a large number of environmental organizations ask us for generous donations. The messages we receive through the year appeal to our emotions.
- **Behavioral** This component is the way people act toward the object. If you read an article on the homeless in your community, and the message appeals to your emotions, you may be inclined to help them in some way. However, in many areas of life, our positive thoughts and supportive emotions are never translated into actions.

Bruce Clarke, president and CEO of a North Carolina based human resource management firm, says, "No one has ever been fired for a bad attitude." He explains that attitude may be the reason given, but the real reason was poor behavior. We cannot know with great certainty another person's attitude, but we can observe and act on behaviors.[4] For example, a traveler visits three bricklayers and asks each one what he's doing. The first mutters, "Working for a buck." The second says, "Making a wall." The third proclaims, "Building a school that will educate children for generations." Each is doing the same work, yet the third bricklayer is working for the future. Chances are the quality of the work performed by the third bricklayer will be superior to the work of the other two.[5]

We should keep in mind that the success of organizations is greatly influenced by the attitudes of its leaders. The traditional purpose of business, according to some economists, is to make money. That narrow focus motivates leaders to maximize short-term profits and deliver good returns to shareholders. Rosabeth Moss Kanter, Professor of Business Administration at Harvard Business School, says great companies generate money, but they are also vehicles for accomplishing societal purposes and providing meaningful livelihoods for those who work for them.[6]

The leader of Panda Express, introduced at the beginning of this chapter, sees the company's growth more in personal rather than professional terms. He says "Forget about return on investment. This is a tremendous overall contribution to society."[7]

Hiring for Attitude

If you are looking for a job, take time to check your résumé, check your look, and check your attitude. Some of the best companies to work for realize that if they don't hire people with the right attitude, the behavioral characteristics that fit their culture, the culture will start to change. Each year, thousands of people apply for jobs at Southwest Airlines. Those who are hired are willing and able to champion the corporate culture: *Warrior spirit*, *servant's heart*, and *fun loving attitude*. The application process includes interviews by a recruiter, the candidate's potential supervisor, and a peer employee.[8]

Healing Jobless Wounds

During the recent economic slump, the U.S. Chamber of Commerce reported that 23 million Americans were unemployed, underemployed, or had given up looking for jobs.[9] After losing a job, it's easy to fall into a funk and become pessimistic about the future. Recent research indicates that during the economic downturn many employers developed a negative work environment that created a sense that "the company doesn't care about me." Seventy-five percent of departing employees who participated in a study conducted by the Corporate Executive Board Company said they wouldn't recommend their employer to others.[10] (See Figure 6.1.)

Figure 6.1 ■ Bad Recommendations Rising

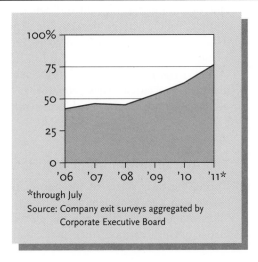

*through July

Source: Company exit surveys aggregated by Corporate Executive Board

Loss of a job and extended periods of unemployment may result in lower self-esteem. As noted in a previous chapter, people with high self-esteem tend to maintain an internal locus of control. They are optimistic in their approach to life and seek to become creative, imaginative problem solvers.

Core Values Revisited

In Chapter 5, we described *core values* as those values that one consistently ranks higher than others. You were introduced to a five-part valuing process that will help you clarify and develop your values (see Table 5.1). Each of us lives our life according to a unique set of *core values*. They are fundamental building blocks of your personality. Examples may include honesty, financial security, healthy spirituality, generosity, or maintaining good health. They represent the clearest answers you can give to these questions:[11]

- What are the highest priorities in my life?
- Of these priorities which do I value most?

Clarifying and developing values is a process that is available throughout our lives. We are constantly choosing from alternatives and considering the consequences of these alternatives. Behavior is more likely to be consistent with attitude when people see the attitude as important and relevant to their lives; that is, when they match their core values.[12] If you are invited, for example, to be active in a campaign to support the rights of gay men and lesbians, you will likely reflect on your core values.

Total Person Insight

"The U.S. job market is showing signs of a sustained recovery. But the country's prolonged struggle with unemployment will leave scars that are likely to remain for years, if not generations."

Source: Ben Casselman, "No Easy Balm for Jobless Wounds," *Wall Street Journal*, January 9, 2012, p. A2.

Your Choice of Attitudes

One of the most significant differences between high and low achievers is choice of attitude. People who go through life with a positive attitude are more likely to achieve their personal and professional goals. People who filter their daily experiences through a negative attitude find it difficult to achieve contentment or satisfaction in any aspect of their lives. Jack Welch, the former chairman and CEO of General Electric, believes that an organization needs people with "positive energy" and needs to get rid of those people who inject the workforce with "negative energy"—even if they are high performers.[13]

The Age of Information Mandates Attitude Changes

During the early stages of the information age, many of the best jobs were filled by people who were proficient at reasoning, logical thinking, and analysis. However, as the information age unfolded and the global economy heated up, organizations discovered that it often takes more than quick and accurate information communicated through advanced technology to retain their clients and customers. In many cases, two competing firms, such as banks, may offer customers the same products at the same prices and use the same information technology. The competitive advantage is achieved through superior customer service provided by well-trained employees with effective interpersonal skills.

Daniel Pink, author of *A Whole New Mind*, says we are moving from the information age to the conceptual age. He predicts that one of the major players in the conceptual age will be the **empathizer**. Empathizers have the ability to imagine themselves in someone else's position and understand what that person is feeling. They are able to understand the subtleties of human interaction.[14] For example, several medical schools have come to the conclusion that empathy is a key element of compassionate medical care. Medical school students at Harvard, Columbia, and Dartmouth are learning that an important part of health care diagnosis is contained in the patient's story. They are trained how to identify the subtle details of a patient's condition through caring, compassionate attitudes.[15]

Technology, in its many forms, will continue to make a major contribution to the workplace. However, we must seek a better balance between "high tech" and "high touch." Leadership, for example, is about empathy. It is about having the ability to relate to and to connect with people. Pink states: "Empathy builds self-awareness, bonds parent to child, allows us to work together, and provides the scaffolding for our morality."[16]

Daniel H. Pink, author of *A Whole New Mind*, predicts that one of the major players in the New Conceptual Age will be the empathizer. These workers have the ability to imagine themselves in someone else's position and understand what that person is feeling.

HOW ATTITUDES ARE FORMED

6-2 Throughout life, you are constantly making decisions and judgments that help form your attitudes. These attitude-shaping decisions are often based on behaviors your childhood authority figures told you were right or wrong, behaviors for which you were rewarded or punished. The role models you select and the various environmental and organizational cultures you embrace also shape your attitudes.

Socialization

The process through which people are integrated into a society by exposure to the actions and opinions of others is called **socialization**. As a child, you interacted with your parents, family, teachers, and friends to learn the skills and social norms necessary to be well-functioning members of society.[17] Children often feel that statements made by these authority figures are the "proper" things to believe.

Peer and Reference Groups

Kurt Mortensen, author of *Maximum Influence—The 12 Universal Laws of Power Persuasion*, says we tend to change our perceptions, opinions, and behaviors in ways that are consistent with group norms. He states that people want to be liked by others and feel connected.[18] As children reach adolescence and begin to break away psychologically from their parents, the **peer group** (people their own age) can have a powerful influence on attitude formation. With the passing of years, reference groups replace peer groups as sources of attitude formation in young adults. A **reference group** consists of several people who share a common interest. Sales and Marketing Executives International would serve as a reference group for persons employed in sales and marketing.

Rewards and Punishment

Attitude formation is often related to rewards and punishment. People in authority generally encourage certain attitudes and discourage others. Naturally, individuals tend to develop attitudes that minimize punishments and maximize rewards. A child who is praised for sharing toys with playmates is more likely to develop positive attitudes toward caring about other people's needs. As an adult, you will discover that your employers will continue to attempt to shape your attitudes through rewards and punishment at work. Many organizations are rewarding employees who take steps to stay healthy, avoid accidents, increase sales, or reduce expenses.

HOW TO RUN AN EMPATHY CHECK ON YOURSELF

Imagine that you are someone who works or lives with you. See how accurately you can describe that person's experience of working or living with you. If you are willing to take a risk, try asking the person you have in mind to listen to your impressions. Ask for feedback on how accurate you are.

Source: Al Siebert, *The Survivor Personality*, New York, New York, Penguin Group, 2010, p. 57.

Role Model Identification

Most young people would like to have more influence, status, and popularity. These goals are often achieved through identification with an authority figure or a role model. A **role model** is that person you most admire or are likely to emulate. As you might expect, role models can exert considerable influence—for better or for worse—on developing attitudes.

> *Role models can exert considerable influence—for better or for worse—on developing attitudes.*

In most organizations, supervisory and management personnel can have the greatest impact on employee attitudes. The new dental hygienist and the recently hired auto mechanic want help adjusting to their jobs. They watch their supervisors' attitudes toward safety, cost control, accuracy, grooming, and customer relations and tend to emulate the behavior of these role models. Employees pay more attention to what their supervisors *do* than to what they *say*.

Cultural Influences

Our attitudes are influenced by the culture that surrounds us. **Culture** is the sum total of knowledge, beliefs, values, objects, and ethnic customs that we use to adapt to our environment. It includes tangible items, such as foods, clothing, and furniture, as well as intangible concepts, such as education and laws. In companies, corporate culture is influenced by all of these factors, and ultimately it is defined by the way people work together to get things done.[19]

Today's organizations are striving to create corporate cultures that attract and keep productive workers in these volatile times. When employees feel comfortable in their work environment, they tend to stay. As noted previously in this chapter, Southwest Airlines has created a company culture that has built an energetic corps of customer-loving employees.

human RELATIONS *in Action*

ATTITUDES SHAPE STEW LEONARD'S CULTURE

Stew Leonard's, a highly profitable four-store supermarket in Connecticut and New York, has developed a distinctive culture that emphasizes teamwork and devotion to customer service. Shortly after opening his first store, Stew Leonard adopted two basic store policies which were chiseled into a 6,000-pound rock next to the front door of his store. The simple message reads:

Rule 1—**THE CUSTOMER IS ALWAYS RIGHT!**

Rule 2—**IF THE CUSTOMER IS EVER WRONG, RE-READ RULE 1.**

Source: Philip Kotler and Gary Armstrong, *Principles of Marketing*, 12th ed. (Upper Saddle River, NJ: Prentice Hall, 2008), p. 20.

The company that sweats together stays together. That is the belief held by Greg Wittstock, CEO of Aquascape, a multi-million dollar pond-supply company based in St. Charles, Illinois. Several years ago, some employees said that they would like the company to build a soccer field. The company was expanding, so Wittstock decided to build a new home for Aquascape. He decreed that about 20 percent of the new headquarters would be dedicated to "fun stuff." He built a racquetball court, an indoor soccer field, a batting cage, a hot tub, and numerous other places of merriment. Greg Wittstock believes that happy workers are productive workers.[20]

ATTITUDES VALUED BY EMPLOYERS

6-3   Many organizations have discovered the link between workers' attitudes and profitability. This discovery has led to major changes in the hiring process. Employers today are less likely to assume that applicants' technical abilities are the best indicators of their future performance. They have discovered that the lack of technical skills is not the primary reason why most new hires fail to meet expectations. Too often new employees are not capable enough in terms of interpersonal skills.[21]

Whether you are looking for your first career position, anticipating a career change, or being retrained for new opportunities, you may find the following discussion helpful concerning what attitudes employers want in their employees.

Basic Interpersonal Skills

In this information-based, high-tech, speeded-up economy, we are witnessing an increase in workplace incivility. Rude behavior in the form of high-decibel cell-phone conversations, use of profanity, or failure to display simple courtesies such as saying "thank you" can damage workplace relationships. As we note in Chapter 11, incivility is the ultimate career killer.

Self-Motivation

People who are self-motivated are inclined to set their own goals and monitor their own progress toward those goals.

People who are self-motivated are inclined to set their own goals and monitor their own progress toward those goals. Their attitude is "I am responsible for this job." They do not need a supervisor hovering around them making sure they are on task and accomplishing what they are supposed to be doing. Many find ways to administer their own rewards after they achieve their goals. Employers often retain and promote those employees who take the initiative to make their own decisions, find better ways of doing their jobs, and keep up to date in their area of specialization.

Openness to Change

In the age of information, the biggest challenge for many workers is adjusting to the rapidly accelerating rate of change. Some resistance to change is normal merely because it may alter your daily routine. However, you will get into trouble if you choose the following three attitudes:[22]

1. *Stubbornness.* Some workers refuse to be influenced by someone else's point of view. They also find fault with every new change.
2. *Arrogance.* Employees who reject advice or who give the impression that they do not want retraining or other forms of assistance send the wrong message to their employer.
3. *Inflexibility.* Displaying a closed mind to new ideas and practices can only undermine your career advancement opportunities.

Team Spirit

In sports, the person who is a "team player" receives a great deal of praise and recognition. A team player is someone who is willing to step out of the spotlight, give up a little personal glory, and help the team achieve a victory. Team players are no less important in organizations. Employers are increasingly organizing employees into teams (health teams, sales teams, product development teams) that build products, solve problems, and make decisions. Chapter 12 contains some tips on how to become a respected team member.

Health Consciousness

The ever growing cost of health care is one of the most serious problems facing companies today. Many organizations are promoting wellness programs for all employees as a way to keep costs in line. These programs include tips on healthy eating, physical-fitness exercises, and stress-management practices, as well as other forms of assistance that contribute to a healthy lifestyle. Employees who actively participate in these programs frequently take fewer sick days, file fewer medical claims, and bring a higher level of energy to work. Chapters 14 and 17 discuss health and wellness in greater detail.

Appreciation of Coworker Diversity

To value diversity in the work setting means to make full use of the ideas, talents, experiences, and perspectives of all employees at all levels within the organization. People who differ from each other often add richness to the organization.

Development and utilization of a talented, diverse work force can be a key to success in a period of fierce global competition. Women and people of color make up a large majority of the new multicultural, global work force. Many people, however, carry prejudiced attitudes against those who differ from them. They tend to "prejudge" others' value based on the color of their skin, gender, age, religious preference, lifestyle, political affiliation, or economic status. Chapter 15 contains specific guidance on how to develop positive attitudes toward joining a diverse work force.

Honesty

Honesty and truthfulness are qualities all employers are searching for in their employees. This is because relationships depend on trust. An honest employee's attitude is "I owe my employer and coworkers the truth." If you cannot be honest with your employer, customers, fellow workers, and friends, they cannot trust you, and strong relationships will be impossible.

HOW TO CHANGE ATTITUDES

6-4   If you are having difficulty working with other team members, if you believe you were overlooked for a promotion you should have had, or if you go home from work depressed and a little angry at the world, you can almost always be sure you need an attitude adjustment. Unfortunately, people do not easily adopt new attitudes or discard old ones. It is difficult to break the attachment to emotionally laden beliefs. Yet attitudes *can* be changed. There may be times when you absolutely hate a job, but you can still develop a positive attitude toward it as a steppingstone to another job you actually do want.

> *It is often said that life is 10 percent what happens to you and 90 percent how you react to it.*

There will be times, as well, when you will need to help colleagues change their attitudes so that you can work with them more effectively. And, of course, when events, such as a layoff, are beyond your control, you can accept this fact and move on. It is often said that life is 10 percent what happens to you and 90 percent how you react to it. Knowing how to change attitudes in yourself and others can be essential to effective interpersonal relations—and your success—in life.

Changing Your Own Attitude

You are constantly placed in new situations with people from different backgrounds and cultures. Each time you go to a new school, take a new job, get a promotion, or move to a different neighborhood, you may need to alter your attitudes to cope effectively with the change. The following attitudes will help you achieve positive results in today's world.

Choose Happiness. In his best-selling book *The Art of Happiness*, the Dalai Lama presents happiness as the foundation of all other attitudes. He suggests that the pursuit of happiness is the purpose of our existence. Survey after survey has shown that unhappy people tend to be self-focused, socially withdrawn, and even antagonistic. Happy people, in contrast, are generally found to be more sociable, flexible, and creative and are able to tolerate life's daily frustrations more easily than unhappy people.[23] Tal Ben-Shahar, Harvard University professor and author of *Happier*, sees a strong link between happiness and success:[24] "All else being equal, happy people have better relationships, are more likely to thrive at work, and also live better and longer."

---

human
RELATIONS
in Action

WHO MOVED MY CHEESE?

Several years ago, Spencer Johnson wrote *Who Moved My Cheese?* In this small book, which has been on the bestseller list for many years, Johnson introduces the reader to a fable on how to cope positively with change. He recognizes that change is a basic fact of life, so learning to cope with it is an important life strategy. Johnson's most important message is that instead of seeing change as the end of something, you need to learn to see it as a beginning. Breaking through your fear of change is a very important attitude shift in our fluid, ever-changing working world.

Source: Tom Butler-Bowdon, *50 Success Classics* (London: Nicholas Brealey, 2004), pp. 168–171.

So, if achieving happiness is truly an important goal, what can we do to achieve it? Here are some important tips:

- *What we choose to focus on largely determines our level of happiness.* The potential for happiness may be all around us, but it may go unnoticed.[25] Let's assume that you are earning an adequate income, but you want to earn more money. Chances are that having more money will not bring greater happiness. It may be time to stop and answer the question: What gives me pleasure? What do I enjoy doing? If earning more money means working longer hours, you may be unable to do things (spend time with family, enjoy more leisure time) that you truly enjoy and bring you happiness.

- *Mentally reframe events or activities that create unhappiness.* Ralph Waldo Emerson once said, "To different minds, the same world is a hell, and a heaven."[26] Beth Zimmerman, a successful entrepreneur, was not comfortable selling strategic planning services. However, without these sales, her business would fail. She viewed selling as *pushing or peddling products*. Then Zimmerman mentally reframed the personal selling process: "Instead of selling, I think of it as listening to the challenges that my customers face and providing them with a way to help solve them."[27] Once she saw herself as a *consultant* and not a *peddler,* she began to enjoy sales.

- *Seek happiness in relationships.* Two leading positive psychologists studied "very happy people" and compared them to those who were less happy. The only external factor that distinguished the two groups was the presence of "rich and satisfying social relationships." We need to share events, thoughts, and feelings in our lives with friends.[28] Have you stopped making contact with a former friend or family member? Do you avoid resolving problems with coworkers or your boss? Are you spending enough time with those who are closest to you?

Embrace Optimism. Optimistic thoughts give rise to positive attitudes and effective interpersonal relationships. When you are an optimist, your coworkers, managers, and—perhaps most important—your customers feel your energy and vitality and tend to mirror your behavior.

It does not take long to identify people with an optimistic outlook. Optimists are more likely to bounce back after a demotion, layoff, or some other disappointment. According to Martin Seligman, professor of psychology at the University of Pennsylvania and author of *Learned Optimism*, optimists are more likely to view problems as merely temporary setbacks on their road to achieving their goals. They focus on their potential success rather than on their failures.[29]

Total Person Insight

> "Research shows that when people work with a positive mindset, performance on nearly every level—productivity, creativity, engagement—improves."
>
> Source: Shawn Achor, "Positive Intelligence," *Harvard Business Review*, January/February 2012, pp. 100–102.

Looking for a job? Research conducted at Duke and Yale universities indicates the importance of optimism during the job search. The research shows that people who have an optimistic outlook on life will have better career prospects than those with a pessimistic disposition.[30]

Pessimists tend to believe bad events will last a long time, will undermine everything they do, and are their own fault. A pessimistic pattern of thinking can have unfortunate consequences. Pessimists give up more easily when faced with a challenge, are less likely to take personal control of their life, and are more likely to take personal blame for their misfortune.[31] Often pessimism leads to **cynicism**, which is a mistrusting attitude regarding the motives of people. When you are cynical, you are constantly on guard against the "misbehavior" of others.[32] If you begin to think that everyone is screwing up, acting inconsiderately, or otherwise behaving inappropriately, cynicism has taken control of your thought process, and it is time to change.

HOW TO DEAL WITH YOUR PESSIMISTIC THOUGHTS

- *Distraction* Some pessimistic thoughts circle through our minds and grab our attention. Habitual pessimistic thoughts are especially serious thought patterns. Find ways to distract yourself from troublesome beliefs.
- *Disputation* In some cases, we need to go on the attack and dispute the beliefs that serve as barriers to an optimistic life. So, after investing a great deal of time and energy, you learn that your class project earned a B. You hoped to earn an A. Reject feelings of despair and reflect on your past accomplishments.

Source: Margin E. P. Seligman, *Learned Optimism*, New York: Alfred A. Knopf, 1990, pp. 217–219.

Think for Yourself. One of the major deterrents to controlling your own attitude is the power of *group think*, which surfaces when everyone shares the same opinion. Individuals can lose their desire and ability to think for themselves as they strive to be accepted by team members, committee members, or coworkers in the same department. You are less likely to be drawn into group think if you understand that there are two overlapping relationships among coworkers. *Personal relationships* develop as you bond with your coworkers. When you share common interests and feel comfortable talking with someone, the bonds of friendship may grow very strong. You form small, intense groups. But there still exists the larger group—the organization. Within this setting, *professional relationships* exist for just one purpose: to get the job done.[33] Maintaining two kinds of relationships with the same people can be challenging.

Let's assume you are a member of a project team working on a software application. The deadline for completion is rapidly approaching, yet the team still needs to conduct one more reliability test. At a team meeting, one person suggests that the final test is not needed because the new product has passed all previous tests, and it's time to turn the product over to marketing. Another member of the team, a close friend of yours, enthusiastically supports this recommendation. You have serious concerns about taking this shortcut but hesitate to take a position that conflicts with that of your friend. What should you do? In a professional relationship, your commitment to the organization takes precedence—unless, of course, it is asking you to do something morally wrong.[34]

Keep an Open Mind. We often make decisions and then refuse to consider any other point of view that might lead us to question our beliefs. Many times, our attitudes persist even in the presence of overwhelming evidence to the contrary. If you have been raised in a family or community that supports racist views, it may seem foreign to you when your colleagues at work openly accept and enjoy healthy relationships with people whose ethnicity is different from your own. Exposing yourself to new information and experiences beyond what you have been socialized to believe can be a valuable growth experience.

In his book *The 100 Absolutely Unbreakable Laws of Business Success*, Brian Tracy suggests reflecting on the "Law of Flexibility." He said, "You are only as free in life as the number of well-developed options you have available to you." The more thoroughly you open your mind to the options available to you, the more freedom you have.[35] This flexibility to see beyond what you thought was true and examine others' perspectives could be one of the most powerful tools you have to inspire the rest of your life.

HELPING OTHERS CHANGE THEIR ATTITUDES

6-5 At some point you may want to help another person change his or her attitude about something. If you try to beg, plead, intimidate, or even threaten him or her into thinking differently, you probably will get nowhere. This process is similar to attempting to push a piece of yarn across the top of a table. When you *push* the yarn in the direction you want it to go, it gets all bent out of shape. However when you gently *pull* the yarn with your fingertips, it follows you wherever you want it to go. Two powerful techniques can help you pull people in the direction you want them to go:

1. Change the *conditions* that precede the behavior.
2. Change the *consequences* that follow the behavior.

Change the Conditions

If you want people to change their attitudes, identify the behaviors that represent the poor attitudes and alter the conditions that *precede* the behavior. Consider the following situation.

A new employee in a retail store is having a problem adjusting to her job. The manager needed her on the sales floor as soon as possible, so he rushed through her job training procedures without taking time to answer her questions. Now she finds there are many customers' questions she cannot answer, and she has trouble operating the computerized cash register. She wants to quit, and her negative attitudes are affecting her job performance and the way she handles her customers.

The manager could easily have prevented this employee's negative attitudes by answering all her questions *before* she was placed on the sales floor. Perhaps he could have asked an experienced salesperson to stay with her as she helped her first few customers. Above all, he could have displayed a caring, supportive attitude toward her.

Change the Consequences

Another way to help other people change their attitudes is to alter what happens *after* they exhibit the behavior you are attempting to change. A simple rule applies: When an experience is followed by positive consequences, the person is likely to repeat the behavior. When an experience is followed by negative consequences, the person is more likely to stop the behavior. For example, if you are a supervisor, and some of your employees are consistently late for work, you might provide some form of negative consequence each time they are tardy, such as a verbal reprimand or reduced pay. Keep in mind, however, that we should not focus attention on the people who exhibit disruptive attitudes and ignore the employees exhibiting the attitudes we want to encourage. Saying "Thank you for being here on time. I really appreciate your commitment" can be an effective reward for those who arrive at work on time. Behaviors rewarded are more likely to be repeated.

An attitude is nothing more than a personal thought process. We cannot control the thinking that takes place in someone else's mind, but we can sometimes influence it. And sometimes we can't do that either, so we have to set certain rules of behavior. Some organizations have come to the conclusion that behavior that offends or threatens others must stop. It may be impossible to stop someone from thinking prejudicial thoughts, but you can establish a zero tolerance policy regarding acts that demean or threaten others.[36]

ORGANIZATIONS' EFFORTS TOWARD IMPROVING EMPLOYEES' ATTITUDES

6-6 When employees have positive attitudes, job performance and productivity are likely to improve. One CEO of a software company has stated, "The way you get superior performance is to get people's passionate loyalty and belief. That means being flexible and giving your people what they need to do a great job."[37]

People who are asked what they most want from their job typically cite mutual respect among coworkers, interesting work, recognition for work well done, the chance to develop skills, and so forth. Of course, workers expect the pay to be competitive, but they want so much more. The late Peter Drucker said, "To make a living is not enough. Work also has to make a life."[38] Organizations are finding creative ways to influence worker attitudes. The following companies made *Fortune* magazine's list of the 100 best companies to work for.[39]

- Plante & Moran is an accounting firm with a human touch and a sense of humor. The company describes itself as "relatively jerk-free." Full-time employees get at least four weeks of paid vacation. Employees are encouraged to bond. During tax season,

Throughout the world, NetApp, a data storage company, has received many "Best Companies" awards. The company ranked on *Fortune* magazine's 2011 list of "100 Best Companies to Work For." NetApp maintains a culture defined by such core values as trust and integrity, effective leadership, teamwork, and fairness. Employees are encouraged to enjoy miniature golf, volleyball, or some other activity available on the campus.

employees get "survival kits" with aspirin, stress balls, and candy, and each office throws an "end of tax season" bash.

- Baptist Health South Florida is a hospital that the competition tries to imitate. Top management maintains close contact with all employees, and employee-led initiatives have resulted in low turnover among registered nurses. Periodic open-forum meetings give employees a chance to voice concerns or make suggestions. Three child-care centers are popular.

- Adobe Systems, a successful Silicon Valley firm, strives to generate camaraderie among its employees. It schedules frequent all-hands meetings, job rotations, and employee councils feed management with ideas. Perks include a fitness center with trainer, seasonal farmers' market, and basketball court.

What do these organizations have in common? Each has given thought to the attitudes that are important for a healthy work environment and has taken steps to shape these attitudes. Many organizations are attempting to improve employee attitudes and productivity by enhancing the quality of their employees' work life.

A Final Word

Viktor Frankl, a survivor of the Auschwitz concentration camp and author of *Man's Search for Meaning*, said, "The last of the human freedoms is to choose one's attitude in any given set of circumstances." Changing an attitude can be a challenge, but the process can also be an important step toward your continued growth and success.

LOOKING BACK: SUMMARY OF LEARNING OBJECTIVES

1. **Understand the impact of attitudes on the success of individuals as well as organizations.**

   Attitudes represent a powerful force in every organization. Employees' attitudes and performance cannot be separated. When employees display a positive attitude toward their work and coworkers, teamwork and productivity improve. When employees display a caring attitude toward their customers, the business is likely to enjoy a high degree of customer loyalty and repeat business. When employees display a serious attitude toward safety rules and regulations, fewer accidents are likely to occur.

2. **List and explain the ways people acquire attitudes.**

   People acquire attitudes through early childhood socialization, peer and reference groups, rewards and punishment, role model identification, and cultural influences. However, attitudes are not set in stone. You always have the power to choose your attitude toward any situation.

3. **Describe attitudes that employers value.**

   Employers hire and attempt to retain employees who have basic interpersonal skills, are self-motivated, accept change, are team players, are concerned about their health, value coworker diversity, and are honest.

4. **Learn how to change your attitudes.**

   You can decide to change your attitudes by choosing to be happy, becoming an optimist, thinking for yourself without undue pressure from others, and keeping an open mind.

5. **Learn how to help others change their attitudes.**

   You can help others change their attitudes by altering the conditions that lead to negative behaviors, such as by providing effective training so that the employee's job performance and personal satisfaction improve. You can also alter the consequences following people's behavior by providing positive consequences if you want them to have a positive attitude toward their behavior and repeat it, and negative consequences to deter them from participating in that behavior again.

6. **Understand what adjustments organizations are making to develop positive employee attitudes.**

   Employers realize that money alone will not make employees happy. Organizations are taking steps to improve employee attitudes by enhancing the quality of their work life.

KEY TERMS

attitudes, 120
empathizer, 123
socialization, 124

peer group, 124
reference group, 124
role model, 124

culture, 125
cynicism, 129

CAREER INSIGHT

Shawn Achor, author of *The Happiness Advantage*, says training your brain to be positive is no different from training your muscles at the gym. He says engaging in one brief positive exercise every day for as little as three weeks can have a lasting impact. Choose one of the five activities below that correlate with positive change and perform it each day for three weeks:[40]

- Jot down three things you are grateful for.
- Write a positive message to someone.
- Meditate at your desk for two minutes.
- Exercise for 10 minutes.
- Take two minutes to describe in a journal the most meaningful experience of the past 24 hours.

TRY YOUR HAND

1. Describe your attitudes concerning
   a. a teamwork environment
   b. health and wellness
   c. learning new skills

   How do these attitudes affect you on a daily basis? Do you feel you have a positive attitude in most situations? Can you think of someone you have frequent contact with who displays negative attitudes toward these items? How might you change this person's attitudes?

2. Identify an attitude held by a friend, coworker, or spouse that you would like to see changed. Do any conditions that precede this person's behavior fall under your control? If so, how could you change those conditions so the person might change his or her attitude? What positive consequences might you offer when the person behaves the way you want? What negative consequences might you impose when the person participates in the behavior you are attempting to stop?

3. For a period of one week, keep a diary or log of positive and negative events. Positive events might include the successful completion of a project, a compliment from a coworker, or just finding time for some leisure activities. Negative events might include forgetting an appointment, criticism from your boss, or simply looking in the mirror and seeing something you don't like. An unpleasant news story might also qualify as a negative event. At the end of one week, review your entries and determine what type of pattern exists. Also, reflect on the impact of these events. Did you quickly bounce back from the negative events, or did you dwell on them all week? Tal Ben-Shahar, a leader in the field of positive psychology, says the potential for happiness is all around us, but may go unnoticed. During the past week, reflect if you failed to recognize or ignored any sources of pleasure and meaning?

4. An important step in changing your attitudes is understanding them. To practice the skill of monitoring your current thought patterns, add four or five different endings to each of the following incomplete sentences. Work as rapidly as possible, and don't worry about whether the ending is reasonable or significant; the object is to build awareness of your attitudes toward your life.[41]

   - I am very thankful for…
   - I am glad I'm not…
   - When I wake up in the morning, my first thoughts are…
   - My most common reaction to an annoying situation is…
   - Personal happiness to me means…
   - I often compare myself to…

CRITICAL THINKING CHALLENGE

Identify at least one strong attitude you have for or against an event, a person, or a thing. How did you acquire this attitude? Is it shared by any particular group of people? Do you spend time with these people?

Now think of an attitude that a friend or coworker holds but that you strongly disagree with. What factors do you believe contributed to the formation of this person's attitude?

SELF-ASSESSMENT EXERCISE

For each of the following statements, circle the number from 1 to 5 that best represents your response to each statement: (1) strongly disagree (never do this); (2) disagree (rarely do this); (3) moderately agree (sometimes do this); (4) agree (frequently do this); (5) strongly agree (almost always do this).

	1	2	3	4	5
A. When forming attitudes about important matters, I maintain an open mind, listen to the views of others, but think for myself.	1	2	3	4	5
B. I make every effort to maintain a positive mental attitude toward other people and the events in my life.	1	2	3	4	5

C. I seek feedback and clarification on the influence of my attitudes and behaviors on others.	1	2	3	4	5
D. I am willing to change my attitudes and behaviors in response to constructive feedback from others.	1	2	3	4	5
E. I consistently monitor the way I shape the attitudes of others through my system of rewards and punishments.	1	2	3	4	5

After identifying your response to each item, select an attitude or skill you would like to improve. Prepare a written goal and then describe the steps you will take to achieve this goal.

YOU PLAY THE ROLE

In this role-play exercise, you will be attempting to mentor a coworker who is a chronic underachiever. She has a great deal of potential, but she does things at work that result in self-sabotage. For example, she tends to procrastinate and often misses deadlines. When she does complete a project, her approach is to get by with the least amount of effort. When things don't go well at work, she tends to blame others. You will meet with another member of your class who will assume the role of your coworker. As a mentor, think about things you might say or do that would help your coworker develop the attitudes that employers value today.

BELOW THE SURFACE | THE POWER OF POSITIVE ATTITUDES

Panda Express is not the only company that supports self-improvement programs that focus on the *total person*. Clif Bar, a California-based energy food maker, helps employees embrace a healthy lifestyle. An on-site gym offers 33 fitness classes and employees enjoy discounts on outdoor gear through partner companies. Workers are allotted 2.5 hours of paid workout time per week. A 40-foot climbing wall is just down the hall. Dogs are abundant and roam freely throughout Clif Bar headquarters.

In 2002, the company pledged to become carbon neutral. It recently installed North America's largest smart solar panel array. Employees are encouraged to go green through clean-energy incentives.

QUESTIONS

1. Andrew Cherng and his wife Peggy ask every employee to make a commitment to continuous learning. They believe this employee development philosophy improves every aspect of their business, and also makes a tremendous contribution to society. Do you agree? Explain your answer.

2. How can the green business practices implemented by Clif Bar benefit employees? Would you enjoy working for a company that embraces green business practices?

3. Clif Bar supports a dog-friendly work environment. What are the pros and cons of this policy?

CLOSING CASE AN A-MAZING WAY TO DEAL WITH CHANGE

Many people have benefited by reading the simple parable presented in Spencer Johnson's book *Who Moved My Cheese? An A-Mazing Way to Deal with Change in Your Work and in Your Life.* The four characters in the book, Sniff and Scurry (two little mice) and Hem and Haw (two little people the size of mice), live in a maze with lots of paths leading nowhere and some leading to rooms filled with cheese that could keep them happy for the rest of their lives. Each of the characters has a unique way of handling the depletion of their cheese supply in Cheese Station C. All four were initially very comfortable thinking that their cheese would always be there. Sniff and Scurry noticed that the cheese was rapidly diminishing and risked exploring the maze to discover a new source for their happiness. Hem and Haw kept doing their daily routine over and over again thinking the situation would improve. They did not acknowledge what was happening around them, and when the cheese was gone, they demanded compensation, declaring that the problem was not their fault. They waited for someone else to replace the cheese and continue to provide their security. They considered going out into the maze, but were afraid they could never find another source of cheese.[42]

QUESTIONS

1. *Who Moved My Cheese?* is the all-time best-selling book in *Amazon.com*'s history and is printed in 42 languages. Analyze why organizations around the world would buy millions of these books for their employees?

2. The book encourages readers to pay attention to what is happening around them, anticipate change, and look at the opportunities that exist outside their comfort zones. How might this advice help people who worry about loss of their jobs or loss of their retirement funds?

3. One of the book's most powerful questions is "What would you do if you were not afraid?" As you look to your future and grasp the attitudes Spencer Johnson suggests, share your answer to that question with your classmates.

CHAPTER 6 ENDNOTES

1. Karl Taro Greenfeld, "The Sharin, Huggin, Lovin, Carin, Chinese Food Money Machine," **Bloomberg Businessweek**, November 22, 2010, pp. 98–103.
2. Ibid.
3. Douglas A. Bernstein, Louis A. Penner, Alison Clarke-Stewart, and Edward J. Roy, **Psychology**, 9th ed. (Belmont, CA: Wadsworth Cengage Learning, 2012), pp. 708–709.
4. Bruce Clark, "Employee's Bad Attitude is Actually Bad Behavior," **News & Observer**, January 15, 2012, p. 3E.
5. Tad Waddington, "Make a Difference!" **Spirituality & Health**, March/April 2009, p. 43.
6. Rosabeth Moss Kanter, "How Great Companies Think Differently," **Harvard Business Review**, November 2011, pp. 66–78.
7. Karl Taro Greenfeld, "The Sharin, Huggin, Lovin, Carin, Chinese Food Money Machine," **Bloomberg Businessweek**, November 22, 2010, p. 103.
8. Alison Beard and Richard Hornik, "It's Hard to Be Good," **Harvard Business Review**, November 2011, pp. 91–92.
9. "It's Time to Get Serious About Jobs!" U.S. Chamber of Commerce Ad, **Wall Street Journal**, January 24, 2012, p. A9.
10. Joe Light, "Exiting Workers Are More Disgruntled," **Wall Street Journal**, August 8, 2011, p. B8.
11. Hyrum W. Smith, **The 10 Natural Laws of Successful Time and Life Management** (New York: Warner Books, 1994), p. 48.

12. Douglas A. Bernstein, Louis A. Penner, Alison Clarke-Stewart, and Edward J. Roy, *Psychology*, 9th ed. (Belmont, CA: Wadsworth Cengage Learning, 2012), p. 708.

13. John Hollon, "The Cult of Welch," *Workforce Management*, October 10, 2005, p. 74.

14. Daniel H. Pink, *A Whole New Mind* (New York: Riverhead Books, 2005), pp. 48–63.

15. Laura Landro, "Compassion 101: Teaching M.D.s to Be Nicer," *Wall Street Journal*, September 28, 2005, p. D1.

16. Daniel H. Pink, *A Whole New Mind* (New York: Riverhead Books, 2005), p. 154.

17. Douglas A. Bernstein, Louis A. Penner, Alison Clarke-Stewart, and Edward J. Roy, *Psychology*, 9th ed. (Belmont, CA: Wadsworth Cengage Learning, 2012), p. 491.

18. Kurt Mortensen, *Maximum Influence: The 12 Universal Laws of Power Persuasion* (New York: AMACOM, 2004), pp. 62–68.

19. William F. Schoell and Joseph P. Guiltinan, *Marketing*, 5th ed. (Boston: Allyn & Bacon, 1992), pp. 166–167; William M. Pride and O. C. Ferrell, *Marketing* (Boston: Houghton Mifflin, 2000), p. 211.

20. Bobbie Gossoge, "And There Was Happiness in Aqualand," *Inc.*, August 2007, pp. 96–101.

21. Kellye Whitney, "New-Hire Failure Linked to Interpersonal Skills," *Chief Learning Officer Magazine*. [cited 5 October 2005]. Available from http://www.clomedia.com; INTERNET.

22. Nathaniel Branden, *Self-Esteem at Work* (San Francisco: Jossey-Bass, 1998), pp. 94–97; "Adjusting an Attitude," *San Jose Mercury News*, August 20, 1997, p. G6.

23. His Holiness the Dalai Lama and Howard C. Cutler, *The Art of Happiness* (New York: Riverhead Books, 1998), pp. 16–17.

24. Tal Ben-Shahar, *Happier*, New York, McGraw Hill, 2007 p. 33. Also see Shawn Achor, "Positive Intelligence," *Harvard Business Review*, January/February, 2012, pp. 100–102.

25. Tal Ben-Sharhar, *Happier* (New York: McGraw-Hill, 2007), p. 107.

26. Ibid.

27. Alison Stein Wellner, "Are You Sales Phobic? Alas, the Cure is to Sell More Often," *Inc.*, March 2007, pp. 52–56.

28. Tal Ben-Sharhar, *Happier* (New York: McGraw-Hill, 2007), p. 111.

29. Patricia Sellers, "Now Bounce Back!" *Fortune*, May 1, 1995, p. 57.

30. Mary Cornatzer, "Study: Optimism Pays in Job Search," *News & Observer*, February 1, 2011, p. 5B.

31. Martin Seligman, *Learned Optimism* (New York: Knopf, 2001), p. 4.

32. Redford Williams and Virginia Williams, *Anger Kills* (New York: Harper Perennial, 1993), p. 12.

33. Bob Wall, *Working Relationships* (Palo Alto, Calif.: Davies-Black, 1999), pp. 11–12.

34. Ibid., p. 17.

35. Brian Tracy, *The 100 Absolutely Unbreakable Laws of Business Success* (San Francisco: Berrett-Koehler, 2000), pp. 67–70.

36. Nathaniel Branden, *Self-Esteem at Work* (San Francisco: Jossey-Bass, 1998), pp. 111–112.

37. Joan Hamilton, "Net Work: At Icarian, It's All Work and Some Play," *BusinessWeek E.BIZ*, April 3, 2000, p. EB116.

38. Quoted in Nancy W. Collins, Susan K. Gilbert, and Susan Nycum, *Women Leading: Making Tough Choices on the Fast Track* (Lexington, Mass.: Stephen Greene Press, 1988), p. 1.

39. "100 Best Companies to Work For," *Fortune*, February 4, 2008, pp. 75–94. Milton Moskowitz, Robert Levering, Christopher Tkaczyk, "100 Best Companies to Work For," *Fortune*, February 7, 2011, pp. 91–101.

40. Shawn Achor, "Positive Intelligence," *Harvard Business Review*, January/February 2012, pp. 100–101.

41. Harry E. Chambers, *The Bad Attitude Survival Guide* (Reading, Mass.: Addison-Wesley, 1998), pp. 6–7.

42. "Dr. Spencer Johnson." [cited 7 December 2005]. Available from http://www.spencerjohnsonpartners.com; INTERNET; Spencer Johnson, *Who Moved My Cheese?* (New York: G. P. Putnam's Sons), 1998.

CHAPTER 7

CHAPTER PREVIEW

LEARNING OBJECTIVES

After studying Chapter 7, you will be able to

7-1 Understand the complex nature of motivation.

7-2 Describe influential theories of motivation.

7-3 List and describe contemporary motivation strategies.

7-4 Identify motivating factors important to individuals from different generations.

7-5 Describe selected self-motivation strategies.

Motivating Yourself and Others

TIP OF THE ICEBERG | TEENAGE RECORD BREAKERS

Jordan Romero, a 13-year-old from Big Bear, California, became the youngest climber to reach the peak of Mount Everest. He hugged his tearful companions and told them he loved them. Then he unpacked his satellite phone and called his mom.

Romero's passion for mountain climbing started at a young age. Prior to reaching the peak of the world's highest mountain, he climbed Mount Kilimanjaro at age nine. His goal is to reach the highest peaks on all seven continents.[1]

At age 16, Laura Dekker became the youngest person to sail solo around the world. After completing her year-long journey, she was met by a jubilant crowd at St. Maarten harbor in the Caribbean. Before embarking on her trip, Dekker had won a court case against Dutch social services who had objected to the record attempt. They thought it would harm her emotionally.[2]

What motivates these young adventurers to pursue their dreams with such determination? The answer may be found in *Drive—The Surprising Truth About What Motivates Us*, by Daniel Pink. He described three basic human needs that have a powerful effect on individual performance and attitude. One of these needs is *autonomy*, the innate desire for self-direction. *Mastery* is the second important need. Most of us yearn for activities that stretch the body and mind in a way that makes the effort rewarding. The urge to master something new and engaging is a powerful force in our lives. The third need is *purpose*. Pink says, "Autonomous people working toward mastery perform at very high levels. But those who do so in the service of some greater objective can achieve even more."[3]

Questions about what motivates anyone are not easily answered, but the research conducted by Daniel Pink is very helpful. This chapter will help you gain additional insights into how your needs motivate you to take action.

According to Daniel Pink's theories, Laura Dekker, the youngest person to sail solo around the world, was probably motivated by both a desire for mastery and a sense of purpose.

THE COMPLEX NATURE OF MOTIVATION

7-1 People are motivated by many different kinds of needs. They have basic needs such as those described by Daniel Pink, but they also need acceptance, recognition, and self-esteem. Each individual experiences these needs in different ways and to varying degrees. To complicate matters more, people are motivated by different needs at different times in their lives. Adults, like children and adolescents, continue to develop and change in significant ways throughout life.

Motivation Defined

People interact with each other in a variety of ways because they are driven by a variety of forces. **Motivation** can be defined as the influences that account for the initiation, direction, intensity, and persistence of behavior. Although the number of possible motives for human behavior seems endless, psychologists have found it useful to organize them into four somewhat overlapping categories:[4]

- *Physiological factors* These include the need for food, water, and sleep.
- *Emotional factors* Panic, fear, anger, love, and hatred can influence behavior ranging from jealously to physical violence.
- *Cognitive factors* These include a person's perceptions of the world, their beliefs about what they can or cannot do, and their expectations about how others will respond to them.
- *Social factors* These are influenced by teachers, family members, friends, media, and other sociocultural forces. Social factors can, for example, influence your views of clothing fashions and organizational memberships.

Total Person Insight

"Sometimes we become so consumed by our daily business that we forget to take a look at the larger picture of who we are and where we are headed in life."

Source: Steven Reiss, *Who Am I?*, New York: Berkley Books, 2000, p. 1.

Although the major focus of this chapter will be motivation in a work setting, it is important to realize that some people find meaning through the obsessions that consume their leisure time. To earn a living, Henry Sakaida helps operate a wholesale nursery in Rosemead, California, but his passion is World War II aviation history. For the past 20 years, he has arranged healing meetings between Japanese and American pilots who once shot at each other over the Pacific.[5] Tatsuo and Yukiko Ono operate a small business in Japan, but they get their greatest satisfaction from following the band The Rolling Stones. They have attended about 300 Stones concerts held at major cities around the world.[6]

In a work setting, it is motivated employees who get the work done. Without them, most organizations would falter.

The Motivation to Satisfy Basic Desires

Steven Reiss, professor of psychology and psychiatry at Ohio State University, conducted a major study to determine what *really* drives human behavior. He asked 6,000 people from many stations in life which values were most significant in motivating their behavior and in contributing to their sense of happiness.[7]

The results of his research showed that nearly everything we experience as meaningful can be traced to one of sixteen basic desires or to some combination of these desires (see Figure 7.1). Each of us has a different combination of the sixteen desires, a mix that can change with time and circumstances. The challenge is to determine which ones (the fundamental values) are most important, and then live your life accordingly. You do not need to satisfy all sixteen desires, only the five or six that are the most important to you.

Reiss and his research team found that most people cannot find *enduring* happiness by aiming to have more fun or pleasure. People who focus primarily on "feel-good" happiness (partying, drinking, etc.) discover that this source of satisfaction rarely lasts more than a few hours. It is "value-based" happiness that gives life meaning over the long run.[8]

Characteristics of Motives

Motives have been described as the "why" of human behavior. An understanding of the following five characteristics of motives can be helpful as you seek to understand the complex nature of motivation.[9]

Motives Are Individualistic. People have different needs. What satisfies one person's needs, therefore, may not satisfy another's. This variation in individual motives often leads to a breakdown in human relationships, unless individuals take the time to understand the motives of others.

Total Person Insight

"A sense of autonomy has a powerful effect on individual performance and attitude."

Source: Daniel H. Pink, *Drive—The Surprising Truth About What Motivates Us*, New York: Riverhead Books, 2009, p. 90.

Figure 7.1 ■ The Sixteen Basic Desires in the Reiss Profile (Order of Presentation Not Significant)

DESIRE	DEFINITION
CURIOSITY	The desire for knowledge
ACCEPTANCE	The desire for inclusion
ORDER	The desire for organization
PHYSICAL ACTIVITY	The desire for exercise of muscles
HONOR	The desire to be loyal to one's parents and heritage
POWER	The desire to influence others
INDEPENDENCE	The desire for self-reliance
SOCIAL CONTACT	The desire for companionship
FAMILY	The desire to raise one's own children
STATUS	The desire for social standing
IDEALISM	The desire for social justice
VENGEANCE	The desire to get even
ROMANCE	The desire for sex and beauty
EATING	The desire to consume food
SAVING	The desire to collect things
TRANQUILITY	The desire for emotional calm

Source: Steven Reiss, *Who Am I?* (New York: Berkley Books, 2000), pp. 17–18.

Motives Change. As noted at the beginning of this chapter, motives change throughout our lives. What motivates us early in our careers may not motivate us later on.

Motives May Be Unconscious. In many cases, we are not fully aware of the inner needs and drives that influence our behavior. The desire to win the "Employee of the Month" award may be triggered by unconscious feelings of inadequacy or the desire for increased recognition.

Motives Are Often Inferred. We can observe the behavior of another person, but we can only infer (draw conclusions about) what motives have caused that behavior. The motives underlying our own behavior and others' behavior are often difficult to understand.

Motives Are Hierarchical. Motives for behavior vary in levels of importance. When contradictory motives exist, the more important motive usually guides behavior. Workers often leave jobs that are secure to satisfy the need for work that is more challenging and rewarding.

INFLUENTIAL MOTIVATIONAL THEORIES

7-2 The work of various psychologists and social scientists has added greatly to the knowledge of what motivates people and how motivation works. The basic problem, as many leaders admit, is knowing how to apply that knowledge in the workplace. Although many theories of motivation have emerged over the years, we will discuss five of the most influential.

---

human RELATIONS *in Action*

THE IDEA THAT SAVED MY COMPANY

Throughout the glory days of the dot-com boom, Chip Conley built Joie de Vivre, a chain of 17 boutique hotels in the San Francisco Bay area. Conley was hailed as one of America's most prominent boutique hoteliers. Then came the dot-com meltdown, the tragedy of 9/11, and a weak worldwide economy. Annual sales fell from $100 million to $75 million. Faced with a desperate situation, Conley began searching for ways to help his business flourish once again. The key to turning his company around was found in the pages of *Toward a Psychology of Being* by Abraham Maslow. This landmark text helped him understand how he could apply Maslow's *Hierarchy of Needs* concept to winning business practices in the workplace.

Source: Chip Conley, *Peak—How Great Companies Get Their Mojo from Maslow*, San Francisco, CA: Jossey-Bass, 2007, pp. 3–7.

Maslow's Hierarchy of Needs

According to Abraham Maslow, a noted psychologist, people tend to satisfy their needs in a particular order—a theory he calls the **hierarchy of needs**. Maslow's theory rests on three assumptions: (1) people have a number of needs that require some measure of satisfaction; (2) only unsatisfied needs motivate behavior; and (3) the needs of people are arranged in a hierarchy of prepotency, which means that as each lower-level need is satisfied, the need at the next level demands attention.[10] Basically, human beings are motivated to satisfy physiological needs first (food, clothing, shelter); then the need for safety and security; then social needs; then esteem needs; and, finally, self-actualization needs, or the need to realize their potential. Maslow's theory is illustrated in Figure 7.2.

Physiological Needs. The needs for food, clothing, sleep, and shelter, or physiological needs, were described by Maslow as survival or lower-order needs. When the economy is strong and most people have jobs, these basic needs rarely dominate because they are reasonably well satisfied. But, needless to say, people who cannot ensure their own and their family's survival, or who are homeless, place these basic needs at the top of their priority list.

Safety and Security Needs. Most people want order, predictability, and freedom from physical harm in their personal and professional lives and will be motivated to achieve these safety needs once their basic physiological needs are satisfied. At this level of the hierarchy, job security is very important.

Figure 7.2 ▪ Maslow's Hierarchy of Needs

Social or Belongingness Needs. Whereas the first two types of needs deal with aspects of physical safety and survival, social or belongingness needs deal with emotional and mental well-being. Research has shown that needs for affection, for a sense of belonging, and for identification with a group are powerful. There are two major aspects of the need to belong: frequent, positive interactions with the same people and a framework of stable, long-term caring and concern.[11]

Esteem Needs. People need respect and recognition from others as well as an inner sense of achievement and self-worth. Promotions, honors, and awards from outside sources tend to satisfy this need. Several esteem-building initiatives that build self-respect and self-confidence are discussed in Chapters 4 and 10.

Self-Actualization Needs. Maslow defined *self-actualization* as a need for self-fulfillment, a full tapping of one's potential. It is the need to "be all that you can be," to have mastery over what you are doing. Self-actualization is people fulfilling their potential or realizing their fullest capacities as human beings (see Table 7.1).

It is worth noting that Maslow's hierarchical arrangement has been questioned and has not always stood up well under actual testing. However, it teaches managers one important lesson: a *fulfilled* need does not motivate an individual.[12] If you have food and shelter, you will likely focus on safety and security needs. Maslow's work is considered a classic in the field of management theory, and his original works have been republished in the book *Maslow on Management*.

Herzberg's Motivation-Maintenance (Two-Factor) Theory

Psychologist Frederick Herzberg proposes another motivation theory called the **motivation-maintenance theory**.[13] **Maintenance factors** represent the basic things people consider essential to any job, such as salaries, fringe benefits, working conditions, social relationships, supervision, and organizational policies and administration. We often take such things for granted as part of the job. These basic maintenance factors *do not* act as motivators, according to Herzberg; but if any of them is absent, the organizational climate that results can hurt employee morale and lower worker productivity. Health insurance, for example, generally does not motivate employees to be more productive, but the loss of it can cause workers to look for employment in another organization that provides the desired coverage.

Table 7.1 ■ Ways of Satisfying Individual Needs in the Work Situation

I NEED	ORGANIZATIONAL CONDITIONS
Physiological	Pay Breakfast or lunch programs Company services
Safety and security	Company benefits plans Pensions Seniority Pay
Social or belongingness	Coffee breaks Sports teams Company picnics and social events Work teams
Esteem	Recognition of work well done Mastery Responsibility Pay (as symbol of status) Prestigious office location and furnishings
Self-actualization	Challenge Purpose Autonomy

Source: Adapted from Judith Gordon, *A Diagnostic Approach to Organizational Behavior*, 3d ed. (Boston: Allyn & Bacon, 1991), p. 144.

Motivational factors are those elements that go above and beyond the basic maintenance factors. They include opportunities for recognition, advancement, or more responsibility. When these are present, they tend to motivate employees to improve their productivity. The workers may seek out new and creative ways to accomplish their organizations' goals as well as their personal goals. Herzberg's list of motivational factors parallels, to some degree, Maslow's hierarchy of needs (see Table 7.2).

Herzberg theorized that if employees' motivational factors are not met, they may begin to ask for more maintenance factors, such as increased salaries and fringe benefits, better working conditions, or more liberal company policies regarding sick leave or vacation time. Critics of Herzberg's theory have pointed out that he assumes that most, if not all, individuals are motivated only by higher-order needs such as recognition or increased responsibility, and that they seek jobs that are challenging and meaningful. His theory does not acknowledge that some people may prefer more routine, predictable work and may be motivated more by the security of a regular paycheck (a maintenance factor) than by the prospect of advancement. Nonetheless, Herzberg made an important contribution to motivation theory by emphasizing the importance of enriched work.

The Expectancy Theory

The **expectancy theory** is based on the assumption that motivational strength is determined by whether or not you *believe* you can be successful at a task. (This theory is an expansion of the self-efficacy concept detailed in Chapter 4.) If you really want something and believe that the probability of your success is high, then your motivation

Table 7.2 ■ Comparison of the Maslow and Herzberg Theories

	MASLOW	HERZBERG
Motivational factors	Self-actualization	Work itself Achievement Responsibility
	Esteem needs	Recognition Advancement Status
Maintenance factors	Social or belongingness needs	Social network Supervision
	Safety and security needs	Company policy and administration
	Physiological needs	Job security Working conditions Salary

increases. *Perception* is an important element of this theory. Research conducted at the University of Kansas found a link between expectations and achievement in college. Students who wanted to complete college and believed they were capable of doing so earned higher grades and were less likely to drop out. In fact, aspirations combined with expectations predicted achievement better than standardized test scores.[14] This somewhat-mysterious connection between what you expect in life and what you actually achieve is sometimes referred to as the **self-fulfilling prophecy**: If you can conceive it and believe it, you can achieve it.

McGregor's Theory X/Theory Y

Theory X managers maintain a pessimistic attitude toward their workers' potential.

Douglas McGregor, author of the classic book *The Human Side of Enterprise,* suggests that managers who are placed in charge of motivating their workers are essentially divided into two groups. Theory X managers maintain a pessimistic attitude toward their workers' potential. These managers believe that workers are basically lazy and have to be goaded into doing things with incentives such as pay or with punishment, that they have little or no ambition, that they prefer to avoid responsibility, and that they do only as much work as they have to keep their jobs. Theory Y managers, on the other hand, maintain an optimistic view of workers' ambition. These managers believe that their subordinates are serious workers who want to work and do their best, are capable of self-direction, and can learn to both accept and seek responsibility if they are committed to the objectives of the organization. Often the expectancy theory kicks in and workers perform to their managers' pessimistic or optimistic expectations.

The Goal-Setting Theory

Successful people and successful organizations have one thing in common: They share the power of purpose. The more you focus on achieving a desired outcome, the greater your likelihood of success.[15] Your goals play a key role in bringing purpose to your life.

Motivation researchers indicate that goals tend to motivate people in four ways (see Figure 7.3). First, goals provide the power of purpose by directing your attention to a

Figure 7.3 ■ A Model of How Goals Can Improve Performance

Goals need to be
• Specific
• Difficult
• Participatively set

Goals motivate by
• Directing attention
• Encouraging effort
• Encouraging persistence
• Fostering goal-attainment strategies and action plans

IMPROVED PERFORMANCE

Feedback on performance

Source: Robert Kreitner and Carlene M. Cassidy, *Management* (12th ed.) Mason, OH: South-Western, 2011, p. 334.

specific target. Second, they encourage you to make the effort to achieve something difficult. Third, reaching a goal requires sustained effort and therefore encourages persistence. Fourth, having a goal forces you to bridge the gap between the dream and the reality; it fosters your creating a plan of action filled with strategies that will get you where you want to go.[16]

If your goal is easy to achieve and requires little effort, it may not serve as a motivator. Goals need to be difficult enough to challenge you but not impossible to reach. Goal setting is an excellent self-motivation strategy. Take a moment and review the goal-setting principles listed in Table 4.2 on page 87.

CONTEMPORARY EMPLOYEE MOTIVATION STRATEGIES

7-3 A healthy, mutually supportive relationship based on trust, openness, and respect can create a work climate in which employees want to give more of themselves. However, creating this type of organizational culture in the age of information may not be easy. How do you motivate employees who work from virtual offices? How do organizations experiencing major upheavals maintain their employees' trust?

Determining the best form of motivation is especially difficult when employees are at different age and economical stages of their lives. It is helpful to ask employees what motivates them personally in their life and what would influence them to perform at a higher level for the organization.[17]

Motivation Through Job Design

Today's workers place a high value on jobs that provide rewards such as a sense of achievement, challenge, variety, and personal growth. It is possible to redesign existing jobs so they will have characteristics or outcomes that are intrinsically satisfying to employees. There are several design options.

Job Rotation. **Job rotation** allows workers to move through a variety of jobs in a predefined way over a period of time. For example, a worker might attach a wheel assembly one week, inspect it the next, organize the parts for assembly during the third week, then return to the original assembly job the fourth week and begin the rotation again.

Job Enlargement. **Job enlargement** means expanding an employee's duties or responsibilities. When a job becomes stale, motivation can often be increased by encouraging employees to learn new skills or take on new responsibilities. In a bank setting, for example, a teller might develop expertise in the area of loan services or opening new accounts.

Job Enrichment. **Job enrichment** is an attempt to make jobs more desirable or satisfying, thereby triggering *internal motivation*. One approach assigns new and more difficult tasks to employees; another grants them additional authority. When American Express decided to give its global customer service division a makeover, it focused on making life better for its 26,000 call center employees. Customer service employees were asked what changes they wanted. The company then provided better pay, flexible schedules, and more career development. To enrich the call center duties, the company switched from a directive to keep calls short and transaction oriented to engaging customers in longer conversations.[18]

Job rotation, job enlargement, and job enrichment appeal to Generation Y workers, who often do not value work for only *external* rewards. These workers are more apt to view work as a valuable learning experience that helps them build a strong résumé.[19]

Motivation Through Incentives

Incentives are often used to improve quality, reduce accidents, increase sales, improve attendance, and speed up production. They often focus on improving behaviors that will cut expenses and improve customer satisfaction. J.A. Frate, Inc., a regional trucking company based in Illinois, tries hard to make sure its drivers feel valued and want to stay with the company. Drivers who show special effort are given recognition and prizes. The recognition plan is based on a point system. Points can be earned for delivery of undamaged freight, carefully prepared log books, and on-time delivery of freight. Points can be redeemed for gift certificates.[20] We are seeing new incentive plans that erase the idea that everyone is motivated by the same thing—a "one-size-fits-all" approach. Incentives and rewards are discussed in more detail in Chapter 10.

Many companies are experimenting with programs that reward the development of new ideas. These programs, known as **intrapreneurships**, encourage employees to pursue an idea, product, or process, with the company providing encouragement and support.

Motivation Through Learning Opportunities

Learning opportunities, both on and off the job, can be a strong motivational force. Employees realize that education and training are critical to individual growth and opportunity. Yuri Kouzmov, director of Web technologies at World Golf Tour, sees working for this company as an "investment" in his career. He is given the opportunity to learn a lot beyond his assigned duties. As an employee in a small company, he has private access to a senior manager at any point.[21]

Many companies are using advanced communications technology to deliver instruction. Some organizations provide tuition reimbursement for online courses offered by colleges and universities across the country.

Motivation Through Empowerment

Empowerment refers to those policies that share information, authority, and responsibility with the lowest ranks of the organization. When employees are empowered to make

"Maybe they didn't try hard enough."

Al Ross/CartoonBank.com

decisions for the good of the organization, they experience feelings of pride, self-expression, and ownership.

TechTarget, a Needham, Massachusetts, interactive media company, has embraced empowerment to a high degree. All of its 210 employees are free to set their own work schedules. There are no set policies mandating working hours or specifying the number of sick, personal, or vacation days. Managers set quarterly goals and timetables, but employees determine how to achieve them. In exchange for the flexibility, employees are expected to stay in contact with their managers. Greg Strakosch, founder and CEO, says the company's "open-leave" policy is credited with attracting and keeping a very talented and dedicated workforce.[22]

Although empowerment efforts are growing in popularity, this motivational strategy should not be viewed as a quick fix. Empowerment requires a long-term commitment of human and financial resources from top management down. Patrick Lencioni, author of *The Three Signs of a Miserable Job*, says an employee's relationship with their direct manager is the most important determinant to employee satisfaction (see Figure 7.4). Yet, many managers are guilty of creating miserable jobs.[23]

Motivation Through Others' Expectations

Research has confirmed that people tend to act in ways that are consistent with what others expect of them.

Earlier in this chapter, you were introduced to the power of your own self-fulfilling prophecy: You will probably get whatever it is you expect. But there is another aspect of the expectancy theory: the power *others'* expectations can have on your motivation.

Research has confirmed that people tend to act in ways that are consistent with what others expect of them. In the classic study *Pygmalion in the Classroom*, Harvard University professors Robert Rosenthal and J. Sterling Livingston described the significant effect of teachers' expectations on students. They discovered that when teachers had high

Figure 7.4 ■ Three Signs of a Miserable Job

Patrick Lencioni, author of *The Three Signs of a Miserable Job*, cites research that indicates many people dislike their jobs. These unhappy workers are costing employers billions of dollars in lost productivity. The primary source of job misery resides in the hands of the direct manager. The three signs of a miserable job are:

■ **Anonymity.** The feeling that employees get when they realize that their manager has little interest in them as human beings; the manager knows little about their lives, their aspirations, and their interests.
■ **Irrelevance.** A condition that takes root when employees cannot see how their job makes a difference in the lives of others.
■ **Immeasurement.** The inability of employees to assess for themselves their contribution or success.

Source: "The Three Signs of a Miserable Job-Q&A with Patrick Lencioni," The Table Group Incorporated, "Cited 7 February 2012" Available from http://www.tablegroup.com.

expectations for certain students who they believed had excellent intellectual ability and learning capacity, those students learned at a faster rate than others in the same group—even though the teachers did not consciously treat the higher-achieving students differently. These teachers had unintentionally communicated their high expectations to the students they *thought* possessed strong intellectual abilities.

The source of low expectations in the workplace is often a boss who perceives an employee as a weak performer and then treats the employee differently than high performers. The employee who thinks he or she is a weak performer in the eyes of the boss will often perform down to expectations.[24]

MOTIVATING THE GENERATIONS

7-4 In Chapter 5, we discussed the variety of historical events that influence the values of various generations (see Table 5.2). It is interesting to discover how those values translate into motivational factors for people in those same generation categories. This information may be helpful in discovering your own motivators, but gaining a greater understanding of these population segments may also be helpful as you learn how to motivate others in your personal and professional life. Figure 7.5 provides a brief summary of motivational factors for each generation.

Learning about the various generations helps you individualize your interactions with them, regardless of your generation. Whether you are a member of one of the older generations or of the younger generations, the majority of the work force of the future will include Generation X and Y workers. If you are one of them, manage them, or are managed by them, it will be critical to your career to adjust your human relations skills accordingly. Some generalizations may be helpful[25]:

■ They are more comfortable with diversity.
■ They seek opportunities for team collaboration and knowledge sharing.
■ They prefer to work with the newest technology.
■ They expect rewards based on productivity, not hours at their desk.
■ They prefer frequent feedback. Coach them, don't lecture them.
■ They are more comfortable with limited bureaucracy. Do not burden them with corporate policies and excessive meetings.

Figure 7.5 ■ Motivational Factors for the Generations

MATURES
Born between
1928 and **1945**

▶

- They are often referred to as *loyalists.*
- They want to build a legacy, both professionally and personally.
- They want to be a part of the company's future.
- Their view of feedback: No news is good news.
- Rewards that are meaningful to them: the satisfaction of a job well done.
- Their motivators: money, public recognition, leadership opportunities, organizational loyalty, responsibility, accomplishment, control.

BABY BOOMERS
Born between
1946 and **1964**

▶

- They are often referred to as the *optimists.*
- They want to build an outstanding career.
- They want to move up within the company and gain personal and financial responsibilities.
- Their view of feedback: performance review once a year, with a lot of documentation.
- Rewards that are meaningful to them: money, title, recognition, the corner office.
- Their motivators: more money, public recognition, desire for subordinates, loyalty to self, promotion, peer recognition, control.

GENERATION X
Born between
1965 and **1976**

▶

- They are often referred to as the *skeptics.*
- They want to build a portable career.
- They want to know exactly what they will be doing and whether they are on the right career path.
- Their view of feedback: they want frequent comments on how they are doing.
- Rewards that are meaningful to them: freedom.
- Their motivators: doing good, meeting organizational goals, recognition from the boss, bonuses, and stock options.

MILLENNIALS
(Generation Y)
Born between
1977 and **2002**

▶

- They are often referred to as the *realists.*
- They want to build a multifaceted career.
- They want help seeing the future and the role they will play in it.
- Their view of feedback: whenever they want it, at the push of a button.
- Rewards that are meaningful to them: work that has meaning for them.
- Their motivators: time off, meeting personal goals, recognition from the boss, skills training, stock options, mentoring.

Source: Adapted from Peggy Blake Gleeson, "Managing and Motivating the Generations: Implications for the Student and the Employee." [cited on 28 December 2005]. Available from http://www.uwsp.edu/education/facets/links_resource/4413.pdf; INTERNET; "Motivating Generation Y," *Management Issue News* [cited on 28 December 2005]. Available from http://www.management-issues.com; INTERNET.

SELF-MOTIVATION STRATEGIES

7-5   The material presented in this chapter explains how, why, when, and where motivation strategies work, and we have identified many organizations that do all they can to motivate their employees to stay on the job and to improve their productivity. However, let's face it—some organizations just don't care if you are motivated or not, as long as you get your job done. If you are satisfied with your life and work, that's great! If you are yearning for a

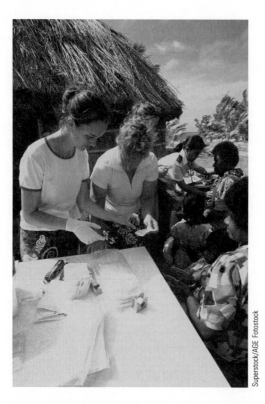

Superstock/AGE Fotostock

Jenny Ice, employed in the Washington office of Ernst & Young LLC, spent 12 weeks in Buenos Aires as a paid volunteer. She provided free accounting services to a small publishing firm. Ms. Ice remained on the company payroll during the time she was gone, and her job as a business advisory services manager was waiting for her when she got back. She describes the experience as among "the best three months of her life."

more exciting professional and/or personal life, guess what? It's up to you! The following self-motivation strategies can help you achieve your potential.

HOW TO KEEP YOUR RESOLUTIONS

The simple act of making a resolution greatly improves your chances of accomplishing a positive change.

- Make a realistic plan in advance.
- Set specific, realistic goals.
- Break each goal into small, measurable steps.
- Alter your surroundings to support your new behavior.
- Plan rewards for yourself as you make progress.

Source: Sue Shellenbarger, "How to Keep a Resolution," *Wall Street Journal*, December 22, 2010, p. D1.

Nurture a Gritty Nature

What factors will contribute most to your future success? A series of recent studies indicate that the quality of **grit**, in the form of hard work and determination, is a major indicator of success. Intelligence accounts for only a fraction of the success formula. Grit has value for people at all levels of ability.[26]

Research conducted by University of Pennsylvania faculty members found that grit is the premier attribute for surviving the grueling first summer of training at West Point. Gritty people tend to be highly self-disciplined and focused on goal achievement. They also bring passion to their tasks. Lance Armstrong entered his first distance running race at age ten. He won, and within three years, he was winning swim meets and other forms of athletic competition. In his autobiography, *It's Not About the Bike,* he says, "If it was a suffer-fest, I was good at it."[27]

How do you nurture grit? Self-discipline, an important part of grit, can be achieved by refraining from doing something. M. Scott Peck, author of the best-selling book *The Road Less Traveled,* told his readers that delaying gratification was "the only decent way to live." Early in life, we are encouraged (or required by our parents) to complete our homework before watching television. Later in life, we have to make hard decisions on our own and become self-disciplined. Should I stay with my diet or throw in the towel? Should I stay home and study for an exam or go drinking with friends? Should I add to my credit-card debt or refrain from buying that wide screen television? With a measure of self-discipline, we can learn to schedule the pain first (using Peck's words) and enjoy the pleasure later.[28]

Total Person Insight

"Genius will get you somewhere, but for the climb to the top you will need grit."

Source: "What's Better than Being Smart? Hanging Tough," *BusinessWeek,* August 17, 2009, p. 6.

Go Outside Your Comfort Zone. Many people do not achieve their full potential because they are afraid to venture outside their "comfort zone." These individuals often earn less than they deserve, exert little effort to win a promotion to a more challenging position, and refuse assignments that might enhance their career.

Self-motivation often decreases when we no longer have a sense of balance in our lives.

Strive for Balance. Self-motivation often decreases when we no longer have a sense of balance in our lives. To achieve balance between your work and personal life, take time to reflect on what is most important to you, and then try to make the necessary adjustments. Employees at Miller & Associates, a Dallas wholesaler of kitchen equipment, complete annual "life-purpose" statements. Each person records the ten most satisfying experiences in his or her life, making note of those that carry special meaning. When David Rogers, a salesperson, finished his "life-purpose" statements, he realized that he wasn't taking time to do some of the things he most valued. He said, "I was so weighted toward work that it was getting in the way of work." Once he cut back on his hours, freeing up time for his social life, his sales actually increased.[29]

Take Action. If you are feeling bored or trapped in a dead-end job, you can enhance your self-motivation by taking responsibility for the situation you are in and then taking action to improve it. Taking personal responsibility for your current situation is not easy because change can be threatening. Don't just wait and hope that things get better. Do something!

- Instead of waiting to see what will happen, volunteer for a project or make a request for an assignment.

- Have lunch with the person in your organization who is doing work that you find intriguing.
- Talk to your boss about the things you want to do.
- Follow up on an idea you have had for a long time.
- Read a book, attend a conference, or do something else that will help you grow and learn.[30]

LOOKING BACK: SUMMARY OF LEARNING OBJECTIVES

1. Understand the complex nature of motivation.

Motivation is a major component of human relations training because it provides a framework for understanding why people do the things they do. Although the number of possible motives for human behavior seems endless, psychologists have found it useful to organize them into four somewhat overlapping categories: physiological factors, emotional factors, cognitive factors, and social factors.

Motives are individualistic and can change over the years. In many cases, people are not aware of the factors that motivate their behaviors. Because there is no valid measure of a person's motives, motives can only be inferred. Motives vary in strength and importance and are therefore hierarchical.

2. Describe influential theories of motivation.

Maslow's hierarchy of needs theory states that physiological needs will come first, followed by safety and security, social, esteem, and then self-actualization needs. According to Maslow, although any need can be a motivator, only higher-order needs will motivate people over the long run.

Herzberg's motivation-maintenance theory contends that when motivational factors such as responsibility, recognition, and opportunity for advancement are not present, employees will demand improvement in maintenance factors such as higher salaries, more benefits, and better working conditions.

Expectancy theory is based on the assumption that personal expectations, as well as the expectations of others, have a powerful influence on a person's motivation. These expectations can become self-fulfilling prophecies. Managers can motivate employees by expressing belief in their abilities and talents.

McGregor's Theory X/Theory Y suggests that managers use two distinct motivational strategies when they attempt to motivate workers toward the goals of the organization. Theory X managers believe that people do not really want to work so they must be pushed, closely supervised, and prodded into doing things. Theory Y managers believe that people want to work and are willing to accept and seek responsibility if they are rewarded for doing so.

Goal-setting theory suggests that people become more focused and persistent if they establish specific, realistic goals in cooperation with their supervisors.

3. List and describe contemporary motivation strategies.

Contemporary organizations attempt to motivate their employees through positive expectations and job design modifications such as job rotation, job enlargement, and job enrichment. They are also discovering the effects of various incentives, intrapreneurship opportunities, additional training, and empowerment.

4. Identify motivating factors important to individuals from different generations.

There are specific strategies that can be used to motivate workers from various age brackets such as the Matures, the Baby Boomers, Generation X, and Millennials (Generation Y). Once you understand their motivating factors, you can individualize your interactions with them and enhance your interpersonal relations skills, regardless of your age.

5. Describe selected self-motivation strategies.

People must make their own plans to keep themselves motivated. They can nurture their grit, move beyond their comfort zone, strive for balance between their professional and personal lives, and take action.

KEY TERMS

motivation, 140
hierarchy of needs, 143
motivation-maintenance
  theory, 144
maintenance factors, 144

motivational factors, 145
expectancy theory, 145
self-fulfilling prophecy, 146
job rotation, 147
job enlargement, 148

job enrichment, 148
incentives, 148
intrapreneurships, 148
empowerment, 148
grit, 152

CAREER INSIGHT

A daily "To Do" list can be a very important part of your self-motivation plan. It can help you set priorities and save time. Some people like hand written to-do lists while others think more clearly when they type, sort, and store tasks in computers, tablets, or smart phones. Julie Morgenstern, an expert on time management, says a to-do list is an essential tool for staying grounded, for saving your energy, and staying focused on high-priority tasks. Keep in mind that effective to-do lists are limited to specific tasks that can be tackled right away and finished fairly soon. Always assign a priority to each task.[31]

TRY YOUR HAND

1. How much grit have you got? On a scale of one to five, rate how well the following statements describe you. In the first section, a five is *strongly agree* and a one is *strongly disagree*. In the second section, the scoring is reversed: One is *strongly agree* and five is *strongly disagree*. Total your score and divide the total by six. If you score over 3.5, consider yourself gritty.[32]

	STRONGLY AGREE	AGREE	MODERATELY AGREE	DISAGREE	STRONGLY DISAGREE
I'm a hard worker.	5	4	3	2	1
Setbacks don't deter me.	5	4	3	2	1
I am now working on a project that may take years to finish.	5	4	3	2	1
I get interested in new pursuits every few months	1	2	3	4	5
People often tell me that I don't perform to my potential.	1	2	3	4	5
New ideas and new projects sometimes distract me from previous ones.	1	2	3	4	5

2. Prepare a list of all the things you wanted to accomplish during the past year but didn't. Think of activities, responsibilities, and commitments, as well as personal and professional goals. Without making excuses for your behavior, or blaming others, identify self-motivating strategies discussed in this chapter that you can implement to improve your chances of completing those tasks successfully.

3. Are you frustrated with any aspect of your personal or professional life right now? Write down a major frustration on a piece of paper, but do not put your name on it. Form a group of four or five class members who have completed the same task. Pass each other's papers randomly from group member to group member, until your instructor says stop. One at a time, each group member can describe his or her ideas on how to overcome the frustration identified on the paper he or she is holding. At the conclusion of this exercise, describe how this "outsider's"

viewpoint of your situation has influenced your thinking.

4. Identify at least one friend or family member from each of the generations discussed in this chapter. Visualize them working for you as you enter a major project with a budget that allows no extra compensation for the additional work you will expect of them. List the ways you would motivate them to put forth their full efforts.

CRITICAL THINKING CHALLENGE

In Chapter 5, you were encouraged to identify and reflect on the values that are important in your life. Return to Table 5.1, and review the five-part values clarification process. Now examine each of the 16 basic desires in Figure 7.1 and identify five or six that seem most important to you. Then apply the five-part valuing process to each of these desires. Do they accurately reflect factors that would motivate you at this point in your life? How might your desires change in the future?

SELF-ASSESSMENT EXERCISE

For each of the following statements, circle the number from 1 to 5 that best represents your response to each statement: (1) strongly disagree (never do this); (2) disagree (rarely do this); (3) moderately agree (sometimes do this); (4) agree (frequently do this); (5) strongly agree (almost always do this).

A. I understand that people interact with each other in a variety of ways because they are driven by a variety of motivational forces.	1	2	3	4	5
B. I accept the premise that motives change, may be unconscious, are often inferred, are individualistic, and are hierarchical.	1	2	3	4	5
C. I am familiar with the most influential motivational theories.	1	2	3	4	5
D. I am able to provide a brief summary of motivational factors that influence each generation.					
E. I can apply a variety of self-motivation strategies.	1	2	3	4	5

After identifying your response to each item, select an attitude or skill you would like to improve. Prepare a written goal and then describe the steps you will take to achieve this goal.

YOU PLAY THE ROLE

You just graduated from a prestigious college with your accounting degree and have accepted a job with a large financial institution that has tremendous career potential. You love your work but hate your job because of Marilyn, your immediate supervisor. Marilyn is highly educated, knows everything there is to know about all of the organization's products and services, but seems to know little about how to manage people. Marilyn is about 20 years older than you are and sincerely believes that you can meet your weekly and monthly goals without any feedback as to how well you are doing. Your daily routine is highly restrictive, with two 15-minute breaks and a 30-minute lunch break that must be taken at specific points on the clock. Because you are new to the organization, you feel insecure and need positive reinforcement. You are losing your self-confidence and considering quitting, but your professional goal is to build a career within this organization. Meet with one of your classmates who will play the role of Marilyn, and discuss your concerns about the lack of feedback. Also, discuss how the organization can make better use of your knowledge, skills, and abilities, which will, in turn, make Marilyn (and you) look good to the executives in charge of promotions and enhance the company's bottom line.

BELOW THE SURFACE | AWAKENING THE DRIVING FORCE WITHIN

At the beginning of this chapter, we described the exceptional accomplishments of Jordan Romero and Laura Dekker. It is interesting to note that both of these young record breakers faced physical, mental, and legal challenges. Romero departed for the Mount Everest peak from the Chinese side of the mountain after Nepal authorities denied him permission on age grounds. Dekker had to go to court after the Dutch social services objected to the record attempt. Government officials thought the trip would harm her emotionally.

Laura Dekker, who was born on a boat, continues to sail and will likely find other records to break. Jordan Romero has already set another record. He reached the summit of Vinson Massif, a 16,067 foot mountain in Antarctica. He is now the youngest person to climb to the summit of the highest mountains on each of the seven continents.[33]

QUESTIONS

1. Daniel Pink has described three basic human needs: *autonomy*, *mastery*, and *purpose*. Which of these needs motivated Laura Dekker? Jordan Romero? Explain your answer.

2. Do you think the power of expectations affected these young adventurers?

3. Your goals play a key role in bringing purpose and direction to your life. Identify the short-term goals that are currently influencing your behavior. What long-term goals do you hope to achieve in the future?

CLOSING CASE | CAN PERSONAL TALES OF ADVERSITY FIRE UP THE STAFF?

Many companies schedule annual meetings to give employees an update on the current status of the organization and involve them in developing plans for the future. At a one-week retreat for 300 Cisco Systems, Inc. finance managers, the first order of business was a series of strategy sessions. This was followed by some team-building activities. Then came a visit by a blind man.

In an after-lunch speech, Erik Weihenmayer described his bitterness as a teenager over losing his sight. He explained how he channeled his anger into rock climbing and dreamed of climbing Mount Everest. After some brief introductory comments, managers of the computer-networking company watched a video that showed Mr. Weihenmayer picking his way past deep crevasses until he reached the top of Mount Everest. Near the end of his presentation, he told the audience it is possible to use adversity to propel you forward.[34]

Several years ago, Plug Power, Inc., an alternative energy company, was facing serious economic problems. The company was an energy success story in 2000, with stock briefly trading at $150 a share. A few years later, the company's shares had declined to single-digit levels. Roger Saillant, CEO, decided Plug Power employees needed to hear an inspirational speaker. He spent $5,000 to bring Trisha Meili to its corporate office in Latham, New York. In 1989, Meili was assaulted in Central Park and left for dead. After a long recovery, she published her memoirs and began her speaking career. She tells her audiences about learning to walk again after spending months in a coma. She had been in a near-death state but was able to make a recovery. Saillant says she struck a chord with Plug Power employees who were working hard to keep the company alive.[35]

Today, organizations are spending hundreds of millions a year on speakers. These speaker lists include Mia Hamm (U.S. Women's Gold Medal Soccer Team), Greg Gadson (decorated U.S. Army Commander), Erin Brockovich (whistleblower), and many others.

QUESTIONS

1. Many inspirational speakers attempt to take the audience on an emotional journey. They try to erase cynicism and complacency and get employees fired up about their jobs. Do you think organizations should rely on inspirational speakers to build passion among their workers during challenging times? Discuss your answer.

2. Let's assume your company has spent a large sum of money to bring in Lance Armstrong. He makes an enthusiastic presentation and receives a standing ovation. Define what steps your company would need to take to ensure that this enthusiasm transfers back on the job during the weeks and months ahead. Be specific as you describe your recommendations.

3. Jordan Romero and Laura Dekker set important records during their teen years. Should they consider a career as an inspirational speaker?

CHAPTER 7 ENDNOTES

1. Cara Anna, "Boy Calls Mom from 'Top of the World'," *The News & Observer*, May 23, 2010, p. 16A; "American Boy, 13, Breaks Everest Record" [cited May 23, 2010]. Available from http://www.cnn.com; INTERNET.

2. "Dutch Teenager Laura Dekker Breaks Solo Around-the-World Sail Record" [cited 23 January 2012]. Available from http://www.metro.co.uk.com; INTERNET; "Laura Dekker: Stubborn, Self Absorbed and a Devil of a Sailor"[cited 21 January 2012]. Available from http://www.DutchNews.nl.com; INTERNET.

3. Daniel H. Pink, *Drive—The Surprising Truth About What Motivates Us*, New York: Riverhead Books, 2009, pp. 84–91; 109–115; 131–135.

4. Douglas A. Bernstein, Louis A. Penner, Alison Clarke-Stewart, and Edward J. Roy, *Psychology*, 9th ed. (Belmont, CA: Wadsworth Cengage Learning, 2012).

5. M. G. Lord, "Raison McÊtre," *New York Times Book Review*, August 18, 2002, p. 13.

6. Jim Carlton, "Wild Horses, Couldn't Drag Them Away from Stones Shows," *Wall Street Journal*, November 22, 2002, p. A1.

7. Data were collected by use of the Reiss Profile, a standardized psychological test used to measure 16 desires.

8. Steven Reiss, "Secrets of Happiness," *Psychology Today*, January/February 2001, pp. 50–56. To learn more about the Reiss Profile, see *Who Am I: The 16 Basic Desires That Motivate Our Happiness and Define Our Personalities* (New York: Berkley Books, 2000).

9. Cynthia Berryman-Fink, *The Managers' Desk Reference* (New York: AMACOM, 1989), pp. 156–157.

10. Robert Kreitner, *Management*, 10th ed. (Boston: Houghton Mifflin, 2007), pp. 378–380.

11. "Belonging Satisfies Basic Human Need," *The Menninger Letter*, August 1995, p. 6.

12. Robert Kreitner and Carlene M. Cassidy, *Management* (12th ed.) Mason, OH: South-Western, 2011, p. 331.

13. Frederick Herzberg, Bernard Mausner, and Barbara Black Snyderman, *The Motivation to Work* (New York: Wiley, 1959).

14. C. R. Snyder, "Hope Helps," *Psychology Today*, November/December 1999, p. 20. Expectancy Theory is discussed in Robert Kreitner, *Management*, 10th ed. (Boston: Houghton Mifflin, 2007), pp. 382–383.

15. Richard Barrett, "The Power of Purpose," *The Inner Edge*, August/September 1999, p. 20.

16. Robert Kreitner and Carlene M. Cassidy, *Management* (12th ed.) Mason, OH: South-Western, 2011, pp. 334–335.

17. Lorri Freifeld, "Why Cash Doesn't Motivate," *Training*, July/August 2011, p. 22.

18. Christopher T. Kaczyk, "American Express," *Fortune*, August 16, 2010, p. 14.

19. Karen Auby, "A Boomer's Guide to Communicating with Gen X and Gen Y," *BusinessWeek*, September 1, 2008.

20. Kelly K. Spors, "Top Small Work Places," *Wall Street Journal*, October 13, 2008, p. R5.

21. Shelly Banjo, "A Perfect Match," *Wall Street Journal*, October 13, 2008, p. R9.

22. Patrick J. Sauer, "Open-Door Management," *Inc.*, June 2003, p. 44.

23. "The Three Signs of a Miserable Job—Q&A with Patrick Lencioni," The Table Group Inc. [cited 7 February 2012]. Available from http://www.tablegroup.com.

24. Janice Love, review of *The Set-Up-to-Fail Syndrome*, by Jean-Francois Manzoni and Jean-Louis Barsoux, *Training*, April 2003, p. 49; Sharon Begley, "Expectations May Alter Outcomes Far More Than We Realize," *Wall Street Journal*, November 7, 2003, p. Bl.

25. Ibid.; Ann C. Humphries, "Motivating Generation X" [cited 27 December 2005]. Available from http://www.christianwomentoday.com/workplace/genx; INTERNET. Karen Auby, "A Boomer's Guide to Communicating with Gen X and Gen Y," *BusinessWeek*, September 1, 2008, p. 63.

26. Peter Doskoch, "The Winning Edge," *Psychology Today*, November/December 2005, pp. 42–45.

27. Ibid., pp. 46–47.

28. M. Scott Peck, *The Road Less Traveled* (New York: Simon & Schuster, 1978), pp. 18–20; Christine B. Whelan, "The Road Is Heavily Traveled Now," *Wall Street Journal*, October 7, 2005, p. W13.

29. G. Pascal Zachary, "The New Search for Meaning in 'Meaningless' Work," *Wall Street Journal*, January 9, 1997, p. Bl.

30. Robin A. Sheerer, *No More Blue Mondays* (Palo Alto, Calif.: Davies-Black Publishing, 1999).

31. Sue Shellenbarger, "Conquering the To-Do List," *Wall Street Journal*, December 28, 2011, pp. D1 and D2.

32. Peter Doskoch, "The Winning Edge," *Psychology Today*, November/December 2005, p. 50.

33. "U.S. Teenager Jordan Romero Sets Seven-Peak Record" [cited 25 December 2011]. Available from http://www.bbc.co.uk.news.

34. George Anders, "At Office Retreats, Tales of Adversity Fire Up the Staff," *Wall Street Journal*, October 13, 2006, pp. A1–A2.

35. Ibid.

PART 3

Personal Strategies for Improving Human Relations

Medioimages/Photodisc/Getty Images

Improving Interpersonal Relations with Constructive Self-Disclosure

TIP OF THE ICEBERG | XEROX CEO SPEAKS HER MIND

CHAPTER PREVIEW

LEARNING OBJECTIVES

After studying Chapter 8, you will be able to

8-1 Explain how constructive self-disclosure contributes to improved interpersonal relationships and teamwork.

8-2 Understand the specific benefits you can gain from self-disclosure.

8-3 Identify and explain the major elements of the Johari Window model.

8-4 Explain the criteria for appropriate self-disclosure.

8-5 Understand the barriers to self-disclosure in an organizational setting.

8-6 Apply your knowledge and practice constructive self-disclosure.

The promotion of Ursula Burns to the top position at Xerox Corporation marked two milestones: the first time an African-American woman was named CEO of a major American corporation and the first time a woman succeeded another woman in the top position at a company of this size. She replaced Anne Mulcahy who held the job for several years.[1]

After the promotion, Burns had to endure countless interviews from media representatives. They wanted to know if she was ready to cope with the pressures that come with the top job. Her response was, "I'm a black lady from the Lower East Side of New York; not a lot intimidates me."[2]

Burns is known to be tough and someone who has the courage to speak her mind. In the early 1990s, her candor at a meeting of the top Xerox executives set the stage for a major promotion. She and other managers were invited to attend the meeting and instructed to sit off to the side. Paul Allaire, then president of the company, would often declare, "We have to stop hiring." Yet Xerox continued to hire new employees, month after month. At one of these meetings, Burns raised her hand and said, "I'm a little confused. If you keep saying, 'No hiring' and we hire a thousand people every month, who can say 'No hiring" and make it actually happen?" Soon after the meeting, Allaire invited her into his office, thanked her for her candor, and made her his executive assistant.[3]

Self-disclosure, when it comes from the heart, can deepen relationships at home and at work. However, this form of communication can be difficult. Expressing personal thoughts and feelings to a coworker, friend, or family member is often very challenging.

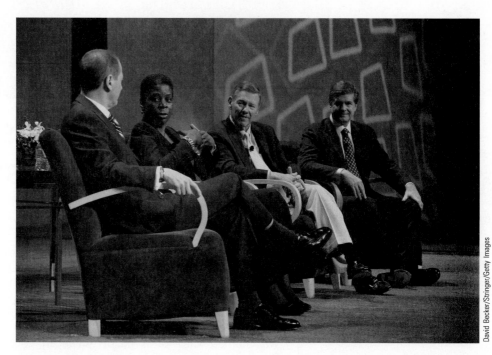

Xerox CEO Ursula Burns is known for her courage to speak openly and candidly, a quality that lies at the heart of self-disclosure.

SELF-DISCLOSURE: AN INTRODUCTION

8-1   As a general rule, relationships grow stronger when people are willing to reveal more about themselves and their work experiences. It is a surprising but true fact of life that two people can work together for many years and never really get to know each other. In many organizations, the culture encourages employees to hide their true feelings. The result is often a weakening of the communication process. Self-disclosure can lead to a more open and supportive environment in the workplace.

In some cases, self-disclosure takes the form of an apology or of granting forgiveness to someone who apologizes to you. If you are a supervisor or manager, self-disclosure may take the form of constructive criticism of an employee whose performance is unsatisfactory. This chapter focuses on constructive self-disclosure and on conditions that encourage appropriate self-disclosure in a work setting.

Self-Disclosure Defined

Self-disclosure is the process of letting another person know what you think, feel, or want. It is one of the important ways you let yourself be known by others. Self-disclosure can improve interpersonal communication, resolve conflict, and strengthen interpersonal relationships.

It is important to note the difference between self-disclosure and self-description. **Self-description** involves disclosure of nonthreatening information, such as your age, your favorite food, or where you went to school. This is information that others could acquire in some way other than by your telling them. Self-disclosure, by contrast, often involves some degree of risk. When you engage in self-disclosure, you reveal private, personal information that cannot be acquired from another source. Examples include your feelings about being a member of a minority group, job satisfaction, and new policies and procedures.

The importance of self-disclosure, in contrast to self-description, is shown by the following situation. You work at a distribution center and are extremely conscious of safety. You take every precaution to avoid work-related accidents. But another employee has a much more casual attitude toward safety rules and often "forgets" to observe the proper procedures, endangering you and other workers. You can choose to disclose your feelings to this person or stay silent. Either way, your decision has consequences.

BENEFITS GAINED FROM SELF-DISCLOSURE

8-2   Before we discuss self-disclosure in more detail, let us examine four basic benefits you gain from openly sharing what you think, feel, or want.

> *Self-disclosure often takes the guesswork out of the communication process.*

1. *Increased accuracy in communication.* Self-disclosure often takes the guesswork out of the communication process. No one is a mind reader; if people conceal how they really feel, it is difficult for others to know how to respond to them appropriately. People who are frustrated by a heavy workload and loss of balance in their life, but mask their true feelings, may never see the problem resolved. The person who is in a position to solve this problem may be oblivious to what's important to you—unless you spell it out.

Total Person Insight

"Vulnerability is often seen as a weakness; it's actually a sign of strength. People who are genuinely open and transparent prove that they have the confidence and self-esteem to allow others to see them as they really are, warts and all."

Source: Patrick Lencioni, "The Power of Saying We Blew It," *Bloomberg Businessweek*, February 22, 2012, p. 84.

2. *Reduction of stress.* Sidney Jourard, a noted psychologist who wrote extensively about self-disclosure, states that too much emphasis on privacy and concealment of feelings creates stress within an individual. Too many people keep their thoughts and feelings bottled-up inside, which can result in considerable inner tension. When stress indicators such as blood pressure, perspiration, and breathing increase, our immune function declines. The amount of stress that builds within us depends on what aspects of ourselves we choose to conceal. If you compulsively think about a painful human relations problem but conceal your thoughts and feelings, the consequence will likely be more stress in your life.[4]

3. *Increased self-awareness.* Chapter 1 stated that self-awareness is one of the major components of emotional intelligence at work. Daniel Goleman, author of *Working with Emotional Intelligence*, defines **self-awareness** as the ability to recognize and understand your moods, emotions, and drives, as well as their effect on others.[5] Self-awareness is the foundation on which self-development is built. To plan an effective change in yourself, you must be in touch with how you behave, the factors that influence your behavior, and how your behavior affects others. A young Asian associate at a financial services firm learned from her supervisor that she was perceived as not being assertive enough in her dealings with clients. As she reflected

Figure 8.1 ■ Self-Disclosure/Feedback/Self-Awareness Cycle

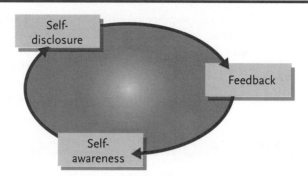

on this feedback and listened to views expressed by her female peers, the associate became aware of how her cultural background influenced her communication with clients. This feedback motivated her to modify her communication style.[6]

The quality of feedback from others depends to a large degree on how much you practice self-disclosure. The sharing of thoughts and feelings with others often sets the stage for meaningful feedback (see Figure 8.1).

4. *Stronger relationships.* Another reward from self-disclosure is the strengthening of inter-personal relationships. When two people engage in an open, authentic dialogue, they often develop a high regard for each other's views. Often they discover they share common interests and concerns, and these serve as a foundation for a deeper relationship.

In too many organizations, workers feel they must be careful about what they say and to whom they say it. David Stewart, organizational consultant, says people long for a work environment in which they can say what is on their mind in an honest and straightforward manner. They yearn for an authentic kind of interaction with their boss and coworkers.[7]

5. *Increased authenticity.* "People trust you when you are genuine and authentic, not a replica of someone else." These words of wisdom come to us from Bill George, noted author and consultant in the area of authentic leadership.[8] Jack Welch, a highly successful CEO at General Electric for many years, says the most powerful thing you can do to get ahead is to be real[9]: "Think of authenticity as your foundation, your center, and don't let any organization try to wring it out of you, subtly or otherwise."

Authenticity has been defined as the unimpeded operation of one's true or core self in one's daily interactions with others. It requires acting in ways congruent with your own values and needs. Authenticity is necessary for close relationships because intimacy cannot develop without openness and honesty.[10]

THE JOHARI WINDOW: A MODEL FOR SELF-UNDERSTANDING

8-3

The first step in understanding the process of self-disclosure is to look at the **Johari Window**, illustrated in Figure 8.2. The word *Johari* is a combination of the first names of the model's originators: Joseph Luft and Harry Ingham. This communication model takes into consideration that there is some information you know about yourself and other information you are not yet aware of. In addition, there is some information that others know about you and some they are not aware of. Your willingness or unwillingness to engage in self-disclosure, as well as to listen to feedback from others, has a great deal to do with your understanding of yourself and with others' understanding of you.[11]

Figure 8.2 ■ Johari Window

Solicit feedback →

	Information known to self	Information not known to self
Information known to others	1 OPEN	2 BLIND
Information not known to others	3 HIDDEN	4 UNKNOWN

Give feedback (self-disclosure) ↓

Source: From Joseph Luft, *Group Processes: An Introduction to Group Dynamics.* Copyright © 1984. Reprinted by permission of The McGraw-Hill Companies.

The Four Panes of the Johari Window

The Johari Window identifies four kinds of information about you that affect your communication with others. Think of the entire model as representing your total self as you relate to others. The Johari Window is divided into four panes, or areas, labeled (1) open, (2) blind, (3) hidden, and (4) unknown.[12]

Open Area. The **open area** of the Johari Window represents your "public" or "awareness" area. This section contains information about you that both you and others know and includes information that you do not mind admitting about yourself. As your relationship with another person matures, the open pane gets bigger, reflecting your desire to be known.

The open pane is generally viewed as the part of the relationship that influences effective interpersonal relations. Therefore, a productive interpersonal relationship is related to the amount of mutually held information. Building a relationship with another person involves working to enlarge the open area. As self-awareness and sharing of information and feelings increase, the open pane becomes larger.

Blind Area. The **blind area** consists of information about yourself that others know but you are not aware of. Others may see you as aloof and stuffy, whereas you view yourself as open and friendly. Or you may view your performance at work as mediocre, and others see it as above average. You may consider your dress and grooming practices appropriate for work, but others feel your appearance is not suitable for such a setting. Information in the blind area is acquired when you learn about people's perceptions of you.

Building a relationship and improving interpersonal effectiveness often involve working to enlarge the open pane and reduce the size of the blind pane. This can be achieved as you become more self-disclosing and thereby encourage others to disclose more of their thoughts and feelings to you (see Figure 8.1). People are more likely to give feedback to a person who is open and willing to share appropriate personal information with them.

Total Person Insight

> "As long as you sit on your power to forgive, you suppress your joy in life."
>
> Source: Thomas Moore, "Finding Freedom in Forgiveness," *Spirituality & Health*, May/June 2008, p. 12.

Hidden Area. The **hidden area** contains information about you that you know but others do not. This pane is made up of all those private feelings, needs, and past experiences that you prefer to keep to yourself. These could be incidents that occurred early in life or past work-related experiences you would rather not share.

Sometimes people spend too much effort building a wall of separation between their inner and outer lives. They conceal too much private information, leading others to ask, "Is this person the same on the inside as he presents himself on the outside?" When you share information about yourself, you allow yourself to be "seen," and it's easier for people to relate to you as a human being with faults, strengths, thoughts, and emotions.[13]

Unknown Area. The **unknown area** of the Johari Window is made up of things unknown to you and others. Because you, and others, can never be known completely, this area never completely disappears. The unknown may represent such factors as unrecognized talents, unconscious motives, or early childhood memories that influence your behavior but are not fully understood. Many people have abilities that remain unexplored throughout their lives. A person capable of rising to the position of department manager may remain a receptionist throughout his or her career because the potential for advancement is unrecognized. You may possess the talent to become an artist or musician but never discover it.

The Importance of Self-Awareness

Marshall Goldsmith, one of America's preeminent executive coaches, was hired to work with a very successful employee who treated direct reports and colleagues like "gravel in a driveway." Goldsmith says, "They were the pebbles; he was the SUV." Although this person was delivering outstanding results for the company, he was offending many of the employees he worked with. During the first meeting with Mike (not his real name), Goldsmith asked, "How do you treat people at home?" Mike insisted he was a great husband and father. He said, "I'm a warrior on Wall Street but a pussycat at home." Goldsmith suggested they call his wife and ask her how she viewed his behavior at home. When she finally stopped laughing at her husband's assessment, she confirmed that Mike was a jerk at home, too. His two sons also agreed with their mother. Once Mike realized how he was perceived by family members and coworkers, he made a commitment to change. Within a year, his treatment-of-people scores on a standardized instrument improved dramatically—and so did his income.[14]

Some of the unknown information that is below the surface of awareness can be made public with the aid of open communication. Input from others (teachers, mentors, or supervisors) can reduce the size of the unknown pane and increase the size of the open area.

HOW TO ACHIEVE GREATER SELF-AWARENESS

- Solicit feedback from multiple persons whose opinions you value.
- Be open to criticism. It is often a gift aimed at helping you.
- Value feedback from persons who have observed your behavior in multiple contexts (classroom, athletic event, etc.).

Self-Disclosure/Feedback Styles

Our relationship with others is influenced by two communication processes over which we have control. We can consciously make an effort to self-disclose our thoughts, ideas, and feelings when such action would improve the relationship. And we can also act to increase the amount of feedback from others. Figure 8.3a represents a self-disclosure/feedback style that reflects minimum use of self-disclosure and feedback processes. This style represents an impersonal approach to interpersonal relations, one that involves minimal sharing of information. Figure 8.3b represents a self-disclosure/feedback style that reflects considerable use of self-disclosure and feedback. Candor, openness, and mutual respect are characteristics of this style.

You can take positive steps to develop a larger open window (Figure 8.3b) by displaying a receptive attitude when others attempt to give you feedback. Openness to feedback from supervisors and coworkers, as opposed to defensiveness, is an important key to success in the workplace. If you become defensive, this behavior is likely to cut off the flow of information you need to be more effective in your job.

360-Degree Feedback. Many organizations are using an assessment strategy known as **360-degree feedback**. With this approach, employees are rated by persons who have had opportunities to observe their performance. The person who completes the feedback form may be the immediate boss, coworkers, team members, and, in some cases, even customers, clients, or patients. The feedback is generally anonymous and often provides valuable insights regarding a worker's talents and shortcomings. If problems are identified, they can be addressed through training and development programs.[15]

Although 360-degree feedback programs are often successful, some poorly planned and implemented programs have resulted in heightened tensions and low morale. Some rating forms look too much like a report card. The multi-rater instrument should give

Figure 8.3 ■ Johari Window at the Beginning of a Relationship (a) and After a Closer Relationship Has Developed (b)

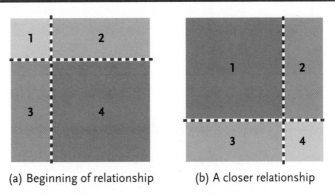

(a) Beginning of relationship   (b) A closer relationship

Source: From Joseph Luft, *Group Processes: An Introduction to Group Dynamics.*

raters an opportunity to designate the areas most in need of development. In an ideal situation, the person being reviewed will receive a feedback-summary report and help to develop a plan for growth in areas that need improvement.[16]

What are some characteristics that might be included in a 360-degree evaluation form? Here are a few examples:[17]

Gratitude: Expresses thanks and gratitude genuinely.

Listening: Listens well to others before speaking.

Unity: Accepts others and works in harmony with a team.

Attention: Pays careful attention in all situations.

Openness: Is approachable to all.

Imagination: Thinks creatively and likes new ideas.

APPROPRIATE SELF-DISCLOSURE

8-4   At the beginning of this chapter, we stated that the primary goal of self-disclosure should be to build stronger relationships. Self-disclosure is also a condition for emotional health, according to Sidney Jourard. These goals (strong relationships and good emotional health) can be achieved if you learn how to disclose in constructive ways. Appropriate self-disclosure is a skill that anyone can learn. However, developing this skill often means changing attitudes and behaviors that have taken shape over a lifetime.

In the search for criteria for developing appropriate self-disclosure, many factors must be considered. How much information should be disclosed? How intimate should the information be? Who is the most appropriate person with whom to share information? Under what conditions should the disclosures be made? In this section, we examine several criteria that will help you develop your self-disclosure skills.

Use Self-Disclosure to Repair Damaged Relationships

Many relationships at work and in our personal life are unnecessarily strained. The strain often exists because people refuse to talk about real or imagined problems. Self-disclosure can be an excellent method of repairing a damaged relationship.

Throughout your career, you will encounter countless workplace problems. Your boss said she would love to give you a salary increase but didn't have the authority to approve raises. Later, you find out that she lied. You miss a team meeting because of an illness. Later, you find out that a team member was highly critical of your work on an important project. Do you confront the foe or suffer in silence?

Most of us revisit the problem numerous times. The process of replaying the incident over and over in our mind is referred to in psychology circles as **rumination**. Some people are inclined to fester in a cycle of anger that results in stress, lost sleep, and loss of concentration.[18]

There will be times when something you say or something you do is highly offensive to someone else. What steps will you take to repair the damaged relationship?

Total Person Insight

"No one can get by in life without being able to issue a sincere apology … [and] without being able to distinguish a sincere apology from something that falls short."

Source: "How not to apologize," *Fort Worth Star-Telegram*, March 7, 2012, page 15-A.

In the heat of the moment, a disagreement can cause harsh words and hurt feelings between friends and coworkers; however, practicing the art of apologizing helps to mend those frayed bonds and restore relationships.

P. Winbladh/Corbis

> *Even in cases where your intention was not to upset or hurt someone, the apology must come from your heart.*

The Art of Apologizing. If your actions have caused hurt feelings, anger, or deep-seated ill will, an apology is in order. A sincere apology can have a tremendous amount of healing power for both the receiver and the giver. Beverly Engle, author of *The Art of Apologizing*, says, "Almost like magic, apology has the power to repair harm, mend relationships, soothe wounds, and heal broken hearts."[19]

Of course some apologies do little to improve interpersonal relations and some make things worse. A *heartfelt apology* demonstrates that you understand and regret the pain you have inflicted. The four apologies described in Table 8.1 are likely to make matters worse.

Do not rely on an e-mail message or a tweet for an important apology. In a private setting, feelings can be exchanged with relative comfort. An effective apology will communicate the three Rs: Regret, Responsibility, and Remedy.[20]

- *Regret.* The regret that you feel must be communicated sincerely. Even in cases where your intention was not to upset or hurt someone, the apology must come from your heart.
- *Responsibility.* Do not make excuses or blame others for what you did. Don't say, "I'm sorry about what happened, but you shouldn't have…" You must accept total responsibility for your actions.
- *Remedy.* A meaningful apology should include a commitment that you will not repeat the behavior. It might also include an offer of restitution.

Table 8.1 ■ Apologies that Make Things Worse

DEFENSIVE APOLOGY	CONTINGENT APOLOGY	TOO-LATE APOLOGY	BULLY APOLOGY
Scenario: "I'm sorry, but..."	**Scenario:** "I'm sorry if I've done something wrong."	**Scenario:** "I realize now that what I did was wrong."	**Scenario:** "Sorry to dump this project on you at 5 p.m."
A self-protective maneuver meant to defend your actions.	Used to appease a person but don't know what you've done wrong—or don't care.	An expression of regret that comes days, weeks, or months too late.	Entirely insincere, offered only to manipulate the recipient into some action.

Source: Adapted from "I'm Very, Very, Very Sorry … Really?" by Elizabeth Bernstein, *Wall Street Journal*, October 19, 2010, p. D1.

The Art of Forgiveness. If someone you work with, a friend, or a family member, offers a sincere apology, be quick to forgive. Forgiveness is almost never easy, especially when you feel you have been wronged. But forgiveness is the only way to break the bonds of blame and bitterness. To forgive means to give up resentment and anger. D. Patrick Miller, author of *A Little Book of Forgiveness*, says: "To carry an anger against anyone is to poison your own heart, administering more toxin every time you replay in your mind the injury done to you." He also says forgiveness provides healing and liberates your energy and your creativity.[21]

When you convey an apology to someone or forgive another person, remember that you reveal a great deal through nonverbal messages. The emotion in your voice, as well as your eye contact, gestures, and body posture, will communicate a great deal about your inner thoughts.

Present Constructive Criticism with Care

Constructive criticism is a form of self-disclosure that helps another person look at his or her own behavior without putting that individual on the defensive. Constructive criticism is not the same as blaming. Blaming people for mistakes will seldom improve the situation.

Many people are very sensitive and are easily upset when they receive criticism. However, giving criticism effectively is a skill that can be mastered through learning and practice. Here are two effective methods for giving constructive criticism. First, avoid starting your message with "You," such as "You didn't complete your monthly inventory report" or "You never take our customer service policies seriously." For better results, replace "You-statements" with "I-statements." Say, "I am concerned that you have not completed your monthly inventory report." Another way to avoid defensiveness is to request a specific change in the future instead of pointing out something negative in the past. Instead of saying, "You did not have authorization to order office supplies," try saying, "In the future, please obtain authorization before ordering office supplies."[22]

"Well, if it doesn't matter who's right and who's wrong, why don't I be right and you be wrong?"

Discuss Disturbing Situations as They Happen

You should share reactions to a work-related problem or issue as soon after the incident as possible. It is often difficult to recapture a feeling once it has passed, and you may distort the incident if you let too much time go by. Your memory is not infallible. The person who erred is also likely to forget details about the situation.

human
RELATIONS
in Action

HELP FOR THE TONGUE-TIED

Research conducted by the Virginia Tech Carilion Research Institute indicates that many people become, in effect, less intelligent in small-group settings. Some of the smartest members of the group, and those best prepared to solve problems, remain silent at meetings for fear of saying something stupid. Here is some help for the tongue-tied:

- Join with someone who is more outgoing than you, or has a higher position in the group. This person can introduce you, bring up your points, and give you an opening into the conversation.

- Talk to the person running the meeting beforehand and indicate the points you want to discuss.

- Be prepared to participate. Know what you want to say, practice your delivery, and bring notes.

Source: Elizabeth Bernstein, "Speaking Up Is Hard to Do: Researchers Explain Why," *Wall Street Journal*, February 7, 2012, p. D1.

If something really bothers you, do not delay expressing your feelings. Clear the air as soon as possible so you can enjoy greater peace of mind. Some people maintain the burden of hurt feelings and resentment for days, weeks, or even years. The avoidance of self-disclosure usually has a negative effect on a person's mental and physical health as well as on-the-job performance.

Accurately Describe Your Feelings and Emotions

People should not be expected to turn off their feelings the moment they arrive at work.

It has been said that one of the most important outcomes of self-disclosure is the possibility for others to become acquainted with the "real" you. When you accurately describe your feelings and emotions, others get to know you better. This kind of honesty takes courage because of the risk involved. When you tell another person how you feel, you are putting a great amount of faith in that person. You are trusting the other person not to ridicule or embarrass you for the feelings you express.[23]

Too often, people view verbalizing feelings and emotions in a work setting as inappropriate. However, emotions are an integral part of human behavior. People should not be expected to turn off their feelings the moment they arrive at work. Experiencing feelings and emotions is a part of being human. If we don't know each other, we can't be close to each other.[24]

What is the best way to report emotions and feelings? Some examples may be helpful. Let's suppose you expected to be chosen to supervise an important project, but the assignment was given to another worker. At a meeting with your boss, you might make the following statement: "For several weeks, I've been looking forward to heading up this project. I guess I didn't realize that anyone else was being considered. Can you tell me why I was not given this assignment?"

Or suppose a coworker constantly borrows equipment and supplies but usually fails to return them. You might say: "Thanks for taking a few minutes to meet with me. I'm the type of person who likes to keep busy, but lately I've spent a lot of time retrieving tools and supplies you've borrowed. I've experienced a great deal of frustration and decided I should tell you how I feel."

As you report your feelings, be sure the other person realizes that your feelings are temporary and capable of change. You might say, "At this point I feel very frustrated, but I am sure we can solve the problem." Expressing anger can be especially difficult. This special challenge is discussed in Chapter 9.

Select the Right Time and Place

Remarks that otherwise might be offered and accepted in a positive way can be rendered ineffective not because of what we say but because of when and where we say it. When possible, select a time when you feel the other person is not preoccupied and will be able to give you his or her full attention. Also, select a setting free of distractions. Telephone calls or unannounced visitors can ruin an opportunity for meaningful dialogue. If there is no suitable place at work to hold the discussion, consider meeting the person for lunch away from work or talking with the person after work at some appropriate location. If necessary, make an appointment with the person to ensure that time is reserved for your meeting.

Avoid Overwhelming Others with Your Self-Disclosure

Although you should be open, do not go too far too fast. Many strong relationships are built slowly. The abrupt disclosure of highly emotional or intimate information may

Dr. Joyce Brothers says we must balance the inclination to be open and honest with the need to be protective of each other's feelings.

actually distance you from the other person, who may find your behavior inappropriate. Unrestricted "truth" can create a great deal of anxiety, particularly in an organization where people must work closely together. Dr. Joyce Brothers says we must balance the inclination to be open and honest with the need to be protective of each other's feelings. Disclosure in such areas as mental illness, domestic violence, fertility problems, or drug abuse is usually off limits at work. To be safe, it is also best to avoid expressing strong political or religious beliefs.[25]

Be careful what you disclose in online networking sites, such as Facebook, LinkedIn, and Twitter. When employers are down to a short list of candidates, they may check these sites to see what kind of public image you have created. Posting inappropriate photos, making bizarre statements regarding a company you worked for in the past, or chronicling your behavior at some wild party may create the image of someone who is not very mature.[26]

BARRIERS TO SELF-DISCLOSURE IN AN ORGANIZATIONAL SETTING

8-5 At this point, you might be thinking, "If self-disclosure is such a positive force in building stronger human relationships, why do people avoid it so often? Why do so many people conceal their thoughts and feelings? Why are candor and openness so uncommon in many organizations?" To answer these questions, let's examine some of the barriers that prevent people from self-disclosing.

Lack of Trust

Trust is an element of both character (which includes integrity) and competence. Although trust is intangible, it is at the core of all meaningful relationships. Low-trust relationships can be very frustrating when you are attempting to get things done in a timely fashion. It often takes a disproportionate amount of time and energy to reach agreements and execute projects when trust is absent.[27]

Total Person Insight

"We won't be able to rebuild trust in institutions until leaders learn how to communicate honestly—and create organizations where that's the norm."

Source: James O'Toole and Warren Bennis, "A Culture of Candor," *Harvard Business Review*, June 2009, pp. 54–61.

Trust is a complex emotion that combines three components: caring, competency, and commitment. Consider the relationship between a doctor and his or her patient. Trust builds when the patient decides that the doctor is competent (capable of diagnosing the health problem), caring (concerned about the patient's health), and committed (willing to find a solution to the medical problem).[28] Trust between a salesperson and a customer is built upon the same three components. Customers want to do business with a salesperson who can accurately diagnose their needs, prescribe the right product, and provide excellent service after the sale.

Lack of trust is the most common—and the most serious—barrier to self-disclosure. Without trust, people usually fear revealing their thoughts and feelings because the

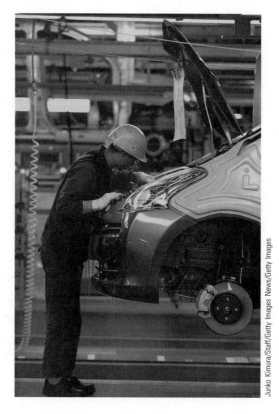

Junko Kimura/Staff/Getty Images News/Getty Images

Toyota Motor Corporation trusts ordinary workers to run its production lines better. The company respects the problem-solving skills of every employee.

perceived risks of self-disclosure are too high. When trust is present, people no longer feel as vulnerable in the presence of another person, and communication flows more freely.[29]

When trust is present, people function naturally and openly. Without it, they devote their energies to masking their true feelings, hiding thoughts, and avoiding opportunities for personal growth.[30] Within many organizations you will find people who spend time building trust and others who spend time destroying trust. Table 8.2 compares behaviors that build trust with behaviors that destroy it. Essentially, the way to build trust is to be trustworthy all the time.

Table 8.2 ■ How Trust Can Be Built and Destroyed

BUILDING TRUST	DESTROYING TRUST
■ Openly share information.	■ Withhold information.
■ Admit your mistakes.	■ Cover up mistakes.
■ Network with coworkers.	■ Keep your distance from coworkers.
■ Display competence.	■ Hide incompetence.
■ Be honest all the time.	■ Be honest only some of the time.
■ Be clear in your convictions.	■ Avoid commitment.
■ Be true to your values.	■ Ignore your values.

Trust Index

The **Trust Index©** and Employee Survey is a research tool that measures the level of trust, pride, and camaraderie within the workplace. It consists of 58 statements that address credibility, respect, pride, fairness, and camaraderie, the five dimensions of the *Great Place to Work* model. The Trust Index is the primary survey instrument used to identify organizations that appear on the annual *Fortune* magazine's *100 Best Companies to Work for List*. After 25 years of research involving millions of employee surveys, Great Place to Work Institute, Inc. says *trust* is the key to great workplaces.[31]

Role Relationships versus Interpersonal Relationships

Self-disclosure is more likely to take place within an organization when people feel comfortable stepping outside their assigned roles and displaying openness and tolerance for the feelings of others. In our society, role expectations are often clearly specified for people engaged in various occupations. For example, some people see the supervisor's role as an impersonal one. Supervisors are supposed to enforce policies, maintain high production, and avoid getting too close to the people they supervise. The advice given to some new supervisors is "Don't try to be a nice guy, or people will take advantage of you." Yet the traits of the most effective supervisors are those who are approachable, display a sense of humor, and take time to listen to employee problems.

Some newly appointed supervisors may deliberately try to build barriers between themselves and subordinates. They draw a sharp distinction between **role relationships** and **interpersonal relationships**. They are too impersonal and aloof, thinking that this is appropriate "role" behavior. Employees usually respond to these actions by becoming defensive or less trusting. Roles are inescapable, but they need not contribute to the depersonalization of relationships.

PRACTICE SELF-DISCLOSURE

8-6   Many people carry around an assortment of hurt feelings, angry thoughts, and frustrations that drains them of the energy they need to cope with life's daily struggles. Although self-disclosure provides a way to get rid of this burden, some people continue through life imprisoned by negative thoughts and feelings. If you avoid disclosing your thoughts and feelings, you make it harder for others to know the real you. You will recall from the beginning of this chapter that self-disclosure involves revealing personal information that cannot be acquired from other sources,improving the quality of your relationships with others.

Becoming a more open person is not difficult if you are willing to practice.

Could you benefit by telling others more about your thoughts, wants, feelings, and beliefs? To answer this question, complete Figure 8.4, which will give you an indication of your self-disclosure style. If you tend to agree with most of these items, consider making a conscientious effort to do more self-disclosing.

Becoming a more open person is not difficult if you are willing to practice. If you want to improve in this area, begin by taking small steps. You might want to start with a nonthreatening confrontation with a friend or neighbor. Pick someone with whom you have had a recent minor problem. Tell this person as honestly as possible how you feel about the issue or problem. Keep in mind that your objective is not simply to relate something that is bothering you, but also to develop a stronger relationship with this person.

Figure 8.4 ■ Self-Disclosure Indicator

	YES	NO
Instructions: Read each statement and then place a checkmark (✔) in the appropriate space.		
1. In most cases, I avoid sharing personal thoughts and feelings with others.		
2. My relationships with others tend to be quite formal.		
3. I would not be comfortable discussing personal problems at work.		
4. I tend to avoid discussing my concerns even when feelings of frustration build inside me.		
5. I tend to avoid giving praise or criticism to others.		
6. I tend to believe that familiarity breeds contempt.		
7. I find it difficult to apologize.		
8. I find it difficult to forgive the wrongdoer.		

As you gain confidence, move to more challenging encounters. Maybe you feel your work is not appreciated by your employer. Why not tell this person how you feel? If you are a supervisor and one of the people you supervise seems to be taking advantage of you, why not talk to this person openly about your thoughts? With practice you will begin to feel comfortable with self-disclosure, and you will find it rewarding to get your feelings out in the open. As you become a more open person, the people you contact will be more likely to open up and share more thoughts, ideas, and feelings with you. Everyone wins!

LOOKING BACK: SUMMARY OF LEARNING OBJECTIVES

1. **Explain how constructive self-disclosure contributes to improved interpersonal relationships and teamwork.**

   Open communication is an important key to personal growth and job satisfaction. Self-disclosure—the process of letting another person know what you think, feel, or want—improves communication. Most people want and need opportunities for meaningful dialogue with coworkers and the person who supervises their work.

2. **Understand the specific benefits you can gain from self-disclosure.**

   Constructive self-disclosure can pave the way for increased accuracy in communication, reduction of stress, increased self-awareness, stronger interpersonal relationships, and increased authenticity.

3. **Identify and explain the major elements of the Johari Window model.**

   The Johari Window helps you conceptualize four kinds of information areas involved in communication: The open area, what you and others know about you; the blind area, what others know about you that you do not know about yourself; the hidden area, what you know but others do not; and the unknown area, what neither you nor others know.

4. **Explain the criteria for appropriate self-disclosure.**

   Always approach self-disclosure with the desire to improve your relationship with the other person. Describe your feelings and emotions accurately, and avoid making judgments about the other person. Use self-disclosure to repair damaged relationships. It is helpful to understand the art of apologizing and the art of forgiveness.

5. **Understand the barriers to self-disclosure in an organizational setting.**

   A climate of trust serves as a foundation for self-disclosure. In the absence of trust, people usually avoid revealing their thoughts and feelings to others. Self-disclosure is more likely to take place within an organization when people feel comfortable stepping outside their assigned roles and displaying sensitivity to the feelings of others.

6. **Apply your knowledge and practice constructive self-disclosure.**

   As with learning any new skill, you can improve your ability to disclose your thoughts and feelings by starting with less threatening disclosures and proceeding slowly to more challenging situations.

KEY TERMS

self-disclosure, 164
self-description, 164
self-awareness, 165
authenticity, 166
Johari Window, 166
open area, 167

blind area, 167
hidden area, 168
unknown area, 168
360-degree feedback, 169
rumination, 170

constructive criticism, 172
trust, 175
trust index, 177
role relationships, 177
interpersonal relationships, 177

CAREER INSIGHT

Many nervous job seekers blabber endlessly about irrelevant information. They create a poor impression and cut short the hiring manager's time for further questions.

"Oversharing in an interview is the most dangerous thing you can do," says Anne Stevens, a managing partner at ClearRock, a Boston executive-coaching firm[32].

TRY YOUR HAND

1. To learn more about your approach to self-disclosure, complete each of the following sentences. Once you have completed them all, reflect on your written responses. Can you identify any changes in your approach to self-disclosure that would improve communications with others? Are there any self-disclosure skills that you need to practice?

   a. "For me, the major barrier to self-disclosure is …"

   b. "To establish a more mutually trusting relationship with others, I need to …"

   c. "In order to receive more feedback from others, I need to …"

   d. "In situations where I should apologize for something or voice forgiveness, I tend to …"

2. On Friday afternoon, a coworker visits your office and requests a favor. She wants you to review a proposal she will give to her boss on Monday morning at 10:00 a.m. You agree to study the proposal sometime over the weekend and give her feedback on Monday before her meeting. You put

a photocopy of the proposal in your briefcase and take it home. Over the weekend, you get busy and forget to review the proposal. In fact, you are so busy that you never open your briefcase. On Monday morning you make a call on a customer before reporting to the office. While sitting in the customer's office, you open your briefcase and see the report. It is too late to study the report and give feedback to your coworker. Which of the following actions would you take?

a. Try to forget the incident and avoid feeling guilty. After all, you did not intentionally avoid your obligation.

b. Call the person's boss and explain the circumstances. Confess that you simply forgot to read the report.

c. Meet with your coworker as soon as possible and offer a sincere apology for failing to read the report and provide the feedback Provide a rationale for your choice.

3. What is the best way for a supervisor to get feedback on his or her performance? One approach is to gather your staff in a meeting room and ask, "Who loves me? Show of hands!" To obtain truly anonymous feedback on your performance, the Internet is a good bet. Several companies offer web-based 360-degree review services. Visit the online clearinghouse HR Guide (*http://www.hr-guide.com*) and review the available resources for 360-degree feedback. Prepare a brief summary of your findings.

CRITICAL THINKING CHALLENGE

Ryan Masanz has developed an online forum for venting work-related complaints. His website, OfficeLeaks.com, lets employees post anonymous comments on their employers. Companies can monitor the comments for a fee. Masanz vows to never reveal employees' identities. He says, "I think great companies want to know honestly what employees think."

Office Leaks was inspired by Masanz's mother. She learned that her company was planning to lay off workers in the weeks ahead, but was not in a position to tell a colleague who was planning to buy a home. Current Office Leaks users can lock their post, allowing only the company's employees to see them.[33]

Glassdoor (www.glassdoor.com) is another online site that provides reviews about companies including an employer's hiring practices, employee opinions, interview information, worker salaries, and CEO reviews. What are some of the strengths and weaknesses of websites like Office Leaks and Glassdoor? Would you consider venting your complaints online? Explain your answer.

SELF-ASSESSMENT EXERCISE

For each of the following statements, circle the number from 1 to 5 that best represents your response: (1) strongly disagree (never do this); (2) disagree (rarely do this); (3) moderately agree (sometimes do this); (4) agree (frequently do this); (5) strongly agree (almost always do this).

	1	2	3	4	5
A. I engage in appropriate self-disclosure in order to achieve improved communication and increased self-awareness.	1	2	3	4	5
B. I am able to share information about myself in appropriate ways, avoiding the extremes of complete concealment and complete openness.	1	2	3	4	5
C. I can identify and explain the major elements of the Johari Window model.	1	2	3	4	5
D. I can explain the criteria for appropriate self-disclosure.	1	2	3	4	5
E. I understand the barriers to self-disclosure in an organizational setting.	1	2	3	4	5

After identifying your response to each item, select an attitude or skill you would like to improve. Prepare a written goal and then describe the steps you will take to achieve this goal.

YOU PLAY THE ROLE

To prepare for this role-play activity, review the second exercise in this chapter's Try Your Hand. You have decided to take action c, which involves a sincere apology. For the purpose of this role-play, you will assume the role of Taite Edwardson, The coworker who requested your help is Tyler Johnson. In order to be well prepared for the role-play, read the text material that describes the use of self-disclosure to repair damaged relationships. Keep in mind that when you apologize to someone, you reveal a great deal through nonverbal messages. The emotion in your voice, as well as your eye contact, gestures, and body posture, will communicate a great deal about your inner thoughts.

BELOW THE SURFACE | SHE'S KNOWN FOR BEING FRANK

At the beginning of this chapter, you were introduced to Ursula Burns, chief executive officer of Xerox Corporation. Ms. Burns has been with Xerox since 1980 when she started as an intern. By the late 1990s, she was part of a dying company, weakened by Japanese competition and less demand for paper copiers. Burns, known as someone who speaks her mind, says, "We had lost complete faith in the leadership of the company. We didn't have any cash and few prospects for making any."[34]

In 2000, Ann Mulcahy was named CEO and helped bring Xerox back from the brink of bankruptcy: Burns was a key player in Xerox's cost-saving efforts. One of her first challenges was planning and initiating an outsourcing program. Outsourcing Xerox's manufacturing would result in the loss of many jobs. She needed to win the support of the Xerox Union, numbering about 4,000 employees. Burns recalls: "I told them the truth, in as much detail as I could, about what was happening." She convinced the union it was going to be either some jobs or no jobs.[35]

Burns is working hard to create a culture of candor where leaders communicate honestly. She doles out radical honesty when needed, but has learned to temper her outspokenness. Burns says she is the beneficiary of good coaching and feedback from her business associates.

QUESTIONS

1. Why is a culture of candor especially important when a company is nearing bankruptcy?

2. Does the first African-American woman to lead a major U.S. corporation face special challenges? Explain your answer.

3. The early years offered Ursula Burns many challenges. She was the middle of three children of a single mother who took in ironing and babysat in a Manhattan project. How can these early life challenges help prepare someone for the executive ranks of a major corporation?

CLOSING CASE | THE IMPORTANCE OF BUILDING TRUST

Within the past few years, we have seen greater recognition that trust is the core of all meaningful relationships. Stephen M.R. Covey, author of *The Speed of Trust*, says that trust is the one thing that changes everything. It is the one thing that, if removed, will destroy the most successful business, the most influential leadership, the greatest friendship, the strongest character, and the deepest love.[36]

Why did Covey include the word "speed" in the title of his book? He says that trust always affects two outcomes—speed and cost. When trust goes down, speed will also go down and costs will go up. Consider the influence of trust in personal selling. When the customer and the salesperson trust each other, they will usually find ways to form a productive relationship and buying decisions will be made without delay. If the trust level is low, the customer will likely be slow to make a buying decision. The response to the salesperson's proposal may be, "I need a little more time to think about your proposal."[37]

Trust is a critical dimension of every productive team. Patrick Lencioni, author of *The Five Dysfunctions of a Team*, says the *absence of trust* is a major threat to team cohesiveness and productivity:

> This occurs when team members are reluctant to be vulnerable with one another and are unwilling to admit their mistakes, weaknesses or need for help. Without a certain comfort level among team members, a foundation of trust is impossible.[38]

The ideal team environment encourages every member to engage in open debate about key issues. When team members do not openly air their opinions, inferior decisions are the result.[39]

Many teams are characterized by great diversity. This is especially true of cross-functional teams staffed by a mix of specialists who represent different departments and job levels. Diverse teams are more likely to become dysfunctional because diverse membership can create communication problems. Jeffrey Polzer, Harvard professor, has examined the fit among team members and how to optimize it. He defines "fit" as interpersonal congruence. This is "… the degree to which members' appraisals of one another are similar to their self-assessments on dimensions relevant to team functioning."[40] For example, if a team member sees himself as someone who is willing to share the credit for team success, do others see him the same way? Polzer's research has shown that high congruence improves the performance of diverse teams.

QUESTIONS

1. Stephen M.R. Covey, author of *The Speed of Trust*, says that every employee in the organization should assume responsibility for building trust. Do you agree? Is this a realistic expectation? Explain.

2. Let's assume you are a member of a productive team that has received considerable praise from top management. You learn that one member of the team has met with the manager who organized the team and taken credit for the team's success. You fear that this individual's behavior will damage the team's future productivity. What should you do to correct this problem?

3. Jeffrey T. Polzer has stated that sharing self-assessments and appraisals of one another through 360-degree feedback can help team members achieve interpersonal congruence. Do you agree with his recommendation? What steps can be taken to be sure the team members are prepared for this type of intervention?

CHAPTER 8 ENDNOTES

1. Adam Bryant, "Xerox's New Chief Tries to Redefine Its Culture," [cited 20 February 2010]. Available from http://www.nytimes.com. INTERNET.
2. Ellen McGirt, "Fresh Copy," *Fast Company*, December 2011/January 2012, p. 134.
3. Alan Murray, "Views from the Top," *Wall Street Journal*, April 21, 2011, p. A11.
4. Martha Beck, "True Confessions," *O, The Oprah Magazine*, June 2002, pp. 183–184.
5. Daniel Goleman, "What Makes a Leader?" *Harvard Business Review*, November/December 1998, p. 95.
6. Cary Cherniss and Daniel Goleman, *The Emotionally Intelligent Workplace* (San Francisco: Jossey-Bass, 2001), p. 258.
7. David Stewart, "Talk at Work: Do You Dialogue?" *Health & Healing*, Vol. 5, No. 6, 2002, p. 2.
8. Bill George, Peter Sims, Andrew N. McLean, and Diana Mayer, "Discovering Your Authentic Leadership," *Harvard Business Review*, February 2007, pp. 129–138.
9. Jack Welch and Suzy Welch, "Get Real, Get Ahead," *BusinessWeek*, May 14, 2007, p. 100.
10. Karen Wright, "In Search of the Real You," *Psychology Today*, May/June 2008, pp. 70–77.
11. Roy M. Berko, Andrew D. Wolvin, and Darlyn R. Wolvin, *Communicating* (Boston: Houghton Mifflin, 1995), p. 46.
12. *Communication Concepts—The Johari Window* (New York: J. C. Penney Company, Consumer Affairs Department, 1979). Roy M. Berks, Andrew D. Wolvin, Darlyn R. Wolvin, *Communicating—A Social and Career Focus*, 8th ed. (Boston: Houghton Mifflin Company, 2001), pp. 73–75.
13. "Self-Disclosure as a Communication Tool," Communication Resource Center [cited 1 January 2011]. Available from http://work911.com/communication/skillsselfdisclosure.htm. INTERNET.
14. Marshall Goldsmith, "How to Learn the Truth About Yourself," *Fast Company*, October 2003, p. 127.
15. Stephen R. Covey, "360-Degree Alignment," *Training*, May 2009, p. 56.
16. Maury A. Peiper, "Getting 360 Feedback Right," *Harvard Business Review*, January 2001, pp. 3–7; William C. Byham, "Fixing the Instrument," *Training*, July 2004, p. 50.
17. "The Path of a Heart-Centered Leader," *Spirituality & Health*, May/June 2005, pp. 53–55.
18. Jared Sandberg, "Do You Hear What I Hear? Telling Off a Colleague—Silently," *Wall Street Journal*, October 23, 2007, p. Bl.
19. Beverly Engel, "Making Amends," *Psychology Today*, July/August 2002, pp. 40–42.
20. Ibid.
21. Sharon Nelton, "The Power of Forgiveness," *Nation's Business*, June 1995, p. 41.
22. Lazarus and Lazarus, *The 60-Second Shrink* (San Luis Obispo, Calif.: Impact, 1997), pp. 76–79.
23. Margery Weinstein, "Office Trust Busters," *Training*, July 2006, pp. 10–11.
24. Bob Wall, *Working Relationships* (Palo Alto, Calif.: Davies-Black, 1999), p. 166.
25. Joyce Brothers, "The Most Important People We Know … Our Friends," *Parade Magazine*, February 16, 1997, pp. 4–6; Sue Shellenbarger, "Ovulating? Depressed? The Latest Rules on What Not to Talk About at Work," *Wall Street Journal*, July 21, 2005, p. Dl.
26. John Murawski, "Stray Remarks Can Hunt Your Job Searchers," *News & Observer*, April 30, 2006, p. El.
27. Stephen M. R. Covey, *The Speed of Trust* (New York: Free Press, 2006), pp. 5–10.
28. Blaine Hartford, "Trust Your Surgeon? Mate? Friends? Colleagues? What Makes Up a Feeling of Trust?" *Health & Healing*, June 2000, p. 36.
29. Aubrey C. Daniels, *Bringing Out the Best in People* (New York: McGraw-Hill, 1994), p. 41.
30. Jack R. Gibb, *Trust: A New View of Personal and Organizational Development* (Los Angeles: Guild of Tutors Press, 1978), p. 29.
31. "Assess Your Organization," [cited 25 February 2012]. Available from http://www.greatplacetowork.com; INTERNET.
32. Joann S. Lublin, "Talking Too Much on a Job Interview May Kill Your Chance," *Wall Street Journal*, October 30, 2007, p. Bl
33. Wendy Lee, "Website Offers Forum for Venting Workers," *News & Observer*, July 31, 2011, p. E2.
34. Ellen McGirt, "Fresh Copy," *Fast Company*, December 2011/January 2012, p. 135.
35. Ibid; See "An Historic Succession at Xerox," by Nanette Byrnes and Robert O. Crockett, *BusinessWeek*, June 3, 2009, pp. 19–21.
36. Stephen M. R. Covey, *The Speed of Trust*, p. 1.
37. Ibid., pp. 13–17.
38. "The Five Dysfunctions of a Team: Book Review" [cited 3 March 2008]. Available from http://www. social-media-university-global.org; INTERNET.
39. Ibid.
40. Jeffrey T. Polzer, "Making Diverse Teams Click," *Harvard Business Review*, July-August 2008, pp. 20–21.

Achieving Emotional Balance in a Chaotic World

TIP OF THE ICEBERG | ACHIEVING A PERSONALITY MAKEOVER

Selina Lo, president and CEO of Ruckus Wireless, is no stranger to doing new things that others can't or won't do. Prior to joining Ruckus, she built a number of successful computer networking startups. Lots of people in Silicon Valley wanted to work at the same company as Selina Lo, but few wanted to work *with* her. Early in her career, she was described as very aggressive and very successful in the areas of sales and marketing. However, anyone who was not part of what Lo deemed the *solution*, she treated as her personal *problem*. Her management tools included yelling, fist pounding, and esteem threatening sarcasm.[1]

When Lo became CEO of Ruckus Wireless in 2004, she realized the need for a personality makeover. She attempted to recruit executives she had known in other jobs. She made generous financial offers, but they refused to work for her. As CEO, Lo also realized that she had an obligation for the lives and happiness of all employees. During an interview with an *Inc.* magazine editor she said, "When the CEO screams, the impact is much greater. I can't build a company with nervous people."[2]

Lo resolved to reform her management style, starting with a commitment to be more patient with employees. She adopted a group decision-making process that forces her to consider the views of others. She tries to take things more slowly, drawing on patience developed while pursuing an important hobby: gardening.[3]

As noted in Chapter 1, our labor force is increasingly geared toward service to clients, patients, and customers. In a service economy, relationships are usually more important than products. Several national training and development organizations are offering educational programs that help workers achieve emotional balance. Fred Pryor Seminars offers *Managing Emotions Under Pressure* and the American Management Association offers *Managing Emotions in the Workplace.*

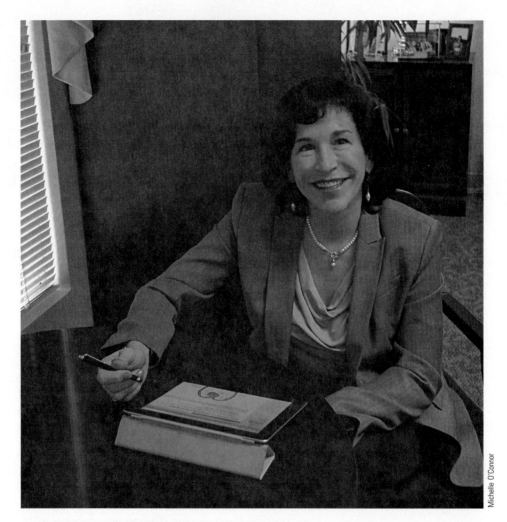

Michelle O'Connor is President and CEO of CMR Institute, a leading provider of educational programs for healthcare representatives employed in the pharmaceutical, biotech, and medical device industries. One of the major challenges facing O'Connor is energizing her staff as they manage the stress of staying informed and responsive to the complex issues affecting healthcare in the United States.

EMOTIONS—AN INTRODUCTION

9-1   An **emotion** is a temporary experience, with positive, negative, or mixed qualities. Emotional experiences tend to alter the thought processes by directing attention toward some things and away from others. Emotions energize our thoughts and behaviors.[4] Anger, fear, love, joy, jealousy, grief, and other emotions can influence our behavior at work and in our personal world. To the extent that we can become more aware of our emotions and assess their influence on our daily lives, we have the opportunity to achieve a new level of self-understanding.

Throughout each day, our feelings are activated by a variety of events (see Figure 9.1). You might feel a sense of joy after learning that a coworker has just given birth to a new baby. You might feel overpowering grief after learning that your supervisor was killed in an auto accident. Angry feelings may surface when you discover that

Figure 9.1 ■ Behavior Is Influenced By Activating Events

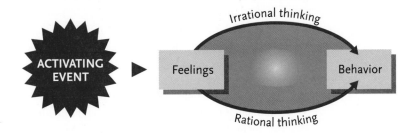

someone borrowed a tool without your permission. Once your feelings have been activated, your mind interprets the event. In some cases, the feelings trigger irrational thinking: "No one who works here can be trusted!" In other cases, you may engage in a rational thinking process: "Perhaps the person who borrowed the tool needed it to help a customer with an emergency repair." The important point to remember is that we can choose how we behave. We can gain control over our emotions.

Achieving Emotional Balance—A Daily Challenge

People make choices dictated primarily by either their heads (reason) or their hearts (feelings).

The need to discover ways to achieve emotional balance has never been greater, thanks to the pace of modern life. To be successful in these complex times, we need to be able to think and feel simultaneously. People make choices dictated primarily by either their heads (reason) or their hearts (feelings). The thinking function helps us see issues logically; the feeling function helps us be caring and human.[5] Many organizations are spawning fear, confusion, anger, and sadness because their leaders lack emotional balance.

The basic emotions that drive us have scarcely changed over the years. However, we are now seeing enormous differences in the expression of emotions. Today, people are much more likely to engage in aggressive driving, misbehave at public events, or become abusive when they are unhappy with service. In the workplace, many people experience emotional pain because of disagreeable bosses or uncooperative team members.

Emotional Intelligence

Daniel Goleman, author of several popular books on emotional intelligence (EQ), challenges the traditional view of the relationship between IQ and success. He says there are widespread exceptions to the rule that IQ predicts success: "At best, IQ contributes about 20 percent to the factors that determine life success, which leaves 80 percent to other forces." **Emotional intelligence** can be described as the ability to monitor and control one's emotions and behavior at work and in social settings. Whereas standard intelligence (IQ) deals with thinking and reasoning, EQ deals more broadly with building social relationships and controlling one's emotions. Several studies indicate that EQ can be increased through a combination of awareness and training.[6] The focus of Goleman's research is the human characteristics that make up what he describes as *emotional-competence*. The emotional-competence framework is made up of two dimensions.[7]

Personal Competence. This term refers to the competencies that determine how we achieve and maintain emotional balance. The essential component of emotional intelligence is *self-awareness*, the ability to read one's own emotions and hence be better equipped to assess one's level of emotional maturity. Personal competence involves keeping disruptive emotions and impulses in check.

Social Competence. This refers to the competencies that determine how we handle relationships. Sensing others' thoughts, feelings, and intentions; listening openly and sending convincing messages; and negotiating and resolving disagreements represent some of the competencies in this category.

Although IQ tends to be stable throughout life, emotional competence is learnable and can increase throughout our life span. We can learn to manage the thoughts that influence our behavior. For example, our minds are capable of producing outrageously irrational mental images such as dying in a plane crash. We have the option of reacting to those images with rational thinking.

Emotional Expression

We sometimes suffer from a lack of emotional balance because we learn to inhibit the expression of certain emotions and to overemphasize the expression of others. Some families, for example, discourage the expression of love and affection. Some people are taught from an early age to avoid expressing anger. Others learn that a public display of grief (crying, for example) is a sign of weakness. If as a child you were strongly encouraged to avoid the expression of anger, fear, love, or some other emotion, you may repress or block these feelings as an adult.[8]

Emotional imbalance also develops if we become fixated on a single emotion. Jealousy, for example, can be a very painful emotion. It throws the mind into turmoil and may trigger distressing feelings such as fear, sorrow, anger, and betrayal.[9]

human
RELATIONS
in Action

JEALOUSY IS ASTRONAUT'S DOWNFALL

Feelings of jealousy often flare with great intensity. Lisa Nowak experienced this emotion when she learned that a fellow astronaut with whom she had an affair was dating another woman. Nowak drove nonstop from Texas to Orlando, Florida, and attempted to kidnap the new girlfriend. She was dismissed from the astronaut corps and later retired from the U.S. Navy with an "other than honorable" discharge.

Source: Jeff Weiner, "Ex-Astronaut's Discharge to Be 'Other than Honorable'," *News & Observer*, July 30, 2011, p. 11A; Hara Estroff Marano, "Love's Destroyer," *Psychology Today*, July/August 2009, p. 65.

THE EMOTIONAL FACTOR AT WORK

9-2   Emotions play a critical role in the success of every organization, yet many people in key decision-making positions—leaders with outstanding technical skills—fail to understand the important role emotions play in a work setting. In part, the problem can be traced to leadership training that emphasizes that "doing business" is a purely rational or logical process. Some leaders learn to value only those things that can be arranged, analyzed, and defined. One consultant put the problem into proper perspective when he said, "We are still trying to do business as if it requires only a meeting of the minds instead of a meeting of the hearts."[10]

Tim Sanders, former chief solutions officer at Yahoo!, says, "How we are perceived as human beings is becoming increasingly important in the new economy." He notes that compassion is an important key to long-term personal success. This is the human ability to reach out with warmth through eye contact, physical touch, or words. It is a quality machines can never possess.[11]

Relationship Strategy

Emotional labor, which taxes the mind, is often more difficult to handle than physical labor, which strains the body.

Emotional undercurrents are present in almost every area of every organization. Most banks, hospitals, retail firms, hotels, and restaurants realize that they need a relationship strategy—a plan for establishing, building, and maintaining quality relationships with customers. Cisco Systems, for example, measures itself by the quality of its relationships with customers. Salespeople achieve their bonuses based in large part on customer satisfaction instead of on gross sales or profit.[12]

Front-line employees, those persons responsible for delivering quality service and building relationships, engage in **emotional labor**, and those who have frequent contact with the public often find the work very stressful.[13] When a company's competitive advantage is tied to the spontaneous warmth of its employees, the job involves emotional labor. Work that taxes the mind is often more difficult to handle than physical labor, which strains the body. A customer service representative or flight attendant who is told to maintain a smile throughout the day may experience emotional exhaustion and withdrawal.[14]

Fuse/Jupiter Images

People who work as clerks and servers are often a business's "face" to its customers, which is why managers should try to help those employees feel fulfilled, valued, and supported in their work.

Toxic Emotions

Peter Frost, author of *Toxic Emotions at Work*, notes that many organizations and their leaders generate emotional pain, which is a form of *toxicity*. Some toxicity can demoralize employees, damage performances, and ultimately contaminate the health of the organization.[15] Worker humiliation is a common toxin in the workplace; lack of recognition for work well done is another.

Toxicity often creates the kind of pain that shows up in worker's diminished sense of self-worth. One or more workers who are depressed or angry can poison team or department morale. How people feel can rub off on others. If the boss is feeling optimistic and enthusiastic, these feelings are often transmitted to staff members.[16] Later in this chapter, we will discuss how toxicity creates worker anger.

FACTORS THAT INFLUENCE OUR EMOTIONAL DEVELOPMENT

9-3 The starting point in achieving greater emotional control is to determine the source of emotional difficulties. Why do we sometimes display indifference when the expression of compassion would be more appropriate? Why is it so easy to put down a friend or coworker and so hard to recognize that person's accomplishments? Why do we sometimes worry about events that will never happen? To answer these and other questions, it is necessary to study the factors that influence our emotional development.

Temperament

At the time of birth, we can observe that infants differ from one another in the emotions they express most often. Some infants are happy, active, and vigorous. Others are very quiet. These characteristics make up the infant's **temperament**— the infant's individual style and frequency of expressing needs and emotions. Although temperament mainly reflects nature's contribution to the beginning of an individual's personality, it can also be affected by environmental factors after birth. For example, the stress experienced by the mother after the baby's birth can affect the baby's temperament. Many events take place between infancy and adulthood that can shift an individual's development.[17]

Unconscious Influences

The **unconscious mind** is a vast storehouse of forgotten memories, desires, ideas, and frustrations, according to William Menninger, founder of the famed Menninger Foundation.[18] He noted that the unconscious mind can have a great influence on behavior. It contains memories of past *experiences* as well as memories of *feelings* associated with past experiences. The unconscious is active, continuously influencing conscious decision-making processes.

Although people cannot remember many of the important events of the early years of their lives, these incidents do influence their behavior as adults. Joan Borysenko offers this example:

> *Inside me there is a seven-year-old who is still hurting from her humiliation at summer camp. Her anguish is reawakened every time I find myself in the presence of an authority figure who acts in a controlling manner. At those moments, my intellect is prone to desert me, and I am liable to break down and cry with the same desolation and helplessness I felt when I was seven.*[19]

This example reminds us that childhood wounds can cause us to experience emotions out of proportion to a current situation. Also, we often relive the experience in a context very different from the one we experienced as a child.

HOW TO ACHIEVE A FEARLESS LIFE

Jeff Golliher has written extensively about the power of fear. He says, "Fear can close our hearts, shape our emotional life, and freeze our emotions, but the only power fear has is the power we give it." Here are some tips on how to take that power back:

- Adopt behavioral techniques aimed at replacing upsetting thoughts with alternative thinking patterns. Focus on altering self-defeating thoughts. If you have a fear of flying, remind yourself that flying is much safer than driving. If you fear getting fired, reflect on your recent raise, a positive performance review, or past accomplishments.
- Move through your fear with activities that are relatively stress free. If you have a fear of public speaking, consider attending a "guest" program offered by Toastmaster Club. This organization provides guests with an easy and relatively stress-free forum for persons who want to conquer their fear of public speaking.

Source: Douglas A. Bernstein, Louis A. Penner, Alison Clarke-Stewart, and Edward J. Roy, *Psychology*, 9th ed. (Mason, OH: Wadsworth Cengage Learning); Jeff Golliher, "Five Insights for Fearless Living," *Spirituality & Health*, May–June 2011, p. 80.

Transactional Analysis. A promising breakthrough in understanding the influence of the unconscious came many years ago with the development of the **Transactional Analysis** (TA) theory by Eric Berne.[20] After years of study, Berne concluded that, from the day of birth, the brain acts like a two-track stereo tape recorder. One track records events, and the other records the feelings associated with those events.

To illustrate how feelings associated with early childhood experiences can surface later in life, picture in your mind's eye a three-year-old walking around his mother's sewing room. He picks up a pair of sharp scissors and begins walking toward the staircase. The mother spots the child and cries, "Tommy, drop those scissors! Do you want to kill yourself?" Tommy's tape recorder records both the event (walking with scissors) and the emotions (fear and guilt). Ten years later, Tommy is taking an art class and his teacher says, "Tommy, bring me a pair of scissors." As he begins to walk across the room, his mind is flooded by the feelings of fear and guilt attached to that earlier childhood event.

The practical applications of TA were discussed in such books as *I'm OK—You're OK*, written by Thomas Harris; *Staying OK*, by Amy Bjork Harris and Thomas Harris; and *Born to Win*, by Muriel James and Dorothy Jongeward. TA concepts have been incorporated into many corporate training programs.

Cultural Intelligence

Culture can be defined as the accumulation of values, rules of behavior, forms of expression, religious beliefs, and the like, for a group of people who share a common language and environment. Culture helps shape just about every aspect of our behavior and our mental processes. Culture is frequently associated with a particular country; but actually, most countries are *multicultural.* African Americans, Hispanic Americans, Asian Americans, and American Indians represent a few of the subcultures within the United

States.[21] Companies also have cultures. Persons who join a new company will often spend several weeks deciphering its cultural code.

The ability to interpret human actions, gestures, and speech patterns in a foreign culture is called **cultural intelligence** or (CQ). A person with a high CQ quickly analyzes an unfamiliar cultural situation and then responds appropriately.[22] The merits of CQ are highlighted in the movie *Outsourced*. A call center based in the United States is outsourced to India. The U.S. manager, Todd Anderson, is sent to Mumbai to train his successor. He received no cross-cultural training prior to his arrival. Serious cultural clashes soon arise as Anderson tries to explain American business practices to befuddled new employees.[23] Management professors P. Christopher Earley and Elaine Mosakowski have studied more than 2,000 managers in 60 countries. They have identified three sources of cultural intelligence.[24]

Head. Before visiting India, Todd Anderson should have learned as much as possible about the host country's customs, religion, politics, morals, social structure, food, table manners, and the roles of men and women. He should have been more open-minded and willing to suspend judgment—to think before acting.

Body. You can win the respect of foreign hosts, guests, or colleagues by showing you understand their culture. The way you shake hands, order coffee, or accept a gift, can demonstrate, to some degree, you have already entered their world. Talking business

Cultural intelligence means taking the time to learn and understand some of the customs and traditions of cultures other than your own, such as the proper way to bow when you greet someone in Japan.

over lunch is a common practice in the United States, but it would be offensive in some countries. Research conducted at the University of Michigan found that job candidates who adopted some of the mannerisms of recruiters with cultural backgrounds different than their own were more likely to receive an offer.[25]

Heart. Adapting to a new culture is much easier when you have confidence in yourself. In Chapter 4, we introduced *self-efficacy*, the belief that you can achieve what you set out to do. A major source of *self-efficacy* is the experience of mastery in your area of specialization. Past successes give us the confidence and motivation needed to increase our cultural intelligence. Our head, body, and heart can work together to help us act appropriately in new cultures or among people with unfamiliar backgrounds.

COPING WITH YOUR ANGER AND THE ANGER OF OTHERS

9-4   **Anger** may be defined as the thoughts, feelings, physical reactions, and actions that result from unacceptable behavior by others. Anger is almost always a response to *perceived* injustice, and may dissolve with a deeper understanding of the cause. Learning to effectively deal with anger (anger management) is a key component of any healthy lifestyle.[26]

Anger is almost always a response to perceived injustice.

Managing Your Anger

Learning to address your own anger and the anger of other people is one of the most sophisticated and mature skills people are ever required to learn. Intense anger takes control of people and distorts their perceptions, which is why angry people often make poor decisions.[27]

Intense anger often takes the form of rage. Examples include road rage, air rage, and customer rage. Research indicates that 70 percent of customers who have problems with a product or service are in a *rage* by the time they talk with a customer-service worker.[28] We are also witnessing more incidents of "workplace rage." Workplace rage can take the form of yelling, verbal abuse, and physical violence. It is more likely to occur when workers are stressed by long hours, unrealistic deadlines, cramped quarters, excessive electronic messages, lack of recognition, bullying incidents, or some combination of these factors.

Anger Management

Melissa Hoistion was enjoying dinner with her husband and their three children at a nice restaurant until the waiter disappeared for about 20 minutes. Her husband became increasingly agitated and suddenly screamed, "Excuse me!" at another waiter across the room. He then stormed off to complain to the manager. When the original server finally returned to the table the man yelled, "Where the hell have you been for the last 45 minutes?"[29] Where would you place him on the National Anger Management Association scale? (See Figure 9.2.)

Scream at your boss? Throw your cell phone at your computer monitor? Drive recklessly on a crowded highway? If so, you may find yourself headed to an anger

Figure 9.2 ■ National Anger Management Association Scale of Anger

Source: Melinda Beck, "When Anger is an Illness," *Wall Street Journal*, March 9, 2010.

management class. Some organizations are not waiting for anger problems to surface. Several hospitals have programs for "disruptive" physicians and a few state bar associations now require "civility" training for lawyers renewing their licenses. And some fit-throwing celebrities, road ragers, and delinquent teens are embracing anger management classes as an alternative to jail sentences.[30]

Keeping Cool in Angry Times

These are stressful times, so it is imperative that you develop an anger management program that works for you. Here are some ways to keep your temper in check.[31]

1. Keep an anger diary or journal. Monitor what makes you angry so you can find ways to cope with your triggers. Record not only the source of irritation, but the feelings that surface when you become angry.
2. Reframe the situation that triggered anger. Try not to see every inconvenience or frustration as a personal affront.
3. Be aware of how you talk to yourself. Do you keep telling yourself how "awful this is" and making yourself feel like a victim?
4. If you feel a blow-up coming on, give yourself a time-out before acting on it. For example, wait 15 minutes before you say something, or an hour before you send an e-mail.
5. Pay more attention to the important things in life and recognize that most frustrations, inconveniences, and indignities are trivial and temporary.

Effective Ways to Express Your Anger

Buddha said, "You will not be punished for your anger, you will be punished by your anger." Buddhist teachings tell us that patience is the best antidote to aggression.[32] Intense anger that is suppressed will linger and become a disruptive force in your life unless you can find a positive way to get rid of it. Expressing feelings of anger can be therapeutic, but many people are unsure about the best way to self-disclose this emotion.

To express anger in ways that will improve the chances that the other person will receive and respond to your message, consider these suggestions:

1. *Avoid reacting in a manner that could be seen as emotionally unstable.* If others see you as reacting irrationally, you will lose your ability to influence them. Jared Sandberg, writing in the *Wall Street Journal*, describes a major sale that faltered when only half the order arrived. When the bad news was delivered by the receiving clerk, the salesperson lost his temper and told the clerk, "I will ruin your life." He then threw the clerk against the wall and kicked his own cubicle wall, which in turn collapsed onto his neighbor's cubicle wall.[33] Lesson learned: Don't shoot the messenger.

2. *Do not make accusations or attempt to fix blame.* It would be acceptable to begin the conversation by saying, "I felt humiliated at the staff meeting this morning." It would not be appropriate to say, "Your comments at the morning staff meeting were mean spirited and made me feel humiliated." The latter statement invites a defensive response.[34]

3. *Express your feelings in a timely manner.* The intensity of anger can actually increase with time. Also, important information needed by you or the person who provoked your anger may be forgotten or distorted with the passing of time.

4. *Be specific as you describe the factors that triggered your anger, and be clear about the resolution you are seeking.* The direct approach, in most cases, works best.

---

human
RELATIONS
in Action

ANGER POISONS DECISION MAKING

Recent research has documented the psychological effects of residual anger. Let's assume you have a serious quarrel with your spouse before going to work. This anger-fueled event will likely color your decisions throughout the day and your work will suffer for it. Angry people tend to rely on cognitive shortcuts rather than engaging in systematic reasoning. They are also quick to blame individuals rather than study all aspects of the problem situation.

Source: Jennifer S. Lerner and Katherine Shonk, "Decision Making," *Harvard Business Review*, September 2010, p. 26.

How to Handle Other People's Anger

Dealing with other people's anger may be the most difficult human relations challenge we face. The following skills can be learned and applied to any situation where anger threatens to damage a relationship.

1. *Recognize and accept the other person's anger.* The simple recognition of the intense feelings of someone who is angry does a lot to defuse the situation.

2. *Encourage the angry person to vent his or her feelings.* By asking questions and listening carefully to the response, you can encourage the person to discuss the cause of the anger openly. Zane Bond, team leader at a software company help desk, never takes an angry call personally. He listens intently and tries to start building a relationship. After learning the details of the customer's problem he tells them confidently, "We are going to fix this."[35]

3. *Do not respond to an angry person with your own anger.* To express your own anger or become defensive will only create another barrier to emotional healing. When you

respond to the angry person, keep your voice tone soft. Keep in mind the old biblical injunction, "A soft answer turns away wrath."[36]

4. *Give the angry person feedback.* After venting feelings and discussing specific details, the angry person will expect a response. Briefly paraphrase what seems to be the major concern of the angry person and express a desire to find ways to solve the problem. If you are at fault, accept the blame for your actions and express a sincere apology.

VIOLENCE IN THE WORKPLACE

9-5   Any discussion of workplace violence is likely to bring to mind a lone employee walking into the office or plant and shooting coworkers or supervisors. These are the images most often presented by the media. The Workplace Violence Research Institute has developed a definition of **workplace violence** that may be more appropriate for today's work environment:

> *Any act against an employee that creates a hostile work environment and negatively affects the employee, either physically or psychologically. These acts include all types of physical or verbal assaults, threats, coercion, intimidation, and all forms of harassment.*[37]

Violence in the workplace is often triggered by loss of a job, conflict between the employee and management, or a personal tragedy, such as divorce or separation. Michele Coleman Mages, Senior Vice President at Pitney Bowes, a mail- and document-management company, says, "People bring all sorts of demons to work—from problems with spouses and kids to bipolar disease—that they shouldn't think they can solve on their own."[38]

Employee Sabotage

Employee sabotage is a problem that is causing nightmares throughout corporate America. It is often described as employee misconduct tinged with an edge of revenge. Employee sabotage may involve deliberate nonperformance, financial fraud, slander, destruction of equipment, arson, or some other act that damages the organization or the careers of people within the organization. Computer crimes have become a common form of sabotage. Computer sabotage by ex-workers is increasing.[39]

Preventing Workplace Violence

Incidents of workplace violence cost employers and others several billion dollars each year. This figure does not, of course, reflect the human suffering caused by acts of violence. Although violence cannot be eliminated, some steps can help curb violent behavior in the workplace.

1. *Use hiring procedures that screen out unstable persons.* In-depth interviews, drug testing, and background checks can help identify signs of a troubled past.
2. *Develop a strategy for responding to incidents before they actually occur.* Establish policies that make it clear that workplace violence incidents will not be tolerated. Every organization should establish a strong expectation of workplace civility. After an employee at Lockheed Martin's airplane-parts plant shot six coworkers to death, they formed a task force on workplace violence. One outcome of this action is a zero-tolerance policy (violators can be fired) for hostile or intimidating speech or actions.[40]

> *As the workplace gets leaner, it need not become meaner.*

3. *When employees are demoted, fired, or laid off, do it in a way that does not demoralize the employee.* When Intel reduced its workforce by 10,500, it used a highly structured process. Intel spokesman Chuck Mulloy says, "The key to making it work is very clear communications, what's going to happen and when."[41]

4. *Provide out-placement services for laid-off or terminated employees.* These services may include development of job-search skills, retraining, or, in cases where the employee is displaying signs of aggression, counseling.

5. *Establish a systematic way to deal with disgruntled employees.* This might involve providing a forum for employees who feel they have been treated unfairly.

6. *Provide supervisors and managers with training that will help them prevent workplace violence and deal effectively with violence if it does occur.* Workplace violence is a growing problem in America, but it is not a problem without solutions. As the workplace gets leaner, it need not become meaner.

EMOTIONAL STYLES

9-6 A good starting point for achieving emotional control is to examine your current emotional style. How do you deal with emotions? Your style started taking shape before birth and evolved over a period of many years. As an adult, you are likely to favor one of four different emotional styles when confronted with events that trigger your emotions.

Suppressing Your Emotions

Some people have learned to suppress their feelings as much as possible. They have developed intellectual strategies that enable them to avoid dealing directly with emotional reactions to a situation. In response to the loss of a loved one, a person may avoid the experience of grief and mourning by taking on new responsibilities at work. This is not, of course, a healthy way to deal with grief.

Hale Dwoskin, author of *The Sedona Method*, says suppression is "keeping a lid on our emotions, pushing them back down, denying them, repressing them, and pretending they don't exist."[42] He says habitual suppression is unhealthy and unproductive. Dwoskin says an alternative to inappropriate suppression and expression is releasing emotions, an approach he calls the Sedona Method (see Figure 9.3).

To continually suppress feelings, hide fears, swallow annoyances, and avoid displaying anger is not healthy. If suppressing your feelings becomes a habit, you create opportunities for mental and physical health problems to develop.

Capitulating to Your Emotions

People who display this emotional style see themselves as the helpless victims of feelings over which they have no control. By responding to emotion in this manner, one can assign responsibility for the "problem" to external causes, such as other people or unavoidable events. Some people would rather endure feelings of helplessness than find a positive solution to a problem. People who capitulate to their emotions are often overly concerned about the attitudes and opinions of others.[43]

Overexpressing Your Emotions

In a work setting, we need to be seen as responsible and predictable. One of the quickest ways to lose the respect and confidence of the people you work with is to frequently

Figure 9.3 ■ The Sedona Method

Hale Dwoskin, author of *The Sedona Method* and CEO of Sedona Training Associates *(http://www.sedonapress.com)*, developed a unique program for making positive changes in your life. He encourages everyone to let go of or release their unwanted emotions. A brief introduction to the process of releasing follows.

Step 1: Focus on an issue you would like to feel better about. You may be experiencing guilt or fear. Allow yourself to feel whatever you are feeling at this moment.

Step 2: Ask yourself one of the following questions:
- Could I let this feeling go?
- Could I allow this feeling to be here?
- Could I welcome this feeling?

Each of these questions points you to the experience of letting go.

Step 3: Ask yourself this basic question: Would I? Am I willing to let go?
Step 4: Ask yourself this simpler question: When?

Dwoskin suggests repeating these four steps as often as needed to feel free of a particular feeling.

Source: Hale Dwoskin, *The Sedona Method* (Sedona, AZ: Sedona Press, 2003), pp. 36–44.

display a lack of emotional control. Frequent use of foul and vulgar language, flared tempers, raised voices, and teary eyes are still regarded as unacceptable behavior by most coworkers and supervisors.

One acceptable way to cope with fear, anger, grief, or jealousy is to sit down with pen and paper and write a letter to the person who triggered these emotions. Don't worry about grammar, spelling, or punctuation—just put all your thoughts on paper. Write until you have nothing more to say. Then destroy the letter. Once you let go of your toxic feelings, you will be ready to deal constructively with whatever caused you to become upset.[44] Another approach is to express your feelings through daily journal entries. Studies indicate that a significant emotional uplift and healing effect can result from spending as little as five to ten minutes a day writing about whatever issues or problems are getting you down.[45]

Accommodating Your Emotions

At the beginning of this chapter, we said an emotion can be thought of as a feeling that influences our thinking and behavior. Accommodation means you are willing to recognize, accept, and experience emotions and to attempt to react in ways appropriate to the situation. This style achieves an integration of one's feelings and the thinking process. People who display the accommodation style have adopted the "think before you act" point of view. It would be normal to feel defensive or angry during a negative performance review by your boss. However, career coaches advise against acting on these emotions. They suggest taking a day or two to digest the feedback and create an appropriate response.[46]

Do we always rely on just one of these four emotional styles? Of course not. Your response to news that a coworker is getting a divorce may be very different from your response to a demeaning comment made by your boss. You may have found appropriate ways to deal with your grief but have not yet learned to cope with the fear of making a team presentation. Dealing with our emotions is a very complex process.

STRATEGIES FOR ACHIEVING EMOTIONAL CONTROL

9-7 Each day, we wake up with a certain amount of mental, emotional, and physical energy that we can spend throughout the day. If we allow toxic thoughts and unpleasant feelings to deplete our energy, we have no energy to change our life or to give to others.[47] Our emotions do have an impact on our health. The link between emotions and health is quite strong for negative feelings that are associated with anger, anxiety, and depression. Some 30,000 heart attacks each year are triggered by momentary anger, according to research conducted at Harvard University.[48] We can learn to discipline the mind and banish afflicting thoughts that create needless frustration, waste energy, and deplete our immune system. In this, the final part of the chapter, we share with you some practical suggestions for achieving greater control of the emotions that affect your life.

Identifying Your Emotional Patterns

We could often predict or anticipate our response to various emotions if we would take the time to study our emotional patterns—to take a running inventory of circumstances that touch off jealousy, fear, anger, or some other emotion. Journal entries can help you discover emotional patterns. Record not only your conscious feelings, such as anxiety or guilt, but feelings in your body, such as a knot in your stomach or muscle tension.

If you don't feel comfortable with journal writing, consider setting aside some quiet time to reflect on your emotional patterns. A period of quiet reflection will help you focus your thoughts and impressions. Becoming a skilled observer of your own emotions is one of the best ways to achieve greater emotional control.

Becoming a skilled observer of your own emotions is one of the best ways to achieve greater emotional control.

In addition to journal writing and quiet reflection, there is one more way to discover emotional patterns. At the end of the day, construct a chart of your emotional landscape. Make a chart (see Table 9.1) of the range of emotions you experienced and expressed during the day.[49] Your first entry might be "I woke up at 6:00 a.m. and immediately felt ___." The final entry might be "I left the office at 5:30 p.m. with a feeling of ___." What emotions surfaced throughout your workday? Resentment? Creative joy? Anxiety? Boredom? Contentment? Anger? Reflect on the completed chart and try to determine which patterns need to be changed. For example, you might discover that driving in heavy traffic is a major energy drain. Repeat this process over a period of several days in order to identify your unique emotional patterns.

Fine-Tuning Your Emotional Style

Once you have completed the process of self-examination and have identified some emotional patterns you want to change, it is time to consider ways to fine-tune your emotional style. Bringing about discipline within your mind can help you live a fuller, more satisfying life. Here are four things you can begin doing today.

Table 9.1 ■ Charting Your Emotional Landscape

TIME	CIRCUMSTANCE	EMOTION
6:00 a.m.	Alarm goes off. Mind is flooded by thoughts of all the things that must be done during the day.	Anxiety
7:10 a.m.	Depart for work. Heavy traffic interferes with plan to arrive at work early.	Anger and helplessness
8:00 a.m.	Thirty-minute staff meeting scheduled by the boss lasts fifty minutes. No agenda is provided. Entire meeting seems a waste of time.	Anger and frustration
9:35 a.m.	Finally start work on creative project.	Contentment
10:15 a.m.	Progress on project interrupted when coworker enters office, sits down, and starts sharing gossip about another coworker.	Anger and resentment
11:20 a.m.	Progress is made on creative project.	Contentment
1:45 p.m.	Creative project is complete and ready for review.	Joy and contentment
2:50 p.m.	Give project to boss for review. She says she will not be able to provide any feedback until morning. This delay will cause scheduling problems.	Frustration
4:00 p.m.	Attend health insurance update seminar sponsored by human resources department. No major changes are discussed.	Boredom
5:40 p.m.	Give up on a search for a missing document, turn off computer, and walk to parking lot.	Relief and fatigue

- *Take responsibility for your emotions.* How you view your emotional difficulties will have a major influence on how you deal with them. If your frustration is triggered by thoughts such as "I can never make my boss happy" or "Things always go wrong in my life," you may never achieve a comfortable emotional state. By shifting the blame to other people and events, you cannot achieve emotional control.

- *Put your problems into proper perspective.* Why do some people seem to be at peace most of the time, while others seem to be in a perpetual state of anxiety? People who engage in unproductive obsessing (irrational thinking) are unable or unwilling to look at problems realistically and practically, and they view each disappointment as a major catastrophe. To avoid needless misery, anxiety, and emotional upsets, use an "emotional thermometer" with a scale of 0 to 100. Zero means that everything is going well, and 100 denotes something life-threatening or truly catastrophic. Whenever you feel upset, ask yourself to come up with a logical number on the emotional thermometer. If a problem surfaces that is merely troublesome but not terrible, and you give it 60 points, you are no-doubt overreacting. This mental exercise will help you avoid seeing every inconvenience or frustration as a "big deal."[50]

- *Take steps to move beyond toxic emotions such as envy, anger, jealousy, or hatred.* Some people are upset about things that happened many years ago. Some even nurse grudges against people who have been dead for years. The sad thing is that the negative feelings remain long after we can achieve any positive learning from them.[51] Studies of divorce, for example, indicate that anger and bitterness can linger a long time. Distress seems to peak one year after the divorce, and many people report that it takes at least two years to move past the anger.[52] When negative emotions dominate one's life, whatever the reason, individual talk therapy can provide relief.

■ *Give your feelings some exercise.* Several prominent authors in the field of human relations have emphasized the importance of giving our feelings some exercise. Leo Buscaglia, author of *Loving Each Other*, says, "Exercise feelings. Feelings have meaning only as they are expressed in action."[53] Sam Keen, author of *Fire in the Belly*, said, "Make a habit of identifying your feelings and expressing them in some appropriate way."[54] If you have offended someone, how about sending that person a note expressing regret? If someone you work with has given extra effort, why not praise that person's work? Make a decision to cultivate positive mental states, such as kindness and compassion. A sincere feeling of empathy, for example, will deepen your connection to others.

LOOKING BACK: SUMMARY OF LEARNING OBJECTIVES

1. Describe how emotions influence our thinking and behavior.

We carry inside us a vast array of emotions that can help us cope with our environment. An emotion can be thought of as a feeling that influences our thinking and behavior. Feelings are activated by a variety of events. Angry feelings may surface when another employee borrows something without your permission. Feelings of grief will very likely follow the loss of a close friend. The need to discover ways to achieve emotional balance has never been greater. We sometimes suffer from a lack of emotional balance because we learn to inhibit the expression of certain emotions and to overemphasize the expression of others.

2. Explain the critical role of emotions in the workplace.

Emotions play a critical role in the success of every organization. Emotional undercurrents are present in almost every area of the organization, and they influence employee morale, customer loyalty, and productivity.

3. Describe the major factors that influence our emotional development.

Our emotional development is influenced by temperament (the biological shaper of personality), our unconscious mind, and cultural intelligence. These influences contribute to the development of our emotional intelligence. Throughout the long process of emotional development, we learn different ways to express our emotions.

4. Learn how to cope with your anger and the anger of others.

Appropriate expressions of anger contribute to improved interpersonal relations, help us reduce anxiety, and give us an outlet for unhealthy stress. We must also learn how to handle other people's anger. It takes a great deal of effort to learn how to deal with our own anger and the anger of others.

5. Understand the factors that contribute to workplace violence.

Workplace violence encompasses a wide range of activities, including homicides, hostile remarks, physical assaults, and sabotage directed toward the employer or other workers. Although violence cannot be eliminated, steps can be taken to curb violent employee behavior in the workplace.

6. Identify and explain the most common emotional styles.

To achieve emotional balance, we need to start with an examination of our current emotional style. When confronted by strong feelings, we are likely to display one of four different emotional styles: suppressing emotions, capitulating to them, overexpressing them, or accommodating them.

7. Describe strategies for achieving emotional control.

Emotional control is an important dimension of emotional style. The starting point in developing emotional control is to identify your current emotional patterns. One way to do this is to record your anger experiences in a diary or journal. Additional ways to identify emotional patterns include setting aside time for quiet reflection and developing a chart of your emotional landscape.

KEY TERMS

emotion, 186
emotional intelligence, 187
emotional labor, 189
temperament, 190

unconscious mind, 190
Transactional Analysis, 191
culture, 191
cultural intelligence, 192

anger, 193
workplace violence, 196

CAREER INSIGHT

Some job interviews are mismanaged by the employer. Poorly trained interviewers often talk too much. They may want to tell you endless details about the job and the company. You may learn only what the interviewer wanted you to hear, and the company learned very little that's useful about you. During the interview you should talk most of the time. Be prepared to assert yourself if the interviewer is talking too much. Here are some points you need to make during the interview:

- Why do you want this job?
- What makes you a good candidate for this job?
- What are your career plans? How does this job fit those goals?

Of course you do not want to talk too much about yourself. After you make your points, invite questions and do your best to create a real dialogue.

Source: Bruce Clark, "Speak Up or You'll Blow the Interview," *News & Observer*, January 9, 2011, p. 3E.

TRY YOUR HAND

1. Recall the last time you were angry at another person or were a victim of a situation that made you angry. For example, someone you trusted divulged some personal information about your family history or accused you of an unethical practice at work. Then answer the following questions:
   a. Did you express your anger verbally? Physically?
   b. Did you suppress any of your anger? Explain.
   c. What results did you experience from the way you handled this situation? Describe both positive and negative results.
   d. If you could relive the situation, would you do anything differently? Explain.

2. To learn more about the way you handle anger, record your anger responses in a journal for a period of five days. When anger surfaces, record as many details as possible. What triggered your anger? How intense was the anger? How long did your angry feelings last? Did you express them to anyone? At the end of the five days, study your entries and try to determine whether any patterns exist. If you find this activity helpful, consider keeping a journal for a longer period of time.

3. To learn more about how emotions influence your thinking and behavior, complete each of the following sentences. Once you have completed them all, reflect on your written responses. Can you identify any changes you would like to make in your emotional style?
   a. "When someone accuses me of a wrongdoing, I usually ..."
   b. "When I feel frustrated, my response is ..."
   c. "When I am fearful, I ..."
   d. "My response to a lack of recognition is ..."
   e. "When I am disappointed, my response is to ..."

4. Many people have an anger-management problem. Although anger is a natural human emotion, the mismanagement of anger can result in serious interpersonal-relations problems. The National Anger Management Association is an organization dedicated to the advancement of anger management. NAMA recognizes there are varied techniques and methods for treating anger management. The NAMA Anger Management Specialist Certification Program has been popular in recent years. Visit the NAMA website at www.namass.org and become acquainted with this certification program and the other services offered by NAMA.

CRITICAL THINKING CHALLENGE

Anger builds when we perceive an injustice. Take time to remember a few occasions when someone's behavior triggered a torrent of anger in you. With pen and paper (not your computer), start writing about the reasons for your anger. Keep writing until your feelings become more focused and the reasons for your anger more clear. Keep writing until the anger is fully voiced. Then reflect on what you have learned that can be applied to anger management situations in the future.

SELF-ASSESSMENT EXERCISE

For each of the following statements, circle the number from 1 to 5 that best represents your response to each statement: (1) strongly disagree (never do this); (2) disagree (rarely do this); (3) moderately agree (sometimes do this); (4) agree (frequently do this); (5) strongly agree (almost always do this).

	1	2	3	4	5
A. I am able to solve problems and make decisions in a logical manner without allowing my emotions to interfere.	1	2	3	4	5
B. My relationships with people at home, school, and work do not suffer because of my expressions of anger or impatience.	1	2	3	4	5
C. I have developed effective ways to cope with my own anger and the anger of others.	1	2	3	4	5
D. I am familiar with, and can apply, several strategies for achieving emotional control.	1	2	3	4	5

After identifying your response to each item, select an attitude or skill you would like to improve. Prepare a written goal and then describe the steps you will take to achieve this goal.

YOU PLAY THE ROLE

You are currently manager of a bank branch that employs 26 people. About three weeks ago, you learned that one of your employees, Wesla Perez, needed time off to spend with a parent who was very ill. You approved the time off without hesitation. Soon, you learned that the parent (mother) had died. On Monday morning, Wesla will return to work. You plan to meet with Wesla and express your condolences. In this role-play exercise, a member of your class will play the role of Wesla Perez. The name you will use during the role-play is Evony Hillison.

BELOW THE SURFACE | THE ULTIMATE MAKEOVER

This chapter opens with an introduction to Selina Lo, president and CEO of Ruckus Wireless. After establishing several computer networking startups she was offered the top job at Ruckus. She was well-known for identifying new markets and then building products based on new technologies to exploit those markets. Born in Hong Kong, Selina Lo received here B.S. in Computer Science from the University of California at Berkeley.

Throughout the 1990s, Lo was one of Silicon Valley's most aggressive and successful salespeople. Later, when she assumed management positions, she maintained her aggressive style. After working two years for Lo, a vice president begged her to please let him report to someone else. He said, "I can't handle working for you. You cause me huge amounts of anxiety."

Lo was also stingy with praise because she didn't need it. She explains that in Chinese culture, it's considered bad manners to praise your children. Lo knows that one way to build rapport with her employees is to be a good listener. A skilled multi-tasker, she now forces herself to stop everything when employees come into her office. Lo is also better able to control her temper. "I've found if you control your temper, it dies down a little bit at a time, like a fire."[55]

QUESTIONS

1. At some point in your life, you will likely work for a boss who is very capable, but lacks patience, seldom gives praise, and often becomes angry. What steps can you take to help this person become a more effective manager?

2. Selina Lo says her management style includes unflinching transparency about all aspects of performance. In the realm of employee performance, how can a manager achieve a high degree of transparency?

CLOSING CASE | IS ROMANCING A COLLEAGUE OKAY?

Romance at work has become more common in recent years, but some relationships do have unintended consequences. Several years ago, Wal-Mart Stores sent an investigator to Guatemala City on a top secret assignment: spy on a factory inspection manager who was suspected of having intimate relations with a female colleague who traveled with him. After four days of surveillance, the investigator confirmed that sexual relations between the two employees did occur. In accordance with Wal-Mart's "no fraternization" policy, the inspection manager was fired.[56] More recently, Harry Stonecipher, Boeing Company's former president and CEO, lost his job when the board of directors learned about his consensual extramarital affair with a female executive.

Today, men and women often work alongside each other in almost equal numbers, sharing long hours and job pressures. Although romance at work is more acceptable today, it is still viewed as a major productivity disrupter by many consultants, human-resource professionals, and executives. Consider the romance that developed at Slingshot, a Dallas interactive-advertising agency.

A pair of workers who started dating were equals on the job and behaved appropriately at work (no giggling in the break room or making eyes at each other across the room). However, when they started going out to lunch with each other every day, coworkers on their seven-person team "felt excluded and it created a lot of negativity" according to Owen Hannay, chief executive at Slingshot.[57]

Critics of romance at work say companies should be concerned when relationships create conflicts of interest and lower job performance. The use of pet names, kissing, and hand-holding can be distracting to other workers. Many workers take an "adult" approach to romance in a work setting. Andrea Holland met her boyfriend when she interviewed him two years ago for a job at Access Communications, a public relations firm. The attraction was immediate. After working together on the same team for three months, they began dating. They kept their relationship quiet. Several months later, they told their bosses that the relationship was serious. They were put on separate teams and sit across the office from each other.[58]

Although critics of romance at work make some valid points, the truth is corporate America is getting more comfortable with love in the workplace. Statistics show that one-third of employees will date someone at work, and up to 20 percent will find their spouse or partner at work.

QUESTIONS

1. Should organizations establish policies that prevent dating a coworker? A supervisor? Explain your answer.

2. Can you think of a situation where employment of married couples would create problems for a firm? Explain your answer.

CHAPTER 9 ENDNOTES

1. Leigh Buchanan, "The Ultimate Business Makeover," *Inc.*, March 2009, p. 60; Selina Lo President & CEO [cited 8 March 2012]. Available from info@ruckuswireless.com; INTERNET.

2. Leigh Buchanan, "The Ultimate Business Makeover," *Inc.*, March 2009, pp. 60–61.

3. Ibid.

4. Douglas A. Bernstein, Louis A. Penner, Alison Clarke-Stewart, and Edward J. Roy, *Psychology*, 9th ed. (Mason, OH: Wadsworth Cengage Learning 2012), p. 446.

5. Carol S. Pearson, "The Emotional Side of Workplace Success," *The Inner Edge*, December 1998/ January 1999, p. 3.

6. Daniel Goleman, *Emotional Intelligence* (New York: Bantam Books, 1995), pp. 34 and 43; Stephen R. Covey, "Questions for Covey," *Training*, July/ August 2007, p. 40.

7. Daniel Goleman, *Working with Emotional Intelligence* (New York: Bantam Books, 1998), pp. 24–28; Robert Kreitner, *Management*, 10th ed. (Boston: Houghton Mifflin, 2007), p. 447.

8. John Selby, *Conscious Healing* (New York: Bantam Books, 1989), p. 32.

9. Hara Estroff Marano, "Love's Destroyer," *Psychology Today*, July/August 2009, p. 65.

10. James Georges, "The Not-So-Stupid Americans," *Training*, July 1994, p. 90.

11. Tim Sanders, *Love Is the Killer App* (New York: Crown Business, 2002), pp. 17–18.

12. Ibid., p. 23.

13. Ron Zemke, "Contact! Training Employees to Meet the Public," *Service Solutions* (Minneapolis: Lake-wood Books, 1990), pp. 20–23.

14. Monika Rice, "The Perils of a Fake Smile," *Spirituality & Health*, July/August 2011, p. 27.

15. Peter J. Frost, *Toxic Emotions at Work* (Boston: Harvard Business School Press, 2007), pp. 5–7.

16. Ibid., p. 3.

17. Douglas A. Bernstein, Louis A. Penner, Alison Clarke-Stewart, and Edward J. Roy, *Psychology*, 9th ed. (Mason, OH: Wadsworth Cengage Learning 2012), pp. 484–485.

18. William C. Menninger and Harry Levinson, *Human Understanding in Industry* (Chicago: Science Research Associates, 1956), p. 29.

19. Joan Borysenko, *Guilt Is the Teacher, Love Is the Lesson* (New York: Warner Books, 1990), p. 70.

20. Visit the Wikipedia (http://www.wikipediea.org) or Businessballs (http://www.businessballs.com) Web sites for a comprehensive overview of TA Theory.

21. Bernstein et al., *Psychology*, p. 25–26.

22. P. Christopher Earley and Elaine Mosakowski, "Cultural Intelligence," *Harvard Business Review*, October 2004, p. 139. Also see "Cultivating Cultural Intelligence," by Neal Goodman, *Training*, March/April 2011, p. 38.

23. *Outsourced* [accessed 8 December 2008]. Available from http://www.netflix.com; INTERNET.

24. P. Christopher Earley and Elaine Mosakowski, "Cultural Intelligence," pp. 141–142.

25. Ibid., p. 141.

26. Harold H. Bloomfield and Robert K. Cooper, *The Power of 5* (Emmaus, Pa.: Rodale Press, 1995), p. 334; Redford Williams and Virginia Williams, *Anger Kills* (New York: HarperCollins, 1993), p. 3; Redford Williams, "Why Anger Kills," *Duke Medicine Healthline*, Winter 2007, p. 11.

27. Kimes Gustin, *Anger, Rage, and Resentment* (West Caldwell, N.J.: St. Ives' Press, 1994), p. 1.

28. Sue Shellenbarger, "How to Keep Your Cool in Angry Times," *Wall Street Journal*, September 22, 2010, p. D3.

29. Elizabeth Bernstein, "This Loved One Will Explode in Five, Four…," *Wall Street Journal*, December 14, 2010, p. D1.

30. Melinda Beck, "When Anger Is An Illness," *Wall Street Journal*, March 9, 2010, p. D1.

31. Ibid., p. D6.

32. Pemna Chödrön, "The Answer to Anger and Other Strong Emotions," *Shambhala Sun*, March 2005, p. 32.

33. Jared Sandberg, "Shooting Messengers Makes Us Feel Better But Work Dumber," *Wall Street Journal*, September 11, 2007, p. Bl.

34. Rolland S. Parker, *Emotional Common Sense* (New York: Barnes & Noble Books, 1973), pp. 80–81.

35. Sue Shellenbarger, "How to Keep Your Cool in Angry Times," *Wall Street Journal*, September 22, 2010, p. D3.

36. Les Giblin, *How to Have Confidence and Power in Dealing with People* (Englewood Cliffs, N.J.: Prentice-Hall 1956), p. 37.

37. "Workplace Violence: An Employer's Guide" [accessed 12 December 2008]. Available from http:// www.workviolence.com; INTERNET.

38. Carol Hymowitz, "Bosses Have to Learn How to Confront Troubled Employees," *Wall Street Journal*, April 23, 2007, p. Bl.

39. Jennifer J. Laabs, "Employee Sabotage: Don't Be the Target," *Workforce*, July 1999, pp. 32–42; Michelle Conlin and Alex Salkever, "Revenge of the Downsized Nerds," *BusinessWeek*, July 30, 2001, p. 40.

40. Anne Fisher, "How to Prevent Violence at Work," *Fortune*, February 21, 2005, p. 42.

41. Pete Carey, "Economic Instability May Lead to Danger," *The Roanoke Times*, November 28, 2008, p. 8.

42. Hale Dwoskin, *The Sedona Method* (Sedona, Ariz.: Sedona Press, 2003), p. 30.

43. Walton C. Boshear and Karl G. Albrecht, *Understanding People: Models and Concepts* (San Diego: University Associates, 1977), pp. 41–46.

44. Chris Hill and Toby Hanlon, "Twenty-Six Simple Ways to Change How You Feel," *Prevention*, August 1993, p. 63.

45. Bloomfield and Cooper, *The Power of 5*, p. 368; Jill Neimark, "Open Mind Open Heart," *Spirituality & Health*, May/June 2008, p. 14.

46. Erin White, "Review Went Badly? Stay Cool, Find a Fix or Look to Move On," *Wall Street Journal*, May 23, 2006, p. B7.

47. Don Miguel Ruiz, *The Four Agreements* (San Rafael, Calif.: Amber-Allen Publishing, 1997), p. 111.

48. Daniel Goleman, Editor *Healing Emotions* (Boston: Shambhala Publications, Inc., 1997), p. 33; Melinda Beck, "When Anger Is An Illness," *Wall Street Journal*, March 9, 2010, p. D6.

49. Sam Keen, *Fire in the Belly—On Being a Man* (New York: Bantam Books, 1991), p. 242.

50. Arnold A. Lazarus and Clifford N. Lazarus, *The 60-Second Shrink* (San Luis Obispo, Calif.: Impact, 1997), pp. 10–11.

51. Borysenko, *Minding the Body, Mending the Mind*, p. 169.

52. Ellen Safier, "Our Experts Answer Your Questions," *Menninger Letter*, May 1993, p. 8.

53. Leo F. Buscaglia, *Loving Each Other* (Thorofare, N.J.: Slack, 1984), p. 160.

54. Keen, *Fire in the Belly*, p. 242.

55. Leigh Buchanan, "The Ultimate Business Makeover," *Inc.* March 2009, pp. 59–61; Selina Lo President & CEO [cited 8 March 2012]. Available from info@ruckuswireless.com; INTERNET.

56. Spencer Morgan, "The End of the Office Affair?" *Bloomberg Businessweek*, September 20, 2010, pp. 73–75.

57. Sue Shellenbarger, "For Office Romance, the Secret's Out," *Wall Street Journal*, February 10, 2010, p. D2.

58. Rachel Beck, "Take Tips to Heart Before Romance at Work," *News & Observer*, February 14, 2010, p. 3E.

Anderson Ross/Blend Images/Getty Images

Building Stronger Relationships with Positive Energy

TIP OF THE ICEBERG | THE LINSANITY PHENOMENON

Jeremy Lin played high school basketball in a gymnasium near the Stanford University campus. But coaches there did not seriously recruit him. He was a good student and a good player, but coaches from major universities did not see his potential. Lin sent film of himself to programs in the Ivy and Patriot Leagues, but only Harvard and Brown showed serious interest in him. No Division I school offered Lin a scholarship.[1]

Lin, a Taiwanese-American economics major, played point guard for the Harvard University Crimson from 2006 to 2010. After earning his economics degree from Harvard, Jeremy Lin was not drafted by any NBA teams. He did play briefly for the Golden State Warriors and the Houston Rockets, but was later dumped by both teams. His play time at the New York Knicks was minimal until he replaced some stars who were sidelined due to injuries. Almost overnight, the legend of Lin started growing. Lin scored 136 points in his first five starts, the most by any NBA player since 1976.

While Jeremy Lin was living the dream, a wave of positive energy enveloped Madison Square Garden (home of the Knicks) and the entire New York Knicks organization. Attendance at Knicks games increased sharply, TV viewer average increased 66 percent, and Lin's jersey sales ranked number 1 on NBAstore.com.[2]

Then, without warning, the Linsanity phenomenon came to an end. The popular Knicks point guard damaged his knee and needed surgery. He missed the rest of the season. At the end of the season in 2012, Lin was acquired by the Houston Rockets.

Our work should provide a major source of positive energy, but too many workers are not fully engaged or satisfied. This chapter provides groundbreaking information that will help you reenergize your life and achieve a higher level of contentment at work and at home.

This chapter discusses the impact of positive energy on both individual and group behavior. **Energy** can be defined as the capacity for work, or the force that helps us do things with vitality and intensity. The chapter examines the field of positive psychology, the power of positive feedback, various types of positive reinforcement, and the reasons why many people have difficulty

Popular basketball player Jeremy Lin serves as one example of how positive energy can rapidly spread among teammates and the outside community. During his time with the New York Knicks, game attendance skyrocketed, and his achievements inspired others who yearned to live their dreams.

expressing positive thoughts and feelings. A section of the chapter is devoted to awards and incentive programs that a variety of organizations use.

POSITIVE ENERGY CONTRIBUTES TO IMPROVED INTERPERSONAL RELATIONSHIPS

10-1 It is positive energy that helps us cope with disappointments, uncertainty, and work that is physically and mentally demanding. In the presence of positive energy, people feel uplifted, encouraged, and empowered. Positive energy helps us remain balanced in a work environment that is increasingly characterized by change and uncertainty[3].

Energy: An Important Force in Our Lives

Judith Orloff, author of *Positive Energy* and pioneer in the field of energy psychiatry, says *energy* is a term with many intriguing dimensions. In basic terms, it is the "get-up-and-go," the stamina that gets you through the day. Envision energy as having one of two qualities: either positive or negative. Positive energy is supportive, loving, and nurturing. Negative energy is fearful, judgmental, and depleting. How you respond to people and places determines, to a large degree, your energy level. Dr. Orloff makes an interesting observation regarding the impact of relationships on our energy level: "Each millisecond of our relationships is governed by a give and take of energy. Some people make us more electric or at ease. Others suck the life right out of us."[4]

POSITIVE PSYCHOLOGY: THEORY AND INITIATIVES

10-2 **Positive psychology** is a recent branch of psychology that focuses on positive human functioning. Marty Seligman, former president of the American Psychological Association, founded positive psychology. He challenged the field to look at what makes life worth living; what a healthy person acts like, rather than a suffering one. Positive psychologists seek to discover what makes life more fulfilling.[5]

Seligman, in his best-selling book *Authentic Happiness*, states that the field of psychology has been consumed by the study of mental illness. He wanted the field to focus more heavily on happiness and fulfillment.

Positive psychology finds its roots in the research conducted by Abraham Maslow, Carl Rogers, Erich Fromm, and other humanistic psychologists. They developed theories and practices that focus on aspects of the human condition that lead to happiness and fulfillment.[6]

The Happiness Advantage

After more than a decade of groundbreaking research in the field of positive psychology, an important principle surfaced: We become more successful *when* we are happier and more positive. Most people think happiness is achieved once they reach a certain goal, thinking that a promotion at work, a raise in pay, or some other accomplishment will result in happiness. The research is finding, however, that happiness and optimism *fuel* performance and achievement. When people work with a positive mindset, performance on nearly every level—productivity, creativity, engagement—improves.[7]

Total Person Insight

"All else being equal, happy people have better relationships, are more likely to thrive at work, and also live better and longer."

Source: Tal Ben-Shahar, *Happier*, New York: McGraw-Hill, 2007, p. 33.

Tal Ben-Shahar, one of Harvard University's most popular lecturers, defines happiness as the overall experience of pleasure and meaning. This definition does not pertain to a single moment but to a generalized aggregate of one's experiences. Several studies show that happy people are successful across multiple life domains, including friendship, marriage, work performance, income, and health.[8]

Developing the Happiness Advantage

Shawn Achor, author of *The Happiness Advantage*, says training your brain to be positive is not so different than training your muscles at the health club. As you develop new habits, you rewire the brain. Achor says there are several simple activities that correlate with positive change.[9]

- Jot down three things you are grateful for. Most of us have many things to be grateful for in our lives.
- Write a positive message to someone who has given you support in some way.
- Meditate at your desk for two minutes.
- Exercise for 10 minutes.
- Take two minutes to record in a journal the most meaningful experience of the past 24 hours.

One brief exercise a day can generate a greater sense of well-being. Achor says one of the most effective activities is engaging positively with coworkers. Team leaders who recognize the accomplishments of team members, for example, encourage them to work with a positive mind-set.

POSITIVE EMOTIONS: PREREQUISITE FOR A FULFILLING LIFE

10-3 Throughout recent periods of great uncertainty and turbulence, negative energy became a powerful force. Many people went to work every day wondering if they would be the next victim of a merger, buyout, downsizing effort, or business closing. Some wondered if they would be able to cope with rapid technological changes. Stressful working conditions caused by rising productivity demands and long hours can also be the source of negative energy. In a negative, stressful work climate, these pressures often result in physical fatigue, decreased optimism, and less happiness.

As noted earlier in this chapter, most scientists in the field of psychology have focused on negative states such as depression, fear, and anxiety. Psychologist Barbara Fredrickson has spent the past two decades investigating the influence of positive emotions. Her findings are the subject of an important book entitled *Positivity*. Fredrickson and other researchers in the field of positive psychology have given us lab-tested tools needed to counter the powerful force of negative energy.

Gratitude

Gratitude is one of those human qualities that benefits the giver and the receiver. Grateful people experience higher levels of positive emotions such as joy, enthusiasm, happiness, and optimism. The practice of gratitude protects us from destructive impulses such as envy, resentment, and bitterness. One way to develop positive energy is to keep a "gratitude journal." Each day, write down three to five things for which you are grateful.[10]

Take time to notice small gestures of goodwill and learn to thank the givers of such gifts. Write thank-you notes frequently. Linda Kaplan, author of *The Power of Nice*, says, "In business, being nice has been underrated."[11]

Total Person Insight

"Gratitude opens your heart and carries the urge to give back—to do something good in return, either for the person who helped you or someone else."

Source: Barbara Fredrickson, *Positivity*, New York: Crown Publishers, 2009, p. 41.

Pride

Pride is the emotional high that follows performance and success. This definition was developed by Jon Katzenbach, author of *Why Pride Matters More Than Money*. He notes that the power of pride is obvious when you observe the high-performing work forces at Southwest Airlines, Marriott, the U.S. Marine Corps, and Zappos. "Pride is a natural by-product of the successes of those organizations," says Katzenbach.[12]

Katzenbach notes that pride-builders can be found at all levels of the organization. They often get involved in the everyday problems of their employees. Roy Pelaez leads a work force of 426 people who clean airplanes for Delta Airlines and Southwest Airlines. Many of his staff are recent immigrants, so he brought in an English-language teacher to tutor employees twice a week on their own time. He scheduled Friday citizenship classes to help employees become U.S. citizens. To help single mothers, Pelaez arranged for certified babysitters subsidized by government programs.[13]

Serenity

Our lives are so filled with stimuli it's very difficult to relax and replace tension with feelings of peace. Barbara Fredrickson says **serenity** is a mindful state that carries the urge to savor your current circumstances and find ways to integrate them into your life more fully.[14] It can come with rewarding work in your garden or curling up with a good book. Try to carve out a little quiet time each day for meditation or spending time in nature.

Interest

From time to time something new or different draws your attention. These circumstances require effort and increased attention on your part. When you uncover a new set of challenges you may need to build new skills, and engage in new learning. Depending on the new interest you may once again feel open and alive.[15] New interests motivate us to use our brain in different ways.

Social Support

Shawn Achor says one of the most effective ways to train the brain to be positive is to engage positively with people in your social support network (friends and coworkers for example). A study conducted at Ochsner Health System, a large medical provider serving southeast Louisiana, helps illustrate the effectiveness of social support as a tool for employee happiness. Achor worked with the medical staff to develop an approach called the "10/5 Way."

- When employees walk within 10 feet of another person in the hospital, they must make eye contact and smile.
- When they walk within 5 feet, they must say hello.

The training involved 11,000 employees, leaders, and physicians. Since the introduction of 10/5, Ochsner employees have experienced higher job satisfaction scores and more satisfied patients.[16]

These are just a few examples of the tools available to help you get in touch with your positive emotions. With a little creative thinking you can discover additional activities.

THE POWER OF THE 3-TO-1 RATIO

Dr. Barbara Fredrickson, world-renowned researcher in the area of positive psychology, encourages us to seek a 3-to-1 positivity ratio. This means that for every negative emotional experience you endure, you need to experience at least three positive emotional experiences that uplift you. Persons who can experience positive emotions in a 3-to-1 ratio with negative ones create a healthier, more vibrant, and flourishing life.

Source: Barbara Fredrickson, *Positivity*, New York: Crown Publishers, 2009, pp. 31–33.

WORKPLACE CULTURES THAT CREATE POSITIVE ENERGY

10-4   It is positive energy that helps us cope with disappointments, uncertainty, and work that is physically and mentally demanding. In the presence of positive energy, people feel uplifted, encouraged, and empowered.

Research conducted by Leadership IQ, a Washington D.C. based consulting firm, indicates that cultures that foster a high level of employee engagement maintain a high level of employee satisfaction.[17] Consider these examples:

Joie de Vivre boutique hotels. Chip Conley, founder of this successful hotel chain, says half of his workers clean toilets all day. To encourage them to feel meaning in their work, he schedules training programs that bring together small groups of housekeepers from different hotels. They are asked to describe what would happen if they weren't on the job each day. Carpets wouldn't be vacuumed, trash would pile up, and bathrooms would fill up with wet towels. Then based on the answers, they are encouraged to come up with alternative names for housekeeping. The suggestions are great:

- "Serenity Keepers"
- "Clutter Busters"
- "Peace-of-mind Police"

At the end of the training session, workers develop a real sense of their contribution to customer satisfaction.[18]

Dirt Pros. Dirt Pros is an integrated facilities maintenance company dedicated to improving the health, appearance, and operation of the built environment. Marcell Haywood, a former point guard for the Florida State Seminoles, founded the company. He says his management style is to engage employees as much as possible. The decision to switch to using only environmentally friendly chemicals and products was influenced by employee feedback. Haywood says:

> *"Rather than tell them what to do, I ask a lot of questions about what we should be doing. Our turnover rate is one-third of what is typical in the industry. I'm proud of that."*[19]

Borrego Solar Systems. Most organizations are searching for new ideas—ways to improve products and services, cut costs, and increase revenue. Mike Hall, CEO of Borrego Solar Systems, realized that workers could be a source of new ideas, but they needed encouragement. Some were introverted and reluctant to come forward with suggestions. Hall decided to organize an internal contest he called the innovation challenge. All 55 of Borrego's employees were encouraged to submit ideas for improving the business. Two quarterly employee contests were introduced to employees, each with a $500 prize. All Borrego Solar Systems employees review the contest entries and winners are determined by a company-wide secret ballot. Several of the winning ideas have already been put in place.[20]

Total Person Insight

"Most great ideas for enhancing corporate growth and profits aren't discovered in the lab late at night, or in the isolation of the executive suite. They come from the people who daily fight the company battles, who serve the customers, explore new markets, and fend off the competition."

Source: J. C. Spender and Bruce Strong, "Who Has Innovative Ideas? Employees." *Wall Street Journal*, August 23, 2010, p. R5.

The Container Store. At Container Store, a 39-store retail chain, emphasis is placed on taking care of employees. Kip Tindell, CEO of this progressive company, says, "If

Figure 10.1 ■ Important Elements of a Successful Small Workplace Culture

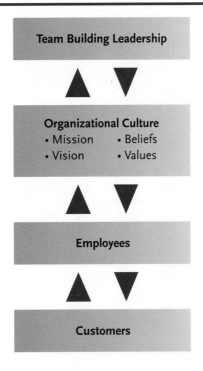

you take care of your employees, they'll take care of your customers." Sales staff receive 241 hours of training; the industry average is 8. Health-care coverage is offered to part-timers. Employees with children can work a special schedule: 9 a.m. to 2 p.m. Employees heaped praise on management for avoiding layoffs during the recent recession.[21]

These examples indicate that many small businesses have developed a workplace environment where employees feel engaged. They realize that when you maximize the talents of your workers, the customer wins. Figure 10.1 indicates the features of a work-place culture that emphasizes cooperation, information sharing, and mutual respect.

POSITIVE REINFORCEMENT—CREATING POSITIVE ENERGY

10-5   In recent years, researchers have quantified the cost of negativity in the workplace, and the results are quite shocking. Negative, or "actively disengaged," workers cost the U.S. economy between $250 and $300 billion a year according to the Gallup International Research and Education Center. The costs associated with negativity are even higher when you add on the expenses associated with employee turnover, absenteeism, fraud, and workplace injuries.[22]

A brief book entitled *How Full Is Your Bucket?* (*http://www.bucketbook.com*), written by Gallup Practice Leaders Tom Rath and Donald Clifton, provides a simple yet compelling strategy for reducing negativity in the workplace. After more than 50 years of comprehensive psychological and workplace research, they were inspired to develop the Theory of the Dipper and the Bucket (see Figure 10.2). According to Rath and Clifton, each of us has an invisible bucket. It is constantly being emptied or filled, depending on what others say or do to us. When our bucket is full, we feel great. A full bucket increases

Figure 10.2 ■ How Full is Your Bucket?

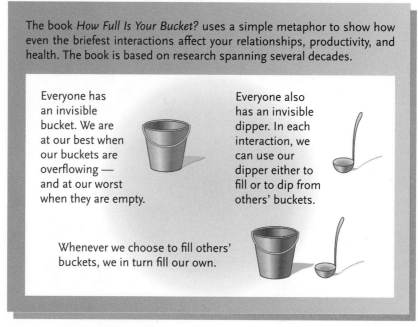

The book *How Full Is Your Bucket?* uses a simple metaphor to show how even the briefest interactions affect your relationships, productivity, and health. The book is based on research spanning several decades.

Everyone has an invisible bucket. We are at our best when our buckets are overflowing — and at our worst when they are empty.

Everyone also has an invisible dipper. In each interaction, we can use our dipper either to fill or to dip from others' buckets.

Whenever we choose to fill others' buckets, we in turn fill our own.

Source: Tom Rath and Donald O. Clifton, *How Full Is Your Bucket?* (New York: Gallop Press, 2004), p. 25.

our positive emotions and renews our energy. When it is empty, we feel awful. There are a lot of empty buckets in today's work force. Survey after survey has found that more than half of the workers in America say they do not feel appreciated in their current jobs.[23]

Each of us also has an invisible dipper. We can use that dipper to fill other people's buckets or our own bucket. When we use that dipper to dip from another person's bucket, we diminish that person and ourselves.

Positive Reinforcement Defined

The goal of positive reinforcement is to encourage productive behaviors. At PaeTec Communications, located near Rochester, New York, everything revolves around respect for the employee. Arunas Chesonis, CEO, sets an example for every employee by sharing financial information, acquisition plans, profits, and other information usually discussed only in the boardroom. He answers e-mails from every employee and expects everyone else to do the same. He rewards information sharing with personal thank-you notes, e-mails, and visits. This pattern is followed in other important areas such as customer service and honoring family life.[24] Positive reinforcement has never been more important than it is today. Large numbers of workers at all levels of organizations encounter energy-draining experiences at work and in their personal lives.

Support from Skinner

The research of B. F. Skinner at Harvard University has contributed to our understanding of reinforcement as a factor influencing the behavior of people in a work setting. Skinner maintained that any living organism will tend to repeat a particular behavior if that behavior is accompanied or followed by a reinforcer. A **reinforcer** is any stimulus that follows a response

Monty Rakusen/Cultura

Nearly all workers appreciate recognition for their accomplishments. They respond positively to notes, letters, gifts, awards, and comments that express appreciation.

and increases the probability that the response will occur again. **Positive reinforcers** strengthen a response if they are experienced after that response occurs.[25]

The Power of Recognition

No one should have to wait for an annual performance review for recognition and performance feedback. This is especially true for Generation Y workers (Millennials). Ron Alsop, author of *The Trophy Kids Grow Up: How the Millennial Generation Is Shaking Up the Workplace*, notes that many Millennials grew up receiving a great deal of affirmation and positive reinforcement. Now, they come into the workplace needy for more.[26] For this generation, frequent feedback is vital and often more important than salary or a company's name recognition.

Giving recognition is one of the easiest and most powerful ways to make an employee feel important and needed. When handled correctly, recognition can be an effective reinforcement strategy that ensures repetition of desired behaviors. The authors of *The One Minute Manager*, a book that has sold more than 13 million copies, point out that recognition in the form of praise need not take a great deal of time. The key is to pay attention to what others are doing and try not to miss an opportunity to use praise to generate positive energy. Table 10.1 provides some excellent tips on planning and delivering praise.

Total Person Insight

"A person's true character can be judged by how he treats those who can do nothing for him."

Source: Roy Chitwood, "Still Trying to Slip Past Gatekeepers? Forget it!" *Value-Added Selling 21*, December 26, 2003, p. 1.

Table 10.1 ■ One-Minute Praisings

ONE-MINUTE PRAISING CAN WORK WELL WHEN YOU:
1. Inform people up front that you'll be giving them feedback.
2. Offer positive reinforcement immediately.
3. Let them know specifically what they did well.
4. Pause for a moment of silence to let them understand how good you feel.
5. Tell them that you feel good about what they did right and that it positively influences the organization and its workers.
6. Offer a handshake or similar physical gesture that lets them know you support them.
7. Ask them to keep up the good work.

Source: "One Minute Praisings" from *The One Minute Manager* by Kenneth Blanchard and Spencer Johnson. 1981, 1982 by Blanchard Family Partnership and Candle Communications Corp., Inc. Reprinted by permission of HarperCollins Publishers, Inc.

Courtesy Can Be Contagious

The poet Alfred Tennyson once said, "The greater the man, the greater the courtesy." Courtesy means being considerate of others in small ways, showing respect for what others revere, and treating everyone, regardless of position, with consideration. In today's fast-paced world, the impact of courtesy can easily be overlooked. Rudeness flourishes in our society, so it is not surprising that common courtesies are sometimes forgotten. Someone arrives late for an important meeting but does not see the need to apologize or even explain why he is late. You schedule an important meeting with your team, and suddenly a member is talking to a friend on her cell phone. These behaviors create negative energy.

Active Listening

As discussed in Chapter 2, everyone feels a sense of personal value when speaking with a good listener. Active listening can be a powerful reinforcer. Active listening is the process of sending back to the speaker what you as a listener think the speaker meant in terms of both content and feelings.

People long for more authentic interactions with coworkers or bosses who are good listeners. *Dialogue*, as a specific practice, is being implemented in a number of progressive organizations. A *dialogue group* is a meeting where all participants agree to be especially aware of what they say, how well they listen, and how well they give feedback to others. This training activity is designed to promote self-reflection and increased self-awareness.[27]

Thank You

Two little words can greatly enhance your ability to improve interpersonal relations with friends, coworkers, and complete strangers: *thank you*. Thanking people isn't simply a matter of common courtesy. A major study involving 200,000 managers and employees showed that saying "thank you" correlates with the economic success of an organization. Giving thanks is a great motivational tool.[28]

Figure 10.3 ■ Job Interview Note

Dear Ms. Jarrett:

Thank you for taking the time to interview me for your upcoming opening in account development. I enjoyed meeting you and learning more about your successful publication.

As noted during our meeting, I managed the advertising department for the University of North Carolina student newspaper, print and on-line editions, over a two-year period. In the area of account development, my goal was to build long-term partnerships with our customers.

Please tell your assistant, Tina Jones, I appreciate her help in scheduling the interview. If a second interview is planned, please contact me at 643-292-9230 (cell).

Sincerely,

Paul L. Mason

Paul L. Mason

Peter Post, coauthor of *The Etiquette Advantage in Business* shares an experience he had while conducting a seminar. A young lady in the audience said, "Have I got a story for you." She applied for a job and was one of three finalists. The other applicants were in-house candidates. She got the job and later her new boss explained why she was hired. He said that after the interview, she was the only candidate who wrote a note to each person on the interview committee. The importance of a thank you cannot be overstated.[29]

A carefully prepared thank you note (see Figure 10.3) provides a great opportunity to gain a competitive edge in today's job market. If possible, link your skills to solving workplace problems you learned during the interview.

BARRIERS TO POSITIVE REINFORCEMENT

10-6   The material in this chapter is based on two indisputable facts about human nature. First, people want to know how well they are doing. Second, they appreciate recognition for their accomplishments. Performance feedback, encouragement, and positive reinforcement can satisfy these important human needs. People often say they prefer negative feedback to no feedback at all. "Don't leave me in the dark" is a common plea (spoken or unspoken) of most people.

If you want attention and appreciation, you must learn to give attention and appreciation.

Preoccupation with the Self

One of the major obstacles to providing positive reinforcement is preoccupation with the self. The term **narcissism** is often used to describe this human condition. Narcissism is a Freudian term alluding to the mythical youth who wore himself out trying to kiss his own reflection in a pool of water.

Deepak Chopra, author of *The Seven Spiritual Laws of Success*, encourages everyone to practice the "Law of Giving." This law states that you must give in order to receive. If you want attention and appreciation, you must learn to give attention and appreciation. If you want joy in your life, you must give joy to others. He says the easiest way to get what you want is to help others get what they want.[30]

The publication of *Random Acts of Kindness* and many people's acceptance of its central theme may have signaled a movement away from self-preoccupation. Random acts of kindness are those little things that we do for others without receiving payback. They involve giving freely, purely, for no reason.[31] Here are some examples from the book:

- Send a letter to a teacher you once had letting him or her know about the difference he or she made in your life.
- Write a card thanking a service provider for his or her care and leave it with your tip.

HOW TO WRITE A THANK YOU NOTE

Should thank you notes or notes in general be handwritten and sent via USPS or sent via electronic message? Peter Post, director of the Emily Post Institute, offers these suggestions.

- If you are in doubt, send a short electronic message right away and follow up with a handwritten note.
- An electronic message may be received, read, and then deleted, while a handwritten note may be opened, read, and might stay on the desk—a reminder of you—for hours or even days.
- Make an effort to write and send your note within 24 hours whenever possible.
- If you send a handwritten note, use quality notepaper.
- If your handwriting is not legible, it's OK to type the note and sign it.

Source: Peter Post, "The Note," *Training*, September/October 2010, p. 44.

Misconceptions About Positive Reinforcement

Some people fail to use positive reinforcement because they have misconceptions about this human relations strategy. One misconception is that people will respond to positive feedback by demanding tangible evidence of appreciation. "Tell people they are doing a good job, and they will ask for a raise" seems to be the attitude of some managers. Actually, just the opposite response will surface more often than not. In the absence of intangible rewards (such as praise), workers may demand greater tangible rewards.

A few managers seem to feel they will lose some of their power or control if they praise workers. Yet, if managers rely on power alone to get the job done, any success they achieve will no doubt be short-lived.

The "Too Busy" Syndrome

Ken Blanchard says, "We're often too busy or too stressed to remember that the recognition we crave, others crave as well."[32] When you are under a great deal of pressure to get your work done, and you are struggling to achieve some degree of work/life balance, it is easy to postpone sending a thank-you note or contacting someone simply for the purpose of saying "Thank you."

The key to solving this problem is planning. A consciously planned positive reinforcement program will ensure that recognition for work well done is not overlooked. One approach might be to set aside a few minutes each day to work on performance feedback and positive reinforcement activities (see Table 10.1).

Failing to Identify Commendable Actions

There are numerous opportunities to recognize the people you work with. By exercising just a little creativity, you can discover many actions that deserve to be commended.

Table 10.2 ■ Job Performance Behaviors to Be Reinforced

1. **Performance Related to Interpersonal Relations**
   a. Demonstrates empathy for customer needs and problems
   b. Is able to handle customer complaints effectively
   c. Is able to keep all employees well informed
   d. Cooperates with supervisory personnel in other departments
   e. Recognizes the accomplishments of employees
   f. Exhibits effective supervision of employees
2. **Personal Characteristics.**
   a. Is honest in dealings with people throughout the organization
   b. Is punctual
   c. Does not violate policies and procedures
   d. Maintains emotional stability
   e. Maintains a neat appearance
   f. Is alert to new ways to do the job better
3. **Management Skills.**
   a. Avoids waste in the use of supplies and materials
   b. Maintains accurate records
   c. Spends time on short- and long-range planning
   d. Takes steps to prevent accidents
   e. Delegates authority and responsibility
   f. Maintains quality-control standards

Assume you are the manager of a large auto dealership. One of the key people within your organization is the service manager. This person schedules work to be performed on customers' cars, handles customer complaints, supervises the technicians, and performs a host of other duties. If you want to give your service manager performance feedback and positive recognition, what types of behavior can you praise? Table 10.2 lists some examples.

Not Knowing What to Say or Do

Bob Nelson, author of *1001 Ways to Reward Employees*, reminds us that we can provide encouragement, praise, recognition, and rewards in a variety of ways. He encourages us to use thoughtful, personal kinds of recognition that signify true appreciation.[33] Many words and phrases can communicate approval. Here are several examples:

- "Good thinking!"
- "Thank you."
- "Excellent idea."
- "Keep up the good work."

And you can give recognition to others through some type of action. Here are some activities that show approval:

- Sending an employee to a workshop or seminar that covers a topic he or she is interested in

- Asking for advice
- Asking someone to demonstrate the correct performance or procedure for others
- Recognizing someone's work at a staff meeting

REWARDING INDIVIDUAL AND TEAM PERFORMANCE

10-7   In recent years, we have seen expanded use of positive reinforcement strategies in the workplace. In the past, we viewed positive reinforcement as the responsibility of supervisors and managers. This view was much too narrow. As shown in Figure 10.4, everyone in the organization has opportunities to recognize the accomplishments of others. Persons in supervisory and management positions can benefit from positive reinforcement initiated by subordinates.

Employees can also be encouraged to recognize the accomplishments of coworkers. In some cases, praise from a respected colleague is more important than praise from the boss. This is especially true when employees work together on a team.

The concept of teamwork and the growing popularity of various types of teams are changing the way companies structure their reward systems. If a work force is reorganized into self-directed work teams (discussed in Chapter 12), it makes sense to consider various types of team recognition plans. Such plans often emphasize the recognition of group performance rather than the recognition of individual performance.

Incentive Programs

Every year, organizations spend billions of dollars for incentives and awards given to their employees. This money is spent on televisions, vacation trips, rings, plaques, pins, certificates, stock options, merit pay, cash bonuses, and a host of other items. An **incentive program** is a planned activity designed to motivate employees to achieve an organizational objective.[34]

One of the most widespread developments in recent years has been the introduction of innovative incentive plans that reward increased productivity, improved quality, improved customer service, lower operating costs, or some combination of these factors. These plans include cash and noncash awards. The most common noncash awards include merchandise, travel opportunities, and recognition in the form of a plaque, trophy, pin, or letter of commendation.

Although the vast majority of U.S. companies use some type of incentive program, many do not achieve positive results. It is possible to design programs that provide

Figure 10.4 ■ Shared Responsibilities for Positive Reinforcement

benefits to the organization and the individual employee, but care must be taken during the planning stage. Here are a few incentive plan fundamentals:

- *Do not assume that financial rewards provide the most powerful incentive.* Stephen J. Dubner, coauthor of the best-selling book *Freakonomics*, says social and moral incentives are often more powerful.[35] An employee who is working excessive hours may value more time with family, socializing, and recreation. Rewards must satisfy individual needs.
- *Avoid incentives that might foster unethical behavior.* Some retail companies encourage sales personnel to push extended warranties—a high-profit item that many customers don't want or need. In some cases, these sales become the basis for measuring employee performance. Employees who don't meet established incentive goals may lose their job.[36]
- *Always field test incentive plans.* Several questions need to be answered: Is the plan easy to administer? Will employees support the plan? Employee input during the planning stage is very important.[37]

CHIPOTLE'S INCENTIVE PROGRAM

Steve Ells, founder of the popular Chipotle's restaurant chain, recognizes the importance of a good manager. The best Chipotle managers get the title "restauranteur" and a $10,000 bonus for each person they hire who starts as crew and goes on to become a manager.

Source: Jessica Shambora, "Chipotle's Rise," *Fortune*, October 18, 2010, p. 72.

Reexamining Our Ideas About Productivity

As a nation, we have progressed from a society of farmers, to a society of factory workers, to a society of knowledge workers. And now, according to Daniel Pink, author of *A Whole New Mind*, we are progressing yet again—to a society of creators and empathizers. He says the information age is giving way to a new world in which creative abilities and high-touch abilities mark the fault line between who gets ahead and who falls behind.[38] What type of organizational culture will bring out the best in these employees?

The Critical Importance of Environment

Positive energy flourishes in a supportive environment. Within the organization, there should be respect for each person, regardless of job title, duties performed, or earnings. The prevailing climate within the organization should also be positive. People must feel good about the organization, its leadership, and other employees. Positive energy comes naturally in a positive work environment. But positive energy will almost never flourish in a negative work environment.

LOOKING BACK: SUMMARY OF LEARNING OBJECTIVES

1. **Explain how positive energy contributes to improved interpersonal relationships.**

   Positive energy can have a major influence on employee morale and productivity. Encouragement, positive feedback, and other types of practices that create positive energy are important factors in improving interpersonal relationships.

2. **Describe the fundamentals of positive psychology.**

   Positive psychology is a recent branch of psychology that focuses on positive human functioning. Marty Seligman is considered the founder of the positive psychology movement. It is based on theories and practices that focus on aspects of the human condition that lead to happiness and fulfillment. Research indicates we become more successful when we are happier and more positive.

3. **Identify and discuss the positive emotions that contribute to a fulfilling life.**

   Research in the field of positive psychology has identified lab-tested tools needed to counter the powerful force of negative energy. The tools discussed in this chapter include gratitude, pride, serenity, interest, and social support.

4. **Describe workplace cultures that generate positive energy.**

   In the presence of positive energy, people feel uplifted, encouraged, and empowered. Organizations that foster a high level of employee engagement tend to maintain a higher level of employee satisfaction. Some of the best ideas for improving the organization come from front line employees.

5. **Understand how to use positive reinforcement to improve relationships and reward behavior.**

   Although many studies indicate that recognition of their accomplishments is important to employees, often more so than monetary rewards and job security, many people seem unable or unwilling to reward a job well done. Praise, pride, courtesy, active listening, written thank-you notes, incentives, and awards can be used to instill positive energy.

6. **Describe the major barriers to the use of positive reinforcement.**

   Preoccupation with self is a major obstacle to providing reinforcement to others. Self-centered persons are likely to overlook the accomplishments of others. Some people say a busy schedule does not allow them time to give recognition to others, and some people have difficulty identifying commendable actions. These and other barriers tend to minimize the use of positive reinforcement.

7. **Explain how to reward individual and team performance.**

   Individual and team performance are often rewarded through the use of incentive programs. Some of the most common incentive programs involving cash payments are gain sharing, profit sharing, production incentives, pay for knowledge, and suggestion programs. Employee stock options have also been popular in recent years.

KEY TERMS

energy, 207
positive psychology, 209
pride, 210

serenity, 211
reinforcer, 214
positive reinforcers, 215

narcissism, 217
incentive program, 220

CAREER INSIGHT

Information-age workers sometimes spend an entire day at work and little seems to get done. It is hard to feel a sense of accomplishment from work that is largely *invisible*. How do you define success in today's increasingly paperless work environment? When work is done in teams, it is difficult to pinpoint individual productivity. Even your boss may have difficulty recognizing your accomplishments. So, think about the type of work that will offer you a sense of accomplishment. How can you get in touch with your positive emotions when your work is largely invisible?

Source: Jared Sandberg, "A Modern Conundrum: When Work Is Invisible, So Are the Satisfactions," *Wall Street Journal*, February 19, 2008, p. B1.

TRY YOUR HAND

1. Organizations are continually searching for ways to reward various employee behaviors. Pretend you are currently working at an upscale retail clothing store and the manager asks you to help her design an incentive plan that would result in improved sales of clothing and accessories. She asks you to review and comment on the following options:
   a. Employee-of-the-month awards for highest sales. (A special plaque would be used to recognize each monthly winner.)
   b. Commission on sales. All employees would be given a 5 percent commission on all sales. Each salesperson would receive an hourly wage plus the commission.
   c. Time off. Employees who achieve sales goals established by management could earn up to four hours of paid time off each week.
   d. Prizes. Employees who achieve weekly sales goals established by management would be eligible for prizes such as sports or theater tickets,

dinner at a nice restaurant, gift certificates, or merchandise sold by the store.

   Rank these four options by assigning "1" to your first choice, "2" to your second choice, "3" to your third choice, and "4" to your fourth choice. Provide a written rationale for your first choice.

2. The authors of *Random Acts of Kindness* tell us that the little things we do for others can have big payoffs. These acts give us an outward focus that helps us move away from self-preoccupation. Plan and initiate at least two acts of kindness during the next week, and then reflect on the experience. What impact did the act have on the other person? How did you feel about this experience?

3. O. C. Tanner Company, founded in 1927, offers a wide range of awards and recognition programs. Visit www.octanner.com and review the various employee recognition strategies. Prepare a written summary of findings.

CRITICAL THINKING CHALLENGE

Throughout life we form habits that can have a major impact on our ability to develop positive relationships with others. Take a few minutes and reflect on the dipper and bucket metaphor. Do you find it easy or difficult to fill someone else's bucket? Your own bucket? Do you frequently dip from others' buckets?

SELF-ASSESSMENT EXERCISE

For each statement, circle the number from 1 to 5 that best represents your response: (1) strongly disagree (never do this); (2) disagree (rarely do this); (3) moderately agree (sometimes do this); (4) agree (frequently do this); (5) strongly agree (almost always do this).

	1	2	3	4	5
A. I can describe the fundamentals of positive psychology.	1	2	3	4	5
B. I understand how positive emotions contribute to a fulfilling life.	1	2	3	4	5
C. I understand and can apply several forms of positive reinforcement.	1	2	3	4	5
D. I make every effort to recognize the accomplishments of others and celebrate my own successes.	1	2	3	4	5

After identifying your response to each item, select an attitude or skill you would like to improve. Prepare a written goal and then describe the steps you will take to achieve this goal.

YOU PLAY THE ROLE

Peggy Klaus, author of *Brag! The Art of Tooting Your Own Horn Without Blowing It*, says, "You have to let the people above you know what you are doing, what skills you're developing, which goals you're achieving." She says, "Don't make them guess." Self-promotion has become more important today because many careers are being buffeted by downsizing, mergers, and business closings. For the purpose of this role-play, assume the role of Britten Higgins, a full-time employee in the computer electronics department of Best Buy. You have heard rumors that your department manager may be promoted. You hope to move up within the Best Buy organization, and advancing to department head would be an important first step. You have decided to meet with your manager and discuss two things: (1) your interest in becoming department head and (2) your accomplishments and the steps you have taken to prepare for advancement. Feel free to ad-lib the information you present during the role-play.[39]

BELOW THE SURFACE | DEVELOPING POSITIVE ENERGY

At the beginning of this chapter, you were given a brief introduction to the Linsanity phenomenon. A little known graduate of Harvard University suddenly becomes an NBA star playing for the New York Knicks. Prior to sustaining a major injury, he achieved success on and off the basketball court. He was named "Brand Ambassador" for Volvo Car Corporation and was involved in other marketing activities.

If you own a Chevrolet Volt or a Nissan Leaf, you get in the habit of checking your energy reserves. And you learn driving habits that permit you to drive further between battery recharges. Get in the habit of checking your own energy reserves. When it's time to recharge your personal batteries, consider these options:

- *Stop paying attention to bad news.* Reduce TV watching and cut back on time spent surfing the Web for non-professional reasons.

- *Stay connected to others.* Reconnect with those you love and stay in touch with friends. Stop eating alone. Humans are not wired to work solo.[40]

- *Restore your sleep.* Daytime stress can steal hours of deep sleep from you at night. The loss of deep sleep makes tomorrow more stressful. Before you go to bed, relax with a good book and some deep breathing.[41] Skip watching the evening news.

- *Give yourself a walk break.* Walking, biking, swimming, or some other exercise reduces stress and increases "feeling good" brain chemicals.[42]

- *Shake off dark moods.* Use happiness-inducing techniques such as meditation, expressing gratitude, writing in your journal about things you are thankful for, or reflecting on past events that make you feel good.[43]

QUESTIONS

1. This case problem describes a few ways to renew your energy at work or at home. Which of these activities would appeal to you?

2. In addition to the above activities, have you discovered other ways to renew energy in your life?

CLOSING CASE | THE ROLE OF PRIDE IN BUILDING HIGH MORALE

Paetec Communications wants its employees to engage in exceptional efforts to make customers happy. Arunas Chesonis, CEO of Paetec, realizes that high morale among his employees is an important key to good customer service. He wants each employee to feel a sense of pride in the company, so he makes every effort to recognize work done well. Rewards range from a personal note to a cruise vacation.

Jon R. Katzenbach, author of *Why Pride Matters More Than Money*, says employee pride is what drives high-performing organizations like Southwest Airlines, SAS Institute, the U.S. Marine Corps, and the Container Store. He offers the following tool kit for those who want to become effective pride builders:

- *Personalize the workplace.* This means get involved in the everyday problems of your employees. Managers at some Marriott hotels work with employees from several different countries. These workers often need help learning the English language, preparing to become American citizens, and finding affordable childcare services. Marriott realizes that any problem that affects employees will eventually affect their on-the-job performance.

- *Always have your compass set on pride, not money.* There is no doubt that financial rewards can help an organization attract and retain good people. However, monetary incentives motivate only a narrow set of behaviors and place an emphasis on self-interest that may not be in the best interests of the company. In recent years, monetary rewards have proven to be a risky source of motivation. Compensation programs can be manipulated by clever employees to their advantage.

- *Localize as much as possible.* "Don't wait for your organization or its leaders to instill pride," says Katzenbach. The best pride builders are quick to spot and recognize the small achievements that will instill pride in their people.

- *Make your messages simple and direct.* A pride building program should not be built on needless complexity. In some cases, a good story about an employee who went the extra mile to help a customer solve a problem can stir up feelings of pride.[44]

QUESTIONS

1. Some human resource department employees voice concerns when supervisors or team leaders get involved with the everyday problems of their workers. Discuss your thoughts regarding this issue.

2. Some leaders in business and industry say that worker pride is the byproduct of achievement. What are your thoughts? What factors constitute achievement at your local McDonald's restaurant? Your local community hospital?

3. Do you agree that pride building can be localized throughout the organization?

CHAPTER 10 ENDNOTES

1. Mark Viera, "Lin Proves Recruiting Is Still an Inexact Science," **News & Observer**, February 15, 2012, p. 3C.
2. Jason Gay, "The Likability of Jeremy Lin," **Wall Street Journal**, February 13, 2012, p. B10.
3. Marshall Goldsmith and Kelly Goldsmith, "How Happiness Happens," **Bloomberg Businessweek**, December 21, 2009, p. 92.
4. Judith Orloff, "Accessing Sacred Energy," **Spirituality & Health**, May/June 2004, pp. 48–51; Judith Orloff, **Positive Energy** (New York: Harmony Books, 2004), pp. 1–15, 288. More information regarding positive energy can be found in Barbara Frederickson, **Positivity** (New York: Random House, Inc., 2009).

5. Angela Winter, "The Science of Happiness," *The Sun*, May 2009, pp. 5–8.

6. "Positive Psychology," [accessed 24 March 2012] Available from www.en.wikipedia.org; INTERNET.

7. Shawn Achor, *The Happiness Advantage*, New York: Crown Publishing Group, 2010, pp. 15–16; Shawn Achor, "Positive Intelligence," *Harvard Business Review*, January–February 2012, pp. 100–102.

8. Tal Ben-Shahar, *Happier*, New York: McGraw-Hill, 2007, pp. 32–33.

9. Shawn Achor, "Positive Intelligence," *Harvard Business Review*, January–February 2012, pp. 100–101.

10. Sheldon Lewis, "Another Reason to List What You're Grateful For," *Spirituality & Health*, March/April 2008, p. 27. To learn more about the powerful influence of gratitude, read *Thanks! How the New Science of Gratitude Can Make You Happier*, by Robert Emmons (Boston: Houghton Mifflin, 2007).

11. "Have a Nice Day," *American Way*, January 1, 2007, p. 18.

12. Jon R. Katzenbach, *Why Pride Matters More Than Money* (New York: Crown Business, 2003), pp. 23–24.

13. John A. Byrne, "How to Lead Now," *Fast Company*, August 2003, pp. 62–70.

14. Barbara Fredrickson, *Positivity*, New York: Crown Publishers, 2009, p. 42.

15. Ibid., p. 43

16. Shawn Achor, "Positive Intelligence," *Harvard Business Review*, January–February 2012, p. 102.

17. Lauren Weber, "Workplace Cultures Come in Four Kinds," *Wall Street Journal*, February 7, 2012, p. B6.

18. Chip Conley, "The Idea That Saved My Company," *Inc. Magazine*, October 2007, pp. 43–44.

19. "Inc. 5000 Update: Dirt Pros," [accessed 30 March 2012] Available from www.info@dirtpros.com, INTERNET.

20. Darren Dohl, "Pipe Up, People! Rounding Up Staff Ideas," *Inc.* February 2010, pp. 80–81.

21. Kip Tindele, "The Professional Organizer," *Fortune*, September 3, 2007, p. 26; Milton Moskowitz and Robert Levering, "The 100 Best Companies to Work For," *Fortune*, February 6, 2012, p. 120.

22. Tom Rath and Donald O. Clifton, *How Full Is Your Bucket?* (New York: Gallup Press, 2004), pp. 31–33; "Employee Engagement" [accessed 3 December 2008]. Available from http://www.gallup.com; INTERNET.

23. Holly Dolezalek, "Don't Go," *Training*, July/August 2003, p. 52; Rath and Clifton, *How Full Is Your Bucket?*, pp. 39–40.

24. David Dorsey, "Happiness Pays," *Inc. Magazine*, February 2004, pp. 89–94.

25. Douglas A. Bernstein, Louis A. Penner, Alison Clarke-Stewart, and Edward J. Roy, *Psychology*, 9th ed. (Belmont, CA: Wadsworth, 2012), p. 209.

26. Ron Alsop, "The Trophy Kids Go to Work," *Wall Street Journal*, October 21, 2008, pp. Dl and D4. Profiles of several Generation Y employers can be reviewed in "Cool, Determined, and Under 30," *Inc.*, October 2008, pp. 97–105.

27. David Stewart, "Talk at Work: Do You Dialogue?" *Health & Healing*, Volume 5, 6 2002, pp. 2.

28. Nancy Lublin, "Two Little Words," *Fast Company*, November 2010, p. 56.

29. Peter Post, "The Note," *Training*, September/October 2010, p. 44.

30. Deepak Chopra, *The Seven Spiritual Laws of Success* (San Rafael, Calif.: Amber-Allen, 1994), pp. 30–31.

31. *Random Acts of Kindness* (Berkeley, Calif.: Conari Press, 1993), pp. 1, 54, 68, and 91.

32. Bob Nelson, *1001 Ways to Reward Employees* (New York: Workman, 1994), p. ix.

33. Ibid., p. xv.

34. "How to Run an Incentive Program," *Incentive*, July 1990, p. 2.

35. Stephen J. Dunbar, "The Freaky Side of Business," *Training*, February 2006, p. 8.

36. Joel Spolsky, "Employees Will Always Game Incentive Plans—Because the Geniuses Who Design Them Don't Anticipate How Employees Will Respond," *Inc.*, October 2008, p. 85.

37. Dave Murphy, "If You Want Gold, Give Them a Goal," *San Francisco Chronicle*, April 14, p. Jl; Jeff Barbian, "Golden Carrots," *Training*, July 2002, p. 18.

38. Daniel H. Pink, *A Whole New Mind* (New York: Riverhead Books, 2005), pp. 48–53.

39. Anne Fisher, "Show Off, Without Being a Blow-hard," *Fortune*, March 8, 2004, p. 68.

40. Michael Roizen and Mehmet Oz, "7 Ways to Recharge Your Personal Batteries," *Roanoke Times*, October 11, 2011, p. 3.

41. Ibid.

42. Ibid.

43. Sue Shellenbarger, "Thinking Happy Thoughts at Work," *Wall Street Journal*, January 27, 2010, p. D2.

44. John A. Byrne, "How to Lead Now," *Fast Company*, August 2003, pp. 62–70; Katzenbach, *Why Pride Matters More Than Money*, pp. 13–19, 47–67; Dorsey, "Happiness Pays," pp. 89–94.

Noel Hendrickson/Photographer's Choice RF/Getty Images

Developing a Professional Presence

TIP OF THE ICEBERG | PERSONAL BRAND DEVELOPMENT

During the summer, 23-year old Ashley Wilson worked as an intern for real estate attorney Michael Sandman; she had no intentions of getting into real estate herself. She always thought she would be a teacher. But Sandman gave her $400 to get a real estate license because he saw her potential. "Her personality is magnetic—though it's hard to put your finger on any one personal quality that makes Ashley so easy to connect with."

In her first real estate job, where the firm had sold only 18 houses during the previous two years, Ashley sold 16 houses in four months. In the next four years, she sold 270 new homes for total sales of $92.6 million. Not bad since this was her first job outside of babysitting. After Ashley took the real estate class, she began seeing herself as the next big realtor. She is now at Keller Williams Realty, a Raleigh, North Carolina firm, where she started the Wilson Realty Group. She reported a 380 percent increase in production during a down period that was perhaps the lowest for most realtors.[1]

Ashley's personal brand is described as high energy, knowledgeable, professional, and charismatic. Her LinkedIn profile contains nearly 40 referrals from clients and colleagues she has worked with who recommend her services. According to her clients, Ashley's top qualities are described as "high integrity, great results, personable, and expert." Ashley's personal brand is a result of her unique attributes, the professional presence she has worked hard to develop, and the ways she promotes her brand on networks like LinkedIn.

Branding can play a crucial role in your success. The authors of *Be Your Own Brand: A Breakthrough Formula for Standing Out from the Crowd* say branding can have a significant impact on your relationships, career, and life. Developing a strong personal brand involves all the small yet significant ways you express what you believe and how you present yourself to others. This chapter presents an abundance of personal brand development information.[2]

227

Developing an effective brand takes time and results in a loyal customer following. Over the past decade, the word "Apple" has evolved into much more than just a company name; it is a global brand that permeates through its products and into the customers it serves, creating a strong demand from those customers to be among the first to experience their "next big thing."

PROFESSIONAL PRESENCE—AN INTRODUCTION

11-1   There are many personal and professional benefits to be gained from a study of the concepts in this chapter. You will acquire new insights regarding ways to communicate positive impressions during job interviews, business contacts, and social contacts made away from work. You will also learn how to shape an image that will help you achieve your fullest potential in the career of your choice.

This is not a chapter about ways to make positive impressions with superficial behavior and quick-fix techniques. We do not discuss the "power look" or the "power lunch." The material in this chapter will not help you become a more entertaining conversationalist or win new customers by pretending to be interested in their hobbies or families. In his book *The Seven Habits of Highly Effective People*, the late Stephen Covey says that the ability to build effective, long-term relationships is based on character strength and not quick-fix techniques. He notes that outward attitude and behavior changes do very little good in the long run *unless* they are based on solid principles governing human effectiveness. These principles include service (making a contribution), integrity and honesty (which serve as a foundation of trust), human dignity (every person has worth), and fairness.[3]

Professional Presence and Personal Branding—A Definition

Professional presence is a dynamic blend of poise, self-confidence, control, and style that empowers us to be able to command respect in any situation.[4] Once acquired, it

Harley-Davidson has thrived by creating a strong brand image that appeals to baby boomers. Jay Leno says big Harleys will always be seen as older guys' bikes. Today, Harley-Davidson realizes that women are a growing segment of the market. The challenge is meeting the needs of smaller, less muscular riders, but avoiding creating brand confusion.

permits us to project a confidence that others can quickly perceive the first time they meet us. Obviously, to *project* this confidence, you need to *feel* confident.

Your **personal brand** describes the attributes and the image you wish to portray to others when they think of you. For example, words like dependable, passionate, loyal, creative, and professional are all attributes that portray a positive image. Your personal brand is comprised of many things including your unique strengths and abilities, the value and service you provide to others, and your personal values.

Your personal brand is manifested through the actions and behaviors you communicate to others. It shines through in everything you do, from face-to-face meetings to your online presence. In situations like a job interview or being considered for a promotion, your personal brand may be the only differentiator that helps you stand out from others with similar skills. Throughout your career, your personal brand is an asset to manage and protect, and the information you learn in this chapter will help you develop your personal brand, and reinvent it throughout your career.

THE IMPORTANCE OF MAKING A GOOD FIRST IMPRESSION

11-2   As organizations experience increased competition for clients, patients, or customers, they are giving new attention to the old adage "First impressions are lasting ones." Research indicates that initial impressions do indeed tend to linger. Therefore, a positive first impression can be thought of as the first step in building a long-term relationship.

Ann Demarais and Valerie White, authors of *First Impressions*, say the secret to a good first impression is "social generosity"—helping others feel good about themselves. This requires shifting your focus from your own feelings to making others feel good. When you meet someone for the first time, you need to put others' needs and feelings before your own.[5]

The Primacy Effect

> *The development of professional presence begins with a full appreciation of the power of first impressions.*

The development of professional presence begins with a full appreciation of the power of first impressions. The tendency to form and retain impressions quickly at the time of an initial meeting illustrates what social psychologists call a **primacy effect** in the way people perceive one another. The general principle is that initial information tends to carry more weight than information received later. First impressions establish the mental framework within which a person is viewed, and information acquired later is often ignored or reinterpreted to coincide with this framework.[6]

Demarais and White note that in a first impression, others see only a very small sample of you, a tiny percentage of your life. But to them, that small sample represents 100 percent of what they know of you. And they will weigh initial information much more heavily than later information.[7]

The First Few Seconds

Malcolm Gladwell, best-selling author of several books including *The Tipping Point* and *Blink*, learned a great deal about the power of first impressions a few years ago when he let his close-cropped hair grow wild. His life changed immediately. He got far more speeding tickets and was routinely pulled out of airport security lines for special attention. People he met knew nothing about him except that he had shaggy hair, but they were ready to think the worst.[8]

Gladwell was inspired to try to understand what happens beneath the surface of rapidly made decisions. His findings later appeared in *Blink: The Power of Thinking Without Thinking*. He says most of us would like to think our decision making is the result of rational deliberation, but in reality, most decisions are made subconsciously in a split second.[9]

Total Person Insight

> "At its heart, branding addresses a hard professional reality: For a successful long-term career, do not look to your company or industry to take care of you. As in every other arena of life, you must take care of yourself. A well-built brand will be your life raft."
>
> Source: Estée Lauder executive Phebe Port; Judith Sills, "Becoming Your Own Brand," *Psychology Today*, January/February, 2008, p. 62.

Most people assess another person very quickly and then settle on a general perception of that individual. Research conducted at Carleton University in Ottawa indicates that people are registering like and dislikes in as little as 1/20th of a second.[10] It is very difficult for us to reverse that first impression. For example, Paula rushed into a restaurant for a quick lunch—she had to get back to her office for a 1:30 p.m. appointment. At the entrance of the main dining area was a sign reading "Please Wait to Be Seated." A few feet away, the hostess was discussing a popular movie with one of the waitresses. The hostess made eye contact with Paula but continued to visit with the waitress. In this situation,

Brad Barket/Getty Images

Malcolm Gladwell, author of the best-selling book *Blink The Power of Thinking Without Thinking*, discovered that wearing long, shaggy hair has consequences. Some people who knew nothing about him were ready to think the worst.

Paula immediately formed a negative impression of the hostess, even though no words were exchanged. She quickly left the restaurant. Unfortunately, the hostess may not have been fully aware of the negative impression she communicated to the customer.

Assumptions versus Facts

The impression you form of another person during the initial contact is made up of both assumptions and facts. Most people tend to rely more heavily on **assumptions** during the initial meeting. If a job applicant sits slumped in the chair, head bowed, and shoulders slack, you might assume the person is not very interested in the position. If the postal clerk fails to make eye contact during the transaction and does not express appreciation for your purchase, you may assume this person treats everyone with indifference. Needless to say, the impression you form of another person during the initial contact can be misleading. The briefer the encounter with a new acquaintance, the greater the chance that misinformation will enter into your perception of the other person. The authors of a popular book on first impressions state that "depending on assumptions is a one-way ticket to big surprises and perhaps disappointments."[11]

Cultural Influence

Cultural influences, often formed during the early years of our life, lead us to have impressions of some people even before we meet them. People often develop stereotypes

"I'm not wasting my life online—I'm building my brand."

of entire groups. Although differences between cultures are often subtle, they can lead to uncomfortable situations. We need to realize that the Korean shopkeeper is being polite, not hostile, when he puts change on the counter and not in your hand. Some Asian students do not speak up in class out of respect for the teacher, not boredom.[12]

Norine Dresser, author of *Multicultural Manners—Essential Rules of Etiquette for the 21st Century*, notes that it is becoming more difficult for organizations to develop policies that do not offend one ethnic group or another. She argues that it is the collective duty of the mainstream to learn the customs and practices of established minority groups.[13]

THE IMAGE YOU PROJECT

11-3 **Image** is a term used to describe how other people feel about you. In every business or social setting, your behaviors and appearance communicate a mental picture that others observe and remember. This picture determines how they react to you. Think of image as a tool that can reveal your inherent qualities, your competence, your attitude, and your leadership potential. If you wish to communicate your professional capabilities and create your own brand, begin by investing the time and energy needed to refine and enhance your personal image.

In many respects, the image you project is very much like a picture puzzle, as illustrated in Figure 11.1. It is formed by a variety of factors, including manners, self-confidence, voice quality, versatility (see Chapter 3), integrity (see Chapter 5), entrance and poise, facial expression, surface language, competence, positive attitude, and handshake. Each of these image-shaping components is under your control, though some are harder to develop than others. As you reflect on the image you want to project, remember that a strong personal brand is built from the inside out.

Figure 11.1 ■ Major Factors That Form Your Image

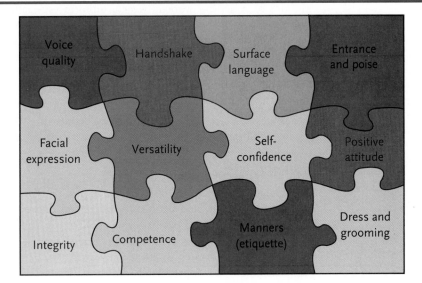

Surface Language

As noted earlier, we base opinions about other people on both facts and assumptions. Unfortunately, assumptions often carry a great deal of weight. Many of the assumptions we develop regarding other people are based on **surface language**, a pattern of immediate impressions conveyed by what we *see*—in other words, by appearance. The clothing you wear, your hairstyle, the fragrances you use, and the jewelry you display all combine to make a statement about you to others.

A good rule to follow is to dress for the job you want, not the job you have

According to many writers familiar with image formation, clothing is particularly important. Although a more relaxed dress code has evolved in some employment areas, people judge your appearance long before they judge your talents. It would be a mistake not to take your career wardrobe seriously. When making career wardrobe decisions, keep in mind these basic guidelines:[14]

1. *If you want the job, you have to look the part.* Establish personal dress and grooming standards appropriate for the organization where you wish to work. Before you apply for a job, try to find out what the workers there are wearing. When in doubt about what to wear, always dress a level up, never down.
2. *If you want the promotion, you have to look promotable.* A good rule to follow is to dress for the job you want, not the job you have. If you are currently a bank teller and want to become a branch manager, identify the successful branch managers and emulate their manner of dress.
3. *If you want respect, you have to dress as well as, or better than, your industry standards.* One would expect to find conservative dress standards in banking, insurance, accounting, and law, and more casual dress standards in advertising, sports entertainment, and agriculture.

Selecting Your Career Apparel

Millions of American workers wear a uniform especially designed for a particular job. The judges on the U.S. Supreme Court and the technicians at the local Midas Auto Service Shop have one thing in common—both groups wear a special uniform to work. Companies that have initiated extensive career apparel programs rely on uniforms to project an image of consistent quality, good service, and uniqueness.

Enterprise Rent-A-Car, the nation's largest recruiter of college students, requires its workers to follow conservative dress and grooming policies. Why? The company maintains that its personal appearance and grooming standards give it a marketing advantage.[15]

In addition to special-design uniforms, there is another type of **career apparel**, somewhat less predictable, worn by a larger number of people in the labor force. Here are two examples:

- A male bank loan officer would be appropriately dressed in a tailored gray or blue suit, white shirt, and tie. This same person dressed in a colorful blazer, sport shirt (without collar), and plaid slacks would be seen as too casual in most bank settings.
- A technician employed by an auto dealership that sells new luxury cars would be appropriately dressed in a matching gray, tan, or blue shirt and pants. The technician would be inappropriately dressed in jeans and a T-shirt.

Many organizations seek advice about career apparel from image consultants who have received certification from the Association of Image Consultants International or Global Protocol, Inc. The demand for etiquette and protocol consultants has increased in recent years.[16]

Clothing and accessories project a certain image, so you should give careful attention to the image you wish to convey to others. The information in Table 11.1 outlines four factors

Table 11.1 ■ Factors Influencing Your Choice of Clothing for Work

Dress codes are undergoing changes, and this complicates the selection of clothing for work. Use the four factors described here for guidance.

1. *Products and services offered.* In some cases, the organization's products and services more or less dictate a certain type of dress. For example, a receptionist employed by a well-established law firm is likely to wear clothing that is conservative, modest, and in good taste. These same dress standards would apply to a pharmaceutical sales representative who calls on medical doctors.

2. *Type of person served.* Research indicates that first impressions created by dress and grooming are greatly influenced by unconscious expectations. Throughout life, we become acquainted with real estate salespeople, nurses, police officers, and others employed in a wide range of occupations. We form mental images of the apparel common to each of these occupations. When we encounter someone whose appearance does not conform to our past experiences, we often feel uncomfortable.

3. *Desired image projected by the organization.* Some companies establish dress codes that help shape the image they project to the public. Walt Disney Company, for example, maintains a strict dress and grooming code for all its theme-park employees.

4. *Geographic region and countries.* In the U.S., dress in the Midwest, South, and Southwest tends to be more casual than dress in the Northeast. Employees who work in multi-national organizations must be aware that what they typically wear to work in one office is not necessarily appropriate in an office located in a different region or country. For example, employees in a southern California office may tend to dress more casually than their colleagues in London, Paris, or New York City.

that influence choices in career apparel. Use this information as a guide and do not give in to blind conformity. As noted by one consultant, "Effective packaging is an individual matter based on the person's circumstances, age, weight, height, coloring, and objectives."[17]

What is Business Casual?

The term **business casual** is used to describe the movement toward dress standards that emphasize greater comfort and individuality. Business casual is clothing that allows you to feel comfortable at work but looks neat and professional. For men, it usually means slacks, khaki pants, collared long-sleeved shirts, and shoes with socks. It usually does not include tattered, frayed, or wrinkled jeans; T-shirts with logos; sneakers or sandals; tank tops; sweat pants; or garish print sport shirts.[18]

Many companies have relaxed dress codes, allowing workers to dress casually. The trend for companies to adopt a "casual Friday" day has extended into a seven-days a week policy for several companies, especially those who work in high-tech jobs. Although the late Steve Jobs "uniform" of a black tee shirt, jeans, and sneakers are the uniform of choice for many Silicon Valley workers, it's hard for most people to carry off this look. Unless you are a billionaire or the next Mark Zuckerberg, you would be advised to steer clear of jeans and sneakers until you earn the clout to dress as you please.

Although no precise definition of business casual exists, the following guidelines will help you make wise choices.

1. *Wear dressier business clothing when meeting with customers or clients.* Avoid creating inconsistencies between your message and your appearance.
2. *Respect the boundary between work and leisure clothing. Don't let advertising dictate your choices.* Victoria's Secret once sold body-hugging spandex tube tops as "workplace wear." As a rule, people should avoid wearing anything that shows so much skin that it distracts other people from their work. Dress that is too casual sends the message you care more about your looks than what you know.
3. *Not all trends should be adopted.* Love body piercing and tattoos? If you can't live without it, do it in a discrete place. You might work at a Tokyo Joe's restaurant today, where body piercing is embraced as part of the "uniform," but you need to think about your career a few years from now. Regrets and collared shirts won't cover up that tattoo you've outgrown. And even though three-day stubble looks great on Bradley Cooper and Brad Pitt, it may not on other men.
4. *Wear clothing that is clean and neat and that fits well.* Casual dress codes tend to emphasize the importance of this guideline.
5. *Be discreet with jewelry, perfume, and cologne.* Nothing is more offensive to people than overbearing perfume and cologne, and many people have allergic reactions from it. When in doubt it's best to avoid it altogether at work and in the gym. Do not let "dress-down" influences rob you of common sense. You don't get a second chance to make a good first impression, so select your casual clothing with care. If you have to ask yourself, "Is this clothing acceptable?" you probably shouldn't wear it to work.

Your Facial Expression

Facial expressions are the cues most people rely on in initial interactions.

After your overall appearance, your face is the most visible part of you. Facial expressions are the cues most people rely on in initial interactions. They provide the clues by which others read your mood and personality and strongly influence people's reactions to each other. The expression on your face can quickly trigger a positive or negative reaction from those you meet. How you rate in the "good-looks" department is not nearly as important as your ability to communicate positive impressions with a pleasant smile and eye contact. Facial expressions usually reflect inner emotions more accurately than words. The smile is the most recognizable signal in the world. People everywhere tend to trust a smiling face.[19]

Your Entrance and Poise

The way you enter someone's office or a business meeting can influence the image you project. A nervous or apologetic entrance may ruin your chances of getting a job, closing a sale, or getting the raise you have earned. If you feel apprehensive, try not to let it show in your body language. Hold your head up, avoid slumping forward, and try to project self-assurance. To get off to the right start and make a favorable impression, follow these words of advice from Susan Bixler: "The person who has confidence in himself or herself indicates this by a strong stride, a friendly smile, good posture, and a genuine sense of energy. This is a very effective way to set the stage for a productive meeting. When you ask for respect visually, you get it."[20] Bixler says the key to making a successful entrance is simply believing—and projecting—that you have a reason to be there and have something important to present or discuss.

Your Voice Quality and Speech Habits

The tone of your voice, the rate of speed at which you speak (tempo), the volume of your speech, your ability to pronounce words clearly (diction), and your speech habits contribute greatly to the image you project. Consider these real-world examples:

- Kristy Pinand, a youthful-looking 23-year-old, routinely used "teen speak" when talking to colleagues and clients. Words such as "cool" and "like" were frequently part of her speech pattern. With feedback from her supervisor, she was able to correct the problem.[21]
- A senior project manager at a major financial-service company was surprised when his boss blamed his thick Brooklyn accent for his stalled advancement in the company. Despite his MBA, the project manager was speaking too fast and skipping many consonants. Rapid speech patterns can be very irritating to some people. His frequent use of "deez" and "doze" created the impression that he was poorly educated and inarticulate.[22]

A conscious effort to improve your voice begins with awareness. A tape or video recording of your conversations will help you identify problem areas. If you hear a voice that is too monotone, too nasal, too high-pitched, too weak, too insincere, or too loud, you can target the problem for improvement. A voice or speaking coach can provide helpful feedback to improve diction and delivery.

Your Handshake

When two people first meet, a handshake is the most typical physical contact between them. A handshake is a friendly and professional way to greet someone or to take leave, regardless of gender. The handshake can communicate warmth, genuine concern for the other person, and strength. It can also communicate aloofness, indifference, and weakness. Generally speaking, a firm (but not viselike) grip communicates a caring attitude, whereas a weak grip communicates indifference. Maintain eye contact and smile during a handshake to increase the positive impact of your handshake.

Throughout your career, you will likely meet people from many ethnic backgrounds. Each may have a ritual, which might include bowing, kissing, hugging, or giving a "high five." In Jamaica, for example, approval of someone or someone's idea may involve hitting fists.[23]

Total Person Insight

"Young people need to take charge of their career, people's perceptions of them, be self aware, network, and not wait for someone to do it for you."

Source: Estée Lauder executive Phebe Port, Emily Glazer, "Create a Positive Image," *News & Observer,* October 3, 2010, page 3.

HOW ONLINE PRESENCE INFLUENCES YOUR PERSONAL BRAND

11-4   When Scott Monty joined Ford Motor Company as the global digital and multimedia communications manager, he brought 3,500 Twitter followers with him and kept his Twitter handle @scottmonty rather than adding the Ford brand name. He now has 41,000 followers. He says, "I was Scott Monty before I came to Ford and I'll be Scott Monty after I leave Ford."[24]

Employees who work for large companies need to establish their own brand that stays with them throughout their career, but do so carefully when building upon the brand of their employer. When it's done right, both the employer and individual win. But getting it right is increasingly difficult. "The personal branding process can create stress within a corporation. People will wonder if you are merely trying to advance your own career, as opposed to contributing to the success of the organization," says[25] Jerry Wilson, senior vice president at Coca-Cola.

The challenge is using social media to add value to your current employer while you also transition into the next career move. Hubert Rampersad, founder of Amsterdam-based Personal Branding University says, "The focus should be on developing yourself not on promoting yourself."[26] Remember your online brand is directly linked to your off-line brand. People don't see your intensions. They can only judge you by what you say and post, and the behavior they observe.

Companies like Estee Lauder offer training programs to help employees navigate the challenges of social media while establishing and building their personal brands. *Brand You* is a year-long course for 30 Estee Lauder "emerging leaders" who are less than five years out of college to assist them with building their brand and taking charge of their career.[27]

HOW TO MAKE YOUR SOCIAL MEDIA PROFILE CONSISTENT WITH YOUR BRAND

- Your photo should look professional. It does not need to be taken by a professional photographer and in fact may look better if it is not. It's more important to capture your smile, warmth, and energy in the moment.
- Do your online profiles reflect the image you wish to portray, both in content and design? What you wear should be consistent with the profession that you are in or hope to join. Include recommendations from other people when appropriate. Save the photos of your dog, friends, siblings, or your boyfriend for your personal site.

- Ask yourself: Is this the image I want my future employer to see when he/she reviews my site? It's likely that an HR department will review your social media profile during a reference check.
- Keep your website and profiles current by posting blogs regularly, commenting on news, and sharing links to informative articles.

Building and Managing Your Personal Brand

Social media networks like LinkedIn, Facebook, and Twitter are very important tools for building your brand image. If you are currently using any of these social networks, you are already (intentionally or unintentionally) establishing your personal brand.

One of the best ways to establish and build your online brand is to write a blog. A blog is like a personal branding portal where you share your knowledge and perspective on topics you find interesting and that you care about. Many students establish blogs during college as a way to promote their brand to future employers. Sometimes it is part of a website where additional types of content such as articles, photos, videos, résumés, and testimonials can be posted. Consider obtaining a website domain through a provider like GoDaddy.com in your own name, such as www.JaneDoe.com, and a Twitter handle in your own name (@JaneDoe) to further establish your brand.

Social media provides so many ways to build your personal brand, but it must be used with great care. Everything you say or do online either adds or detracts from your personal brand. As you learned in previous chapters, what you say in e-mails, social media networks and forums, and anywhere else online is forever etched in digital history. Many people have regretted posting a photo of a night out drinking with friends on Facebook.

Be wary of not only what you post online, but what your friends and complete strangers may post about you. A friend may tag you in an unsavory photo. Or a stranger might record a video of you having a "private" conversation with your girlfriend, or record the regretful insult you hurled at a store clerk—and post them on YouTube. If you saw the movie *Social Network*, you may recall that even Mark Zuckerberg learned a hard lesson about posting remarks in haste. Whatever you say and do can be held against you. Never mind the court of law. It's the court of social media you need to worry about.

HOW TO RUIN YOUR CAREER IN 10 SECONDS OR LESS

Never, ever make a hasty decision to post a picture, write a Tweet, compose a blog, or respond on Facebook when you are angry or without considering the following:

1. All the potential audiences that will see it now and in the future
2. The long-term implications of your message and how it could be misinterpreted by others
3. How you will be perceived professionally
4. Before you hit the "send" or "post" button, double check to see if you are using your personal or your company account.

Social Media Monitoring

You must be just as diligent about monitoring your personal brand as you do creating and building it. The social media monitoring market is growing quickly as firms like Radian6, Reputation.com, and others track and monitor the online **social reputation** of individuals and businesses. There are also free services like Google Alerts that permit you to track where and how your name is mentioned. Keep an eye on the photos where you are tagged. If they don't reflect the brand persona you wish to portray, un-tag it.

ETIQUETTE FOR A CHANGING WORLD

11-5 Why are so many guides to etiquette crowding bookstore shelves? And why are many organizations hiring consultants to conduct classes on etiquette guidelines? One reason is that we need advice on how to avoid annoying other people, and what to do if they annoy us. In today's fast-paced, often tense, work environment, we have to work a little harder to maintain a climate of fairness, kindness, and mutual respect.[28]

Total Person Insight

"If I had only one piece of advice to offer, it would be to be on time. When you're on time, you start to build the relationship. When you're late, you start by having to recover from a mistake."

Source: Peter Post, Director of The Emily Post Institute and co-author of *The Etiquette Advantage in Business; Training*, March/April 2011, p. 44.

Etiquette (sometimes called *manners* or *protocol*) is a set of traditions based on kindness, efficiency, and logic.[29] Letitia Baldrige, author and etiquette consultant, says, "It's consideration and kindness and thinking about somebody other than oneself."[30] Sometimes we need new etiquette guidelines to deal with our changing world. Today, smoking at work is usually prohibited or restricted to a certain area. Meetings often begin with the announcement "Please silence your cell phones and beepers." And the nearly universal use of e-mail has spawned hundreds of articles on e-mail etiquette (see Chapter 2). A diverse work force has created many new challenges in the area of protocol.

Although it is not possible to do a complete review of the rules of etiquette, we will discuss those that are particularly important in an organizational business setting.

Dining Etiquette

Job interviews and business meetings are frequently conducted at breakfast, lunch, or dinner, so be aware of your table manners. To illustrate decisions you might need to make during a business meal, let's eavesdrop on Tom Reed, a job candidate having a meal with several employees of the company he wants to work for. After introductions, the bread is passed to Tom. He places a roll on the small bread-and-butter plate to the right of his dinner plate. Soon, he picks up the roll, takes a bite, and returns it to the plate. Midway through the meal, Tom rises from his chair, places his napkin on the table, and says, "Excuse me; I need to make a potty run." So far, Tom has made four etiquette blunders: The bread-and-butter plate he used belongs to the person seated on his right; his own is to the left of his dinner plate. When eating a roll, he should break off one piece at a time and butter the piece as he is ready to eat it. The napkin should have been placed on his chair, indicating his plan to return. (When departing for good, leave it to the left of your plate.) And finally, the words *potty run* are too casual for a business meal. A simple statement such as, "Please excuse me; I'll be back in just a moment," would be adequate.

"Fine. Sit there and check your messages. Perhaps it will give you something to contribute to the conversation."

William Haefeli/CartoonBank.com

There are some additional table manners to keep in mind. Do not begin eating until the people around you have their plates. If you have not been served, however, encourage others to go ahead. To prevent awkward moments during the meal, avoid ordering food that is not easily controlled, such as ribs, spaghetti, chicken with bones, or lobster.

Meeting Etiquette

Business meetings should start and end on time, so recognize the importance of punctuality. Anne Marie Sabath, owner of a firm that provides etiquette training for business employees, says, "We teach people that if you're early, you're on time, and if you're on time, in reality, you're late." Showing up late for any meeting will be viewed as rudeness by coworkers, your boss, and your clients. Do not feel obligated to comment on each item on the agenda. Yes, sometimes silence is golden. In most cases, you should not bring up a topic unless it is related to an agenda item. If you are in charge of the meeting, end it by summarizing key points, reviewing the decisions made, and recapping the responsibilities assigned to individuals during the meeting. Always start and end the meeting on a positive note.[31]

Cell Phone Etiquette

Cell phone contempt surfaces in offices, restaurants, houses of worship, and many other places.

New technologies often bring new annoyances, and the cell phone is no exception. *Cell phone contempt* surfaces in offices, restaurants, houses of worship, and many other places. Cell phone etiquette is based on a few simple guidelines. First, it is not acceptable to use

Communication technologies can create annoyances. If you are trying to enjoy a meal at your favorite restaurant, you probably do not want to sit next to someone who is talking loudly on their cell phone. If you are making an important presentation at a team meeting, and some members are busy sending out text messages, you will likely feel some frustration. Is anyone listening to me?!

your cell phone at business meetings, in elevators, or at restaurants. If you receive a call at a restaurant, take the call outside the dining area. When making or receiving a call, talk in a normal speaking voice. Too often cell phone users talk louder than normal because they feel the need to compensate for the size of small phones. Try to confine your calls to private areas; it is rude to inflict your conversation on people near you.[32] Finally, if a coworker or friend insists on "staying connected" at all times, and you find this behavior annoying, confront the person respectfully.

Conversational Etiquette

When you establish new relationships, avoid calling people by their first name too soon. Never assume that work-related associates prefer to be addressed informally by their first names. Use titles of respect—Ms., Mr., Professor, or Dr.—until the relationship is established. Too much familiarity will irritate some people. When the other person says, "Call me Ruth" or "Call me John," it is all right to begin using the person's first name.

A conversation that includes obscene language can create problems in the workplace. Although the rules about what constitutes profanity have changed over the years, inappropriate use of foul language in front of a customer, a client, or, in many cases, a coworker is a breach of etiquette. An obscenity implies lack of respect for your audience. Also, certain language taboos carry moral and spiritual significance in most cultures. Obscene language is often cited by persons who file sexual harassment charges.[33]

Total Person Insight

"Profanity will always offend someone, but the lack of profanity will never offend anyone."

Source: This quote was attributed to Rand Corporation. See Jared Sandberg, "In the Workplace, Every Bleeping Word Can Show Your Rank," *Wall Street Journal*, March 21, 2006, p. Bl.

Networking Etiquette

Networking—making contact with people at meetings, social events, or other venues—is an effective job search method. Networking is also important to salespeople searching for prospects and to professionals (accountants, lawyers, consultants, etc.) who need to build a client base.

When you meet people at an event, tell them your name and what you do. Avoid speaking negatively about any aspect of your current job or your life. In some cases, you will need to make a date to call or meet with the new contact later. After the event, study your contacts and follow up.

Send a *written* thank-you note if someone has been helpful to you or generous with his or her time. You might also consider sending a newspaper or magazine article that is relevant to the conversation you had with someone, since one goal of networking is providing something of value to another person.

We have given you a brief introduction to several areas of etiquette. This information will be extremely helpful as you develop a strong personal brand. Remember that etiquette is based on consideration for the other person. If you genuinely respect other people, you will have an easier time developing your personal approach to workplace manners. You will probably also agree with most of the etiquette "rules" we have been discussing. Nancy Austin, coauthor of *A Passion for Excellence*, says, "Real manners—a keen interest in and a regard for somebody else, a certain kindness and at-ease quality that add real value—can't be faked or finessed."[34] Real manners come from the heart.

Incivility—The Ultimate Career Killer

Civility in our society is under siege. In recent years, we have witnessed an increase in coarse, rude, and obnoxious behavior. Unfortunately, some of the most outrageous behavior by athletes, coaches, politicians, and business leaders has been rewarded with wealth and influence.

As noted in Chapter 1, civility is the sum of the many sacrifices we are called upon to make for the sake of living together. At work, it may involve refilling the copier paper tray after using the machine or making a new pot of coffee after you take the last cup. It may mean turning down your radio so workers nearby are not disturbed or sending a thank-you note to someone who has helped you complete a difficult project. Small gestures, such as saying "Please" and "Thank you" or opening doors for others, make ourselves and others more content. Learning to discipline your passions so as to avoid obnoxious behavior will demonstrate also your maturity and self-control.

Professional Presence at the Job Interview

Professional presence has special meaning when you are preparing for a job interview. In most cases, you are competing against several other applicants, so you can't afford to make a mistake. A common mistake among job applicants is failure to acquire background information on the employer. Without this information, it is difficult to prepare questions to ask during the interview, and decisions about what to wear will be more difficult.

Keep in mind that regardless of the dress code of the organization, it is always appropriate to dress conservatively. If you arrive for an interview wearing torn jeans and a T-shirt, the person conducting the interview may think you are not serious about the job. The expectation of most employers is that the job applicant will be well groomed and dressed appropriately.

Joann Lublin, columnist for the *Wall Street Journal*, says interview etiquette begins the minute you walk in the door. Employers are building a picture of you piece by piece. You will always lose credibility if you are late or if you fail to give your full attention during the interview. Don't even think about peeking at your Blackberry.[35]

LOOKING BACK: SUMMARY OF LEARNING OBJECTIVES

1. **Explain the importance of professional presence.**

   Professional presence is a dynamic blend of poise, self-confidence, control, and style. Once acquired, it permits you to be perceived as self-assured and competent. These qualities are quickly perceived the first time someone meets you.

2. **Understand the importance of a favorable first impression.**

   People tend to form impressions of others quickly at the time they first meet them, and these first impressions tend to be preserved. The impression you form of another person during the initial contact is made up of assumptions and facts. Assumptions are often based on perceptions of surface language—the pattern of immediate impressions conveyed by appearance. Verbal messages also influence the impression you make on others.

3. **Define image and describe the factors that form the image you project to others.**

   Image is a term used to describe how other people feel about you. In every business or social setting, your behaviors and appearance communicate a picture that others observe and remember. This picture determines how they react to you. Image is formed by a variety of factors, including manners, self-confidence, voice quality, versatility, integrity, entrance and poise, facial expression, surface language, competence, positive attitude, handshake, and the clothing you wear.

4. **Understand how your online presence will help or hinder your personal brand.**

   Everything you do and say online either adds or detracts from your personal brand. Give careful attention to how you build and maintain your social media profiles and other types of online content. Monitor your social reputation regularly.

5. **Understand how life and workplace etiquette contributes to improved interpersonal relations.**

   Etiquette, sometimes called manners or protocol, is tradition based on kindness, efficiency, and logic. Dining, meeting, cell phone, conversational, and networking etiquette are all important in the workplace.

KEY TERMS

professional presence, 228
personal brand, 229
primacy effect, 230
assumptions, 231

cultural influences, 231
image, 232
surface language, 233
career apparel, 234

business casual, 235
social reputation, 238
etiquette, 239

CAREER INSIGHT: HANDYMAN ETIQUETTE

Andy Bell, founder of Handyman Matters Franchising Corporation, manages 134 franchises in 37 states and three countries. He has implemented strict initial contact guidelines for all of his technicians. Technicians must take two steps back after ringing a doorbell and wear a clean, neat uniform (collared shirt and slacks) with identifying logo. When the homeowner comes to the door, the technician immediately presents a business card.

Handyman technicians receive training in all areas of in-home conduct.[36]

Handyman Matters training is focused on many "small" things because they understand how they ultimately reflect the company's image and create a brand that consumers trust. In an industry such as this, quality is expected but personal customer care is not, and this is what helps to create the Handyman Matters brand image.

TRY YOUR HAND

1. Many people complain that interrupting has become a major annoyance. You begin speaking and someone finishes your sentence. Marilyn Vos Savant, author of the "Ask Marilyn" column, recommends a technique that can stop interrupters. When someone interrupts you, stop speaking abruptly and say "What?" This will highlight the interruption, and the person who interrupts you will be forced to repeat himself or herself too, which is an unpleasant experience. Repeat this method, if necessary, until the offender lets you complete your sentences. Marilyn Vos Savant says you should save this method for *chronic* interrupters.[37]

2. The first step toward improving your voice is to hear yourself as others do. Listen to several recordings of your voice on a cell phone message, tape recorder, or digital recording, and then complete the following rating form. Place a checkmark in the appropriate space for each quality.

QUALITY	MAJOR STRENGTH	STRENGTH	WEAKNESS	MAJOR WEAKNESS
Projects confidence	_____	_____	_____	_____
Projects enthusiasm	_____	_____	_____	_____
Speaking rate is not too fast or too slow	_____	_____	_____	_____
Projects optimism	_____	_____	_____	_____
Voice is not too loud or too soft	_____	_____	_____	_____
Projects sincerity	_____	_____	_____	_____

3. You have assumed the duties of sales manager at a new Lexus automobile dealership that is scheduled to open in three weeks. You will hire and train all salespeople. What types of career apparel would you recommend to members of your sales team? What grooming standards would you recommend?

4. Many employers say that Generation Y job applicants arrive at the job interview with an overblown sense of entitlement—an enhanced view of their self-importance. To avoid sending this message, what behaviors should be avoided during the interview?

CRITICAL THINKING CHALLENGE

The authors of *First Impressions* say that making a good first impression means making the person you meet feel positive toward you. When you have contact with someone, do you think about how the other person is feeling during the initial contact, or do you stay focused on yourself? What can you do to make someone feel positively about you?[38]

SELF-ASSESSMENT EXERCISE

For each of the following statements, circle the number from 1 to 5 that best represents your response: (1) strongly disagree (never do this); (2) disagree (rarely do this); (3) moderately agree (sometimes do this); (4) agree (frequently do this); (5) strongly agree (almost always do this).

A. I project to others an image that matches my talents and aspirations.	1	2	3	4	5
B. The factors that form my image (career apparel, manners, facial expression, etc.) are appropriate and do not detract from the image I project to others.	1	2	3	4	5
C. The personal brand I project to others is consistent with my core values.	1	2	3	4	5
D. When I post content on social media, I consider the long-term impact on my personal brand.					
E. I understand the importance of creating and managing my personal brand, and do so intentionally.	1	2	3	4	5

After identifying your response to each item, select an attitude or skill you would like to improve. Prepare a written goal and then describe the steps you will take to achieve this goal.

YOU PLAY THE ROLE

After spending a number of years working for a prestigious CPA firm, you established your own company. Cameron, Stanley, and Robert is the area's top accounting firm. You cater to an upscale business clientele who appreciate your outstanding customer service and the quality of your firm's work. Currently, you employ ten associates. The newest member of your accounting firm is Annika Johnson, a young CPA who is proud to be a member of Generation Y. Her intelligence, self-confidence, and image impressed you during the hiring process; however, you are now noticing an image change. Although she is well paid, Annika likes to shop at discount clothing stores, always searching for a great bargain. Very often her clothing and accessories communicate a "thrift store" image that clashes with the upscale image of CSR. You have decided to meet with Annika and try to encourage her to adopt a wardrobe that is more appropriate for the clientele she serves. You will meet with another class member who will assume the role of Annika Johnson.

BELOW THE SURFACE | CREATING YOUR PERSONAL BRAND

Diane Keng shares the same passion for brand building as Ashley Wilson, the young realtor portrayed in the opening story of this chapter. Diane is an 18-year-old freshman at Santa Clara University. Like many other young career-focused adults, Diane understands she must establish her professional brand early in her career, and continue to build it throughout her life. She manages two accounts on Facebook, one is personal and the other is professional. Her personal account is strictly for family and friends and her professional account is regularly updated with information about her tech start-up called MyWeboo.com where she regularly posts information about women entrepreneurs and engineers. Diane's goal is to establish a personal brand and create a positive image early in her career. She says that people like to look up others on Facebook before they actually meet them in person, and once first impressions are made, they're really tough to change.[39]

Your personal brand is derived from your core values. Personal brand development begins with self-management practices that help you create and strengthen relationships with other people. Early in his career, Jerry Seinfeld decided he would never use profanity in his comedy routines. This personal decision forced him to use more creativity, and he became a stronger comedian. Jeff Bezos, founder ofAmazon.com, recalls an early life experience that changed the way he viewed relationships. He made a comment to his grandmother that hurt her feelings. Later, his grandfather met with him privately and said, "You'll learn, one day, that it's much harder to be kind than clever."[40] This insight has helped Bezos in his professional life.

Developing a distinctive brand that will help you in your interactions with others may require making some changes in your life. To become distinctive, you must stand for something. What you stand for relates to your values. Thus, a strong personal brand is generally built from the inside out. But, to some extent, you can also decide what type of image you want these values to project. This may require changes in your manners, dress, voice quality, facial expression, posture, or behaviors that reflect your integrity.

QUESTIONS

1. Judith Sills, clinical psychologist who writes a column for Psychology Today, says your brand is the professional identity you create in the minds of others. What personal qualities will give you greater visibility, recognition, and acceptance in the labor market? These qualities should send the message, "Pick me; I'm special."

2. This chapter described several different ways to use social media to build and grow your personal brand identity. What are some of the ways that you would like to develop your online presence? Summarize a brief action plan that describes the activities and steps you will put in place to build and promote your personal brand.

CLOSING CASE | MAKE YOURSELF MEMORABLE

The words *magnetism, charisma, authenticity,* and *class* are used to describe persons who are admired and respected. These special individuals are also memorable. Some say class and charm are fading fast from the American scene, replaced by bad behavior displayed by professional athletes, movie stars, radio and TV commentators, and politicians. Yet, there are some role models worth remembering. The late Paul Newman was a serious actor, a successful racer, and a generous philanthropist. He established Newman's own brand of food and condiments and then directed more than $250 million to charity. He was dedicated to helping make the world a better place for all.[41]

Arthur Ashe was the first African-American male to win the U.S. Open and Wimbledon tennis tournaments and the first African-American on the U.S. Davis Cup team. He was also the first African-American male ranked number one in the tennis world. He displayed a unique combination of grace and class. His life was marked by personal modesty, civility, and generosity. Ashe led an exemplary family and professional life until his untimely death from AIDS, which he had contracted after heart bypass surgery.

The late Payne Stewart, killed in the bizarre crash of a Learjet, is remembered as a vicious competitor and a classy hero to many golf fans.

Cellist Yo-Yo Ma and talk-show host Oprah Winfrey display magnetism and charm.

The authors of *Make Yourself Memorable* say that memorable people have style. They describe the four interlocking elements of style as *look, conduct, speech*, and *presentation*. Ann Landers, the late advice columnist, used to say that if you had class, success would follow. She described some of the elements of class:[42]

- Class never tries to build itself up by tearing others down.

- Class never makes excuses.

- Class knows that good manners are nothing more than a series of small, inconsequential sacrifices.

- Class is comfortable in its own skin. It never puts on airs.

- Class is real. It can't be faked.

QUESTIONS

1. Some social critics say that too many people these days are rude, crude, and inconsiderate of others. Do you agree? Explain.

2. Make a list of prominent people who, in your opinion, have class. Also, make a list of friends or coworkers who have class. List and evaluate the personal qualities displayed by these individuals you most admire.

3. If you want to become a more memorable person—someone with class—what type of self-improvement program would you undertake? Explain. If you decided to develop a strong personal brand, would class be a major component of your brand?

CHAPTER 11 ENDNOTES

1. Iris June Vinegar, "Here Comes Ashley," *News & Observer*, February 25, 2010, p. 8D.

2. David McNally and Karl D. Speak, *Be Your Own Brand—A Breakthrough Formula for Standing Out from the Crowd* (San Francisco: Berrett—Koehle Publishers, Inc., 2002), p. 112.

3. Stephen R. Covey, *The Seven Habits of Highly Effective People* (New York: Simon & Schuster, 1989), pp. 22, 34.

4. Susan Bixler, *Professional Presence* (New York: G. P. Putnam's Sons, 1991), p. 16. For more information on professional presence see Judith Sills, "Becoming Your Own Brand," *Psychology Today*, January/February 2008, p. 62.

5. Ann Demarais and Valerie White, *First Impressions* (New York: Bantam Books, 2004), pp. 22–23.

6. Ibid., p. 16.

7. Ibid.

8. Gordon Anders, "Hey, Not So Fast," *Wall Street Journal*, January 11, 2005, p. D9.

9. Danielle Sacks, "The Accidental Guru," *Fast Company*, January 2005, pp. 69–70.

10. Jeffrey Zaslow, "First Impressions Get Faster," *Wall St. Journal* February 16, 2006, p.D4.

11. Leonard Zunin and Natalie Zunin, *Contact—The First Four Minutes* (New York: Ballantine Books, 1972), p. 17.

12. Clyde Haberman, "No Offense," *New York Times Book Review*, February 18, 1996, p. 11.

13. Norine Dresser, *Multicultural Manners: Essential Rules of Etiquette for the 21st Century* (Hoboken, NJ: John Wiley and Sons, Inc., 2005). This book provides comprehensive coverage of multicultural etiquette.

14. Susan Bixler and Nancy Nix-Rice, *The New Professional Image*, 2nd ed. (Avon, Mass: Adams Media Corporation, 2005), p. 311; Susan Bixler and Lisa Scherrer Dugan, 5 *Steps to Professional Presence* (Avon, Mass: Adams Media Corporation, 2001), pp. 4–8.

15. Suein L. Hwang, "Enterprise Takes Idea of Dressed for Success to a New Extreme," *Wall Street Journal*, November 20, 2002, p. Bl.

16. "GPA Licensee Certification/Train-the-Trainer" [cited 16 January 2006]. Available from http://www.globalprotocol. com; INTERNET. See "Overview of Image Consulting" [cited January 14, 2009.] Available from http://www.aici. org; INTERNET.

17. Dave Knesel, "Image Consulting—A Well-Dressed Step Up the Corporate Ladder," *Pace*, July/August 1981, p. 74.

18. Cora Daniels, "The Man in the Tan Khaki Pants," *Fortune*, May 1, 2000, p. 338; Susan Bixler and Nancy Nix-Rice, *The New Professional Images*, 2nd ed. (Avon, Mass: Adams Media Corporation, 2005), pp. 133–144.

19. Deborah Blum, "Face It!" *Psychology Today*, September/October 1998, pp. 34, 69.

20. Susan Bixler, *The Professional Image* (New York: Perigee Books, 1984), p. 219.

21. Joann S. Lublin, "To Win Advancement, You Need to Clean Up Any Bad Speech Habits," *Wall Street Journal*, October 5, 2004, p. Bl.

22. Ibid

23. Susan Bixler and Lisa Scherrer Dugan, 5 *Steps to Professional Presence* (Avon, Mass: Adams Media Corporation, 2001), pp. 65.

24. Josh Hyatt, "Building your brand (and keeping your job)," *Fortune*, CNN Money July 30, 2010, Retrieved from http://money.cnn.com/2010/07/30/news/economy/building_your_brand.fortune/index.htm

25. Ibid.

26. Ibid.

27. Emily Glazer, Create a Positive Image, *News & Observer*, October 3, 2010, p. 3.

28. Cynthia Crossen, "Etiquette for Americans Today," *Wall Street Journal*, December 28, 2001, p. W13.

29. Barbara Pachter and Mary Brody, *Complete Business Etiquette Handbook* (Englewood Cliffs, NJ: Prentice-Hall, 1995), p. 3.

30. Amy Gamerman, "Lunch with Letitia: Our Reporter Minds Her Manners," *Wall Street Journal*, March 3, 1994, p. A14.

31. Ann Marie Sabath, "Meeting Etiquette: Agendas and More," *DECA Dimensions*, January/February 1994, p. 8; "Is Etiquette a Core Value?" *Inc.*, May 2004, p. 22.

32. Leila Jason, "Are There Rules of Etiquette for Cell-phone Use?" *Wall Street Journal*, September 10, 2001, p. R16; Dana May Casperson, "Tactfully Respond to Cell Phone Intrusion," *Selling*, April 2005, p. 5.

33. Gene Veith, "Curse of the Foul Mouth," *Wall Street Journal*, January 24, 2003, p. Dl; Tara Parker-Pope and Kyle Pope, "When #@%&@ Is—and Isn't—Appropriate," *Wall Street Journal Sunday*, featured in *The News & Observer*, January 21, 2001, p. D4.

34. Nancy K. Austin, "What Do America Online and Dennis Rodman Have in Common?" *Inc.*, July 1997, p. 54.

35. Joann S. Lublin, "Interview Etiquette Begins the Minute You Walk in the Door," *Wall Street Journal*, August 1, 2006, p. Bl.

36. Gwendolyn Bounds, "Handyman Etiquette: Stay Calm, Avert Eyes," *Wall Street Journal*, May 10, 2005, p. Bl.

37. Marilyn Vos Savant, "Ask Marilyn," *Parade*, May 30, 2002, p. 19.

38. Ann Demarais and Valerie White, *First Impressions* (New York: Bantam Books, 2004), p. 22.

39. Emily Glazer, Create a Positive Image, *News & Observer*, October 3, 2010, p. 3.

40. "The Right Words at the Right Time," *O, The Oprah Magazine*, May 2002, p. 202.

41. Joe Morgenstern, "Paul Newman: So Much More Than Just a Pretty Face," *Wall Street Journal*, September 30, 2008, p. B17; Mark Vaughn, "Paul Newman 1925–2008," *Autoweek*, October 6, 2008, p. 43.

42. Stephanie G. Sherman, *Make Yourself Memorable* (New York: American Management Association, 1996), pp. 3–4; "People in the News," *U.S. News & World Report*, November 8, 1999, p. 12; Ann Landers, "If You've Got Class, Nothing Else Matters," *The News & Observer*, July 11, 1998, p. E2; Carlin Flora, "The Superpowers," *Psychology Today*, May/June 2005, pp. 40–50.

PART 4

If We All Work Together...

Jupiterimages/Comstock Images/Getty Images

Odilon Dimier/PhotoAlto/Getty Images

Team Building: A Leadership Strategy

TIP OF THE ICEBERG | NEW FORMS OF TEAM DEVELOPMENT

After 20 years at PepsiCo, Mike White made an industry-changing career move to become the CEO of DirectTV. White needed a quick indoctrination to learn about the industry and what better way than working on the front line as an installer. To make sure he got an unbiased view, he went undercover on the television show *Undercover Boss*.

Being an installer was harder than he imagined. The technology is complex and configuration was different in every home. On top of that, he had to crawl around on roof tops in the humid 98 degree Alabama heat. White says, "You have to get as close as you can to where your employees interact with the customers to find out how things really work, and that takes hard work and lots of curiosity. You've got to create trust between the front lines and middle management. You have to understand that you're not there to embarrass anyone or to find out what they're doing wrong. You're there to learn."[1]

As a white-collar executive, White has had very different experiences than the hard-working front-line team. But as a result of his undercover experience, White now understands what it's like, and he is more committed than ever to understanding how to help the front line. "In this economy, empathy is very important to motivate a team, and you can't have empathy if you haven't walked in their shoes for a bit."[2]

Companies of all sizes have embraced the use of teams to work on many types of projects because it is proven to be an effective strategy. At ICU Medical, Inc., maker of medical devices, any worker can form a team to tackle a project. Team members define the problem, assign tasks, and create deadlines themselves. Over the years, teams have altered production processes, set up 401(k) plans, and solved logistical problems in the movement of parts. George Lopez, CEO at ICU, says letting employees form teams has helped him spread out the decision-making and encourages input from people closest to the problems.[3]

As competition increases and work-related problems become more complex, organizations are seeking more input from their employees. However, there is an enormous vacuum in leadership today. Bill George, author of *True North, Authentic Leadership*, and other publications, says too

Every second counts in a NASCAR race. Each team member is responsible for a task or series of tasks. A small mistake can result in the loss of several positions on the race track. Crew training, with emphasis on teamwork, is essential.

often the wrong people are attaining leadership roles. He states that there are leaders throughout organizations who are waiting for opportunities to lead. Too often these people do not feel empowered to seek leadership roles.[4]

The focus of this chapter is team-building leadership strategies and understanding the characteristics that make a strong team. It is important to understand the difference between leadership and management. **Leadership** is the process of inspiring, influencing, and guiding employees to participate in a common effort.[5] Stephen Covey, in his book *The 8th Habit*, says, "Leadership is communicating people's worth and potential so clearly that they come to see it in themselves only."[6]

Thanks to the efforts of James Kouzes and Barry Posner, we know a great deal about the practices of exemplary leaders. Kouzes and Posner have summarized and reported on many years of research on this topic in *The Leadership Challenge*, a best-selling book.[7] They found that the most effective leaders engage in five practices of exemplary leadership (see Figure 12.1).

Leadership is expected from people in senior roles in a company; however, leadership can be exhibited by anyone in an organization. The saying "*Leaders are made, not born*" is true. Leadership is a series of skills that can be acquired through study and practice.

Management is the process of coordinating people and other resources to achieve the goals of the organization. Most managers focus on four kinds of resources: material, human, financial, and informational.[8] Most leaders achieve their goals by combining effective leadership and management.

Figure 12.1 ■ Five Practices of Exemplary Leadership

The Leadership Challenge is considered to be the definitive field-guide on leadership. There are over a million copies in print, in fifteen languages. The authors have devised the following five practices of exemplary leadership.

- **Model the Way.** Leaders must model the behavior they expect from others.
- **Inspire a Shared Vision.** The leader's dream or vision is the force that invents the future. It is the employees' belief in and enthusiasm for the vision that motivates them to give their best.
- **Challenge the Process.** Leaders do not accept the status quo. They search for opportunities to innovate, grow, and improve processes.
- **Enable Others to Act.** Effective leaders make people feel confident, strong, and capable of taking action.
- **Encourage the Heart.** Through good times and bad, leaders encourage the heart of their employees to carry on and do their best.

Source: James M. Kouzes and Barry Z. Posner, *The Leadership Challenge*, 3rd ed. (San Francisco, CA: Jossey-Bass, 2002), pp. 13–20.

LEADERSHIP CHALLENGES IN A CHANGING WORKPLACE

12-1 The New Economy is characterized by rapid change and demand for increased productivity. As the pace of change quickens and the pressure to work harder increases, the result is greater employee stress and tension. How can a supervisor motivate employees who are tired and frustrated? Some of the most important leadership strategies, such as building trust, empowering employees, and developing the spirit of teamwork take time. How do managers respond to leaders at the top of the organization who want changes implemented overnight?

Diversity and globalization have also become prominent characteristics of today's work force. Supervising a multicultural and multilingual work force can be very challenging, especially when workers are scattered across multiple time zones. We are seeing greater use of part-time and temporary workers. Companies today are increasingly looking to attain specific skills as well as operational efficiencies by hiring independent contractors and outsourcing work. Add to this the challenges of managing a multi-generational work force and you can see that managers have more challenges than they once did.

Team Building: An Introduction

Can the element of teamwork make a difference between the successful and unsuccessful operation of an organization? Yes, research indicates that a leadership style that emphasizes **team building** is positively associated with high productivity and profitability. Problems in interpersonal relations are also less common where teamwork is evident. Teamwork ensures not only that a job gets done but also that it gets done efficiently and harmoniously.

There is also evidence that team building can have a positive influence on the physical and psychological well-being of everyone involved. When employees are working together as a team, the leader and members often experience higher levels of job satisfaction and less stress.

Another positive outcome of teamwork is an increase in synergy. **Synergy** is the interaction of two or more parts to produce a greater result than the sum of the parts taken individually.[9] Mathematically speaking, synergy suggests that two plus two equals five. Teamwork synergy is especially important at a time when organizations need creative solutions to complex problems.

Total Person Insight

"True leadership is about making *other* people better as a result of your presence—and making sure your impact endures in your absence."

Source: Stop Holding Yourself Back, by Anne Morriss, Robin J. Ely, and Frances X. Frei, *Harvard Business Review*, January–February 2011, p. 160.

Characteristics that Influence Team Dynamics

Teamwork and collaboration are required across all parts of an organization. Managing and leveraging the diversity of knowledge in teams enables companies to make decisions, solve complex problems, and quickly respond to continuously changing market and customer needs. However, managing and leading a team is not easy, and it requires work and commitment to continuously improve both technical skills and soft skills.

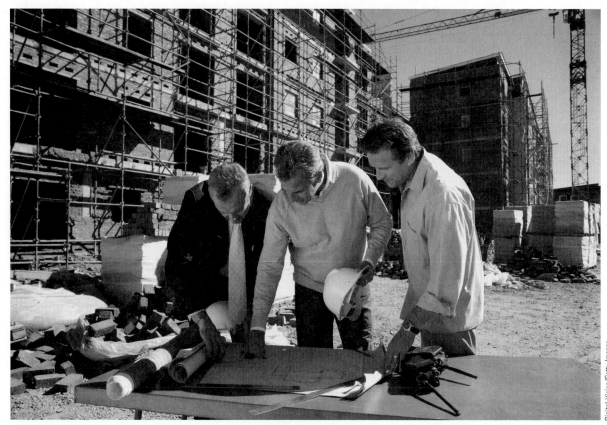

Digital Vision/Getty Images

Each aspect of our lives, from the clothes we wear to the buildings in which we work, is the direct result of team dynamics.

The corporate culture at Zappos is so effective that it has developed a training division, Zappos Insights, to teach other companies how to create remarkable company cultures.

Understanding the key characteristics that drive teamwork and collaboration will help managers focus on the most important aspects of creating a high performance team. They include having a shared vision and values, clear goals and objectives, and establishing team practices in the areas of accountability, communication, and decision-making. Leaders must also continuously build trust among team members so they share ideas and knowledge without fear of being criticized. Nurturing trust is the result of open, honest communication, and team members following through on their commitments.

Team Core Values

One of the most effective ways to align how a department or business unit team will work together is to create team core values. This creates a sense of ownership, shared vision, and commitment for how people will work together as a team to achieve objectives. The leader facilitates team involvement through developing values that are congruent with the company values, yet are unique to an individual team.

In Chapter 5 we introduced the Zappos Core Values (see Figure 5.1). These values help employees stay focused on what is truly important in their daily work. Zappos has become so successful with their company culture they created a separate training division called Zappos Insights to teach other organizations how to create a great company culture.

COMMON TYPES OF WORK TEAMS

12-2 Teams are the primary way organizations get things done. There are all kinds of teams including cross-functional teams, department teams, management teams, project teams, virtual teams, and special project teams. This section focuses on three of the most common types of teams: self-managed, cross-functional, and virtual teams.

Self-Managed Teams

Self-managed teams, also known as high performance work teams, assume responsibility for traditional management tasks as part of their regular work routine. Examples include decisions about production quotas, quality standards, and interviewing applicants for team positions. A typical self-managed team usually has 5 to 15 members who are responsible for producing a well-defined product (such as an automobile) or service (such as processing an insurance claim). Team members usually rotate among the various jobs and acquire the knowledge and skills to perform each job. Employees formerly concerned only with their own jobs suddenly become accountable for the work of the total team.[10]

Cross-Functional Teams

Cross-functional teams are task groups staffed with a mix of specialists, focused on a common objective.[11] These teams are often temporary groups with members from different departments and job levels. The teams are often involved in developing new work procedures or products, devising work reforms, or developing new technology. Team members often provide a link among separate functions, such as production, distribution, finance, and customer service. Hypertherm Incorporated, a metal-cutting equipment maker based in Hanover, New Hampshire, has developed cross-functional teams for each of its five product lines. Team members represent engineering, marketing, production, and sales. Salespeople and marketers know customers best, so they make an important contribution to new product development. During the hiring process, every effort is made to screen out persons who would not be effective team players.[12]

Virtual Teams

In a competitive global marketplace, virtual teams composed of employees physically dispersed throughout the nation or around the world are now common. It is no longer necessary to go to a *place* to get work done. For virtual workers, the workplace is not a building, but the *networks*.[13] Technology makes it possible for employees to collaborate on projects and effectively draw talent with specialized skills and intellectual capital from various departments and locations around the world. The advantages of virtual teams include speed, agility, expanded expertise, improved communication, and real-time collaboration.

Trina Hoefling, an expert on managing virtual work teams and author of *Working Virtually* says the real purpose of virtual work is to *create synergy* for mission accomplishment *without the limitations* of time or space.[14]

Managing and working with virtual team members in different time zones and different cultures has its challenges, but with the right leadership there is no reason why virtual workers cannot be just as effective as those that meet face-to-face. The guidelines in Figure 12.2 help leaders overcome the challenges of managing virtual teams.

Patrick Lencioni, author of *The Five Dysfunctions of a Team*, has spent many years researching factors that contribute to unproductive teams. In his best-selling book, he provides a five-part model that explains how teams typically hurt themselves (see Figure 12.3).

Figure 12.2 ■ How to Effectively Manage a Virtual Team

- Make sure everyone has a clear concept of the overall goal. If it is not possible to meet in person, host a virtual web conference with webcams for the team to get to know each other and to learn each other's roles.
- Communicate why each team member was selected to be on the team; share strengths and passions. Structure ways for them to get to know each other as both team members and individuals.
- Redefine roles and reassign tasks within the team in order to ensure better outcomes for the project as a whole.
- Require detailed status reports and meeting results, and find structured methods to stay abreast of deadlines and the completion of milestones. This keeps the manager and entire team up-to-date.
- Encourage peer collaboration to continuously improve work structure.

Source: Adapted from GroupONE Solutions/Trina Hoefling's "Practical Tips for Virtual Managers," and Trina Hoefling, *Working Virtually.*

BEHAVIORAL SCIENCE PRINCIPLES SUPPORTING TEAM BUILDING

12-3   One approach to the study of leadership is examining the careers of successful leaders who have demonstrated their ability to develop teamwork. A second approach to the study of leadership is reviewing the findings of scholars who have identified the characteristics of successful leaders. What do successful leaders have in common? See in the sections that follow, how Douglas McGregor, Robert Blake, Jane S. Mouton, and Robert K. Greenleaf have answered this question.

Influential Thought Leaders

In his book *The Human Side of Enterprise,* Douglas McGregor presented convincing arguments that management had been ignoring important facts about how people work effectively in teams. The author said that managers often failed to recognize the potential for growth of most workers and their desire for fulfillment. He identified several characteristics of an effective work team which included an informal, comfortable work environment where people are engaged and freely express their feelings and ideas; there are few "hidden agendas" and constructive disagreement is encouraged; and tasks or objectives of the group are well understood and accepted by the members.[15] McGregor's views on the characteristics of effective work teams have merit today as many authors continue to build on his thinking.

Warren Bennis is another influential thought leader. More than 30 years ago he argued that democracy would dominate the workplace. He predicted that the pyramid shaped organization chart with top management in a position of absolute power and decision-making would become obsolete.[16] He envisioned an organization where employee ideas were not only respected but encouraged because this helped the entire organization to improve.

Peter Drucker is widely regarded as the most well-known and respected management expert of our time. His lectures pragmatically linked organizations and society, and predicted changes in our "age of discontinuity," most of which came true. He warned us of the

Figure 12.3 ■ Five Dysfunctions of a Team

Patrick Lencioni believes that effective teamwork is not common in most organizations. Too often teams fall prey to five interrelated dysfunctions:

Absence of Trust: Trust is the foundation of effective teamwork.

Fear of Conflict: Teams that lack trust are not capable of engaging in open, unfiltered debate.

Lack of Commitment: When team members fail to voice their views openly during passionate debate, they rarely buy in and commit to decisions.

Avoidance of Accountability: Without commitment and buy in, team members are often hesitant to call their peers on actions and behaviors that seem counterproductive to the good of the team.

Inattention to Results: Failure to hold one another accountable creates an environment where team members put their own needs above the collective goals of the team.

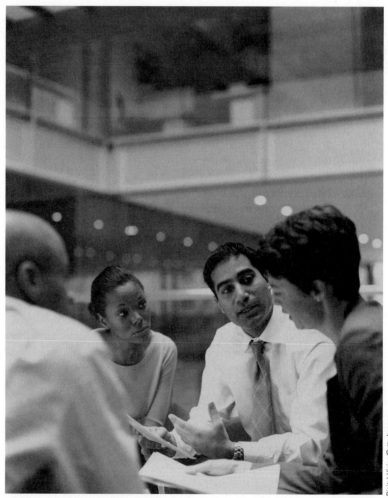

Digital Vision/Getty Images.

In order to achieve effective results, team members must be willing to openly voice their concerns and collectively hold themselves accountable for the results of their decisions.

disparity between executive pay and front-line workers. He articulated why leaders should not make decisions based on short-term gain, but the long-term future of the company.

Drucker helped leaders think differently. An advocate of innovation, Drucker said, "The best way to predict the future is to create it," meaning companies must be attuned to society changes in order to drive innovation to meet unmet customer needs. He was famous for asking simple, yet powerful questions such as "What should an organization stop doing?" Drucker became the first management guru whose advice was sought by executives trying to figure out how to manage in increasingly turbulent times.[17]

Drucker's contributions to management and leadership were significant. He said leaders must motivate knowledge workers, not simply with money, but by communicating core values and a higher purpose. His ideas of pay for performance and management by objectives have been embraced by companies around the world.

When Peter Drucker died in 1995 at the age of 95, he had the satisfaction of not only seeing so many of his predications come true, but witnessed companies transform their organizations as a result of his influential thinking.

Total Person Insight

"It is teamwork that remains the ultimate competitive advantage, both because it is so powerful and so rare."

Source: Patrick Lencioni, *The Five Dysfunctions of a Team* (San Francisco: Jossey-Bass, 2002), p. vii.

The Ohio State Model

The wide range of types of leadership positions may cause you to ask: Do people in these positions have much in common? Will team-building strategies work in most situations? The answer to both questions is yes. A great majority of successful leaders share certain behavior characteristics. Two of the most important dimensions of supervisory leadership—*consideration* and *structure*—have been identified in research studies conducted by Edwin Fleishman at Ohio State University[18] and validated by several additional studies. By making a matrix out of these two independent dimensions of leadership, the researchers identified four styles of leadership (see Figure 12.4).

Consideration

The dimension of **consideration** reflects the extent to which a leader's relationships with subordinates are characterized by mutual trust, respect for the employees, consideration of their feelings, and warmth in interpersonal relationships. When consideration is present, the leader-subordinate relationship is characterized by a climate of good rapport and two-way communication.

Structure

The dimension of **structure** reflects the extent to which a leader is likely to define and direct his or her role and the roles of subordinates toward goal attainment. Individuals who incorporate structure into their leadership style actively direct group activities by planning, setting goals, communicating information, scheduling, and evaluating performance. People who work under the direction of a highly structured leader know what is expected of them.

Figure 12.4 ■ Basic Leadership Styles from Ohio State Study

This matrix is similar to the Leadership Grid (formerly called the Managerial Grid) developed by Robert Blake and Jane Mouton. The Leadership Grid is based on two leadership style dimensions: concern for people and concern for production.

Source: James M. Kouzes and Barry P. Posner *The Leadership Challenge,* 3rd ed. (San Francisco, CA: Jossey-Bass, 2002), pp. 13–20.

It is interesting to note that the dimensions of consideration and structure are independent of each other. A leader may be well qualified in one area but lack competence in the other. Anyone who assumes a leadership role can consciously work to develop competence in both areas.

Improving Consideration Skills

Brian Tracy says that effective leaders are guided by the *law of empathy:* "Leaders are sensitive to and aware of the needs, feelings, and motivations of those they lead."[19] This is good advice for anyone who wants to become an outstanding leader. To improve the dimension of consideration, one should adopt the following practices:

Recognize Accomplishments. When individual achievements are overlooked, leaders miss a valuable opportunity to boost employee self-confidence and build morale. As noted in Chapter 10, people need recognition for good work, regardless of the duties they perform or the positions they hold. Of course, recognition should be contingent on performance.

> *A supervisor should provide each employee with as many opportunities to succeed as possible.*

Provide for Early and Frequent Success. According to an old saying, "Nothing succeeds like success." A supervisor should provide each employee with as many opportunities to succeed as possible. The foundation for accomplishment begins with a carefully planned orientation and training program. Supervisors and managers should review job duties and responsibilities, organizational policies and procedures, and any other pertinent information with their employees early in the relationship. Successful leaders are successful teachers.

Take a Personal Interest in Each Employee. Everyone likes to be treated as an individual. Taking a personal interest means learning the names of spouses and children, finding out what employees do during their leisure time, asking about their families, and acknowledging birthdays. The more you learn about the "whole person," the better you will be able to help employees balance their work lives with the rest of their lives.

> *Therefore, efforts to improve the communication process represent a good use of the supervisor's time and energy.*

Establish a Climate of Open Communication. To establish a climate of open communication, the leader must be available and approachable. Employees should feel comfortable talking about their fears, frustrations, and aspirations. Communication is closely linked to employee morale—morale is directly linked to productivity. Therefore, efforts to improve communication are a good use of a supervisor's time and energy.

Discover Individual Employee Values. Today's lean, flatter organizations offer employees fewer opportunities for promotion, smaller raises, and less job security. As a result, many workers no longer feel secure or identify with the company. Leaders should encourage employees to explore their values and determine whether there is a match between what matters most to them and the work they are doing. If a value conflict turns up, determine whether it is possible to redesign the job or give the employee a new assignment.[20]

Improving Structure Skills

The leader who incorporates structure into his or her leadership style plays an active role in directing group activities. The team builder gives the group direction, establishes performance standards, and maintains individual and group accountability. The following practices can be used to develop the dimension of structure:

Communicate Your Expectations. Members of the group or team must possess a clear idea of what needs to be accomplished. The law of expectations, according to Brian Tracy, states, "Whatever you expect, with confidence, becomes your own self-fulfilling prophecy."[21] Leaders must effectively formulate their expectations and then communicate them with conviction.

Bob Hughes, a consultant in the area of team building, suggests establishing baseline performance data so progress can be assessed.[22] In an office that processes lease applications, where accuracy and speed are critically important, the baseline data might include the number of error-free lease applications the team processes in one day. In an ideal situation, team members will be involved in setting goals and will help determine how best to achieve the goals. The goal-setting process is described in Chapter 4.

Provide Specific Feedback Often. Feedback should be relevant to the task performed by the employee and should be given soon after performance. Feedback is especially critical when an employee is just learning a new job. The supervisor should point out improvements in performance, no matter how small, and always reinforce the behavior she or he wants repeated. The most relevant feedback in a self-managed work team usually comes from coworkers, because team members are accountable to one another.

> *A person can make a mistake and still be a valuable employee.*

The Center for Creative Leadership (CCL®) creates comprehensive solutions that deliver consistent, proven results in **three key development areas.**

Leadership Strategy

Talent Development

Organizational Leadership

Center for
Creative
Leadership

www.ccl.org

CCL - Americas
+1 336 545 2810
info@ccl.org

Effective leaders never stop learning. Programs offered by the Center for Creative Leadership help managers and executives learn how to work more effectively with people.

Deal with Performance Problems Immediately. As a leader, you must deal quickly with the person who does not measure up to your standards of performance. When members of the group are not held accountable for doing their share of the work or for making mistakes, group morale may suffer. Other members of the group will quickly observe the poor performance and wonder why you are not taking corrective action.

To achieve the best results, focus feedback on the situation, issue, or behavior, not on the employee. A person can make a mistake and still be a valuable employee. Correct the person in a way that does not create anger and resentment. Avoid demoralizing the person or impairing his or her self-confidence.[23]

Coaching for Peak Performance. Coaching and developing people to become effective leaders is a critical competency required by leaders in every organization. In the book *Leading at a Higher Level*, Ken Blanchard defines coaching:[24]

> *Coaching is a deliberate process using focused conversations to create an environment that results in individual growth, purposeful action, and sustained improvement.*

Foreseeing a leadership shortage in coming years, Blanchard says it is important to shift from managing performance to focusing on development. He describes five areas where coaching can be applied:[25]

- **Performance Coaching** is used when individuals need help returning their performance to acceptable standards.
- **Development coaching** is used when high performing individuals are ready to become more fully rounded in their current role.
- **Career coaching** is employed when individuals are ready to plan their next career moves.
- **Coaching to support learning** occurs when managers or direct reports need support, encouragement, and accountability to sustain recent training and turn insights into action.
- **Creating an internal coaching culture** is what happens when leaders recognize the value of coaching and use it to develop others.[26]

HOW TO COACH FOR PERFORMANCE IMPROVEMENT

1. Document the performance problem.
2. Talk with and help the employee to recognize and agree that there is a need to improve performance in a specific area. Leaders should never assume the employee sees the problem in the same way they do.
3. Explore options. Let the employee suggest ways to improve performance.
4. Get a commitment from the employee to take action.

Source: Adapted from Kenneth R. Phillips, "The Achilles' Heel of Coaching," *Training and Development*, March 1998, p. 41; Anne Fisher, "In Praise of Micromanaging," *Fortune*, August 23, 2004, p. 40.

Situational Leadership

The **Situational Leadership Model**, developed by Paul Hersey and his colleagues at the Center for Leadership Studies *(www.situational.com)*, is a leadership model widely used in several organizations. **Situational leadership** is based on the theory that the most successful leadership occurs when the leader's style matches the situation. Situational leadership theory emphasizes the need for flexibility.[27]

Paul Hersey says that the primary behaviors displayed by effective managers in the Situational Leadership Model can be described as *task behavior* and *relationship behavior*. Task behavior, as Hersey describes it in his book *The Situational Leader,* is very similar to the "concern for production" dimension of the Leadership Grid. And relationship behavior is very similar to the "concern for people" dimension.[28]

Hersey says that, when attempting to influence others, you must (1) diagnose the readiness level of the follower for a specific task and (2) provide the appropriate leadership style for that situation. In other words, given the specific situation, you must decide how much task behavior and how much relationship behavior to display. Readiness is defined as the extent to which an employee has the ability and willingness to accomplish a specific task. If an employee has the experience and skill to perform a certain task or activity, this information will influence the leader's style. However, the leader must also consider the employee's confidence level, commitment, and motivation to accomplish the task or activity. Hersey reminds us that readiness levels often vary greatly among members of the work group.[29]

SERVANT LEADERSHIP

One of the most important leadership principles is the idea of *servant leadership,* a concept developed by Robert K. Greenleaf. He said, "The servant-leader is servant first. It begins with the natural feeling that one wants to serve, to serve first." Greenleaf believed that true leadership emerges from those whose *primary* motivation is a deep desire to help others. Servant-leadership encourages collaboration, trust, and the ethical use of power and empowerment.

Source: "What Is Servant Leadership?" [cited 11 February 2009]. Available from http://www.greenleaf.org/whatissl/index.html; INTERNET.

Additional Leadership Qualities

In addition to consideration and structure skills, leaders need some additional qualities (see Figure 12.5). One of these is character. As noted in Chapter 5, character is composed of personal standards of behavior, including honesty, integrity, and moral strength. Effective leadership is characterized by honesty, truthfulness, and straight dealing with every person.[30] Without character it is impossible to build a trusting relationship with the people you lead.

A second important quality is emotional intelligence, a concept that was discussed in Chapter 9. Emotional intelligence is a much more powerful predictor of leadership success than IQ, because it gives you the ability to monitor your own and others' emotions and deal with them effectively.[31] A leader with high emotional intelligence is more likely to detect friction and eliminate conflict among team members. This leader is also more flexible, and therefore better able to use situational leadership.

Character and emotional intelligence are leadership qualities that can be developed. Leaders develop themselves—they are not born. One very important key to growth in both of these areas is self-awareness. Without self-awareness we may behave in ways that are potentially ineffective, limiting our potential for growth and opportunity[32]

Figure 12.5 ■ Additional Leadership Qualities

TEAMWORK: THE EMPLOYEE'S ROLE

12-4   Each member should assume an active part in helping the work unit achieve its mission. This means that every member of the work group can and should be a team member and a team builder. These dual roles are achieved when employees assume greater responsibility for the success of the work unit. Today's most valued employees are those who are willing to assume leadership responsibilities.

Dynamics of Leadership-Team Behavior

Jim Collins, author of bestsellers *Good to Great* and *Built to Last,* was curious why some of the companies profiled in his books had lost their prominence, and a few even failed. Although these companies were at the height of their success during the research study, Collins wanted to learn what caused the companies to go from great to mediocre.[33] The result of this study was outlined in his book *How the Mighty Fall.* One of the areas Collins and his research team studied was the dynamics of leadership-team behavior, and the characteristics that differentiate a low-performing team (left side of chart in Figure 12.6) from a high-performing team (right side this chart).

Figure 12.6 ■ The Dynamics of High Performance Teams

Low Performing Teams Teams on the Way Down	High Performing Teams Teams on the Way Up
People shield those in power from unpleasant facts, fearful of penalties and criticism for shining light on the rough realities	People bring forth grim facts "Come here and look, man this is ugly"—to be discussed; leaders never criticize those who bring forth harsh realities
People assert strong opinions without providing data, evidence, or a solid argument	People bring data, evidence, logic, and solid arguments to the discussion
The team leader has a very low questions-to-statements ratio, avoiding critical input and/or allowing sloppy reasoning and unsupported opinions	The team leader employs a Socratic style, using a high questions-to-statements ratio, challenging people, and pushing for penetrating insights
Team members acquiesce to a decision but don't unify to make the decision successful—or worse, undermine it after the fact	Team members unify behind a decision once made, then work to make the decision succeed, even if they vigorously disagreed with it
Team members seek as much credit as possible for themselves, yet do not enjoy the confidence and admiration of their peers	Each team member credits other people for success, yet enjoys the confidence and admiration of his or her peers
Team members argue to look smart or to further their own interest rather than argue to find the best answers to support the overall cause	Team members argue and debate, not to improve their personal position but to find the best answers to support the overall cause
The team conducts "autopsies with blame" seeking culprits rather than wisdom	The team conducts "autopsies without blame," mining wisdom from painful experiences
Team members often fail to deliver exceptional results and blame other people or outside factors for setbacks, mistakes, and failures	Each team member delivers exceptional results, yet in the event of a setback each accepts full responsibility and learns from mistakes

Source: Excerpt from Jim Collins, How the Mighty Fall, *BusinessWeek*, May 25, 2009.

Employees as Leaders

In traditional organizations, there were leaders and followers, and the followers were not expected to develop leadership skills. Today, the most effective leaders are helping their work-team members develop leadership skills so that individuals can develop their capacity to lead, and the team's success will not ride on one person. At a time when most organizations are attempting to compete in a complex, ever-changing global market, there is real merit in establishing a diversity of leadership within the work group. If we are willing to expand our definition of leadership, we can see leaders everywhere:[34]

- The quiet "worker bee" frequently serves as a leader when the issue is how to get the work done during a crisis situation.
- The "corporate counselor," who informally guides coworkers through stressful problems by merely listening, is an emotional leader.
- The rigid "rule follower" keeps our creativity from becoming irresponsible.

BECOMING A VALUED TEAM MEMBER

12-5   Throughout your working life, your success is very likely to depend on your ability to be an effective team member. Here are some tips on how to become a respected team member in any organizational setting.[35]

1. *Avoid becoming part of a clique, or subgroup within the team.* As a member of a clique, you are very likely to lose the trust and respect of other team members.
2. *Avoid any action that might sabotage the team.* By engaging in frequent criticism of other team members, gossip, or other unconstructive behaviors, you undermine team efforts.
3. *Keep in mind that effective team participation depends on honest, open communication among team members.* Use the fundamentals of constructive self-disclosure discussed in Chapter 8.
4. As *a team member, do not feel the need to submerge your own strong beliefs, creative solutions, and ideas.* If the team members are about to make a decision that in your opinion is not "right," do not hesitate to speak up and express your views.

Total Person Insight

"Great challenges require great teamwork, and the quality most needed among teammates amid the pressure of a difficult challenge is collaboration... Each person brings something to the table that adds value to the relationship and synergy to the team."

Source: John C. Maxwell, *The 17 Essential Qualities of a Team Player* (Nashville, Tenn.: Thomas Nelson Publishers, 2002), pp. 13–14.

Teamwork can be a very satisfying experience. It can generate positive energy and contribute to a sense of optimism about the future. As a team member, you have the opportunity to assume a very important leadership role.

Managing the Relationship with Your Boss

The idea that you should manage the relationship with your boss may sound a little unusual at first. But it makes a lot of sense when you consider the advantages of assuming this responsibility. When the subordinate and the boss are both working to maintain a good relationship, conflict is less likely to surface. The boss-subordinate relationship is

An increased emphasis on social responsibility has prompted companies such as Salesforce.com to promote its 1%/1%/1% model which represents employees donating 1% of their time to volunteer initiatives, the company donating 1% of its technology products to nonprofits, and the company donating 1% of its equity to social-improvement initiatives. Here, Orlando Magic President Alex Martins is partnering with a Palmetto Elementary School student for a community beautification project during the 2011 Magic Volunteer Program (MVP).

not like the one between parent and child—the burden for managing the relationship *should not* and *cannot* fall entirely on the one in authority.

When you take time to manage the relationship with your boss, he or she will become more effective in performing his or her job. In many cases, managers are no more effective than the combined competence of the people they supervise. Some employees do not realize how much their boss needs assistance and support from them. How do you go about managing your boss? Here are some general considerations:

Assess Your Own Strengths. The boss represents only one-half of the relationship. The development of an effective working relationship also requires reflecting on your own strengths. As noted in Chapter 4, the first step towards strength building is to discover your greatest talents.

Develop an Understanding of Your Boss. Become familiar with this person's strengths, weaknesses, work habits, communication style, and needs. Spend time studying your boss. In some cases, the direct approach is best. Ask your boss, "How would you like me to work with you?" Try to determine his or her goals and expectations. What is the person trying to accomplish? Does your boss enjoy casual meetings to discuss business matters or formal meetings with written agendas?

Flex Your Communication Style. In terms of communication style, is your boss supportive, emotive, reflective, or directive? Once you have answered this question, begin thinking of how to flex your style in ways that will build rapport and avoid unnecessary stress. Remember, style flexing is a temporary effort to act in harmony with another person's preferred communication style (see Chapter 3).

Be Frank and Candid. Suppose that to avoid conflict, you almost never disagree with your boss—even when your boss is obviously wrong. Are you making a contribution to his or her growth and development? Obviously not. And don't hesitate to speak up regarding your contributions. Learn how to point out your accomplishments gracefully. You might say, "I know you're busy, so why don't I send you an e-mail explaining what I'm working on and what I've done?"[36]

As organizations become flatter, with fewer layers of management and more projects carried out by teams, collaboration has become more important. Effective team members are those who collaborate actively with their leader and other members of the team.

---

human RELATIONS *in Action*

TIPS FOR YOUNG LEADERS

Wanted: A new breed of boss who can provide strong leadership, handle technology, inspire teamwork, and cope with uncertainty. The person who fits this description may be quite young and inexperienced. Many of today's leaders are no longer molded solely by seniority and experience. Here are some tips for the young manager:

- Keep in mind that watching your own bosses in action is not enough to teach you to be one.
- Never assume that others are motivated by the same things you are.
- Don't ask for suggestions or opinions that you are not seriously prepared to consider.
- Give before you take. Approach relationships (with your employees, your boss, and customers) with what you have to offer, not with what you want.
- Reach out to people with more age and experience.

Source: Dimitry Elias Legger, "Help! I'm the New Boss," *Fortune*, May 29, 2000, p. 281.

LOOKING BACK: SUMMARY OF LEARNING OBJECTIVES

1. Explain the importance of teamwork in an organizational setting.

Teamwork ensures not only that a job gets done but also that it gets done efficiently. Therefore, successful teamwork can often make the difference between the profitable and the unprofitable operation of an organization. The team-building leadership style is effective because it is suited to the needs of most of today's employees.

2. Identify and explain common types of work teams.

Many companies are forming specific types of teams. Three of the most common are self-managed, cross-functional, and virtual teams. Self-managed teams assume responsibility for traditional management tasks as part of their regular work routine. Team members are responsible for producing a well-defined product or service. They usually rotate among the various jobs and acquire

the knowledge and skills to perform each one. Cross-functional teams are task groups staffed with a mix of specialists focused on a common objective. These teams are often temporary units with members from different departments. Virtual teams are comprised of employees who work from a variety of locations. The advantages of virtual teams include speed, agility, expanded expertise, improved communication and collaboration.

3. Explain the behavioral science principles that support team building.

One way to learn about team building is to study leaders who promote teamwork and scholars who discuss it; examples are McGregor, Blake, Mouton, and Greenleaf. Two important dimensions of supervisory leadership contribute to team building. One of these dimensions, *consideration,* reflects the extent to which a supervisor maintains relationships with employees that are characterized by mutual trust, respect, and rapport. The other dimension, *structure,* reflects the extent to which a supervisor is likely to direct group activities through planning, goal setting, communication, scheduling, and evaluating. The Leadership Grid® and the Situational Leadership Model help clarify these two dimensions of leadership. Effective leaders must also develop the qualities of character and emotional intelligence.

4. **Describe the attributes of a high performance team.**

   Managers must learn to leverage the diversity of knowledge, skills, and abilities to enable teams to make decisions and solve complex problems. High performing teams have a shared vision and values, clear goals and objectives, keep commitments, and are accountable to each other and the team. Open, honest communication encourages differing ideas, asking tough questions, and learning from mistakes—all factors that build trust and continuous improvement.

5. **Describe the team-member skills that employees need.**

   Members of an effective work group should assume effective leadership and membership roles. Each team member helps the group achieve its mission. Everyone assumes the role of team member and team builder. Employees are in a unique position to give guidance and support to their supervisor or manager. Most bosses need this assistance and support to achieve success.

KEY TERMS

leadership, 252	self-managed teams, 256	structure, 259
management, 252	cross-functional teams, 256	coaching, 262
team building, 253	virtual teams, 256	Situational Leadership Model, 263
synergy, 254	consideration, 259	situational leadership, 263

CAREER INSIGHT

Harness Your Emotions

Emotions drive performance, and leaders who do not acknowledge their own or their employee's temperaments can't inspire the best work from their staffs. Employees who work for intimidating or self-absorbed bosses become guarded and are reluctant to share information or new ideas. Daniel Goleman, in his book *Social Intelligence*, says emotional distress can impair the brain's mechanism to learn and think clearly.

Source: Carol Hymowitz, "Business is Personal, So Managers Need to Harness Emotions," *Wall Street Journal*, November 13, 2006, p. B1.

TRY YOUR HAND

1. Business publications such as the *Wall Street Journal, Fortune, Bloomberg Businessweek,* and *Fast Company* frequently feature articles describing problem bosses. Managers with high-tech backgrounds (computer science, electrical engineering, mathematics, etc.) sometimes create employee frustration through insensitive or impersonal behavior. These so-called nerd managers are often more focused on technology than on people. They have high IQs but rank low in emotional intelligence, and they lack people skills. The result is often high employee turnover. Let's assume that you are working for a small business and the owner is often described by employees as the "nerd boss from hell." What steps might you take to influence your boss, who seems to spend all his time obsessing about technology and ignoring the needs of his employees? Review the material featured in this chapter, and then develop a plan that would help your boss develop a strong team-building leadership style.[37]

2. There is increasing pressure on organizations to allow employees' personal problems to be brought to the attention of the supervisor or manager.

Personal problems that can disrupt people's lives include dealing with a teenager on drugs, coping with the needs of a sick parent, losing a babysitter, or getting a divorce. Schedule an interview with two persons who hold supervisory-management positions and ask these questions:

  a. Do you assume the role of mentor and counselor when an employee brings a personal problem to your attention?

  b. Should you give the person with a serious problem some special consideration, such as time off, less demanding work, or professional help that is paid for by the company?

3. The skills needed to be an effective leader can be developed by anyone who is willing to invest the time and energy. It is possible to practice important leadership skills before you assume the duties of a supervisor or manager. Review the various ways to improve consideration and structure skills discussed in this chapter, and then begin searching for opportunities to practice these skills. Here are some opportunities for practice:

  a. Volunteer for assignments in your community

  b. Group assignments at work, at college, or at your place of worship

  c. Involvement in political, professional, or social activities

4. The authors of *The Leadership Challenge* have identified five practices of exemplary leadership (see Figure 12.1). Review these practices and select the two that you feel present the greatest challenge to someone who has been promoted to a leadership position for the first time. Provide a rationale for your choice.

CRITICAL THINKING CHALLENGE

Reflect on your work experience and experiences in high school or college. Recall situations when you felt like a member of an effective team. What did the supervisor, manager, teacher, or coach do to develop the spirit of teamwork? What were the specific characteristics of individual team members that contributed to team performance? Compare your answers to those in Figure 12.6: The Dynamics of High Performance Teams.

SELF-ASSESSMENT EXERCISE

For each of the following statements, circle the number from 1 to 5 that best represents your response: (1) strongly disagree (never do this); (2) disagree (rarely do this); (3) moderately agree (sometimes do this); (4) agree (frequently do this); (5) strongly agree (almost always do this).

	1	2	3	4	5
A. As a team member, I help create an atmosphere of mutual trust and respect.	1	2	3	4	5
B. In the role of team member, I listen carefully to the views of others and speak frankly about the issues that are on my mind.	1	2	3	4	5
C. I practice being a servant-leader, meaning my primary desire is to help others.	1	2	3	4	5
D. As a team member, I get behind a decision once made, and work to make the decision succeed, even if I disagreed with it.	1	2	3	4	5
E. I enjoy arguing and debating issues with team members, not to improve my personal position, but to find the best possible solution to a problem or challenge.	1	2	3	4	5

After identifying your response to each item, select an attitude or skill you would like to improve. Prepare a written goal and then describe the steps you will take to achieve this goal.

YOU PLAY THE ROLE

You are currently a computer technician employed by Tech Assistance, Inc. The company provides a wide range of services, including computer system setup, PC and server repairs and upgrades, virus and spyware removal, data recovery services, and Internet security. The company was founded by Erin Wilson about five years ago. You are one of five technicians who make service calls and occasionally work in the repair center when needed. You like your work, but feel a sense of frustration when fellow employees fail to give their best efforts. The owner is very effective in solving technical problems but often displays poor people skills. She simply does not pay attention to employees; to what they are doing, or to how they are feeling. She knows almost nothing about their hobbies, family status, or personal concerns. There are times when you feel like quitting, but you like solving technical problems and helping customers with their computer needs. You have decided to meet with Erin and provide some suggestions on how to become a more effective leader. Use the name Reagan Simpson during the role play.

BELOW THE SURFACE | ENGAGING EMPLOYEES

t's amazing how much more you can learn when you don't think you're the smartest person in the room,"[38] says Kimberly Schaefer, CEO of Great Wolf Resorts. Schaefer's response is similar to that of Mike White, the CEO of DirectTV who went undercover in the opening story of this chapter. Their experiences were eye-opening, like other CEOs who have gone undercover, disguised as a front-line worker in their own companies in the television show *Undercover Boss*.

Schaefer, whose undercover role at Great Wolf Resorts was that of a line cook, experienced a high level of teamwork in the kitchen. It was an unexpected and inspiring experience. "The seven guys on the line worked with precision. How many pancakes are we going to make? How much fruit should we put in, at the same time keeping costs in mind? All those things were happening in this little unit without a supervisor. If you could spread that teamwork spirit throughout the company, you'd become so much more productive."[39]

As a result of the experience, Schaefer is now actively looking for ways to engage more employees to improve personal experience for customers. Schaefer's lesson was one some CEOs never learn. If managers are looking for ways to improve their business, the most effective first step to take is to ask employees how to do it.

QUESTIONS

1. If you were one of the line cooks at Great Wolf Resorts, and you worked with little supervision from your manager, what skills and abilities would you need to learn in order to feel completely at ease with your job? What skills would you need to work effectively with your coworkers? What do you consider to be the major arguments for and against involving CEOs in undercover roles? Do you think this would be positively received by most people in an organization? Could it be perceived as a threat to some workers? Explain your answers.

2. Schaefer said that as a result of her experience, she wants to engage employees to improve customer experiences and company procedures. Reflect on a job you currently have or previously worked in. If your boss asked you how to improve customer service or company policies, what would you want him or her to know? Would you be willing to openly share your thoughts and ideas or would you feel uncomfortable or afraid to share your thoughts?

CLOSING CASE   VIRTUAL TEAMWORK: MAKING IT WORK

Virtual teams are composed of employees who are physically dispersed throughout the nation or around the world. They are linked by various forms of electronic technology. Face-to-face contact is usually minimal or nonexistent. Virtual teams face several challenges: time zone differences, which make quick information exchanges difficult, and cultural miscues, which can cause misunderstandings. When teams don't meet in person, its less likely they will develop the kind of chemistry common to productive teams that have face-to-face meetings. Many virtual teams are in continuous danger of becoming dysfunctional.[40]

Recent research has identified certain traits and practices common to most virtual teams. Here are a few important rules for making these teams productive.[41]

- Choose a few team members who already know each other. This will speed up the process of building networks among team members. Invest in online resources that help all team members quickly learn about one another.

- Ensure the task is meaningful to team members and the company. Assign tasks that are challenging and interesting.

- The virtual team should include "boundary spanners," persons who have many connections to useful people outside of the team.

- Develop a team mission statement along with teamwork expectations, project goals, and deadlines.

- Create an online site where team members can collaborate, exchange ideas, and motivate one another. The team should have a shared online workspace that all members can access 24 hours a day.

- Encourage frequent communication and try to reach agreement about preferred communication tools.

- If you are a virtual team leader, find ways to mark team progress toward goals.

QUESTIONS

1. Which of the five dysfunctions of a team (presented in Figure 12.3) would be the greatest barriers to virtual team productivity? Defend your answer.

2. What can be done to avoid information overload when the virtual team is made up of 25 to 30 members?

CHAPTER 12 ENDNOTES

1. "Secrets of an Undercover Boss," *Fortune*, Career, p. 41–44, September 27, 2010.
2. Ibid.
3. Erin White, "How a Company Made Everyone a Team Player," *Wall Street Journal*, August 13, 2007, p. Bl.
4. Bill George (with Peter Sims), *True North* (San Francisco: John Wiley & Sons, Inc., 2007), p. xxiv.
5. Robert Kreitner, *Management*, 11th ed. (Boston: Houghton Mifflin, 2009), p. 402.
6. "Stephen Covey Talks About the 8th Habit: Effective Is No Longer Enough," *Training*, February 2005, pp. 17–19.
7. James M. Kouzes and Barry Z. Posner, *The Leadership Challenge*, 3rd ed. (San Francisco: Jossey-Bass, 2002), pp. 3–12.
8. William M. Pride, Robert J. Hughes, and Jack R. Kapoor, *Business*, 8th ed. (Boston: Houghton Mifflin, 2005), p. 198.
9. Robert Kreitner, *Management*, 11th ed. (Boston: Houghton Mifflin, 2009), p. 182.
10. Robert Kreitner, *Management*, 11th ed. (Boston: Houghton Mifflin, 2009), pp. 353–354.
11. Ibid., pp. 482–483.
12. Scott Thurm, "Teamwork Raises Everyone's Game," *Wall Street Journal*, November 7, 2005, p. B8.

13. GroupONE Solutions / Trina Hoefling's "Master Virtual Work Presentation" based on Hoefling's book, *Working Virtually.*

14. Ibid.

15. Adapted from a list in Douglas McGregor, *The Human Side of Enterprise* (New York: McGraw-Hill, 1960), pp. 232–235, 21.

16. Bennis,Warren, *An Invented Life—Reflections on Leadership and Change*, pp. 37–38. Addison-Wesley Publishing Company, 1993.

17. Rosabeth Moss Kanter, "What Would Peter Drucker Say," *Harvard Business Review*, Nov. 2009, pp. 65–70.

18. These two dimensions can be measured by the *Leadership Opinion Questionnaire* developed by Edwin A. Fleishman and available from Pearson Performance Solutions. Available from http://www.pearsonps.com; INTERNET.

19. Brian Tracy, *The 100 Absolutely Unbreakable Laws of Business Success* (San Francisco: Berrett-Koehler, 2000), pp. 138–139.

20. "Making a Nickel Do a Dime's Work," *Training*, April 1994, p. 12.

21. Brian Tracy, *The 100 Absolutely Unbreakable Laws of Business Success* (San Francisco: Berrett-Koehler, 2000), pp. 19–20.

22. "Tips for Teams," *Training*, February 1994, p. 14.

23. David G. Baldwin, "How to Win the Blame Game," *Harvard Business Review*, July/August 2001, pp. 1–7 (Reprint RO107C).

24. Blanchard, Ken and the Founding Associates and Consulting Partners of The Ken Blanchard Companies, *Leading at a Higher Level: Blanchard on Leadership and Creating High Performing Organizations*, (Upper Saddle River, NJ: FT Press, 2010), p. 150.

25. Ibid., pp. 150–151.

26. Blanchard, Ken and the Founding Associates and Consulting Partners of The Ken Blanchard Companies. *Leading at a Higher Level: Blanchard on Leadership and Creating High Performing Organizations*, (Upper Saddle River, NJ: FT Press, 2010).

27. Robert Kreitner, *Management*, 11th ed. (Boston: Houghton Mifflin, 2009), p. 409.

28. Paul Hersey, *The Situational Leader* (Escondido, Calif.: Center for Leadership Studies, 1984), pp. 29–30. To obtain current information on the Situational Leadership Model, visit http://www.situational.com.

29. Ibid.

30. Brian Tracy, *The 100 Absolutely Unbreakable Laws of Business Success* (San Francisco: Berrett-Koehler, 2000), p. 121.

31. Cary Cherniss and Daniel Goleman, *The Emotionally Intelligent Workplace* (San Francisco: Jossey-Bass, 2001), pp. 22–23.

32. Will Schutz, *The Human Element* (San Francisco: Jossey-Bass, 1994), pp. 237–238.

33. Collins,Jim, "How the Mighty Fall," *BusinessWeek*, May 25, 2009, pp. 26–33.

34. Margaret Kaeter, "The Leaders Among Us," *Business Ethics*, July/August 1994, p. 46.

35. Peter Koestenbaum, *Leadership—The Inner Side of Greatness* (San Francisco: Jossey-Bass, 1991), pp. 179–183; Stephen Covey, "Why Is It Always About You?" *Training*, May 2006, p. 64.

36. Rachel Leibrock, "Manage Your Manager, Keep Your Job," *News & Observer*, October 12, 2008.

37. Michaele Weissman, "Nerd Alert!" *Wall Street Journal*, May 14, 2001, p. R14; Peter Frost and Sandra Robinson, "The Toxic Handler: Organizational Hero—and Casualty," *Harvard Business Review*, July/August 1999, pp. 97–106.

38. "Secrets of an Undercover Boss," *Fortune*, Career, pp. 41–44, September 27, 2010.

39. Ibid.

40. Lynda Gratton, "Working Together… When Apart," *Wall Street Journal*, June 16, 2007, p. R4.

41. Ibid.

Resolving Conflict and Dealing with Difficult People

TIP OF THE ICEBERG | WHEN FEAR OF CONFLICT IS A FATAL DECISION

Jetta Productions/Iconica/Getty Images

As Flight 90 prepared to take off from Washington National Airport during a snowstorm, the copilot looked out the window and noticed that ice had built up on the wings and engines of the aircraft. The plane had been waiting in a taxi line on the runway for 49 minutes. The concerned copilot thought the pilot would see the obvious, but when it appeared he did not and continued the pre-flight check, the copilot began to make nervous comments. "See all those icicles on the back there and everything? Boy, it's a losing battle here trying to deice those things, it [gives] you a false sense of security, that's all it does." As the pilot taxied down the runway, the copilot continued his remarks, but seemed to be careful not to question the authority of the pilot. "That doesn't seem right, does it?" The pilot ignored his concerns and continued to taxi down the runway.[1] The 737 jet was only airborne for 30 seconds before crashing into the 14th Street Bridge linking Washington and Virginia, killing 74 of the 79 people on board, plus four motorists on the bridge.[2]

The official report said the disaster was caused by pilot error. But what was the *real cause* of the pilot error? Inadequate deicing is certainly one cause. Another is the inability of the copilot to confront the pilot and clearly and firmly say that he thought the pilot was putting the lives of 79 people in danger.

For many people, the idea of dealing with conflict or having a difficult conversation sounds about as much fun as a three-hour visit to the dentist. But conflict does not need to escalate into a stressful situation if you know how to deal with it. Managing conflict is a learned skill, and this chapter offers specific guidelines for effectively resolving a wide range of conflicts.

Difficulty with managing conflict led to the tragedy of
Flight 90 and the loss of 74 lives onboard.

A NEW VIEW OF CONFLICT

13-1   Most standard dictionaries define **conflict** as a clash between incompatible
people, ideas, or interests. These conflicts are almost always perceived as negative experiences in our society. But when we view conflict as a negative experience, we may be
hurting our chances of dealing with it effectively. In reality, conflicts can serve as opportunities for personal growth if we develop and use positive, constructive conflict resolution
skills.[3]

Much of our growth and social progress comes from the opportunities we have
to discover creative solutions to conflicts that surface in our lives. Dudley Weeks,
professor of conflict resolution at American University, says
conflict can provide additional ways of thinking about the *source*
of conflict and open up possibilities for improving a relationship.[4] When people work together to resolve conflicts, their
solutions are often far more creative than they would be if only
one person addressed the problem. Creative conflict resolution
can shake people out of their mental ruts and give them a new
point of view.

> *Much of our growth and social progress comes from the opportunities we have to discover creative solutions to conflicts that surface in our lives.*

Meaningful Conflict

Too much agreement is not always healthy in an organization. Employees who are anxious to be viewed as "team players" may not voice concerns even when they have doubts
about a decision being made. Meaningful conflict can be the key to producing healthy,
successful organizations because conflict is necessary for effective problem solving and
for effective interpersonal relationships.[5] The problem is not with disagreements, but
with how they are resolved.

FINDING THE ROOT CAUSES OF CONFLICT

Throughout this text, we have often compared the challenges of interpersonal relations to an iceberg. The tip of the iceberg is in plain view and readily available for consideration. However, most of the iceberg exists below the surface and can create problems if we choose to ignore it. Let's assume that the owner of your company has initiated a new policy on sexual harassment. This behavior has been carefully defined by the company lawyer, and the message seems very clear: Employees who are guilty of sexual harassment will be terminated. The Iceberg of Conflict, Figure 13.1, reveals a wide range of factors that will influence each employee's perception of the new company policy.

When you are in conflict, each level of the iceberg represents something that may influence the conflict-resolution process. It is important that we go deep enough to understand the influence of our emotions, self-perceptions, needs, unresolved issues from the past, and other things that exist at each level of the iceberg. The Iceberg of Conflict helps you better understand yourself and how to respond to create a positive outcome.

Conflict Triggers

A **conflict trigger** is a circumstance that increases the chances of intergroup or interpersonal conflict. People encounter many different types of conflicts in any given day or week, so it is wise to learn to handle conflict in a fast, efficient manner. Later in this

Figure 13.1 ■ Iceberg of Conflict

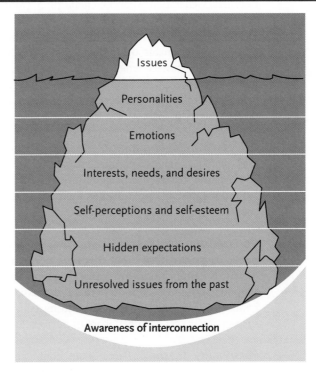

Source: From Kenneth Cloke and Joan Goldsmith, *Resolving Conflicts at Work: A Complete Guide for Everyone on the Job*, pp. 114–116, copyright © 2000 by Jossey-Bass. Reprinted with permission of John Wiley & Sons, Inc.

chapter, you will learn techniques for doing this. First, we will look at some of the most common types of conflicts.

Organizational Change. Organizational change is one of the seven root causes of conflict. In most organizations, there is tension between opposing forces for stability (maintain the status quo) and change. For example, if management wants to shift more health-care costs onto workers, tension may surface. With too much stability, no change in healthcare cost allocation, the organization may lose its competitive position in the marketplace. With too much change, the mission blurs and employee anxiety develops.[6]

Ineffective Communication. A major source of personal conflict is the misunderstanding that results from ineffective communication. In Chapter 2, we discussed the various filters that messages must pass through before effective communication can occur. In the work setting, where many different people work closely together, communication breakdowns are inevitable. Achieving effective two-way communication is always a challenge.

Value and Culture Clashes. In Chapter 5, you read that differences in values can cause conflicts between generations, between men and women, and between people with different value priorities. Today's diverse work force reflects a kaleidoscope of values and cultures, each with its own unique qualities. The individual bearers of these different values and traditions could easily come into conflict with one another.

As noted in previous chapters, generational influences are among the most powerful forces shaping values in our work force. Value differences among Matures, Baby Boomers, Generation X, and Generation Y (Millennials) can lead to conflict.

Work Policies and Practices. Interpersonal conflicts can develop when an organization has unreasonable or confusing rules, regulations, and performance standards. The conflicts often surface when managers fail to tune in to employees' perceptions that various policies are unfair. Managers need to address the source of conflict rather than suppress it. Conflict also surfaces when some workers refuse to comply with the rules or neglect their fair share of the workload.

Adversarial Management. Under adversarial management, supervisors may view their employees and even other managers with suspicion and distrust and treat them as "the enemy." Employees usually lack respect for adversarial managers, resenting their authoritarian style and resisting their suggestions for change. This atmosphere makes cooperation and teamwork difficult.

Competition for Scarce Resources. It would be difficult to find an organization, public or private, that is not involved in downsizing or cost-cutting. The result is often destructive competition for scarce resources such as updated computers, administrative support personnel, division and/or department budgets, salary increases, or annual bonuses. When budgets and cost-cutting efforts are not clearly explained, workers may suspect coworkers or supervisors of devious tactics.

Personality Clashes. There is no doubt about it: Some people just don't like each other. They may have differing communication styles, temperaments, or attitudes. They may not be able to identify exactly what it is they dislike about the other person, but the bottom line is that conflicts will arise when these people have to work together. Even

"I cooked us a lovely dinner for two—you could at least do the dishes!"

Carolita Johnson/CartoonBank.com

people who get along well with each other in the beginning stages of a work relationship may begin to clash after working together for many years.

RESOLVING CONFLICT ASSERTIVELY

13-2 Conflict is often uncomfortable whether it is in a personal or professional setting. People sometimes get hurt and become defensive because they feel they are under personal attack. Because we have to work or live with certain people every day, it is best to avoid harming these ongoing relationships. But many people do not know how to approach and manage conflict in a positive way. Many professionals advise going directly to the offending person and calmly discussing his or her irritating behavior rather than complaining to others.[7] Figure 13.2, "Dealing with People You Can't Stand," offers specific strategies you might use. By taking those steps to change *your* behavior, you can facilitate a powerful change in theirs. Keep in mind that some people are unaware of the impact of their behavior, and if you draw their attention to it, they may change it.

Whereas these strategies may be comfortable for some people, such a direct approach may be very uncomfortable for many others. People who attempt to avoid conflict by simply ignoring things that bother them are exhibiting **nonassertive behavior**. Nonassertive people often give in to the demands of others, and their passive approach makes them less likely to make their needs known. If you fail to take a firm position when such action is appropriate, customers, coworkers, and supervisors may take advantage of you, and management may question your abilities.

Figure 13.2 ■ Dealing with People You Can't Stand

THE BULLY ▶	Bullies find ways to manipulate or control others. They are pushy, ruthless, loud, and forceful and tend to intimidate you with in-your-face arguments. They assume that the end justifies the means. **Strategy:** Keep your cool. Immediately respond calmly and professionally to let the bully know you are not a target: "When you're ready to speak to me with respect, I'll be ready to discuss this matter." Walk away from a ranting bully. Ask the bully to fully explain what he or she is trying to say or do, and then paraphrase your understanding of the bully's real intentions.
THE BACKSTABBER ▶	They present themselves as your friend but do everything in their power to sabotage your relationships with your supervisors, coworkers, and clients. They use tactics such as withholding information from you and then suggesting to others that you are incompetent, witless, and worthy of demotion. **Strategy:** Once you've discovered your saboteur, tell key people that the person is, in fact, not a friend, which takes power from the backstabber and reveals the smear campaign.
THE WHINER ▶	They wallow in their woe, whine incessantly about the injustices that surround them, and carry the weight of the world on their shoulders. **Strategy:** Listen so you can identify and focus on possible solutions. If they remain in "it's hopeless" mode, walk away saying, "Let me know when you want to talk about a solution." Communicate how their behavior brings down others on the team.
THE JERK ▶	They tend to be self-centered, arrogant, manipulative, and goal-oriented. They trust no one and refuse to collaborate with others. They may take pot-shots at you during meetings, but avoid one-on-one confrontations. They lack empathy, but can be great sweet-talkers to the boss. **Strategy:** They often do not respond to normal pleas to change their behavior, so just back off. Do not take their bait, limit your contact with them, avoid conflict when possible, and always be on guard.
THE KNOW-IT-ALL ▶	They will tell you what they know, but they will not bother listening to your "clearly inferior" ideas. Often, they really don't know much, but they don't let that get in the way. They exaggerate, brag, and mislead. **Strategy:** Acknowledge their expertise, but be prepared with your facts. Use "I" statements, such as "From what I've read and experienced . . ."
THE COWARD ▶	When faced with a crucial decision, they keep putting it off until it is too late and the decision makes itself, or they say yes to everything but follow through on nothing. **Strategy:** Help them feel comfortable and safe in their rare decisions to move forward, and stay in touch until the decision is implemented. Arrange deadlines and describe the consequences that will result when they complete the tasks and what will happen if they don't.
THE EXPLODERS ▶	They throw tantrums that can escalate quickly. When they blow their tops, they are unable to stop. When the smoke clears and the dust settles, the cycle begins again. **Strategy:** When an explosion begins, assertively repeat the individual's name to get his or her attention, or repeat a neutral comment such as "Stop!" Calmly address what they said in their first few sentences, which usually reveals the real problem. Give them time to regain self-control. Suggest that they take time out to cool down, and then listen to their problems in private.

Source: Adapted from *Dealing with People You Can't Stand* by Rick Brinkman and Rick Kirshner. Copyright © 1994 by McGraw-Hill, Inc. Reprinted by permission of The McGraw Hill Companies.

Table 13.1 ■ Behaviors Exhibited by Assertive, Aggressive, and Nonassertive Persons During Conflict

	ASSERTIVE PERSON	**AGGRESSIVE PERSON**	**NONASSERTIVE PERSON**
In conflict situations	Communicates directly	Dominates	Avoids the conflict
In decision-making situations	Chooses for self	Chooses for self and others	Allows others to choose
In situations expressing feelings	Is open, direct, honest, while allowing others to express their feelings	Expresses feelings in a threatening manner; puts down, inhibits others	Holds true feelings inside
In group meeting situations	Uses direct, clear "I" statements: "I believe that ..."	Uses clear but demeaning "you" statements: "You should have known better ..."	Uses indirect, unclear statements: "Would you mind if ... ?"

Assertive behavior, on the other hand, provides you the opportunity to stand up for your rights and express your thoughts and feelings in a direct, appropriate way that does not violate the rights of others. It is a matter of getting the other person to understand your viewpoint.[8] People who exhibit appropriate assertive behavior skills are able to handle their conflicts with greater ease and assurance while maintaining good interpersonal relations.

Some people do not understand the distinction between being aggressive and being assertive. **Aggressive behavior** in conflict situations involves expressing your thoughts and feelings and defending your rights in a way that *violates* the rights of others. Aggressive people may interrupt, talk fast, ignore others, and use sarcasm or other forms of verbal abuse to maintain control.

Table 13.1 may give you a clearer understanding of how nonassertive, assertive, and aggressive individuals respond when confronted with conflict situations.

How to Become More Assertive

Entire books have been written that describe how to improve your assertiveness skills. Several years ago, the American Management Association (*www.amanet.org*) began offering skill-development seminars that focus on assertiveness training, including Assertiveness Training for Managers and Assertiveness Training for Women in Business.[9] Enrollees have the opportunity to achieve greater credibility by learning how to handle tough situations with composure and confidence. Whether you choose to read books or participate in assertiveness training, know that you can communicate your wants, dislikes, and feelings in a clear, direct manner without threatening or attacking others. Here are three practical guidelines that will help you develop your assertiveness skills.

In the Beginning, Take Small Steps. Being assertive may be difficult at first, so start with something that is easy. You might decline the invitation to keep the minutes at the weekly staff meeting if you feel others should assume this duty from time to time. If you are tired of eating lunch at Joe's Diner (the choice of a coworker), suggest a restaurant that you would prefer. If someone insists on keeping the temperature at a cool 67 degrees and you are tired of being cold all the time, approach the person and voice your opinion. Voicing your needs or requests is not necessarily a bad thing.

Use Communication Skills That Enhance Assertiveness. A confident tone of voice, eye contact, firm gestures, and good posture create nonverbal messages that say, "I'm serious about this request." Using "I" messages can be especially helpful in cases where you want to assert yourself in a nonthreatening manner. If you approach the person who wants the thermostat set at 67 degrees and say, "You need to be more considerate of others," the person is likely to become defensive. However, if you say, "I feel uncomfortable when the temperature is so cool," you will start the conversation on a more positive note.

Be Soft on People and Hard on the Problem. The goal of conflict resolution is to solve the problem but avoid doing harm to the relationship. Of course, relationships tend to become entangled with the problem, so there is a tendency to treat the people and the problem as one. Your coworker, Terry, is turning in projects late every week, and you are feeling a great deal of frustration each time it happens. You must communicate to Terry that each missed deadline creates serious problems for you. Practice using tact, diplomacy, and patience as you keep the discussion focused on the problem, not on Terry's personality traits.

LEARN TO NEGOTIATE EFFECTIVELY

13-3   In the past, the responsibility for negotiating an effective resolution to conflicts was often given to supervisors, department heads, team leaders, shop stewards, mediators, and other individuals with established authority and responsibility. Today, many companies have organized workers into teams that are empowered to solve their own problems whenever possible. This means that every employee needs to learn how to effectively negotiate satisfactory resolutions to conflicts. Danny Ertel, author and consultant in the area of negotiations, says, "Every company, today, exists in a complex web of relationships, and the shape of that web is formed, one thread at a time, through negotiations."[10] Team assignments, compensation, promotions, and work assignments are just a few of the areas where you can apply negotiation skills.

Think Win/Win

There are basically three ways to approach negotiations: win/lose, lose/lose, and win/win. When you use the **win/lose approach**, you are attempting to reach your goals at the expense of the other party's. For example, a manager can say, "Do as I say or find a job somewhere else!" The manager wins; the employee loses. Although this approach may end the conflict on a short-term basis, it does not usually address the underlying cause of the problem. It may simply sow the seeds of another conflict because the "losers" feel frustrated.

When the **lose/lose approach** is used to settle a dispute, each side must give in to the other. If the sacrifices are too great, both parties may feel that too much has been given. This strategy can be applied when there is little time to find a solution

Soon after celebrating their 15th wedding anniversary, Elaine and Michael Honig decided to get a divorce. As joint owners of the successful Honig Vineyard, the divorce could have created serious problems. However, they decided to remain friends as well as business partners after the divorce.

through effective negotiation techniques, or when negotiations are at a standstill and no progress is being made. Union-management disputes, for example, often fall into the lose/lose trap when neither side is willing to yield. In these cases, an arbitrator, a neutral third party, may be called in to impose solutions on the disputing parties.

In general, the win/lose and lose/lose approaches to negotiating create an "us versus them" attitude among the people involved in the conflict, rather than a "we versus the problem" approach. "Us versus them" (or "my way versus your way") means that participants focus on whose solution is superior, instead of working together to find a solution that is acceptable to all.

> *The basic purpose of the win/win approach to negotiating is to fix the problem—not the blame!*

The basic purpose of the **win/win approach** to negotiating is to fix the problem—not the blame! Don't think hurt; think help. Negotiating a win/win solution to a conflict is not a debate where you are attempting to prove the other side wrong; instead, you are engaging in a dialogue where each side attempts to get the other side to understand its concerns, and both sides then work toward a mutually satisfying solution. Your negotiations will go better when you shift your emphasis from a tactical approach of how to counter the other person's every comment to discovering a creative solution that simple haggling obscures.[11]

Perhaps the most vital skill in effective negotiations is listening. When you concentrate on learning common interests, not differences, the nature of the negotiation changes from a battle to win, to a discussion of how to meet the objectives of everyone involved in the dispute (see Figure 13.3).

Figure 13.3

Rob Walker reviewed several of the best-selling books on negotiation, including *Getting to Yes, You Can Negotiate Anything, The Negotiation Tool Kit*, and *The Power of Nice*. He discovered a few basic negotiating tips that recur in these popular advice books:

- Stay rationally focused on the issue being negotiated.
- Exhaustive preparation is more important than aggressive argument.
- Think through your alternatives.
- The more options you feel you have, the better a negotiating position you will be in.
- Spend less time talking and more time listening and asking good questions. Sometimes silence is your best response.
- Let the other side make the first offer. If you are underestimating yourself, you might make a needlessly weak opening move.

Source: Rob Walker, "Take It or Leave It: The Only Guide to Negotiating You Will Ever Need," *Inc.*, August 2003, p. 81.

Beware of Defensive Behaviors

Effective negotiations are often slowed or sidetracked completely by defensive behaviors that surface when people are in conflict with each other. When one person in a conflict situation becomes defensive, others may mirror this behavior. In a short time, progress is slowed because people stop listening and begin thinking about how they can defend themselves against the other person's comments.

We often become defensive when we feel our needs are being ignored. Kurt Salzinger, Executive Director for Science at the American Psychological Association, reminds us that conflicts are often caused by unfulfilled needs for things such as dignity, security, identity, recognition, or justice. He says, "Conflict is often exacerbated as much by the process of the relationship as it is by the issues."[12] Determining the other person's needs requires careful listening and respect for views that differ from your own. If you feel you are trapped in a win/lose negotiation and can hear yourself or the other person becoming defensive, do everything in your power to refocus the discussion toward fixing the problem rather than defending your position.

PARABLE OF THE ORANGE

Two people each want an orange, but negotiations drag on without a solution. Finally, they agree to split the orange in half. But it turns out that one person simply wanted the juice, and the other person wanted only the rind. In this case, haggling obscured the solution. If they had engaged in a true dialogue, each side could have gotten what it wanted.

Source: Rob Walker, "Take It or Leave It: The Only Guide to Negotiating You Will Ever Need," *Inc.*, August 2003, p. 77.

Know That Negotiating Styles Vary

Depending on your communication style, assertiveness skills, and past experiences in dealing with conflict in the workplace, individuals naturally develop their own negotiating styles. But negotiating is a skill, and people can learn how and when to adapt their style to deal effectively with conflict situations.

Total Person Insight

> Any method of negotiation may be fairly judged by three criteria: It should produce a wise agreement if agreement is possible. It should be efficient. And it should improve, or at least not damage, the relationship between parties.
>
> Source: Roger Fisher and William Ury, *Getting to Yes* (New York: Penguin Books, 1981), p. 4.

Robert Maddux suggests there are five different behavioral styles that can be used during conflict situations. He takes the position that different styles may be appropriate in different situations.

Avoidance Style (Uncooperative/Nonassertive). This style is appropriate when the conflict is too minor or too great to resolve. Any attempt to resolve the conflict might result in damaging a relationship or simply wasting time and energy. Avoidance might take the form of diplomatically sidestepping an issue or postponing your response until a more appropriate time.

Accommodating Style (Cooperative/Nonassertive). This style is appropriate when resolving the conflict is not worth risking damage to the relationship or general disharmony. Individuals who use this approach relinquish their own concerns to satisfy the concerns of someone else. Accommodating might take the form of selfless generosity or blind obedience to another's point of view.

Win/Lose Style (Uncooperative/Aggressive). This style may be appropriate when the conflict involves "survival of the fittest," when you must prove your superior position, or when your opinion is the most ethically or professionally correct. This power-oriented position allows you to use whatever means seem appropriate when it is time to stand up for your rights.

Problem-Solving Style (Assertive/Cooperative). This style is appropriate when all parties openly discuss the issues and a mutually beneficial solution can be found without anyone making a major concession. Problem solvers attempt to uncover underlying issues that may be at the root of the problem, and then focus the discussion toward achieving the most desirable outcome. They seek to replace conflict with collaboration.

Compromising Style (Moderately Aggressive/Moderately Cooperative). This style is appropriate when no one person or idea is perfect, when there is more than one good way to do something, or when you must give to get what you want. Compromise attempts to find mutually acceptable solutions to the conflict that partially satisfy both sides. Never use this style when unethical activities are the cause of the conflict.

How to Have a Crucial Conversation

An important book that describes a process for how to resolve conflict is *Crucial Conversations: Tools for Talking When Stakes Are High*. The authors summarize 25 years of

Figure 13.4 ■ The Crucial Conversations Model

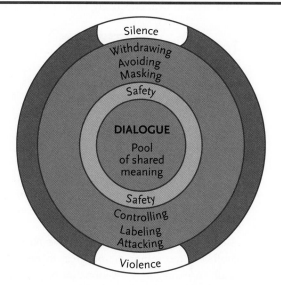

Source: Crucial Conversations: Tools for Talking When the Stakes Are High, "The Dialogue Model," Kerry Patterson, Joseph Grenny, Ron McMillan, and Al Switzler, 2002, p. 182.

research and evaluations of 25,000 people in high-stakes conversations. Companies that are practicing these methods have experienced significant improvements in innovation, teamwork, and change management.

The authors define a *crucial conversation* as a discussion between two or more people where stakes are high, opinions vary, and emotions run strong. Figure 13.4, illustrates a powerful model anyone can use to create a meaningful dialogue based on mutual understanding.

At the center of the model is a circle called the *Pool of Shared Meaning*, the focus of having an effective dialogue with others. The authors contend that the single most important factor of a crucial conversation boils down to this: People must find a way to get all relevant information (from themselves and others) out into the open. People must be willing and capable of expressing their thoughts, feelings, and emotions openly and honestly, *and they must be willing to do so even when their ideas are controversial.*[13]

Unfortunately, the more crucial the conversation, the less likely people are to handle it well. When people move into the realm of *silence* or *violence*, conflict resolution tends to break down. *Silence* occurs when we suppress our thoughts, withhold information, or avoid a topic, limiting the amount of information needed to resolve conflict. *Violence*, which does not imply physical violence, occurs when we begin attacking others' ideas, trying to manipulate them, or hurting their feelings.

To steer the conversation back to a *meaningful dialogue*, the most important area to focus on is creating a safe environment. When we feel safe with others, open communication is possible and the dialogue stimulates ideas and shared meaning. Lack of safety keeps us from moving into the pool of sharing meaning. As soon as you identify that others may not feel safe, the best way to deal with the conflict is to step out of the content of the issue being discussed, and rebuild safety. For example, saying "Can we shift gears for a moment and talk about [the bigger picture of the discussion topic]? It seems we are both trying to force our viewpoints. Can we continue talking to find a solution that will make both of us happy?"

People who are gifted communicators keep a close eye on safety. They learn to step back and ask themselves, "Are we in or out of dialogue?" "Where am I?" "Where are others?" If safety feels weak, they step out of the content of the conversation, focus on increasing safety, then step back into the conversation.

It is also important to understand the interpretations and judgments that people often place on the behavior they observe in others. In a heated discussion, emotions can quickly overrule facts, causing them to *"make up" a story* in their mind to explain what they *see and hear*. This causes them to *feel* a strong emotion and to *act* in a way that is not productive to resolving conflict. Critical thoughts are really stories you have created; they are not necessarily true. For example, let's say Susan works for a boss that constantly cuts her off mid-sentence. The story she "makes up" might be "George always cuts me off during staff meetings—I bet he doesn't think I'm smart enough to lead this team… Or maybe he's thinking that just because I'm a woman, people won't listen to me or respect me." In this case, Susan just made up a negative story in her mind, based on what she saw and heard, that made her feel less safe. She needs to challenge underlying thoughts that may be distorted.[14]

CONFLICT RESOLUTION PROCESS

13-4 The **conflict resolution process** consists of five steps that can be used at work and in your personal life. To apply the five steps requires understanding and acceptance of everything we have discussed up to this point in the chapter: application of assertiveness skills, understanding how to deal with various types of difficult people, support for the win/win approach to conflict resolution, and learning how to negotiate.

> *A misunderstanding is a failure to accurately understand the other person's point. A disagreement, in contrast, is a failure to agree, which would persist despite the most accurate understanding.*

Step One: Decide Whether You Have a Misunderstanding or a True Disagreement

David Stiebel, author of *When Talking Makes Things Worse!*, says a misunderstanding is a failure to accurately understand the other person's point. A disagreement, in contrast, is a failure to agree, which would persist despite the most accurate understanding. In a true disagreement, people want more than your explanation and further details; they want to change your mind.[15] When we fail to realize the distinction between these two possibilities, a great deal of time and energy may be wasted. Consider the following conflict situation.

As Sarah entered the driveway of her home, she could hardly wait to share the news with her husband Paul. Late that afternoon, she had met with her boss and learned she was the number-one candidate for a newly created administrative position. Sarah entered the house and immediately told Paul about the promotion opportunity. In a matter of seconds, it became apparent that he was not happy about the promotion. He said, "We don't need the extra money, and you do not need the headaches that come with an administrative position." Expecting a positive response, Sarah was very disappointed. In the heat of anger, Sarah and Paul both said things they would later regret.

If Sarah and Paul had asked each other a few questions, this conflict might have been avoided. Before arriving home, Sarah had already weighed the pros and cons of

Cartoon Features Syndicate

"There's no denying the conflict around here, J.B., but a flak jacket?"

the new position and decided it was not a good career move; however, she wanted her husband's input before making the final decision. This conflict was not a true disagreement in which one person tries to change the other person's mind; it was a misunderstanding that was the result of incomplete information. If Sarah and Paul had fully understood each other's position, it would have become clear that a true disagreement did not exist.

Step Two: Define the Problem and Collect the Facts

The saying "A problem well defined is a problem half solved" is not far from the truth. It is surprising how difficult this step can be. Everyone involved needs to focus on the real cause of the conflict, not on what has happened as a result of it.

As you begin collecting information about the conflict, it may be necessary to separate facts from opinions or perceptions. Ask questions that focus on who is involved in the conflict, what happened, when, where, and why. What policies and procedures were involved?

Conflict resolution in the age of information offers us new challenges. As we are faced with information overload, we may be tempted to use the information we already have rather than search for the new information needed to guide a decision.[16]

Step Three: Clarify Perceptions

Your perception is your interpretation of the facts surrounding the situations you encounter. Perceptions can have a tremendous influence on your behavior. In a conflict situation, it is therefore very important that you clarify all parties' perceptions of the problem. You can do this by attempting to see the situation as others see it. Take the case of Laura, a sales representative who was repeatedly passed over for a promotion although her sales numbers were among the best in the department.

After a period of time, Laura became convinced that she was the victim of gender discrimination. She filed charges with the Equal Employment Opportunity Commission (EEOC), and a hearing was scheduled. When Laura's boss was given a chance to explain his actions, he described Laura as someone who was very dedicated to her family. He said, "It's my view that she would be unhappy in a sales management position because she would have to work longer hours and travel more." He did not see his actions as being discriminatory. Laura explained that she valued the time she spent with her husband and children but achieving a management position was an important career goal.

Step Four: Generate Options for Mutual Gain

Once the basic problem has been defined, the facts surrounding it have been brought out, and everyone is operating with the same perceptions, everyone involved in the conflict should focus on generating options that will fix the problem. Some people, however, do not consider generating options to be part of the conflict resolution process. Rather than broadening the options for mutual gain, some individuals want to quickly build support for a single solution. The authors of the best-selling book *Getting to Yes* say, "In a dispute, people usually believe that they know the right answer—their view should prevail. They become trapped in their own point of view."[17] Group members should be encouraged to generate a wide variety of ideas and possibilities.

Step Five: Implement Options with Integrity

The final step in the conflict resolution process involves finalizing an agreement that offers win/win benefits to those in conflict. Sometimes, as the conflict resolution process comes to a conclusion, one or more parties in the conflict may be tempted to win an advantage that weakens the relationship. This might involve hiding information or using pressure tactics that violate the win/win spirit and weaken the relationship. Even the best conflict solutions can fail unless all conflict partners serve as "caretakers" of the agreement and the relationship.[18]

Establish timetables for implementing the solutions, and provide a plan to evaluate their effectiveness. On a regular basis, make a point to discuss with others how things are going to be sure that old conflict patterns do not resurface.

THE ROLE OF LABOR UNIONS IN CONFLICT RESOLUTION

13-5   Since the 1930s, labor unions have had the authority to negotiate disputes between union members and management. This arrangement serves as an equalizing factor that allows organized workers the power necessary to challenge managers' decisions. Most management-labor union disputes escalate when the employment contracts that establish the workers' wages, benefits, and working conditions expire and need to be renegotiated. The overwhelming majority of employment contracts are settled through **collective bargaining**, a process that defines the rights and privileges of both sides involved in the conflict and establishes the terms of employment and length of the contract (usually from three to five years). However, if labor and management cannot settle their differences, they may submit their disputes to one of the following:

- **Mediation**—A neutral third party listens to both sides and suggests solutions. It carries no binding authority. Both parties are free to reject or accept the mediator's decision.
- **Voluntary arbitration**—Both sides willingly submit their disagreements to a neutral party. The arbitrator's decision must be accepted by both sides.
- **Compulsory arbitration**—When the government decides that the labor-management dispute threatens national health and safety, or will damage an entire industry, it can appoint an arbitrator who dictates a solution that is binding on both sides and can be enforced in a court of law.

Harvard scholar Henry Louis Gates, Jr. returned from a trip and had difficulty opening the door to his home. A passerby thought Gates might be a burglar and called police. Sgt. James Crowley arrived on the scene and a major conflict ensued. The conflict became a national issue when president Obama publicly criticized the police officer. The "beer summit" was an attempt at reconciliation.

When collective bargaining, mediation, and arbitration are not enough to settle disputes, union leaders may recommend, and members may vote, to go on strike against their employers. A strike generally results in a lose/lose situation in which workers lose paychecks, employers lose sales, customers lose products or services, and communities lose economic stability. In the fall of 2008, the International Association of Machinists and Aerospace Workers staged an eight-week strike against Boeing Company. The strike cost an estimated $100 million a day in deferred revenue and production delays.[19]

LOOKING BACK: SUMMARY OF LEARNING OBJECTIVES

1. **List and describe some of the major causes of conflict in the workplace.**

   Conflicts among people at work happen every day and can arise because of changes within the organization, poor communication, values and culture clashes, confusing work policies and practices, competition for scarce resources, or adversarial management. Often, however, conflicts come from coworkers who refuse to carry their fair share of the workload or have a difficult personality. Although unresolved conflicts can have a negative effect on an organization's productivity, a difference of opinion sometimes has a positive effect by forcing team members toward creative and innovative solutions to problems.

2. **Use assertiveness skills in conflict situations.**

   Assertiveness skills are necessary when you want to maintain your rights during a conflict with someone else but want to avoid being overly aggressive, which means interfering with others' rights. Begin building assertiveness skills by tackling relatively minor issues first until you gain the confidence to take on those who try to take away your power. Use "I" statements rather than "you" statements so that the other person does not become defensive. Focus on fixing the problem rather than attacking the other person.

3. **Understand when and how to implement effective negotiation skills.**

   You can vastly improve your human relations skills when dealing with difficult people by learning when and how to intentionally implement Robert Maddux's five negotiating styles: avoidance style, accommodating style, win/lose style, problem-solving style, and compromising style. TheCrucial Conversations model, Figure 13.4 describes a helpful process to create a meaningful dialogue based on mutual understanding when opinions vary and emotions run strong.

4. **Identify key elements of the conflict resolution process.**

When employees cannot solve their conflicts in an informal manner, many organizations create solutions through a conflict resolution process. The five-step conflict resolution process is described in this chapter.

5. **Discuss the role of labor unions in conflict resolution.**

Labor leaders and business owners are finding new ways to cooperate with each other rather than negotiating with a nonproductive "us versus them" attitude. They are finding that flexibility and innovation are far more effective than old adversarial styles. If labor and management cannot settle their differences, they may submit their disputes to mediation, voluntary arbitration, or compulsory arbitration. When these methods cannot settle disputes, union members may vote to go on strike. This may cause workers to lose paychecks, employers to lose sales, customer to lose products and services, and communities to lose economic stability.

KEY TERMS

conflict, 276
conflict trigger, 277
nonassertive behavior, 279
assertive behavior, 281
aggressive behavior, 281

win/lose approach, 282
lose/lose approach, 282
win/win approach, 283
conflict resolution process, 287
collective bargaining, 289

mediation, 289
voluntary arbitration, 289
compulsory arbitration, 289

CAREER INSIGHT: DEALING WITH WORKPLACE BULLIES

Building a civilized workplace involves getting rid of workplace bullies. Workplace bullying can include sarcastic comments, physical threats, social exclusion, or work sabotage. Unlike sexual or racial harassment, this aggressive behavior is not necessarily illegal. But it does violate company policies that prohibit intimidation. Abusive supervisors and coworkers who cause emotional distress should not be tolerated. One of the most underutilized weapons in the arsenal against bullies is telling them the truth about the way they make you feel.

Source: Robert Kreitner, *Management*, 11th ed. (Boston: Houghton Mifflin, 2009), p. 182.

TRY YOUR HAND

1. Has there been someone in your life (now or in the past) that you just can't (or couldn't) stand? Explain the behaviors this person exhibits that get on your nerves. Carefully examine Figure 13.2, determine which category fits the person best, and then describe what you might do to help this person change his or her behavior. Be specific.

2. Describe a conflict that is disrupting human relations at school, home, or work. It might involve academic requirements at school, distribution of responsibilities at home, or hurt feelings at work. Identify all the people involved in the conflict, and decide who should be involved in the conflict resolution process. Design a conflict resolution plan by following the steps given in this chapter. Implement your plan using The Dialogue Model, Figure 13.4 and report the results of this conflict resolution process to other class members.

3. To learn more about your level of assertiveness, complete the short quiz below. Simply answer "yes" or "no" to each question and then interpret your score.

ARE YOU ASSERTIVE ENOUGH?

Take this short quiz from *The Instant Manager* to find out.

Being assertive is not the same as being aggressive. Assertiveness is confidence translated into action. It is neither bullying nor brow-beating, but simply allowing your convictions to carry a conversation. Honesty combined with a non-confrontational manner will make assertiveness one of the most valuable tools in your managerial tool kit.

Answer "Yes" or "No" to each question. Do you…

Yes❑   No❑   1. Apologize when you don't have an instant solution to a problem?

Yes❑   No❑   2. Frequently apologize for your decisions?

Yes❑   No❑   3. Feel that you do not have the right to change your mind?

Yes❑   No❑   4. Feel guilty when you make mistakes, even when they can be fixed?

Yes❑   No❑   5. Automatically say "yes" when someone makes a request?

Yes❑   No❑   6. Feel foolish asking questions when you do not understand something?

Yes❑   No❑   7. Follow instructions without question?

Yes❑   No❑   8. Think your opinion does not count, especially if it differs from the majority?

Yes❑   No❑   9. Feel that you do not have the right to ask people to change their behavior towards you?

Yes❑   No❑   10. Feel guilty delegating or deferring tasks?

Yes❑   No❑   11. Have trouble walking away from an argument?

Total number of "Yes" ☐

HOW TO INTERPRET YOUR SCORE.
If you answered "Yes" to:

8 to 11 of the questions: You need serious improvement. Take an acting or public speaking course, review your accomplishments—whatever will boost your self-confidence.

4 to 7 of the questions: You are just squeaking by. Try some speaking and body-language techniques and learn to keep your cool.

0 to 3 of the questions: You are just about right. Keep it up!

Excerpted from *The Instant Manager—More than 100 Quick Tips & techniques for Great Results*, by Cy Charney (AMACOM 2004).

---

4. To develop your assertiveness skills, find a partner who will join you for a practice session. The partner should assume the role of a friend, family member, or coworker who is doing something that causes you a great deal of frustration. (The problem can be real or imaginary.) Communicate your dislikes and feelings in a clear, direct manner without threatening or attacking. Then ask your partner to critique your assertiveness skills. Participate in several of these practice sessions until you feel confident that you have improved your assertiveness skills.

CRITICAL THINKING CHALLENGE

Think about and briefly summarize the various conflicts you witnessed among workers within an organization in which you worked as an employee or volunteer. Carefully examine each conflict scenario and determine if the root cause is the same as the generally perceived cause for the disagreements. What did you discover?

SELF-ASSESSMENT EXERCISE

For each of the following statements, circle the number from 1 to 5 that best represents your response: (1) strongly disagree (never do this); (2) disagree (rarely do this); (3) moderately agree (sometimes do this); (4) agree (frequently do this); (5) strongly agree (almost always do this).

	1	2	3	4	5
A. In my attempts to resolve conflict, I strive for a solution that all parties can accept.	1	2	3	4	5
B. I will put off certain discussions that I know will be difficult longer than I should, rather than get into an argument.	1	2	3	4	5
C. When others don't deliver on a promise, there are times when I judge them more quickly than I should.	1	2	3	4	5
D. In a conflict situation, I make every effort to clarify perceptions.	1	2	3	4	5
E. In a conflict situation, I try to distinguish between a misunderstanding and a true disagreement.	1	2	3	4	5

After identifying your response to each item, select an attitude or skill you would like to improve. Prepare a written goal and then describe the steps you will take to achieve this goal.

YOU PLAY THE ROLE

Assume the role of a business manager for a large hospital. About three weeks ago, you received some incomplete medical records from Ashley Mason, the physician in charge of the emergency room. With a red pen, you marked the areas that were incomplete and sent the forms back to the doctor. You attached a terse note that requested the forms to be returned within 24 hours. Three days passed without a reply, and your anger increased each day. Finally, you sent the doctor an e-mail that basically accused Dr. Mason of incompetence in the area of medical record keeping. The doctor phoned you immediately and said the entire emergency room staff had been extremely busy and did not have a moment to spare. You replied that timely and accurate record keeping is the responsibility of every physician employed by the hospital. Unfortunately, your tone of voice and your selection of words were totally inappropriate. Basically, you treated Dr. Mason like a child who had misbehaved, and the doctor hung up on you. You immediately felt like a fool and regretted your behavior. The next day, the completed forms were returned to you. You have decided to meet with Dr. Mason. Your goal is to repair the damaged relationship and set the stage for effective communications in the future. Before meeting with another class member who will assume the role of Dr. Mason, review the information on the art of apologizing in Chapter 8 and information in this chapter on resolving conflicts.

BELOW THE SURFACE

EVEN ROCKET SCIENTISTS NEED TO LEARN CONFLICT RESOLUTION SKILLS

Seventy-three seconds after the space shuttle Challenger launched on January 28, 1986, the world watched in horror as the shuttle exploded in the sky. The initial investigation revealed faulty O-rings as the cause. Unfortunately, just as there was a "cause behind the cause" in the opening case that described the Flight 90 airline disaster, there was a similar cause behind the Shuttle disaster. Both disasters were the result of employees unable to have a crucial conversation with a person of higher authority. Howard Schwartz, in his book *Narcissistic Process and Corporate Decay*, described the Challenger disaster as a tragic example of the "exportation of conflict."[20]

Four years **before** the tragedy, several NASA engineers discovered O-rings may malfunction if the temperature dropped below 53 degrees, but these concerns were disregarded. Ignoring NASA regulations, engineers did not report the problem to senior management at NASA, but chose to keep the problem within their reporting channels with Thiokol, the contractor that built Shuttle parts. Although the O-rings were reclassified as "Criticality 1"—meaning that their failure would result in the destruction of the Challenger—no one suggested that the shuttle be grounded until the flaw could be fixed.[21]

According to the Presidential Commission Report, "The decision to launch the Challenger was flawed. Those who made the launch decision were unaware of the recent history of problems concerning the O-rings and were unaware of the initial written recommendation of the contractor advising against the launch at temperatures below 53 degrees Fahrenheit.... If the decision makers had known all of the facts, it is highly unlikely that they would have decided to launch 51-L [the Challenger] on January 28, 1986."[22]

Upon evaluating the space shuttle Challenger launch you may reach the conclusion that it is difficult to challenge authority, especially in jobs with high levels of responsibility and where the stakes are high.

QUESTIONS

1. If you were one of the NASA engineers who knew of the safety risk from the O-rings, would you have responded differently than the engineers who adhered to the "chain of command" which is so commonly used in organizations as a process to solve problems?

2. If you answered yes to the question above, how would you handle the situation to avoid a confrontation with your boss? Use the Crucial Conversations skills you learned in this chapter.

3. NASA's organizational culture was said to be one of the causes for the Challenger shuttle disaster. What changes should NASA make to its organizational culture to avoid critical situations related to authority and decision-making?

CLOSING CASE | NOT WHAT THE DOCTOR ORDERED

When a Brazilian man went to the doctor to seek treatment for his hearing problem, he walked out the door with a vasectomy instead. How could this happen? It's easy when the patient doesn't think to question authority. "The strangest thing is that he asked no questions when the doctor started preparations in the area which had so little to do with his ear," said a spokesperson for the Clinic.[23]

When people go to a hospital or clinic, quality health care from qualified medical care professionals is an expectation, right? It is rare when people question the decisions of doctors or the care they receive. But maybe they should. An average of 195,000 Americans die annually from potentially preventable, in-hospital medical errors. The equivalent of 390 jumbo jets full of people are dying each year due to likely preventable, in-hospital medical errors, making this one of the leading killers in the U.S. said Dr. Samantha Collier.[24]

In addition to deaths, more than two million infections occur in hospitals each year, many of which could be prevented by people simply washing their hands or by speaking up when they observe incompetence. Studies reveal that a majority of health-care workers regularly see colleagues take dangerous shortcuts, make mistakes, and appear critically incompetent, yet fewer than one in ten speak up and share their full concerns.

QUESTIONS

1. You are a new nurse in a hospital who is preparing to assist in the operating room. You observe the primary surgeon scrubbing for the surgery and just before he enters the OR, he stops to sign some papers. How would you approach the surgeon?

2. You work for a tyrant of a doctor who has fired several nurses in your department. You just saw him make an error that might endanger the patient, but you are afraid to speak up. You need the job. What would you do?

3. You are a doctor in a reputable hospital and work with a physician who you regard as incompetent in many areas. Do you speak to the doctor directly or opt to speak to your boss? What are the advantages and disadvantages of each approach?

CHAPTER 13 ENDNOTES

1. Kilroy, Chris. AirDisaster.com, retrieved on March 1, 2012 from http://www.airdisaster.com/special/special-af90.shtml.

2. Air Florida Flight 90, Wikipedia, retrieved February 29, 2012 from http://en.wikipedia.org/wiki/Air_Florida_Flight_90.

3. Dudley Weeks, *The Eight Essential Steps to Conflict Resolution* (New York: G. P. Putnam's Sons, 1992), p. 7.

4. Ibid., pp. 7–8.

5. Susan M. Heathfield, "Fight for What's Right: Ten Tips to Encourage Meaningful Conflict" [cited 7 February 2006]. Available from http://www. about.com

6. Robert Kreitner, *Management*, 9th ed. (Boston: Houghton Mifflin Harcourt Publishing Company, 2004), pp. 529–530.

7. Carol Kleiman, "How to Deal with a Co-worker Who's Getting on Your Nerves," *San Jose Mercury News*, October 3, 1999, p. PCI.

8. "Assertiveness: More Than a Forceful Attitude," *Supervisory Management*, February 1994, p. 3.

9. American Management Association, *Catalog of Seminars* (New York: American Management Association) [cited 1 January 2006]. Available from http://www. amanet.org.

10. Danny Ertel, "Turning Negotiation into a Corporate Capability," *Harvard Business Review*, May/June 1999, p. 3.

11. Rob Walker, "Take It or Leave It: The Only Guide to Negotiating You Will Ever Need," *Inc.*, August 2003, pp. 65–77.

12. Kurt Salzinger, "Psychology on the Front Lines," *Psychology Today*, May/June 2002, p. 34.

13. Kerry Patterson, Joseph Grenny, Ron McMillan, and Al Switzler, *Crucial Conversations: Tools for Talking When Stakes Are High*, McGraw Hill, 2002, p. 20. For more information about the crucial conversations model, visit www.crucialconversations.com

14. Ibid., p. 98.

15. David Stiegel, *When Talking Makes Things Worse!* (Dallas: Whithall & Nolton, 1997), p. 17

16. Roger Fisher and Alan Sharp, *Getting It Done* (New York: Harper Business, 1998), pp. 81–83.

17. Roger Fisher and William Ury, *Getting to Yes* (New York: Penguin Books, 1981), p. 59.

18. Dudley Weeks, *The Eight Essential Steps to Conflict Resolution* (New York: G. P. Putnam's Sons, 1992), p. 228.

19. Rory Marshall, "Boeing Factories to Get Back to Work," *The News & Observer*, November 3, 2008, p. 5A

20. Adam Hanft, "The Joy of Conflict," *Inc.*, August 2005, p. 112; Adam Hanft, "Down with Bossocracy," *Inc.*, April 2004, p. 126

21. Rogers Commission Report (1986). "Report of the Presidential Commission on the Space Shuttle *Challenger* Accident," Volume 1, Chapter 6.

22. Ibid., Chapter 5.

23. "Earache Brazilian loses more than hearing," *BBC News*, Wednesday, 20 August, 2003. http://news.bbc.co.uk/2/hi/health/3169049.stm.

24. "Study Finds Nearly 200,000 Deaths Annually from Hospital Errors," Consumer Affairs, August 12, 2004, retrieved from http://www.consumeraffairs.com/news04/hospital_errors.html

PART 5

Special Challenges in Human Relations

Jupiterimages/Comstock Images/Getty Images

Responding to Personal and Work-Related Stress

TIP OF THE ICEBERG | WELCOME TO WORLD OF "WORK OVER-LOAD"

Tammy DePew Smith, a single mother of three, starts her work day from the desk in her bedroom around 6:30 a.m. after getting her daughter off to school. During the next hour, she works as a customer-service agent for Santa Clara based LiveOps, a call-center company. At the rate of 25 cents per minute, she has just earned $15.00. By the time Smith gets another child off to school, homeschools her young son, and squeezes in another three shifts, she must tackle her evening "job" of making dinner, helping with homework, getting kids off to bed, and attending to other tasks.

As an independent contractor, Smith does not have health insurance, nor is she entitled to sick days, vacation, or other company benefits. But during the long economic downtown, Smith considers herself lucky to have a job.[1]

Tammy is not alone. Many people confess to feeling stressed out from constant, never ending work. In a 24/7 "always on" economy, people need to learn how to manage the stress caused by information overload, a demanding workload, and the desire for some personal time.

During a period of economic uncertainty, many workers feel they should always be "on the job." And various forms of technology gives them a 24/7 link to work. Many companies have broadened the use of company-owned mobile devices to allow more flexible work schedules. If your employer provides you with a laptop, smartphone, personal digital assistant (PDA) or some other compact mobile device, the implicit message may be "stay in touch." As your work bleeds into evenings and weekends, you may feel like you are on the job all the time. Welcome to the world of *electronic overtime.*[2]

Throughout your career, you will encounter many anxiety-provoking and stressful events. We live in a world of continuous change that often creates a heightened sense of urgency. Many organizations are searching for ways to wring more productivity from a smaller number of employees. Tensions build as people work longer hours and live with the possibility that they may be part of the next round of layoffs.

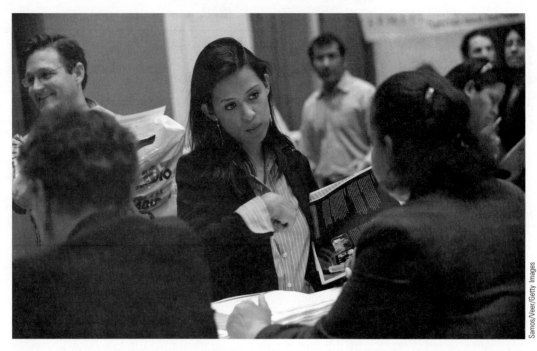

These job applicants are no doubt feeling a great deal of stress. During a period of high unemployment, the competition for fewer jobs is more intense.

THE STRESS FACTORS IN YOUR LIFE

14-1   **Stress** refers to two simultaneous events: an external stimulus, called a stressor, and the physical and emotional responses to that stimulus (anxiety, fear, muscle tension, surging heart rate, and so on). Stress can come from your environment, your body, or your mind.[3] Environmental stress at work may be caused by noise, safety concerns, windowless settings, long hours, or unrealistic deadlines. Some bodily stress can be attributed to poorly designed workstations that produce eye strain, shoulder tension, or lower-back discomfort. However, the stress that comes from our minds is the most common type of stress.

There can be positive aspects of mental stress. Stress *can* be a powerful stimulus for growth if it motivates you to do your best work. It can build within you the energy and desire needed to perform effectively. It can also promote greater awareness and help you focus on getting tasks completed quickly and efficiently. However, a great deal of the mental stress we encounter every day is caused by our negative thinking and faulty reasoning. For example, someone with large house payments and a great deal of personal debt may begin to worry excessively about the possibility of a layoff; the individual who lacks self-confidence may fear each technology change that is introduced at work; or workers in organizations being merged may mentally anguish over who will be laid off next.

> *However, a great deal of the mental stress we encounter every day is caused by our negative thinking and faulty reasoning.*

Responding to Stress

Stress responses consist of three elements: the event or thought (stressor) that triggers stress, your perception of it, and your response to it.[4] In his book *Stress for Success*, James Loehr suggests that as you are exposed to new stressors, you should try to respond in ways that help you establish mental, physical, and emotional balance.[5] Unfortunately, most of us do not take the time to train our minds and bodies so that we build our capacity to handle the stress in our lives.

Total Person Insight

"Most people seem to agree that these are high pressure times. Employees complain of being burned out. Used up. Overloaded. Too many of us are just plain tired, overdosed on change, sick of ambiguity and uncertainty."

Source: Price Pritchett and Ron Pound, *The Stress of Organizational Change* (Dallas: Pritchett, LP, 2005).

Our natural response to stress is as old as life itself—adapted by almost all species as a means of coping with threats to survival. When faced with an unexpected or possibly threatening situation, human beings—like animals—instinctively react with the **fight or flight syndrome**: The amygdala, located in the limbic region of the brain, sounds an alarm and adrenaline pours into the bloodstream, heart rate and blood pressure increase, breathing accelerates, and muscles tighten. The body is poised to fight or run. Ironically, the same instincts that helped our ancestors survive are the ones causing us physical and mental health problems today. When we are stressed out, the body builds up too much cortisol, the toxic chemical associated with stress. When stress continues to build and reaches a critical point, it can trigger an amygdala response, which affects our coping, reasoning, and decision-making abilities. As continuous stress builds in a work environment, it may cause a person to respond harshly to a colleague, feel overwhelmed or helpless, and to lose motivation to work on projects, resulting in lost productivity and effectiveness.[6]

Repeated or prolonged stress can trigger complex physiological reactions that may involve several hundred chemical changes in the brain and body.[7] Everyone reacts differently to stress, so there is no single best way to manage it. You must train yourself to respond effectively to the stressors in your personal and professional life so that you will not only survive, but thrive. The first step is to understand what might cause or trigger stress.

MAJOR CAUSES OF STRESS

14-2   A study by the National Institute for Occupational Safety and Health found that half the working people in the United States view job stress as a major problem in their lives.[8] Some say the pace at work is so dizzying that it takes them hours to finally relax after the workday ends. Most of us can benefit from learning how to pinpoint the sources of stress in our life, and learn to respond to them in a more effective manner.

Some say the pace at work is so dizzying that it takes them hours to finally relax after the workday ends.

Work-Life Balance

What do workers want most from their job? Many surveys indicate that work-life balance is the most important employment benefit.[9] Unfortunately, an economic downturn forces many workers to defer efforts to strike a better work-life balance. During a recession, workers may feel obligated to work longer hours, take less vacation, or postpone taking a sabbatical.

A few companies are taking steps to help employees achieve more control over their time. Dow Corning has a "No-Meetings Week" once a quarter, an attempt to call a halt to all nonessential internal meetings. IBM has established a companywide "Think Fridays," a block of Friday-afternoon time free of nonessential meetings and interruptions. Some companies encourage workers to schedule family time or time for leisure activities.[10]

Long Hours/Irregular Schedules. The New Economy, sometimes referred to as the 24/7 economy, is a nonstop "We never close" economy. Companies increasingly need employees who can work flexible schedules. Evening shifts, rotating shifts, 12-hour workdays, and weekend work often add stress to workers' lives. Tess Mateo, a director in the CEO's office at PricewaterhouseCoopers, recalls an early morning conference call with eight coworkers who were working in six time zones.[11] Working in a global economy often requires a very flexible work schedule.

In recent years, a growing number of workers call workloads excessive and say that they are bothered by increased pressure on the job. Many of the companies that have slashed their payroll now spread the same amount of work over fewer people. Years of multitasking and workaholism have left workers across the American economic and geographic spectrum feeling exhausted.[12]

DRAWING THE LINE

Denzil Samuels was an executive for Siemens Enterprise Communications, a company headquartered in Munich, Germany. On most weeks, while at Siemens, a normal commute would be from Denver to Munich. As he had a global role, he would also travel to Tokyo, Australia, various locations in the U.S., and anywhere the role required.

Soon after joining Siemens, Denzil was approached by his boss who asked why he hadn't replied to an important e-mail over the weekend. He said, "I usually work 12 to 18 hours each day and despite a brutal travel regime, make myself available 24 hours a day Monday through Friday. I think it's fair that I take a small amount of personal time to be with my family on the weekend. Would that be okay with you?" His boss quickly realized this request was more than fair and now respects his personal time on weekends.

In a 24/7 economy, it's important for employees to take the initiative to set limits and expectations on demanding work schedules when they can.

Source: Author interview with Denzil Samuels.

Change

Changes in the workplace come in many forms, including the need to do a job faster, to master advanced technology, or to take on a new work assignment. Consider employees

"Please! Have a seat!"

who have been accustomed to working alone and now must work with a team, or employees who have held jobs that required little contact with the public and now must spend a great deal of time with clients, patients, or customers. When companies restructure in an attempt to meet demands of the marketplace, they often do not take into consideration the life demands of the employees.

As we look to the future, there are two realities to keep in mind. First, management personnel above you are trying to cope with their own high-pressure responsibilities, so you are not likely to get much emotional handholding from them. Second, the pace of change is not likely to slow down. The authors of *The Stress of Organizational Change* say the secret to coping with high-velocity change is *surrender:* "Surrendering to change does the most to eliminate the stress. It creates the opportunity for *breakthrough* rather than *breakdown.*" They note that much of the pressure we are feeling these days is self-induced stress. Resisting change, or hanging on to old habits and beliefs, requires the investment of a great deal of emotional energy.[13] Surrendering to change demands a higher level of adaptability to our ever-changing workplace.

Multitasking

It's Monday morning, and you just finished a one-hour meeting with a cross-functional team. You promised the team members you would send them an e-mail that summarizes the decisions made during the meeting. As you walk back to your office, you glance at your iPhone and 39 e-mails are waiting for a response. A text message from your boss indicates she wants an updated product shipping report ASAP. Your afternoon includes three meetings, and you must leave the office at

4:30 p.m. to attend your daughter's soccer game.[14] Welcome to the world of multitasking.

While multitasking is common for most people, research finds that it can be counterproductive and can actually lower productivity. Researchers at the University of California found that many workers experience frequent distractions throughout the day; it often takes up to 25 minutes to return to an abandoned task.

Although multitasking can be stressful, we must find ways to embrace it. We are now living in a complex, fast-response world, and our challenge is to immediately prioritize and address whatever task is most critical. The good news is we are able to get someone's attention at a moment's notice. In today's environment, not being able to multitask would probably be highly stressful.[15]

Work Environment

The place a person works—office, cubicle, or remote location—matters very little because computers are the center of our lives. As countless workers spend the majority of their day sitting in front of a computer, they may remain oblivious to the physical stress this causes on our body over time. It may cause back pain, spine and neck problems, aching shoulders, sore elbows, eye fatigue, and carpal tunnel syndrome (a repetitive stress wrist injury). Sitting in a chair that offers little support, hunched over a laptop, or staring at a poorly positioned monitor takes its toll.

Experts in **ergonomics**—techniques for adapting the work environment to the human body—say that anyone spending hours in front of a computer should get the right equipment and use it properly.

Work environment stressors can include other factors such as a windowless work area, a small workspace, feeling uncomfortable from working in close proximity to other people, or a cubicle that lacks privacy. If you don't have much control over your work environment, then you need to focus on the things you can change, such as putting pictures of family and friends around your computer, adding flowers or a plant, and taking short breaks to walk outside. All these things help contribute to a positive mood and work performance.

Noise Pollution

Noise is unwanted sound, such as the roar of traffic, your neighbor's loud music, or the loud voice of the person who occupies the cubicle nearby. It can increase your stress level without your conscious awareness. It is the uncontrollability of noise, rather than its intensity, that often is the greatest irritant. The noise you can't shut off is likely to have a negative effect on your emotional well-being. Persistent exposure to noise can cause headaches, sleep disturbances, anxiety, and depression. Research indicates that noise affects people more than any other work area pollutant.[16]

"QUIET, PLEASE!"

Noise is the enemy of any worker who requires concentration in a space (such as a cubicle) that can't be soundproofed with the closing of a door.

- If you have an exceptionally loud voice, get in the habit of speaking more softly, especially in open spaces.

- Many people tend to unconsciously talk louder when they're on the phone. Place a Post-it reminder next to your phone to lower your voice while talking on the phone.

- Never shout a request or response to a nearby worker.

- If you must listen to music at your desk, keep it low or use headphones if your company allows them.

- When you ask someone to quiet down, do it as politely as possible.

Source: Adapted from *The Etiquette Advantage in Business (2nd Ed) Peggy Post and Peter Post*, William Morrow, 2005, 68–69.

Incompetent Leaders

Organizations often promote individuals into supervisory positions when they exhibit extraordinary talents in a specific technical field. The most talented electrician becomes maintenance supervisor. The most efficient surgical nurse is promoted to nursing supervisor. The top salesperson is made sales manager. But technical superstars may be poor supervisors. And studies indicate that incompetent supervisors are a major source of stress in the workplace.[17]

Work and Family Transitions

In our fast-moving world, most of us have learned that certain transitions are inevitable. A **transition** can be defined as the experience of being forced to give up something and face a change. Author Edith Weiner states, "People are now in a constant state of transitioning. It is difficult for anyone to say with any degree of certainty where he or she will be maritally, professionally, financially, or geographically five years from now."[18]

When a single person marries or a married couple divorces, the transition can be extremely stressful and can affect job performance. A new baby and the challenge of child care can cause stress in working mothers and fathers. As double-income parents attempt to meet the needs of the family, they often feel guilty about the time spent away from their children.

Rumination

Throughout your career, you will face countless disappointments and defeats. Your boss said she would like to give you a salary increase but didn't have the authority to approve raises. Later, you find out that she lied. You miss a team meeting because of an illness. Later you find out that a team member was highly critical of your work on an important project. Do you confront these foes or suffer in silence?

Most of us revisit personal and work-related problems too often. The process of replaying the incident over and over in our mind is referred to in the field of psychology as **rumination**. Ruminative thinking, the recurring intrusion of thoughts about negative events, can result in loss of concentration, loss of sleep, and feelings of depression.[19]

HOW TO BE PRESENT AND ENJOY THE MOMENT

Stress is often caused by thinking about something that has happened in the past, or *might* happen in the future. Either way, you can't control the outcome, nor can you enjoy life in the current moment.

- If you are the type of person that obsesses about the past and what could have happened, or what you should have done, try to spend only a few minutes thinking about what you learned as a result of the experience and what you might change next time if you encounter a similar situation. Then let it go.

■ If you tend to worry about the future, remind yourself of what you can and cannot control. Focus only on the things you do have the power to change, and create an action plan.

Another way to escape rumination is to select a meditation you can say to yourself during a time of stress. One of the best meditations is the "Serenity Prayer" in Figure 14.1 that is practiced by thousands of people around the world who attend daily AA meetings. There is a lot of wisdom in this one sentence that can be applied to many situations.

Warning Signals of Too Much Stress

In today's stress-filled world, it makes sense to become familiar with the signals that indicate you are experiencing too much stress in your life. Table 14.1 offers information regarding physical, emotional, and relational symptoms that may need your attention. When these symptoms persist, you are at risk for serious health problems because stress can exhaust your immune system, making you more vulnerable to colds, flu, fatigue, and infections. Recent research demonstrates that 90 percent of illnesses are stress related.[20]

Figure 14.1 ■ Serenity Prayer

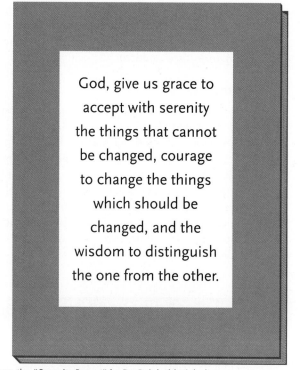

God, give us grace to accept with serenity the things that cannot be changed, courage to change the things which should be changed, and the wisdom to distinguish the one from the other.

Source: Adapted from the "Serenity Prayer" by Dr. Reinhold Niebuhr

Table 14.1 ■ Symptoms of Stress

PHYSICAL	EMOTIONAL	RELATIONAL
■ Sleep disturbances	■ Nervousness, anxiety	■ Increased arguments
■ Tension or migraine headaches	■ Depression, moodiness	■ Isolation from social activities
■ Hair loss	■ Irritability, frustration	■ Conflict with coworkers or employers
■ Sweaty palms or hands	■ Lack of concentration	■ Overreactions
■ Skin problems	■ Substance abuse	■ Road rage
	■ Memory problems	

Source: Adapted from Sheila Hutman, Jaelline Jaffe, Robert Segal, Heather Larson, Lisa F. Dumke, "Stress: Signs and Symptoms, Use and Effects," *Helpguide: Expert, Non-Commercial Information on Mental Health & Lifelong Wellness,* Reprinted with permission from *http://www.helpguide.org.* © 2006 Helpguide.org. All rights reserved.

STRESS-MANAGEMENT STRATEGIES

14-3   Ideally, we should do everything in our power to eliminate those elements that cause us stress—lack of work-life balance, change, multitasking, noise pollution, long hours/irregular schedules, incompetent leaders, work/family transitions, and rumination—but

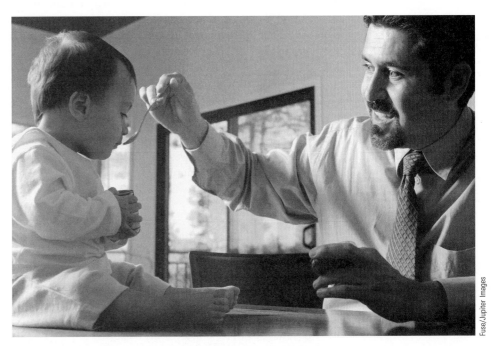

Fuse/Jupiter Images

In today's high-stress work environment, it's important to set aside uninterrupted time to enjoy the most important aspects of your life, including family, friends, and time for yourself.

this is not generally a realistic option. We can try to reduce them, but eliminating them is often not possible. We can, however, learn ways to manage our reactions to the stressors in our daily lives and minimize their negative impact.

There is no one-size-fits-all way to reduce stress. You have to become aware of what works best for you. Do not wait until you are feeling stressed before you employ stress-management techniques; make them part of your daily routine. Once you become aware of what creates a stressful response in you (stress is very individualized), begin looking for stress-management strategies that will help you cope with the stressful situations.

Sleep

Perhaps one of the most effective strategies for managing the negative aspects of stress is getting enough quality sleep. Growth hormones and repair enzymes are released and various chemical restoration processes occur during sleep. (This explains why children need considerably more sleep than adults.) To train your body so that you can deepen your capacity to handle stress, follow these guidelines to improve your sleep recovery periods:

- Develop a sleep ritual: Go to bed and get up at the same time as often as possible.
- Mentally wind down before going to bed. Avoid stressful activities.
- Avoid central nervous system stimulants such as caffeine, chocolate, alcohol, or nicotine near bedtime.
- Keep your bedroom cool, well ventilated, and dark.[21]

Many workers get less than the recommended amount of sleep (seven to eight hours) at night and therefore experience daytime drowsiness. This problem is so widespread that many employers encourage employees to take a short nap. Most employees are more productive and less apt to make fatigue-induced errors after waking from a short nap.[22]

Exercise

Study after study has proven that exercise, for most people, is the number one treatment for stress and tension because it releases pleasure-inducing chemicals called endorphins. Exercise designed to reduce stress is not necessarily strenuous and may include aerobic exercise such as walking, swimming, low-impact aerobics, tennis, or jogging. Even gentle exercise such as yoga or tai chi will help you manage your daily stress and improve motivation.

Unfortunately, about 70 percent of Americans do not exercise regularly, and nearly 40 percent are not active at all. Too many people fail to take advantage of the physical and mental benefits of exercise. These benefits include lower cholesterol, weight loss, increased mental alertness, and a stronger heart.

Several companies understand the importance of fun and exercise. They might place foosball or ping pong tables in the lunch room to not only give employees a quick energy boost, but also to improve employees' performance by making them happier. Many companies have on-site exercise facilities or provide reimbursement for joining a neighborhood athletic club. Coors Brewing Company reported a $6.15 return in profitability for every $1 spent on its company fitness program.[23]

Companies such as Playworks are combining employees' needs for recreation with socially-responsible initiatives, allowing employees to interact with local children in team-building activities. Here, Mattel and Playworks volunteers are enjoying a Winter Wonderland with LA kids at Mattel's 2011 event.

Deep Breathing

When you participate in deep-breathing exercises, you are encouraged to focus on the present moment rather than those things that are causing you stress. In his book *Breathe Smart: The Secret to Happiness, Health, and Long Life*, Aaron Hoopes describes techniques that can effectively calm your body.[24]

Complete Cycle Breathing. Start and end your day with three rounds of a complete cycle of breathing: Inhale, then pause while gently holding the breath in; exhale, then pause while holding the breath out. When you pause with your breath in, it creates a moment of stillness in which the whole body is focused on processing oxygen. When you suspend breathing out for a moment, it allows the body to use all the oxygen remaining in your lungs. Normally, we take 14 to 19 breaths a minute while at rest. The goal of deep-breathing programs is to lower that rate to under ten.[25]

Abdominal Breathing. Press your abdominal muscles out and down as you inhale, which creates a vacuum that pulls the lungs down, allowing them to expand beyond the typical shallow breath that uses only the top third of the lungs. As you exhale, pull the abdominal muscles up and in so that the lungs empty from the bottom up, which clears the stale air out of your body and brings in fresh oxygen.

Meditation

Meditation is a relaxation technique that slows your pulse, respiration, and brainwave activity and lowers your blood pressure. It produces feelings of contentment, calmness, and heightened awareness. Meditation is sometimes called the smart person's bubble bath. About ten million Americans say they practice some form of meditation.[26]

Scientific studies show that meditation can have a profound stress-reducing effect because it trains and conditions the mind in the same way exercise trains and conditions the body. Neuroscientists found that monks who spend years meditating actually grow their left prefrontal cortex, the part of the brain most responsible for feeling happy. Practicing meditation regularly can permanently rewire the brain to raise levels of happiness, lower stress, and improve immune function.[27]

Richard Davidson's research at the University of Wisconsin in Madison suggests that through regular meditation, the brain is reoriented from a stressful fight or flight mode to one of acceptance, a shift that increases contentment with the realities of life. The process effectively deactivates the frontal areas of the brain, where sensory information is received and processed. Meditation allows people to quietly and intentionally detach from their emotional reactions so that they can respond appropriately. It allows them to peacefully observe their stress-producing thoughts and then choose to release them.[28] Most meditation techniques involve these elements:

1. Sit or lie down in a comfortable, quiet place where you are not likely to be disturbed.
2. Intentionally relax the muscles of your body from your toes to your head.
3. Focus on the sound of each breath, using the abdominal breathing techniques mentioned earlier.
4. Train yourself to think about the calm and peaceful present. If your mind drifts, just slowly bring it back to focusing on the present.

HOW TO MEDITATE IN ONE MINUTE

Many type-A people don't meditate because they don't want to take 10–20 minutes (or sit still that long) to meditate. Martin Boroson, author of *One Moment Meditation*, discovered a solution for people like this that is just as effective—and it only takes one minute a day. All you need is a timer.

Find a quiet place and set the timer for one minute. Sit in a relaxed position, close your eyes and focus on your breathing. When the alarm sounds, stop.

Most people find that they are able to turn down the volume of thinking in their mind. The more they practice, the more quickly and deeply they can drop into a peaceful space. Executives, managers, doctors, and lawyers find the exercise immensely useful. They use the one-minute meditation just prior to making a presentation or making a difficult phone call, or at the end of the day to leave stress at work. Try it and see how this one minute can change your state of mind.

Source: Martin Boroson, author of "One-Minute Meditation: Stillness for People on the Go." *Spirituality & Health*, September–October, 2011, p. 57.

Solitude

Although some people feel uncomfortable when alone, many others feel "over-connected" because of the need to constantly respond to cell phone, e-mail, Facebook, Twitter, and text messages. Those who are constantly in touch with others can benefit from the

Those who are constantly in touch with others can benefit from the therapeutic effect of solitude.

therapeutic effect of solitude. Solitude can be viewed as an emotional breather, a restorer of energy, and a form of rest similar to sleep. Ester Buchholz, author of *The Call of Solitude*, says alone-time is a great protector of the self and the human spirit. She also notes that solitude is often required for the unconscious to process thoughts and events.[29] To experience the benefits of solitude, get up 20 minutes earlier in the morning. Use this time for meditation, journal writing, or just sitting in silence. Enjoy this period of solitude free from the current pressures and demands on your life.

Resilience

Resilience means being capable of bouncing back when you are confronted with stressful situations. At 3M's headquarters in Maplewood, Minnesota, more than 7,000 employees have completed a "Resilience at Work" training program that covers such diverse topics as financial planning, time management, and parenting. These topics represent those factors in a person's life that could cause stress if they got out of control. Participants are taught to determine what issues are within their control and how to deal with them when they get out of control.

Resilience is not just a personal characteristic; it applies to teams as well. When people have confidence in themselves, in one another, and in an organization, it motivates people to push the boundaries and strive to achieve more without fear of making a mistake. Rosabeth Moss Kanter says that teams that are immersed in a culture of accountability, collaboration, and initiative are more likely to believe that they can weather any storm.[30]

HOW TO BEAT STRESS IN 10 MINUTES OR LESS

- **Pet a dog**. Not only will it lower your blood pressure, it will lower the dog's too.
- **Take a 10-minute walk.** It's the simplest, most effective way to reduce anxiety and improve your mood.
- **Call your mom.** Research proves that calling your mom (or getting a hug) is a powerful way to lower your stress. It floods the system with oxytocin and washes away cortisol caused by stress.
- **Socialize.** There is a good reason you feel so good when you hang out with friends. Your body needs it. Research has shown that the more social connections a person has, the healthier they are. It reduces anxiety, improves concentration and focus, and strengthens your heart and immune system.

Source: Adapted from Monika Rice, "The Mother of All Stress Relief," *Spirituality & Health*, November–December 2010.

USING POSITIVE PSYCHOLOGY TO COMBAT STRESS

14-4 In this section, we will revisit some of the positive psychology concepts covered in Chapter 10. We will describe how you can apply a positive mindset to reduce stress in all areas of your life. Happiness is more than just a mood; it's a way of living and working. Each person has a different "happiness baseline" and fortunately, it's a baseline that can be raised. Over time, by learning how to raise your baseline, you can achieve higher levels of happiness. The highs and lows of emotions can be influenced with positive thoughts and experiences.

Laugh and Have Fun

Laughter is a gentle exercise of the body, a form of "inner jogging." When you laugh, your immune system is given a boost, stress-related hormones such as cortisol are reduced, and your respiratory function is improved.[31] Having fun while you are on the job does not exclude being serious about your work and caring about doing a good job. People can have fun at work without being silly or inappropriate. The goal is to create a positive, fun-loving atmosphere that helps reduce stress levels. Businesses do this in unique ways. Lego Systems holds an annual "Stress Free Day" for its 600 employees who are encouraged to take a break from work to get massages or manicures, or play basketball or volleyball. Other companies create a playful and relaxing environment by having open and creative workspaces, or by allowing people to bring their dogs to work.

Some employers even provide employees with individual help and guidance to improve stress and help them achieve their goals. For example, Zappos.com has a personal coach to assist employees with both personal and professional issues. This might include managing stress, setting and attaining goals, advice about setting budgets to manage personal finances, or creating a career path that provides more personal fulfillment.

Many people have lost touch with what is fun for them. Ann McGee-Cooper, author of *You Don't Have to Go Home from Work Exhausted*, recommends making a list of things that are fun for you and then estimating the time they take.[32] This exercise may help you realize that there is plenty of time for fun things in your life. A walk in the park will require only 20 minutes, and reading the comics takes only 5 minutes out of your day.

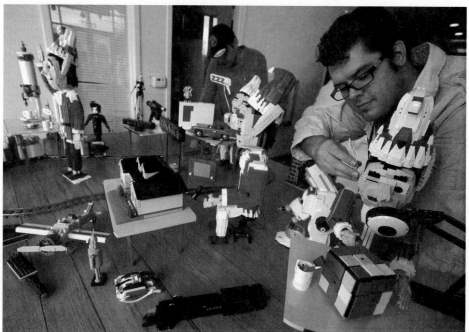

Many employers such as Lego encourage their employees to take adequate personal time for themselves, even instituting an annual dedicated "Stress Free Day" where employees are encouraged to take a break from work to have massages or participate in recreational activities.

Commit Random Acts of Kindness

Many studies have proven that acts of kindness toward friends, family, or even strangers, decreases stress levels and improves mental health. In one research study, participants that were told to complete five acts of kindness toward others felt much happier throughout the course of the day, and continued to feel happier in the days following the experiment.[33]

Regain or Let Go of Control

Another way people experience stress is when they feel they have no control in a situation. They worry and feel stressed by things beyond their control such as the stock market, the price of housing, or losing their job. Needless worry about things outside of our control is not only a waste of time, it robs people of energy and time that can be put toward other, more productive things they can control.

Try this exercise the next time you feel worried and anxious.

1. On a sheet of paper draw lines to make three columns. In the first column, make a list of all the things that you feel stressed about.
2. When you are done with this, write the words "Control" in the header of the second column and write "Can't Control" at the top of the third column.
3. Go through each item on the list and put a check in the column that corresponds to either what you can control, or cannot control.
4. Cross off the things that have a "can't control" check next to them. This should actually give you some relief—and renewed energy.
5. Review the list of items you can control. Develop goals and an action plan for each item that will help you cope or deal more effectively with the stress it causes.

Dogs are best friends and co-workers to employees at Silicon Valley-based Zynga.

David Paul Morris/Bloomberg/Getty Images

Total Person Insight

"It is impossible to live without failing at something, unless you live so cautiously that you might as well not have lived at all."

Source: J. K. Rowling, *Harvard Business Review*, April 2011, page 103.

COPING WITH PSYCHOLOGICAL DISORDERS

14-5 In the ideal scenario, when a stressful situation ends, hormonal signals switch off the fight or flight response, and the body returns to normal. Unfortunately, stress does not always let up. If you are under stress day after day and year after year, your hormonal response never shuts down. This can have a hazardous, even lethal, effect on your body and mental health.[34]

Once every ten years, the National Institute of Health (NIH) conducts a national study to assess mental illness in America. The findings of the most recent study, published in 2005, indicate that mental illness, in its many forms, affects one-quarter of the U.S. population.[35] In the final pages of this chapter, we will briefly examine three common psychological disorders and discuss therapy options.

Anxiety

Anxiety is a condition in which intense feelings of apprehension are longstanding and usually disruptive. Millions of Americans struggle with unwanted anxiety, and the cost in terms of suffering and lost productivity is very high. For most people, anxious feelings surface from time to time, but they are neither longstanding nor disruptive. If you have ever been tense before taking an exam or making an oral presentation, you have some idea of what anxiety feels like.[36]

Anxiety becomes a *disorder* only when it persists and prevents you from leading a normal life. Psychiatrists have found that there are several different anxiety disorders. A *phobia*, an irrational fear of a specific object or situation, represents one type of anxiety. Claustrophobia (fear of confined spaces) and agoraphobia (fear of crowds and public places) are two of the many phobias that can have a disruptive effect on a person's daily life.[37]

What is the best treatment for anxiety? Many anxious states are caused by stress, so consider using the stress-management methods described in this chapter. Various methods of relaxation, for example, can lessen the severity of anxiety symptoms. However, when self-help methods do not bring the desired results, seek professional help (see Figure 14.2).[38]

Depression

Depression is a mood disorder. Nearly 19 million American adults experience it. This psychological disorder costs U.S. businesses nearly $70 billion annually in lost productivity, medical expenditures, and other related expenses. People of all ages can experience depression, but it primarily impacts workers in their most productive years: the 20s through 40s.[39]

Figure 14.2 ■ Getting Professional Help

Anxiety Disorders Association of America http://www.adaa.org	▶ The mission of the ADAA is to promote the prevention, treatment, and cure of anxiety disorders and to improve the lives of all people who suffer from them.
Depression and Bipolar Support Alliance http://www.dbsalliance.org	▶ This organization runs local support groups around the country for people coping with depression and bipolar disorder.
National Alliance on Mental Illness http://www.nami.org	▶ NAMI offers support groups and courses to help people with psychiatric disorders, as well as family members living with and caring for the mentally ill.
The Therapy Directory http://therapists.psychology today.com/rms/prof_search.php	▶ *Psychology Today* magazine maintains a searchable database people can use to find a therapist in their area.
The Mental Health Association http://www.depressionscreening.com	▶ The Mental Health Association offers a free depression screening test, which may help identify depressive symptoms and determine whether a further evaluation by a medical or mental health professional is necessary.
Online Clinics http://www.onlineclinics.com	▶ Online Clinics was created to serve clinics, clinicians, and patients who want to find quality health care services online.

Source: Adapted from Leila Abbound, "Mental Illness Said to Affect One-Quarter of Americans," *Wall Street Journal*, June 6, 2005.

When depression seriously affects a person's productivity on the job or in interpersonal relationships, psychiatrists consider that individual to have a depression. Symptoms such as withdrawal, overwhelming sadness, or hopelessness may persist for weeks or months.

In most cases, depression is a treatable disorder, but it often requires a variety of approaches. An important U.S. study on depression found that two-thirds of patients achieve remission if they stick with therapy. Persisting in treatment is very important.[40] Many employers have found that investing in therapy for depressed employees can reduce absenteeism while improving workers' health.[41] To learn more about therapy options, see Figure 14.2.

Burnout

Burnout is a gradually intensifying pattern of physical, psychological, and behavioral dysfunction that evolves in response to a continuous flow of stressors.[42] When you experience burnout, you feel that your energy fuel tank is operating on empty. Just as the engine of a car literally stops running without fuel and oil, a complete mental

"No, no, that's not a sin, either. My goodness, you must have worried yourself to death."

Charles Barsotti/The New Yorker Collection

or physical breakdown can result from burnout. The most common symptoms of burnout include the following:

- Increased detachment from coworkers, customers, or clients
- Increased tardiness, absenteeism, cynicism, and moodiness
- Increased disorientation: forgetfulness or low concentration
- Increased personal problems: drug or alcohol abuse, decreased social contacts, or marital discord

All individuals experience one or two of these symptoms from time to time. But a person experiencing burnout exhibits these behaviors with increasing frequency and intensity. A candidate for burnout is likely to be someone who can't seem to "turn work off," needs to feel in control of their work, puts work before their families and personal lives, and puts in long hours at work.[43]

Popular Therapy Options

Many organizations offer various **employee-assistance programs (EAPs)** aimed at overcoming anxiety, depression, burnout, alcohol abuse, and drug abuse. These programs are designed to address the negative effects of psychological disorders before employees become dysfunctional.

In addition to EAPs, millions of people choose to participate in one or more relevant **twelve-step programs** for help with drug and alcohol addiction, eating disorders, and gambling addiction. All twelve-step programs rely on the same fundamentals:

- *Working the steps.* This means admitting the problem, recognizing that life has become unmanageable, and turning life over to a higher power.
- *Attending meetings.* Meetings of twelve-step programs are held in convenient locations throughout communities across the country. Members describe their own problems and listen to others who have experienced similar problems. In most cases, members form strong support groups.

Web-based counseling is growing in popularity. Some licensed therapists give their clients a choice of face-to-face counseling or online counseling. In addition, there are thousands of support groups organized around various psychological disorders and moderated by therapists—some are licensed, some are not. Web-based therapy may be risky. There is often no guarantee that the self-proclaimed therapist is legitimate or licensed to practice in your state, and no online therapist can promise confidentiality.[44]

LOOKING BACK: SUMMARY OF LEARNING OBJECTIVES

1. **Understand the stress factors in your life.**

   Stress refers to two simultaneous events: an external stimulus, called a stressor, and the physical and emotional response to that stimulus. Stress at work may be caused by many factors. Our stress response consists of three elements: the event or thought (stressor) that triggers stress, your perception of it, and your response to it.

2. **Explain the major personal and work-related causes of stress.**

   When individuals cannot adequately respond or successfully adapt to change, stress is usually the result. Major causes of stress include failures to achieve work-life balance, long hours and irregular schedules, multitasking, change, poorly designed computer work stations, noise, incompetent leaders, work and family transitions, and rumination.

3. **Learn how to identify and implement effective stress-management strategies.**

   You are more likely to handle the ever-increasing stress of today's demands when you maintain a sleep routine and exercise program, practice the relaxing effects of deep breathing and meditation, laugh and have fun, seek out moments of solitude,

   and learn how to physically and mentally recover once the stress is reduced or ended.

4. **Learn how to use positive psychology to combat stress.**

   Positive psychology can be learned and applied to change and improve your life in countless ways. Small things like taking time to laugh and having fun produce big benefits. Other stress relievers include expressing kindness toward others and training yourself to view situations with optimism. It's also helpful to make a list of the stressors in your life to understand what you can and cannot control, and accept those things you cannot control.

5. **Identify stress-related psychological disorders and therapy options.**

   When stress becomes persistent and overwhelming, it can lead to debilitating psychological disorders such as anxiety, depression, and burnout. While self-management techniques sometimes help, there may come a time when medication and one-on-one or group therapy with a licensed therapist is necessary. Employee assistance programs at work and community-based twelve-step programs may offer additional support.

KEY TERMS

stress, 300
fight or flight syndrome, 301
ergonomics, 304
transition, 305
rumination, 305

meditation, 310
resilience, 311
anxiety, 314
depression, 314
burnout, 315

employee-assistance programs (EAPs), 316
twelve-step programs, 316

CAREER INSIGHT: WANT TO GET MORE DONE? GET MORE SLEEP AND TAKE A BREAK

After breathing, sleep is our most fundamental need and should be our highest priority, says Tony Schwartz, CEO of the Energy Project. Most people need seven to eight hours of sleep, yet sleep is usually the first thing people will give up when they feel like they need to get more done. Sleep deprivation actually makes us much less efficient, so if you want to get more done, give up something other than sleep.

Another way to sustain your energy throughout the day is to take frequent breaks, approximately every 90 minutes throughout your day to keep your body in alignment with its natural rhythms. Just as we cycle through various stages of sleep at night, our body clock cycles every 90 minutes throughout the day, moving between periods of high and low energy. A short nap can also help you sustain your energy.

Source: http://www.theenergy project.com/tips. Retrieved April 17, 2012.

TRY YOUR HAND

1. Determine what circumstances are causing the most stress in your life. For example, are you trying to work too many hours while going to school? Are you experiencing parental or peer pressure? Do you feel burdened with things you cannot control? Then answer the following questions:
   a. What aspects of the situation are under your control?
   b. Are there any aspects of the situation that are out of your control? Explain.
   c. What steps can you take to help eliminate the stress?
   d. What individual stress-management strategies could you use to counteract the effects of this stress?
2. Consider the following company-sponsored stress-management programs. List them in order from most beneficial to you to least beneficial. Explain your reasoning.
   a. Access to on-site exercise facilities or company-sponsored health club membership
   b. A workshop on stress management sponsored by the company
   c. A cafeteria where healthy, nutritionally balanced foods are served

   d. Access to a soundproof audiovisual room for viewing relaxing videotapes, listening to soothing music, or taking a nap
3. Stress often increases as we struggle with time management. How well do you manage your time? Take a few minutes and answer each question below. Then spend time developing a time-management program that meets your individual needs.
   a. Do you develop a daily "to do" list that indicates the activities you hope to work on?
   b. Do you maintain a planning calendar—a single place to record daily appointments, deadlines, and tasks?
   c. Do you have a series of personal and professional goals that guide you in setting priorities for use of your time?
   d. Have you learned to say no to proliferating requests for your participation in team activities, projects, social activities, and so on, that may complicate your life?
4. Try a one-day "news fast." Do not read, watch, or listen to any news for a day and see how you feel.

CRITICAL THINKING CHALLENGE

The best way to cope with stress is to develop a process for coping with it before it disrupts your life. The more systematic you can make this process, the more effective it will be. Try using these steps to create your own personal plan for dealing with stressful events in your life:

1. Assess the sources of stress and the effect it has on you.

2. Identify which stressors you want to address, and those that can be changed.
3. Create a plan to deal with each stressor and the specific steps you will take.
4. Evaluate the outcomes you have as a result of implementing changes to deal with stress, and adjust strategies as needed.

SELF-ASSESSMENT EXERCISE

For each of the following statements, circle the number from 1 to 5 that best represents your response: (1) strongly disagree (never do this); (2) disagree (rarely do this); (3) moderately agree (sometimes do this); (4) agree (frequently do this); (5) strongly agree (almost always do this).

	1	2	3	4	5
A. I understand what causes or triggers stress in my life.	1	2	3	4	5
B. I make every effort to screen out negative thoughts and accentuate positive thinking.	1	2	3	4	5
C. I manage stress and tension so I am not overwhelmed by the negative stressors in my life.	1	2	3	4	5
D. I have developed good habits of diet, sleep, and exercise in order to cope more effectively with the negative stressors in my life.	1	2	3	4	5
E. I apply positive psychology strategies and activities to cope stressful situations.	1	2	3	4	5

After identifying your response to each item, select an attitude or skill you would like to improve. Prepare a written goal and then describe the steps you will take to achieve this goal..

YOU PLAY THE ROLE

Assume you are the spouse of Terry, a call-center customer-service representative. Terry routinely comes home from work stressed out and in a surly mood. Each representative at the center handles up to 120 calls per day and faces more frequent personal attacks than workers in most other occupations, with little or no opportunity to respond. The management of the organization is inflexible when it comes to accommodating its customers' needs, so the call-center personnel have little power to make the customers happy. Many times they are forced to refuse the customers' requests and respond, "It's corporate policy." Terry has become irritable, impatient, and emotionally unavailable to you and your three elementary-school-aged children. The job pays better than any other opportunities in the area, and your family has become dependent on Terry's income. Upon returning home from work today, Terry walked past you and the kids, went into your bedroom, closed the door, turned on the TV, and began rapidly consuming a cold beer. You've had enough! Rather than escalate the stress by mentioning the divorce option, you have decided to try to talk with Terry about reducing the stress in your lives. Role-play this discussion with one of your classmates, who will play the role of Terry.

BELOW THE SURFACE | IS GOOD STRESS "BAD?"

David Sacks is the CEO of Yammer, a successful social networking software company. He experiences a different type of work-related stress than Tammy, the person portrayed in the opening vignette. David's stress is "good stress" driven by his passion for the company he created.

David's "typical" day is challenging and long, leaving him with very little downtime. He usually starts by checking e-mail from home, and if he gets drawn into it, he might still be sitting at home in his boxers three hours later. Sometimes David enjoys a quick breakfast with his wife and two young children before heading to the office—which is good because he usually gets home too late in the evening to see them.

"I have to make a special effort to make it home for dinner. I wish I were more disciplined," Sacks confesses. "I don't have a set time that I go to bed or leave the office. I just do all the work that's in front of me, and then I look up and say, "Oh, wait, it's midnight, I should get home." Although Sacks doesn't go into the office on weekends, he's still thinking about work. "Disconnecting is very hard for me. I think about work constantly. I wish I had an on/off switch."[45]

QUESTIONS

1. David is obviously a successful entrepreneur who enjoys his work. Although his stress is described as "good stress," is there a potential downside to the type of life he leads? If so, what would this be?

2. David's schedule is similar to the long and challenging work days of many people. If he enjoys what he does, is there anything wrong with working 10-12 hour work days? Explain your answer.

3. If you could advise David about making changes to his life, what would they be?

CLOSING CASE ACHIEVING A MORE BALANCED LIFE

Katherine Garrigan has worked full time at a Chicago museum for almost two years. During that time, the 24-year-old has taken just two short vacations totaling about eight days.[46] Jacqueline Piatt, a 26-year-old account executive at PJ, Inc., a New York-based public-relations firm, described her upcoming trip to Barcelona: she plans to spend time at the beach, eat tapas, see the sights, and party until 5 a.m. Unfortunately, she has to squeeze it all into one weekend. Her work schedule does not allow for a longer vacation.[47]

Many Americans have adopted a demanding work ethic that leaves little time for a well-rounded life. U.S. workers tend to work long hours and spend less time on vacation than do workers in many other industrialized countries. Long hours at work usually result in loss of leisure time and less time with family and friends. Consider these characteristics of the U.S. workforce:

- A full 35 percent of the employed workers are not taking all of their paid vacation days. During one recent year, Americans failed to take 438 million days of paid vacation.[48]

- McDonalds Corporation offers salaried employees an eight-week paid sabbatical for every

ten years of employment. Sabbaticals, which originated in academia, provide employees time for rest and reflection—a break from 50-hour work weeks. Yet, only 5 percent of American companies offer paid sabbaticals.[49]

- Some companies discourage use of sick days. Nearly half of the full-time workers in America do not have paid sick days and those who do have this benefit are often discouraged from using it.[50]

Most workers want to succeed and advance at work, yet schedule time for family, friends, and leisure activities. Many fail in their attempt to achieve this level of work-life balance.

QUESTIONS

1. Many workers do not use all of the paid vacation time they have earned. Assess which factors may influence workers to make this decision.

2. Some companies feel vacation can have a positive effect on the personal health of their workers. They believe that workers asked to do more with fewer resources may need their vacation time more than ever. Argue whether employers

should require workers to take all of their paid vacation days. Why or why not?

3. Several companies, including Accenture, Cisco Systems, and Wells Fargo, offer paid sabbaticals

to employees so they can work as volunteers, improve their education, or learn new skills, for example. Evaluate the advantages and disadvantages of this approach to sabbaticals.

CHAPTER 14 ENDNOTES

1. Peter Coy, Michelle Conlin, and Moira Herbst, "The Disposable Worker," **Bloomberg Businessweek**, January 18, 2010, p. 33.

2. Kelly Yamanouchi, "Working Anywhere at Any Time Creates Overtime Problems." **News & Observer**, July 8, 2012, P. 3E.

3. Bruce Cryer, Rollin McCraty, and Doc Childre, "Pull the Plug on Stress," **Harvard Business Review**, July 2003, pp. 1–2.

4. Richard Laliberte, "Lighten Up," **New Choices**, June 2001, p. 65.

5. James E. Loehr, **Stress for Success** (New York: Times Books, 1997), p. 4.

6. Shawn Achor, **The Happiness Advantage** (New York: Crown Business, 2006), p. 133–134.

7. Harold H. Bloomfield and Robert K. Cooper, **The Power of 5** (Emmaus, Pa.: Rodale Press, 1995), p. 18.

8. Cora Daniels, "The Last Taboo," **Fortune**, October 28, 2002, p. 138.

9. "Work-Life Balance Tops Pay," **USA Today**, March 13, 2008, p. IB.

10. Sue Shellenbarger, "Another Casualty Emerges from the Crisis: Family Time," **Wall Street Journal**, October 15, 2008, p. Dl.

11. Sue Shellenbarger, "Time-Zoned: Working Around the Round-the-Clock Workday," **Wall Street Journal**, February 15, 2007, p. Dl.

12. Sonja Steptoe, "Ready, Set, Relax!" **Time**, October 27, 2003, pp. 38–41; Sue Shellenbarger, "Are Saner Workloads the Unexpected Key to More Productivity?" **Wall Street Journal**, March 10, 2000, p. Bl.

13. Price Pritchett and Ron Pound, **The Stress of Organizational Change** (Dallas, Tex.: Pritchett, 2005), pp. 3–8.

14. This hypothetical example was adapted from Mary Donato, "Workplace Stress: A Survival Guide," **Sales & Marketing Management**, November/December 2006, p. 24.

15. David H. Freedman, "Why Interruption, Distraction, and Multitasking Are Not Such Awful Things After All," **Inc.**, February 2007, p. 68.

16. "Sound Bites," **UC Berkeley Wellness Letter**, September 2004, pp. 6–7; Jane Spencer, "Behind the Music: iPods and Hearing Loss," **Wall Street Journal**, January 10, 2006, p. Dl; Steve Thompson, "Straight Pipes and Street Civility," **Autoweek**, March 20, 2006, p. 10.

17. Kenneth Labich, "Psycho Bosses from Hell," **Fortune**, March 18, 1996, p. 123; Vanessa Ho, "Companies Get the Message That Happy Workers Help Bottom Line," **Roanoke Times & World News**, November 13, 1995, p. E6.

18. Edith Weiner, "The Fast Approaching Future," **Retail Issues Letter**, July 1994, p. 3.

19. Douglas A. Bernstein, Louis A. Penner, Alison Clarke-Stewart, and Edward J. Roy, **Psychology**, 7th ed. (Boston: Houghton Mifflin, 2006), pp. 515 and 605.

20. Art Ulene, **Really Fit Really Fast** (Encino, Calif.: Health-Points, 1996), pp. 56–58.

21. Loehr, **Stress for Success**, pp. 179, 183; Eilene Zimmerman, "Sleep Less, Feel Better," **Sales & Marketing Management**, June 2004, p. 49.

22. Arlene Weintraub, "Napping Your Way to the Top," **BusinessWeek**, November 27, 2006, pp. 97 and 99.

23. J. Loehr and T. Schwartz, "The Power of Full Engagement: Managing Energy, Not Time, Is the Key to Performance and Personal Renewal," **Free Press**, New York, p. 65.

24. Jennifer Derryberry, "The Joy of Breathing," **Spirituality & Health**, July/August 2004, pp. 78–79.

25. Robert J. Davis, "Breathing and Hypertension," **Wall Street Journal**, April 27, 2004, p. D4.

26. Joel Stein, "Just Say Om," **Time**, August 4, 2003, p. 50; Katherine Ellison, "Mastering Your Own Mind," **Psychology Today,** September/October, 2006, pp. 70–77.

27. Shawn Achor, **The Happiness Advantage** (New York: Crown Business, 2006), p. 51–52.

28. Joel Stein, "Just Say Om," **Time**, August 4, 2003, p. 50; Katherine Ellison, "Mastering Your Own Mind," **Psychology Today**, September/October, 2006, pp. 47–56; Richard J. Davidson et al., "Alterations in Brain and Immune Function Produced by Mindfulness Meditation," **Psychosomatic Medicine**, received for publication December 2002 [cited 16 February 2006]. Available from "http://www.psychosomaticmedicine.org"; "Mindfulness Meditation," **Spirituality & Health**, March/April 2004, p. 74; Michelle Conlin, "Meditation," **BusinessWeek**, August 30, 2004, pp. 136–137.

29. Ester Buchholz, "The Call of Solitude," *Psychology Today*, January–February 1998, pp. 50–54; "Loners May Not Fear Others, They Just Need Some Solitude," *Wall Street Journal*, March 1, 2007, p. B7.

30. Rosabeth Moss Kanter, "Cultivate a Culture of Confidence," *Harvard Business Review*, April 2011, p. 34.

31. Megan Satosus, "No Fun of Any Kind," *CIO Magazine*, May 2, 2005 [cited 16 February 2006]. Available from http://www.cio.com.

32. Ann McGee-Cooper, *You Don't Have to Go Home from Work Exhausted* (New York: Bantam Books, 1992), pp. 52–53.

33. Shawn Achor, *The Happiness Advantage* (New York: Crown Business, 2006), p. 52.

34. Sheila Hutman, Jaelline Jaffe, Robert Segal, Heather Larson, and Lisa Dumke, "Stress: Signs and Symptoms, Causes and Effects" [cited 11 February 2006]. Available from http://www.helpguide.org/mental/ stress_signs.htm; INTERNET.

35. Leila Abbound, "Mental Illness Said to Affect One-Quarter of Americans," *Wall Street Journal*, June 7, 2005, p. Dl.

36. Douglas A. Bernstein, Louis A. Penner, Alison Clark-Stewart, and Edward J. Roy, *Psychology*, 7th ed. (Boston: Houghton Mifflin, 2006), pp. 589–590.

37. Ibid.

38. To learn about specific ways to control your fears see Jason Zweig, "How to Control Your Fears in a Fearsome Market," *Wall Street Journal*, July 19, 2008, p. Bl.

39. Paul Raeburn, "Mental Health: Better Beneftis Won't Break the Bank," *BusinessWeek*, December 17, 2001, p. 100; Elyse Tanouye, "Mental Illness: A Rising Workplace Cost," *Wall Street Journal*, June 13, 2001, p. B1.

40. Sharon Begley, "New Hope for Battling Depression Relapses," *Wall Street Journal*, January 6, 2004, p. Dl; Avery Johnson, "Treatment Works for Two-Thirds of the Depressed," *Wall Street Journal*, November 1, 2006.

41. Lindsey Tanner, "Treating Workers' Depression Pays," *News & Observer*, September 26, 2007, p. 4A.

42. Douglas A. Bernstein, Louis A. Penner, Alison Clark-Stewart, and Edward J. Roy, *Psychology*, 7th ed. (Boston: Houghton Mifflin, 2006), p. 495.

43. Dana Mattioli, "When Devotion to Work Becomes Job Obsession," *Wall Street Journal*, January 23, 2007, p. 88.

44. Rebecca Segall, "Online Shrinks: The Inside Story," *Psychology Today*, May/June 2000, pp. 38–43; Joshua Rosenbaum, "The Typing Cure," *Wall Street Journal*, September 16, 2002, p. R10.

45. David Sacks, "The Way I Work," *Inc.*, November 2011, p. 122–124.

46. Erin White, "For Young Workers, Taking Time Off Can Be Stressful," *Wall Street Journal*, March 27, 2007, p. B10.

47. Anjoli Athavaley, "Vacation Deflation: Breaks Get Shorter," *Wall Street Journal*, August 15, 2007, p. Dl.

48. Anjoli Athavaley, "Vacation Deflation: Breaks Get Shorter"; Howard Shapiro, "Vacation Time Going Unused," *News & Observer*, February 17, 2008, p. 8G.

49. Michael Arndt, "Nice Work if You Can Get It," *BusinessWeek*, January 9, 2006, pp. 56–57.

50. Molly Selvin, "Taking Sick Days Often Discouraged," *News & Observer*, May 27, 2007, p. 5E.

Comstock Images/Getty Images

Valuing Work Force Diversity

TIP OF THE ICEBERG | CHARGES OF DISCRIMINATION INCREASE

Throughout the past decade, America has experienced a major demographic transformation. Nearly 92 percent of the nation's population growth—25.1 million people—came from minorities of all types, including those who identified themselves as mixed race.[1] Despite the overwhelming evidence that workplace diversity improves innovation, problem solving, product development, and new customer acquisition, many organizations have been slow to embrace diversity in the work force.

The Equal Employment Opportunity Commission (EEOC) received nearly 100,000 charges of discrimination during the 2011 fiscal year, the most in its 46-year history. Charges of religious discrimination jumped by 9.5 percent, the largest increase of any category. Claims of bias based on ancestry or country of origin rose 5 percent.[2] Federal law restricts employers from discriminating on account of a worker's race, gender, or age, among other protected categories.

During a period of economic decline, companies need to thin their ranks and sometimes unfairly target certain workers, especially older and disabled employees. Laid-off workers who can quickly find another job are more likely to move on with their lives and avoid the hassle of filing a bias claim. But when jobs are scarce, an unemployed person is more likely to sue.[3]

Legal action initiated by the EEOC has involved a wide range of companies. A large-scale employment discrimination lawsuit was filed against Abercrombie & Fitch in 2005. The retailer was accused of refusing to recruit, hire, promote, and retain minorities who did not fit Abercrombie's "All American" look. The retail giant was slapped with a fine of $50 million. The company agreed to institute a range of policies and programs to promote diversity. Today those employees who self-identify as Asians, African Americans, and Hispanics represent more than half of the Abercrombie & Fitch workforce.[4]

Some employers such as Abercrombie & Fitch historically known for promoting a narrow "All-American" male image have begun to scale back those policies and feature more women in their advertising campaigns.

WORK FORCE DIVERSITY

15-1 Diversity can be a source of competitive advantage in the marketplace. It gives organizations an enhanced ability to understand the needs of different market segments. One of the guiding principles at PepsiCo is "Win with diversity and inclusion." The company recognizes that diversity brings new perspectives into the workplace and encourages innovation as well as the ability to identify new market opportunities. New products inspired by members of the diverse PepsiCo workforce include a wasabi-flavored snack aimed at Asian Americans; guacamole-flavored Doritos Chips aimed at Hispanics; and Mountain Dew Code Red, which appeals to African Americans.[5]

America has always served as host to a kaleidoscope of the world's cultures, and the diversity movement will continue. Growing minority and immigrant populations will contribute to increased racial and ethnic diversity. The American work force is becoming more racially and ethnically diverse, increasingly female, increasingly older, and increasingly nonwhite.[6]

Valuing diversity means appreciating everyone's uniqueness, respecting differences, and encouraging every worker to make his or her full contribution to the organization. Organizations that foster the full participation of all workers will enjoy the sharpest competitive edge in the expanding global marketplace.

Figure 15.1 ■ Primary and Secondary Dimensions of Diversity

Source: This model is adapted from *Workforce America!* Authored by Marilyn Loden and Judy B. Rosener.

Dimensions of Diversity

There are primary and secondary dimensions of diversity. The **primary dimensions** are core characteristics of each individual that cannot be changed: age, race, gender, physical and mental abilities, ethnic heritage, and sexual orientation (see Figure 15.1). Together they form an individual's self-image and the filters through which each person views the rest of the world. These inborn elements are interdependent; no one dimension stands alone. Each exerts an important influence throughout life. Marilyn Loden and Judy Rosener describe individual primary dimensions in their book *Workforce America!* They say, "Like the interlocking segments of a sphere, they represent the core of our individual identities."[7]

The greater the number of primary differences between people, the more difficult it is to establish trust and mutual respect. When we add the secondary dimensions of diversity to the mix, effective human relations become even more difficult. The **secondary dimensions** of diversity are elements that can be changed, or at least modified. They include a person's work experience, health habits, religious beliefs, education and training, first language, family status, organizational role and level, communication style, and socio-economic status (see Figure 15.1). These factors all add a layer of complexity to the way we see ourselves and others. The blend of secondary and primary dimensions adds depth to each person and helps shape his or her values, priorities, and perceptions throughout life.[8]

The greater the number of primary differences between people, the more difficult it is to establish trust and mutual respect.

Each of us enters the work force with a unique perspective, shaped by these dimensions and our own past experiences. Building effective human relationships is possible only when we learn to accept and value the differences in others. Without this acceptance, both primary and secondary dimensions of diversity can become roadblocks to further cooperation and understanding.

Global Diversity

A large number of American companies are attempting to develop global diversity initiatives. Many of these programs fail because they are based purely on an American perspective. The primary and secondary dimensions of diversity featured in Figure 15.1

reflect an American perspective. Social class, for example, is often a forgotten component in U.S. based diversity initiatives. However, it is a very important dimension of diversity in some regions such as Latin America.[9]

PREJUDICED ATTITUDES

15-2   **Prejudice** is a premature judgment or opinion that is formed without examination of the facts. Throughout life, we often prejudge people in light of their primary and secondary dimensions. Rather than treat others as unique individuals, prejudiced people tend to think in terms of **stereotypes**—perceptions, beliefs, and expectations about members of some group. In most cases, a stereotype involves the false assumption that all members of a group share the same characteristics. The most common and powerful stereotypes focus on observable personal attributes such as age, gender, and ethnicity.[10]

Total Person Insight

"Understand that diversity initiatives that may make a lot of sense at home, in their current form, could lose their importance abroad, because other nations have different issues and experiences to consider."

Source: Neal Goodman, "Diversity Dimensions," *Training*, November/December 2011, p. 66.

One of the most common stereotypes in the workplace has been labeled "singlism." This stereotype is based on the assumption that singles have lots of time to spend at work because they have no life away from work. Human-resources managers have been trying for years to discredit the notion that heavy travel, weekend work, and overbearing jobs should be reserved for unmarried employees.[11]

How Prejudicial Attitudes Are Formed and Retained

Three major factors contribute to the development of prejudice: childhood experiences, ethnocentrism, and economic conditions.

Childhood Experiences. Today's views toward others are filtered through the experiences and feelings of childhood. Children watch how their family members, friends, teachers, and other authority figures respond to different racial, ethnic, and religious groups. As a result, they form attitudes that may last a lifetime, unless new information replaces the old perceptions. Prejudicial attitudes are not unalterable. Whatever prejudice is learned during childhood can be unlearned later in life.[12]

CLASS-BASED BIAS

Paul C. Gorski, professor in the Graduate School of Education at Hamline University, states that many of us need to examine our own class-based prejudices. We sometimes stigmatize victims of income inequality (children, parents, and coworkers), forgetting that they may have experienced savage inequalities in such areas as education, health care, housing, and employment opportunities. Try to avoid letting class-based prejudices color your assumptions about others.

Source: Paul C. Gorski, "The Question of Class," *Teaching Tolerance*, Spring 2007, pp. 26–29.

Ethnocentrism. The tendency to regard our own culture or nation as better or more "correct" than others is called **ethnocentrism**. The word is derived from *ethnic,* meaning a group united by similar customs, characteristics, race, or other common factors, and *center.* **Ethnic identity** is the part of a person's identity that reflects the racial, religious, or cultural group to which the person belongs.[13] When ethnocentrism is present, the standards and values of our own culture are being used as a yardstick to measure the worth of other cultures.

In their book *Valuing Diversity,* Lewis Brown Griggs and Lente-Louise Louw compare ethnocentrism in an organization to icebergs floating in an ocean. We can see the tips of icebergs above the water level, just as we can see our diverse coworkers' skin color, gender, mannerisms, and job-related talents and hear the words they use and their accents. These are basically "surface" aspects of a person that others can easily learn through observation. However, just as the enormous breadth of an iceberg's base lies beneath the water's surface, so does the childhood conditioning of people from different cultures. As icebergs increase in number and drift too close together, they are likely to clash at their base even though there is no visible contact at the water's surface.[14] As organizations increase the diversity of their work force, the potential for clashes resulting from deep-seated cultural conditioning and prejudiced attitudes also increases.

Economic Factors. When the economy goes through a recession or depression, and housing, jobs, and other necessities become scarce, people's prejudices against other groups often increase. If enough prejudice is built up against a particular group, members of that group may be barred from competing for jobs. The recent backlash against immigrants can be traced, in part, to a fear that the new arrivals will take jobs that would otherwise be available to American workers. Prejudice based on economic factors has its roots in people's basic survival needs, and, as a result, it is very hard to eliminate.

Increasingly, income and wealth inequality in America is viewed by many as a serious barrier to racial harmony. *Fortune* magazine reports that the average net worth of the top fifth of American households has more than doubled in real terms since 1962; the middle class has seen only a 25 percent rise; and the bottom 20 percent is deeper in debt.[15] America is evolving into a two-caste society.

Total Person Insight

"At Prudential, valuing diversity and inclusion is the way we do business. And we take our business very seriously. Our senior leaders are held accountable for promoting an environment that values inclusion."

Source: Emilio Egea, Chief Diversity Officer, Prudential Financial. [Cited 9 March 2010] Available from www.diversityinc.com

Unconscious Prejudices. Many people have biases that they don't know they have. These *implicit biases* are acquired over a lifetime, absorbed from our culture, and work automatically to color our perceptions and influence our choices. A massive national study, *Project Implicit,* investigates thoughts and feelings that exist outside of conscious awareness or conscious control.[16]

Research results based on several million participants in the study were carefully studied before the 2008 presidential election. Findings indicate white voters have an implicit negativity toward African Americans and the elderly. Senator McCain (age 72) and Senator Obama (African American) both had handicaps during the campaign.

THE MANY FORMS OF DISCRIMINATION

15-3 **Discrimination** is behavior based on prejudiced attitudes. If, as an employer, you believe that overweight people tend to be lazy, that is a prejudiced attitude. If you refuse to hire someone simply because that person is overweight, you are engaging in discrimination.

> *Discrimination is behavior based on prejudiced attitudes.*

Individuals or groups that are discriminated against are denied equal treatment and opportunities afforded to the dominant group. They may be denied employment, promotion, training, or other job-related privileges on the basis of race, lifestyle, gender, or other characteristics that have little or nothing to do with their qualifications for a job.

Gender

Discrimination based on gender has been, and continues to be, the focus of much attention. The traditional roles women held in society have undergone tremendous changes in the past few decades. Women enter the work force, not only to supplement family income, but also to pursue careers in previously all-male professions. Men have also been examining the roles assigned them by society and are discovering new options for themselves. Most companies have recognized that discrimination based on gender is a reality and are taking steps to deal with the problem. Chapter 16 is devoted to an in-depth discussion of overcoming gender bias.

Age

People who make up today's work force are working longer and living longer. Meaningful employment is a source of well-being for many of these workers. In light of our extended life span, it's time to rethink the concept of age. Tom Lowry, author of a *BusinessWeek* article entitled "Extreme Experience" says, "If 60 is the new 40, then 80 is the new 60." He describes 25 persons, who range in age from 75 to 100, who run their companies or wield real influence in the business world.[17] CVS Caremark, a large drugstore chain, is currently recruiting baby boomers and other older workers. Stephen Wing, director of CVS workforce initiatives, says, "When you're in your 50s and 60s, you're in your prime."[18]

Of course not every organization has adopted an enlightened view of age. Some companies fail to understand that workers in their 50s and 60s are productive, cost-effective employees. During the recent recession, age-discrimination complaints processed by the Equal Employment Opportunity Commission (EEOC) reached a record high. Some companies replace older workers with younger workers in order to reduce compensation expenses.

GENERATIONAL TENSION

Many of today's younger workers are hoping older Americans will retire and make room for them. Many older workers have seen their retirement funds disappear in the wake of the stock market collapse, and they can't afford to retire. In addition, many of the older workers who lost their jobs during the recent recession face discrimination getting new ones. Add to this complex picture thousands of baby-boomer generation workers who are more interested in *renewal* than *retirement*. They want to secure work with social value—work they can feel proud of. An expanded AmeriCorps may be the answer for some of these people.

Source: Ellen Goodman, "Worker Longer, with Pride," *News & Observer*, March 21, 2009, p. 15A.

Age bias is still pervasive in hiring. Older workers should anticipate the most common fears employers have about older workers and defuse them. This means showing plenty of energy, flexibility, reasonable pay expectations, and up-to-date skills.[19]

Race

Few areas are more sensitive and engender more passion than issues surrounding race. Race denotes a category of people who are perceived as distinctive on the basis of certain biologically inherited traits, such as skin color or hair texture.[20] Because people cannot change these inherited traits, they can easily become victims of discrimination.

There is as much genetic variability between two people from the same "racial group" as there is between two people from any two different "racial" groups.

Throughout American history, we have seen attempts to place people in racial categories and judge them as racial symbols rather than as unique individuals. During World War II, many Americans of Japanese ancestry were confined in concentration camps because they were considered a security threat, merely because of their racial heritage. Because of the war on terrorism, today's "racial" targets often include immigrants from Pakistan, Iraq, and other Middle Eastern countries, as well as their American-born children.

The Myth of Race. Critics of racial categories view them as social inventions that intensify and reinforce racist beliefs and actions. They believe that one way to break down racial barriers and promote a race-free consciousness is to get rid of traditional racial categories. A growing number of geneticists and social scientists reject the view that "racial" differences have an objective or scientific foundation.[21] The American Anthropological Association (AAA) has taken the official position that "race" has no scientific justification in human biology. The AAA position is that, "There is as much genetic variability between two people from the same 'racial group' as there is between two people from any two different 'racial' groups."[22]

It is important to keep in mind that some race categories include people who vary greatly in terms of ethnic identity. The Asian label includes a wide range of groups, such as Vietnamese, Filipino, Chinese, and Korean, with distinct histories and languages. The label "African American" does not take into consideration the enormous linguistic, physical, and cultural diversity of the peoples of Africa.[23]

Multiracial and Multicultural Trends

Marriage across racial and ethnic lines has reached a new high in the United States. About 15 percent of new marriages in 2010 were between individuals of a different race or ethnicity. About 9 million people living in the United States identify themselves as

Barack Obama and golf champion Tiger Woods both have multiracial backgrounds. They share America's changing geography of race, culture, and identity. Millions of Americans have mixed racial origins.

multiracial or multicultural.[24] This large group includes Barack Obama, son of a black man and a white woman.

THE MACACA INCIDENT

George Allen served one term as governor of Virginia and then he was elected to the U.S. Senate. While seeking re-election to the Senate, he used the term "Macaca," an unfamiliar ethnic slur, to describe a dark-skinned man of Indian descent seated in the audience. The use of this sarcastic word triggered an extraordinary fall from political grace. He lost the election.

Source: Frank Bruni, Kim Severson, and Grant Barrett, "Buzzwords are Catchy—and Caustic," *News & Observer*, December 25, 2006, p. 3A.

Race as Social Identity. Although races are not scientifically defensible, they are "real" socially, politically, and psychologically. Race and racism affect our own self-perception and how we are treated by others. Groups that are working to build ethnic pride, such as Native Americans, oppose efforts to get rid of the traditional racial categories, which they consider part of a positive identity.

Religion

Discrimination based on a person's religious preference has been an issue throughout history. Religion has always had the power to fracture and divide people of faith. The authors of a study at Baylor University say, "American religion is startlingly complex and diverse. Though Americans may agree that God exists, they do not agree on much else."[25]

Charges of religious discrimination in the workplace have increased in recent years according to EEOC reports.[26] Muslims face unique challenges as they attempt to balance their prayer schedule with inflexible work schedules. Misunderstandings occur frequently over relatively minor issues, such as Muslim women's right to wear head scarves and Muslim men's right to maintain facial hair.

Readers of *Spirituality & Health* magazine frequently voice concerns regarding lack of tolerance among members of the three major faith groups: Judaism, Christianity, and Islam. Rabbi Rami Shapiro, who writes the "Roadside Assistance for the Spiritual Traveler" column for this publication, offers us this timely advice:[27]

> *We need to understand all three levels of religion and promote the voices of the ethicists and mystics within each faith, rather than the shrill and fearful screams of fanatics who hew to the tribal vision of their religion.*

Total Person Insight

"People with disabilities comprise the largest minority group in the United States—some 17 percent of the population. Behind this statistic are more than 45 million individuals who are human beings first, and who have special needs second."

Source: Peggy Post and Peter Post, *The Etiquette Advantage in Business* (second edition), New York: HarperCollins Publishers, 2005, p. 62.

Disability

The Americans with Disabilities Act (ADA) bans discrimination against workers and customers with disabilities and requires employers to make "reasonable accommodations" so that the disabled can access and work in the workplace.

National Sports Center for the Disabled

The National Sports Center for the Disabled's mission is to positively impact the lives of people with any physical or mental challenge. Today, the NSCD is one of the largest outdoor therapeutic recreational agencies in the world. Thousands of lessons are provided each year.

The ADA covers a wide range of disabilities, including learning impairments, AIDS, diabetes, alcoholism, visual impairments, and physical impairments that require use of a wheelchair (visit *http://www.adata.org*). Although legal protection is in place, the unemployment rate for people with disabilities has outpaced those of the overall working population. Also, persons with a disability earn much less than those employees without a disability.[28]

Successful implementation of diversity and ADA initiatives may require changes in corporate culture, attitudes, and policies. The starting point should be a review of all job descriptions and qualification standards. Staff training on nondiscrimination practices, disability etiquette, and awareness may be needed. Diversity initiatives should include the active recruitment and retention of individuals with disabilities.[29]

human
RELATIONS
in Action

MEETING SOMEONE WITH A DISABILITY

Here are a few suggestions for making a good impression. If the person …

… **is in a wheelchair.** Sit down, if possible. Try to chat eye to eye. Don't touch the wheelchair. It is considered within the boundaries of an individual's personal space.

… **has a speech impediment.** Be patient and carefully listen; resist the urge to finish his or her sentences.

… **is accompanied by a guide dog.** Never pet or play with a guide dog; you will distract the animal from its job.

… **has a hearing loss.** People who are deaf depend on facial expressions and gestures for communication cues. Face the person and speak clearly and slowly. Speak directly to the person, not to an interpreter or assistant if one is present.

Source: "When Meeting Someone with a Disability." Adapted from "Communication Solutions." Used by permission of Progressive Business Publications.

Sexual Orientation

Discrimination based on a person's sexual orientation is motivated by *homophobia,* an aversion to homosexuals. Not long ago, gays and lesbians went to great lengths to keep their sexuality a secret. But today many gays, lesbians, bisexual, and transgender people are "coming out of the closet" to demand their rights as members of society. Indeed, many young people entering the work force who are used to the relative tolerance of college campuses refuse to hide their orientation once they are in the workplace.

Gay rights activists are working hard to create awareness that discrimination based on sexual orientation is no less serious than discrimination based on age, gender, race, or disability. Activist groups, such as the Human Rights Campaign, the Interfaith Alliance, and the Southern Poverty Law Center, are also working to rid the workplace of antigay behaviors, such as offensive jokes, derogatory names, or remarks about gays. An atmosphere in which gays and lesbians are comfortable being themselves is usually more productive than an atmosphere in which they waste their time and energy maintaining alternate, and false, personalities.

In recent years, we have witnessed several workplace trends favorable to gay and lesbian employees. More than 80 percent of *Fortune* 500 companies include sexual orientation in their antidiscrimination policies, and some companies have established lesbian and gay resource groups—known in some companies as affinity groups—that provide a point of contact for previously invisible employees. Also, a majority of the nation's top 500 companies now extend medical benefits to same-sex partners.[30]

in Action

THE PAIN OF GROWING UP GAY

At age 14, Mitchell Gold harbored a secret that he felt would forever ruin his chances of happiness and success in life. He was gay and afraid his family would disown him if they knew his secret. Today he is owner of a fast-growing furniture company located in Taylorsville, North Carolina, and he is working hard to make sure no other teenager has to experience what he did. He has launched an educational campaign called Faith in America to combat religion-based prejudices directed toward the gay community. The centerpiece of his campaign is a book entitled *Youth in Crisis: What Everyone Should Know About Growing Up Gay.* These personal stories describe the pain being inflicted on many gay teens.

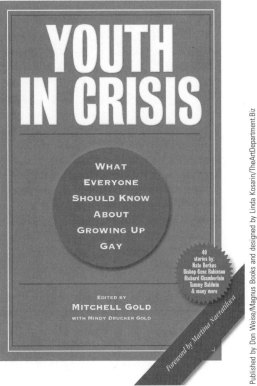

Source: Yonat Shimron, "Passion for Justice," *News & Observer*, November 20, 2008, p. Dl. For additional information, visit http://www.crisisbook.org.

Progress on the Legal Front. Gay and lesbian advocates heralded the passage of important federal legislation. In 2009, President Obama signed an historic hate crimes bill into law. This law gives the federal government the authority to investigate and prosecute hate crimes when local authorities can't or don't. Until this law was passed, the federal government had no way to respond to crimes motivated by the victims' sexual orientation. In 2011 the president repealed the "Don't Ask, Don't Tell" policy, a form of discrimination in the military.[31]

Figure 15.2 ■ Active Hate Groups 2000–2011

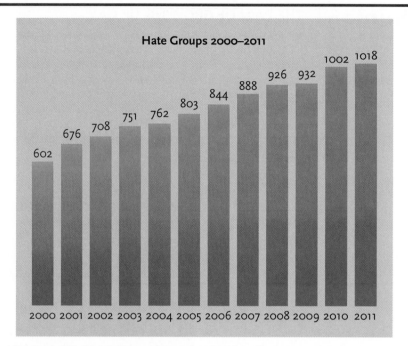

Source: Mark Potok, "The Year in Hate and Extremism," SPLC Intelligence Report, Spring 2012, p. 41.

The Southern Poverty Law Center reports that the number of active hate groups has increased steadily over the past decade (see Figure 15.2). Examples of active hate groups include the Ku Klux Klan, Neo-Nazis, White Nationalists, and Black Separatists.

Policies aimed at preventing verbal and physical harassment of students based on sexual orientation have been adopted by many public schools and colleges. In some cases, these initiatives have generated considerable controversy. Some religious and conservative groups have actively opposed these violence-prevention efforts, believing that they promote homosexuality.[32]

Subtle Forms of Discrimination

A person who feels he or she has been the victim of discrimination based on gender, age, race, abilities, or sexual orientation can take legal action by filing a complaint with his or her state's office of the Equal Employment Opportunity Commission. However, although many state and federal laws protect individuals from discrimination based on these issues, they do not specifically protect workers from the more subtle forms of discrimination. For example, those who graduated from an Ivy League college may treat coworkers who graduated from state-funded colleges as inferior. Overweight employees might experience degrading remarks from coworkers. Those who speak with a distinct regional accent may hear snickers behind their back at work. People who do not value differences often equate a difference with a deficiency.

Discrimination Against the Unemployed. Long-term unemployment has created a new "underclass." Many employers do not want to hire someone who does not have a job. An advocacy group for workers reviewed online job postings and found more than

100 companies that want only applicants who are currently employed. The Equal Employment Opportunity Commission is holding hearings to determine if screening out jobless applicants is a form of discrimination.[33]

What Can You Do?

What should you do if you discover you are the target of some form of subtle, unprotected discrimination because you are different from others at work? If you want to stay in the organization, you will need to determine whether the "difference" is something you can change—your weight, the way you dress, your manner of speaking. If the difference is something you cannot or choose not to change, you may need to address the situation directly. Review the assertiveness skills you studied in Chapter 13. Your assertiveness may help change other people's attitudes and in turn alter their discriminatory behaviors. Another powerful method of eliminating subtle discrimination is to compensate for it by excelling in your work. Become an expert on the job, and work to increase your skills and your value to the organization. As your colleagues gain respect for your talents, they will likely change their attitudes toward you.

human
RELATIONS
in Action

TOOLS FOR TOLERANCE: WORKPLACE

- Hold a "diversity potluck" lunch. Invite coworkers to bring foods that reflect their cultural heritage.
- Suggest ways to overcome any barriers that might prevent people of color and women from succeeding.
- Value the input of every employee. Reward managers who do.
- Push for equitable leave policies. Provide paid maternity and paternity leave.
- Start a mentoring program that pairs employees of different ages, such as seniors with entry-level workers.
- Vary your lunch partners. Seek out coworkers of different backgrounds, from different departments, and at different levels in the company.

Source: "Tools for Tolerance: Workplace," adapted from *101 Tools for Tolerance: Simple Ideas for Promoting Equity and Celebrating Diversity.* Copyright © 2000, Southern Poverty Law Center, Montgomery, AL. Reprinted by permission of Southern Poverty Law Center. *101 Tools for Tolerance* is available free from the SPLC. For more information, visit http://www.splccenter.org.

THE ECONOMICS OF VALUING DIVERSITY

15-4 The new millennium has brought greater understanding that diversity can be a source of competitive advantage. This occurs when a company makes full use of the ideas, talents, experiences, and perspectives of all employees at all levels of the organization. Joe Watson, a recruiter of minorities, believes that if you want to satisfy clients and customers from diverse backgrounds, you need a diverse mix of employees who are more likely to understand them.[34]

A study conducted by the Society for Human Resource Management revealed diversity initiatives within organizations can affect an organization's bottom line by reducing costs associated with turnover, absenteeism, and low productivity. In addition, efforts to value workers' and customers' diversity reduce complaints and litigation and improve the

"Gays and lesbians getting married—haven't they suffered enough?"

Source: Steven Petrow, *Complete Gay & Lesbian Manners*, New York: Workman Publishing, 2011, p. 188.

> *The price tag for not helping employees learn to respect and value each other is enormous.*

organization's public image.[35] Organizations that pursue diversity and make it part of their culture usually outperform companies that are less committed to diversity.

The price tag for *not* helping employees learn to respect and value each other is enormous. Many highly skilled and talented employees will leave an organization that does not value diversity. A comment, gesture, or joke delivered without malice but received as an insult will create tension among workers and customers alike.

MANAGING DIVERSITY

15-5   **Managing diversity** is the process of creating an organizational culture where the primary and secondary dimensions of diversity are respected. This process can be a challenge now that the work force is composed of so many different nationalities. Managers at some Marriott Hotels work with employees from 30 different countries. The employees who are part of the Toyota Formula 1 race team represent 27 nationalities. Even some small retail stores have become a kind of United Nations. The Kroger supermarket in Durham, North Carolina, has employees from ten countries. The issue is further complicated when an organization's diverse work force is in global satellite offices separated by thousands of miles. Microsoft's research unit, for example, is staffed by 700 multinational scientists and engineers working in six laboratories on three continents.[36]

> *Learn to look critically and honestly at the particular myths and preconceived ideas you have been conditioned to believe about others.*

What Individuals Can Do

You cannot totally eliminate prejudices that have been deeply held and developed over a long time. But you can take steps to change those attitudes and behaviors that may have a negative impact on your employer's efforts to enhance diversity.

1. *Recognize the powerful influence of entrenched stereotypes.* Research findings indicate that stereotypes are so well learned and so ingrained that they may be activated automatically and without conscious awareness. Prejudice is ingrained, but it can be reduced.[37]

2. *Learn to look critically and honestly at the particular myths and preconceived ideas you have been conditioned to believe about others.* Contact among people of different races, cultures, and lifestyles can break down prejudice when people join together for a common task. The more contact there is among culturally diverse individuals, the more likely it will be that stereotypes based on myths and inaccurate generalizations will not survive.

3. *Develop sensitivity to differences.* Do not allow gender-based, racist, or antigay jokes or comments in your presence. If English is not a person's native language, be aware that this person might interpret your messages differently from what you intended. When in doubt as to the appropriate behavior, ask questions. "I would like to open the door for you because you are in a wheelchair, but I'm not sure whether that would offend you. What would you like me to do?"

4. *Develop your own diversity awareness program.* The starting point might be creation of a "diversity profile" of your friends, coworkers, and acquaintances. How much diversity do these individuals have in terms of race? Ethnicity? Religion? Assess the cultural diversity reflected in the music you listen to and the books you read. Study Islam, Buddhism, and other faiths that may be different from your own.[38]

What Organizations Can Do

A well-planned and well-executed diversity program can promote understanding and defuse tensions between employees who differ in age, race, gender, religious beliefs, and other characteristics. Programs that are poorly developed and poorly executed often backfire, especially in organizations where bias and distrust have festered for years. A comprehensive diversity program has three pillars:[39] organizational commitment, employment practices, and training and development (see Figure 15.3).

Organizational Commitment. Catalyst, a research and advisory group, conducted a survey of 106 global companies to determine why these companies use diversity strategies as part of their overall business plan. Nearly 90 percent said their diversity program was designed to help them gain a competitive advantage.[40] When the objective of the diversity initiative is to achieve a stronger competitive position, the commitment is usually quite strong. Ron Glover, vice president of global diversity at IBM, says how we think about diversity and how we deliver it has to be directly connected and deeply embedded in the organization's business objectives.[41]

To achieve work force diversity, organizations need to design a plan that actively recruits men and women of different ethnicities, family situations, disabilities, and sexual orientations. Diversity should not be limited to race and gender.

Companies that see diversity programs as a quick-fix *event*—a one-day workshop that promotes the advantages of a diverse work force—often create greater, not less, divisiveness among workers. Companies that see diversity programs as a *process* know that the key to a successful diversity program is long-term commitment.

Employment Practices. To achieve work force diversity, organizations need to design a plan that actively recruits men and

Figure 15.3 ■ Three Pillars of Diversity

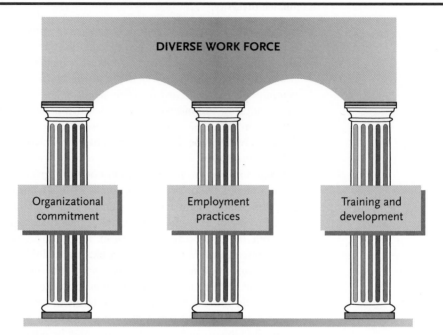

women of different ethnicities, family situations, disabilities, and sexual orientations. Diversity should not be limited to race and gender. One approach is to make a special effort to plug into networks that are often ignored by corporate recruiters.

Organizations must also foster a climate for retention. Newly hired people who are different from the majority must often contend with an atmosphere of tension, instability, and distrust and may soon lose the desire to do their best work. Subtle biases often alienate these employees and create unnecessary stress.

Training and Development. To develop a culture that values and enhances diversity, organizations need training programs that give managers and employees the tools they need to work more effectively with one another regardless of their backgrounds. Unfortunately, most of the diversity training efforts at American companies are ineffective for these reasons:

- Mandatory programs, often undertaken mainly to avoid liability in discrimination lawsuits, are frequently ineffective and may even be counterproductive. Voluntary diversity training, undertaken to advance the organization's goals, is more effective.[42]
- Middle managers, who play a key role in hiring, development, and promotion decisions, often do not support diversity efforts. To overcome this roadblock, top management must champion diversity and model ideal behaviors to middle management. They should also reward middle managers who take steps to enhance diversity initiatives.[43]

Done well, diversity training programs can promote harmony, reduce conflict, and help give the organization a competitive advantage. Participants should learn which specific behaviors will not be condoned and the basic rules of civil behavior. We may not be able to stop people from bringing their prejudices to work, but they can learn to act as though they have none.

AFFIRMATIVE ACTION: YESTERDAY AND TODAY

15-6 The Civil Rights Act of 1964 marked the beginning of antidiscrimination employment legislation. In an attempt to make up for past discrimination in the areas of employment, education, and business, affirmative action policies were initiated by the federal government. **Affirmative action** involves intentionally seeking and hiring employees from groups that are under-represented.[44]

The Equal Employment Opportunity Commission (EEOC) is charged with enforcing employment-related laws. One recent EEOC lawsuit filed against Lockheed Martin Corporation illustrates the high cost of discrimination. Charles Daniels, an African-American electrician at the company, said he was subjected to racial harassment by coworkers on a daily basis and death threats once he complained to supervisors. After a long trial, Mr. Daniels was awarded $2.5 million.[45]

Although affirmative action has stirred controversy for many decades, there is no doubt that this initiative has helped minorities gain access to large corporations and top universities. The number of African Americans at the nation's top 50 colleges and universities has doubled in recent decades. Women have also benefited, especially in the 1970s and 1980s, when they began breaking into traditionally male-dominated fields.[46] The flow of controversy over affirmative action sometimes includes references to quotas. Quotas are not legal in the United States.[47]

Affirmative Action Issues. Many people say it is time to rethink affirmative action or even eliminate it. Recent political and legal interpretations of affirmative action have stimulated a nationwide debate over the merits of any program that grants preferential treatment to specific groups. The following are some factors that should guide decisions related to the implementation of affirmative action policies:

- Affirmative action's purpose is not to give unqualified people special rights.[48]
- Affirmative action in the best sense promotes equal consideration, not reverse discrimination.[49]
- One of the most significant changes brought about by affirmative action laws has been the publication of job announcements.[50]
- The definition of employment selection tests has been expanded to include any procedure used as a basis for an employment decision. Informal and formal interviews, performance tests, physical requirements, and other procedures qualify as "tests."[51]

Those who say affirmative action causes companies to hire and promote less qualified people fail to realize that the hiring process usually goes beyond the abilities, knowledge, and skills of the job candidate and includes additional merit-based factors, such as education and experience. When these factors are included in the hiring process, recipients of affirmative action are less likely to feel stigmatized. The way people react to a preferential selection procedure will often depend on how well it is structured and implemented.[52]

LOOKING BACK: SUMMARY OF LEARNING OBJECTIVES

1. **Define the primary and secondary dimensions of diversity.**

   Primary dimensions of diversity include gender, age, race, physical and mental abilities, sexual orientation, and ethnic heritage. Secondary dimensions include religious beliefs, work experience, communication style, organizational role and level, family status, socio-economic status, first language, education and training, and health habits.

2. **Discuss how prejudiced attitudes are formed.**

   Prejudice is a premature judgment or opinion based partly on observation of others' differences and partly on ignorance, fear, and cultural conditioning. Prejudiced people tend to see others as stereotypes rather than as individuals. Prejudicial attitudes are formed through the effects of childhood experiences, ethnocentrism, and economic factors. Many people have unconscious prejudices, biases they don't know they have.

3. **Develop an awareness of the various forms of discrimination in the workplace.**

   Discrimination is behavior based on prejudicial attitudes. Groups protected by law from discrimination in the workplace include people who share characteristics such as gender, age, race, disability, religion, and sexual orientation. More subtle discrimination can arise when individuals have different appearances or educational backgrounds. These subtle forms of discrimination may not be illegal, but they are disruptive to a productive work force.

4. **Understand why organizations value diversity.**

   The issue of valuing diversity is an economic one for most organizations. The work force will soon be made up of a minority of white men and a majority of women, people of color, and immigrants. To remain competitive, organizations must value the contributions of all of their diverse workers and make full use of their ideas and talents. Only then will they be able to understand their equally diverse customers' needs. Valuing diversity is not just a nice idea, but a business imperative.

5. **Identify ways in which individuals and organizations can enhance work force diversity.**

   Individuals can enhance diversity by letting go of their stereotypes and learning to critically and honestly evaluate their prejudiced attitudes as they work and socialize with people who are different. They will need to develop sensitivity to differences and their own personal diversity awareness programs. Organizations must commit to valuing individual differences and implementing effective employment practices that respect and enhance diversity. Their diversity training programs should be an ongoing process rather than a onetime event. They need to seek out, employ, and develop employees from diverse backgrounds.

6. **Discuss the current status of affirmative action programs.**

   Affirmative action involves intentionally seeking and hiring employees from groups that are under-represented in the organization. Affirmative action guidelines have helped bring fairness in hiring and promotion to many organizations. Today, however, some people believe these guidelines are discriminatory because they allow preferential treatment for the people they were designed to protect.

KEY TERMS

valuing diversity, 324	stereotypes, 326	race, 329
primary dimensions, 325	ethnocentrism, 327	managing diversity, 336
secondary dimensions, 325	ethnic identity, 327	affirmative action, 339
prejudice, 326	discrimination, 328	behavioral profiling, 344

CAREER INSIGHT

Discrimination against persons who are unemployed is a modern day problem. If you have been unemployed for a few months or a few years, here are some tips on how to get hired:

- When you are unemployed, keep your skills up to date. Take a class, become active in a professional group, consider becoming a volunteer.
- Redo your résumé. List only the past 10 years of work experience.

- Explore internships, fellowships, or work for a temp agency.
- Network. Tell everyone you are looking for a job.
- Understand that there might be negative perceptions about you because of your work record. Be proactive and bust the stereotype. Be prepared to show they are wrong.

Source: Adapted from Faye Fiore, "Will I Ever Work Again?" *aarp.org/bulletin*, October 2011, pp. 18–19.

TRY YOUR HAND

1. The "managing diversity" movement has raised the discussion of equal employment opportunity and affirmative action to a higher level. Consider the following comments by R. Roosevelt Thomas, Jr., which appeared in a *Harvard Business Review* article entitled "From Affirmative Action to Affirming Diversity":

   Managers usually see affirmative action and equal employment opportunity as centering on minorities and women, with very little to offer white males. The diversity I'm talking about includes race, gender, creed, and ethnicity but also age, background, education, function, and personality differences. The objective is not to assimilate minorities and women into a dominant white male culture but to create a dominant heterogeneous culture.[53]

   What does "dominant heterogeneous culture" mean to you? Consider your former or current workplace. Assess how the atmosphere at work would be different if Roosevelt got his wish. Be specific.

2. For one week, keep a journal that records instances in which you see actions or hear comments that reflect prejudicial, negative stereotypes. For example, watch a movie or TV show and observe whether the actors are predominantly of a particular race or ethnic group. Listen to your friends' conversations, and notice any time they make irrational judgments about others based on stereotypes. Finally, reflect on your own attitudes and perceptions. Do you engage in stereotyping?

   Share your experiences with a class member, and propose what steps you can take to help rid the environment of negative stereotyping.

3. Arrange a meeting with someone who is a member of a racial or ethnic group different from your own, and attempt to build a relationship by discussing the things that are important to each of you. Perhaps it is another student, coworker, or member of your community. As you get to know this person, become aware of his or her beliefs and attitudes. Try not to be diverted by accent, grammar, or personal appearance; rather, really listen to the person's thoughts and ideas. Search for things you and your new acquaintance have in common, and assess how your differences could be opportunities for personal growth.

4. Before, during, and after the terrorist attacks and the war in Iraq, Muslims became victims of discrimination throughout the world, merely because of their religious beliefs and stereotyped physical appearance. To learn more about the Muslim culture, visit the Muslim Public Affairs Council website at www.mpac.org, the Muslim American Society at www.masnet.org, or www.Islaml01.net, an introductory guide for non-Muslims. What did you learn that would help you respond to someone who displays a bias against Muslims in your presence?

CRITICAL THINKING CHALLENGE

In an ideal world, everyone would be free of prejudiced attitudes and would avoid thinking in terms of stereotypes. However, childhood experiences can shape attitudes that are difficult to change. Do you carry any prejudices that are obvious carryovers from your childhood or adolescence? Are you doing anything to overcome these prejudices? Explain.

SELF-ASSESSMENT EXERCISE

For each of the following statements, circle the number from 1 to 5 that best represents your response: (1) strongly disagree (never do this); (2) disagree (rarely do this); (3) moderately agree (sometimes do this); (4) agree (frequently do this); (5) strongly agree (almost always do this).

A. I refuse to perpetuate negative stereotypes, and I accept each person as a unique individual worthy of my respect.	1	2	3	4	5
B. I make every effort to identify my own prejudiced attitudes and avoid stereotypical attitudes toward people of color, older people, persons with disabilities, and others who are different from me.	1	2	3	4	5
C. I work hard to combat prejudice because it has a negative impact on my self-esteem and the self-esteem of the victim.	1	2	3	4	5
D. When I witness discriminatory behavior, I speak up and/or take action to defend the victim.	1	2	3	4	5
E. I understand the economics of valuing diversity and support my employer's efforts to hire and retain minority employees.	1	2	3	4	5

After identifying your response to each item, select an attitude or skill you would like to improve. Prepare a written goal and then describe the steps you will take to achieve this goal.

YOU PLAY THE ROLE

You are currently supervising 15 employees. Until recently, the work group was working as a productive team and was free of any serious interpersonal relationship problems. Last week, Deaven Erhardt, a relatively new hire, posted an article from the *New York Times* supporting gay marriage on the workroom bulletin board. The article emphasized freedom of marital choice, which some of your senior colleagues find morally offensive. A week later, Erhardt posted another article from the *San Francisco Chronicle* supporting same-sex marriage and a petition to endorse gay marriage in your state. Needless to say, the workroom was becoming a politically contentious environment and was no longer free of interpersonal relationship problems. You explained the situation to your manager, and he suggested that you meet with Erhardt and request that no more articles be displayed in the work area. You will meet with another class member who will assume the role of Deaven Erhardt. Try to convince your role-play partner that these politically sensitive articles are inappropriate in a work setting.

BELOW THE SURFACE | SUBJECTIVE PERCEPTIONS

At the beginning of this chapter, we reviewed a rather alarming trend—charges of discrimination have increased during the past few years. Most leaders in the field of human resource development agree that promoting and retaining a talented, diverse workforce is good business. However, achieving this goal is not easy. Here are a few of the major barriers:

Top management does not always provide strong leadership in the area of diversity. Companies should regularly review their equal employment opportunity (EEO) policies to be sure they comply with all legal requirements. All employees from executives to hourly workers should be trained on the policies and company expectations.

The much publicized case of Wal-Mart Stores, Inc. v. Dukes reminds us of how diversity practices at one company can have repercussions around the country. In 2000, Betty Dukes, a 54-year-old Wal-Mart employee, filed a sex discrimination claim against her employer. She claimed that despite six years of hard work and excellent performance reviews, she was denied the training needed to advance to a higher salaried position. Five other women, with similar grievances, went to court with Dukes. They were seeking class-action status for their lawsuit alleging that Wal-Mart discriminated against women in pay and promotion. They claimed the company created a sex-segregated work setting, where male managers could make staffing decisions with little company oversight. The plaintiffs brought their case on behalf of themselves and 1.6 million other past, present, and future female Wal-Mart employees.[54]

The case moved through the lower court system and was finally reviewed by the Supreme Court. In June 2011, by a 5-4 majority, the court held the case could not proceed as a class-action. The judges who represented the majority opinion stated that a policy of decentralized decision making is not, by itself, enough "commonality" glue to unite a mega-class court case.[55]

QUESTIONS

1. The plaintiffs claimed the degree of discretion given to local managers was a recipe for widespread discrimination. An expert witness said he believed Wal-Mart gave managers too much discretion and let them rely on too many subjective factors in promotion and pay. Do you agree?

2. Making employment decisions based on subjective perceptions of qualifications and performance has always been part of American business. What steps can a company take to ensure that employment decisions are made for legitimate, non-discriminatory reasons?

CLOSING CASE | RACIAL VERSUS BEHAVIOR PROFILING

Racial profiling refers to the use of an individual's race or ethnicity by law enforcement personnel. It is sometimes a key factor in deciding whether to engage in enforcement. Some traffic stops, for example, are based on racial profiling:[56]

- A Hispanic driver is stopped in a "white" neighborhood because he "looks out of place."
- A group of black teenagers is pulled over because of the kind of car they are driving.

The American Civil Liberties Union (ACLU) has taken the position that racial profiling disproportionately targets people of color. This practice, at the Federal level, is challenged by the Fourth Amendment of the U.S. Constitution, which guarantees the right to be safe from unreasonable search and seizure without probable cause.[57]

Behavioral profiling is the process of observing, anticipating, and interpreting a specific behavior. Gestures, body movements, tone of voice, and facial expressions can communicate confidence or fear, trust or mistrust, curiosity or boredom. All U.S. customs agents are required to watch videos teaching them techniques for studying body language in order to identify potential terrorists and drug traffickers.[58]

QUESTIONS

1. Critics of racial profiling argue that the individual rights of a suspect are violated if race is used as a factor in that suspicion. Do you agree or disagree with these critics?

2. Do you believe "behavior profiling" is a viable method of interpreting a person's actions? Why or why not?

3. There is no simple codebook of nonverbal cues that is accepted across all the cultures of the world. How would you enhance the training programs discussed in this case so that they compensate for cultural diversity?

CHAPTER 15 ENDNOTES

1. Sudeep Reddy, "Latinos Fuel Growth In Decade," *Wall Street Journal*, March 25, 2011, p. A2.

2. Sam Hananel, "Job Discrimination Claims Rise at Record Levels," [cited 24 January 2012] Available from www.abcactionnews.com.

3. Nathan Koppel, "Claims Alleging Job Bias Rise with Layoffs," *Wall Street Journal*, September 24, 2010, p. A6.

4. Ericka Jones, Shawn Knapp, and Toya Spencer, "Abercrombie & Fitch: From Sued to Selling," *Diversity Executive*, July/August 2011, pp. 46–48.

5. Carol Hymowitz, "The New Diversity," *Wall Street Journal*, November 14, 2005, pp. R1–R3. "PepsiCo Values & Philosophy," [cited 6 April 2012] Available from www.pepsi.com; INTERNET.

6. Connor Dougherty, "Nonwhites to Be Majority in U.S. by 2042," *Wall Street Journal*, August 14, 2008, p. A3.

7. Marilyn Loden and Judy B. Rosener, *Workforce America!* (Homewood, Ill.: Business One Irwin, 1991), pp. 114–115. Information on primary and secondary dimensions of diversity can also be found in Marilyn Loden, *Implementing Diversity* (Burr Ridge, Ill.; McGraw-Hill, 1996).

8. Ibid., p. 21.

9. Neal Goodman, "Diversity Dimensions," *Training*, November/December 2011, p. 66.

10. Douglas A. Bernstein, Louis A. Penner, Alison Clarke-Stewart, and Edward J. Roy, *Psychology*, 9th ed. (Belmont, CA: Wadsworth, 2012), p. 714.

11. Sue Shellenbarger, "The Stereotypes Behind 'Singlism' Persist," *Wall Street Journal*, December 9, 2008, p. D5.

12. D. Stanley Eitzen and Maxine Baca Zinn, *In Conflict and Order* (Boston: Allyn & Bacon, 2001), p. 237.

13. Douglas A. Bernstein, Louis A. Penner, Alison Clarke-Stewart, and Edward J. Roy, *Psychology*, 9th ed. (Belmont, CA: Wadsworth, 2012), p. 505.

14. Lewis Brown Griggs and Lente-Louise Louw, *Valuing Diversity* (New York: McGraw-Hill, 1995), pp. 3–4, 150–151.

15. Doris Burke, "The Growing Wealth Gap," *Fortune*, November 7, 2011, p. 28.

16. June Kronholz, "How the Unconscious Affects the Truth," *Wall Street Journal*, August 2, 2008, p. W6; "General Information—Project Implicit" [cited 13 April 2009]. Available from http://www.projectim plicit.net; INTERNET.

17. Tom Lowry, "Extreme Experience," *BusinessWeek*, September 8, 2008, p. 46.

18. Joseph Weber, "This Time, Old Hands Keep Their Jobs," *BusinessWeek*, February 9, 2009, p. 50.

19. Sue Shellenbarger, "Work & Family Mailbox," *Wall Street Journal*, April 13, 2006, p. D4.

20. Craig Calhoun, Donald Light, and Suzanne Keller, *Sociology*, 6th ed. (New York: McGraw-Hill, 1994), p. 241.

21. Nicholas D. Kristof, "Is Race Real?" *New York Times*, July 11, 2003; Robert S. Boynton, "Color Us Invisible," *New York Times Book Review*, August 17, 1997, p. 13.

22. Stephen Magagini, "A Race Free Consciousness," *The News & Observer*, November 23, 1997, pp. A25–A26.

23. Carol Mukhopadhyay and Rosemary C. Henze, "How Real Is Race? Using Anthropology to Make Sense of Human Diversity," *Phi Delta Kappa*, May 2003, p. 675.

24. Miriam Jordan, "More Marriages Cross Race, Ethnicity Lines," *Wall Street Journal*, February 17, 2012, p. A2; Natalie Morera, "Shades of Gray," *Diversity Executive*, July/August 2011, p. 30.

25. Yonat Shimron, "God as Fearsome Father," *News & Observer*, October 1, 2006, p. 24A.

26. Phred Dvorak, "Religious-Bias Filings Up," *Wall Street Journal*, October 16, 2008, pp. B1–B2.

27. Rabbi Rami Shapiro, "Can We Reconcile Faiths? Did Jesus Walk on Water?" *Spirituality & Health*, November/December 2007, p. 16.

28. Nadine Vogel, "Know the Facts: The EEOC and the ADA," *Diversity Executive*, January/February 2012, pp. 32–35.

29. Ibid.

30. Sue Shellenbarger, "Amid Gay Marriage Debate, Companies Offer More Benefits to Same-Sex Couples," *Wall Street Journal*, March 18, 2004, p. Dl; Barbara Rose, "Policies to Accommodate Gays Draw Scrutiny," *The News & Observer*, July 3, 2005, p. El2; Rachel Emma Silverman, "Wall Street, a New Push to Recruit Gay Students," *Wall Street Journal*, February 9, 2000, p. Bl.

31. "A Historic Hate Crimes Law," *Equality*, Winter 2010, pp. 8–9.

32. Robert Tomsho, "School & Efforts to Protect Gays Face Opposition," *Wall Street Journal*, February 20, 2003, p. Bl.

33. John Murawski, "Jobs Scarce, But the Stigma Stays," *News & Observer*, February 12, 2012, p. E1.

34. Chuck Salter, "Diversity Without the Excuses," *Fast Company*, September 2002, p. 44.

35. Jessica Marquez, "Survey Says Diversity Contributes to the Bottom Line," *Workforce Management*, November 18, 2005 [cited 23 February 2006]. Available from http://www.workforce.com; INTERNET.

36. Fay Hansen, "Microsoft R&D Seeks Global Tech Talent, Not Bargains," *Workforce Management*, July 2005, p. 39; Kreitner, *Management*, p. 80; "Toyota's Charge Toward the Pinnacle of the Sport," *Canadian Grand Prix Program 2002*, p. 54; Robin Townsley Arcus, "World Market," *The Urban Hiker*, October 2000, p. 34.

37. Douglas A. Bernstein, Louis A. Penner, Alison Clarke-Stewart, and Edward J. Roy, *Psychology*, 9th ed. (Belmont, CA: Wadsworth, 2012, pp. 718–719.

38. *101 Tools for Tolerance* (Montgomery, Ala.: Southern Poverty Law Center), pp. 4–7.

39. Gail Johnson, "Time to Broaden Diversity," *Training*, September 2004, p. 16; Adapted from Leone E. Wynter, "Do Diversity Programs Make a Difference?" *Wall Street Journal*, December 4, 1996, p. Bl.

40. "Time to Diversify," *Sales & Marketing Management*, May 2002, p. 62.

41. Sam Ali, "How IBM Holds People Accountable for Diversity Results," *Diversity Inc. Magazine*, December 6, 2010, Available from www.diversityinc.com; INTERNET.

42. Shankar Vedantam, "Forced Diversity Training Fails," *News & Observer*, July 21, 2008, p. 3A.

43. "Diversity Dilemma," *Training*, July/August 2007, p. 10.

44. Ricky W. Griffin, *Principles of Management* (Boston: Houghton Mifflin Company, 2007), p. 195.

45. Kris Maher, "Lockheed Settles Racial-Discrimination Suit," *Wall Street Journal*, January 3, 2008, p. A4.

46. Jonathon Kaufman, "Fair Enough," *Wall Street Journal*, June 14, 2008, p. A8.

47. "Affirmative Action," [cited 15 April 2012] Available from www.wikipedia.org; INTERNET.

48. Bob Gregg, "Debunking the Affirmative-Action Myth," *Diversity Inc. Magazine*, March 17, 2011. Available from www.diversity.com; INTERNET.

49. Ibid.

50. Ibid.

51. Robert Kreitner and Carlene M. Cassidy, *Management* (12e), Mason, OH: South-Western, 2011, p. 277.

52. Roger O. Crockett, "How to Narrow the Great Divide," *BusinessWeek*, July 14, 2003, p. 104; Sharon S. Brehm, Saul M. Kassin, and Steven Fein, *Social Psychology*, 5th ed. (Boston: Houghton Mifflin, 2002), pp. 478–480.

53. R. Roosevelt Thomas, Jr., "From Affirmative Action to Affirming Diversity," *Harvard Business Review*, March/April 1990, p. 114.

54. Rebecca P. Bromet, "A Stitch in Time," *Diversity Executive*, March/April 2012, p. 48; Ladan Nikravan, "White Men Can Help It," *Diversity Executive*, March/April 2012, p. 24.

55. Ibid.

56. "Racial Profiling," [cited 18 April 2012]. Available from http://en.wikipedia.org; INTERNET.

57. "Racial Profiling," [cited 18 April 2012]. Available from www.aclu.org; INTERNET.

58. Ann David, Joseph Pereira, and William M. Bulkeley, "Security Concerns Bring New Focus on Body Language," *Wall Street Journal*, August 15, 2002, p. A1, A6; "The Power of Body Language," Course Archive. [cited 6 January 2003]. Available from www.presentersuniversity.com/courses/show_archive.cfm?RecordID 539; INTERNET.

The Changing Roles of Men and Women

Image Source/the Agency Collection

TIP OF THE ICEBERG | MASTERS FLAP DOESN'T DETER IBM CHIEF

The famed Masters Tournament held at the Augusta National Golf Club is one of the most unique sporting events in the world. Only the best male golfers are invited to play in this international event that lasts four days. Golf fans enjoy watching the tournament on television because the show is *almost* commercial free. Only four minutes is devoted to commercials each hour.

IBM was one of three sponsors of the 2012 Masters Tournament. The company considers this sporting event to be a great showcase for its technology. In the past, Augusta National has offered membership to a number of IBM chief executive officers. However, the all male golf club did not extend membership to IBM's current CEO, a talented woman. Virginia Rometty was at the center of the debate over Augusta National's all-male membership during the days leading up to the start of the tournament. Should IBM spend a huge amount of money on an event if its CEO lacks equal status with other sponsors?[1]

There is a reason why Virginia Rometty is CEO of a major American corporation. She attended the Masters, spent time with some of IBM's best customers, but maintained a low profile. She wanted the spotlight to be on her company throughout the four-day tournament. Public criticism of Augusta National's male-only membership policy would have been a distraction.[2]

A few weeks after the 2012 Masters Tournament ended, Augusta National Golf Club admitted two women, ending it's male-only status. Throughout this chapter, we will discuss several gender issues that create human relations problems at work and at home.

Strong female executives such as IBM's CEO Virginia Rometty have challenged the traditional notion of males having exclusive rights to positions of power. Here, Rometty receives the key to the city of Rio de Janeiro following the successful launch of IBM's Rio Operations Center.

TRADITIONAL ROLES ARE CHANGING

16-1 All cultures promote one set of behaviors for boys and a separate set for girls. Children generally learn their socially acceptable roles by the time they are five years old, and these roles are often continually reinforced throughout the life cycle by teachers, parents, authority figures, and the media. These traditional roles can be harmful to both men and women. For instance, the expectation that men should be aggressive and unemotional stifles their sensitivity and creativity. The assumption that women are emotional and weak hinders them in reaching leadership positions. Although men and women will always be different, their roles can and should be more nearly equal.

Gender bias (also known as sexism) is discrimination on the basis of gender. When employers base employment, promotion, job-assignment, and compensation decisions on a person's gender, human relations and productivity suffer. Gender bias is no longer a female-only issue, and many organizations are making the necessary adjustments.

Changes in the Role of Women

In the past, children were more likely to see their mothers as homemakers and their fathers as breadwinners. Today, a large number of women have assumed the role of breadwinner or are part of a dual-earner family. The recent economic downturn and the large number of marriages that end in divorce have accelerated this trend.

The women's movement that began in the 1960s with Betty Friedan's book, *The Feminine Mystique*, has helped women make tremendous strides toward equality with men in the workplace. Historians often say this book started women down a path that changed family life and American culture. It made American housewives realize they could grow and fulfill their potentialities as human beings.[3]

Few Women at the Top. Women now make up about half the U.S. work force and just over half of managerial and professional positions. Yet their rise to senior-executive posts and corporate boards has stalled. According to the U.S. Census, women hold only 16 percent of board of director seats, 14 percent of executive officer positions, and 7.5 percent of executive officer top-earner positions. They are earning advanced professional degrees in record numbers, and in some areas, surpassing men. Catalyst, an organization that has spent the past 50 years studying women's advancement in the workplace, makes the following point: "Doing all the right things" to get ahead works well for men, but does not provide as great an advantage for women.[4] Later in this chapter, we will discuss some initiatives that will help women achieve greater parity with men.

Women have made significant gains in a wide range of traditionally male-dominated areas such as marketing, law, medicine, and computer technology. However, some problem areas persist. Studies indicate that men continue to dominate craft, repair, and construction jobs, whereas women hold only a small percentage of these skilled trade jobs. The good news is that research shows that men and women are increasingly moving into, and succeeding in, nontraditional careers. If less than 25 percent of the work force is of one gender, a career is considered nontraditional.[5]

Changes in the Role of Men

As noted in Chapter 4, the transition from childhood to adulthood can be a long and difficult period. This is especially true of young men who are living in a new kind of extended adolescence. Adolescence for males now extends through their 20s and even, for many, into their 30s. Kay Hymowitz, in a recent *Wall Street Journal* article titled "Where Have All the Good Men Gone" makes the following observation:[6]

> *"Not so long ago, the average American man in his 20s had achieved most of the milestones of adulthood: a high-school diploma, financial independence, marriage and children. Today, most men in their 20s hang out in a novel sort of limbo, a hybrid state of semi-hormonal adolescence and responsible self-reliance."*

Hymowitz does not feel that this period of "pre-adulthood" brings out the best in men. Is this criticism too harsh? Data published by the Bureau of Labor Statistics helps explain why many young males are not working. The U.S. jobless rate among males ages 16 to 24 stands at about 22.5 percent, more than double the national average.[7]

John Rosemond, author of the syndicated newspaper column *Parenting*, believes that many underachieving males grew up in homes where the role of father was diminished. The most obvious example is the father-absent home. The high divorce rate has contributed greatly to the diminishment of male influence during the pre-teen and teen years.[8] Many fathers say it's hard to be a breadwinner, which often involves working long hours, and a caretaker at home.

The Burden of Job Loss

The recent recession impacted workers in just about every industry, but men took a much bigger hit than women. Two male-dominated industries—construction and manufacturing—account for about half of the jobs lost since the recession started in 2007. Men account for 87 percent of the workers in manufacturing and 71 percent in construction. Eighty-one percent of health care workers are women, and this industry has logged a net gain in jobs.[9]

A feature article in *Bloomberg Businessweek* began with this ominous headline: "The Hidden Job Crisis for American Men." The article describes a trend of disengagement for male workers that stretches back six decades. The share of American men aged 16 to 64 who are employed has fallen from nearly 85 percent in the early 1950s to less than 65 percent now.[10]

Historically, men are more likely to work full time than women. Many of these full-time male workers have assumed the duties of breadwinner, a role accompanied by a great deal of self-imposed as well as societal stress. The sudden loss of a job can be devastating. Many of these men face long periods of unemployment and when they do return to the labor market, earnings are likely to be much lower.

---

human
RELATIONS
in Action

SECRET SERVICE SCANDAL SHOWS GENDER GAP

On the morning of April 12, 2012, a secret service officer and a prostitute publicly argued over payment in a hotel hallway. During the investigation of this incident it was learned that a dozen secret service employees had hired prostitutes who visited them at their hotel. These agents were part of a large group sent to Colombia ahead of President Barack Obama's visit. Critics of the Secret Service believe that greater diversity would bring more accountability to the agency. Only about 11 percent of agents and uniformed officers are women.

Source: Eric Tucker, "Scandal Shows Gender Gap at Secret Service," *The News & Observer*, April 29, 2012, p. 3A.

PROBLEMS FACING WOMEN IN ORGANIZATIONS

16-2   When women pursue careers, they often face three major challenges: the wage gap, the glass ceiling, and balancing career and family. Many employers are making changes that will accommodate the needs of the growing number of working women and mothers, but more needs to be done.

The Wage Gap

In 1963, John F. Kennedy signed the Equal Pay Act into law. The goal of this law was to end the practice of paying women lower rates for the same job strictly on the basis of their sex. At that time, women with full-time jobs earned an average between 59–64 cents for every dollar their male counterparts earned in the same job.[11]

Fast forward to National Equal Pay Day held on April 17, 2012. President Barack Obama issued a proclamation that noted women who work full time earn only 77 cents for every dollar their male counterparts earn. He also noted that the pay gap was even greater for Latina and African-American women.[12]

Recent data analysis from the American Association of University Women shows that the gap between men and women's wages differs greatly depending on the state where you live. The AAUW numbers show that Washington, D.C., has the narrowest wage gap: women earn 91 percent of what men do on average ($56,127 vs. $61,381). Wyoming was ranked last, with women earning just 64 percent of what their male counterparts do ($32,426 vs. $50,854).[13]

Explaining the Wage Gap

In a great number of occupations, women still earn less than men doing the same job, working the same number of hours, and bringing to the job the same amount of work experience and education. The Institute for Women's Policy Research says the reasons for discrimination vary, but research indicates that women are less likely to be selected for the best jobs. So they begin their career at a lower wage and may not catch up. The

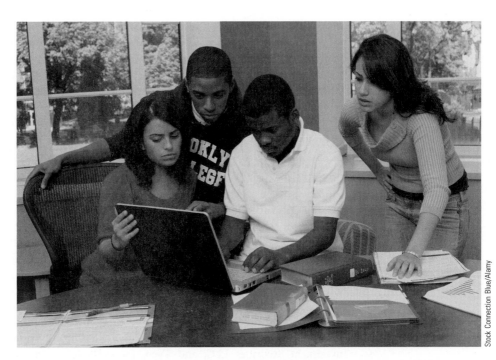

Stock Connection Blue/Alamy

The two female students in this photo are less likely to be selected for the best jobs and may face barriers to career advancement. They are more likely to begin their career at a lower wage and may not catch up.

staff at IWPR says, "Discrimination in who get hired for the best jobs hits all women but particularly black and Hispanic women."[14]

Today, women are more committed to building a career, but many still take time off to have children. This works against them, because continuous work experience tends to increase both productivity and pay in many employment settings.[15]

The Glass Ceiling

There is a condition in the workplace that gives women a view of top management jobs but blocks their ascent. It is often referred to as the **glass ceiling**. Catalyst has studied women in business and has documented widespread limits on female career advancement to the highest levels of our nation's largest corporations. Although we have seen positive change at the middle-management ranks, women are still being held back by some widely held misconceptions. Top male executives say the major barrier for women is a lack of significant general management and line experience and less time in the "pipeline." Women in senior management positions say the *real* problems are (1) preconceptions of women held by men and (2) exclusion of women from informal networks of communication.[16]

Building a Better Pipeline. After many years of aggressive efforts to create opportunities for women who are seeking top management positions, inequality remains entrenched. Companies must come up with better programs to help talented women advance. Here are some suggestions for building a better pipeline:

- Recognize that first jobs set the stage for all the inequities that follow. Women earn, on average, $4,600 less than their male peers in their first post-MBA job—a gap that widens to more than $31,000 as their careers advance.[17]

- Closing the pay gap involves reducing the influence of the Old Boys' Club. Ilene Lang, President and CEO of Catalyst, says the Club is not necessarily malicious, but... "It entails establishing business relationships on high-priced golf courses, at exclusive country clubs, in the executive sky-boxes at sporting events—arenas from which women and minorities are traditionally excluded.[18]
- Smart companies recognize that their high-potential women must be sponsored by top executives, most of whom are men. These companies hold male executives accountable for the success of female rising stars.[19]

The *Wall Street Journal* compiled a list of 10 female executives whose operational expertise and track record make them likely CEO candidates to head a Fortune 1000 company within five years. Nine members of the group have children, and many have husbands who abandoned the fast track to support their wives' careers.[20]

Women who pursue top-level positions must often cope with jobs structured to accommodate the lives of men with wives who do not have full-time careers. They also must cope with the social pressure to fulfill more traditional, "feminine" roles.[21]

Why should we be concerned about the dominance of men in top leadership positions? Cultures that are totally masculine often lack compassion and give rise to rigid, intolerant practices since they lack the intuitive, empathic qualities more common among women. In some cases, a highly competitive masculine culture encourages greed and corruption. The male-dominated hierarchy at Enron, WorldCom, Bernard L. Madoff Investment Securities LLC, and Tyco, for example, fostered unethical practices on a grand scale.

Total Person Insight

"Professors at Pepperdine University conducted a massive 19-year survey of 215 *Fortune 500* companies. By every measure of profitability, the study found that companies with the best records for promoting women to executive positions outperform the competition."

Source: Clair Shipman and Katty Kay, *Womenomics: Write Your Own Rules for Success* (New York: HarperCollins, 2009), pp. 2–3.

Macho leadership styles can also alienate women. The idea is not to push men off the stage but to get more women onto the stage with them. In an ideal situation, women and men will share the stage and create a culture where everyone is able to express the full range of his or her talents.[22]

Balancing Career and Family Choices

Women today know that they will probably be working for pay for part or all of their adult lives. This expectation is quite a departure from previous generations, when most women assumed the responsibilities of wife and mother. The challenge of performing multiple roles, however, can be stressful and tiring. A majority of the women in two-income families not only contribute significantly to their family's income, but also do most of their family's household chores.

The "Mommy Track" and Other Options. The term **Mommy Track** is used to describe the lifestyle of women who choose a career path that allows a mother flexible or reduced work hours. This may slow or block advancement, however it is a lifestyle that many choose in order to pursue childbearing.

Anne Sweeney is Co-Chair of Disney Media Networks and President of Disney ABC Television Group. Her position represents a growing shift in many companies toward diversifying their top-level management.

human RELATIONS *in Action*

WAYS WOMEN CAN HOLD THEIR OWN IN A MALE WORLD

- *Make sure women are valued.* Check to see whether the company values women, and if they are represented on the board and in leadership positions.

- *Identify alpha and beta males.* Separate the two types of men in the office and engage in conversations accordingly. Alpha males have a "get it done" mindset, and beta males are more concerned with "collaboration and partnership."

- *Find a mentor.* Look for a female employee at the company with direct experience in a male-dominated workplace.

- *Speak assertively.* Eliminate the phrase "I'm sorry" from your vocabulary. Apologizing for a situation that you are not responsible for demonstrates weakness. Do not begin a phrase, "*I think,*" as it demeans what you are saying.

- *Socialize with the boys.* Make your best effort to socialize with your male coworkers in formal and informal situations.

- *Do not assume stereotypical roles.* Let others "clean up" after your coworkers and bring coffee to meetings.

Source: Dana Mattioli, "Ways Women Can Hold Their Own in a Male World," *The Wall Street Journal*, August 25, 2008, p. D4. Reprinted by permission.

Women in greater numbers than ever before are combining motherhood and work. Some are willing to trade some career growth and compensation for freedom from the constant pressure to work long hours and weekends. And a growing number of women say, "I want a career and family." By the time women reach age 40, about 25 percent have both careers and children.[23]

Many women want to expand their life choices but are uncertain about the options available. If you are a woman who wants both career and family, then consider the following:[24]

- Choose a career that will give you the gift of time. Some careers provide more flexibility and are more forgiving of interruptions such as parental leave. Sixty percent of pharmacists are now female, a career that offers flexible hours.
- Choose a partner who supports your goal of having a career and family.
- Choose an employer who has given work/life balance a high priority.
- Be prepared to use your negotiation skills to push for policies and practices that are favorable to employees with children.

According to Judith Warner who wrote *Perfect Madness—Motherhood in the Age of Anxiety*, mothers who try to achieve work/family balance (I'm a great mom and a great worker) often feel a sense of frustration as they try to "do it all."[25]

PROBLEMS FACING MEN IN ORGANIZATIONS

16-3 Many men are beginning to realize that they have been as rigidly stereotyped in their role as women have been in theirs. Men encounter resistance from their family, coworkers, and friends when they attempt to break out of their stereotypes. The changes a man makes to alter traditional masculine role characteristics can be threatening to others and can cause serious problems in his relationships. Yet the stress men are under today to conform to the expectations of society often leads to heart disease and other health problems. Many wonder if upholding the male image is worth the price.

Men Working with Women

Male attitudes toward female ambitions have changed over the years. One reason for this change is the dramatic increase of female college classmates. Men have learned that they will be competing with these smart and ambitious women in the workplace. They are also learning that women can be excellent coworkers, team members, and leaders. Those men who are secure in their talents and abilities welcome the opportunity to work beside equally self-assured women. Those men who are threatened by powerful, talented women need an attitude adjustment.

Balancing Career and Family Choices

Henry David Thoreau observed that "the mass of men lead lives of quiet desperation." Does this dire observation apply to men who are pursuing careers and assuming family roles today? The answer is a qualified yes. Men, like women, now have more choices regarding marriage and family life and face many barriers to achieving work/life balance.

- The long-term trend toward wage equality gives families more choices regarding who should assume the roles of breadwinner, child-care provider, and housekeeper. For the first time, men and women in our society have the same desire for jobs with more responsibility.[26] One wife in four now out-earns her husband. Because of their upbringing, most men are often ill-suited to staying at home with their children while their wives become the breadwinners.[27]

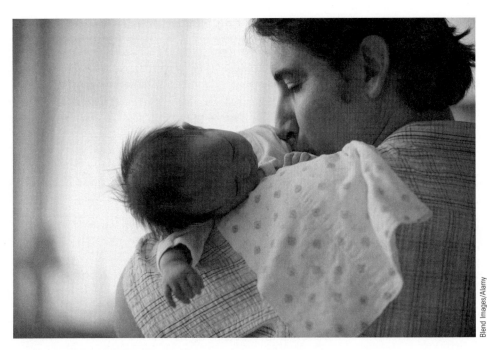

Blend Images/Alamy

The lines between traditional gender roles become blurred as men and women become increasingly integrated within society.

- Men often seek a "package deal" in life that includes four elements: marriage, fatherhood, employment, and homeownership—not necessarily in that order. Yet these goals often conflict. Many men express the desire to be closer to their children than their traditional fathers were to them, but they get caught in the traditional cycle of working long hours to pay for a nice home for the wife and kids.[28] Unfortunately, men are often reluctant to talk openly about personal pressures created by these work/family conflicts, and the cycle continues.
- Working fathers who want to take paternity leave or time off to help raise their children often experience discrimination in the workplace. Women who choose these options are generally seen in a more positive light. Many men still feel that taking parental leave will unofficially penalize them.[29] Just as women struggle with this issue, men must also step forward and encourage employers to commit to family-friendly workplace policies and practices. Table 16.1 provides some tips for the at-home partner and the breadwinner.
- Men are less likely than women to adopt a healthy lifestyle and seek health care when it is needed. As a result, they lead in each of the ten leading causes of death and have a life span shorter than that of their female counterparts.[30]

During life's most stressful transitions, such as divorce or loss of a job, men often spend more time reflecting on things they value in life. Those who feel that their male identity is dependent on what is accomplished at work and that success is measured by the size of their paycheck sometimes reestablish their priorities. In a *Wall Street Journal* article entitled "Who's the New Guy at Dinner? It's Dad …," one dad explains his transition following the loss of his managerial job at AOL. He says he told his young twin daughters, "I'm going to find a new job doing something I love that makes people happy." When he was hired as a fifth-grade teacher, his children were thrilled, and so was he. He can now spend more time with his children.[31]

Table 16.1 ■ Striking a Balance

If You Are the at-Home Partner

- Own the choice you've made while recognizing that traditional gender roles don't always correspond with a couple's actual competencies.

- Inoculate yourself against the loss of identity you may feel, or the isolation you may experience, by forging a strong community of other professionals who have made similar decisions to head home.

- Understand that your partner's work, while providing time away from child-care duties and household chores, is not vacation.

- Talk clearly with your partner about what's going to work for a two-year period, not just for the moment. Recognize that your current arrangement is not forever.

If You Are the Breadwinner

- Some resentments are unavoidable and can convey important information about yourself.

- Be sensitive to your partner's loss of professional identity. Don't take work inside the home for granted.

- Give your partner time to adjust to new duties before swooping in to correct their parenting behavior or housekeeping style.

- Do not assume that because you earn the money, you hold greater decision-making status in your relationship.

Source: Two People, One Breadwinner, sidebar: "Striking a Balance" by Deborah Siegel from *Psychology Today*, July/August 2007. Reprinted with permission from *Psychology Today Magazine* (Copyright © 2007 Sussex Publishers, LLC).

CHALLENGES AND OPPORTUNITIES FOR WORKING MEN AND WOMEN

16-4   As men and women struggle with their career and family choices, many progressive organizations are gearing up to meet the needs of their employees in the 21st century. They are recognizing the demands placed on working parents and are attempting to address the problems associated with quality child care. At the same time, they realize they should provide flexible work schedules that adjust to the changing roles of men and women.

The Challenge of Child Care

The need for affordable, quality child care has never been greater. Mothers and fathers alike face forced overtime and unpredictable hours as their employers attempt to cut costs while improving productivity. At the same time, many day-care providers shut their doors at 6 p.m. and on weekends. Workers who cannot balance the demands of work with available child care are often disciplined or fired.

Eighty percent of employers report that child-care problems force employees to lose work time.

Some companies provide on-site day-care centers and find this fringe benefit a strong factor in retaining valuable employees who are also parents. Eighty percent of employers report that child-care problems force employees to lose work time.[32]

Many of *Fortune's* 100 Best Companies to Work For have made the list because of their sensitivity to the needs of workers with children; consequently, they have provided programs and activities that meet workers' needs. Chesapeake Energy, based in Oklahoma City, was number 18 on the list of 100 Best Companies to Work For in 2012. This company recently built a 63,000-square-foot child-care center that's big enough for 300 children.[33]

human
RELATIONS
in Action

THE FAMILY AND MEDICAL LEAVE ACT

The Family and Medical Leave Act (FMLA) guarantees continuation of any paid health benefits, plus a return to the same or an equivalent job, for employees (men as well as women) who take up to 12 weeks' unpaid time off—all at once or intermittently—so that they can care for themselves or an ailing family member such as a parent, child, or spouse during a serious health condition, or for childbirth or adoption. (Some states are considering providing financial compensation during part or all of the employee's time off.)

To qualify, you must work for an employer with 50 or more employees and at a location with at least 50 employees within 75 miles. Your employer can deny leave if you have not worked there for at least 12 months and for at least 1,250 hours during the past year. You also may be ineligible for protection if you are among your employer's top 10 percent of employees, based on pay. If you feel you have a legitimate family leave dispute, contact the Wage and Hour Division of the United States Department of Labor (*http://www.wageandhour.dol.gov*).

Source: http://en.wikipedia.org [cited 6 May 2012].

Keep in mind, however, the resentment that may build among child-free employees who see employees with children given the opportunity to arrive late or leave early to accommodate the needs of their children. To prevent this potential human relations problem, employers should consider offering flexible schedules to all employees. (See Figure 16.1)

Flexible Work Schedule Opportunities

Men and women who are concerned about balancing personal and work lives say that flexible work schedules rank very high on the list of desired benefits. As a result, many organizations allow various scheduling options so that they can recruit and retain the top talent in the labor market. Indeed, in the recent recession, more employers used flexible setups to save money. On the basis of an April 2009 survey by Towers Perrin of 700 employers, 21 percent to 32 percent are either implementing or considering part-time shifts of four-day workweeks, as a cost-cutting tool.[34]

Figure 16.1 ■ A Two-Way Street

To make flexible scheduling more fair for working parents and child-free employees alike, some employers are:

- Allowing all employees to apply for flexible schedules
- Requiring proposals that outline how the flexible schedule will impact work that must be completed in a timely manner
- Evaluating flexible setups regularly
- Making scheduling a team responsibility
- Cross training workers so that they can take over their coworkers' responsibilities when necessary

Source: Figure adapted from Sue Shellenbarger, "A Two-Way Street," *Wall Street Journal*, November 17, 2005, p. Dl.

Figure 16.2 ■ Flextime in Action

| Flexible 2-hour arrival range | Fixed 6½-hour core time | Flexible 2-hour departure range |

7:00 a.m.   9:00 a.m.   3:30 p.m.   5:30 p.m.

Source: Robert Kreitner and Carlene Cassidy, *Management*, 12th edition (Mason, Ohio: South Western, Cengage Learning, 2011), p. 348.

Flextime. **Flextime** typically includes a core time when all employees work, usually between 9:00 a.m. and 3:30 p.m. Employees can determine their own arrival and departure times within certain limits, which may mean arriving at 7 a.m. or leaving at 5:30 p.m. (see Figure 16.2).[35]

Compressed Workweek. Typically, a **compressed workweek** consists of four 10-hour days—for example, Monday through Thursday or Thursday through Sunday. Employees may be given the opportunity to adjust their work schedules to fit their lifestyle. One of the newest compressed workweek schedules, often called the 9/80, is growing in popularity. Employees work one extra hour each day for nine days, a total of 80 hours in two weeks, and receive a three-day weekend every other week.[36]

Paid-Time-Off (PTO) Banks. With a **PTO bank**, normal paid-time-off days—vacation allotment, sick days, personal days—are lumped together into a time bank that employees can draw from in hourly increments. Employees can draw from their account whenever they need to and for whatever reason. About one-third of the U.S. companies currently have PTO banks.[37]

Job Sharing. With **job sharing**, two employees share the responsibilities of one job. For example, one employee might work the mornings and the other employee might work the afternoons. In some cases, each job sharer works two days alone and one day overlapping with the other person. This means the job is fully covered, and each job sharer knows what the other is doing.[38]

Telecommuting. The availability of powerful home-office computer and communication technologies, the large-scale use of temporary workers as the result of massive downsizing, and the demands of workers who want to blend work and family have fueled an increase in **telecommuting**—employees working at home at a personal computer linked to their employer's computer. The number of corporate telecommuters in 2009 was 8.7 million. Work-at-home employees confer savings on real estate and office costs. Employers who are equipped to measure output against costs often discover that an efficient telecommuter is an asset.[39]

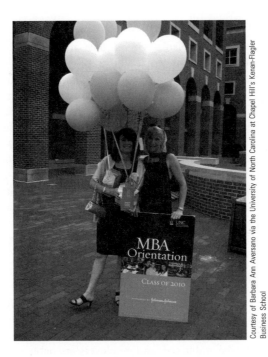

Courtesy of Barbara Ann Aversano via the University of North Carolina at Chapel Hill's Kenan-Flagler Business School

On Mondays, Tuesdays, and half of Wednesdays, Anna Miller is the MBA program associate director at the University of North Carolina Kenan-Flagler Business School. The rest of the time, she is home with her four children. Meghan Gosk has a similar schedule but in reverse. When faced with the option of reducing work hours or sacrificing something in the family schedule, Miller and Gosh chose a flexible job sharing arrangement.

human
RELATIONS
in Action

"DOES A FLEXIBLE WORK SCHEDULE MAKE YOU A TARGET FOR LAYOFFS?"

As the economy continues to fluctuate, employees who have chosen flexible work options often fear loss of job security. Maintaining a flexible work schedule during a recession requires planning—and luck. In an uncertain work force climate, many employers focus on those employees who are there 9-to-5 and whom they see on a daily basis. Other employers evaluate costs and view an efficient part-timer or telecommuter as an asset. In a nontraditional work environment where you have chosen a flexible work option, "you need to be realistic, be flexible, and deliver results." Your schedule may be scrutinized, so it is important to attend meetings and come into the office on a day off. "To improve your survival chances, ask yourself, 'What's most important to my company right now, and how do I make sure I'm contributing to that, and that my achievement is visible to my boss?'"

Source: Sue Shellenbarger, "Does Avoiding a 9-to-5 Grind Make You a Target for Layoffs?" *Wall Street Journal*, April 22, 2009, p. Dl.

HOW TO COPE WITH GENDER-BIASED BEHAVIOR

16-5   Traditional attitudes, beliefs, and practices are not changed easily. If you are a man or a woman breaking into a nontraditional role, you may encounter resistance. In addition, you may be confused about how to act or you may be overly sensitive about the way others treat you. As a result, if you are choosing a new role for yourself, you may have to adopt new behaviors and be prepared to confront some of the very real obstacles you will encounter.

Sexual Harassment in the Workplace

One of the most sensitive problems between men and women in organizations is **sexual harassment**, unwelcome verbal or physical behavior that affects a person's job performance or work environment. Employers have a legal and moral responsibility to prevent sexual harassment, which can occur from men harassing women, women harassing men, or same-sex harassment. As men and women work together on teams, more employers are becoming acutely aware of the increased potential for misinterpreted comments and actions between the genders. When sexual harassment is present in the workplace, the cost of increased absenteeism, staff turnover, low morale, and low productivity can be high.

The number of reported incidents of sexual harassment directed toward men is increasing, according to the US Equal Employment Opportunity Commission (EEOC). "There are positive changes taking place in the workplace that are allowing and encouraging men to report these claims," said Danny Baker, of the Washington-based Gender Public Advocacy Coalition. "This is also related to an increasing dialogue about what we call male-on-male sexual harassment."[40]

Forms of Sexual Harassment. Under the law, sexual harassment may take one of two forms. The first is **quid pro quo** (something for something), which occurs when a person in a supervisory or managerial position threatens the job security or a potential promotion of a subordinate worker who refuses to submit to sexual advances. These kinds of threats are absolutely prohibited, and employers are liable for damages under the Fair Employment Practices section of the Civil Rights Act. These behaviors can take the form of comments of a personal or sexual nature, unwanted touching and feeling, or demands for sexual favors.

The second form of sexual harassment involves the existence of a **hostile work environment**. Supreme Court decisions have held that sexual harassment exists if a "reasonable person" believes that the behavior is sufficiently severe or pervasive to create an abusive working environment, even if the victim does not get fired or held back from a promotion. A hostile work environment exists when supervisors, coworkers, vendors, or customers use sexual innuendo, tell sexually oriented jokes, display sexually explicit photos in the work area, discuss sexual exploits, and so on. Unlike quid pro quo harassment, hostile work environment claims tend to fall in a gray area: What is offensive to one person may not be offensive to another. The bottom line is that most kinds of sexually explicit language, conduct, and behavior are inappropriate in the workplace, regardless of whether such conduct constitutes sexual harassment within the legal meaning of the term. (See Table 16.2.)

Table 16.2 ■ Sexual Boundaries 2.0

20 YEARS AGO	TODAY
Sexually explicit remarks	Sexually explicit emails, IMs
Lewd one-on-one talk	Raunchy office banter
Inappropriate touching	Inappropriate joking
Violating office romance policies or dating subordinates	Violating office company-imposed relationship pacts, aka love contracts

In many workplaces, the definition of harassment has become more nuanced.
Source: Michelle Conlin, "Indiscretions: Harassers in High Places," *BusinessWeek*, November 13, 2006, p. 44. Reprinted by special permission. Copyright © 2006 by The McGraw-Hill Companies, Inc.

In 2012, Marissa Mayer accepted the role of CEO of Yahoo!, a $5 billion company. Mayer was pregnant when she accepted the role, and also the youngest Fortune 500 CEO, breaking several stereotypes.

human
RELATIONS
in Action

PREGNANCY DISCRIMINATION

Discrimination against pregnant women in the work force has increased 23 percent in the past ten years. It is one of the fastest-growing categories of charges filed with the Equal Employment Opportunity Commission.

The charges are coming from women in entry-level jobs as well as executives. Pregnant women claim they have been unfairly fired, denied promotions, and in some cases urged to terminate pregnancies in order to keep their jobs. Several factors may be behind this trend.

- More pregnant women are staying in the workplace rather than quitting their jobs as in previous generations.
- Pregnancy is expensive for employers. The result is a squeeze on maternity leave pay and time off by employers.
- Stereotypes about pregnant women persist. Mounting research indicates that men and women alike view pregnant women as less competent.
- Employers are making honest mistakes or are confused by conflicting laws. Many states have protections for pregnant women that go beyond the federal law, which allows for twelve weeks of unpaid leave.

Source: Sue Shellenbarger, "Downsizing Maternity Leave: Employers Cut Pay, Time Off," *Wall Street Journal*, June 11, 2008, p. Dl; Sue Shellenbarger, "Government Eases Path for Parents to Sue Employers," *Wall Street Journal*, May 24, 2007, p. Dl.

How to Address Sexual Harassment

Ever since Professor Anita Hill accused Supreme Court Judge nominee Clarence Thomas of lewd and overbearing conduct toward her, the country has been trying to determine the difference between innocent comments and sexual harassment.

Indra Nooyi, Chairman and CEO of PepsiCo, is a robust, effective leader whose leadership style has helped to maintain Pepsi's strong status within the ever-evolving food and beverage industry.

The key word is *unwelcome*. Victims of sexual harassment need to tell the harasser, in no uncertain terms, that his or her behavior is inappropriate. Meanwhile, victims should record the occurrence in a journal that includes the date and details of the incident. They should also talk with coworkers who can provide emotional support and help verify instances of harassment. Chances are, if one person is being harassed, others are as well. If the harasser continues the behavior, the victim should go to a higher authority such as the harasser's supervisor or the organization's human resources division. Under the law, companies are legally liable if they do not immediately investigate the situation and take action to eliminate the offensive behaviors. These actions can include reprimand, suspension, or dismissal of the harasser.

Clarification of the Law. The Supreme Court has given employees and employers help in understanding the legal aspects of sexual harassment. The court handed down two landmark rulings that included the following guidelines:[41]

- Companies can be held liable for a supervisor's sexually harassing behavior, even if the offense was never reported to management.
- An employer can be liable when a supervisor threatens to punish a worker for resisting sexual demands—even if such threats are not carried out.

The court also offered employers advice on how to avoid costly legal fees. A company can deflect sexual harassment charges by developing a *zero-tolerance policy* on harassment, communicating it to employees and making sure victims can report abuses without fear of retaliation. If the employer can show that an employee failed to use internal procedures for reporting abusive behavior, the company will be protected in a court of law.

Although the courtroom doors are open for individuals to protect themselves from unwanted behavior, pressing a sexual harassment charge is a lengthy, expensive, and psychologically draining experience. Before you file charges, be sure you have used all the remedies available to you through your employer.

Learn to Understand and Respect Gender Differences

As mentioned in Chapter 2, gender bias often acts as a filter that interferes with effective communication between men and women. These communication barriers, according to Deborah Tannen, are due to linguistic style. **Linguistic style** refers to a person's speaking pattern and includes such characteristics as directness or indirectness, pacing and pausing, word choice, and the use of such elements as jokes, figures of speech, stories, questions, and apologies. Linguistic style is a series of culturally learned signals that we use to communicate what we mean.[42] Communication experts and psychologists have made the following generalizations concerning gender-specific communication patterns:

- Men tend to be more direct in their conversation, whereas women are more apt to emphasize politeness.
- Men tend to dominate discussions during meetings and are more likely to interrupt.
- Women prefer to work out solutions with another person; men prefer to work out their problems by themselves.
- Men tend to speak in a steady flow, free of pauses, interrupting each other to take turns. Women tend to speak with frequent pauses, which are used for turn taking.
- Male-style humor tends to focus on banter, the exchange of witty, often teasing remarks. A woman's style is often based on anecdotes in which the speaker is more likely to mock herself than she is to make fun of another person.
- Women are likely to downplay their certainty; men are likely to minimize their doubts.[43]

Does linguistic style really make a difference? Let's assume that two employees, Mary and John, are being considered for promotion to a management position. The person who must make the decision wants someone who displays a high degree of self-confidence. If John is regularly displaying the "male" communication patterns described previously, he may be viewed as the more confident candidate. But if the person making the promotion decision is searching for someone who is sensitive, an attentive listener, and a consensus builder, Mary may win the promotion. We know that people in positions of power tend to reward linguistic styles similar to their own, so the candidate (male or female) with the greatest versatility may get the promotion.[44] In Chapter 3, we defined *versatility* as acting in ways that earn social acceptance.

Total Person Insight

"The more hours of television a girl watches, the fewer options she thinks she has in life. And the more hours a boy watches, the more sexist his views become."

Geena Davis
Founder, Geena Davis Institute on Gender in Media

Source: Sue Shellenbarger, "What's Holding Women Back?" *Wall Street Journal*, May 7, 2012, p. B11.

A Few Words of Caution

Differences do exist: Most men are somewhat more competitive, assertive, and task-focused, and most women are more sensitive, cooperative, and people-focused than most men. However, our stereotypes about men and women are often too strong and too inflexible.[45] When we place too much emphasis on the ways in which women and

> *When we place too much emphasis on the ways in which women and men differ, we stop viewing them as individuals.*

men differ, we stop viewing them as individuals. As noted in Chapter 3, it is tempting to put a label on someone and then assume the label tells you everything you need to know about that person.

Once you understand the concept that men and women communicate in different ways, you can begin to flex your style. Refer to Table 16.3 for more specific suggestions on how to communicate better with the opposite gender. Keep in mind, however, that an overextension of a strength *can* become a weakness.

Men and women have so much to learn from each other. NYU psychologist Carol Gilligan offers this metaphor: "One can think of the oboe and the clarinet as different, yet when they play together, there is a sound that's not either one of them, but it doesn't dissolve the identity of either instrument."[46]

Learn New Organization Etiquette

As women enter into upper levels of management and men begin to work in support positions, the ways in which men and women deal with each other change subtly. Does this change require new rules of etiquette? In some cases, yes. The following guidelines may help you understand how to act in these new situations:

1. When a woman visits a man's office, he should rise from his desk to greet her. When a man enters a woman's office, she should rise from her desk to greet him.
2. Whoever has a free hand (could be a small woman) should help anyone carrying too heavy a load (could be a large man).

Table 16.3 ■ Workplace Tips for Avoiding Gender-Specific Language Barriers

MEN CAN ...

- think about women as fellow employees rather than sexual objects.
- recognize that, within their gender group, women are as unique as men.
- communicate with women based on their individuality rather than on the characteristics of a stereotyped group.
- use general humor, not sexual humor.
- remember that even when intentions are good, the impact of your communication may be bad.
- follow this rule: When in doubt, do not make the statement or act out the thought.

WOMEN CAN ...

- stay calm when expressing feelings to avoid being labeled as overemotional.
- express feelings verbally rather than nonverbally. Men are not always good at reading behavior.
- avoid male bashing.
- use general humor, not self-effacing humor.
- say what needs to be said concisely, without excessive apologies or disclaimers.
- recognize that a man may not understand the impact of his sexually related comment. When something is offensive, say something right away.

Source: From Anita Bruzzese's, "Working Toward a Truce in the Battle of the Sexes," Springfield *News Leader,* August 9,1994, p. bl. Reprinted by permission.

3. Women resent being "gofers." Meeting participants should not expect a woman to take notes, answer the phone, or type material. Men and women should rotate such clerical duties. A woman should not leap to serve coffee when it is time for a break.

4. Whoever arrives first at a door should open it, and whoever stands in the front row in the elevator should get off first.

5. Whoever extends an invitation to lunch or dinner should, in most cases, pay the tab.

6. Training materials, memos, and so on should be written in gender-free language. Clerical and secretarial personnel should not be referred to only as "she" or "her" and management personnel only as "he" or "him."

The new etiquette provides a means to overcome old stereotypes and traditional ways of setting men and women apart solely on the basis of gender. By practicing these points of etiquette and adopting a positive, helpful attitude toward each other, men and women can help ease the transition from traditional to nontraditional roles. Women and men both will be winners.

LOOKING BACK: SUMMARY OF LEARNING OBJECTIVES

1. **Describe how the traditional roles of men and women are changing.**

   The traditional roles assigned to both genders limit their opportunities to choose careers and lifestyles best suited to their abilities and true interests. Many men and women are breaking out of these traditional roles. During the past few decades, women have entered the job world in increasing numbers and in professions previously considered all male. Also, a large number of women have assumed the role of breadwinner or are part of a dual-earner family. Women now hold over half of the managerial and professional positions. Today men are more likely to accept women in the role of breadwinner.

2. **Understand problems facing women as a result of gender bias in organizations.**

   Women are still subject to a wage gap, earning less than men receive for similar work, but the gap is narrowing. Moreover, the glass ceiling gives women a view of top-level jobs, but blocks their ascent. They are making progress, however, in the mid-management ranks. The real problems seem to be the preconceptions men have of women and the exclusion of women from the informal networks of communication.

3. **Understand problems facing men as a result of gender bias in organizations.**

   Men are working to dispel the myth that men must always be in control, emotionally unexpressive, logical, and achievement oriented. They realize that the rigid male role has had adverse effects on their relationships with their families. Many men are choosing more personally rewarding careers that allow time for family responsibilities even if they must sacrifice some material gain to do so.

4. **Discuss challenges and opportunities for working men and women.**

   The need for affordable, quality child care continues to challenge mothers and fathers alike. Progressive companies are more sensitive to the needs of workers with children. Flexible work schedules rank high on the list of most workers. Flextime, compressed workweeks, PTO banks, job sharing, and telecommuting are popular work schedule options.

5. **Explain the forms of sexual harassment and how to cope with gender-biased behavior.**

   Sexual harassment may be a problem for men as well as women. It may take on two forms: quid pro quo, a threat to job security or promotion if sexual favors are not granted, or sexually explicit language, photos, or innuendo that create a hostile work environment. Most organizations have developed guidelines to help employees avoid harassment or fight it when it occurs. This chapter also provides information that helps us understand and respect gender differences.

KEY TERMS

gender bias, 348	compressed workweek, 358	sexual harassment, 360
glass ceiling, 351	PTO bank, 358	quid pro quo, 360
mommy Track, 352	job sharing, 358	hostile work environment, 360
flextime, 358	telecommuting, 358	linguistic style, 363

CAREER INSIGHT

In these uncertain economic times, it's a good idea to explore all of your options. You may want to consider becoming an entrepreneur. There are numerous tests to help you determine whether you are a good candidate for starting a business. But whether a test can really determine who does or does not make a capable entrepreneur is debatable. There are some personality traits common among successful entrepreneurs, like the tendency to have a higher risk tolerance, drive, and resiliency to overcome failure than the general population according to experts.

Author Bill Wagner offers an *Entrepreneur IQ* test at his Web site, *http://TheEntrepreneurNextDoor.com*, which compares your answers to others. In addition, there are the Strong and MBTI tests used to assess entrepreneurial aptitude.

Many communities have an organization called SCORE (Service Corps of Retired Executives), which includes retired executives who are willing to guide and share their experiences with entrepreneurs and small businesses nationwide.

TRY YOUR HAND

1. The following situations represent either quid pro quo or hostile environment forms of sexual harassment in the workplace. Identify the form represented by each situation, and explain your reasoning. Describe the actions you might take if you were the potential victim in each incident.
   a. Julie thinks David is very handsome. She often stares at him when she thinks he is not looking. David is aware of Julie's staring and is very uncomfortable but is too shy and embarrassed to say anything to her.
   b. While sitting at her desk, Karen receives the following electronic message from her boss on her computer screen: "Can we discuss your possible promotion over dinner this evening?"
   c. At a convention reception, one of Joan's most important clients invites her out for cocktails and dinner. She politely declines. He announces loudly, "She won't go out to dinner with me, and I'm her best customer!" Under his breath he says, "Honey, if you want my business, you'd better cooperate." Joan's boss insists she go to dinner with the client.

2. On a sheet of paper, list and explain the various choices you would make when attempting to balance your career and family responsibilities. For example, will marriage be a part of your future? Will you have children? When? How will you provide care for these children while you and your spouse are at work? Would you prefer home-based work? Which flextime options would you consider valuable? Do you want to work for someone else or own your own business?

3. During a period of one week, analyze your verbal and nonverbal communications with people who are of the opposite gender. Try to determine whether any linguistic style differences are apparent during conversations. If you discover style differences, try to determine if they serve as a barrier or aid effective communication.

4. To examine various flexible work-schedule options, visit *www.workoptions.com*. Write an analysis of how the information available on this site might help individuals make an educated decision about their personal and professional life choices.

CRITICAL THINKING CHALLENGE

1. Do members of your immediate family hold traditional or nontraditional gender roles? If so, have any of these roles undergone changes during the past decade? Examine why there have been changes.

2. Before marriage, each partner should understand the other partner's expectations with regard to careers, family responsibilities, and priorities. What are your expectations of your spouse (if you are married), or what do you imagine they would be (if you are not)?

SELF-ASSESSMENT EXERCISE

For each of the following statements, circle the number from 1 to 5 that best represents your response: (1) strongly disagree (never do this); (2) disagree (rarely do this); (3) moderately agree (sometimes do this); (4) agree (frequently do this); (5) strongly agree (almost always do this).

	1	2	3	4	5
A. I refuse to perpetuate negative stereotypes and I accept each person as a unique individual worthy of my respect.	1	2	3	4	5
B. I make every effort to identify my own prejudiced attitudes and avoid stereotypical attitudes toward people of color, older people, people with disabilities, and others who are different from me.	1	2	3	4	5
C. I work hard to combat prejudice because it has a negative impact on my self-esteem and the self-esteem of the victim.	1	2	3	4	5
D. I encourage my employer to develop flexible work-schedule options.	1	2	3	4	5
E. I understand and respect gender differences.	1	2	3	4	5

After identifying your response to each item, select an attitude or skill you would like to improve. Prepare a written goal and then describe the steps you will take to achieve this goal.

YOU PLAY THE ROLE

If you are looking to use flexible work-schedule options (review the different options listed in this chapter) at your place of work, you need to be prepared when asking for permission. Your supervisor may initially say "no"; however, be prepared with counter arguments. Write a business proposal discussing the benefits of your plan to you and the company. If you select telecommuting, describe the arrangements that you have made for your designated home workspace, the logistics of how often you will "check in" with your supervisor, and a vehicle for feedback to assess your performance. You must show enthusiasm for this approach. Finally, be a good listener and try to determine the major objections to your proposal. Flexible work-schedule options, specifically telecommuting, may be new to this workplace and require additional education and adjustments. Select a class member to play the role of your supervisor as you present your proposal.

BELOW THE SURFACE | HELPING WOMEN REACH THE TOP

I n the opening vignette, you were introduced to Virginia Rometty, the first woman to serve as CEO of International Business Machines. Prior to joining IBM, Rometty earned degrees in computer science and electrical engineering at Northwestern University.

Business and government leaders have been talking for decades about the importance of advancing more women to top leadership roles. Many believe women in technology will be the key drivers of global competitiveness and innovation in the future. Today we are seeing greater investor pressure on boards to diversify corporate management teams. The ranks of female chief executives remain thin, but the pipeline is promising.

A recent *Wall Street Journal* conference, *Women In the Economy*, examined what's holding women back in the workplace. Women are now graduating from college and graduate school in greater numbers than men and entering the work force in equal numbers. However, men are at least twice as likely as women to move forward. What can be done to prepare more women for top positions at major companies? Here are some suggestions:[47]

- Start the talent search early; identify talented female employees with leadership potential and give them support.
- Women often lack sponsors to advocate for them. Members of the "good old boys" network are more likely to enjoy the support of one or more sponsors.

- Guide talented female employees into jobs with bottom line, profit-and-loss impact—experience considered essential for top management positions. Experience serving on a corporate board of directors is also important. Virginia Rometty gained valuable experience while serving on the American International Group, Inc. board of directors.

QUESTIONS

1. Men often enjoy the advantage of continuous employment, which helps keep them on the fast track to the top. Women often take a leave from work for the birth of children or child-care obligations. Should women be given more flexible work options?

2. Madeleine Albright, former U.S. Secretary of State, serve on the Executive Task Force that planned the *Wall Street Journal* "Women In the Economy" conference. She said, "Women are really good at making friends and not good at networking." Do you agree? Explain your answer.

3. At the end of the *Women in the Economy* conference, members agreed that progress for women starts at the top: "Hold senior managers accountable by tying promotion and compensation to meeting diversity goals and requiring regular reports to the board of directors." Is this practice realistic? Explain your answer.

CLOSING CASE | A SANER WORKPLACE

C ompanies everywhere are starting to retool. "The one-size-fits-all workplace doesn't work," says the Alfred P. Sloan Foundation's Christensen. "The idea that you will work full-time year in and year out, that you will be on a career trajectory that is a straight line, is vanishing. Employees increasingly feel more entitled to say: 'I need and I want to work in a certain way'."

In their book, *Womenomics: Write Your Own Rules for Success*, broadcasters Claire Shipman and

Katty Kay cite studies that show the increasing impact of professional women on companies' bottom lines and give practical advice on how to create "a more sane" work life. Women may be driving the work force revolution, but men are realizing the benefits, too.

At Capital One Financial, Judy Pahren, director of human resources, realized that *flexibility* was not just a "woman initiative," but rather, a need across an entire employee base. "We had thought that maybe it was gender-based; however, it was true of the men who worked at Capital One Financial also." A few months later, The Flexible Work Arrangements program was implemented for the entire company. The program allows employees to determine their work schedules with their immediate supervisors; options are flextime, telecommuting, a compressed workweek, or part-time employment.

More and more workers of *both* sexes are willing to scale back career goals, according to Families & Work Institute data. In focus groups, employees say things like "I need to make these choices because my family is a priority" or "I need to make these choices to make my life work."

According to Brenda Barnes, CEO of Sara Lee, "Today's business environment provides the opportunity for work-life balance. This doesn't mean employees work less; instead, it means empowering employees to do their work on a schedule that works for them. So if they want to work from their kitchen table at 3 a.m., as long as the work gets done, who cares when or where they are doing it? Companies need to recognize that this kind of *flexibility* offers employees the ability to manage and balance their own career and lives, which improves productivity and employee morale."[48]

QUESTIONS

1. On the basis of your personal and professional needs, design a flexible work arrangement that would allow you to have work-life balance in your career.

2. Predict the implications of a flexible work arrangement program for the future. Evaluate the impact on business/industry, management, employees, and consumers. Is the Capital One Financial's Flexible Work Arrangement program a realistic option for employees who work in retailing? Manufacturing? The hospitality industry? Explain your answer.

3. Capital One thought work *flexibility* was a key issue only for female employees. They realized, with additional inquiry, that it was true for the men employees as well. Analyze why both sexes are willing to scale back career goals and the implications their decisions will have on their career and life choices.

CHAPTER 16 ENDNOTES

1. Spencer E. Ante, "Masters Flap Won't Deter IBM Chief," **Wall Street Journal**, April 6, 12, p. B1.

2. Ibid.

3. Clyde Frazier, "How Feminine Mystique Shaped Lives in the 1960s," **News & Observer**, March 27, 2011, p. 6D.

4. Nancy M. Carter and Christine Silva, "Women in Management: Delusions of Progress," **Harvard Business Review**, March 2010, p. 19; "What's New," [cited 27 April 2012]. Available from www.catalyst.org; INTERNET.

5. "The Pros and Cons of Non-Traditional Careers" [cited 21 April 2009]. Available from http://www.quintcareers.com/pros-cons_non-traditional_careers.html; INTERNET.

6. Kay Hymowitz, "Where Have All the Good Men Gone?" **Wall Street Journal**, February 19–20, 2011, p. C1.

7. John W. Miller and Matthew Dalton, "U.W. Sales Slump Clouds Outlook for Anheuser," **Wall Street Journal**, March 5, 2010, p. B4.

8. John Rosemond, "Today's Males Need Fathers, Not Friends," **The News & Observer**, November 17, 2009, p. 20.

9. Andrea Coombes, "Men Suffer Brunt of Job Losses in Recession," **Wall Street Journal**, July 7, 2009, p. D6.

10. Peter Coy, "The Hidden Job Crises for American Men," **Bloomberg Businessweek**, April 11–April 17, 2011, pp. 7–8.

11. Borgna Brunner, "The Wage Gap," [Cited 2 May 2012]. Available from www.infoplease.com; INTERNET.

12. Barack Obama, "Presidential Proclamation—National Equal Pay Day, 2012," April 17, 2012, Available from www.whitehouse.gov.

13. "Equal Pay Day: AAWW Releases State by State Gender Wage Gap Rankings," [cited 1 May 2012]. Available from www.huffingtonpost.com, INTERNET.

14. "Women Still Confront Yawning Gender Wage Gap: Study," *Chicago Tribune*, April 18, 2012. Available from http://articles.chicagotribune.com, INTERNET.

15. "A Salary Gap Remains Between Genders, Census Results Indicate," *Wall Street Journal*, March 25, 2003, p. Dl; Charles J. Whalen, "Closing the Pay Gap," *BusinessWeek*, August 28, 2000, p. 38.

16. Gale Duff-Bloom, "Women in Retailing—Is There a Glass Ceiling?" *Retailing Issues Letter*, Center for Retailing Studies, Texas A&M University, May 1996, pp. 1–4; Margaret Hefferman, "The Female CEO," *Fast Company*, August 2002, pp. 60–61.

17. Ilene H. Lang, "Co-Opt the Old Boys' Club: Make It Work for Women," *Harvard Business Review*, November 2011, p. 44.

18. Ibid.

19. Ibid.

20. Joann Lublin and Kelly Eggers, "More Women are Primed to Land CEO Roles," *Wall Street Journal*, April 30, 2012, pp. B1 and B6.

21. Anna Fels, "Do Women Lack Ambition," *Harvard Business Review*, April 2004, pp. 7–8.

22. "The Emancipated Organization," *Harvard Business Review*, September 2002, pp. 1–3 (Reprint F0209B). (This article features an interview with Kim Campbell, Canada's first female prime minister.)

23. Virginia Postrel, "Mommy Track Without Shame," *Wall Street Journal*, March 26, 2011, p. C12.

24. Sylvia Ann Hewlett, "Executive Women and the Myth of Having It All," *Harvard Business Review*, April 2002, pp. 5–11; Margaret Heffernan, "The Female CEO," *Fast Company*, August 2002, pp. 58–66.

25. Judith S. Nulevitz, "The Mommy Trap," *New York Times Book Review*, February 20, 2005, pp. 1, 12–13.

26. Lois Backon, "Making Work Fit," *Diversity Executive*, September/October 2011, p. 14.

27. Dorothy Foltz-Gray, "Bread Winning Wives," *Health*, October 2003, pp. 103–107; Sue Shellenbarger, "As Moms Earn More, More Dads Stay Home: How to Make the Switch Work," *Wall Street Journal*, February 20, 2003, p. Dl.

28. "Today's Dads: Same Old Parenting Trap," *Business-Week*, October 14, 2002, p. 167. (This article summarizes the views of Nicholas Townsend, author of *The Package Deal*, a book about the many life/work conflicts men face.)

29. Jeffrey Winters, "The Daddy Track," *Psychology Today*, September/October 2001, p. 17.

30. David Gremillion, "Men's Health Needs a Heartfelt Change," *The News & Observer*, June 17, 2001, p. A31.

31. Jeffrey Zaslow, "Who's the New Guy at Dinner? It's Dad; Laid-Off Fathers Face Tough Job at Home," *Wall Street Journal*, October 2, 2002, p. Dl.

32. Child Care Connections. Available from http://www.childcareconnections.net/

33. Milton Moskowitz and Robert Levering, "The 100 Best Companies to Work For," *Fortune*, February 6, 2012, p. 118.

34. Sue Shellenbarger, "Does Avoiding a 9-to-5 Grind Make You a Target for Layoffs?" *Wall Street Journal*, April 22, 2009, p. Dl.

35. Sue Shellenbarger, "Bob's Mobile Office and Day-Care Center," *Wall Street Journal*, December 26, 2002, p. Dl.

36. Kathy Bergen, "Compressed Workweek Pays Off—On 10th Day," *Roanoke Times & World News*, March 30, 1997, p. B2.

37. Robert Kreitner and Carlene Cassidy, *Management*, 12th edition (Mason, Ohio: South Western Cengage Learning, 2011), p. 349.

38. Carol Kleiman, "Get Two Workers for the Price of One!" *The News & Observer*, February 26, 2003, p. E14.

39. Sue Shellenbarger, "Does Avoiding a 9-to-5 Grind Make You a Target for Layoffs?" *Wall Street Journal*, April 22, 2009, p. Dl.

40. "More Men Report Sexual Harassment in US Workplace" [cited 25 April 2009]. Available from BNET in partnership with mywire; INTERNET.

41. Susan B. Garland, "Finally, a Corporate Tip Sheet on Sexual Harassment," *BusinessWeek*, July 13, 1998, p. 39.

42. Deborah Tannen, "The Power of Talk: Who Gets Heard and Why," *Harvard Business Review*, September/October 1995, pp. 129–140.

43. Jayne Tear, "They Just Don't Understand Gender Dynamics," *Wall Street Journal*, November 20, 1995, p. A14; Dianna Booker, "The Gender Gap in Communication," *Training Dimensions* (West Des Moines, IA.: American Media Incorporated, Fall 1994), p. 1; Jennifer J. Laabs, "Kinney Narrows the Gender Gap," *Personnel Journal*, August 1994, pp. 83–85; Scot Ober, *Contemporary Business Communication*, 5th ed. (Boston: Houghton Mifflin, 2003), pp. 58–59.

44. Tannen, "The Power of Talk," p. 146.

45. Sharon S. Brehm, Saul M. Kassin, and Steven Fein, *Social Psychology*, 5th ed. (Boston: Houghton Mifflin, 2002), pp. 154–156.

46. Anastasi Toufexis, "Coming from a Different Place," *Time*, Fall 1990, p. 66.

47. Sue Shellenbarger, "What's Holding Women Back?" *Wall Street Journal*, May 7, 2012, p. B7 and B9; Marissa Mayer, "The 100 Most Influential People in the World," *Time*, April 18, 2012, p. 26.

48. "A Saner Workplace," *BusinessWeek*, June 1, 2009, pp. 66–69.

PART 6

You Can Plan for Success

CHAPTER 17
A Life Plan for Effective Human Relations

Jupiterimages/Comstock Images/Getty Images

CHAPTER 17

Jupiterimages/Comstock Imges/Getty Images

CHAPTER PREVIEW

LEARNING OBJECTIVES

After studying Chapter 17, you will be able to

17-1 Learn how to cope with the forces that influence work/life balance.

17-2 Define success by standards that are compatible with your needs and values.

17-3 Discuss the meaning of *right livelihood.*

17-4 Describe four nonfinancial resources that can enrich your life.

17-5 Provide guidelines for developing a healthy lifestyle.

17-6 Develop a plan for making needed changes in your life.

A Life Plan for Effective Human Relations

TIP OF THE ICEBERG | RECLAIMING YOUR LIFE

The perks at Google—a playful work environment, gourmet food, and volleyball court—have helped the company win several Fortune Magazine "Best 100 Companies to Work For" awards. But perks come with a price. Google is also known for its punishing fast-paced work culture with 80-hour workweeks, demanding bosses, and a mantra for maintaining what co-founder and CEO Larry Page calls "a healthy disregard for the impossible." Even employees who have worked in fast-paced technology companies and demanding cultures find that Google pushes them harder than they have ever worked.

When Eric Chang joined Google in 2004 as a software engineer, he was accustomed to a demanding work life. He grew up in Taiwan, a country like many others in Asia that thrive on stress and hard work. But exhausted from years of stress and long workweeks, he began to explode easily at his wife and young son. As he watched colleagues become burned out or even quit from the ongoing stress, he knew he had to make changes.

Help came to Chang in a class he took at Google called "Search Inside Yourself" (SIY). The seven-week class is popular at Google and usually has a waiting list. The course teaches employees how to examine the meaning of success and failure, and how their work and relationships are affected by the choices they make. Like Eric Chang, Richard Fernandez, director of executive development, says SIY has helped him make significant changes. "I'm definitely much more resilient as a leader. I listen more carefully and with less reactivity in high-stakes meetings. I work with a lot of senior executives who can be very demanding, but that doesn't faze me anymore. It's almost an emotional and mental bank account. I've now got much more of a buffer there."[1]

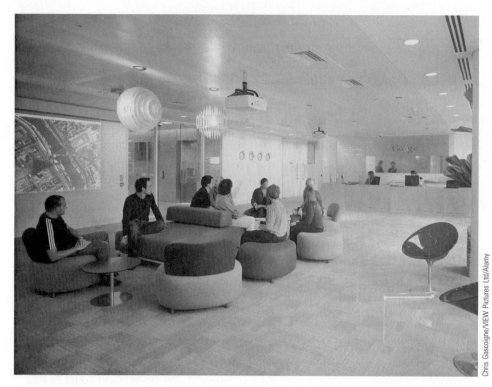

Google provides comfortable areas where employees can get together for informal meetings, or to simply relax. Google offsets demanding work schedules with a variety of programs to encourage intellectual, physical, and emotional growth among its employees.

ACHIEVING BALANCE IN A CHAOTIC WORLD

17-1   In this chapter, we help you construct a life plan that will enhance your relationships with people in your personal life and in your work life. This plan will also help you to better manage the mental, physical, emotional, and spiritual aspects of your life. We discuss the meaning of success and suggest ways to cope with major disappointments that will surface in your work life. You will learn how to avoid being trapped by a lifestyle that offers financial rewards but little else. This chapter also helps you define your relationship with money and describes four nonfinancial resources that give meaning to life. Finally, you will learn how to develop the mental and physical fitness needed to keep up in today's frantic, fast-paced world.

Redefining Our Work Lives

In Chapter 1, we noted that the labor market has become a place of churning dislocation caused by the heavy volume of mergers, acquisitions, business closings, bankruptcies, and downsizings. We also noted that changing work patterns have created new opportunities and new challenges. Millions of American workers are self-employed, working as independent consultants, contractors, landscape gardeners, and financial consultants. Thousands of new small business firms have created rewarding careers for owners and their employees.

It is important to visualize a future filled with sharp detours and several redefinitions of our work lives. Tom Peters, noted author and consultant, was one of the first observers to recognize that a typical career path is no longer linear and is not always upward. He says, "It's more like a maze, full of hidden turns, zigs, and zags that go in all sorts of directions—even backwards sometimes, when that makes sense."[2] The idea of finding job security and knowing that we have "arrived" is obsolete.

TOWARD A NEW DEFINITION OF SUCCESS

17-2   Most of us have been conditioned to define success in narrow terms. Too frequently we judge our own success, and the success of others, by what is accomplished at work or material possessions. Successful people have been described as those who have a "good job," "make good money," or have "reached the top" in their field. From early childhood on, many people are taught to equate success with pay increases and promotions. Too often, unfortunately, people who try to achieve these career goals are forced to give up everything else that gives purpose and meaning to their lives. Bill George, author of books entitled *True North* and *Authentic Leadership*, suggests we forge an integrated life that blends work with such things as family, friends, community service, exercise, church, and whatever else matters in your life.[3]

Po Bronson, author of *What Should I Do with My Life?*, says more people need to search for work they are passionate about. His best-selling book profiles 55 people who struggled to find their calling. One of the persons he interviewed was Ann Miyhares, a Cuban-American who made her family proud by becoming a senior vice president at a bank but lost their respect when she exchanged her banking career for that of a social worker, a career she found much more fulfilling.[4] Everyone defines success differently. What is important is how *you* define it by choosing a career that provides you with personal satisfaction and happiness.

> *From early childhood on, many people are taught to equate success with pay increases and promotions.*

Total Person Insight

"You only have control over three things in your life — the thoughts you think, the images you visualize, and the actions you take (your behavior). How you use these three things determines everything you experience. If you don't like what you are producing and experiencing, you have to change your responses."

Source: Jack Canfield, *The Success Principles* (New York: HarperCollins, 2005), p. 9.

The Need for New Models of Success

In recent years, a growing number of people are angry, disillusioned, and frustrated because they have had to abruptly change their career and life plans. They gave their best efforts, worked long hours, and then the company eliminated their jobs. A variety of economic, social, and demographic forces have combined to create a high level of career distress among all age groups. Young workers, often burdened with student loans, face the prospect of being unemployed or underemployed. Older workers, nearing retirement, have seen the value of their 401(k)s decrease by as much as 50 percent. Others affected by the collapse of financial institutions or unethical corporations like Enron and Qwest have been the victims of corruption and had nearly all of their retirement and savings wiped out. As a result, many of these Baby Boomers are postponing retirement, thus creating a "gray ceiling" that impedes the advancement of younger workers.

*"I really didn't enjoy working five days a week, fifty weeks
a year for forty years, but I needed the money."*

Americans are known for burdening themselves with a very demanding work ethic. They spend more time on the job than employees in any other industrialized nation. U.S. workers not only work long hours, but they spend less time on vacation than do workers in most other industrialized countries. As downsizing efforts have left fewer people to do the same amount of work, many people are working even harder.

Total-Person Model

What is changing is that most workers, especially younger workers, yearn for more leisure time. Some of the most successful and progressive organizations in America recognize the need to create a culture that satisfies both personal and work-related needs. They realize the ideal work environment embraces the *total person*, a concept we discussed in Chapter 1).

When Jeff Soderberg founded Software Technology Group, a technology consulting business based in Salt Lake City, he created a new model of success. His company provides employees with plenty of time to have a life. He does not believe there is a correlation between time spent at work and success. He refuses to hire workaholics, and, in an industry where 80-hour workweeks are common, he tells new hires, "We expect a 40-hour workweek." Soderberg sets a good example by frequently taking time off during the week to enjoy rock climbing in the nearby canyons.[5]

Values-based Organizational Culture

Companies like Southwest Airlines, Zappos, and Starbucks have created new models of success by developing healthy, thriving, company cultures that focus on core values. As a result, these companies have created higher levels of customer service, employee satisfaction, and profitability. Tony Hsieh, founder of Zappos.com, has achieved monetary success, but that is not his goal in life. He wants to unlock the secrets of human happiness, and his company is his research center. His single-minded focus on happiness has resulted in Zappos receiving several "best places to work" awards. His thoughts on achieving happiness are described in his book, *Delivering Happiness.*

Developing Your Own Life Plan

The goal of this chapter is to help you develop a life plan for effective relationships with yourself and others. The information presented thus far has, we hope, stimulated your thinking about the need for a life plan. We have noted that personal life can seldom be separated from work life. The two are very much intertwined. We have also suggested that it is important for you to develop your own definition of success. Too frequently, people allow others (parents, teachers, friends, a spouse) to define success for them. Finally, as you begin work on your life plan, keep in mind the following advice from Jack Canfield, author of *The Success Principles:*

> *If you want to be successful, you have to take 100% responsibility for everything that you experience in your life. This includes the level of your achievements, the results you produce, the quality of your relationships, the state of your health and physical fitness, your income, your debts, your feelings—everything!*[6]

Because work is such an important part of life, we will now move to a discussion of items that will help you in your career planning and the concept of "right livelihood."

TOWARD RIGHT LIVELIHOOD

17-3   Ann Rea studied fine arts in college. She enjoyed painting and drawing but put those interests aside in order to pursue a career in information technology. This was a practical choice because jobs in this field were available. However, IT work was not rewarding. While working as an IT project management consultant in Davis, California, she met pop artist Wayne Thibaud, who urged her to start painting again. Later, she worked on another project management job under the supervision of a terrible boss, a "real jerk" in her words. That experience motivated her to try to make a living as a painter. Today she is widely known for her paintings of California vineyards.[7]

Ann Rea, like many other people, has been searching for "right livelihood." The concept of right livelihood is described in the core teachings of Buddhism.[8] In recent years, the concept has been described by Michael Phillips in his book *The Seven Laws of Money* and by Marsha Sinetar in her book *Do What You Love ... The Money Will Follow.* **Right livelihood** is work consciously chosen, done with full awareness and care, and leading to enlightenment. Barbara Sher, author of *Wishcraft* and *I Could Do Anything If I Only Knew What It Was*, says right livelihood means that you wake up in the morning and spend all day working at something you really want to do.[9]

For Stephen Lyons, the search for right livelihood began when he fell on hard times— divorce, unemployment, and bankruptcy. He came from a family of blue-collar tradesmen, none of whom had attended college. He trained as an electrician and had steady work until a recession created large-scale unemployment in the San Francisco area. Finally, he convinced a small college that he could repair their cranky air-conditioning system and ended up with a job and the opportunity to earn a business degree at the school. With more education, he felt confident to start a business installing home solar-power systems. Creating renewable energy has turned out to be a form of right livelihood for Lyons.[10]

There are three characteristics to right livelihood: choice, emphasis on more than money, and personal growth.

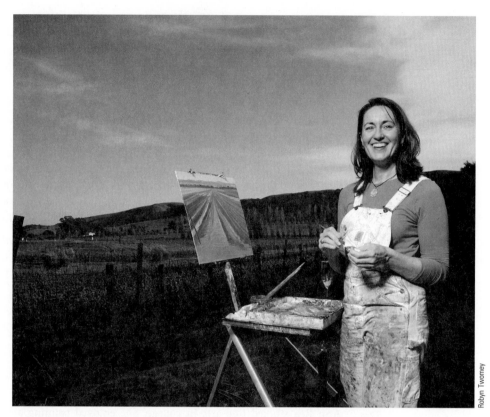

Robyn Twomey

After graduating from the Cleveland Institute of Art, Ann Rea embarked on a "practical" career in investments and IT project management. After seven miserable years, time spent mostly in corporate cubicles, she opted for a major career makeover and started painting full time.

Right Livelihood Is Based on Conscious Choice

Marsha Sinetar says, "When the powerful quality of conscious choice is present in our work, we can be enormously productive."[11] She points out that many people have learned to act on what others say, value, and expect and thus find conscious choice very difficult:

> It takes courage to act on what we value and to willingly accept the consequences of our choices. Being able to choose means not allowing fear to inhibit or control us, even though our choices may require us to act against our fears or against the wishes of those we love and admire.[12]

To make the best choices, you must first figure out what you like to do, as well as what you are good at doing—your strengths. What you like doing most is often not obvious. It may take some real effort to discover what genuinely motivates you. Students often get help from career counselors, mentors or explore a career option during a summer internship. If you are employed, consider joining a temporary project team. A team assignment provides an opportunity to work with persons who perform very different types of duties. You might also consider reassignment within your organization, especially if you have the opportunity to work in another country and experience living in a different culture.

Right Livelihood Places Money in a Secondary Position

People who embrace right livelihood accept that money and security are not the primary rewards in life. Michael Phillips explained that "right livelihood has within itself its own rewards; it deepens the person who practices it."[13] For example, people who work in social services usually do not earn large amounts of money, but many of them receive a great deal of personal satisfaction from their work. You may need to trade some income for self-expression, mental rewards, or some other form of personal satisfaction. People who have made this choice, like Ann Rea, may not make large sums of money, but the work provides enormous personal satisfaction.

Many people who once viewed success in terms of wealth, material possessions, and status are realizing that something is missing from their lives. They once felt pressured to "have it all" but now feel disappointed that their achievements have not brought them real happiness.

Right Livelihood Recognizes That Work Is a Vehicle for Personal Growth

Most of us spend from 40 to 60 hours each week at work. Ideally, we should not have to squelch our real strengths and abilities, ignore our personal goals, and forget our need for stimulation and personal growth during the time we spend at work.[14] Most employees know intuitively that work should fulfill their need for self-expression and personal growth, but this message is not embraced by all leaders. Too few organizations truly empower workers and give them a sense of purpose. When employees feel that the company's success is their own success, they will be more enthusiastic about their work.

The search for right livelihood should begin with a thoughtful review of your values. The values clarification process (see Table 5.1 in Chapter 5) should be completed *before* you interview for a job. Your values should be reassessed throughout your life as your values evolve and your work preferences change. For example, Frank Harrington spent 13 years climbing the ranks at a California-based semiconductor maker. Throughout that period, he gradually realized he hated his job, so he changed careers. Preparing for a new career took years, but today he is a nurse and much happier.[15]

When a job fails to fulfill your expectations, consider changing jobs, changing assignments, or changing careers. If the job is not right for you, your body and your mind will begin sending you messages. When you begin feeling that something is lacking, try to answer these basic questions: What is making me feel this way? What, exactly, about my current position is unpleasant? Choosing a satisfying career and lifestyle requires understanding what contributes to your job satisfaction, and your needs will change over time. Self-exploration and continual evaluation of your needs, goals, and job satisfaction are important. Don't wait for a crisis (layoff) to clear your vision.[16]

> *Most employees know intuitively that work should fulfill their need for self-expression and personal growth, but this message is not embraced by all leaders.*

Defining Your Relationship with Money

Money is a compelling force in the lives of most people. It often influences the selection of a career and the commitment we make to achieve success in that career. Sometimes we struggle to achieve a certain economic goal only to discover that once we get what we want, it does not fulfill us in the way we had hoped. Money does not create or sustain happiness. Happiness comes from social relationships, enjoyable work, fulfillment, a sense that life has meaning, and membership in civic and other groups.[17] As you learned in earlier chapters, research has proven that financial success does not make us happy, but the reverse is true. The happier you are, the more likely it is you will become successful.

"Don't give me too much, I'm not good with money."

Many people struggle with money management decisions and seem unable to plan for the future. The personal savings rate in America is at a record low, and the household debt burden is at a record high. Many people are ill prepared to cope with the financial drain that comes with the loss of one's job or a serious health problem that is not covered by medical insurance. For decades Americans have been known as a "nation of hyper-consumers, living way beyond their means." While the recession and slow economic recovery has curtailed an appetite for reckless spending, many in the U.S. continue to struggle with this issue.[18]

> The happier you are, the more likely it is you will become successful.

True Prosperity. The way we choose to earn, save, and spend our money determines, in large measure, the quality of our lives. For example, if you think that having more money is going to produce happiness or peace of mind, will you ever earn enough? Shakti Gawain, author of *Creating True Prosperity*, says that more money does not necessarily bring greater freedom, fewer problems, or security. Rather, "prosperity is the experience of having plenty of what we truly need and want in life, material and otherwise." Gawain says, "The key point to understand is that prosperity is an *internal* experience, not an *external* state, and it is an experience that is not tied to having a certain amount of money."[19] Many of us go through life unconscious of our own real needs and desires. We must learn to predict more accurately what will give us lasting pleasure instead of short-term pleasure.[20] How do we do this? Steven Reiss (see Chapter 7) says that nearly everything we experience as meaningful can be traced to one of sixteen basic desires or to some combination of those desires (see Figure 7.1). Now would be a good time to revisit this list of basic desires and identify the five or six that seem most important to you. This review may help you understand your relationship with money.

Mature Money Management. Many people do not have a mature relationship with money. They spend everything they earn and more, and then they have bouts of financial anxiety. People who are deep in debt often experience symptoms of depression. Money issues continue to be the number one cause of divorce in the United States.[21]

Space does not permit a comprehensive examination of money management, but here are some important suggestions from Jonathan Clements, an expert on financial planning:[22]

- *Develop a personal financial plan.* With a financial plan, you are more likely to achieve your financial goals. A key element of your plan is determining where your income is going. With a simple record-keeping system, you can determine how much you spend each month on food, housing, clothing, transportation, and other things. Search for spending patterns you may want to change. Create a budget and stick to it.

- *Spend less than you earn.* Many people constantly strive to raise their standard of living by purchasing a better car, a bigger house, or expensive clothes. Academics refer to this as the *hedonic treadmill.* Credit comes easy, so it is hard to discipline yourself against going into debt. The cost of credit is often much more than we realize. A three-year auto loan (for a $35,195 loan) at a 5.89 percent rate has $3,287 in financing costs. Extend this loan to five years, and the financing cost will exceed $5,000.[23] Whenever possible, charge only what you can afford to pay off each month and keep your balance at zero.

- *Maintain a cash cushion.* If you lost your job today, how long could you live on your current cash reserves? Financial consultants suggest that cash reserves should be equal to the amount you earn during a three-to-six-month period.

Achieving Wedded Bliss. Many people do not think about financial compatibility before or after marriage. When couples talk about financial issues and problems, the result is usually less conflict and smarter financial decisions. David Bach, author of several books on financial planning, helps couples achieve financial compatibility. He has the partners start by writing down what is most important to each of them—their five top values. They are also instructed to write down what the purpose of money is. He says, "Smart financial planning is more than a matter of numbers; it involves values first and stuff second."[24]

HOW TO SAVE MONEY IN PAINLESS WAYS

Let's assume you have decided to develop a three-year savings plan for a major purchase. The following "incidental expenses" provide some saving options.

	Savings
Take lunch to work three days per week and save $6.50 per day.	$3,000
Rent your movies instead of going to the theater.	$450
Skip the coffee shop and brew your own at home.	$4,000
Buy frozen gourmet pizza instead of ordering delivery.	$1,500
Total Savings	$8,950

Source: Adapted from "Calculate Your Savings Possibilities," SunTrust Banks, Inc. 2009.

DEFINING YOUR NONFINANCIAL RESOURCES

17-4   It is often the **nonfinancial resources** that make the biggest contribution to a happy and fulfilling life. A strong argument can be made that the real wealth in life comes in the form of good health, peace of mind, time spent with family and friends, learning

Figure 17.1 ■ Put Balance in Your Life

FINANCIAL RESOURCES
- Compensation from work
- Business profits
- Income from interest earned
- Income from investments

NONFINANCIAL RESOURCES
- Physical and mental health
- Education and training
- Leisure time
- Healthy spirituality

(which develops the mind), and healthy spirituality. Paul Hwoschinsky, author of *True Wealth*, makes this observation about nonfinancial resources: "If you are clear about who you are, and clear about what you want to do, and bring your financial and nonfinancial resources together, it's extraordinary what can happen. I encourage people to really honor their total resources, and magical things happen. New options occur."[25]

If you focus most or all of your attention on work and you suffer a major work-related disappointment, then the result is likely to be feelings of depression and despair. Thoughts such as "Now I have lost everything" can surface when you fail to get a promotion, find out that you were not selected to be a member of a special project team, or learn that your job has been eliminated. But if you fully understand the power of your nonfinancial resources, then work-related disappointments are easier to cope with. The starting point is to realize that *most* of your resources are nonfinancial. During periods of great uncertainty, it is especially important that you think about all your nonfinancial assets and consider ways to enhance them. We briefly discuss four nonfinancial resources that can enrich your life: physical and mental health, education and training (intellectual growth), leisure time (time for family, socializing, recreation), and healthy spirituality (see Figure 17.1).

Physical and Mental Health

Is the statement "Health means wealth" just a worn-out cliché, or is this slogan a message of inspiration for people who want to get more out of life? If good health is such an important nonfinancial asset, then why are so many people flirting with self-destruction by eating the wrong foods, drinking too much, exercising too little, and generally choosing unhealthy lifestyles? The answer to the second question may be lack of awareness of the benefits of physical fitness. Here are a few benefits of a modest exercise program.[26]

■ There is an interrelationship between health and outlook on life. For example, when the physical body is fit, toned, and strong, this condition has a positive effect on the mind. We are more likely to experience higher levels of self-esteem, feel a greater sense of self-confidence, and have a more positive outlook on life.

- Regular exercise and a healthy diet produce greater mental clarity, a higher energy level, and a more youthful appearance. Even low-intensity exercise such as walking can result in weight loss and reduction in the death rate from coronary artery disease and stroke.

More than 80 percent of the companies with 50 employees have wellness programs. Healthy employees file fewer insurance claims and are less likely to call in sick.[27] Increasingly, incentives are being used to encourage employee participation in various programs.

Education and Training (Intellectual Growth)

The New Economy thrives on a well-educated and well-trained work force. It rewards workers who take personal responsibility for their learning. The need to continually update, train, and develop yourself involves becoming a *career activist*, someone who writes your own script rather than waiting for someone else to write it for you.[28]

Develop your unique brand. In Chapter 11, we noted that branding can play a crucial role in your career success. Developing a strong personal brand requires knowledge and competence in the areas where you want to become an expert. To do this you must clarify, confirm, and build your strengths (see Chapter 4). Developing your expertise requires commitment, whether it is playing a musical instrument, playing a sport, computer programming, or consulting in a certain field.

Be selective in what you learn. Learning often requires large amounts of time and energy, so consider carefully what knowledge or skill will generate the most improvement.

Take advantage of various learning pathways. It helps to think of your job as a learning resource. Take full advantage of instructional programs offered by your employer. Volunteer for team assignments that will provide new learning opportunities. Peter Senge, author of *The Fifth Discipline*, says the fundamental learning unit in any organization is a team.[29]

Find a mentor(s) inside or outside of the company you work for and seek advice from her/him in several areas. And look outside the company for opportunities. Learning is a life-long adventure. Continue to learn and acquire new skills and knowledge after you have finished a college degree. Universities, community colleges, and organizations like the Learning Annex offer individual classes and programs to expand your knowledge and personal growth. Also consider learning soft skills in programs offered by Toastmasters, Dale Carnegie, or other organizations that offer seminars, conferences, and workshops.

Total Person Insight

"Practice isn't the thing you do once you're good. It's the thing you do that makes you good."

Source: Malcolm Gladwell, *Outliers: The Story of Success*, Little, Brown and Company; November, 2008.

Leisure Time

Leisure time can provide an opportunity to relax, get rid of work-related stress, get some exercise, spend time with family and friends, or simply read a good book. Many people cherish leisure time but experience schedule creep. *Schedule creep* is the tendency of work to expand beyond the normal work schedule and replace available leisure time. It often surfaces in small symptoms—an extra hour or two here, a weekend worked there.[30]

If you are working for a workaholic, someone who may have given up all or most of his or her leisure time, you may be pressured to work at the same pace. If your boss is constantly trying to meet impossible deadlines and deal with last-minute rushes, you may feel the need to give up time for recreation or family. Often a busy, overworked boss may not realize the effect his or her behavior has on others in the organization. If this happens, try to talk to your boss to find a solution that is agreeable to both of you. Identify the consequences of being overworked. Look at the situation from all points of view. If you refuse to work longer hours, what will be the consequences for your relationship with the boss, your relationship with other employees, or your future with the organization?[31]

We have discussed the growing number of studies that show that if you have strong and fulfilling relationships, you are happier, may live longer, decrease your chances of becoming sick, and cope more successfully when illness strikes.[32] Time spent with friends and family can be a powerful source of mental and physical renewal.

Spencer Platt/Getty Images

Everybody needs the occasional break. Amazon CEO Jeff Bezos finds that isolated relaxation helps him reenergize and refocus so that he can continue to drive the Amazon empire forward.

One of the best ways to feel satisfied about your work is to get away from it when you begin to feel worn out. People who take time off from work often return with new ideas, a stronger focus, and increased energy. For Jeff Bezos, CEO of Amazon, the best way he renews his energy and stimulates new ideas for his company is to get away for a solo retreat. "I just lock myself up," he says. "There are no distractions from the office. No phones ringing. It's just because with a little bit of isolation I find I start to get more creative. I do spend a lot of time web surfing during those two or three days and just looking at what hobbyists and hackers are doing. What are the sorts of things that are on the cutting edge?"[33] He then writes up his observations in memos to himself, and sometimes to his executive team who then build on his ideas.

Find some quiet time for yourself each day. You might use it to meditate, take the dog for a walk, or just sit quietly. Use this time to nourish yourself and bring balance to your life.

If you want more leisure time, then you must establish your priorities and set your goals. This may mean saying no to endless requests to work overtime or rejecting a promotion. Sometimes you must pull back from the endless demands of work and "get a life."

Healthy Spirituality

Spirituality is receiving greater attention in education and in the workplace. More business and professional schools are offering courses dealing with spirituality and *personal fulfillment*. Patricia Aburdene, author of *Megatrends 2010*, says the number one megatrend is spirituality. She defines a megatrend as the large, overarching direction that shapes our lives. Aburdene explains how integrity, trust, doing good deeds, and giving back can translate into high performance and healthy profits.[34]

WHAT IS THE DIFFERENCE BETWEEN RELIGION AND SPIRITUALITY?

"Religion is often about who's in and who's out, creating a worldview steeped in 'us *against* them.' Spirituality rejects this dualism and speaks of us *and* them. Religion is often about loyalty to institutions, clergy, and rules. Spirituality is about loyalty to justice and compassion. Religion talks about God. Spirituality helps to make us godly. The two need not be at odds. Religion at its best is spirituality in community."

Source: Rabbi Rami Shapiro, "What is the difference between religion and spirituality?" *Spirituality & Health*, May-June 2012, page 17.

Spirituality can be defined as an inner attitude that emphasizes energy, creative choice, and a powerful force for living. It involves opening our hearts and cultivating our capacity to experience reverence and gratitude. It frees us to become positive, caring human beings.[35]

Spirituality encompasses faith, which can be described as what your heart tells you is true when your mind cannot prove it. For some people, faith exists within the framework of a formal religion; for others, it rests on a series of personal beliefs such as "Give others the same consideration, regard, kindness, and gentleness that you would like them to accord you."[36] Many people think of spirituality as a remote, abstract concept. But traditional teachings suggest that spirituality is directly connected to the most ordinary human activities.[37]

An understanding of the many aspects of spirituality can give us an expanded vision of what it means to be human. Although spirituality is often associated with religion, it should be viewed in broader terms. Robert Coles, of Harvard Medical School, likes a definition of spirituality given to him by an 11-year-old girl:

> *I think you're spiritual if you can escape from yourself a little and think of what's good for everyone, not just you, and if you can reach out and be a good person—I mean live like a good person. You're not spiritual if you just talk spiritual and there's no action. You're a fake if that's what you do.*[38]

> *An understanding of the many aspects of spirituality can give us an expanded vision of what it means to be human.*

The words of this young girl remind us that one dimension of spirituality involves showing concern and compassion for others. Thomas Moore, author of the best selling book *Care of the Soul*, says, "To be spiritual means to mature to a point beyond limited self-interest and anxiety about self."[39] Harvard psychiatrist George Vaillant, author of *Adaptation to Life*, says that defining spirituality is like trying to define Shakespeare's genius. Everyone knows it exists, but no two people would describe it in the same way. "I think spirituality involves qualities like patience, tolerance, kindness, honesty, and humility—and always, love. It's the universal response to things we all deeply appreciate—love, fresh water, music, sunrise, human connection, and a power greater than ourselves."

Total Person Insight

> "Spirituality I take to be concerned with those qualities of human spirit—such as love and compassion, patience, tolerance, forgiveness, contentment, a sense of responsibility, a sense of harmony—which bring happiness to both self and others."
>
> Source: The Dalai Lama, Co-Author, *The Art of Happiness*, "Teaching Tolerance," Spring 2005, p. 28.

Spirituality at Work. In many ways, large and small, work can be made more spiritual. The philosophy of Worthington Industries is expressed in a single sentence: "We treat our employees as we would like to be treated."[40] Herr Foods, Inc. promises, "An atmosphere that enhances the moral and spiritual integrity of each individual."[41]

Research indicates that the new generation of workers, Generation Y, will be looking deep inside companies to see what makes them tick. The person with a passion for environmental issues will be drawn to companies like outdoor apparel maker Patagonia, which contributes one percent of sales to environmental causes.[42] Patagonia also appeals to persons who seek an employer who maintains high ethical standards. Patagonia has made the "World's Most Ethical Companies" list six years in a row.

Many activities can be considered spiritual. Visiting an art gallery, listening to a concert, or walking near the ocean can stimulate healthy spirituality. Table 17.1 describes some ways to begin your journey to healthy spirituality.

For many people, a commitment to a specific religion is an important dimension of spirituality. Active membership in a religious group provides an opportunity to clarify spiritual values and achieve spiritual direction. It also provides social connections—an extended family that you can depend on for social support.[43]

Table 17.1 ▪ Ways to Achieve Healthy Spirituality

As interest in healthy spirituality grows, people are searching for ways to become more spiritual. The following spiritual practices draw our focus away from ourselves and the anxieties in our lives.

- *Meditation* Oprah Winfrey described the powerful influence of meditation this way: "There is no greater source of strength and power for me in my life now, than going still, being quiet, and recognizing what real power is." (See Chapter 14 for a step-by-step guide to meditation.)

- *Prayer* Dr. Larry Dossey, physician and author of numerous books on the role of spirituality in medicine, says prayer can be a powerful force in our lives. Prayer groups have been established at many organizations.

- *Spiritual Reading* In addition to sacred readings, consider *Healing and the Mind* by Bill Moyers, *10 Secrets for Success and Inner Peace*, by Dr. Wayne Dyer, and *The Hungry Spirit*, by Charles Handy.

- *Time with Nature* Spiritual contemplation during a walk in the woods or a visit to a quiet lake can help us balance mind, body, and spirit.

Source: David Elkins and Amanda Druckman, "Four Great Ways to Begin Your Spiritual Journey," *Psychology Today*, September/October 1999, p. 46; Larry Dossey, M.D., "Can We Change the World?" *The Inner Edge*, June/July 2000, pp. 22–23.

DEVELOPING A HEALTHY LIFESTYLE

17-5 Earlier in this chapter, we noted that a healthy lifestyle can provide a higher energy level, a greater sense of self-confidence, and, generally, a more positive outlook on life. People who maintain good health usually have more endurance, spend less time feeling tired or ill, and miss less work than persons who are not healthy. Good health is receiving greater attention today because many Americans are investing more time and energy in their work. They are being asked to work longer hours and to do more in less time. Good health can help combat stress and tension at work and at home. In this section, we offer guidelines that form the framework for a good diet and a good exercise program.

Guidelines for a Healthy Diet

Eating the right foods is a choice you make every day that directly impacts your health and energy level, and, in some cases, extends your life. We will review several important dietary guidelines.

The U.S. Department of Agriculture (USDA) published a new *"My Plate"* diagram in June, 2011, replacing the old MyPyramid, a picture crowded with captions that seemed to confuse most Americans (see Figure 17.2). In recent years, obesity in America has risen at an alarming rate. Nearly one in five children ages 6 to 19 is obese, a number that is up sharply from approximately 1 in 20 in 1980.[44] The goal of My Plate is to make health-sustaining food choices easy to understand because it shows how the American plate should look.

Fruits and vegetables cover half the plate. Whole grains make up one-quarter of the plate and the remaining portion is protein-rich foods. The category once called "meat and beans" is now simply "proteins" to make way for other options like seafood and vegetarian foods such as tofu. Next to the plate is a blue circle for dairy, which means milk, soymilk, cheese, or yogurt.

Figure 17.2 ■ U.S. Department of Agriculture's MyPlate

Maintain a Healthy Weight

Everyone should monitor their body weight and exercise to determine whether they need to adjust calorie intake.[45] More than 65 percent of Americans are overweight, and these added pounds increase the risk of heart disease, cancer, and diabetes. Inactivity combined with diets high in calories, salt, and fats result in serious health problems. Maintaining a healthy weight is all about balance—*calories in versus calories out*. If you consume more calories a day than you burn you will gain weight. To maintain your ideal body weight, the number of calories consumed must equal the calories burned through exercise and physical activity. If you want to lose weight, the number of calories you consume need to be less than the number of calories you burn (see Figure 17.3).

Eating a variety of foods is important because you need more than forty different nutrients for good health: vitamins and minerals, amino acids (from proteins), essential fatty acids (from fats and oils), and sources of energy (calories from carbohydrates, fats, and proteins). The type of foods you eat is also very important. Whole grains should be substituted for refined grains, and dark leafy greens such as spinach, kale. and Swiss chard are packed with vitamins A, C, and K, folate, potassium, magnesium, calcium, iron, and fiber.

Figure 17.3 ■ Balancing Calories in and Calories Out

The Hidden Dangers of Eating Out

The foods that are popular with many Americans are high in calories and fat, especially saturated fat, which contributes to high blood cholesterol levels. Many seemingly harmless choices are in disguise. A large tuna melt at Quiznos has 2,090 calories and 175 grams of fat.[46] A Chipotle Chicken Burrito (with tortilla, rice, chicken, pinto beans, cheese, salsa, and sour cream) is 970 calories, 18 grams of saturated fat, and 2,200 mg of sodium. Forget the cheese and sour cream and it drops to 750 calories and only 5.5 grams of saturated fat. A cup of black coffee has zero calories. If you want something fancier, say a Starbucks Venti White Chocolate Mocha, your "coffee" is now 580 calories and 15 grams of saturated fat—worse than a McDonald's Quarter Pounder with Cheese![47]

Heart disease and certain kinds of cancer are byproducts of foods that contain highly saturated fats. Avoid foods that include partially hydrogenated oils—better known as *trans fats*. These artery-clogging fats can be very harmful to your health.

Exercise Fuels a Healthy Body

There is an interrelationship between health and outlook on life. For example, when a person feels their body is fit, toned, and strong, this physical condition has a direct correlation to a strong, positive effect on the mind. We are more likely to experience higher levels of self-esteem, feel a greater sense of self-confidence, and have a more positive outlook on life. Regular exercise and a healthy diet produce greater mental clarity, higher energy levels, and a more youthful appearance.

"Sedentary living is so dangerous that it is simply not an option." This is the conclusion of research conducted at Duke University. An inactive life style (sedentary sickness) results in an array of risk factors such as weight gain, increases in bad cholesterol and blood sugar levels.[48] **Physical fitness**, which involves the performance of the lungs, heart, and muscles, can also have a positive influence on mental alertness and emotional stability. Research indicates that even a moderate level of physical activity can have a surprisingly broad array of health benefits on virtually every major organ system in the body.[49] For most people, a program that involves regular physical activity at least three or four times a week and includes sustained physical exertion for 30 to 35 minutes during each activity period is adequate.[50] This modest investment of time and energy will give you a longer and healthier life. Even low-intensity exercise such as walking 30 minutes a day can result in weight loss and reduction in the death rate from coronary artery disease and stroke.

To achieve lifesaving benefits from exercise, start slowly with an aerobic fitness activity you will enjoy. Swimming, running, low-impact aerobics, and jogging are aerobic exercises. When we engage in aerobic exercise, the body is required to improve its ability to handle oxygen.[51] These exercises strengthen the heart, burn up calories, increase stamina, and help release tension.

Energy Recovery

To state the obvious, sleep is not optional. But sometimes we treat it as if it were so. When schedules are booked to capacity and we feel like we need to get more done, we have a natural tendency to think we should push harder and longer to get more done. If we sacrifice two hours of sleep, we think we will get two hours of additional productivity. In fact the opposite may occur. When people deprive themselves of sleep it depletes their energy and reduces productivity. What we need to do instead is learn to manage our energy.

Tony Schwartz, CEO of The Energy Project, says the body operates in "ultradian rhythms every 90 minutes, during which we move from alertness to fatigue."[52] For optimal performance, he recommends we adjust our schedule to focus for periods of no longer than 90 minutes, and then take a break to refresh and renew. When people operate in a manner consistent with their natural rhythm, they will get more done in less time, and at a higher level of quality.[53]

Total Person Insight

> "Build Energy Rituals—specific behaviors done at precise times—for your most difficult challenges. Try beginning the day by focusing without interruption on the most important challenge in front of you, for no more than 90 minutes, and then take a real renewal break."
>
> Source: Tony Schwartz, www.theenergyproject.com/tips

PLANNING FOR CHANGES IN YOUR LIFE

17-6 Throughout this book, we have emphasized the concept that you can control your own behavior. In fact, during these turbulent times, changes in your behavior may be one of the few things under your control. What are some behaviors you can adopt (or alter) that will make an important positive change in your life? Once you have identified these behaviors, you can set goals and do what is necessary to achieve them.

The Power of Habits

Let's take a look at the powerful influence of habits. Some habits, like taking a long walk three or four times a week, can have a positive influence on our well-being. Simply saying "Thank you" when someone does a favor or pays a compliment can be a habit. Other habits, such as smoking, complaining, feeling jealous, or constantly engaging in self-criticism, are negative forces in our lives. Stephen Covey makes this observation: "Habits are powerful factors in our lives. Because they are consistent, often unconscious patterns, they constantly, daily, express our character and produce our effectiveness ... or ineffectiveness."[54]

Breaking deeply embedded habits, such as impatience, procrastination, or criticism of others, can take a tremendous amount of effort. The influences supporting the habit, the actual root causes, are often repressed in the subconscious mind and forgotten.[55] How do you break a negative habit or form a positive habit? The process involves five steps.

Motivation. Once you are aware of the need to change, you must develop the willingness or desire to change. After making a major commitment to change, you must find ways to maintain your motivation. The key to staying motivated is to develop a mindset powerful enough that you feel compelled to act on your desire to change.

Knowledge. Once you clearly understand the benefits of breaking a habit or forming a new one, you must acquire the knowledge you need to change. Seek information, ask for advice, or learn from the experiences of others. This may involve finding a mentor, joining a group, or gathering sufficient material and teaching yourself.

Practice. Information is only as useful as you make it. This means that to change your behavior you must *practice* what you have learned. If you are a shy person, does this mean you need to volunteer to make a speech in front of several hundred people? The answer is no. Although there is always the rare individual who makes a major change seemingly overnight, most people find that the best and surest way to develop a new behavior is to do so gradually. It usually takes at least 21 days of consistent behavior change to change a habit.

Feedback. Whenever you can, seek feedback as you attempt to change a habit. Dieters lose more weight if they attend counseling sessions and weigh-ins. People who want to improve their public speaking skills benefit from practice followed by feedback from a teacher or coach. Everyone has blind spots, particularly when trying something new.

Reinforcement. When you see yourself exhibiting the type of behavior you have been working to develop—or when someone mentions that you have changed—reward yourself! The rewards can be simple, inexpensive ones—treating yourself to a movie, a bouquet of flowers, a favorite meal, or a special event. This type of reinforcement is vital when you are trying to improve old behaviors or develop new ones.

The Choice is Yours

Are you ready to develop a life plan for effective human relations? We hope the answer is yes. One of the positive aspects of personal planning is that you are making your own choices. You decide what kind of person you want to be and then set your own standards and goals. The results can mean not only career advancement and financial benefits, but also greater happiness and personal fulfillment, and the development of strong, satisfying relationships with others. These relationships may be the key to future opportunities, and you in turn, may be able to help others reach their goals.

In the opening chapter of this text, we talked about the *total person* approach to human relations. By now, we hope you realize that you are someone special! You have a unique combination of talents, attitudes, values, goals, needs, and motivation—all in a state of development. You can decide to tap your potential to become a successful, productive human being however *you* understand those terms. We hope this book helps you to develop your human relations skills and to become what you want to be. You can turn the concepts and guidelines presented here into a plan of action for your own life and career. We'll leave you with this inspiring poem by Dawna Markova, author of *I Will Not Die an Unlived Life*—and we wish you the best!

I Will Not Die an Unlived Life

I will not die an unlived life.
I will not live in fear
of falling or catching fire.
I choose to inhabit my days,
to allow my living to open me,
to make me less afraid,
more accessible;
to loosen my heart
until it becomes a wing,
a torch, a promise.
I choose to risk my significance,
to live so that which came to me as seed
goes to the next as blossom,
and that which came to me as blossom,
goes on as fruit.

Source: Dawna Markova, *I Will Not Die an Unlived Life—Reclaiming Purpose and Passion*, Conari Press, 2000, San Francisco, CA.

LOOKING BACK: SUMMARY OF LEARNING OBJECTIVES

1. **Learn how to cope with the forces that influence work/life balance.**

   The labor market has become a place of great uncertainty due to the heavy volume of mergers, acquisitions, business closings, and downsizing. There is increasing pressure to work harder, work longer hours, and give up more leisure time. Learning how to cope with the forces that influence work/life balance has never been more challenging.

2. **Define success by standards that are compatible with your needs and values.**

   The traditional definitions of success that most of us know are too confining. They describe success almost entirely in terms of measurable job achievements. These definitions leave out the intangible successes to be had in private and professional life. Many people today are discovering that true success is a combination of achievements.

3. **Discuss the meaning of *right livelihood*.**

   Achieving right livelihood is a very important dimension of success. Right livelihood is work consciously chosen and done with full awareness and care that leads to enlightenment. Right livelihood recognizes that work is a vehicle for self-expression, and places money in a secondary position.

4. **Describe four nonfinancial resources that can enrich your life.**

   A person's nonfinancial resources often make the biggest contribution to a happy and fulfilling life. Each of us has four nonfinancial resources that can enrich our lives: physical and mental health, education and training (intellectual growth), leisure time (time for friends and family, socializing, recreation), and healthy spirituality.

5. **Provide guidelines for developing a healthy lifestyle.**

   Many Americans are working to achieve healthy lifestyles. Healthy lifestyles can give us a higher energy level, a greater sense of self-confidence, and, generally, a more positive outlook. People who maintain good health usually have more endurance, spend less time feeling tired or ill, and miss less work than those who are not physically fit.

6. **Develop a plan for making needed changes in your life.**

   Planning for changes in your life often requires breaking negative habits or forming positive habits. The process of breaking habits and forming new ones involves five steps: motivation, knowledge, practice, feedback, and reinforcement.

KEY TERMS

right livelihood, 377

nonfinancial resources, 381

spirituality, 385

physical fitness, 389

TRY YOUR HAND

1. The concept of *right livelihood* is based on conscious choice, placing money in a secondary position, and work as a vehicle for personal growth. Take time to reflect on the past six months and evaluate if *right livelihood* principles have guided you in your decision-making. If so, discuss the influence of the concept, and if not, evaluate its importance in future decision-making.

2. Throughout this chapter, you were encouraged to take control of your life and establish your own definition of success. This chapter has a strong "all development is self-development" theme. Can we really control our own destinies? Can we always make our own choices? Mike Hernacki, author of the book *The Ultimate Secret of Getting Absolutely Everything You Want*, says yes:

   To get what you want, you must recognize something that at first may be difficult, even painful to look at. You must recognize that you alone are the source of all the conditions and situations in your life. You must recognize that whatever your world looks like right now, you alone have caused it to look that way. The state of your health, your finances, your personal relationships, your professional life—all of it is your doing, yours and no one else's.[56]

Do you agree with this viewpoint? Take a position in favor of or in opposition to Hernacki's statement. Prepare a short one- or two-paragraph statement that expresses your views.

3. There are many ways to deepen and extend your spirituality. One way is to begin placing a higher value on silence, tranquility, and reflection. If your life is extremely busy, you may not be taking time for thought or reflection. If you are accustomed to living in the presence of noise throughout the day, quiet times may make you feel uncomfortable at first. During a period of one week, set aside a few minutes each day for your own choice of meditation, prayer, contemplation, or reflection. Try to find a quiet place for this activity. At the end of the week, assess the benefits of this activity, and consider the merits of making it part of your daily routine.[57]

CRITICAL THINKING CHALLENGE

For most people, true success is a combination of achievements. These achievements might relate to such things as leisure time, earnings, job status, health, or relationships.

1. On a piece of paper, describe your personal definition of success.

2. If you could design the most ideal way to make a living by doing what you love, what would this be? Would doing this help you achieve your personal definition of success you described above?

SELF-ASSESSMENT EXERCISE

For each of the following statements, circle the number from 1 to 5 that best represents your response: (1) strongly disagree (never do this); (2) disagree (rarely do this); (3) moderately agree (sometimes do this); (4) agree (frequently do this); (5) strongly agree (almost always do this).

A. I stay connected with family and friends and network with professional and business associates.	1	2	3	4	5
B. I try to maintain a balance in my life by avoiding an addiction to work and by engaging in leisure-time activities.	1	2	3	4	5
C. I envision my existence in a larger context and view healthy spirituality as a positive, enlightening force in my life.	1	2	3	4	5
D. I avoid rigid individualism (self-centered behavior) by investing time and energy in helping others.					
E. I constantly strive to improve my knowledge, skills, and sense of purpose in my life's work.	1	2	3	4	5
F. I have established well-thought out goals for my life and these goals are tied to my values.	1	2	3	4	5

After identifying your response to each item, select an attitude or skill you would like to improve. Prepare a written goal and then describe the steps you will take to achieve this goal.

YOU PLAY THE ROLE

Ambry Waller, one of your closest friends, used to go fishing quite often, and he loved to hike in the mountains. After getting married, his life changed dramatically. He and his wife purchased a new home, and soon they were raising a family. Once the bills started piling up, he abandoned his leisure-time activities and started working long hours at his job. He eagerly volunteered for overtime in order to increase his earnings. As the years passed, Ambry and his wife adopted many trappings of middle-class life: a big house, two cars, a huge flat screen TV in the family room, and a motorboat

that sits idle for most of the year. One afternoon, you meet Ambry for a beer at a local bar. The conversation quickly turns serious as Ambry describes his frustration: "I love my wife and children, but I am so tired of working long hours and worrying about my financial obligations. My credit-card debt is now over $7,000."

In this role-play activity, you will meet with another class member who will assume the role of Ambry Waller. Your goal is to help Ambry identify some ways he can achieve greater work/life balance. Your name for this role-play will be Corey Cell.

BELOW THE SURFACE | RELEARNING THE MEANING OF LIFE

At the beginning of this chapter, we described how employees at Google benefited from Search Inside Yourself (SIY), a class that teaches employees how to deal with stress and burn-out from a demanding work culture. The class teaches employees to reexamine their choices, both at work and at home. The employees who complete SIY learn how to identify and talk about their emotions, and how to apply new skills that expand their mental, physical, and emotional well being in a challenging work environment.

Like the employees who complete SIY, students at Columbia Business School are learning similar skills in a popular class that "requires thinking about the 'meaning of life,' and not infrequently convinces MBA students that—surprise!—money isn't everything."[58] Srikumar Rao, an ex-marketing executive from Wall Street and Hollywood is the creator of the class. It has such a long waiting list that Rao had to invent a rigorous application process that requires students to submit a résumé, seven essays, and participate in an interview. As more people struggle to balance demanding jobs and an uncertain economy, it's doubtful that the class will become less popular anytime soon.

While many people are learning how to cope more effectively with the stress of challenging jobs,

others have opted out of crazy work schedules to choose work that offers them a lifestyle that makes them much happier.

In 2002, Richard Binder quit his job as a software engineer to become a "pen doctor." He repairs fountain pens sent to him from customers around the world. His gross income is less than what he earned as a software engineer, but he is happier. He says, "Basically, I get my pleasure from making people happy with their pens." For Richard Binder, the search for right livelihood is over.[59]

QUESTIONS

1. Given the changes taking place in our economy, you may need to return to the classroom at age 30, 40, or 50. How would you feel about the prospect of becoming a middle-aged student?

2. Mary Lou Quinlan spent 20 years climbing the ladder in the field of advertising. Finally she became CEO of N.W. Ayer, a successful advertising company. She achieved "success" but she was not happy. She then decided to become an entrepreneur. That decision was made after completing the following steps:

   I got a piece of paper and divided it in half. On the left side, I wrote down what I love to do and what I'm good at, and on the right side, I wrote down what I don't like to do and what I stink at. Unfortunately, what I don't like to do and what I stink at were my job descriptions as CEO.[60]

Quinlan founded a consulting company named Just Ask a Woman, a firm that helps companies market to women. Evaluate the advantages and disadvantages of the decision making model used by Quinlan.

3. Many companies are reducing the contribution made to employee retirement programs and others are eliminating these contributions. Briefly describe the retirement program you would like to establish and maintain during the years ahead. Predict the major barriers to achieving your goal.

CHAPTER 17 ENDNOTES

1. Caitlin Kelly, "Google class asks employees to take a deep breath," New York Times, published in **News & Observer**, Business, May 6, 2012.
2. Thomas J. Peters and Robert H. Waterman, Jr., **In Search of Excellence: Lessons from America's Best-Run Companies** (New York: Harper & Row, 1982), p. 14; Tom Peters, "Tom Peters' True Confessions," **Fast Company**, December 2001, p. 80.
3. Bill George (with Peter Sims), **True North** (San Francisco: John Wiley & Sons, Inc., 2007), p. xxiv; Bill George, Peter Sims, Andrew N. McLean, and Diana Mayer, "Discovering Your Authentic Leadership," **Harvard Business Review**, February 2007, pp. 129–138.
4. Po Bronson, **What Should I Do with My Life?** (New York: Random House, 2002), p. 365; Patricia Kitchen, "Seeking Your Calling," **The Record**, March 9, 2003, p. Dl.
5. Ethan Watters, "Come Here, Work, and Get Out of Here, You Don't Live Here. You Live Someplace else," **Inc.**, October 30, 2001, pp. 56–61; "Why We're Different" [cited 27 April 2009]. Available from http://www.stgutah.com; INTERNET.
6. Jack Canfield, **The Success Principles** (New York: HarperCollins, 2005), p. 3.
7. Anne Fisher, "The Practical Painter," **Fortune**, May 14, 2007, p. 124.
8. See His Holiness the Dalai Lama and Howard C. Cutler, **The Art of Happiness at Work** (New York: Riverhead Books, 2003), pp. 157–173.
9. Yvonne V. Chabrier, "Focus on Work," **New Age**, 1998, p. 95.
10. Bronson, **What Should I Do with My Life?** pp. 68–72.
11. Marsha Sinetar, **Do What You Love ... The Money Will Follow** (New York: Dell, 1987), p. 11.
12. Ibid., pp. 11–12.
13. Michael Phillips, **The Seven Laws of Money** (Menlo Park, Calif.: Word Wheel and Random House, 1997), p. 9.
14. Sinetar, **Do What You Love**, pp. 14–15.
15. Erin White, "Profession Changes Take Time But May Be Worth Wait," **Wall Street Journal**, November 27, 2007, p. B6.
16. Carole Kanchier, "Dare to Change Your Job and Your Life in 7 Steps," **Psychology Today**, March/April 2000, pp. 64–67.
17. Suze Orman, "The Pursuit of Cold, Hard Happiness," **O, The Oprah Magazine**, March 2004, pp. 54–56; Sharon Begley, "Wealth and Happiness Don't Necessarily Go Hand in Hand," **Wall Street Journal**, August 13, 2004, p. Bl.
18. Geoffrey Colvin, "We're a Nation Helpless to Save Ourselves," **Fortune**, April 18, 2005, p. 52.
19. Shakti Gawain, **Creating True Prosperity** (Novato, Calif.: New World Library, 1997), p. 7.
20. Carlin Flora, "Happy Hour," **Psychology Today**, January/February 2005, p. 48.
21. "Why Money Matters Are a Leading Cause of Divorce," **Spirituality & Health**, November/December 2006, p. 32.
22. Jonathan Clements, "If You Didn't Save 10% of Your Income This Year, You're Spending Too Much," **Wall Street Journal**, December 22, 2004, p. Dl; Jonathan Clements, "Rich, Successful—and Miserable: New Research Probes Midlife Angst," **Wall Street Journal**, October 5, 2005, p. Dl.
23. Jonathan Clements, "Amid Losses, 12 Financial Truths Persist," **Wall Street Journal**, Sunday, June 18, 2006, p. 7E; Jonathan Welsh, "When a $38,000 Car Costs $44,000," **Wall Street Journal**, May 22, 2007, p. Dl.
24. Toddi Gutner, "Talk Now, Retire Happily Later," **BusinessWeek**, April 2, 2001, p. 92.
25. "A Field Is Born," **Harvard Business Review**, July/August 2008, p. 164.
26. Michael Toms, "Money: The Third Side of the Coin" (interview with Joe Dominguez and Vicki Robin), **New Dimensions**, May/June 1991, p. 7.

27. Dee Gill, "Get Healthy…Or else," *Inc.*, April 2006, p. 36.

28. *The Career Activist* concept is described in Barbara Moses, *Career Intelligence: The 12 New Rules for Work and Life Success* (San Francisco: Berrett-Koehler Publishers, Inc., 1998).

29. Ron Zemke, "Why Organizations Still Aren't Learning," *Training*, September 1999, p. 43.

30. Sue Shellenbarger, "Working 9 to 2: Taking Steps to Make Part-Time Job Setups More Palatable," *Wall Street Journal*, February 17, 2005, p. Dl.

31. Jay T. Knippen, Thad B. Green, and Kurt Sutton, "Asking Not to Be Overworked," *Supervisory Management*, February 1992, p. 6.

32. Art Ulene, *Really Fit Really Fast* (Encino, Calif.: HealthPoints, 1996), pp. 198–199.

33. John Byrne, "The 12 Greatest Entrepreneurs of Our Time—and What You Can Learn from Them, *Fortune*, April 9, 2012, p. 74.

34. Anne Fisher, "Catch the New MBA Craze: Raoism," *Fortune*, February 8, 2006, p. 36; "The #1 Megatrend in Business Today Is…Spirituality," *Spirituality & Health*, March/April 2006, p. 30.

35. Leo Booth, "When God Becomes a Drug," *Common Boundary*, September/October 1991, p. 30; David N. Elkins, "Spirituality," *Psychology Today*, September/October, 1999, pp. 45–48.

36. Harold H. Bloomfield and Robert K. Cooper, *The Power of* 5 (Emmaus, Pa.: Rodale Press, 1995), p. 484.

37. Thomas Moore, "Sacred Time with Children," *Spirituality & Health*, November/December 2007, p. 12.

38. "Making the Spiritual Connection," *Lears*, December 1989, p. 72.

39. Thomas Moore, "Will We Take the Moral Values Challenge?" *Spirituality & Health*, January/February 2005, pp. 10–11.

40. "Career Opportunities" [cited 1 May 2009]. Available from http://www.worthingtonindustries.com

41. "Our Philosophy" [cited 1 May 2009]. Available from http://www.herrs.com

42. Ann States, "Get Ready for a Pickier Workforce," *BusinessWeek*, September 18, 2006, p. 82.

43. Kevin Helliker, "Body and Spirit: Why Attending Religious Services May Benefit Health," *Wall Street Journal*, May 3, 2005, p. Dl.

44. John Rosemond, "Parents can solve kids' obesity," *The News and Observer 2D*, Tuesday, January 11, 2011.

45. Sara Schaefer Munoz, "The Food Pyramid Gets Personalized," *Wall Street Journal*, April 20, 2005, p. Dl; "Johanns Reveals USDA's Steps to a Healthier You" [cited 24 February 2006]. Available from http://www.mypyramid.gov; INTERNET.

46. Michael Orey, "A Food Fight Over Calorie Counts," *BusinessWeek*, February 11, 2008, p. 36.

47. Nutrition Action Newsletter, Center for Science in the Public Interest, 2011, www.cspineet.org.

48. "Just Move," *Duke Medicine HealthLine*, Winter 2007, p. 6.

49. Robert Langreth, "Every Little Bit Helps," *Wall Street Journal*, May 1, 2000, p. R5; Tara Parker Pope, "Health Matters," *Wall Street Journal*, August 9, 2004, p. R5.

50. John Swartzberg, "Exercise: It's Not Just Physical," LIC *Berkeley Wellness Letter*, November 2002, p. 3.

51. Robert A. Gleser, *The Healthmark Program for Life* (New York: McGraw-Hill, 1988), p. 147.

52. Tony Schwartz, "Energy-the X factor in engagement, productivity & performance" (white paper) www.theenergyproject.com

53. Ibid.

54. Stephen R. Covey, *The Seven Habits of Highly Effective People* (New York: Simon & Schuster, 1989), p. 46.

55. James Fadiman, *Be All That You Are* (Seattle: Westlake Press, 1986), p. 25.

56. Mike Hernacki, *The Ultimate Secret of Getting Absolutely Everything You Want* (New York: Berkley Books, 1988), p. 35.

57. Adapted from Bloomfield and Cooper, *The Power of 5*, pp. 492–493.

58. Anne Fisher, "Catch the New MBA Craze: Raoism, *Fortune*, VOL. 153, No. 3, February 8, 2006.

59. Kate Bonamici, "Fountain Pen Doctor," *Fortune*, January 23, 2006, p. 40.

60. Mary Lou Quinlan, "Just Ask a Woman," *Fast Company*, July 2003, p. 50.

Glossary

360-degree feedback   With this approach, employees are rated by persons who have had opportunities to observe their performance. The person who completes the feedback form may be the immediate boss, coworkers, team members, and, in some cases, even customers, clients, or patients.

A

Active listening   Active listening is fueled by curiosity and requires your complete concentration on what you are hearing, body language that exhibits your listening attitude, and feedback as to what you think the speaker is trying to tell you.

Affirmative action   Involves intentionally seeking and hiring employees from groups that are under-represented.

Aggressive behavior   Aggressive behavior in conflict situations involves expressing your thoughts and feelings and defending your rights in a way that *violates* the rights of others.

Anger   The thoughts, feelings, physical reactions, and actions that result from unacceptable behavior by others.

Anxiety   A condition in which intense feelings of apprehension are longstanding and usually disruptive.

Assertive behavior   Assertive behavior provides you the opportunity to stand up for your rights and express your thoughts and feelings in a direct, appropriate way that does not violate the rights of others.

Assumptions   The impression you form of another person during the initial contact is made up of both assumptions and facts. Most people tend to rely more heavily on assumptions during the initial meeting.

Attitudes   Thoughts that you have accepted as true and that lead you to think, feel, or act positively or negatively toward a person, idea, or event.

Authenticity   The unimpeded operation of one's true or core self in one's daily interactions with others.

B

Behavioral profiling   The process of observing, anticipating, and interpreting a specific behavior. Gestures, body movements, tone of voice, and facial expressions can communicate confidence or fear, trust or mistrust, curiosity or boredom.

Blind area   The blind area consists of information about yourself that others know but you are not aware of. Others may see you as aloof and stuffy, whereas you view yourself as open and friendly.

Blog   A discussion or information site, usually written by one person, used to communicate perspectives and information about certain topics.

Burnout   A gradually intensifying pattern of physical, psychological, and behavioral dysfunction that evolves in response to a continuous flow of stressors.

Business casual   The movement toward dress standards that emphasize greater comfort and individuality.

C

Career apparel   A type of job-specific uniform worn by a collective group of workers such as UPS drivers or airport security agents.

Character   Character is composed of personal standards of behavior, including honesty, integrity, and moral strength.

Coaching   Coaching and developing people to become effective employees is a critical competency required by leaders in every organization.

Codes of ethics   Written statements of what an organization expects in the way of ethical behavior can give employees a clear indication of what behaviors are acceptable or improper.

Collective bargaining   A process that defines the rights and privileges of both sides involved in the conflict and establishes the terms of employment and length of the contract (usually from three to five years).

Communication style model   The communication style model will help you identify your most preferred style.

Communication style   The patterns of behavior that others can observe.

Communication   The means by which we come to an understanding of ourselves and others.

Communication-style bias   A state of mind that most of us experience from time to time, but we may find it difficult to explain the symptoms.

Compressed workweek   A situation where employees may be given the opportunity to adjust their work schedules to fit their lifestyle. One of the newest compressed workweek schedules, often called the 9/80, is growing in popularity. Employees work one extra hour each day for nine days, a total of 80 hours in two weeks, and receive a three-day weekend every other week.

Compulsory arbitration   When the government decides that the labor-management dispute threatens national health and safety, or will damage an entire industry, it can appoint an arbitrator who dictates a solution that is binding on both sides and can be enforced in a court of law.

Conflict resolution process   The conflict resolution process consists of five steps that can be used at work and in your personal life.

Conflict resolution   If your job includes supervisory-management responsibilities, you will spend a great deal of time in conflict resolution, attempting to resolve conflicts among members of your staff.

Conflict trigger   A circumstance that increases the chances of intergroup or interpersonal conflict.

Conflict   A clash between incompatible people, ideas, or interests.

Consideration   The dimension of consideration reflects the extent to which a leader's relationships with subordinates are characterized by mutual trust, respect for the employees, consideration of their feelings, and warmth in interpersonal relationships.

Constructive criticism   A form of self-disclosure that helps another person look at his or her own behavior without putting that individual on the defensive.

Core values   Those values that you consistently rank higher than others. When you are able to identify your core values, you have a definite picture of the kind of person you want to be and the kind of life you want to have.

Critical listening   The attempt to see the topic of discussion from the *speaker's* point of view and to consider how the speaker's perception of the situation may be different from your own.

Cross-functional teams   Task groups staffed with a mix of specialists, focused on a common objective. These teams are often temporary groups with members from different departments and job levels.

Cultural influences   Cultural influences, often formed during the early years of our life, lead us to have impressions of some people even before we meet them.

Cultural intelligence   The ability to interpret human actions, gestures, and speech patterns in a foreign culture.

Culture   The accumulation of values, rules of behavior, forms of expression, religious beliefs, and the like, for a group of people who share a common language and environment.

Cynicism   A mistrusting attitude regarding the motives of people. When you are cynical, you are constantly on guard against the "misbehavior" of others.

D

Depression   A mood disorder. Symptoms such as withdrawal, overwhelming sadness, or hopelessness may persist for weeks or months.

Developmental psychology   A branch of psychology concerned with the course and causes of developmental changes over a person's lifetime.

Directive style   A communication style that combines high dominance and low sociability.

Discrimination   Behavior based on prejudiced attitudes. If, as an employer, you believe that overweight people tend to be lazy, that is a prejudiced attitude. If you refuse to hire someone simply because that person is overweight, you are engaging in discrimination.

Dominance continuum   Every person falls somewhere on the low or high spectrum of the dominance continuum.

Dominance   The tendency to display a "take-charge" attitude.

E

Emotion   A temporary experience, with positive, negative, or mixed qualities.

Emotional intelligence   The ability to monitor and control one's emotions and behavior at work and in social settings.

Emotional labor   Those persons responsible for delivering quality service and building relationships, engage in emotional labor.

Emotive style   A style of communication that combines high sociability and high dominance.

Empathic listening   Listening with your ears, your eyes, and your heart.

Empathizers   People who have the ability to imagine themselves in someone else's position and understand what that person is feeling. They are able to understand the subtleties of human interaction.

Employee-assistance programs (EAPs)   A program aimed at overcoming anxiety, depression, burnout, alcohol abuse, and drug abuse, designed to address the negative effects of psychological disorders before employees become dysfunctional.

Empowerment   Refers to those policies that share information, authority, and responsibility with the lowest ranks of the organization.

Energy   Energy can be defined as the capacity for work, or the force that helps us do things with vitality and intensity.

Ergonomics   Techniques for adapting the work environment to the human body.

Ethics   Principles that define behavior as right, good, and proper.

Ethnic identity   The part of a person's identity that reflects the racial, religious, or cultural group to which the person belongs.

Ethnocentrism   The tendency to regard our own culture or nation as better or more "correct" than others.

Etiquette   A set of traditions based on kindness, efficiency, and logic.

Excess zone   Characterized by a high degree of intensity and rigidity. It can also be labeled the "danger" zone.

Expectancy theory   Based on the assumption that motivational strength is determined by whether or not you *believe* you can be successful at a task.

External locus of control   People who maintain an external locus of control believe that their life is almost totally controlled by outside forces and that they bear little personal responsibility for what happens to them.

F

Feedback   If interpersonal communication is to be effective, some type of feedback, or understood response, from the person receiving the information is necessary.

Fight or flight syndrome   The amygdala, located in the limbic region of the brain, sounds an alarm and adrenaline pours into the bloodstream, heart rate and blood pressure increase, breathing accelerates, and muscles tighten. The body is poised to fight or run.

Flextime   Typically includes a core time when all employees work, usually between 9:00 a.m. and 3:30 p.m. Employees can determine their own arrival and departure times within certain limits, which may mean arriving at 7 a.m. or leaving at 5:30 p.m.

G

Gender bias   Discrimination on the basis of gender.

Glass ceiling   A condition in the workplace that gives women a view of top management jobs but blocks their ascent.

Grapevine   An informal communication channel that carries unofficial information.

Grit   A form of hard work and determination that is a major indicator of success.

Guided imagery   Provides you with a way to harness the power of the mind and imagination to succeed at something.

H

Hawthorne studies   Became a sweeping investigation into the role of human relations in group and individual productivity. These studies also gave rise to the profession of industrial psychology by legitimizing the human factor as an element in business operations.

Hidden area   Contains information about you that you know but others do not. This pane is made up of all those private feelings, needs, and past experiences that you prefer to keep to yourself.

Hierarchy of needs   A theory whereby people tend to satisfy their needs in a particular order.

Horizontal channels   Ways to move information among people on the same level of authority, such as all the store managers of a national retail clothing store chain, all department chairpersons within a college, or all the administrative assistants within an organization.

Hostile work environment   Exists when supervisors, coworkers, vendors, or customers use sexual innuendo, tell sexually oriented jokes, display sexually explicit photos in the work area, discuss sexual exploits, and so on.

Human relations   Covers all types of interactions among people—their conflicts, cooperative efforts, and group relationships.

I

Image   A term used to describe how other people feel about you.

Impersonal communication   A one-way process that transfers basic information such as instructions, policies, and financial data.

Incentive program   A planned activity designed to motivate employees to achieve an organizational objective.

Incentives   A type of reward used to improve quality, reduce accidents, increase sales, improve attendance, and speed up production.

Informal organization   A network of relationships that exerts considerable influence on workers' performance.

Inner critic   Negative thought that take place in your internal conversation.

Integrity   The basic ingredient of character that is exhibited when you achieve congruence between what you know, what you say, and what you do.

Intensity zones   An indicator of communication style, such as a person who is either moderately or strongly dominant.

Internal locus of control   People who believe they are largely responsible for what happens to them maintain an internal locus of control. They make decisions for their own reasons based on their standards of what is right and wrong.

Internal values conflict   Occurs when a person is forced to choose between two or more strongly held values.

Interpersonal communication   The exchange of information between two or more people.

Interpersonal relationships   The personal dynamics that exist between people, not necessarily defined by the more rigid role relationships.

Intrapreneurships   Programs that encourage employees to pursue an idea, product, or process, with the company providing encouragement and support.

J

Job enlargement   Expanding an employee's duties or responsibilities.

Job enrichment   An attempt to make jobs more desirable or satisfying, thereby triggering internal motivation.

Job rotation   Allows workers to move through a variety of jobs in a predefined way over a period of time.

Job sharing   Two employees share the responsibilities of one job.

Johari Window   The word Johari is a combination of the first names of the model's originators: Joseph Luft and Harry Ingham. This communication model takes into consideration that there is some information you know about yourself and other information you are not yet aware of.

L

Leadership   The process of inspiring, influencing, and guiding employees to participate in a common effort.

Linguistic style   A series of culturally learned signals that we use to communicate what we mean.

Lose/lose approach   When the lose/lose approach is used to settle a dispute, each side must give in to the other.

M

Maintenance factors   Represent the basic things people consider essential to any job, such as salaries, fringe benefits, working conditions, social relationships, supervision, and organizational policies and administration.

Management   The process of coordinating people and other resources to achieve the goals of the organization.

Managing diversity   The process of creating an organizational culture where the primary and secondary dimensions of diversity are respected.

Meaningful dialogue   A type of discussion that stimulates ideas and shared meaning.

Mediation   A neutral third party listens to both sides and suggests solutions. It carries no binding authority. Both parties are free to reject or accept the mediator's decision.

Meditation A relaxation technique that slows your pulse, respiration, and brainwave activity and lowers your blood pressure.

Mentor Someone who develops another person through tutoring, coaching, and guidance.

Mirroring Describes situation where one person intentionally matches the communication style of the person he or she is meeting with.

Modeling Shaping your behavior to resemble that of people you admire and embracing the qualities those people demonstrate.

Mommy track A term used to describe the lifestyle of women who choose a career path that allows a mother flexible or reduced work hours.

Moral intelligence Our mental capacity to determine how universal human principles such as responsibility, compassion, forgiveness, and humility should be applied to our personal values, goals, and actions.

Motivation The influences that account for the initiation, direction, intensity, and persistence of behavior.

Motivational factors Those elements that go above and beyond the basic maintenance factors. They include opportunities for recognition, advancement, or more responsibility.

Motivation-maintenance theory A theory proposed by Psychologist Frederick Herzberg whereby employees are not directly motivated by certain maintenance factors (such as health insurance), but the absence of such a benefit would cause the employee to look for a job elsewhere.

N

Narcissism A Freudian term describing someone obsessed with his or her own self-image, alluding to the mythical youth who wore himself out trying to kiss his own reflection in a pool of water.

Nonassertive behavior Characterized by people who attempt to avoid conflict by simply ignoring things that bother them.

Nonfinancial resources Factors that contribute to a happy and fulfilling life, such as good health, peace of mind, time spent with family and friends, learning (which develops the mind), and healthy spirituality.

Nonverbal messages The messages (other than spoken or written words) we communicate through facial expressions, voice tone, gestures, appearance, posture, and other nonverbal means.

O

Observational learning Learning by watching others.

Open area The area of the Johari Window that represents your "public" or "awareness" area. This section contains information about you that both you and others know and includes information that you do not mind admitting about yourself.

Organizational culture The collection of shared values, beliefs, rituals, stories, and myths that foster a feeling of community among organizational members.

P

Peer group As children reach adolescence and begin to break away psychologically from their parents, the peer group (people their own age) can have a powerful influence on attitude formation.

Personal brand The attributes and the image you wish to portray to others when they think of you.

Personality A unique pattern of enduring thoughts, feelings, and actions that characterize a person.

Physical fitness A set of wellness factors that involves the performance of the lungs, heart, and muscles that can also have a positive influence on mental alertness and emotional stability.

Positive psychology   A recent branch of psychology that focuses on positive human functioning.

Positive reinforcers   A type of reward that is given after a response occurs.

Prejudice   A premature judgment or opinion that is formed without examination of the facts.

Pride   The emotional high that follows performance and success.

primacy effect   The tendency to form and retain impressions quickly at the time of an initial meeting.

Primary dimensions   Core characteristics of each individual that cannot be changed: age, race, gender, physical and mental abilities, ethnic heritage, and sexual orientation.

Professional presence   A dynamic blend of poise, self-confidence, control, and style that empowers us to be able to command respect in any situation.

PTO bank   A bank of paid-time-off days—vacation allotment, sick days, personal days—that employees can draw from in hourly increments.

Q

Quid pro quo   Occurs when a person in a supervisory or managerial position threatens the job security or a potential promotion of a subordinate worker who refuses to submit to sexual advances.

R

Race   Denotes a category of people who are perceived as distinctive on the basis of certain biologically inherited traits, such as skin color or hair texture.

Reference group   Consists of several people who share a common interest. Sales and Marketing Executives International would serve as a reference group for persons employed in sales and marketing.

Reflective style   A type of communication style that features a combination of low dominance and low sociability.

Reinforcer   Any stimulus that follows a response and increases the probability that the response will occur again.

Resilience   Being capable of bouncing back when you are confronted with stressful situations.

Right livelihood   Work consciously chosen, done with full awareness and care, and leading to enlightenment.

Role model   A person you admire or are likely to emulate.

Role relationships   Rigid relationships developed between groups such as supervisors and subordinates that are defined by their expected roles and may result in communication barriers.

Rumination   The process of replaying an incident over and over in our mind.

S

Scientific management   A movement initiated by Frederick W. Taylor that continues to influence the workplace today.

Secondary dimensions   Elements that can be changed, or at least modified. They include a person's work experience, health habits, religious beliefs, education and training, first language, family status, organizational role and level, communication style, and socio-economic status.

Self-acceptance   The foundation of successful interaction with others.

Self-awareness   The ability to recognize and understand your moods, emotions, and drives, as well as their effect on others.

Self-concept   The bundle of facts, opinions, beliefs, and perceptions about yourself that are present in your life every moment of every day.

Self-description Involves disclosure of non-threatening information, such as your age, your favorite food, or where you went to school. This is information that others could acquire in some way other than by your telling them.

Self-disclosure The process of letting another person know what you think, feel, or want. It is one of the important ways you let yourself be known by others.

Self-efficacy The learned expectation of success.

Self-esteem Characterized by the relationship between a person's self-efficacy and self-respect.

Self-fulfilling prophecy The somewhat mysterious connection between what you expect in life and what you actually achieve: If you can conceive it and believe it, you can achieve it.

Self-managed teams High performance work teams that assume responsibility for traditional management tasks as part of their regular work routine.

Self-respect What you think and feel about yourself.

Self-talk Takes place in the privacy of your mind. It can be rational and productive, or it can be irrational and disruptive.

Semantics The study of the relationship between a word and its meaning(s).

Serenity A mindful state that carries the urge to savor your current circumstances and find ways to integrate them into your life more fully.

Sexual harassment Unwelcome verbal or physical behavior that affects a person's job performance or work environment.

Situational Leadership Model A model developed by Paul Hersey and his colleagues at the Center for Leadership Studies that is widely used in several organizations.

Situational leadership Based on the theory that the most successful leadership occurs when the leader's style matches the situation.

Sociability continuum Characterizes the extent to which a person is friendly and expresses feelings openly.

Sociability The tendency to seek and enjoy social relationships.

Social media Refers to the use of Web-based and mobile technologies to turn communication into an interactive dialogue.

Social reputation Represents the extent to which a company or individual's online profile reflect a brand.

Socialization The process through which people are integrated into a society by exposure to the actions and opinions of others.

Spirituality An inner attitude that emphasizes energy, creative choice, and a powerful force for living.

Stereotypes Perceptions, beliefs, and expectations about members of some group.

Strength A consistent, near perfect performance of an activity; you can see yourself doing it repeatedly, happily and successfully.

Stress Refers to two simultaneous events: an external stimulus, called a stressor, and the physical and emotional responses to that stimulus (anxiety, fear, muscle tension, surging heart rate, and so on).

Structure Reflects the extent to which a leader is likely to define and direct his or her role and the roles of subordinates toward goal attainment.

Style flexing The deliberate attempt to change or alter your style to meet the needs of another person.

Supportive style A type of communication that combines low dominance and high sociability.

Surface language A pattern of immediate impressions conveyed by what we *see*—in other words, by appearance.

Synergy   The interaction of two or more parts to produce a greater result than the sum of the parts taken individually.

T

Talent   Any naturally recurring pattern of thought, feeling, or behavior that can be productively applied.

Team building   A leadership initiative associated with high productivity and profitability. Problems in interpersonal relations are also less common where teamwork is evident. Teamwork ensures not only that a job gets done but also that it gets done efficiently and harmoniously.

Telecommuting   Employees working at home at a personal computer linked to their employer's computer.

Temperament   An infant's individual style and frequency of expressing needs and emotions.

Total person   A person's collective single system that is composed of several separate characteristics such as emotional control, self-awareness, or physical fitness.

Transactional Analysis   A theory developed by Eric Berne whereby he concluded that, from the day of birth, the brain acts like a two-track stereo tape recorder. One track records events, and the other records the feelings associated with those events.

Transition   The experience of being forced to give up something and face a change.

Trust index   A research tool that measures the level of trust, pride, and camaraderie within the workplace.

Trust   The building block of all successful relationships with coworkers, customers, family members, and friends.

Twelve-step programs   Initiatives that help with drug and alcohol addiction, eating disorders, and gambling addiction.

U

Unconscious mind   A vast storehouse of forgotten memories, desires, ideas, and frustrations.

Unknown area   The area of the Johari Window made up of things unknown to you and others. Because you, and others, can never be known completely, this area never completely disappears.

Upward communication   The process of encouraging employees to share their feelings and ideas with their managers.

V

Values conflicts   Problem areas that cause organizational issues such as declining quality, absenteeism, and poor customer service.

Values drift   The slow erosion of your core values over time.

Values   The personal beliefs and preferences that influence your behavior.

Valuing diversity   Involves appreciating everyone's uniqueness, respecting differences, and encouraging every worker to make his or her full contribution to the organization.

Versatility   Acting in ways that earn other people's approval of our behavior.

Vertical channels   Represent the means whereby information can move up and down through all levels of authority within an organization.

Virtual office   Networks of workers connected by the latest technology.

Virtual teams   Virtual teams composed of employees physically dispersed throughout the nation or around the world.

Visualize   Forming a mental image of something.

Voluntary arbitration   Both sides willingly submit their disagreements to a neutral party. The arbitrator's decision must be accepted by both sides.

W

Whistleblower   A person who reveals wrongdoing within an organization to the public or to those in positions of authority.

Win/lose approach   Occurs when someone attempts to reach his or her own goals at the expense of the other party's.

Win/win approach   An approach whereby both parties negotiate to fix a problem.

Workplace violence   Any act against an employee that creates a hostile work environment and negatively affects the employee, either physically or psychologically. These acts include all types of physical or verbal assaults, threats, coercion, intimidation, and all forms of harassment.

Name Index

Note: Page numbers in italic type indicate illustrations. Figures and tables are indicated, respectively, by *f* or *t* following the page number.

Subject Index

Note: Page numbers in italic type indicate illustrations. Figures and tables are indicated, respectively, by *f* or *t* following the page number.